P9-CEQ-241

South African Dialogue

SOUTH AFRICAN DIALOGUE
Contrasts in South African Thinking on Basic Race Issues

Edited by N. J. Rhoodie

The Westminster Press, Philadelphia

PUBLISHED BY THE WESTMINSTER PRESS ®
PHILADELPHIA, PENNSYLVANIA

PRINTED IN THE UNITED STATES OF AMERICA

Library of Congress Cataloging in Publication Data

Rhoodie, N. J.
South African dialogue.

1. Africa, South—Race question—Addresses, essays, lectures. I. Title.
DT763.R473 1973 301.45'1'0420968 73-4205
ISBN O-664-20979-3

Contents

Preface

This book is in two respects an historic text : firstly, no publication dealing with local race relations can boast of a more impressive line-up of contributors. Secondly, this is the first comprehensive publication in which proponents and opponents of the National Party's race policies have voluntarily participated in a dialogue.

Since Mr John Vorster became premier of South Africa in 1966, the National Party (N.P.) has on several occasions demonstrated its willingness to establish contact with friendly and neutral Black African states. Until now this *outward* policy has met with no mean success. Dialogue, as opposed to confrontation, is today one of the cornerstones of the Republic's Africa policy. The Government is anxious to see that dialogue does not remain limited to senior diplomatic level but expands to include non-governmental persons and institutions. It is true, unfortunately, that dialogue is still mainly limited to other African states, while the local Non-White groups are largely excluded. Critics of the Government claim that those local Non-White leaders involved in a dialogue with the 'Establishment' are either pro-apartheid or, due to their official connection with Government-created Non-White political institutions, unable to adopt a forthright anti-apartheid posture. These critics also contend that dialogue has hitherto been handled as though it were the exclusive preserve of the N.P. Government.

Currently there is an increasing consensus of opinion among informed Whites that the dialogue policy should not be limited to foreign policy in Africa, that locally it should not only involve Government institutions but that it be expanded to promote increasing contact also in the broader strata of the population. Increasing dialogue in academic, professional and other non-official circles is urgently needed to act as a catalyst in the promotion of better race relations. And dialogue must most certainly not involve only those Non-Whites who support the policy of separate development as currently conceived.

The present book offers clear proof that dialogue of this kind is possible. In fact, the contributors run practically the whole gamut of political sentiment in South Africa and their contributions cover an ideological spectrum spanning the polarities of integration and separation. This example of dialogue in action augurs well for the future of race relations in South Africa. Dialogue in South Africa might well prove to be the precursor of cross-ethnic negotiation, a prime requisite for institutional adjustments and experimentation aimed at a workable political accommodation for the country's diverse groups.

Non-South African observers of the local racial scene are often confused by the apparent inconsistencies in the White establishment's handling of the Republic's socio-political minorities as a result of incidents which are grouped under the colloquial phrase *petty apartheid.* These observers, and a growing number of local Whites, cannot fail to notice the contradictions between positive policy actions such as promises of Bantu homeland independence, considerable economic aid to neighbouring Black states, the cordial treatment of visiting foreign Black dignitaries, increasing multiracial international sports meetings, dispensing equal treatment to visiting Blacks participating in scientific symposia, and other instances of colour blind services and facilities accessible to eminent foreign visitors, and the blatant colour-discriminatory laws such as job reservation, segregated public service facilities of the most basic kind, making sexual relations between White and Non-White a criminal offence but not between the different Non-White groups themselves, preventing Non-White doctors from giving orders to White hospital personnel, refusing a world-renowned coloured-American entertainer permission to perform before White audiences in a major South African city, official threats to prohibit private sport involving cross-racial participation, the policy of several Performing Arts Councils that prohibits a Coloured tenor (the only South African ever to make his debut in the Metropolitan Opera House in New York) not only from sharing the operatic stage with Whites, but even from sitting in the White audience, and the distressing petty apartheid measures pertaining to social and residential segregation and race classification.

Urbanization and urbanism, university education and economic progress have over the last two decades combined to create a new class of Afrikaner – a development destined to play no mean role in the future shaping of race relations in South Africa. This development created the social, cultural, economic and psychological conditions that brought about the genesis of the *verligte* Afrikaner, *verlig* in the sense of being more open-minded than earlier Afrikaner generations, less resistant to change, more willing to establish cross-cultural contacts and, of special significance in South Africa, manifesting a genuine preparedness to discard blatant colour and race discrimination. The *verligtes* are becoming increasingly critical of a system in which – so many of them believe – the basic political and civil rights of the individual are determined by his colour. In South Africa, therefore, *petty apartheid* can generally be equated with *colour* discrimination, that is, the determination of rights and privileges on the basis of a colour or racial differential alone.

On the other hand, though, *verligte* Afrikaners are at pains to point out that many petty apartheid measures are merely of an interim nature, temporary regulatory devices designed at best (a) to obviate the numerous conflicts and frictions that are unavoidably engendered in situations of direct contact between groups involving incompatibilities created by considerable differences in living and educational standards, life style, norms, values and physically identifiable racial traits; and (b) to smooth the way for a system of socio-political and cultural partnership based on the reciprocally recognized principle of self-determination. They maintain that separate development is a pragmatic, flexible policy with sufficient in-built adjustment potential to meet the demands of the day. They claim that this inherent dynamism renders the policy capable of absorbing even radical adjustments provided these do not militate against the central principle of separate development: self-determination for the Afrikaner as a separate *volk*. For the Afrikaner this includes the right to exist as a separate socio-political and cultural entity and the claim to indigenous status in the land of his birth.

The responsible Afrikaner is prepared to negotiate a workable accommodation with his Non-White neighbour but not at the cost of lowered living standards and national capitulation. And in view of the fact that the Afrikaners will form the strongest socio-political category in the subcontinent in the foreseeable future, it is self-evident that they will be the deciding factor in any accommodation negotiated on a cross-racial basis. Those ignorant of Afrikaner history and the Afrikaners' emotional make-up are inclined to underestimate their single-minded determination to preserve their ethno-national identity. They fail to realize that Afrikaner nationalism precipitated the first anti-colonial wars in Africa, namely the Anglo-Boer Wars of 1880-81 and 1899-1902. Moreover, Afrikaners claim to be ethnically indigenous to Africa: the only White African nation on the Continent. As proof of this claim they argue that theirs is the only language containing in its name the name of the Continent which created their ethnic identity. They also underscore the fact that they are the only White nation outside Europe which has evolved its own language.

Politically sophisticated Non-Whites in South Africa are convinced that the disqualifications to which they are subjected are primarily manifestations of *colour* prejudice. Even incumbents of Government-created Non-White political institutions often indict the dominant White nation of entrenching a socio-political structure designed to perpetuate an exclusively White reward and power system. They concede though that this indictment does not generally apply to the Bantu homelands – an admission qualified with the counter argument that, theoretically at least, non-racialism does therefore operate in only 13 per cent of South Africa's land area. In the rest of the country a person's basic rights are determined by a central colour bar separating White society from *all* Non-Whites irrespective of the latter's ethnic composition. Because all Non-Whites are exposed to a common set of discriminatory practices Black consciousness has extended its radius to encompass also Non-Bantu Africans such as Coloureds and Asians.

Confronted with these accusations, Afrikaner leaders contend that although a race and colour differential has historically played an overwhelming causal role in the crystallization of South Africa's socio-political structure, there is no reason to believe that it will in future continue to do so. Historically the cultural and socio-political differences between the two main racial groups of South Africa have always corresponded to a general colour polarization. The average White has consequently been conditioned to associate these differences with race and vice versa. The wide gap between the relevant groups in terms of levels of civilization and socio-political development has thus for generations imbued the dominant society with a sharp colour consciousness. And this is a psycho-social reality which will not evaporate overnight.

From the Whites' point of view colour differences have, naturally, considerably heightened the 'social visibility' of the Non-White 'out-groups'. In the event of group friction high social visibility is invariably a complicating factor. Imagine, for example, a colour differential superimposed upon the cultural and religious disputes in Canada and Ireland respectively. In a contact situation like the one obtaining in South Africa the matter of 'social visibility' is of crucial importance in order to grasp the dynamics of local intergroup relations. The more pronounced the cultural and socio-political differences between the dominant and minority groups and the stronger the survival drive of the dominant group, the more prominent will be the role played by high social visibility in the handling of intergroup relations.

Most Bantu-African sophisticates harbour ambivalent sentiments with regard to the political future of the Bantu homelands. While they do not reject the concept of independent Black nation states in principle, they nonetheless contend that these embryonic Black states do not satisfy the minimum requirements for economic viability and thus lack the one ingredient without which no meaningful political development can materialize. Political development is doubly hamstrung due to the geo-political fragmentation of the homelands. They point out that the homelands are economically depressed areas, accommodating the less sophisticated Bantu and are unable to satisfy the minimum material needs of even their own natural increase. And even should these territories become independent, so they argue, the Republic of South Africa would still be left with a national population consisting of a dominant White group and several Non-White minorities, including the denationalized, westernized Bantu-Africans residing permanently in the White urban areas. In fact, they demand that the latter should be recognized as a new socio-political category, constituting a permanent sub-system within the wider South African population structure.

Everything considered, it appears as though the non-Whites, generally speaking, prefer a geo-politically unified South Africa to a Balkanized sub-continent apportioned along racial or ethnic lines. The concept of Black consciousness is deliberately utilized with a view to uniting all Non-Whites in the common cause of obtaining full citizenship and political rights in an unpartitioned South African state.

Bantu-Africans, Asians and Coloureds naturally realize that the *Non-Blacks* are not prepared to organize the political accommodation of the *Blacks* on a one-man-one-vote basis. In fact, these Blacks realize, frustrating as it may be to them personally, that they would best serve their ideal of a colour-blind universal adult suffrage if they initially adopt the more pragmatic approach associated with concepts such as race confederation, ethnic commonwealth and supra-nationality. Basically these concepts all embody a socio-political dispensation (a) providing for cross-communal or cross-racial participation in central decision making; (b) structured and institutionalized on a group or communal basis; (c) guaranteeing protection for legitimate group interests, *inter alia* by means of entrenched group autonomy; (d) geared to phasing out colour discrimination; (e) providing for future institutional changes through negotiated adjustments. In a nut-shell this system boils down to a South African nation composed of several socio-political categories interacting as autonomous units that participate at central government level in respect of matters that transcend local group needs.

To those Whites and Non-Whites (or Non-Blacks and Blacks) sensitive and responsive to the follow-through effect of historical realities, and in particular the dictates of contemporary *realpolitik,* the great internal dialogue of the foreseeable future will not centre on the introduction of deliberate mass integration, but on the basic design of the multi-communal system sketched in the foregoing paragraph, including the political mechanics, constitutional formulae and institutional apparatus required for such an ambitious but by no means impossible accommodation. Basic to this realism is the fact that South Africa is inhabited by several historically evolved socio-political groups whose *common* interests and needs could be accommodated within a centralized decision making institution, but whose *disparate group-centred* interests and needs would have to be handled on the basis of separate but interacting autonomous units co-existing within a wider multi-communal society.

An objective study of the 35 chapters comprising this book cannot fail to underscore in the mind of the reader the labyrinthine complexity of South Africa's race and ethnic problems. For those both physically and emotionally removed from these problems the snares of oversimplification are manifold. And oversimplification spawns instant solutions. South Africans by and large are wary of slot-machine solutions, fully knowing that should a particular solution fail, they would have to live with it. Conversely, it is equally wrong for South Africans simply to assume that all critics outside the country's borders are ignorant of the local race situation. There is evidence pointing to a growing number of well-informed observers of the South African racial scenario.

The socio-political structure of South Africa may appear to many 'outsiders' to be irrational. Many social scientists in particular are wont to describe Afrikaner nationalism as a phenomenon that defies rational analysis. However, the scepticism of social scientists who enlist text-book models in order to prove that this nationalism is ideologically outdated, politically dangerous and incapable of definition in operational terms, nevertheless fails to neutralize the fact that Afrikaner nationalism is still very much alive. Therefore, model solutions which may sound impressively convincing from a lecturer's podium in the often make-believe atmosphere of a university auditorium, will not necessarily pass the acid test of viability *in loco.*

In conclusion, to the men and women who made this book possible I should like to express my deepest appreciation for their generous application to a worthwhile task. I know that all of them had to interrupt heavily loaded work programmes in order to write their contributions. I also know that they did so not only because of their genuine interest in local race relations but also because each and everyone of them is strategically positioned to considerably influence the relationship between the several socio-political categories in South Africa. All of them are dedicated to the promotion of sound race relations despite differences in ideological orientation and disparate views on cross-racial accommodation at both the aspirational and operational level.

N.J. RHOODIE,
Pretoria

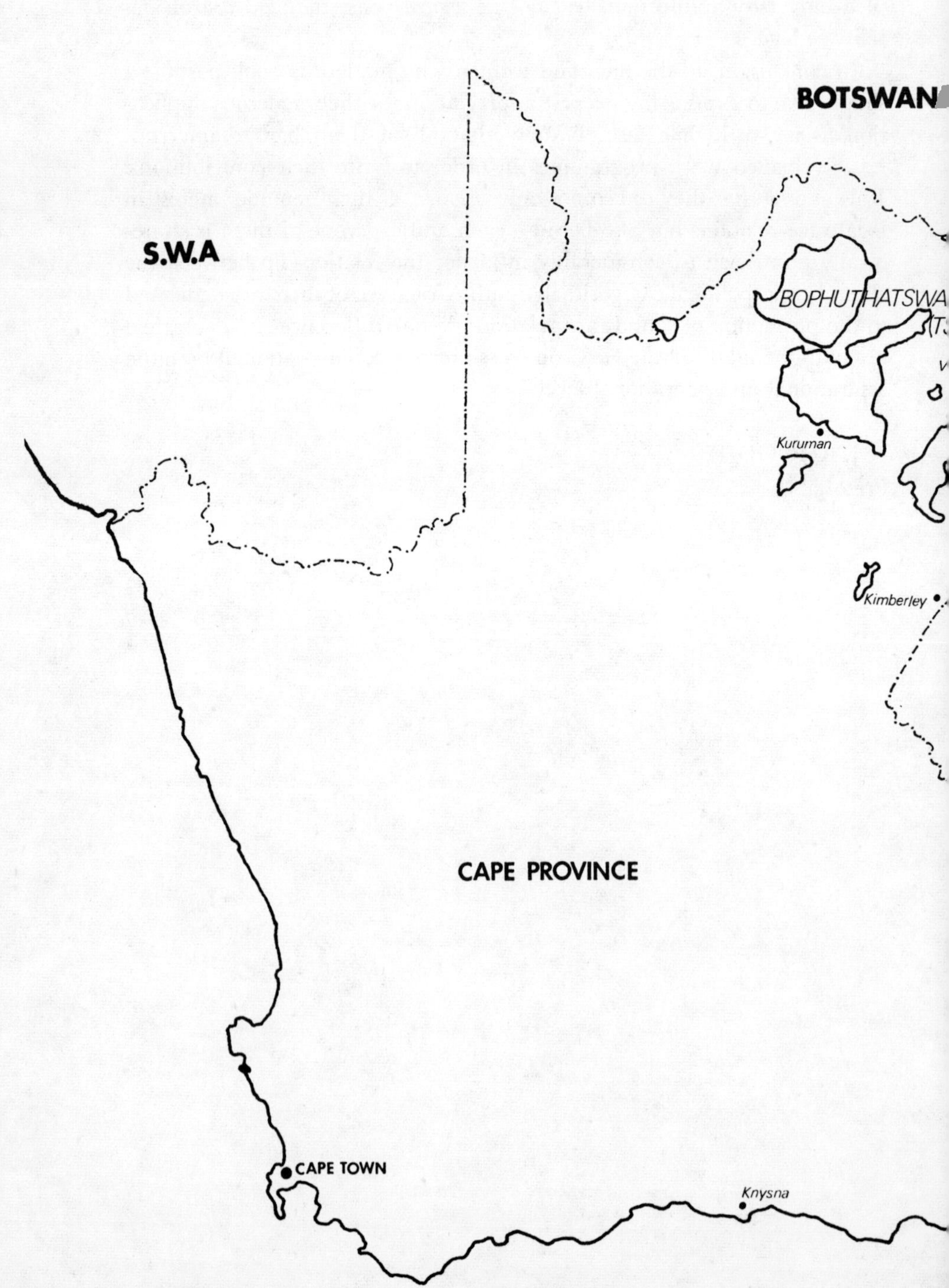

BOTSWAN
S.W.A
BOPHUTHATSWA
Kuruman
Kimberley
CAPE PROVINCE
CAPE TOWN
Knysna

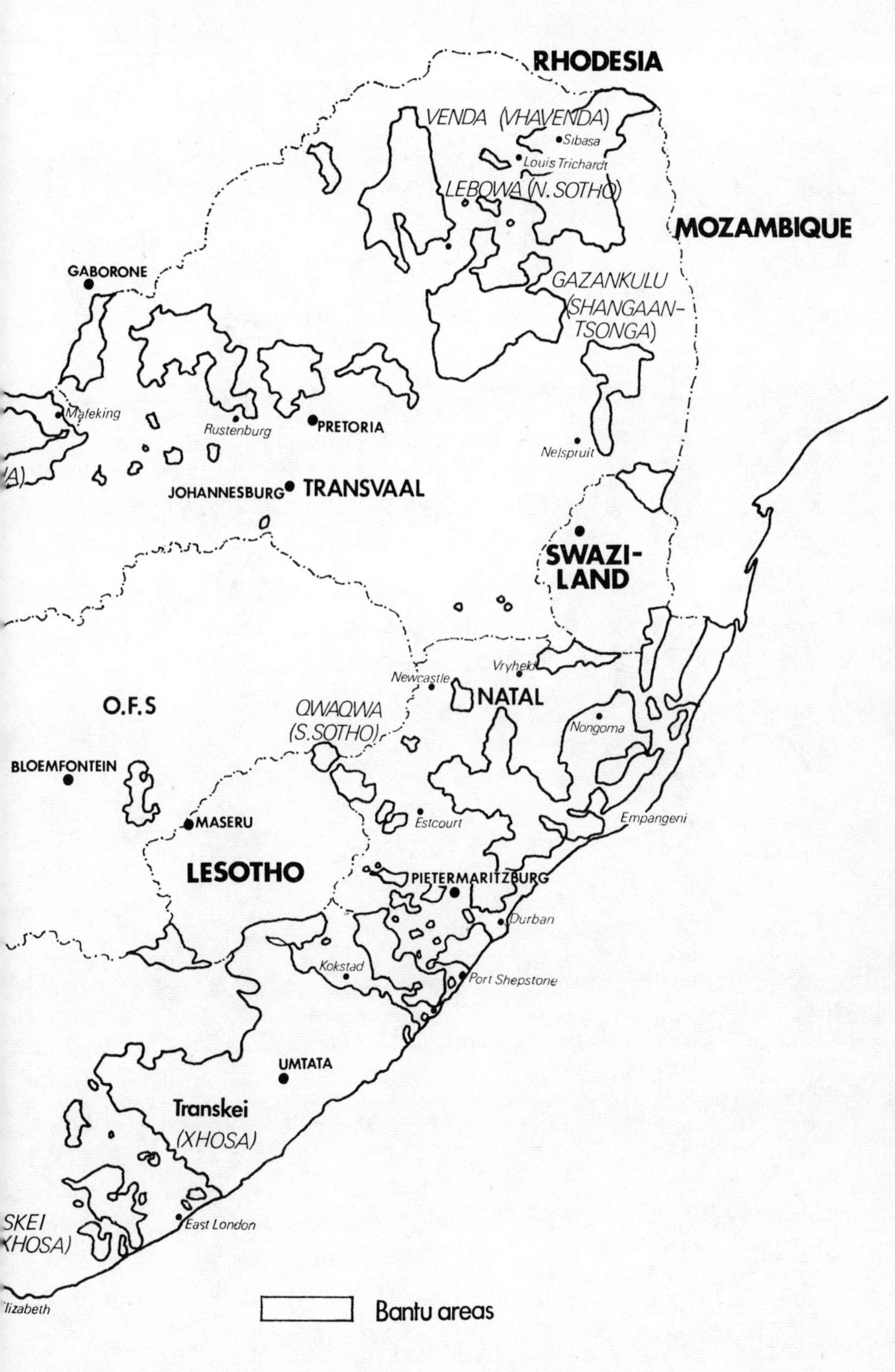
RHODESIA
VENDA (VHAVENDA)
Sibasa
Louis Trichardt
LEBOWA (N. SOTHO)
MOZAMBIQUE
GABORONE
GAZANKULU
(SHANGAAN-
TSONGA)
Mafeking
Rustenburg
PRETORIA
Nelspruit
JOHANNESBURG
TRANSVAAL
SWAZI-
LAND
Vryheid
Newcastle
NATAL
O.F.S
QWAQWA
(S. SOTHO)
Nongoma
BLOEMFONTEIN
MASERU
Estcourt
Empangeni
LESOTHO
PIETERMARITZBURG
Durban
Kokstad
Port Shepstone
UMTATA
Transkei
(XHOSA)
East London
Bantu areas

The General Race Relations Structure

The Basic Race Structure

C. J. Jooste

Chris Jooste is director of the pro-separate development South African Bureau of Racial Affairs. He holds a Ph.D. from the University of Natal and has numerous publications to his credit, mainly on race relations. He is one of the top Afrikaans-speaking authorities on the South African Government's ethnic and race policies.

The view that South Africa is a single nation state is incorrect. It overlooks two fundamental features, namely the past history of the sub-continent (especially its political history) and the course of future development on which it is set. The trend of future development has become crystallized over the past two decades and can be characterized as a form of decolonization, of the regaining of independence by peoples who lost their sovereignty in the period of British expansion and administration which lasted for over a century from 1806 to 1910.

'South Africa', as a political concept, dates back to the time when almost the entire sub-continent, i.e. Africa south of the Limpopo River, was under British control (excluding only South West Africa on the West Coast and the Portuguese province of Mozambique on the East Coast). This expansion took place in terms of the 'greater Britain' policy which aimed at making Britain the 'paramount power' in Southern Africa. National boundaries disappeared in the wake of this policy, different peoples were incorporated and territories were annexed and administered as parts of the growing Empire.

A smaller South Africa emerged in 1910 when Britain granted independence to its former colonies, the Cape of Good Hope and Natal, and to the conquered Republics of the Orange Free State and the Transvaal, under a constitution uniting the four territories into a Union of South Africa. Three territories remained under British control until recently when they were granted sovereignty separately as the independent Republic of Botswana (formerly Bechuanaland) in 1966, the Kingdom of

Lesotho (formerly Basutoland) in 1966 and the Kingdom of Swaziland in 1968.

The constitution of the Union of South Africa, approved by the British Parliament in 1909, placed the administrative responsibility for the entire territory in the hands of the White population. The transfer of responsibility for deciding on the political development of the Non-White peoples of South Africa to the Afrikaners had started earlier, in 1906 and 1907 when Britain granted responsible government to the former Republics of Transvaal and the Orange Free State. The draft peace treaty which ended the war of independence contained an important clause concerning the Non-White franchise which was framed by Lord Alfred Milner, the British High Commissioner and chief negotiater of the treaty: '. . . the franchise will not be given to Natives until after the introduction of self-government'. This draft was not acceptable to General Smuts as it implied granting the franchise to Non-Whites on a common roll once self-government was regained by the Republics. Milner then agreed that the whole question should be settled eventually by the Afrikaners themselves and thus ceded any responsibility for Non-White development which Britain might have gained as a result of the war. In 1906 and 1907 the Liberal Government in Britain gave responsible government to the Transvaal and the O.F.S. under constitutions which restricted the franchise to Whites. This principle was maintained in the draft constitution of the Union and was approved by the British Parliament in 1909.

The Union Government was a White government, ruling over the former Afrikaner Republics of the Transvaal and the Orange Free State, the White territories in the Cape of Good Hope and Natal, Bantu territories which had been annexed and incorporated into British South Africa over the years, as well as over Non-White peoples domiciled in White territories, principally Indians and Coloureds living in Natal and the Cape Province respectively.

The political destiny of the Bantu peoples and their territories and of other Non-White peoples was thus entrusted to the White nation in South Africa, a nation composed of Afrikaners, predominantly from the former Republics, and Englishmen who had settled more or less permanently in the country. The Afrikaners were numerically stronger and exerted a powerful influence on political events in Southern Africa. The conquest of peoples was foreign to them. Their approach was to occupy vacant land and to leave the Bantu peoples to govern themselves in their respective national territories. This approach was also dominant in the Union Government and in all governments since 1910, with the possible exception of General Smuts' second regime during the World War II period.

This Afrikaner approach has influenced the political evolution of South Africa significantly. It was logical in terms of this policy that the White government should have set itself the task of restoring the independence of those peoples who had lost their freedom to Britain and who had been placed under the Union Government as subject peoples in 1910. The first survey of Bantu territories was carried out in 1913 and these lands have been protected against alienation to foreign persons ever since; the scattered territories have been consolidated and expanded to form viable geographical homelands for the respective nations who are now moving towards self-government.

Britain's granting of independence to Botswana, Lesotho and Swaziland will therefore be followed by the granting of sovereign independence to her other former Bantu territories which she handed over to the Union of South Africa in 1910. This process, which now rests with the Government of the Republic of South Africa, has already reached an advanced stage. The term 'South Africa' is thus losing its political significance and is assuming a predominantly geographical meaning.

The future map of South Africa, south of the Limpopo, will include the countries and peoples listed in the table. A brief description of the non-independent nations may serve to clarify the emerging political structure.

THE PEOPLES OF SOUTH AFRICA – GENERAL INFORMATION

Territory	*Population (1970)*	*Head of State*	*Head of Government*
Independent Territories			
Botswana	593 000	President Sir Seretse Khama	The President
Lesotho	880 000	King Moshoeshoe II	Prime Minister Chief Leabua Jonathan
Mozambique	6 950 000	Province of Portugal	
Republic of South Africa	3 750 716 White 2 018 533 Coloured 620 422 Indian	State President J. J. Fouché	Prime Minister B. J. Vorster
Swaziland	395 138	King Sobhuza II	Prime Minister Prince Makhosini Dlamini

Territory	*Population (1970)*	*Head of State*	*Head of Government*
*Non-Independent Territories (Bantu Homelands)**			
Bophuthatswana (Tswana)	1 718 508	State President R.S.A.	Chief Councillor Chief Lucas M. Mangope
Ciskei (Xhosa)	900 000	State President R.S.A.	Chief Councillor Chief Justice Mabandla
Lebowa (North Sotho)	1 603 530	State President R.S.A.	Chief Councillor Chief M. M. Matlala
Gazankulu (Shangana-Tsonga)	736 978	State President R.S.A.	Chief Councillor Prof. H.W.E. Ntsanwisi
Qwaqwa (South Sotho)	1 453 354	State President R.S.A.	Chief Councillor Chief Wessels Mota
Transkei (Xhosa)	3 030 000	State President R.S.A.	Chief Minister Chief Kaiser Matanzima
Venda (Vhavenda)	357 875	State President R.S.A.	Chief Councillor Chief P.R. Mphephu
Kwazulu (Zulu)	4 026 082	State President R.S.A	Chief Councillor Chief G. Buthelezi

* These are the official names for these territories and their peoples.
South West Africa (Namibia) has not been included.

THE SOTHO PEOPLES

The *Tswana* belong to the Sotho linguistic community and are most closely related to the people of the Republic of Botswana. Their country, which they have decided to call Bophuthatswana, is composed of a number of territories in the north-western parts of South Africa. These territories are in the process of being consolidated into one or two large blocks on the Botswana border.

The 1,7 million Tswanas have achieved a large measure of local self-government which will be extended during the next year or two to a status closely approximating that of the Transkei Xhosas. The Tswana Legislative Assembly, under Chief Lucas Mangope, controls six government departments, viz. Authority Affairs and Finance, Justice, Education and Culture, Agriculture, Community Affairs and Welfare and Works. A Chief Councillor and five Councillors are elected by the Legislative Assembly as the political heads of the respective departments. The civil service includes a number of officials on loan from the government of the Republic of South Africa.

Bophuthatswana is rich in mineral resources and its secondary industrial development benefits greatly from the proximity of the Witwatersrand market as well as from industrial development on the borders of Tswana territories near Rosslyn, Brits and Rustenburg. The Legislative Assembly has decided to move its headquarters from Montshiwa near Mafeking to a new capital city to be developed at Heystekrand.

The *South Sotho* and the people of the Lesotho kingdom have a common origin. They speak the same language and share other cultural characteristics. The national territory, Qwaqwa (Witsieshoek), is a small mountainous area adjacent to Lesotho, on the main railway, road and air routes between Durban and the Witwatersrand. The population is about one and a half times the size of the Lesotho population but the vast majority of the people are still living outside Qwaqwa, in the adjoining territories of the Transkei and the Republic of South Africa.

A territorial authority was established in 1969 under Chief Wessels Mota, became a Legislative Assembly in 1971 and will advance to Transkei-status in the next year or two. The country is headed for intensive industrial and tourist development.

The *North Sotho* nation of the Lebowa is the third member of the Sotho family and occupies land in the northern parts of South Africa, near the Portuguese province of Mozambique. It has advanced politically along with the other Sotho peoples and negotiations for further advancement towards parliamentary government have started already. The Lebowa consists of a few blocks of land which will be consolidated by way of exchange with the Republic of South Africa.

The three Sotho nations, viz. Tswana, South Sotho and North Sotho, have many cultural characteristics in common, but there are also important differences between them, especially with respect to language and political and tribal organization. Their respective Departments of Education and Culture are active in the promotion of literature and art and in providing for various kinds of cultural expression and participation. As in the case of Botswana, Lesotho and Swaziland, the three Sotho territories are served by a single university, located in the Lebowa. Plans are, however, under way for the expansion of university training to Bophuthatswana and to Qwaqwa.

THE VHAVENDA

The Vhavenda of Venda is a small nation in the northern part of the sub-continent. The national language, Chivenda, is related to languages found in Rhodesia. The Legislative Assembly, with its headquarters at Sibasa, has started negotiations with the Republic of South Africa with a view to advancement towards parliamentary government. Venda has a considerable agricultural, mining and tourist potential.[1]

SHANGANA-TSONGA

Gazankulu is a small country in the north, near Venda and Mozambique. The name Shangana originated when the Tsonga people were dominated by the Zulu Chief Soshangane after he fled from Shaka and established his Gasa empire in Mozambique in 1835. Many Tsonga migrated when this happened and the descendants of these early immigrants still prefer the name Tsonga. They were followed by others who were true subjects of Soshangane – hence the name Shangana. Their settlement in what has since become the Republic of South Africa is, therefore, of fairly recent origin, the latest settlers having arrived in 1895 after the defeat of their chief, Ngungunyane, by the Portuguese. The Gazankulu Legislative Assembly has set up its headquarters at Giyane, and has started negotiations for a parliamentary form of government.[2]

THE NGUNI PEOPLES

The *Xhosa* of the Transkei and the Ciskei belong to the Nguni-speaking peoples, viz. the Xhosa, Zulu and Swazi who have established themselves along the east coast of the sub-continent. The Ciskei Xhosa have reached further south than any of the other major Bantu migrations, and have established themselves in territories between 26½° and 28° east and 30° and 34° south. One of these territories, Glen Grey, adjoins the Transkei.

The Ciskei (on the western side of the Great Kei River) has its own Legislative Assembly under Chief Justice Mabandla, and is pursuing a course towards self-government independently of the Transkei (east of the Kei River). It seems possible, however, that politically these two territories may move closer towards each other in the future.

1. Cf., 'The Vhavenda of Vendaland' in the *Journal of Racial Affairs,* 22:1 (Jan., 1970), for a brief description of Venda and its present political status.
2. Cf., 'The Shangana-Tsonga' in the *Journal of Racial Affairs,* 22:2 (April, 1970).

The Transkei Xhosa have already achieved a large measure of independence. They have a parliament composed of hereditary chiefs and elected representatives. A Chief Minister and five Ministers control the administrative and executive functions. The powers of the Transkei government can be extended by the transfer of further departments of the civil service to it, until it achieves full sovereign independence. The Transkei development sets the pattern for the transfer of power to the other developing nations in South Africa.

The *Zulu* nation of Kwazulu has established itself between the eastern seaboard and the mountain range, the Drakensberg, in territories east and south-east of Mozambique and Swaziland. Political development has lagged behind largely as a result of internal tribal strife, but considerable progress has been made over the past two years. Constitutional development will probably follow a different course from that outlined in respect of the other nations in view of the special position of the Zulu royal family.

COLOUREDS AND INDIANS

The Coloured population is of mixed origin, the main elements being Hottentot, Slave (Negroid, Mongoloid, Australoid), Bushman, Bantu and European. According to a Cape census, in 1860 there were little over 100 000 Coloured persons, living mostly on White-owned farms and on mission stations. Today they are over two million in number and they are rapidly assuming metropolitan characteristics.

Coloured areas which can be regarded as national territories are scattered over a wide area and accommodate no more than three per cent of the total Coloured population. The percentage living on White-owned farms is declining and a growing percentage is being accommodated in urban areas adjoining White cities and towns.

Politically, they have attained a large measure of community autonomy, mainly in the sphere of education, local government, rural development and welfare. A partly elected, partly nominated Coloured Representative Council is functioning already and controls its own civil service. These functions are carried out within and under the jurisdiction of the Republic of South Africa. The future development of the Coloureds towards self-government has not been spelt out in detail.

The 620 000 Indians are the descendants of indentured labourers who came to Natal from India over 100 years ago, and of others who have settled in South Africa as traders. More than four-fifths of them are resident in Natal and they are mainly concentrated in and around metropolitan Durban. They are particularly active as entrepreneurs in trading undertakings and also as entrepreneurs and employees in secondary industry and certain types of tertiary activity.

Indians can advance to local self-government in their living areas, and there is a nominated Advisory Council which represents the Indian community in negotiations with the central government on matters such as education, welfare, residential development, local government, economic affairs, etc. This nominated Council is expected to develop into an elected body.

The racial factor manifests itself more strongly in Southern Africa than in other parts of the world. Practically all the human sub-species are represented here; differences between sub-species coincide with cultural, including socio-political differences, and these subdivisions (racial, cultural, political) have been in interaction here for 600 years or more. Racial mixing, cultural conflict, political grouping and regrouping, etc., have been taking place over a long period and have given rise to a complex situation in which it is hard to identify the respective roles of race and culture.

The complexity, which is rooted in history and tradition, is complicated still further by an unsatisfactory terminology, e.g. the generalized, unsystematic and indiscriminate use of terms such as race, ethnic group, nation, people, liberal, democratic, etc., in contemporary literature and thinking about South Africa. In the period before and during World War II it was customary to refer to the relations between Afrikaners and South Africans of British descent as race relations. Today this terminology is used principally for White/Non-White relations. Popular references to the Coloured race, Black races (meaning the respective Bantu peoples), people of British stock in South Africa, etc., are far removed from the scientific usage of race terminology and from the basic principles on which human relationships in the sub-continent have developed.

The foregoing outline of the development of nation states has shown that race classification is by no means the only or even the major determining factor in the 'race relations structure', although it is agreed that the Bantu, White and Asian populations exist as three clearly identifiable bio-genetic groups. Ethnic differentiation is largely a cultural process which has given rise to a variety of tribes, peoples or nations the world over, each with its own particular identity and its characteristic cultural features. The process was facilitated by long residence of a group or a tribe, etc., in a defined geographical area. It is under such conditions of relative isolation that a national identity emerges, which is different from those of peoples of other regions, apart from the fact that they have a common racial origin.

The Afrikaners, for example, have emerged as a distinct ethnic group over a period of almost two and a half centuries. They lived together in comparative isolation from Europe at first and moved towards their republics in the north subsequently, where they maintained a way of life apart from that of the British colonies to the south and the east. The Afrikaner identity has survived in spite of the fact that there are many other White people in South Africa – people of diverse cultural origin but racially of the same sub-species.

The Coloured people on the other hand, have a diverse racial origin. They live predominantly in the South and Western Cape, and have most of the features of a people in the early stages of differentiation. The Bantu and Indian populations in these predominantly Coloured regions are small, and the White population has been declining now for several decades, relatively on the whole, but absolutely in certain regions. These circumstances will favour the development of an identifiable ethnic group.

The Bantu nations have a common racial origin. Their history of ethnic differentiation has stretched over more than one and a half centuries and has therefore reached an advanced stage. The emergence of a Zulu national identity played a major part in the location and character of most of the other peoples and it may be of value to give a brief outline of its history at this stage.

Not more than 160 years ago a large number of small Nguni tribes lived side by side in the area known as the Natal province of the Republic of South Africa. One of these tribes, under its chief, Shaka Zulu, adopted a policy of expansion around 1810 and subjected one tribe after the other to its power until the authority of Shaka Zulu was recognized by practically all the Nguni tribes of the Natal region.

The process of Zulu nation-building was facilitated greatly by the military system of drawing young people of all tribes into the regiments as well as by the fact that cultural differences between tribes were small. Language differences have disappeared almost altogether. Those who refused to accept the authority of Shaka Zulu had to move far out of his reach and several of the tribes aligned themselves to form new national units in entirely different territories far removed from Kwazulu.[3]

Some of the Nguni tribes in Natal, for example, fled towards present-day Lesotho to combine with Sotho tribes under Moshoeshoe I and grew into a South Sotho nation. Moshoeshoe was a strong ruler who, not unlike Shaka, was able to gather a large number of small groups under his authority successfully. Other tribes fled to Mozambique under Soshangane to start a Shangaan people, which in turn resulted in the Shangana-Tsonga people of South Africa. A few tribes joined the Fingo of the Ciskei and a number moved northwards to form the Matabele of Rhodesia and the Ngoni of Malawi. This northward movement also unsettled and redistributed the Tswana, Northern Sotho and other tribes in the northern and western parts of the Transvaal.

The expansive policies of Shaka Zulu thus influenced the political landscape of Southern Africa profoundly. They gave rise to the emergence of a cohesive Zulu nation, numerically stronger than any of the other nations south of the Limpopo and with a strong sense of national pride. It is a people which is still striving towards greatness as a nation and which is now advocating the institution of Shaka Day as its national day.

Indirectly, Shaka's policies also influenced the rise of almost every other nation in Southern Africa. Settlement and resettlement of tribes took place; tribes were compelled to join forces to protect their respective identities and their national territories; and they had to seek the protection of Afrikaner or British authorities. The more settled conditions brought about by Afrikaner and British powers during the latter parts of the nineteenth century, and especially development since the transfer of power to the Union Government in 1910, have made it possible for the various peoples and cultures to consolidate themselves in their respective national territories.

Trends in Southern Africa are, therefore, not as unique as they may appear from a distance. They are not contrary to world trends and they are not heading for revolution any more than those in any other part of the world. Relationships in this sub-continent are built on the principle of recognizing the right of a people to maintain its identity and to strive towards sovereign independence in its own fatherland. The practical appli-

3. Cf., J.S. Malan, 'The Rise of the Zulu Nation and its possible future Development'. Lecture to the S.A. Bureau of Racial Affairs, July, 1971.

cation of this principle can be seen in the appearance of more and more nation states, starting with the Union of South Africa in 1910, then Botswana and Lesotho in 1966 and Swaziland in 1968. It can also be seen in the rapid progress towards political emancipation of the remaining non-independent states in recent years, viz. the Transkei, Ciskei, Bophuthatswana, Qwaqwa, Lebowa, Venda, Gazankulu and Kwazulu.

Relationships which were characterized by dominant and subordinate peoples – Britain and her former Protectorates and the Republic of South Africa and her presently non-independent peoples – have changed and are still changing towards international relationships – relationships between good neighbours. It is envisaged that a commonwealth relationship will develop between the already independent and the emerging states in the sub-continent which will provide the machinery for handling matters of common interest. The commonwealth ties will be characterized by respect for the sovereignty of each nation in internal affairs.

The political development outlined above has progressed so far that some form of commonwealth arrangement is already a practical proposition. As it was possible for Malta, the former Federation of Rhodesia and Nyassaland and others to be members of the British Commonwealth while they were still dependent, so it seems feasible that the developing nations in South Africa can be drawn into an international relationship which has the expressed purpose of promoting the advancement of all concerned. Such a relationship will be especially valuable for advancing the economic progress of the respective countries. It is a general ideal to move towards an urban-industrial type of economy so that living levels may be raised, that political status may gain a fuller meaning, and that the realization of national ideals may be facilitated.

The Crux of the Race Problem in South Africa

Ellen Hellmann

The author holds a D.Phil. from the University of the Witwatersrand and is an internationally recognized authority on South Africa's urban Africans. She has many publications to her credit, most of which deal with the urban African. A past-president of the South African Institute of Race Relations and chairman of its general purposes committee, she was awarded the medal for dedicated service to Africa in 1970 by the Royal Africa Society.

Crucial to any attempt to resolve the race problem in South Africa, as I see it, is the preparedness of the majority of the 3,8 million Whites to realize and to accept that South Africa is, by reason of its historical development, its present population composition and distribution, and its economic structure, destined for all time to be a multi-racial society; that its present discriminatory political, economic and social structure cannot be maintained, and that radical changes on a broad front will have to be made to accommodate this multi-racial population on a basis of greater justice.

I refer only to the Whites in this context not because they have a monopoly of racial prejudice,[1] and not even because they alone have the political power to bring about peaceful change, but because by inclination, by customary usage, and by their constant exposure to the official dogma of separate development, they are the one racial group which evades, and is encouraged to evade, this realization. The Africans in South Africa, unlike those in the newly independent countries in sub-Saharan Africa, do not envisage South Africa as an all-Black country. They regard the

1. The worst racial riots in recent South African history occurred in Durban in 1949, when Africans rioted against Indians and 142 lives were lost.

Whites as a permanent and indispensable part of the social universe. Both the Coloured and the Indian leaders are unequivocally committed to non-racialism. Moreover, by the very nature of their vulnerability as minority groups midway in the South African racial hierarchy, they can have no other goal than to become full citizens of one South African nation.

South Africa has been compared with other colonial powers, with this difference : that her colonial subjects lived within the physical boundaries of the mother country.[2] The general apparatus of colonialism, as it had developed by the twentieth century, had likewise evolved in South Africa. People of European descent ruled the indigenous peoples, who were admitted into the White dominated society to the extent that they were required as low-paid workers. In the post-war era, the culmination of those changes, which elsewhere led to the dismantling of empires and the liquidation of colonialism, did not leave South Africa unaffected. Until then, segregation had been the name given to South Africa's racial policy, a system of White domination and privilege. During the war years, this policy had increasingly been subjected to reassessment. General Smuts, as early as 1942, publicly acknowledged the need for change, and in his 1948 election campaign committed his party to accepting certain recommendations of the Fagan Commission[3] which, while they certainly did not herald an end to racial discrimination, did offer substantially increased rights to urban Africans.

Instead, South Africa opted for the National Party's policy of apartheid. This differed from segregation in the weight it gave not only to safeguarding White racial identity, but to preserving the identity of the different Non-White peoples and encouraging them to develop their own national ethos. This was the first response to the manifest need to modify a policy of undisguised White supremacy. Whether voters appreciated this subtle refinement I, for one, doubt. I believe they voted then, as they have since, for the continuance of the comfortable status quo : comfortable, that is, for Whites, each one of whom, without exception, benefits from the existing system. An important change in policy and in emphasis came in 1959, when the concept of eventual independence for the Bantu national units was born. Apartheid was out : separate development was in.

Since then the theoretical basis of the policy has been elaborated, and

2. See Leo Marquard, *South Africa's Colonial Policy,* Presidential Address, S.A. Institute of Race Relations, 1957.

3. *Report of the Native Laws Commission,* 1946-8, U.G. No. 28, 1948.

rapid progress has been made in building the political structure for limited self-government in the traditional African homelands. More and more stress has been laid on what I think can fairly be called the sanctity of the concept of separate development, on this 'transcendental principle',[4] on assertions that this implies only differentiation, recognition of differences which have to be respected and preserved, but no judgment of worth. Addressing the U.N. in 1964, the Minister for External Affairs explicitly rejected 'the idea of domination by any one nation over another' and affirmed that of 'equality and mutual respect for human dignity'. He said, 'The crucial difference (between South Africa and other countries with multi-racial populations) is this – that our task in South Africa is not primarily that of solving a problem of races, it is a problem of nations, a problem of bringing about a situation where peaceful co-existence of the various nations living in our country will be possible. We believe that this can only be achieved by the independent development of each people towards the full realization of its separate nationhood and the recognition of the right of each nation to govern itself in accordance with its own national traditions and aspirations.'[5]

Put in these broad terms, the moral basis of this approach appears to be unexceptionable. It could be taken to imply that the territory of South Africa is to be divided among these different nations: the 3,8 million Whites, the two million Coloured people, the 614 000 Asians, and the 15 million Africans divided into eight Bantu nations. But this is not what it means. What is planned is that the White territory will consist of over four-fifths of the total area of South Africa, with the Coloured and Asian 'nations' living in demarcated group areas widely dispersed within the White national homeland. The White 'nation' will have sole political control through its central legislature elected only by Whites, and consequently sole control of the country's fiscal resources. In the remaining 13,7 per cent of South Africa's land area, eight Bantu-African nations are to develop to ultimate sovereignty.

4. J.A. Lombard, in address to SABRA Congress on 'Homeland Development – a Programme for the Seventies,' p. 4, Port Elizabeth, 7 August, 1970.

5. Quoted from Prof. J.L. Boshoff, address at SABRA Congress, and printed in *Bantu,* December, 1970, Dept. of Information, Pretoria.

THE COLOUREDS AND ASIANS : AN APARTHEID DILEMMA

While the application of the concept of 'nation' to eight incipient African nations on the basis of linguistic criteria and certain cultural differences may have a certain, though I believe limited, validity, in the case of the other three 'nations' in South Africa – the White, the Coloured and the Asian – the label 'nation' is clearly an artifice to evade the unpalatable and morally embarrassing necessity of calling these groups what they are: namely, racial groups. Among the Whites there are tribes, at the very least the Afrikaners and the English-speaking group, probably more different from each other than the North Sotho and the Tswana, who are to become separate nations. The Asians consist of people with a multiplicity of languages, and marked cultural and religious differences. On any criteria other than those of descent and the physical characteristics of race – and these so difficult to define clearly that members of the same family have been classified in different racial categories in terms of the Population Registration Act – the Coloured people, 86 per cent of them Afrikaans-speaking, belong to the Whites from whom they are in part descended, and whose languages and culture they share.

The Government has acknowledged that it is not possible to provide national homelands for the Coloured people and the Asians. The Prime Minister, pressed to state how the Coloured people are to become a nation without a homeland, and how the problem of a White and a Coloured nation in one area is to be resolved, said : 'Our children after us will have to find a solution. We must now lay the foundation.' He was convinced that 'the development must be away from each other' and that the future did not lie in bringing the Coloured people into Parliament.[6]

But where does the future for the Coloured and Asians lie? The Government is adamant that it is not to be in integration. It also helplessly concedes that a national homeland is a geographical impossibility. The Minister of Coloured Affairs, confronted by this intractable choice, scuttles separate development and takes refuge in 'parallel development'.[7] Meanwhile the appearance of nationhood must be given. Accordingly an elaborate political structure is being tinkered into shape. Different types of local affairs committees, nominated consultative and elected management committees are being set up in the different Coloured and Indian group areas. Apart from those in the small town of Verulam, which has been pro-

6. *Hansard,* 1969, No. 1 col. 369.
7. *Rand Daily Mail,* 5 December, 1970.

claimed an Indian group area and has an all-Indian elected autonomous town board, and Pacaltsdorp, which has a similar Coloured local authority, all these local bodies are subordinate to, and dependent on, the White local authorities. The Coloured people of the Cape Province are to lose their municipal franchise rights in 1972. Eventually, so it is announced, independent town or city councils are to emerge in the Coloured group areas. Meanwhile, the administrative complications of setting up 'sub-budgets' for Coloured group areas, as the (White) local authorities have been asked to do, and trying to make the functions of what are basically powerless Indian and Coloured local bodies appear meaningful, are immense. And the Member who holds the portfolio of local government (budget R2 420 for 1969-70) on the Coloured Persons Representative Council has to await the recommendations of an inter-departmental committee of senior officials to find out what his functions are.

The Indians have been given a South African Indian Council consisting, at this stage, of 25 nominated members with advisory powers only. There is a Coloured Persons Representative Council consisting of 40 elected and 20 nominated members, with executive powers in respect of certain matters, such as education and community development, which will be financed from money made available annually by the South African Parliament – in which Coloured people are in no way represented. The first elections for the Coloured Persons Representative Council were held in 1969. Though the Labour Party (opposed to separate development) won 26 out of the 40 elective seats, the members nominated by the Government (which included 13 candidates defeated in the election, amongst them the man appointed to be Chairman of the Executive Council) put the Federal Party, which supports parallel development, into power.[8] Is it unfair to ask how this squares with the assurance that there will be 'no domination by any one nation over another'?

The brutal fact is that Brown-White relationships are regulated by apartheid pure and simple. The moral and practical untenability of this situation is coming into ever sharper focus in public debate.[9] Race dis-

8. For details, see Muriel Horrell, *A Survey of Race Relations in South Africa*, 1969, S.A. Institute of Race Relations, pp. 6 ff.

9. See *Rapport*, 3 January, 1971, for a discussion of conflicting views and a summary of an editorial in *Woord en Daad*, reflecting the views of the Afrikaans Calvinist Movement, which calls for clarification of government policy towards the Coloured people and stresses the unacceptability of the present policy.

crimination, particularly the results of large-scale uprooting[10] and compulsory resettlement under the Group Areas Act, is causing the Coloured people and the Indians immense hardship. It is officially claimed that there have been benefits in the form of slum clearance and improved housing. But these benefits could have been secured without destroying whole communities, compelling people to abandon long-established homes and businesses, and depositing them in new, often distant, undeveloped areas lacking in services and amenities. They could have been brought about without forcing whole peoples into an acute sense of continuing insecurity, exacerbated by the spectacle of group areas already proclaimed for Indians, as in Ladysmith and in Newcastle, being re-proclaimed as White group areas. But the Indian people, I believe, suffer less spiritual hurt under the present dispensation than does the Coloured community. Their roots do not go as deep in South African history and they can derive some support from being descendents of peoples of age-old cultures, rich in their heritage. But the Coloured people, particularly in the Cape where 85 per cent of them live, whose lives and destinies have always been inextricably linked with the White group, and whose loyalties to South Africa have been unshakeable, are being spiritually lacerated by the rejection they are now experiencing.

The occasions of colour discrimination are multiplying – beach apartheid, cultural apartheid, job reservation, discrimination in salary scales for jobs demanding equal qualifications, separate and inferior amenities. The humiliations are recurrent, as are the assaults on personal dignity. The hope the Coloured people formerly held of being accepted on a basis of personal attainment is fading. Despite the fact that their economic position is improving because of the shortage of White workers and the restrictions on Africans, anger, bitterness and anti-White resentment are growing.[11]

10. The number of families 'disqualified' by declarations made in terms of the Group Areas Act, which means being required to move, is, according to the Minister of Community Development: 1 578 White, 70 889 Coloured, 38 180 Indian and 933 Chinese. *Rand Daily Mail,* 5 February, 1971.

11. See Statement by Fred van Wyk, director of the S.A. Institute of Race Relations, warning of impending 'racial disaster', *Sunday Times,* 7 February, 1971.

SEPARATE AFRICAN NATIONS : DIVIDE AND RULE ?

The idea of bringing separate African nations into being has a territorial basis, although the fragmented nature[12] of the Bantu homelands raises problems as yet far from resolution, and a claim to ethno-cultural justification, far from unassailable though it is. The Transkei, for example, consists of a number of tribal groups, the overwhelming majority admittedly Xhosa-speaking, who were in the not so distant past at war with each other. A number of these tribal groups have, on the grounds of cultural differences, as good or as bad a claim to be regarded as separate 'nations' as other tribal groups now regarded as national units and allocated to separate homelands. But let this be. The fact is that the idea of Bantu nationhood has been made real. A wide network of vested interests in the new political structures has been created. A process has been set in motion which is probably now already irreversible. It may appear as feasible to carve eight African states out of South Africa's territory (and ten more in South West Africa) as to have a Lesotho, a Botswana and a Swaziland on its borders. In this connection it should be remembered that at the time of Union, and for long thereafter, it was believed that these three former British dependencies would become part of South Africa. The fact that racial discrimination in South Africa did not become less but, incorporated in discriminatory legislation, increased in scope and severity, ruled out any possibility that these territories might be incorporated in South Africa.

Regional and national loyalties are undoubtedly growing under the stimulus of government policies. Whether one is to call these loyalties national or tribal is clearly open to debate. Within a unified South Africa, divided loyalties are the equivalent of tribalism. In a divided South Africa, they become nationalisms. Elsewhere in Africa, the newly independent nations are struggling to subdue tribalism and to develop an over-riding national unity within their arbitrarily defined borders. But in South Africa, the national South African consciousness that was developing is deliberately being undermined and a fading tribalism is being revitalized. If divide and rule is the final objective, then success is undoubtedly being

12. The Tomlinson Commission said the homelands comprise some 280 separate areas (p. 46). In 1970, the Minister, in answer to a question in the House, said there were 81 'pieces of land' (not necessarily compact areas) constituting the homelands, Zululand alone having 29. In addition there are 'black spots' i.e. African-owned land surrounded by White-owned farms, which are earmarked for removal by voluntary sale or expropriation.

achieved. If one's vision is that of one South Africa, as mine is, then it is comfortless indeed to be the impotent spectator to tribal divisiveness making itself felt – even in the urban areas. In the predominantly modern industrial environment of the towns tribal origin was becoming irrelevant, until the government introduced it as a category of classification, compelling local authorities to house people in ethnic group areas, to conduct elections to the urban Bantu councils on tribal electoral rolls, and so on.

The dangers inherent in the creation of a multiplicity of new nationalisms which might well have been subsumed under one South African nationalism but which, once quickened into life, may become bitterly assertive, are obvious. I realize that in the world as a whole the two ongoing processes of Balkanization and of coalition, economic and political, on a regional and continental basis are not necessarily mutually exclusive. But to me it appears as the height of folly for a country, which has for the best part of a century functioned as one nation – and considered the advantages of Union sufficiently weighty to bring it into being despite the differences between its formerly separate constituents – to decide to hive off eight nations: and thereafter confront the problems of instituting a workable coalition – if indeed that is by then at all feasible.

THE TRANSKEI: BANTUSTAN PROTOTYPE

Meanwhile the ship of state appears to be heading full steam ahead towards the creation of new nations. However, though the public is being prepared by official Ministerial pronouncement for the 'ultimate possible independence'[13] of new African nations, the precise meaning of this independence has not, as far as I am aware, been spelt out. It would surprise me, and I believe it would be unacceptable to large sections of the electorate, if autonomy for the Transkei – apparently envisaged to be brought about soon – entailed the right to control its external relations, which is a logical correlate of genuine sovereignty. I am assuming that in this regard the Government is not contemplating the pattern of dominance exercised over its satellite states by the rulers of the Soviet Union. But if this is not the shape of things to come, then is the Transkei which, unlike the totally South African encircled and hence captive Lesotho, has a coast line of its own, to be free, for example, to negotiate with any foreign power to develop a port of its own, to grant air bases to a foreign power? At present the Transkei is

13. See 'Homelands Policy Outlined', *South African Digest,* 19 February, 1971, Department of Information, Pretoria.

dependent on South Africa for grants of R18,2 million towards its total estimated revenue of R23,9 million for 1970-1. Under present conditions this amounts to complete dependency. But within the framework of the international power struggle, and the means at the disposal of the major powers, this relatively paltry sum could easily be outbid to assist a fellow member of the U.N.

Nor has there been any agreement on the question of economic viability. Until now the African areas have been no more than rural slums neglected by successive governments. The people resident there, in the main engaged in farming on traditional lines based on communal tenure, cannot support themselves on their low output. The African areas have been, and still are, reservoirs of labour, dependent on the earnings of their migrant workers. Of the total population in the Transkei estimated to number 1 579 000 in 1967-8, 233 000 were migratory workers employed in the 'White' areas.[14] Their estimated earnings were R23 million, of which half found its way back to the Transkei. By mid-1969, only 42 401 were employed in the Transkei (excluding a small number of self-employed professional persons), of them roughly a third in government employ and a mere 1 280 engaged in manufacturing.[15]

Until a few years ago it was generally assumed that economic viability would be a prerequisite for political independence. Now official thinking appears to have changed. The Minister of Bantu Administration and Development has said that help would be required after independence had been attained, and spoke of future 'inter-dependent independence'. But Paramount Chief Kaiser Mantanzima, Chief Minister of the Transkei, is reported to have stated that 'his Government would not make any move to demand full independence until his country was economically independent.'[16]

Increasingly, the need to promote the rapid economic development of the homelands is coming to the fore and is being stressed by a number of Cabinet Ministers. Officials in the field are engaged in arduous and dedicated work to bring about agricultural rehabilitation and to stimulate other economic activities. Planners, academics, and other intellectuals,

14. A further 1 029 000 were permanently outside the Transkei but nevertheless regarded as 'citizens' of the Transkei, giving the Transkei what the Minister called a *de jure* population totalling 2 841 000. *Hansard,* 1969, No. 17, col. 7138.

15. Muriel Horrell, *A Survey of Race Relations in South Africa,* 1970, S.A. Institute of Race Relations, p. 138.

16. *Rand Daily Mail,* 16 January, 1971.

whose commitment to the ideal of separate development is as sincere as it is convinced, make eloquent pleas for sacrifice by the White community. Whether the electorate at large, which, like any other electorate, is unwilling to foot a bill likely to encroach on its own requirements, will be prepared to respond to these calls is extremely doubtful. But even those who most dauntlessly assail the problems of economic development in terms of actual population numbers and projections, have got no further than to plan, over the next ten years, for the provision of employment in industrial centres to be developed in the homelands and in border areas for the men actually resident in the homelands who reach the age of gainful employment within this period. Moreover, the realization of these plans depends on efforts of great magnitude involving large-scale expenditure, vision and co-operative White entrepreneurship. Even if all these forces are successfully mustered, at the end of a decade an estimated 410 700 men (the women are left out of account altogether) will find gainful employment in the homelands and border areas. But within the same period 478 700 men will reach working age in the White areas. No planner has suggested that they will be able to work anywhere but in the so-called White homelands.[17]

URBAN AFRICANS IN WHITE AREAS

This leads to what I am convinced is the heart of the problem: the treatment of Africans *outside* the Bantu homelands. And the order of numbers involved. In other words, postulating that, contrary to initial expectations, the necessary territorial adjustments are made, the economic development of the homelands is dramatically speeded, and eight fully independent fledgling Bantu nations are born, what then? Will South Africa then be securely set on the road to a reasonably equitable racial accommodation? It is my contention that the facts allow of no answer but an unqualified 'No': and that the emergence of a number of separate African states will in no way bring the resolution of South Africa's basic racial problems any nearer.

The total African population in 1970, according to preliminary census figures, was 14 893 000. Of these 7 975 000 (53,5%) were in the so-called White areas and 6 918 000 in the homelands. According to the Department of Statistics, the percentage in the homelands has increased during the

17. From tables prepared by P.J. v.d. Merwe, attached to paper by Professor J.A. Lombard, Pretoria University, given at SABRA Congress in Port Elizabeth, August, 1970.

past decade by 68,7%, while that in the White areas increased by only 16,8% – the overall increase in the African population being 36,3%.[18] Partly the greater increase in the homelands is accounted for by what is generally accepted to have been under-enumeration in the African homelands in 1960, and in 1970 in the urban areas because unknown, but certainly appreciable, numbers of Africans were there illegally. Partly it is due to the removal of Africans in urban townships in the White areas to towns in the homelands, to the compulsory removal of unauthorized dependants of men working in the White areas, and to the 'endorsement out' of widows, unmarried mothers, divorced and deserted wives and their children who have no urban residential qualifications, or cannot prove that they have them. Such people have had to move to resettlement areas in the homelands, usually not within daily commuting distance of centres of employment, which have earned themselves, not unjustifiably, the appellation 'dumping grounds'. In the vigorous drive to decrease the number of Africans in the White areas, 69 new homeland towns have been established, and more are planned. But despite what appears to be an impressive increase in the homeland population, the all-important fact is that there are eight million Africans in the White homeland as against less than four million Whites, a proportion of more than 2 to 1. And there are no grounds whatsoever to infer that this proportion will ever be substantially reduced.

'White' South Africa could not function for a day without the army of African workers to man its industries and commercial undertakings, its mines and services. In 1960, the number of Africans employed in the White areas was 2 342 371, excluding 548 317 employed in mining and quarrying (over 60 per cent of whom were foreign workers coming from countries outside the Republic). Since then, in a period of massive economic expansion, the figures have risen sharply.[19] In manufacturing, the number of Africans employed rose from 308 583 in 1960 to 615 700 by August 1970. Since then, too, African workers have increasingly moved out of purely unskilled work into operative and other semi-skilled categories of

18. Muriel Horrell, *op. cit.*, pp. 134-5.

19. Cf. series in *Sunday Times,* commencing 31 January, 1971, dealing with Non-White economic integration. The figures for 1970 show 1 283 000 Whites and 3 733 000 Non-Whites employed in all sectors of the economy, but excluding agriculture, i.e. Whites form 25,6% of the total labour force – a percentage that would be lower if the 778 725 African farm labourers and domestic servants employed (in 1963) on farms in the White area were included.

work. This has come about mainly because of job reclassification and 'placing more jobs outside the hierarchy to which the "closed shop" applies and from which Africans are automatically excluded because they may not belong to registered trade unions.'[20] Growth and diversification have taken place despite job reservation, despite the Physical Planning Act which prevents employers outside Natal and the industrial border areas from increasing their African industrial labour force without express permission, and despite strict influx control. One does not have to don a prophet's mantle to be able to state categorically that industrial colour bars will yield to the imperative need for increasing the number of African workers, just as they are now visibly breaking down as Coloured workers take on jobs in the building and other industries formerly reserved for Whites – for the simple and unanswerable reason that there are no Whites available to do these jobs. Faced by the inexorable choice between putting the economy into reverse and relaxing the colour bar, White self-interest finds itself better served by up-grading Non-Whites.[21] Government spokesmen, headed by the Minister of Labour, continue to proclaim, 'No economic integration'. If that means faithful obedience to the two basic South African commandments: Never shall a White man be subordinate to a Black man; and never shall a Black man get a job when a White man is available, it cannot be gainsaid. If it means that the South African economy is not irrevocably dependent on a racially mixed labour force, then the visible reality of factory and shop provides the living refutation.

But despite the indispensability of Africans to the economy of the White homeland, despite the fact that a growing proportion of the urban African population – which now numbers over four million – are second and third generation townsmen, ethnically inter-married and strangers to the homelands, their status in the White homeland is that of rightless aliens. Any White immigrant, from the day he sets foot in South Africa is accorded rights of employment, of freedom of movement and of association, to ownership of property, and of security of residence, which are denied to every African in the White areas, irrespective of his educational attainments and the length of time he and his forebears have lived in the White area.

20. Sheila T. van der Horst, *Progress and Retrogression in South Africa,* Presidential Address, 1971, S.A. Institute of Race Relations.

21. Cf. series of articles in *The Star* in February 1971 dealing with economic integration.

In 1960 there were three million Africans in the White rural areas, the overwhelming majority squatters, labour tenants or full-time agricultural workers on White-owned farms. The present numbers will be known when the census results are available. It is government policy to abolish both squatting (on White-owned farms and State lands) and the labour tenancy system (whereunder men work on a farm for part of the year, usually six months, in return for the right to live there with their dependants, and, generally, to run stock and cultivate a plot of land) in favour of full-time farm employment. At the end of 1968, there were 82 629 registered squatters, 7 301 having been resettled during the year. The number of registered African labour tenants at the end of 1969 was 24 957. During that year 3 380 had been found redundant.

While the desirability of gradually bringing into being a full-time African agricultural labour force is generally accepted, there is no doubt that the implementation of this policy is subjecting Africans to great hardship. A grave problem of homelessness exists, particularly in certain districts in Natal, where Africans evicted from farms 'are living in squalid shacks on the outskirts of Natal towns'.[22] Low productivity due to lack of training and, in some instances, inefficient White management and supervision, and the prevalence of low wages[23] form part of a vicious circle from which only some progressive White farmers and a small minority of efficient African farm workers have as yet found an escape. But compounding the problems of an African labour force in the early stages of training and development are the restrictions on freedom of movement and the status of rightlessness in the White homeland.

THE GOVERNMENT'S TREATMENT OF URBAN AFRICANS

The National Party came to power in 1948 pledged to regard Africans in urban areas as migrant workers, to arrest the process of detribalization, to control 'the entire migration of Bantu into and from the cities' by the State with the co-operation of local bodies, to return 'redundant Bantu in the urban centres to their original habitat', to permit the entry of Africans into the urban areas only as temporary employees compelled to return to their homes on the expiry of their employment, and to introduce what its 1948 manifesto called 'a convenient identification and control

22. Muriel Horrel, 1969, *op. cit.*, p. 102.

23. Cash wages (i.e. excluding accommodation, rations and other tangibles) according to the latest available Agricultural Census (1963-64) averaged R83 p.a., varying from R57,5 in the Orange Free State to R94 in Natal. Sheila T. van der Horst, *op. cit.*

system'.[24] In the intervening 23 years the National Party has elaborated this policy and has applied it relentlessly.

New and greatly increased controls over entry into the urban areas and the right to remain there were introduced in 1952, African women being included for the first time under what are usually called the pass laws. But briefly, the position is that no African may be in an urban area without a permit for more than 72 hours (onus of proof resting on him) unless he was born there, worked for one employer there for ten years or was lawfully resident in the area for 15 years, and in each case continued to reside there. The wife, son under eighteen years or unmarried daughter of such a qualified African may also be in the town provided he or she ordinarily resides with him and entered the area lawfully. This latter, obviously paradoxical, provision has over recent years been interpreted to mean that a married man whose wife is not already lawfully in the town will only be permitted to have his wife join him if she has herself acquired these qualifications in an urban area. Even such a residentially qualified African may lose his right to remain in the town if unemployed for a specific period, or in terms of one or other of the numerous regulations which can be invoked. But even these residential rights, already diminished, are recurrently rumoured to be under threat of extinction. An earlier draft Bill of the Bantu Affairs Administration Act of 1971 contained a clause extinguishing the qualifications whereby Africans could acquire urban residential rights. The ideal, it is bluntly reiterated by Government spokesmen, is that all African labour in the White areas should be there on a migratory basis.[25]

Clearly enough this 'ideal' demands that there be no addition to the residentially qualified urban African population from areas outside the towns. The 1968 Bantu Labour Regulations provide for this. They lay down that no African man – women are virtually prohibited from coming to a town to work – may leave his homeland unless, after registering with his tribal labour bureau, he has been offered and has accepted a specific job in the White area. Such contract workers are required to return to their tribal area on the expiry of the job or at the end of twelve months. Provision is made for the renewal of the contract, if employer and employee

24. D.W. Krüger, *South African Parties and Policies 1910–1960,* Human & Rousseau, Cape Town, 1960, p. 405.

25. For example, *Rand Daily Mail,* 5 February, 1971, reporting the Minister of Community Development.

both so desire, but the continuity of residence necessary to qualify for the right to remain in a town is broken.

Another means used to increase the proportion of migrant workers in the towns is the sharp reduction of loan funds for family housing to local authorities, which are responsible for the accommodation of Africans authorized to be in their area. The local authorities, which are in effect no more than agents of the central government Department of Bantu Administration and Development, are being subjected to strong pressure to make them confine their building to hostel accommodation for 'single' workers – or to agree to build houses for the families of their workers in the homelands, be they even as far as 400 kilometres away! Hostels for workers compelled to live under single conditions are being built, while the shortages in family housing mount. On the outskirts of Johannesburg, in an area 2,5 square kilometres in extent, the first few of the planned 12 barrack-like hostels are in the course of erection. Each hostel will accommodate 2 500 'single' workers, ten for men and two for women. Johannesburg has a housing backlog of over 13 000 for the families of legally qualified Africans. In Port Elizabeth the shortage of family houses is 12 000, and slum conditions are developing in townships once regarded as models. And it must be remembered that unless accommodation is available, even a legally qualified African is not permitted to have his family join him. But this process of the deliberate break-up of families with its attendant disruption of family life and the other all too predictable social consequences grinds on inexorably.

There has certainly been no attempt to camouflage the policy being followed in the White areas. The Minister put it plainly enough. 'In White areas here', he said, 'the Bantu are not being granted equality or potential equality with the White man in respect of any single aspect of social life whatsoever; not as far as the say as regards the government of this country is concerned, not as far as proprietary rights are concerned, not as far as labour status is concerned, not as far as social amenities are concerned; they have no potential or actual equality.' [26] Of actual equality the Minister need not have bothered to speak. There never was such. And the actions of his Department, both under his direction and that of his predecessor, have spoken louder even than his words in their systematic elimination of such potentiality for equality as existed. The rights of urban Africans,

26. *Hansard,* 3 February, 1970, No. 1, col. 117.

limited as they were before 1948, have since then been eroded to an extent that in 1948 would have seemed inconceivable.

Freehold rights to land have been extinguished. Townships where Africans owned land since the turn of the century and built their own houses have either been zoned as White group areas, or, as in Alexandra to the north of Johannesburg, are being cleared of family housing to make way for hostels. Three years ago a departmental directive ordered local authorities to stop the sale of houses on easy terms on leasehold land and of the home ownership scheme whereunder Africans in the higher-income group built their own homes on 30 years' leasehold plots – a body blow aimed at the emerging middle class, robbing them of incentive and security, and counteracting the stabilizing influence of home ownership. Traders have been limited to a one-man-one-site principle in the municipal African townships, have had their right to erect their own premises on leasehold plots taken from them, have been denied the right to form companies or enter into partnerships, and prohibited from establishing new dry-cleaning establishments, garages and filling stations. Local authorities were reminded that 'trading by Bantu in White areas[27] is not an inherent primary opportunity for them' and were told that Bantu traders must confine themselves to the provision 'of the daily essential domestic necessities'. 'Moneyed Bantu and Bantu companies and partnerships ought to establish themselves in the Bantu homelands.' [28]

The *quid pro quo* is citizenship of a homeland. A Bantu Homelands Citizenship Act was passed in 1970. It is not yet in operation, but when the necessary machinery has been set up, citizenship of a particular homeland, whether at the 'self-government' stage of the Transkei or at the territorial authority stage of the other national units, will be conferred on every African, regardless of his own wishes. Undoubtedly there are Africans who seek to express their national identity. But it is indisputable that many Africans, particularly townspeople, want no truck with this form of citizenship, the value of which eludes them – as, indeed, it eludes me. The only right this citizenship seems to give is the right to vote in a homeland with which these urban Africans have long ceased to have any connection.

The Act expressly denies that a citizen of a territorial authority area will be regarded as an alien in the Republic. He will be accorded full

27. This refers to trading in municipal African townships. Africans are not permitted to carry on any form of trade outside these townships.

28. Circular Minute No. A.12/1-A8/1, 14 February, 1963 from Secretary for Bantu Administration and Development.

protection by the Republic according to international law. In his second reading speech, the Minister undertook that 'such a homeland citizen . . . will be regarded as a South African citizen for purposes of foreign relations and protection. The Republic can also at any time, by way of legislation or administratively grant all kinds of privileges to the citizens of the Bantu homelands, such as opportunities for employment, residence and visits in the white homeland.' [29] It couldn't be clearer. South African citizenship for an African means the right to apply for a passport, and nothing more : everything else is privilege under suffrance.

There is, moreover, no provision for any form of naturalization. Immigration is reserved for Whites only.[30] Blacks are migrants-in-perpetuity. It is, I think, relevant to note the practice of those countries in western Europe with migrant workers drawn from countries with a manpower surplus, the example of which is officially quoted from time to time in justification of the South African dispensation. Switzerland, West Germany, Holland, Belgium and France all provide, on differing conditions, for naturalization; France after five years, providing there has been assimilation into the French community and knowledge of the French language is adequate. Western Germany, at the other extreme, makes naturalization possible only after 10 to 25 years, depending on the country of origin. It is also worth noting that not one of these countries totally bans the entry of the dependents of foreign workers.[31]

The theory that, by some means or other, the total African population can be attached to the homelands is nothing more than an extended exercise in make-believe. It is abundantly clear that the homelands, overcrowded and under-developed as they are, helplessly dependent on the export of labour, can never hope to do more than support their present population and its natural increase. Even this is a wildly extravagant hope, realizable only if extensive industrial development in the homelands and a vast acceleration in the establishment of border industries can be brought about. At this stage, ten years after the programme was introduced, the border industries give employment to some 110 000 Africans.

But the real evil stems from the two riders to the initial theory : that all

29. *Hansard,* 23 February, 1970, No. 1. col. 1787.

30. See the Minister's reply given to a question put in the House, whether only White immigrants are permitted to settle in the Republic? 'Yes, they must be of White descent.' *Hansard,* 2 July, 1970, No. 1. col. 91.

31. See Information Papers B1 and B2 prepared by the Runnymede Trust, Runnymede Industrial Unit, Background Notes, October 1970, for details.

Africans in the White area are to become migratory workers, and that urban Africans are in the towns on a temporary basis. The harmful economic effects are obvious. To attempt to meet the requirements of a modern economy, which needs an increasingly skilled and stable labour force, on the basis of migrant workers is a practical impossibility. But the extent of family disruption and social demoralization eroding the very fabric of African existence in the towns and villages and farms of White South Africa is less visible. 'The convenient identification and control system' pledged by the National Party in 1948 has over the years been moulded into a documentation and permit system of monstrous dimensions, administered by an ever-growing bureaucracy. Like a Kafka nightmare, it engulfs the eight million Africans in the White homeland, reaching into work and domestic life, governing the entry of a wife into a home and of a child into a school.[32] It has contributed to swelling the daily average number in prison, sentenced and unsentenced, to 88 979 for the year 1968-9. In the same year, 632 077 persons were sent for trial for infringements of the various Acts and regulations collectively known as the pass laws. They constituted 26,5 per cent of the total number of prosecutions of persons of all races, for all offences. This means that the number of prosecutions under the pass laws averaged 1 732 every single day of the year.[33]

The Press, particularly the English-medium newspapers, carry occasional reports of the operation of influx control and the human tragedies it causes. Individual cases suddenly impact on the public conscience and consciousness. But this is only the tip of the iceberg. A system of this nature, which conflicts with economic realities and defies the elementary principles of sound social development, must inevitably churn out victims. It is, moreover, my impression that it is the naïve more than the sophisticated, the ignorant and the illiterate more than the educated, and, above all, the poor, who find themselves helplessly ensnared in it. Inevitably too, a system of this nature, involving a vast army of officials, lends itself to bribery and corruption, and engenders the acceptance of illegality. The townships are corroded with corruption. The law itself is falling into disrepute. What moral stigma can be expected to attach to a prison sentence imposed under laws which carry the brand of discrimination? Increasingly White employer and Black employee are becoming accomplices in evading the law.

32. See *Memorandum on the Application of the Pass Laws and Influx Control,* The Black Sash, 1971.

33. Muriel Horrell, 1970, *op. cit.*, p. 164.

Illegality is contagious, and this contagion is disastrously evident in the African townships. I do not suggest that the high incidence of crimes of violence, the assaults and thefts and robberies, the consequent insecurity of life and property, are solely attributable to the system of oppression and injustice embodied in laws which no people could be expected to do other than reject. I do suggest that it is a potent contributory cause of the normlessness of present-day urban African society.

At this period of traumatic cultural transition, the State should be endeavouring to facilitate cultural adaptation to a modern urban environment, to protect the nuclear family units in the African townships in their poverty and in their striving to adapt to new roles and functions, and to encourage stability of residence and community development. Instead, it is following policies which conflict with all these needs and undermine growth processes already in being. This is, on my assessment, the poignant tragedy of the present position. There has been massive change and development. Millions of workers have adapted themselves to the requirements of a modern industrial system. An African middle class has emerged with broadly the same indices of status as those of the White middle class. It is developing a similar life-style, in general regarding the White middle class as its reference group. It functions as standard-setter for the whole community. There has been a preparedness, even an eagerness, on the part of the urbanizing[34] African community to accept and adapt to what is generally called Western culture.[35] This growth is being stunted by a government which tells the people concerned to look to their own, to value their own traditions and culture, not to stray into forbidden green pastures. It is small wonder that a Black Power movement, pregnant with the constructive possibilities of self-help and the explosive dangers of racial exclusiveness, is coming into being.

Former growth-points of inter-racial co-operation have been destroyed or forced into a twilight existence. Once there was active co-operation in the field of social welfare. Now it has been made impossible for multiracial voluntary committees to operate. The dictate is that each race group must conduct and control its own social services, and that those for Afri-

34. See F.v.Z. Slabbert, 'Modernization and Apartheid', in *Anatomy of Apartheid,* Spro-cas publications, No.1, 1970, for an analysis, applied to the Transkei, of the conflict between the requirements of modernization and the structure of traditional societies.

35. I elaborate these cursory generalizations in 'Social Change among Urban Africans' in *South Africa: Sociological Perspectives,* Eds. Heribert and Kogila Adam, O.U.P., 1971.

cans should operate mainly in the homelands. Homes for the aged and the handicapped have had to close or be re-located in the homelands, where White volunteers are denied entry. White advisory and finance committees are still allowed to function, but the main-spring of incentive has been destroyed. The loss in constructive inter-racial co-operation and understanding occasioned by this gross official interference is incalculable. So, too, in the field of the creative arts, the insistence on rigid apartheid has stultified development. The outcome of enforced isolation is cultural impoverishment. The implications of forbidding the existence of mixed political parties in terms of the Prohibition of Political Interference Act of 1968 speak for themselves.

The challenge to which the supporters of separate development have conspicuously failed to respond is to indicate how they visualize the destiny of the millions of Africans who will live their lives outside the Bantustans. The politicians in the National Party, who frame the laws, give no answer. Certain academics and others outside the ranks of the professional politicians make what I claim is the completely unwarranted assumption that, once the Bantustans have become independent, White fears of being swamped and of eventual Black political domination will diminish. That, they believe, will reduce the level of racial prejudice, make the relaxation of racial discrimination possible, and finally lead to its elimination. Why? With Whites constituting, as they do, only 26 per cent of the population of the White homeland, what grounds are there for such an assumption? Why, if the Bantustans of to-day become the sovereign African nations of tomorrow, will the White minority then be prepared to dismantle the structure of racial domination if it considers this structure necessary now for its protection and the exercise of its privileges? Why should this change alone act as the solvent of the basic problems of racial injustice, the existence of which these proponents of separate development do not deny?

I return to my contention that no matter how determined the efforts to camouflage South Africa's race problem under the guise of multinationalisms, it remains stubbornly, implacably and unyieldingly a problem of *race* relations. For South Africa, no less than for the other multiracial nations of the world, there is no magical solution to hand. South Africa will, together with mankind as a whole, have to rejoin the mainstream of human striving in the arduous endeavour to evolve a social structure in which all its peoples may develop and fulfil their innate potential as members of one nation.

Crucial Facets of South Africa's Race Problem

Willem van Heerden

Willem van Heerden was for many years one of South Africa's top newspaper editors. Currently retired, he is still an active writer and keen observer of the South African scene. An objective approach to race relations, and a constant call on South Africans as well as on critics of his country to adjust their thinking to the realities of the South African situation are features of many of his writings.

There are many crucial facets to what has popularly become known as the 'racial problem' of South Africa, and the relative importance of each depends largely on one's angle of approach. This is only to be expected when one of the most complex human situations of the present-day world is involved. Not man-made, not wilfully planned, but begotten by and inherited from centuries of bygone events, the human and political set-up at the southern end of Africa has developed into one of the greatest challenges to statemanship in all history. It is a situation that has unleashed some of the most ignoble of human passions and in the process South Africa has become the hapless pawn in the cynical game of international politics.

In the main, attacks on the White South African nation since the end of World War II have come from three sources.

Firstly, some of Africa's Black political leaders have been conducting a vendetta against the White governments of the South so clearly racist in nature that it defies every element of reason. Their campaign amounts to mere blanket condemnation directed at everything White, and does not distinguish between policies that have little in common. The commonwealth of free and equal nations that is the declared object of the Republic of South Africa, the communal equality that is Rhodesia's aim, and Portugal's policy of integration between White and Black citizens are equally unacceptable to these detractors, seemingly because of one common denominator – the three otherwise completely different policies are all intent on providing security in Southern Africa for Whites as well as for Blacks.

Whether this African censure is inspired by real hatred of Whites, or whether the leaders in question merely fan anti-White sentiment in order to divert the attention of their own peoples from the poverty, tribal animosities and other domestic problems that are still the fate of most of Africa, is not always easy to tell. What is fairly clear, however, is that the anti-White activities beyond the Zambesi have little relation to genuine concern for the Black people of the South.

After all, rulers who have to secure themselves by suppressing elementary liberties at home, can hardly convincingly condemn supposed violation of those liberties in lands far away. One of the most striking features of the political emancipation of Black Africa since 1960 has been the speed at which free institutions disappeared from the scene. Democratic constitutions, laboriously prepared for the evolving colonies in London and Brussels, have largely been ignored. In the greater part of what used to be British and Belgian colonial Africa, so-called 'one-party' governments (the African version of dictatorship) have now firmly entrenched themselves. The exceptions, strangely enough, are those states bordering on the Republic of South Africa. In Tanzania Dr Nyerere has even established a 'peoples' army' to protect his government against a possible *coup d'etat* by officers of the regular army, as happened in Uganda and elsewhere. And Dr Kaunda of Zambia has announced heavy penalties for even members of his own ruling party who henceforth criticize members of his government.

In the Republic of South Africa, by contrast, anyone of any colour can and does criticize freely, although activities to further Communism are illegal and sedition is, of course, punishable as everywhere else. It is, therefore, rather incongruous that the liberties of Black Africans who enjoy freedom of thought and speech, should have become the subject of concern to leaders of Black Africans who have no such freedom. It is also illogical for the leaders of peoples in the shackles of poverty and ignorance to rush from one Heads of State meeting to another on behalf of peoples who are comparatively well-off and who are advancing at a rate faster than any elsewhere on the African continent. It is significant that it is those Black African countries where steady progress has been a feature of independence, countries like the Ivory Coast and Ghana which have taken the lead towards establishing dialogue between Black Africa and White South Africa.

The Communist empires of Europe and Asia are the second source from which attack on South Africa is directed. There is good reason for the intense interest of these regimes in what happens in this country, although in this case it bears no closer relationship to humanitarian motives than it does in the subjected countries of Eastern and Central Europe. Remember the fleets of tanks that are kept constantly at the ready to patrol the streets of Budapest or Prague when these highly civilized peoples move to extricate themselves from under the heel of the oppressor. Real concern about the liberties of peoples many thousands of kilometres away is inconsistent with machine-gunning of Germans who reach for freedom by scaling the infamous Berlin Wall. Can genuine humanitarian interest in the Black peoples of South Africa come from a regime that forcibly detains Jews who wish to emigrate to Israel?

In South Africa everybody, White and Non-White alike, is at liberty to leave the country at any time should he or she prefer to live somewhere else. The only exceptions, totalling not more than a few hundred, are individuals who have been convicted in court or are being held under the security laws of the country.

The Communists' real concern about what is happening and what does not happen in South Africa derives from their only too obvious objective of establishing Communist domination over the whole of the African continent from Suez to Cape Point. To this end Moscow and Peking are vying with each other, and for this purpose they have found undeveloped territories populated by illiterate and impoverished masses with ambitious and vain rulers practically 'ready-mixed' material.

The exceptions are the sophisticated Western states at the southern end of the continent. These are hurdles the Communists do not expect to negotiate by diplomatic means. As a result they resort to every ruse they can think of to discredit the White governments of the sub-continent, and to isolate their settled Western communities. South Africa comes under heavier fire for reasons that are obvious. In the first place it is most generously endowed with natural resources; secondly, its strategic position is all-important from the point of view of control of the seas, and, finally, it is a serious competitor for diplomatic influence in Africa south of the Sahara.

Infinitely more difficult to understand than either African or Communist animosity, however, is the third source of attack on South Africa. This is the antipathy towards the White peoples of the sub-continent which has suddenly and unexpectedly sprung up during the past two decades amongst fellow Western nations in Europe and the New World.

It is not suggested that there is nothing wrong in South Africa or that there are not many things that will change (are in the process of changing, in fact). But whatever blame this country can be expected to accept for not solving its problems fast enough, fails to explain the severity of Western hostility that has descended upon it as if overnight. It would seem as if nothing that South Africa could have done would have averted the suddenness with which Western clerics, academics, and governments became conscious of the *abhorrence* of White authority in the African sub-continent. This is the term for which Western chancelleries have developed a noticeable preference – after White authority has existed here for well over three centuries!

Western governments, of course, and more particularly the great powers, have international considerations to take care of. It is not surprising, therefore, to find them going all the way to emulate the Communist drive for favour on the African continent. Part of 'going all the way' – the cheapest part – is to butter up African rulers by subscribing to their likes and dislikes in language as extravagant as that employed by Communist spokesmen. And it is perhaps only to be expected that Western statesmen should adjust their moral concepts to the dictates of diplomatic expediency.

What is surprising is the violent condemnations of the White people of South Africa and their policies which have come from pulpits, editorial chairs and debating chambers since 1945. And it is particularly puzzling when men of the cloth solemnly denounce South Africans, not as fallible humans, but as spokesmen of the Almighty. With many Church dignitaries it is almost a catch-phrase to call on Westerners' 'Christian conscience' to bear witness against South Africa. Similarly, Christians in South Africa itself are exhorted to 'obey God' rather than follow their country's policy.

One hesitates to sound disrespectful, but one must question the divine origin of ministrations that ally themselves so closely with changing political concepts. After all, moral values based on Christian teachings did not originate in the second half of the twentieth century. It was only then, however, that churchmen found South African political policy to be in conflict with these values. Colonialism, which prevailed in Africa for hundreds of years, never troubled the conscience of even the princes of the Church. Only after the political 'wind of change' since the Second World War and the leftist revolution started sweeping the world has the very presence of White men in Africa been denounced on Christian pulpits no less than on the Red Square.

Terrorists are being trained and armed by the Communist countries for the express purpose of sending them into South Africa, Rhodesia and the Portuguese territories to murder White families and to disrupt order. Hardly a word of protest is raised against this in the West. But mere mention of the sale of arms to South Africa is enough to outrage 'world opinion', with the Organization of African Unity, Communist governments, Western socialist parties and the World Council of Churches united in uproar. There is only one possible inference to be drawn from this – most Western opinion, Church opinion included, would approve of armed Non-White, and if need be non-Christian, insurrection against an unarmed White government and defenceless White communities. Such is the degree to which Western Christian values seem to have been affected by the 'wind of change' blown up by the Second World War.

One hesitates to succumb to cynicism, no matter how strong the temptation may at times tend to become. For it would be tantamount to loss of faith in mankind not to accept innate sincerity also amongst South Africa's detractors. After allowing for an obvious amount of prejudice and also the degree to which Western thinking has been influenced by leftist intellectuals during the post-war years, one has still to look for another explanation of the double standards that seem to be applied whenever this country is concerned. How does one explain the strange phenomenon of people who are horrified at the thought of a murderer being hanged in Europe, calmly and purposefully assisting towards planned murder of peaceful White families in Africa?

And that leads straight to what must undoubtedly be considered if not *the* crux, one of the crucial elements of South Africa's 'racial' situation – its unfathomableness from a distance. It is well-nigh impossible to acquire a real understanding of the South African scene without first-hand acquaintance with it and its background. A famous Dutch editor once told me: 'When I arrived here a month ago, I had a ready answer to all your problems. After a fortnight I began to feel less certain. Now, quite frankly, I no longer know.' It is an experience that has been shared by many an open-minded visitor to South Africa.

Lack of knowledge and understanding did not prevent the world at large from drawing its conclusions, however. Those with hostile intentions invented pictures of the situation in South Africa to suit their purpose. The Communists (and their fellow-travellers elsewhere) have purposely drawn a picture as repulsive as possible to Western minds. Hostile African politicians rely on artificial comparisons with former colonial territories elsewhere on the continent and talk of South Africa as a country still to be 'liberated'.

But the most harmful of all the erroneous impressions about South Africa are those which have been doing the rounds in Western countries since 1950. The impressions are partly produced by the fruitful imaginations of the ignorant, partly created by biased reporting in profit-hungry news media, but are for the most part brought about by wrongly equating the South African multi-national situation with the bi-racial structure of the United States. This comparison with the totally different situation in America has resulted in a completely false picture in many Western minds of the South African problem. It has also resulted in failure to distinguish between the long-term aims of South African policy and certain current social practices, generally lumped together under the label 'apartheid', which have their roots in history and are real enough, but inevitably destined to disappear.

It would make for a better appreciation of the real situation if the distinction were sharply drawn. South Africa, it needs to be stressed, has never been a country with a politically integrated population consisting merely of Coloureds and Whites, with the White minority the ruling class, and the Coloureds a suppressed and downtrodden majority. The country's population is a community, not of individuals but of peoples, consisting of a White nation, eight separate Bantu nations, nearly two million Coloureds (persons of mixed blood) and some half-a-million Indians. The Cape Coloureds and the Indians will be dealt with presently. Let us first consider the position in respect of the Whites and Blacks.

Basic to a proper understanding of the South African set-up is an appreciation of the fact that the present Republic of South Africa is not the outcome of colonialism in the sense that a distant White power has imposed its authority over a local Black people or peoples. Although the settling of parts of South Africa by Whites was the outcome initially of

Dutch and afterwards British colonial rule, both have long since disappeared from the scene. The resultant White nation has never at any time employed force, with the sole purpose either of establishing colonial authority over Black peoples, or of conquering territory that belonged to the latter.

Space permits of only a very brief account of how this White African nation came into being, and of the events that established its present relationship with its Black neighbours. What follows are therefore only the broad outlines of the story. Both the White and Black peoples of South Africa are settlers from elsewhere, the Whites coming from beyond the seas, and the Blacks crossing the frontiers from the north. Both arrived during comparatively recent times, the Blacks preceding the Whites in some parts of the country, and vice versa, an important fact to bear in mind. Available evidence has it that the forebears of the present Bantu nations, or some of them at any rate, were the first to arrive on what is now South African soil, but history is not clear on how far these Black immigrants had penetrated southwards by the time the first Whites arrived at the Cape in 1652 and started their advance northwards and eastwards. What is known, is that the Blacks advancing from the north, and the Whites, advancing from the south, first met more than a century later at the Great Fish River in the Eastern Cape Colony. Here the contact led to a series of what later became known as 'Kaffir Wars', which resulted in no more than halting both advances. On the whole the point of first contact remains to this day the dividing line between White territory to the west and Bantu territory to the east.

At the northern and north-western frontiers of the present Cape Province there was no contact between White and Black prior to 1836, the year of the Great Trek of Whites into the interior, almost two centuries after their forebears had first set foot on the sub-continent. It was this exodus from the erstwhile Cape Colony that brought extensive contact between nations of different colours in South Africa. On the whole, the contact was peaceful. Apart from two severe battles there were only occasional skirmishes as a result of what was called 'punitive expeditions' following stock thefts on a big scale. Minor adjustments excepted, the establishment of the present homeland pattern took place without the use of force between White and Black. Both contributed to the extermination and expulsion of the Bushmen, a Khoisan race of wild little men who dwelt in the caves and hunted on the plains of the sub-continent before the arrival of either Whites or Bantu, and whose complete inability to distinguish between game and stock made them unacceptable neighbours to both. But never were the rights to land as established through occupation by Blacks violated by Whites.

It is true, of course, that the White pioneers of 1836 settled in country which had previously been occupied by Black peoples. When these Voortrekkers, as they have since become known, moved in, however, the territory, comprising many thousands of square kilometres, had been vacated long before their arrival. This happened as a result of one of the bloodiest events in history – the so-called *Mfecane* during the first decade of the nineteenth century.

At that time a man of destiny became chief of a small tribe called the Zulu in present-day Natal. Savagely ambitious and a military genius, Shaka transformed his peaceful tribe into a mighty war machine. Within a matter of years it attacked and destroyed all human life within its reach practically as fast as its armies could march. An offshoot of Shaka's military empire, led by a run-away commander called Mzilikazi, fled across the Drakensberg and repeated the human slaughter amongst the peaceful Sotho, Tswana and other communities in the present-day Orange Free State and Transvaal. As a result when the White Voortrekkers arrived, thousands upon thousands of square kilometres of land were covered with no more than the bones of the two tyrants' victims to tell the tale.[1]

The White newcomers to this land were also attacked by the armies of both Mzilikazi and of Shaka's successor, Dingane, but both were defeated and their military power destroyed. The former moved across the Limpopo River into present-day Rhodesia where he founded the Matabele nation. In Natal the Whites took possession only of that portion of the present

1. Professor Omar-Cooper of the University of Zambia who has made a special study of the *Mfecane,* has this, *inter alia,* to say about it: 'The colossal upheaval was accompanied by carnage and destruction on an appalling scale. Whole tribes were massacred and even more died in the famine and anarchy which followed in the wake of the desolating hordes. Still greater numbers abandoned their ancestral lands and sought refuge in difficult mountain country or elsewhere where geographical features held out hope of asylum. The pattern of the population distribution in South Africa was radically changed.'

province that Dingane had ceded to them by freely negotiated treaty before the defeat and destruction of his army.[2]

This, very briefly, is how the settlement pattern of the area south of the Limpopo came to be established. The Cape Province as far as the Fish River, those parts of the present-day Orange Free State and the Transvaal that were occupied by the Voortrekkers after having been laid waste by the armies of Shaka and Mzilikazi, and Natal without Zululand became what is now the homeland of the White South African nation. The Black nations are in possession of homelands stretching in a horse-shoe pattern round this White area. These Black homelands consist of, amongst others, the Ciskei, the Transkei, Lesotho, Zululand and Swaziland in the east, the Tswana homeland in the northern Transvaal, with Botswana completing the 'shoe' in the west. Of these, Lesotho, Swaziland and Botswana, formerly British protectorates, are now fully independent, the Transkei is on the way to independence and the others have reached various stages of development towards the same goal.

Some acquaintance with this background is essential in order to appreciate how utterly untenable any comparison of the South African situation with that of the United States must necessarily be and why South African policy, to be correctly understood, must also be dissociated from the concept 'colonialism'. Decisive to the issue is that in the course of the centuries a White nation has developed on the southern end of the African continent with an identity distinct from that of any other nation, White or Non-White.

Even then if there had been no more to the problem than merely distinction between a White nation and a homogeneous Black nation, the White South African nation would still have been entitled to the same right as that which every other nation on earth justly claims – to maintain the composition that determines its national character, and to protect its political independence against both physical violence and being overwhelmed by an unlimited intake of foreign elements. If poets sing the

2. Dingane entered into a treaty with the Pioneer leader Pieter Retief in which he ceded to the Voortrekkers land south of the Tugela River down to the sea on condition that they retrieve cattle stolen from the Zulus by Sikonyela, a chief from beyond the Drakensberg Mountains, out of reach of Dingane's armies. Retief retrieved the cattle but on delivering them, he and 70 of his men were overpowered and brutally murdered. Dingane thereupon attacked a number of unsuspecting and isolated Voortrekker camps and men, women and children were butchered. Several hundred White immigrants were killed before the remainder could organize themselves and defeat Dingane's army at what has since been known as Blood River.

virtues of nations who have, and still are, prepared to face death in order to protect their own identity and freedom, by what virtue are South Africans condemned by all manner of men in the world at large when they refuse to freely and meekly surrender both?

There is, however, as already indicated, more to it than merely a question of Whites as distinct from a homogeneous mass of Non-Whites. Not only has a White nation developed and established itself in South Africa, but so too have the different Black nations of the sub-continent maintained their historic separate identities.

Admission of this is to be found in the separate freedoms that Britain has granted to her three former dependencies. For it was merely incidental that Swaziland, Lesotho and Botswana remained under the authority of Britain after 1910, and that the Transkei, Zululand and other Bantu territories came to be administered by South Africa. Put differently, South Africa is not inhabited by an atomistic conglomeration of individuals, but by a complex of historic Black and White nations, the one hardly less conscious and less proud of its identity than the others. A far cry then from the simplistic conception of a 'minority' White government suppressing a 'voteless' Black majority.

For these different nations to be suddenly transformed into a single workable democracy is unthinkable to anyone with any real knowledge of South African conditions and not pre-occupied with ideological theories. It cannot be done with the Blacks alone, let alone together with almost four million Whites, two million Coloured and half-a-million Indians. The only change that could possibly be effected, would be replacement of what is now called 'minority' government by a Non-White dictatorship. But as no possible dictatorship of this nature would have enough support to maintain itself and to maintain order, any attempt at change, if successful, could only succeed in creating chaos.

The central fact about the South African situation is that there is not, and never has been, a single political nation. National identities and national boundaries have always existed and still exist. By arrangement in 1910, some of the Bantu national territories came to be administered by the White South African Union while some continued to be ruled by Britain, but in both cases their separate national existences have been respected, and in both cases they have been prepared and are being prepared for national independence, in the same way as has happened with colonial dependencies elsewhere on the African continent.

Also, as a result of the origin of the different homelands by means of occupation at the dawn of contemporary South African history, problems of consolidation still have to be faced by the White and the Non-White governments concerned. This is the subject of study by a committee of experts at the present moment. Consolidation of homelands into geographic units is not the only problem. Equally, if not more important is the underdeveloped state of the homelands, those formerly ruled by Britain as well as those administered by South Africa. The Whites have in the past concentrated on the development of their own territory, while the Blacks have shown little interest in the economic development of their homelands. They have preferred to sell their labour to the Whites. Ten years ago, however, the emphasis of Government policy shifted almost completely from growth of the White metropolitan areas to industrial development of the Bantu homelands themselves and the White areas bordering on these homelands. These bordering areas aim at providing work for neighbouring Bantu close to their homes, thus not only assuring them of an income, but stimulating primary, secondary and tertiary industries in the Bantu homelands.

The large numbers of Bantu who, for more than a century, have moved from their own areas (not only those administered by South Africa but also from Lesotho, Swaziland, Botswana, Rhodesia, Malawi and Zambia) to sell their labour to and settle as labourers amongst the Whites, now pose economic and political problems. Some of these people have lived in the White area for generations, although many have retained the links with their homelands and maintained the 'tribal' or national ties.

It is important to note that these peoples were admitted as labourers, not as immigrants. No matter how shortsighted it may have been, they were rarely, if ever, looked upon by their White employers as potential citizens. Nor did they so regard themselves. As a result their descendants were left in mid-air by subsequent political and economic developments. Only one White political party has come to accept the idea that these Bantu expatriates have to be absorbed into the White body politic. This party enjoys the support of probably less than ten per cent of the White population, however. As the application of its policy must inevitably lead to abandonment of political control by the Whites in favour of a Black majority, it is extremely unlikely that the policy will ever find favour with anything near a majority of White voters.

The alternative being applied by the present Government is to arrange that these Bantu acquire extra-territorial citizenship of their respective homelands, and consequently the protection of their home governments. While a considerable percentage of the White population is not sure how this will work, it is difficult to visualize any other practical solution that would be compatible with democratic practices. South African political leaders and thinkers have repeatedly pointed out that the concern of the policy of separate development is not only with territorial borders but also with the borders of national consciousness. In 1965 the late Dr Verwoerd defined it thus: 'The basic standpoint is that the Bantu and the Whites will have their political future apart from one another; territorial separation is important, but not the crux of the policy of separation.' And recently the editor of the bi-quarterly journal *RSA World* described it as a policy based on 'the recognition of nationhood and citizenship as something transcending geography, . . . as something which belongs to and cannot be separated from each and every member of the nation wherever he may live and move and have his being'.

It is a conception that has its shortcomings from the White as well as from the Non-White point of view and it may be without precedent, but neither has the situation that has to be dealt with a counterpart.

The South African political set-up is further complicated by the presence of two groups that do not fit easily into the homeland pattern. These groups are the Coloureds and the Indians, domiciled largely in the Western Cape and Natal respectively. They constitute a different problem. Their histories and backgrounds, the attitudes of other population groups towards them and the variety of views held by politicians (and others) about their place in the sun, warrant, if not a separate volume, then at least a separate chapter. Here it will have to suffice to state that, even if they do not fit in readily, it is more than likely that these two groups will ultimately be politically and economically accommodated with the Whites. This will have to happen, if for no other reason – and there are other reasons as well – than that there is no other way. They, and especially the Coloureds, are far too important a part of South Africa's peoples to remain wandering, politically speaking, in some sort of no-man's land between Blacks and Whites.

Failure to distinguish sufficiently between the original Black settlers and these Non-White population groups that are by-products of White South Africa's history, is perhaps the weak point of present South African policy. As I have already said, however, some facets of the South African situation must inevitably change and are in the process of changing. Most in need of change, it would probably be correct to state, are the basic attitudes of the different colour groups towards one another, i.e. of Coloureds towards Blacks, and vice versa, as well as that of Whites and Blacks towards each other. There are historic reasons for these time-honoured attitudes. Since their initial contact, for example, there has been a master-servant relationship between White and Black. For generations Whites have come to associate a Non-White skin with dependence and servitude, and Non-Whites have looked upon a White skin as the hallmark of authority that had either to be resisted or obeyed. Both these historic attitudes have to be replaced by a new approach to each other as fellow-Africans if there is to be a happy settlement of the complex human situation that is their common heritage from what has gone before. Responsible opinion, both White and Non-White, actively encourages the breaking down of mental attitudes that clearly can have no place in a peaceful Africa of the future. But much has still to be done. And it takes time. Americans, surely, should need no convincing of the time it takes to bring about fundamental changes in human relationships established through the centuries.

It takes time, and what is equally important, it requires a readiness to accept realities. The differences between the peoples of South Africa, not only the differences between Blacks and Whites, but also the differences between the divergent Non-White nations and communities cannot simply be erased, either by internal policy or by outside pressure. Union into a single democratic nation of human elements so profoundly different and so conscious of difference as is the case in South Africa, cannot be pulled out of the conjurer's hat, or dictated from theorists' armchairs. Outsiders who insist on this type of solution, only succeed in retarding real progress, because of the atmosphere of make-believe that they create, the confused thinking that they give rise to and the consequent resistance to any change which they cause to develop.

Neither would it be a solution to merely reverse the roles, i.e. by substituting the present White government with a Black dictatorship. However much such a change might suit those with ulterior motives outside South Africa, it would certainly benefit nobody in the country itself, White, Black or Brown. It would, in fact, not even benefit whoever the prospective dictator might be, because in South Africa's circumstances he would be unlikely to outlast his first months of office.

The Fabric of Apartheid

The Rationale of Separate Development

C. P. Mulder

The Honourable C. P. (Connie) Mulder, M.P., is one of the top half-dozen leaders in the National Party hierarchy. Young by Parliamentary standards, he is expected to play a major role in shaping the political future of South Africa. Connie Mulder is a natural leader, a good debater and brilliant politician. Endowed with the charismatic qualities that come naturally to popular leaders, he might easily one day become Prime Minister of his country. He holds a Ph.D. from the University of South Africa and is at present Minister of Information, Social Welfare and Pensions in the South African Government.

The opponents of South Africa's policy of separate development usually base their criticism on the contention that it is by its very nature racialistic and oppressive and designed to favour the White population at the expense of the other ethnic groups. Far from this being the case, it is in accordance with both the wording and the spirit of the United Nations Charter, when it speaks of the self-determination 'of peoples', in that it respects the identity and dignity of the diverse peoples of the Republic and seeks to lead them each and all to a state in which they may competently manage their own affairs.

Furthermore, in the unique conditions obtaining in South Africa, separate development is the only policy yet devised which meets the situation. The various alternatives based on unitary government and a common franchise for the whole country cannot but end in chaos, which all right-thinking men wish to avoid. In other words, the policy is not based on ideology but on pragmatism.

That is why the majority of South Africans, White and Non-White, takes strong exception to the fact that many people in other countries are not even prepared to try to find out what the policy of separate development is, and what it aims to achieve. Many foes, and even well-meaning friends, accept as a foregone conclusion that this policy is oppressive, abhorrent and inhuman, without ever having made a real study of it. They base their attitude on superficial impressions which they have gathered from the sensational, one-sided, negative reporting of mass news media.

This policy is accepted every day by more and more South Africans of all racial groups, as was clearly demonstrated by the latest election results in the Transkei, where the Xhosa people, in the Transkei as well as in the urban areas of South Africa, voted in favour of Mr Kaiser Matanzima's party on a basis of universal suffrage. The policy of separate development was one of the main issues during his election campaign, while his opponent supported the policy of integration.

Why should a policy be abandoned if its ultimate aim is to safeguard the national identity of separate nations in free and sovereign states with full independence and self-determination in every sphere of life? Why should a policy be totally rejected if it encourages each individual, in his own country, to develop to the maximum of his abilities, and opens new avenues of progress to him?

The hard core of the problem lies in the diversity of South Africa's population. There are not just two peoples, as some imagine, one Black and one White, the former indigenous, the latter immigrant, but a mosaic of many different and distinct peoples of whom all but a mere handful are immigrants.

Prior to the seventeenth century, South Africa was very sparsely populated by Cappoid peoples, totally distinct from the mixed Negro-Hamitic stocks, now known as Bantu, who came from the north. The Cappoids were yellow-skinned people who included the Bushmen and Hottentots Van Riebeeck encountered when he landed at the Cape in 1652. They exhibited many Mongoloid characteristics – broad, high cheek bones, slanting eyes with epicanthic folds, short statures and very short legs. They spoke Khoisan languages whose characteristic clicks were adopted by some of the Bantu as they advanced southwards and absorbed more and more Cappoid blood.

Though the Cappoid peoples were once widely but sparsely dispersed over vast areas of the African savannah, very few now remain. As a primitive hunting and gathering people, they could not stand up to the

Bantu pastoral and agricultural tribes. Those not slaughtered or absorbed by the Bantu migrating south, retreated before them, often into inaccessible arid regions where some of their descendants, the present Bushmen, still live.

Another branch of the Cappoid peoples, the Hottentots, who were pastoralists, occupied parts of South Africa in the seventeenth century, living well ahead of the vanguard of the migrating Bantu; and it was these Hottentots who the early White settlers met on landing at the Cape. At that time, in the more southern parts, the Hottentot population probably numbered 40 000, while the Bushmen were some 25 000 strong. Constant feuding between the two groups killed off many and resulted in most of the Bushmen being driven into the arid regions of South West Africa. Epidemic disease decimated the Hottentots, but there is a large proportion of Hottentot blood in the Cape Coloured people.

In the seventeenth century the Dutch landed at the Cape of Good Hope, by which time certain Bantu groups had entered South Africa, then a virtually empty land, from the north, but had established few settlements. Their migration was still in progress but it was not until 150 years later that a group of these immigrants from the north, the Xhosa, met the Whites, migrating from the south, at the Fish River, more than 800 kilometres from Cape Town in what is now the Eastern Cape Province. Boundaries were fixed between the two groups, but raids by the Xhosa provoked a series of frontier wars and caused the British colonial authorities to annex the Xhosa territories (the Transkei and the Ciskei) which the Cape Colonial government administered as native dependencies. Today these same territories are the homelands of the self-governing Xhosa nation.

The Xhosa nation, numbering 3 929 922, is, however, only one of South Africa's Bantu nations. The others are:

Zulu	4 026 082	Shangaan	736 978
South Sotho	1 453 354	Swazi	498 704
Tswana	1 718 508	Venda	357 875
North Sotho	1 603 530		

Each of the eight nations mentioned above insists on maintaining its identity, using its own language, managing its own affairs and avoiding any interference by the other seven. A Tswana is as different from a Zulu as a Swede is from a Belgian. Thus, when people speak of the Black or

Bantu population of South Africa, they no more refer to a homogeneous group than they do when they speak of the White people of Europe as Europeans.

Other features of the ethnic picture are 3 779 000 Whites, about 2 018 533 Coloureds of mixed African (chiefly Hottentot), European and Asian descent, and 620 422 Asians whose ancestry and culture stem from the Indian sub-continent. That brings the number of nations in South Africa to eleven. The fundamental question – and it underlies all government planning – is, how can these nations advance peacefully to the full realization of their potential?

Further complicating the picture is marked cultural diversity. The nations range from a highly sophisticated Western-type urban-technological society, to peoples of the most unsophisticated type to whom witchcraft is still very real, folk who, whatever their, as yet, unproved potential may be, are at present practising a very primitive and precarious form of subsistence agriculture, and in many cases resist efforts to change their mode of life. The latter are dependent on the advanced societies for technological and educational progress without which they cannot emerge from their age-old cultural pattern and take their place as economically viable communities in the modern world. Therefore the worst calamity that could befall the unsophisticated – and they form the large majority – would be the economic and cultural collapse of the sophisticated groups.

Economic statistics make this clear. The Whites contribute the vast proportion of South Africa's revenue, and subsidize the Bantu peoples very heavily indeed in many ways, directly and indirectly. Therefore, were the Whites ever to lose control of their economy by allowing it to pass into the hands of those unable to use power wisely, each and every person of every race would inevitably end up in penury, and many would starve.

For this reason alone South Africa cannot afford to introduce the political system some have urged upon her, that of a unitary government based on a universal franchise; and it is undoubtedly significant that none but a mere handful of people in South Africa itself support such a system. The Whites, the Indians, the Coloureds and each Bantu nation alike reject this alleged panacea. Furthermore, in the context of South Africa, the concept of majority rule of the whole country is not only impracticable but meaningless, for there exists no majority that could rule, the population being, in effect, a collection of different nations which one and all form minority groups.

At the same time, even those most dependent on others often fervently wish to manage their own affairs. This is a common phenomenon in Africa today where independence so often takes precedence over economic viability. The South African Government respects these political aspirations and is doing its best to satisfy them within the framework of reality.

It is fortunate that the aim of these peoples' political aspirations is to control their own affairs, for that is precisely what people usually do best. A Xhosa Minister may be expert at deciding on situations in the Transkei which is his homeland, whereas the White businessman from nearby East London would not know where to start. The converse is also true. Therefore, the South African Government pursues a policy of separate political development based on the simple notion of encouraging the different nations to manage their own affairs, and preventing them from meddling in the affairs of others – in short, self-determination in a very practical sense. Separate development is not a denial of human rights and values. On the contrary, it flows, in a multi-national country like South Africa, from the acceptance and recognition of human rights and values. It is furthermore not a policy designed for export, but to meet the specific circumstances and conditions prevailing in South Africa.

SAFEGUARDING BLACK INTERESTS

Adverse comment on the policy usually concentrates on its negative aspects, on what people may not do, rather than on the many constructive things they are encouraged to do. It concentrates only on the prohibitions that limit the freedom of action of the Non-White groups, but overlooks the fact that prohibitions are reciprocal. Thus, for example, a member of the Xhosa nation may not buy property in a White area. This, though important, is not as important as the fact that the Whites are prohibited from acquiring land in the Transkei. Could they do so, this most land-conscious community would undoubtedly buy up vast tracts of Bantu land, much of which is excellent. It would be a matter of months, rather than years, before a huge landless Black proletariat flocked to the cities, flooding the labour market, thereby, because of the impossibility of housing them, causing economic and social chaos. This explains why the sanctity of the Bantu homelands has been one of the cornerstones of the policy of all South African governments, irrespective of the party in power, and of the Colonial government before them.

Much the same applies to commerce. The Bantu trader in the homelands cannot as yet compete with the White or Indian merchant with his background of generations of expertise. It is therefore in the interests of the slowly developing Bantu commercial class that it be afforded protection from fierce competition, which the policy of separate development provides by excluding White and Indian merchants in Bantu homelands.

Mineral rights belong to the group in whose area the minerals are found. Already gold and platinum have been discovered in Bantu homelands and belong to the Bantu nation in question, in this case the Tswana, who draw the mining royalties. In a highly mineralized country like South Africa, minerals could well prove a decisive factor in developing the homelands, and a source of great wealth to their inhabitants.

These few examples, covering agriculture, commerce and mining – many others could be quoted – will serve to show how important differentiation is to the Bantu nations, how it underpins the very foundations of their economy. One cannot but conclude that far from the Bantu advancing and achieving an ever rising standard of living *in spite of* separate development, as South Africa's critics aver, their situation compares so favourably with the rest of Africa *because of* the policy and the protection they enjoy as result of it.

It is noteworthy that the policy of allocating separate homelands to the Bantu nations is no invention of the National Party. Britain inaugurated it. At the time of Union in 1910, 1 205 000 km^2 (467 716 sq. miles) were excised from South Africa – the three British Protectorates of Basutoland, Bechuanaland and Swaziland, now the independent states of Lesotho, Botswana and Swaziland. South Africa is continuing that policy and applying it to those Bantu nations which in 1910 were allowed to remain within her borders. The final result of this policy will be the creation of eight further independent states in this sub-continent which will be as sovereign and as free as Lesotho, Botswana or Ghana.

Just as the rulers and people of the three erstwhile Protectorates are jealous of their territories, so are the Bantu nations of South Africa, fast moving to full independence, of theirs – so much so that any attempt to reverse the policy now would meet with bitter opposition from each and every one of them.

To understand the situation aright, it is essential to appreciate that no Bantu nation wants to rule the Whites in the White area any more than the Whites wish to rule the Bantu nations in their territories. Each group seeks self-determination, the right to manage its own affairs in its own way, free from outside interference; and that is precisely what separate development provides.

This explains why appeals from abroad, exhorting the 'Bantu majority', in the interests of 'Black Freedom and Power', go unheeded. They fail to make sense because the concept on which they are based is fictitious. There is no 'Black mass of people' in the country, but there are various Bantu nations which are being helped by the Government to attain self-sufficiency and independence at a rate commensurate with their ability.

It will interest those wedded to the principle that the will of the majority must always prevail that the vast majority of South Africa's people, Black, and White and Brown, subscribes to the policy of separate parallel nations and has no taste for an integrated free-for-all in which one nation may meddle in the internal affairs of another. On the other hand, those who champion minority rights – so important in a country of minorities – may rest assured that the whole South African system is based on preserving such rights – not merely of one or two minorities, but for all.

Granted, there are people of all races in South Africa who claim to be 'anti-apartheid'. However, when one carefully examines their views, it becomes evident that they oppose some facets of the policy, not parallel development *holus bolus.*

For instance, many Coloureds deplore the distinction made between them and the Whites. At the same time they draw a rigid line between themselves and the Bantu, and bitterly resent any encroachment by the Indians into their society.

The Indian for his part would consider it an unpardonable insult to be equated with the Zulu, and *vice versa,* while the Zulu's antagonism to the Indian has flared up in bloodshed on more than one occasion. Nor will the Zulu or the Xhosa identify himself with, say, the Tswana. They have been known to demonstrate this antagonism at week-end faction fights. For this reason the ethnic groups have to be separated in mining compounds and housing estates. The Whites, in common with the rest, wish to exclude others from their society – and so it goes on.

Although the rights and wrongs of this universal exclusiveness in South Africa are debatable – the world press shows that – national identity and exclusiveness are an undeniable reality which all South Africa's peoples do take into account when going about their daily business and planning their future. Any policy that refuses to recognize national differences can only result in chaos. Indeed, the peace, prosperity and accord that prevail in South Africa today are evidence that her peoples are realists who refuse to close their eyes to the inescapable facts of the situation.

DIALOGUE ON DEGREE OF SEPARATION

Differences of opinion and the never-ending dialogue on parallel development in South Africa, therefore, do not stem from whether there should or should not be separation, as opposed to full integration, *but on the degree of separation desirable, what form it should take and how it should be implemented to the benefit of all,* with the minimum of inconvenience to the individuals immediately concerned.

The situation of the Bantu nations, each with a traditional homeland of its own and its right of control therein, is straightforward. That of the Whites is similarly uncomplicated. They also control their own area. Bantu within the White area are regarded as foreign nationals temporarily there to work but exercising their political rights, rights to acquire land, etc. in their own homelands. The White man in a Bantu homeland, like the Transkei, is in a similar position. He is a citizen of White South Africa, and it is there, not in the Transkei, that he may exercise his rights of citizenship.

The position of the half-million Indians, most of whom live in Natal, has been a more complicated problem. Originally imported a hundred years ago as indentured labourers on the sugar estates, they have multiplied and prospered. Today some are immensely rich. But their riches have been built up by their attachment to the White economy to which they have contributed notably. The way has always been open for them, with governmental financial assistance, to return to India, where they were deemed to belong. Few took advantage of this. They were doing too well in South Africa.

In 1960 their status was changed when the Government acknowledged them as South Africans with a permanent place in the country, and set up a department with a Minister of its own to attend to their affairs. They had no traditional homeland in South Africa, as had the Bantu and White nations. The oriental origin of their culture and the adherence of most of them to Hinduism or Islam set them apart from the Whites, on the one hand, and the Bantu nations, on the other. Absorption by either is neither practicable nor desired. They are a people apart, a very gifted people with more than 4 000 years of cultural achievement behind them – an industrious people with a bright future.

Naturally, they have political aspirations. The view of present Indian leaders is that the small representation in Parliament that their numbers would justify, could avail them little. They are therefore supporting and enthusiastically implementing the policy of an Indian Council to manage their own domestic affairs.

The Council, at present (1971) a nominated body, will be an elected one in time to come. It has an executive committee of Indians which functions as a 'cabinet', the members holding portfolios, such as finance, education, social welfare, local government and such other matters as the South African Parliament should delegate to it. In this way the Indians will control matters that most affect them.

The precise relationship between the Indian Council and the South African Parliament has not yet been finally determined. The important thing is that the latter sincerely wishes Indian affairs to be handled by the Indians themselves and is giving them every assistance to shoulder these responsibilities, while the Indians, for their part, are determined to make the scheme work. Their enthusiasm and undoubted gifts should ensure that it does.

The Coloureds are in a similar situation, and for them a Coloured Council has been set up on much the same lines as that for the Indians. Their Council consists of twenty appointed members and forty representatives elected on the basis of universal suffrage by all Coloureds over the age of 21.

The Coloureds, like the Indians, have no traditional homeland and are closely tied to the White economy. Both communities, however, have numerous areas specifically for their own occupation. In some cases one group has been moved to enable the other group to move in. For instance, the exclusive seaside resort of Isipingo Beach in Natal was given to Indians, the Whites being moved out and compensated. In District Six, on the other hand, Coloureds are being moved out while Whites move in.

The Department of Community Development, working under the Group Areas Act, determines such resettlement of populations, which has contributed greatly to the ultimate good of all groups and to peaceful relations between them. Naturally, individuals from all groups suffer inconvenience in the process, which certain organs of publicity exploit, often quite unfairly. Meanwhile everything possible is being done to minimize the inconvenience and to compensate for financial loss.

In this regard, the movement of urban populations in particular has been seized upon and used to South Africa's detriment. There can be no exception taken to pictures being published of insanitary shanty towns being bulldozed away, while the inhabitants look on, watching their homes being destroyed by the Government, *provided* similar pictures are published of the modern housing estates to which the people are moved. Publication of the former without the latter, however, is apt to mislead.

WORK OPPORTUNITIES AND JOB RESERVATION

As far as is practicable, bearing in mind the existing level of Bantu skills, the Bantu homelands are regarded as the preserve of the Bantu worker. As yet, however, the number of Bantu entrepreneurs is exceedingly small, and therefore opportunities of salaried employment in the homelands are scarce. To remedy this, White-owned industries have been set up just outside the borders of the Bantu areas to provide Bantu from the homelands with work and cash wages. Meanwhile Bantu development corporations are stimulating commerce and industry in the homelands. As yet, however, most Bantu wage earners work in the White areas, and take a proportion of their earnings back to their respective homelands.

This has raised a problem. There is a danger of certain Whites being displaced by Bantu workers, and this has led to the application of what is known as 'job reservation'. Just as the rights of the Bantu are regarded as paramount in his homeland, so are those of the White in his. When it comes to employment opportunities, each takes precedence over the other in his own area. It is considered that this policy, besides protecting the White worker in his own area, will encourage the more progressive Bantu to use their skills in their own homelands where enterprise is badly needed, rather than to rely exclusively on the White economy. The Bantu areas have great agricultural and industrial potential and also in some cases mining prospects, and therefore need all the skilled men they can raise.

The case of the Indians and Coloureds is quite different. They have no traditional homelands of their own, and they therefore participate in the White economy where they are usually highly successful in finding remunerative employment. Some have become prosperous entrepreneurs. Thus, we find Indians and Coloureds engaged in a wide variety of skilled occupations in the White area – in agriculture and mining, the motor industry, clothing and textile manufacture, the footwear industry; in building as bricklayers, plasterers, painters, plumbers; as welders, burners, riggers and boilermakers in the engineering industry; in radiotronics, dealing with circuitry and cabinet construction; in the furniture trade, in catering, etc. They staff their own educational establishments, run their own libraries and clubs, own businesses and reach high standards of skill. Their contribution to South Africa is a valuable one which is recognized and recompensed.

It would be foolish to claim that in implementing the policy of separate development no mistakes have been made. There are certain things which could have been done better, we now know in the light of experience. It must be remembered, however, that the South African situation is unique. There has been no precedent to follow. South Africa has therefore had to invent methods as she went along, and because of the complexity of human nature, some things have not turned out as well as could reasonably have been expected; others have developed much better than the most sanguine dared to hope. Yet other matters have developed in a manner no man could have predicted, world opinion being one of them.

The reader may by now be baffled, as South Africans of all races are, by the virulent attacks made on South Africa in the U.N. and by various foreign powers and their presses. He will recall charges of oppression and inhumanity and even worse. He will recollect that South Africa has been stigmatized as a 'threat to world peace', that an embargo has been placed on supplying arms for her external defence, lest submarines supplied be used to decimate her Black inhabitants, the bulk of whom live far inland, and supersonic aircraft to destroy their scattered thatched huts.

Many critics go on to predict dire results from the policy – riot, wholesale insurrection. 'Blood bath' is a term commonly used to describe the 'inevitable' future.

It is important to realize that though many of these critics have political axes to grind, others are good, sincere, honest folk who firmly believe what they say. Furthermore, their prediction of catastrophe would be well justified if conditions in South Africa were what they believe them to be. But they are not.

A great deal of misconception arises because most people abroad quite naturally judge matters by their own experience in their own society. For example, they may look upon White and Bantu in South Africa as two groups in one society, rather like employers and employees in a European country. They cannot conceive of them constituting ten distinct nations, speaking different languages, each jealous of its own identity, wedded to its own particular customs and resenting the intrusion of other people –

in short, demanding diversification and the right to practise differentiation in some form or other.

The problem has been to devise a social, political and economic system which will work in these conditions, not in those of some other country, and the answer – or perhaps one should say, the solution that has grown out of the situation – is social and political separation coupled with the greatest degree of economic co-operation possible.

Policies can only be judged rationally by results. No policy, however well-intentioned, no matter on what a high moral or ideological basis it be founded, can possibly be 'right' if it brings the 'wrong' results. It must succeed to be acceptable. This pragmatic view implies a goal, which South Africa regards as the betterment of all her diverse peoples. If we examine the improvement in living standards during the last fifty or sixty years, the growth of the economy, the rising level of education, the degree of literacy, the development of health services, soil and water conservation, etc., we find that all the peoples of South Africa have progressed further and faster than similar communities anywhere else on the African Continent. This goal is being achieved. That being so, South Africa can see no reason whatsoever why she should abandon her proven policy, least of all for an alternative which has failed to bring comparable results anywhere else.

Separate development must therefore be regarded as permanent policy, not as an experiment which may be abandoned in the face of foreign pressure. The only valid reason for changing the basic policy would be if a better one were forthcoming. So far, this has not occurred. All suggested alternatives have been proved impracticable and would inevitably lead to chaos for all, if applied in the South African situation.

However, although the basic principle of separate development will not be changed, its method of application is continually being modified. This is possible because the approach is pragmatic, and essential because changing circumstances demand modifications in method and detail from time to time. Thus, ever greater powers are rapidly being handed over to the Bantu nations. More and more avenues for employment are opening up for Non-Whites as their skills and abilities increase, both in the public services – for example, the railways – and in the private sector.

The provision of education, including higher education, is transforming certain groups, and so affecting their relationship with other groups. Economic advance is producing similar results. For example, a wealthy entrepreneur or qualified professional man is obviously in a different social position than was his illiterate penurious grandfather. So things are changing constantly.

In the process, the Non-White peoples are borrowing much from Western technology and a certain amount from Western culture, and no impediment is placed in the way of their doing so. This does not necessarily mean that they will eventually become culturally indistinguishable from the Whites. On the contrary, most of them cling tenaciously to what they deem valuable in their own culture, to their language and not infrequently to the religion of their ancestors. Indeed, in some of South Africa's largest towns one hears European, Bantu and Asiatic languages spoken, while places of worship include Christian churches, Jewish synagogues, Hindu temples and Moslem mosques. No attempt is made to force anyone into an alien world.

'PETTY APARTHEID'

And what about 'petty apartheid'? This concept is usually accepted to mean separate schools, residential areas, buses, taxis, train coaches, hospitals, etc.

Surely many of these practices are not only found in South Africa? In some countries, for example, separate residential areas are maintained by an undertaking of all owners not to sell their property to a person of another group or colour, without the consent of the remaining residents. In South Africa we are honest enough to say quite frankly that we find these practices still necessary to prevent unnecessary friction between the different groups. *It is based on pragmatism and realism, and the fruit of this realism is reaped in peaceful co-existence, with an excellent record of stable government, and dynamic growth and development in the interest of all our peoples.*

We believe that the differences in colour, language, culture and general outlook cannot be argued away, but we do aim to minimize friction in the interim before achieving our ultimate aim of eliminating discrimination as far as possible. The Honourable B.J. Vorster, Prime Minister of South Africa referred to these differences in an interview on 11 March, 1971 :

> 'In a multi-national country cognizance must be taken of that fact. It then becomes essential that you must minimize friction as much as possible. Taking into account the relation between English- and French-speaking Canadians, between Flemish- and French-speaking

Belgians, Roman Catholics and Protestants in Ireland, Greeks and Turks in Cyprus, Black and White in Britain, Negroes and Whites in America, it will be realized that in South Africa we have more *potentially explosive material than in any other country I know of*, especially if international propaganda, and propaganda within this country, which tries to stir trouble between the various groups and sections, is taken into account. In spite of all that, I can say in all sincerity that *the lack of tension between the various national groups is visible in South Africa.* I ascribe it to the fact that we have the policy of separate development here.'

Separate or parallel development is founded on the basic concept of diversity. While it is not based on the concept of one people being 'superior' or 'inferior' to another, 'better' or 'worse', of a 'higher' or 'lower' culture, as we have seen, it definitely recognizes people's differences – differences they freely acknowledge and choose to preserve. Even theoretically, the only alternative would be to ignore these differences or to stamp them out. The former would amount to basing policy on myth, the latter to denying South Africa's peoples their cherished identities and different ways of life, and thus to inviting chaos by refusing them the self-determination the present policy provides. Both are unthinkable – and yet in most cases that, in effect, is what the statements of opponents of separate development inevitably imply.

This is slowly dawning upon an increasing number of people abroad. Some have visited South Africa and seen things for themselves. Many have become convinced that the present policy stems from the local situation and is a fair, rational and pragmatic attempt to solve South Africa's problems; that it has succeeded till now and promises well for the future. Others do not go so far as this, but most would agree with Dr Donald Coggan, the Archbishop of York, who is reported as telling a press conference in 1970, after he had paid a two-and-a-half month visit to South Africa: 'There is no easy solution to the problem . . . I think visitors to South Africa, and still more those who have never visited the country, should be cautious in what they say. The position of those who are fighting for a more liberal approach in South Africa could be made more difficult by what we say when we get home.'

His Grace's remarks imply three things with which most thinking South Africans will agree. In the first place, South Africa's problems are extremely complex. Secondly, there are people, some of whom have never so much as set foot on South African soil, who broadcast what they mistakenly consider is best for the country and its diverse peoples. And thirdly, their misinformed comments and criticisms do nothing to assist South Africans in their sincere efforts to make their land a better place for all its inhabitants.

The South African situation obviously does not lend itself to 'instant' imported solutions. The processes of social and political change cannot be hurried, because what is required and what is being undertaken is evolutionary, not revolutionary – and that takes time. Meanwhile, what the world should understand is that South Africans of all population groups are very far from complacent, and are grappling with their complex problems with tremendous vigour.

A Critique of Separate Development

Joel Mervis

Editor of the Sunday Times, *South Africa's best selling newspaper, Joel Mervis is widely recognized as one of the Continent's top newspapermen. He is a brilliant writer and an astute student of the South African political scene. He studied at the Universities of Cape Town and the Witwatersrand and has several publications to his credit, most of them spiced with delightful witticisms aimed at the local political set-up.*

The concept of separate development is intriguing, the policy ingenious. The very title, 'separate development', is noteworthy. The words are significant because they bear no physical resemblance to the word 'apartheid', which for policy-makers is certainly an advantage. Apartheid, once a magic touchstone for electoral victory, acquired ugly connotations and a disreputable character, and was wisely abandoned. It remains to be seen whether 'separate development' is anything more than apartheid in modern dress; and, for those who care to gaze more closely, whether the new attire does not follow the current fashion of being a see-through dress or perhaps even one that is topless.

The basic ingredients and the fundamental principles of separate development are certainly no mystery. These can be summarized as follows: the White man shall remain master in his own country. There is no middle course in reconciling the aspirations of the racial groups in the White areas. South Africa must to some extent defer to world pressure on racial matters, and separate development represents that accommodation with world opinion. South Africa's race policy needs to have a moral basis, and this is provided by the creation of self-governing, independent Bantu homelands.

Many important official pronouncements have been made on the subject, and the question arises which of these should be selected to give a clear, accurate picture of the rationale of separate development. The fairest method would be to allow an ardent, distinguished supporter of separate development himself to make the choice. This has conveniently been done by Professor J.L. Boshoff, Principal of the University of the North (an African university). He is a former Secretary for Education in the Transkei, and before that was an inspector of schools in the department of Bantu Education.

In an address to the congress of the South African Bureau of Race Affairs (Sabra) in 1970, Professor Boshoff stressed that it was of crucial importance for the delegates to understand precisely what was involved in the policy of homeland development. In order to bring clarity and understanding to this question, said Professor Boshoff, he knew of no better review of what homeland development stood for, and above all what its purpose was, than that contained in the speech of the South African Minister of Foreign Affairs (Dr Hilgard Muller) at the United Nations on December 21, 1964. At that time, it will be recalled, Dr Verwoerd, the grand architect of separate development, was Prime Minister. The voice heard at the United Nations was the voice of Dr Muller, but it is not unreasonable to suppose that the hand was the hand of Dr Verwoerd. Professor Boshoff gave Dr Muller's statement the warmest praise, describing it as 'a brilliant exposition and defence of the policy of separate development'. Professor Boshoff added: 'It satisfies me as Afrikaner and Christian. It satisfies me emotionally and intellectually.' For an authentic pronouncement on what separate development means, we turn then to the important statement made by Dr Muller at the United Nations. This is what he said:

'Mr President, let me say first of all that those who belong to the South African nation of European descent hold no brief for the domination of any nation over another. On the contrary, we are strongly opposed to it, with an opposition that is rooted in our traditions and history. For a large section of this nation was itself for a long time in the past subjected to foreign domination.

'We are, however, not the only nation within the borders of South Africa living in a traditional territory of its own. For South Africa is in fact and in the first place a multi-national country, rather than merely a multi-racial country. Apart from the South African nation of European descent it includes the homelands of a number of other nations having their own separate identities, each with its own undeniable right to separate nationhood in a land which has likewise been its own.

'The crucial difference (between South Africa and other countries with multi-racial populations) is this – that our task in South Africa is not primarily that of solving a problem of races; it is a problem of nations, a problem of bringing about a situation where peaceful co-existence of the various nations in our country will be possible. We believe that this can only be achieved by the independent development of each people towards the full realization of separate nationhood and the recognition of the right of each nation to govern itself in accordance with its own national traditions and aspirations. This, Sir, is a principle fundamental in our policy of separate development – a policy which is profoundly different from the caricature of apartheid which is commonly presented by our critics.

'With this in view (that all nations in South Africa should be free to develop as they themselves may wish to develop) and taking into account the history, the culture and the psychology of each of the nations in South Africa, it is our objective to provide to every individual the fullest chance of development within his own nation, and where possible in his own homeland. And not only that, for it is similarly our objective to enable all our national groups increasingly to come together to consult on problems of mutual interest and concern, and on the basis of mutual equality and respect for human dignity, through the establishment of high-level consultative machinery. In this way we are confident of our ability also to eliminate discrimination among the various national groups. For when each of these groups has reached a stage of effectively administering and controlling its own affairs, both the practical and psychological basis for discrimination will rapidly disappear.

'What I have been saying, Sir, is certainly nothing new. It has been stated repeatedly by my Prime Minister (Dr Verwoerd) and by other members of the South African Government. There are, of course, those critics of our policy who, in many cases, with questionable motives, reject our declarations as empty words or as political propaganda.'

That impressive statement by Dr Muller certainly justifies Professor Boshoff's glowing praise. The professor, however, made one other notable observation to the Sabra delegates. He expressed his surprise – several times – that Dr Muller's important remarks, at the time they were made, were completely ignored by the South African Press. According to Professor Boshoff, Dr Muller's speech was not 'published or emphasized or discussed'. It is indeed astonishing that this important speech should be ignored, and Professor Boshoff could give no explanation for the omission.

A cynic might perhaps offer this explanation: the Opposition Press regarded the speech as too good to be true and the Government Press thought it too true to be good.

The formulation of the policy of separate development springs from certain fundamental attitudes and beliefs. These are considered to be unshakeable and immovable, so that whatever conflicts with them must bend, or defer, or give way. These basic attitudes are the cornerstone of separate development and they have been clearly set out by Government leaders.

First, there is the basic postulate that the Whites shall retain supremacy. It was enunciated by Dr Verwoerd in these words: 'I want to state unequivocally that South Africa is a White man's country and he must remain the master here. In the reserves we are prepared to allow the Bantu to be the masters, but within the European areas we, the White people of South Africa, are and shall remain masters.'

This theme has often been repeated, and quite recently by Mr M.C. Botha, Minister of Bantu Administration and Development, who said: 'The most important criterion which should always be mentioned is that there should be a guarantee that the say of the White nation should remain undisturbed for all time. In fact, we do guarantee it for all time if we remain in power with our policy of separate development in South Africa . . . Under our policy all so-called rights which could lead to equality with Whites in South Africa on a basis of integration will in due course be removed by us.'

The second basic postulate is that, in the White area, there can be no possible compromise or accommodation with the Non-Whites. The policy was firmly stated by Dr Verwoerd, in 1964, in these words: 'One either follows the course of separation, when one must accept the logical consequences right up to the final point of having separate states, or else one believes in the course of assimilating the various races in one state and then one must also accept the eventual consequences. These are, domination by the majority, that is, Black domination. There is no middle course except during a transitional period.'

These twin factors – an unshakable determination to maintain White supremacy and the firm belief that there can be no middle course – are the fount and inspiration of separate development. While the Government is not prepared to budge one inch in the White area, it is prepared to make generous concessions in the Non-White areas by creating eight homelands, all of which are earmarked for self-government and eventual independence.

THE ACHILLES' HEEL OF SEPARATE DEVELOPMENT

The maintenance of White supremacy is therefore being achieved at a price – the surrender of large tracts of South Africa to eight other nations. The plan is perfectly straightforward. As Dr Verwoerd pointed out, you either have separation or you have integration. The homelands plan, its protagonists contend, marks the doom of integration and the entrenchment of separation. That is unquestionably how the Government sees the policy of separate development.

Unfortunately, life isn't as simple as all that; and the policy is seriously defective because it glosses over unpleasant facts as if they did not exist. The policy refuses to accept the inescapable truths that economic integration in the White area is deep-rooted and irrevocable, and that the Non-White population is permanent and irremovable. Only by ignoring those realities, or by treating fact as if it were fiction, can the homelands programme be said to make any kind of sense. This can hardly be described as a wise or statesmanlike approach.

It is not the homeland Africans which constitute the problem, but the vast, urbanized, integrated African proletariat in the White area. The homelands certainly have nothing to complain about in the new deal, but they provide no more than an interesting auxilliary to the main issue. The complex politico-constitutional edifice being built on their behalf could almost as well be taking place in Australia for all the relevance it will have in solving the critical confrontation that is steadily building up in the White area. This is how many Whites would be looking at the matter, for they have most to lose; and if uncertainty is created it is their stability which would be imperilled.

Because separate development throws the spotlight on the homelands, it tends to obscure the important fact that the main purpose of separate development is to provide a solution for the White area rather than the homelands where no serious racial conflict exists at all. The conditions in the White area and events that may or could develop in the White area, rather than those in the homelands, are of paramount importance in judging the validity, the realism or the adequacy of the policy of separate development. It will hardly console the Whites if separate development brings peace and stability to the Transkei but strife and turmoil to the Transvaal.

In some respects separate development can be compared to the curate's egg in the famous *Punch* joke. The scene, it will be recalled, was at the breakfast table, and the formidable bishop asked the nervous curate how his boiled egg was. The nervous curate replied: 'Parts of it, your Grace, are excellent.' Parts of separate development, like the curate's egg, are also excellent. But, as is well known, the parts of an egg that are excellent will unfortunately not prevent the egg from being tainted as a whole. The parts of separate development consist, on the one hand, of a gratifying liberal programme of political emancipation and, on the other, an intensified campaign of illiberal, intolerant restriction. The bad part could well taint the whole.

Separate development purports to have as its main aim the maintenance of White supremacy, and it is therefore the White area which needs close scrutiny to see how it may or could be affected by separate development. In the melting pot that constitutes the White area, with people and ideas inextricably mingled, political, economic and sociological forces are on the move. These forces cannot be stilled but, by the exercise of wisdom and statecraft, they could be channelled and controlled in an environment of peace, stability and security. It is to be doubted whether separate development is even remotely geared to achieve this result.

Whatever people may say to the contrary, and whatever a policy may claim, it remains an incontrovertible fact that the White area, consisting of Whites, Africans, Coloureds and Indians, is now an economically integrated society. So deep-rooted is the integration that it has become permanent and irrevocable. The population consists of approximately four million Whites, eight million Africans, two million Coloureds and 600 000 Asians (preponderantly Indians). There are in fact about one million more Africans in the White area than in the homelands. The prospect of any substantial move of Africans to the homelands is remote, largely because the homelands cannot support their existing population and Africans in the White area are desperately needed where they are.

If the pattern of twenty years of National Party rule is any criterion, the number of Africans in White South Africa can be expected to rise rather than drop. For two decades the Government has used every means at its disposal – and it has powerful resources – to halt the flow of Africans to the White areas. These prodigious efforts have met with failure on the grand scale. During the sixties – a decade of intense activity to keep the Africans out – the African population in the White area rose by about one million. In the two decades of Nationalist rule the number of Africans in the White area rose from two million to eight million – a 300 per cent increase. The figure of two million was given by Dr Verwoerd, speaking at Naboomspruit on August 4, 1952.

In the context of Government policies in general, and of separate development in particular, a vitally important lesson can be learned from this vast flow of people across the massive barriers created to halt them. The lesson is that policies, edicts, warnings, promises, threats and regulations are powerless against economic and sociological forces when these really get to work. In this instance we had the full weight of Government power thrown into the fight to reverse the flow of Africans. The campaign failed. This failure should serve as a warning to those who place their faith in confident Government assurances that White supremacy will be maintained. High-sounding guarantees which ignore facts can be dangerously misleading. We have already seen how the assurances about restricting African migration and integration were easily defeated by events. The influx of Africans supplies the proof that the Government – any government – is incapable of eliminating the economic and sociological forces that are unleashed in a developing, expanding society. Thus, that maintenance of White supremacy will not be guaranteed by forceful ministerial statements, but rather by a willingness to recognize change and the forces of change, and to make the adjustments needed to channel those forces along a peaceful course. The policy of separate development does not inspire confidence that the Government will be any more successful in maintaining White supremacy than they were in stopping the flow of migrants.

TREATMENT OF THE URBAN AFRICAN

Another grave weakness in the policy of separate development is its assumption that, if full rights are granted to the homelands, then Africans in the White area will somehow regard this as a vicarious grant of rights to themselves, and will be content to be treated as non-persons. The whole concept ignores even the most rudimentary principles upon which human rights and human dignity are based.

The picture of what is happening in the White area is not pleasant. The Africans acquire a status that is imposed upon them and decided for them, without consultation, and in a manner that can only be described as showing a contemptuous disregard for their right to have any feelings or aspirations at all. They are to be denied citizenship of their own country. Their status will be that of a temporary sojourner. They are denied property rights. Restraints are placed on the entrepreneur class in African townships. Husbands are denied the right to live with their wives. A woman needs a permit to live with her husband. Labour in the urban areas will be there on a migratory basis. A migrant worker has no rights in the area, he cannot bring his wife there, nor can he rent a house. As for parents, the burden of having to prove the right of their own children to live with them in their own home is frightening in its enormity and complexity. But Africans in the White area will have a vote – in a homeland. For some it will be a homeland they have never seen and in which they have no interest.

These conditions are not accidental or haphazard. They are designed to ensure that Africans are kept in their place. The key to this approach was supplied by Mr M.C. Botha, Minister of Bantu Administration and Development, when he told Parliament in February, 1970: 'In White areas the Bantu are not being granted equality or potential equality in respect of any single aspect of social life whatsoever; not as far as the say in the Government of this country is concerned, not as far as property rights are concerned, not as far as social amenities are concerned. They have no potential or actual equality.' It is hard to believe that a ministerial utterance could be couched in terms so scornful and contemptuous and apparently with so little regard to the humiliation and indignity they inflict upon eight million people, half of whom comprise the bulk of the country's labour force.

But these ministerial utterances, and their message, must be noted with care, for they are indispensable in shedding light upon the policy of separate development. In this instance Mr Botha shed light on what might perhaps be described as the 'positive' aspects of separate development in the White area. The 'positive' plan is that eight million Black people are to live indefinitely in conditions so impersonal that they resemble human ciphers – and they are expected to accept this without demur. One does not need to be reminded that the economy depends absolutely on the labour of about four million Africans and could not function without them. The country's prosperity, indeed its very existence, depends upon the continued presence of this integrated group. Yet they are being deprived of so many rights and amenities that they scarcely have the status of people. It is open to serious question whether this is a sound way of implementing separate development and maintaining White supremacy. Forces of resentment and bitterness are being created, and stimulated, in a manner that will surely make a difficult situation worse. It cannot be reasonable or just or humane to expect Africans in the White area to accept a personal non-status or, alternatively, the status of a non-person, simply because the homelands are gaining independence. The fact that citizens in the homelands are getting something gives one no reason to believe that urban Africans will be satisfied with nothing.

The dangers of this situation did not escape the notice of leading Afrikaner Nationalists. One of them is Dr G.D. Scholtz who, while editor of the official National Party paper *Die Transvaler,* referred to the matter in his important book *'n Swart Suid-Afrika?* That was in 1964. Dr Scholtz noted with some alarm that the dependence of White South Africa on Non-White labour had become more deeply entrenched than ever. Unless the Whites freed themselves from this dependence, he wrote, 'their children will pay with their blood for the destruction of White civilization'. Dr Scholtz followed this up with a leading article in *Die Transvaler,* in which he referred to the growing preponderance of Africans in all major industries. He stressed the need 'to get rid of the threatening stranglehold of the Non-White proletariat' and to eliminate the economic integration of the Bantu 'which must of necessity lead to political integration and eventually political domination'. In another article soon afterwards, Dr Scholtz supported a Cabinet Minister who called for sacrifices to halt this process. Dr Scholtz warned of 'the extremely detrimental consequences . . . when individuals are blinded by their own economic interests'.

Nearly seven years have elapsed since Dr Scholtz uttered his warning, and if he was fearful then he must be desperately alarmed now. For the 'threatening stranglehold' to which he referred has become even tighter. In these seven years nearly a million more Africans have been integrated into the White economy. At many levels they now hold jobs requiring higher skills. If they were indispensable before, they are doubly so now. The 'threatening stranglehold' to which Dr Scholtz referred has ceased to 'threaten'. It has become a reality – a plain, straightforward stranglehold.

The significance of Dr Scholtz's observation lies in his desperate cry to get rid of these Non-White workers – for only in that way, as he sees it, will our children be able to avoid paying with their blood for the destruction of White civilization. I do not believe that Dr Scholtz was being unduly alarmist. The disaster he fears could happen – and, by discussing it with such frankness, Dr Scholtz has really got to the heart of the matter.

Dr Scholtz's anxieties expose the extent of the Government's dilemma; they reveal the inadequacy of separate development as a solution, and shed light on some of the irreconcilable conflicts in Nationalist thinking. The primary objective, of course, is to entrench the White man as master in his own area. The way to do that, according to Dr Scholtz, is to 'get rid' of the Africans. This would certainly be an effective solution, if it could be done. But Dr Scholtz is asking for the impossible and the unattainable. We cannot 'get rid' of the Africans. Therefore, if we cannot get rid of them, and Dr Scholtz is correct in his prognostication, conditions are ripe for the ultimate destruction of White civilization. The Government, equally alive to this danger, seeks to avoid it by separate development. Yet this policy, if anything, will surely intensify the dangers that already make Dr Scholtz extremely apprehensive about the future. The Africans will still remain in the White areas, but with their rights steadily eroded. They will gradually be transformed into a sullen, resentful proletariat, living in a country in which they have no stake and are deprived of the right to have a stake.

BANTU HOMELANDS : A RED HERRING?

As has been indicated, the policy of separate development tends to obscure these dangers by throwing the spotlight on the homelands, and thereby creating the impression that if these are a success, the whole problem is largely solved. To some extent, this may actually be what Dr Verwoerd had in mind when he unfolded his master plan for Bantu states. In 1961 he told Parliament: 'The development of Bantu states is not what we would have liked to see. It is a form of fragmentation which we would not have liked if we were able to avoid it. In the light of the pressure being exerted on South Africa there is, however, no doubt that this will eventually have to be done, thereby buying for the White man his freedom and the right to retain domination in what is his country, settled for him by his forefathers.'

The rationale of separate development is thus explicitly stated. It could be described as a kind of bargain – full rights for Africans in the homelands in exchange for no rights for Africans in the White area. The fact that this bargain is dictated by the Whites and thrust upon the Non-Whites whether they like it or not is, again, another matter; but for the present let us examine the homelands, on their merits, and see what part they play in the wider plan.

The homelands, it is hoped, will make an important contribution to the maintenance of White supremacy. They could do this by siphoning off a substantial number of Africans from the White area and absorbing them into the Bantustans. Present indications are that it will take a long time for the homelands to become viable states. Nor can one place much reliance on their ability, in the foreseeable future, to perform their vital function of attracting Africans from the White area. As matters stand they face a formidable task in finding employment for their existing population.

Even the most advanced homeland, the Transkei, is still an undeveloped, backward country. As recently as two years ago, Mr George Matanzima, a Transkei Cabinet Minister, pleaded with the South African Government 'not to throw people back into the wastepaper basket'. These were his words: 'In the homelands we have no factories or other immediate sources of employment, so that people are just thrown back into a wastepaper basket to add to the rest of them. Avenues of employment in the homelands must first be made available before these endorsed-out Africans (from the Western Cape) are sent there.'

Since Mr Matanzima's plea two years ago there has of course been some development, but compared to the needs of the territory it is trifling. About 2 000 Africans in the Transkei are employed in industry; and industries are sparse. They include three furniture factories, three bakeries, three vehicle repair shops, a brewery (for Bantu beer) and a meat-processing plant. Of the 1 600 000 Africans in the Transkei, about 42 000 are in employment. Of these, about half are employed in Government service. The Bantu Investment Corporation, since its establishment in 1959, has invested R13-million in the development of the homelands. It has been particularly active in the retail trade, enabling Africans to take over about 400 shops at approximately R18 000 a shop. Up to 1969 it had financed 1 100 businesses through direct loans and 1 300 by-trade credit on stock. It established 12 wholesale distribution organizations and 28 savings banks. The upshot is that, in ten years, after spending R13-million, the corporation has enabled 5 000 people to be employed in the homelands. The process is clearly slow, and the progress made has certainly not impressed Sir de Villiers Graaff, Leader of the Opposition. In February 1970, he told Parliament: 'Inside the reserves there is virtually no industrial development at all. The Prime Minister's policy of separate development is a farce and a colossal bluff.'

These are strong words, but they do not appear to be altogether unjustified. The fact is that although the homelands, politically and constitutonally, present a splendid picture of freedom, liberation and emancipation, they are in a parlous economic condition. Nor is the development able to keep pace even remotely with the projected programme.

The Tomlinson Report, published about fifteen years ago, envisaged the creation of 50 000 jobs a year. In fact, the average is at most 5 000 a year. Further, Tomlinson gave us until 1981 to create the jobs, because a population of 15 000 000 was projected by 1981. The projected 1981 population figure has already been reached, which places the number of jobs even further behind in the race for economic viability. The Tomlinson Report anticipated the creation of 1 250 000 jobs by 1981 at the rate of 50 000 a year. As we have already reached the 1981 population figure, and as only 75 000 jobs have so far been created, it could be said that we have already fallen behind by 1 175 000 jobs.

Many other facts and statistics have been widely quoted to show that economic development in the homelands is necessarily slow. This is not of itself a reflection upon Government policy or Government inadequacy. Government revenues are not unlimited and the State spends on the homelands only as much as it can afford. The significance of slow economic progress is that if, for decades to come, the homelands are unable to provide employment for their own citizens, what real hope can there be that they will attract Africans from the White areas? To the extent, therefore, that the homelands could solve the problem by attracting the Africans from White South Africa, they are of no value whatever.

Nor is the ancillary device known as 'border industries' likely to meet with any substantial success in drawing off Africans from the White urban areas. An excellent authority on this subject is Professor Jan Moolman, who was a member of the Tomlinson Commission.

He studied a border area, Rosslyn, in the Tswana homeland, and (in August 1970) came to the conclusion that a border area, instead of pumping development into a homeland, actually 'sucks a homeland dry'. The economic problems of the homelands are further illustrated by Professor Moolman in a reference to Mabopane, a potentially big city in the Tswana homeland near Pretoria. This city, claims Professor Moolman, will not have the 'economically active machine' needed to drive it and, adds Professor Moolman, 'Pretoria will suck Mabopane dry of development'. He points out that Ga-Rankuwa, near Mabopane, with 40 000 inhabitants, has existed for ten years and shows no signs of developing an economic heart. 'There is no growth of trade, but instead unmistakable signs of over-population and slum formation.'

Although border industry development is proceeding more rapidly than development in the homelands, there is still a lack of infra-structure in many of these areas, and the inducements to industrialists to shift to the border areas are not generally attractive. But even if the border areas are developed adequately, they do not contribute substantially to implementing separate development. They represent merely an extension of the existing system of employing African workers as migrant workers in the White areas.

All the available evidence indicates that the homelands offer little chance of bringing about separation in South Africa. They will acquire the attractive trappings of autonomous states, but the population pattern will remain the same throughout South Africa – and the problem will remain the same. In so far as the homelands can be said to be an important part of the policy of separate development, they make little or no contribution to solving the dangerous problems that must arise from the presence of eight million Africans in White South Africa. It is this vital gap in the machinery of separate development that constitutes its fundamental weakness. There is no bridge between the homelands and the White area. On the contrary, the creation of the homelands has had the effect of exacerbating the difficulties in the White area. The Government, morally uplifted by the new ethical basis it has found for apartheid, apparently believes that the more it liberates and emancipates the homelands, the more it is entitled to tighten restrictions in the White areas. It is almost as if the Government had decided to swap a paradise in the Transkei for a powder keg in the Transvaal.

Only an optimist can believe that the Black population of the White area will decrease. The probabilities are that the number of Africans (eight million at present) will have risen substantially by the end of the century. Demographers' projections are not always reliable, and these tend to vary from demographer to demographer. The projection for the year 2000 is that the African population in the White area will be at least 13 million. Some projections go as high as 20 million, but if we take the lower figure that is plenty to go on with, particularly as the White population is expected to be no more than seven million. These figures, in themselves, are a denial and a negation of 'separation'. They show that all the arts of influx control and other restraints are powerless to halt the inexorable increase of the Black population.

But it is not necessary to look as far ahead as the year 2000. At any given moment between then and now the Africans will outnumber the Whites by about two to one. By virtue of the policy of separate development this will mean that the White citizens of South Africa, in their own country, will be outnumbered two to one by 'foreigners' living permanently there. It is to be doubted whether this is a healthy condition for any country, or whether it really forms a sound basis for a stable society. But, as we have seen, the policy of separate development provides for this contingency. The Government plan is to keep the Africans in a permanent state of inferiority. They will enjoy neither citizenship nor political rights; their status will be that of temporary sojourners; and they will be governed by a mass of restrictions which to a greater or lesser extent, for a larger or smaller number, will curtail their freedom of movement, their right to seek jobs, their right to live together as a family and so on. This procedure is a very positive and a very definite part of separate development.

Before considering the impact this is likely to make on the Africans, it is desirable to consider its probable effect on the Whites. They are always ready to make sacrifices, but are unlikely to be willing to do so when they see no reason for it. One sacrifice they are not prepared to make is to see their economy disrupted and their living standards lowered by a mass of restrictions directed not against them, but against the Africans. They have learned something about co-existence with Africans. The twin cities of Johannesburg and Soweto live harmoniously together; in the factories men and women of all races work together in harmony; in the streets, in the shops, in offices, in homes there is an atmosphere of tolerance and goodwill. The Whites can have no possible interest in seeing their labour force curtailed and their economy hurt. Above all, they can only view with alarm a deterioration in race relations that must inevitably arise from unduly harsh restrictions imposed upon millions of people who have an undeniable right to a fair deal from the country they help to sustain. Like Dr Scholtz, whom we quoted above, the White citizens also have fears for the future. But they do not seek to 'get rid' of the Africans. In the first place, they need the Africans and, secondly, they know it would be impossible to get rid of them anyway. For them, the implications of separate development have become serious indeed.

What, then, of the Africans themselves? Can they reasonably be expected to accept a status of perpetual inferiority – a status so degrading that an African whose father and grandfather were born in Johannesburg, and who has never seen a homeland in his life, is regarded as a 'temporary sojourner' in the only country he has ever known? This is asking a good deal of anybody – and those who believe that the Africans will accept such a status indefinitely are living in a fool's paradise. Thus, where it has become essential to consult with the Africans, to find some method which will take cognizance of their aspirations, but without endangering the security of the Whites, the policy of separate development takes exactly the opposite course: No consultation and no concessions. Far from making conditions more amenable for Africans, the few rights they may still be said to hold are also being whittled away.

INTEGRATION: POLICY OR PROCESS?

Those who believe that such a harsh, restrictive, impersonal policy will produce stability bear an awful responsibility. In his famous report Professor Tomlinson used this phrase: 'It is clear that a continuation of the *policy of integration* (my italics) would intensify racial friction and animosity . . .' This concept of a 'policy of integration' – so often repeated by politicians – represents the ultimate fallacy in political thinking. It is a grotesque fiction, for in the past sixty years, since Union, a 'policy of integration' has never existed. What has occurred is a *process* of integration, but this was not done as a matter of policy. Even a 'policy' *against* integration did not help. Integration was the inevitable consequence of economic and sociological forces that could not be stopped. The vast integration of Black labour was not the product of a 'policy'. The official policy in fact was exactly the opposite – non-integration plus apartheid. Yet, in spite of that, integration took place on a vast scale.

The custom or habit of equating a 'policy' with 'reality', or of believing that one has only to state a policy for it to have the force, substance and effect of reality is the great illusion at the root of separate development. It is a dangerous illusion. We have seen that the 'policy' of separation did not alter the 'fact' of integration. Now we have a firm 'policy' of 'no middle course' for Whites and Africans being applied to a country whose entire prosperity and economic survival rests on the backs of those Africans. Economic and social forces do not recognize a policy; they create the conditions for change and they decide events. A policy of White supremacy, in these circumstances, is an absurdity.

The Whites can maintain their supremacy not by declaiming a policy but by recognizing the forces for change and the need for change, and by adjusting themselves to meet the challenge of a changing world. They have surely been given adequate warning, by the mass migration of Africans, and by widespread economic integration, that policies cannot stop the inexorable march of economic and sociological forces.

So we turn back now to the statement by Dr Hilgard Muller at the United Nations, quoted above. Here, to remind you, are some of the phrases he used: 'Those who belong to the South African nation hold no brief for the domination of any nation over another . . . This, Sir, is a principle fundamental in our policy of separate development – a policy which is profoundly different from the caricature of apartheid which is commonly presented by our critics . . . it is our objective to provide to every individual the fullest chance of development within his own nation and, where possible in his own national homeland . . . respect for human dignity.' Dr Muller was able to make these observations because he was speaking specifically about *nations* and not about *races*. When, therefore, he spoke of granting 'every individual the fullest chance of development within his own nation', he was excluding eight million Africans in White South Africa because they are not 'individuals within their own nation'. When he spoke about 'respect for human dignity' he excluded them again because they are not a nation. This is a form of sophistry to make one blush, but at any rate it is the device by which the denial of rights to Africans in the White area is being justified.

South Africa, it would appear, is no longer multi-racial but multi-national, and only a national in his own home is entitled to any rights at all. This is the kind of argument that could make for spirited discussion in a university debate, but it is quite irrelevant as far as the feeling and aspirations of the large Non-White urbanized proletariat are concerned.

The constitutional distinction between multi-racial and multi-national will not be readily apparent to a man prevented from living with his wife. But, into whatever category the urban Africans may be placed, they are still people, with wants, desires, feelings, ambitions, families, loves and hates. The concept that such feelings can be utterly stifled by a policy is, of itself, an affront to human dignity. But, worse still, it is an act of folly whose ultimate effect could be to produce conditions precisely the opposite of those which the policy of separate development seeks to preserve.

The Legal Framework of Apartheid

John Dugard

Christopher John Robert Dugard is one of South Africa's top legal academicians. He holds the degrees of B.A., LL.B. (University of Stellenbosch) and LL.B. and the Diploma in International Law (Cantab.). He has written extensively on the legal aspects of various South African issues. He was a visiting Professor of Public and International Affairs at Princeton in 1969 and is currently Professor of Law at the University of the Witwatersrand. John Dugard is also Vice-President of the South African Institute of Race Relations.

INTRODUCTION

Racial discrimination in modern South Africa is not a system of social conventions and taboos as it was, to a large extent, in pre-1948 South Africa. It is a carefully constructed legal order which prescribes in minute detail the discriminatory expectations of the governing White oligarchy. This is what distinguishes South Africa from most other societies in which discriminatory practices are legally prohibited, although socially condoned. After World War II the South African legislative history of accelerated discrimination and differentiation in race relations stands in sharp contrast to the experience of other states which during the same period have invoked legal processes on both the national and the international plane to prohibit racial discrimination.

The legislative endorsement of racial discrimination not only results in the substitution of a legal sanction for societal censure in order to coerce those individuals who are unwilling to comply with discriminatory prescriptions and expectations, but at the same time it gives an aura of respectability and legitimacy to discriminatory practices. The prevailing positivist attitude of most White South Africans to the nature of law assists the Government in this respect. Although the common law of South Africa is Roman-Dutch law[1] the country's guiding legal philosophy is English positivism, which was exported to the Cape after the British annexation of 1806. Legal positivism, which is characterized by the theory of command – viz. that law is simply the command of a political superior to a political inferior – and the insistence on a rigid separation of law and morality, induces unquestioning obedience to Parliament's will and discourages the examination of laws against moral standards. Failure on the part of White South Africans to question the morality of legislative enactments paradoxically results in the equation of Parliament's will with justice once that will has been constitutionally certified and published at the Government's expense in the *Government Gazette.* The Government has not hesitated to exploit this deep-rooted respect for the law by regulating racial discrimination by law rather than by social convention. It is interesting that recent studies suggest that the firm adherence to positivism by the German legal profession of the thirties greatly assisted Hitler in the construction of a legal order based on immoral injunctions.[2]

Institutionally, positivism manifests itself in the doctrine of parliamentary sovereignty, according to which Parliament's will is supreme and may not be subjected to judicial review. This cardinal feature of English constitutional law was adopted by the Founding Fathers of the Union of 1910 when the four British colonies in Southern Africa joined together under a flexible constitution which might be altered by a simple majority vote of those present and voting in both legislative chambers (the House of Assembly and the Senate) sitting separately, except where the equal rights of the English and Afrikaans languages and the voting rights of the Cape Non-Whites were affected. In the latter cases constitutional amendment required a two-thirds majority vote of the total number of members of both houses of Parliament sitting together. No express provision was made for judicial review of legislation and, after the courts had exercised this power in respect of legislative attempts to deprive the Cape Coloured voters of their rights in the fifties,[3] the Constitution was amended to exclude the judicial testing right. The Republican Constitution of 1961[4]

1. See following page.
2. Lon L. Fuller, 'Positivism and Fidelity to Law' (1958) 71 *Harvard Law Review* 630 at 658-61.
3. See page 90.
4. Act 32 of 1961.

which is modelled on the Constitution of 1910 reiterates this point. Section 59(2) declares that

> 'No court of law shall be competent to enquire into or to pronounce upon the validity of any Act passed by Parliament . . .'[5]

This provision reduces the judiciary to a subordinate status in the constitutional structure of South Africa. The courts have no power to test apartheid legislation against ideal standards of equality resembling those contained in the American Bill of Rights. They are constitutionally denied the power to play the activist, egalitarian role that the American Supreme Court has played in the past twenty years.

THE LAW OF APARTHEID

The South African common law consists of a blend of principles of Roman-Dutch law, developed by the courts and jurists of the Netherlands during the seventeenth and eighteenth centuries, and principles of the English common law which have been absorbed into the Roman-Dutch system during its sojourn in South Africa. It does not permit racial discrimination: on the contrary it places full emphasis on the importance of equality before the law. The 'law of apartheid' therefore is not the product of the common law, but the creation of a host of legislative enactments, most of which have been passed by Parliament since 1948 when the National Party Government came into office. The 'law of apartheid' can broadly be divided into two categories: first, those laws which prescribe the social, economic and educational status of the individual in society and which give legal endorsement to practices of racial discrimination; secondly, those laws which construct the institutions of separate development and determine the political status of the individual.

A: PERSONAL STATUS OF THE INDIVIDUAL UNDER APARTHEID

As a person's political, civil, economic and social rights are determined by his race it is of primary importance to establish the racial group to which he belongs. This is not left to societal determination because this might allow persons to cross from a less privileged racial group to a more privi-

5. The only exception to this rule concerns the equal language rights. Here the courts are empowered to enquire whether the correct, special Parliamentary procedure for amending such rights has been followed.

leged group if their physical appearance permitted it. Instead, an elaborate legislative scheme has been established to identify each person racially.[6] The central statute is the Population Registration Act of 1950[7] which is the corner-stone of the whole system of apartheid. It provides for the compilation by the Secretary for the Interior of a population register of the entire South African population, which is to reflect the classification of each individual 'as a White person, a Coloured person or a Bantu, as the case may be, and every Coloured person and every Bantu whose name is so included shall be classified . . . according to the ethnic or other group to which he belongs'.[8] The legislature has had considerable difficulty in finding a definition which will defy all attempts to cross the colour line and the definitions of 'White', 'Coloured' and 'Bantu' have frequently been amended. The current definitions, which are based on the three criteria of appearance, social acceptance and descent, are as follows: a White person is one who is in appearance obviously White – and not generally accepted as Coloured – or who is generally accepted as White – and is not in appearance obviously Non-White, provided that 'a person shall not be classified as a White person if one of his natural parents has been classified as a Coloured person or a Bantu'; a Bantu is a person 'who is, or is generally accepted as, a member of any aboriginal race or tribe of Africa'; and a Coloured is 'a person who is not a White person or a Bantu'.[9] A person who is aggrieved by the classification by the Secretary for the Interior may lodge an objection with an administrative tribunal – viz. a race classification board – from which a limited appeal lies to the Supreme Court. Thousands of objections have been lodged against the Secretary's classification, particularly by persons classified as 'Coloured'. Statistics, however, cannot capture the misery and human suffering caused by this legislative scheme which sometimes even results in division of families owing to the different racial classifications of members of the same family.[10]

6. See, further, on this subject, Arthur Suzman, 'Race Classification and Definition in the Legislation of the Union of South Africa, 1910-1960' (1960), *Acta Juridica* 339 and Elizabeth S. Landis, 'South African Apartheid Legislation' (1961), 71 *Yale Law Journal* 1 at 4-16.

7. Act 30 of 1950.

8. Section 5(1).

9. Sections 1 and 5(5).

10. See Muriel Horrell, *Race Classification in South Africa: Its Effects on Human Beings,* Fact paper No. 2 (1958), published by the S.A. Institute of Race Relations.

The purpose of the Population Registration Act is to place each individual in a particular racial group. Other statutes then prohibit sexual, residential, social, educational and economic intermingling.

Before the National Party came to power in 1948 marriages between persons of different races were very rare, but in 1949 the Prohibition of Mixed Marriages Act[11] was passed forbidding marriages between Whites and Non-Whites and rendering unions entered into in contravention of this law 'void and of no effect'. At the time of its introduction Government spokesmen justified the Act on the ground that some thirty of the States of the United States retained similar laws. Since then, however, the United States Supreme Court has held such statutes to be unconstitutional,[12] and declared that 'the freedom to marry has long been recognized as one of the vital personal rights essential to the orderly pursuit of happiness by free men'.[13]

Persons belonging to different racial groups are not only denied the right to marry each other, but they are also forbidden to live together, or to have any sexual contact. The Immorality Act of 1957,[14] confirming previous laws of this kind, makes it a criminal offence for a White person to have sexual intercourse with a Non-White person or to commit any 'immoral or indecent act' with such a person. The maximum penalty for this offence is seven years' imprisonment[15] but the maximum is never imposed. The Act is, however, vigorously enforced and convictions have risen rapidly from 1950 when there were only 265 to 1969 when there were 679.[16] Only about half of those charged are convicted but in most cases the social disgrace attached to prosecution under the Act is tantamount to conviction and imprisonment. Although the Act is ostensibly designed to protect White women from the lust of Black men, statistics suggest that Black women are in greater need of protection. Of the 679 convicted in 1969 336 were White men and 319 Non-White women, while only nine White women and fifteen Non-White men were convicted.[17]

Pre-1948 housing and residential patterns were clearly determined by the accepted practice of social segregation, buttressed by legislation in cer-

11. Act 55 of 1949.
12. *Loving* v *Virginia* 388 US 1 (1967).
13. Act 12.
14. Act 23 of 1957, section 16.
15. Sections 16 and 22.
16. *House of Assembly Debates,* vol. 29, col. 2493 (25 August, 1970).
17. *Ibid.*

tain cases. Inevitably there was a certain amount of overlapping, particularly between the Whites and the Coloureds in Cape Town and the Whites and the Indians in Natal. In furtherance of its rigid, ideological policies the National Party Government resolved to eliminate all residential integration. The result was the Group Areas Act of 1950[18] which empowers the State President, after an investigation by the Group Areas Board – an administrative tribunal established under the Act – to proclaim any area a 'group area' for a particular racial group and to compel residents not belonging to the chosen group to move elsewhere. In theory all racial groups are equally affected by this scheme, but in practice Whites are less affected. By the end of 1968 only 656 White families had become disqualified from remaining in their homes while 58 999 Coloured families, 784 Chinese families, 35 172 Indian families and 25 156 African families had been disqualified.[19] The inequalities of the system have recently been highlighted by the case of District Six, a suburb near the centre of Cape Town, which had a population of 61 000 Coloureds and 800 Whites. The area has been proclaimed 'White', with the result that the Coloured population will be compelled to leave District Six, which is within walking distance of the city and move to a suburb sixteen kilometres outside Cape Town.[20]

The Group Areas Act is essentially designed to segregate urban areas. Human removals in the rural areas are effected by the Bantu Land Act of 1913[21] and the Bantu Trust and Land Act of 1936[22] which provide for the setting aside of certain areas for the exclusive occupation of Africans, but, at the same time, prohibit Africans from owning land outside these areas and authorize the expropriation of African-owned land (described as 'black spots') acquired before 1936, after which date Africans were prohibited from purchasing land in White areas.[23] Before 1948 only three small 'black spots' had been 'cleared' but since then 106 'spots' have been 'cleared' and 75 810 people moved from their homes to other areas[24] which often lack the necessary facilities for human habitation and are far from

18. Act 41 of 1950, re-enacted as Act 36 of 1966. See further Landis, *op. cit.* 20-29.
19. *House of Assembly Debates,* vol. 25, col. 312 (7 February, 1969); *A Survey of Race Relations in South Africa,* 1969, p. 166.
20. Leo Marquard, *The Peoples and Policies of South Africa,* 4th ed. (1969), p. 74.
21. Act 27 of 1913.
22. Act 18 of 1936.
23. Section 13(2) of Act 18 of 1936.
24. *A Survey of Race Relations in South Africa,* 1968, p. 121.

sources of employment.[25] According to Government spokesmen some 276 'black spots' are still to be moved.[26]

Separate development demands that separate areas be set aside for exclusive occupation by different groups, but it does not prohibit Blacks from working in White areas as migrant labourers. The impermanent nature of their sojourn is, however, repeatedly brought home to them by laws which restrict their entrance to White areas, oblige them to account for their presence there and threaten them with arbitrary expulsion. The two most formidable laws regulating the status of the Black man in the White urban areas are the Bantu (Urban Areas) Consolidation Act[27] and the Bantu (Abolition of Passes and Co-ordination of Documents) Act.[28] In terms of the former statute it is an offence – punishable by a fine or imprisonment and 'repatriation' (deportation to rural homeland) – for an African to remain for longer than 72 hours in an urban area, unless he is able to prove that (a) he has resided in such area continuously since birth; or (b) he has worked continuously in such area for the same employer for ten years; or (c) he has lawfully resided continuously in such area for at least fifteen years and has not been convicted of a serious offence; or (d) the African is the wife, unmarried daughter, or minor son of a male falling under (a) (b) or (c); or (e) permission to remain has been granted to him by a labour bureau. In any criminal prosecution for this offence the accused is presumed, until the contrary is proved, to be unlawfully within the urban area.[29] The same statute permits an African who is lawfully entitled to reside in an urban area to be removed by administrative means if he is found to be 'idle' (habitually unemployed) or 'undesirable' (has previously been convicted of certain offences) or if his presence is seen as 'detrimental to the maintenance of peace and order in any such area'. Such a person is then sent back to his homeland, to a rehabilitation centre or to a work or farm colony for a period not exceeding two years.[30]

The control of movement of Africans throughout the Republic is effected by the 'pass system'. A pass has been defined as a document 'required for lawful movement into, out of, or within a specified area' which 'must be

25. *Ibid.*, 1968, pp. 124-137.
26. *Ibid.*, p. 121.
27. Act 25 of 1945, as amended. See, further, Landis, *op. cit.* 43-52.
28. Act 67 of 1952. Landis, (1962) 71 *Yale Law Journal* 437 at 457-62.
29. Section 10.
30. Sections 20 and 29 *bis*.

produced on demand of a specified person, failure of production constituting an offence'.[31] The pass laws are of pre-Union vintage and were inherited by the National Party when it came to power. In 1952 the Government sponsored a statute with the misleading title of the Bantu (Abolition of Passes and Co-ordination of Documents) Act which did *not* repeal the pass laws but simply co-ordinated them by providing for the carrying of 'reference books' instead of passes and extended them by requiring women to carry reference books as well as men. In terms of the Act every African over the age of sixteen must be fingerprinted and furnished with a reference book which contains his identity card and, *inter alia,* information about his employment. The reference book must be carried on the person of the African and failure to produce it on demand constitutes a criminal offence punishable by a fine not exceeding R20 or imprisonment not exceeding one month.

The 'pass laws' and the Bantu (Urban Areas) Consolidation Act are vigorously enforced. During the twelve-month period from mid-1968 to mid-1969, 632 077 persons were arrested and tried for offences under these laws, representing 26,5 per cent of the total number of prosecutions of persons of all races for all offences.[32] In the Johannesburg municipal area alone there were about 245 persons arrested daily for such offences.[33] As a result of these laws a large number of law-abiding Africans are brought into contact with the enforcement of the criminal law. Such contact, for offences which can at best be described as 'technical', hardly induces respect for the law.

Laws dictating sexual and residential separation are supplemented by laws prescribing separate public amenities designed to prohibit social contact between persons of different racial groups. Since 1953 it has not been necessary to provide equal amenities for different races – whereby hangs a forensic tale. At the time that American courts were prepared to accept the constitutionality of separate but equal facilities for different races,[34] South African courts were reluctant to recognize the competence of sub-

31. E. Kahn in *Handbook on Race Relations in South Africa* (edited by Ellen Hellmann) (1949), p. 275.

32. *Report of the Commissioner of South African Police, 1968/9* RP 59/1970; *A Survey of Race Relations in South Africa,* 1970, p. 164.

33. *House of Assembly Debates,* vol. 26, col. 5364 (6 May, 1969).

34. Following the approval of this doctrine by the Supreme Court in *Plessy* v *Ferguson* 163 US 537 (1896).

ordinate law-making bodies to provide for separate facilities.[35] Only in 1934 did the Appellate Division decide, in *Minister of Posts and Telegraphs* v *Rasool*,[36] that equal separate facilities for different races complied with the test of reasonableness, used for judging the constitutionality of subordinate or delegated legislation. (On this subject it must be pointed out that while the courts have no power to test Acts of Parliament they may scrutinize the laws of subordinate law-making bodies – such as municipal councils – to ascertain whether such laws discriminate unreasonably, but only where the enabling Act of Parliament itself is silent on the subject of such discrimination. Our courts have adopted the view that delegated legislation is unreasonable if it is 'found to be partial and unequal' in its operation between different races.[37]) In the early fifties the courts incurred the wrath of the Government when they declared invalid by-laws and regulations of subordinate law-making bodies which provided for substantially unequal facilities for different races.[38] The Government's response was to produce the Reservation of Separate Amenities Act[39] which permits authorities to reserve separate but unequal facilities and accommodation for different races and expressly denies courts the power to declare such reservations invalid. Ironically this Act was passed at about the same time as the American Supreme Court ruled against separate facilities on the ground that they are 'inherently unequal'.[40]

Racial division is maintained at all levels of education. Separate schooling was practised long before 1948, but at two of the Universities – the Universities of Cape Town and the Witwatersrand – there was no racial test for admission. The National Party Government has tightened its control over separate educational facilities by removing African schools from provincial control and subjecting them to the control of the central government,[41] and by prohibiting Non-Whites from studying at 'open universi-

35. Alfred Avins, 'Racial Separation and Public Accommodations: Some Comparative Notes between South African and American Law', (1969) 86 *South African Law Journal* 53.

36. 1934 AD 167.

37. This is the test contained in the English decision of *Kruse* v *Johnson* [1898] 2 QB 91 at 99.

38. *R* v *Abdurahman* 1950 (3) SA 136 (AD) and *R* v *Lusu* 1953 (2) SA 484 (AD).

39. Act 49 of 1953; Landis, *op cit.* 450.

40. *Brown* v *Board of Education of Topeka* 347 US 483 (1954).

41. Bantu Education Act 47 of 1953; Landis, *op. cit.* 489.

ties'.[42] Separate universities now exist for each ethnic group – Whites, Coloureds, Indians, Xhosas, Zulus and Sothos.

The law of apartheid in the field of labour is the most difficult to describe, as here law[43] and convention combine to ensure that both the status and the salary of the Non-White remain subordinate to those of his fellow White worker. The most notorious statutes reserving certain jobs for Whites are the Mines and Works Act[44] and the Bantu Building Workers Act[45] which prohibit Africans from performing skilled work on the mines and in the building trade. The inevitable disparity in wages then follows. For instance, to cite an extreme example, in 1967 the average monthly remuneration of a White miner was R282 and that of an African miner was R17 (excluding board and lodging).[46] Africans are deprived of the normal bargaining power in industrial relations as a result of the non-recognition of African trade unions[47] and the prohibition on their right to strike.[48]

B: INSTITUTIONAL APARTHEID

At the time of Union the four colonies, which were to become the four provinces, were divided over the part to be played by the Non-White in the political process. While the Cape favoured a non-racial, qualified franchise based on individual merit, the other three colonies pressed for the total exclusion of the Non-White from the franchise. The result was a compromise, with each province retaining its pre-Union franchise and the Non-White vote in the Cape protected by an entrenchment procedure which provided that no change might be made to these voting rights without a two-thirds majority vote of both Houses of Parliament sitting together, but only Whites could sit in Parliament. In the long run the northern philosophy was to prevail. In 1936 African voters in the Cape were removed from the common electoral roll by the required two-thirds majority[49] and placed on a separate roll to elect three White representa-

42. Extension of University Education Act 45 of 1959; Landis, *op cit.* 496.

43. For a survey of these laws see Landis, *op. cit.* 437.

44. 27 of 1956. Section 12 permits the State President to issue regulations reserving certain jobs for certain races.

45. 27 of 1951, section 15.

46. *A Survey of Race Relations in South Africa,* 1968, p. 104.

47. The Industrial Conciliation Act 28 of 1956 governing labour relations in South Africa does not provide for the recognition of African unions.

48. Bantu Labour (Settlement of Disputes) Act 48 of 1953, section 18.

49. Representation of Natives Act 12 of 1936.

tives to the House of Assembly. At the same time provision was made for four White Senators elected by electoral colleges to represent Africans throughout the Union. The Coloureds in the Cape were left on the common roll until the National Party came to power in 1948 determined to purge all Non-Whites from the political process. But the National Party was not able to command the neccessary two-thirds majority vote and, after its attempts to remove the Coloured voters by a simple majority vote had been ruled unconstitutional by the Appellate Division,[50] it enlarged the Senate in order to obtain the required majority.[51] So it was that in 1956 the Coloureds too were placed on a separate roll to elect four White representatives to the House of Assembly.[52]

The first decade of National Party rule was marked by the constitutional struggle over the Coloured vote and the construction of an apartheid society based upon discriminatory measures of the kind described under sub-heading A. No real effort was made to provide an institutional framework for the promised vertical separate development, although the seed of future developments was to be found in the Bantu Authorities Act of 1951[53] which gave its approval to traditional, tribal authorities. The legislative implementation of the Grand Design of a commonwealth of nations in South Africa was left to Dr Verwoerd, who became Prime Minister in 1958. The first step was to remove the White representatives of the African people in Parliament and to give legislative approval to the separate homelands policy. This was effected by the Promotion of Bantu Self-Government Act[54] which declared in its preamble that the Bantu peoples of South Africa do not constitute a homogeneous people, but form eight separate national units on the basis of language and culture – namely the Northern Sotho, Southern Sotho, Swazi, Shangana-Tsonga, Tswana, Venda, Xhosa and Zulu – which would one day form '*self-governing* Bantu national units'.[55] In the meantime, the Government explained, there was no place for representation in the White Parliament be-

50. *Harris* v *Minister of the Interior* 1952 (2) SA 428 (AD) and *Minister of the Interior* v *Harris* 1952 (4) SA 769 (AD).

51. For an account of this 'constitutional crisis', see H.R. Hahlo and Ellison Kahn, *South Africa: The Development of its Laws and Constitution* (1960), pp. 151-163.

52. The South Africa Act Amendment Act 9 of 1956 revalidated the Separate Representation of Voters Act 46 of 1951.

53. Act 68 of 1951.

54. Act 46 of 1959.

55. White Paper 3 of 1959, p. 7. Italics added.

cause 'participation in the government of the guardian territory does not form part of the preparation of the subordinate units for the task of self-government'.[56]

Although tribal, regional and territorial authorities – viz. the traditional authorities provided for in the Bantu Authorities Act of 1951 – have been extensively developed in the Bantu homelands, only one had received the constitutional stamp of partial self-government before 1971, namely, the Transkei.

The Transkei was hurriedly – by South African standards but not by those of other colonial powers – given the legal trappings of self-government in 1963 in order to impress on the International Court of Justice the sincerity of the Government's intentions in respect of separate development at the time of the legal proceedings between South Africa and Ethiopia/Liberia over South West Africa. The constitution[57] cleverly adopts the rhetoric of advanced self-government and the uninitiated might be forgiven for believing that the Transkei was given powers similar to those of a state under a federation. The Transkei is expressly described as self-governing[58] and is given its own flag, anthem and official language.[59] Transkeian citizenship is conferred on black Transkeians.[60] A Legislative Assembly is created with powers over local matters such as inferior courts, finances, agriculture, education and soil conservation.[61] Furthermore it is expressly provided that the Assembly may repeal Republican laws which deal with matters falling under its control[62] and that no Acts of Parliament which deal with matters transferred to the control of the Legislative Assembly will apply to citizens of the Transkei.[63]

But these provisions must be seen in their true legal perspective. Transkeian 'citizens' remain South African citizens for external purposes and for the purposes of international law – the most important attribute of

56. *Ibid.*, p. 6.

57. Act 48 of 1963. See further on this constitution, Ellison Kahn, 'Some Thoughts on the Competency of the Transkeian Legislative Assembly and the Sovereignty of the South African Parliament', (1963) 80 *South African Law Journal* 473.

58. Section 1.

59. Sections 4, 5 and 6. Xhosa is recognized as an official language in addition to English and Afrikaans.

60. Section 7.

61. First Schedule.

62. Section 37(1)(*b*).

63. Section 37(3).

citizenship. Although the Transkeian Legislative Assembly is given wider legislative powers than the provincial councils it remains firmly subordinate to the central White Parliament and Government. Parliament may legislate at will for the Transkei – and even repeal the whole Transkeian Constitution – and no South African court could question the validity of such enactments by reason of section 59(2) of the South African Constitution,[64] while the Government retains an ultimate veto over legislation because all enactments of the Legislative Assembly require the approval of the State President acting on the advice of his White Cabinet.[65] Further limitations on the Legislative Assembly's power arise from the express exclusion from its jurisdiction of such vital matters as defence, military units, external affairs, the control of any Republican police force charged with the maintenance of internal security, postal, telephone and radio services, immigration, aviation, railways, harbours and national roads.[66] The composition of the Legislative Assembly and the manner of its election ensure that Government policy will be pursued. Of the 109 members, 64 are chiefs – many of whose appointment and status is dependent upon the Government – and 45 are elected. In the first election anti-Government Chief Victor Poto captured 38 of the 45 elected seats but was still defeated in his bid for Chief Minister of the Transkeian Cabinet by Chief Kaiser Matanzima, who enjoyed the support of the pro-Government tribal chiefs. In the second election in 1968, however, Chief Kaiser Matanzima secured the support of 28 of the elected members. Suspicion is cast over the whole election process in the Transkei by the emergency regulations promulgated in 1960 in Proclamation 400[67] which are still in force today and which seriously inhibit free elections. *Inter alia* these regulations prohibit gatherings of more than ten persons (subject to certain exceptions, such as church services) without special permission, make it an offence to treat a Chief with disrespect, and permit persons to be held indefinitely without trial for the purpose of police questioning.[68]

The Transkeian experiment is cherished with pride by the Government

64. See above p. 82.

65. Section 40.

66. Section 39.

67. Proc No. R400, *GGE* No. 6582 of 30 November 1960, amended by Proc No. R413 *GGE* No. 6594 of 14 Decembeer 1960.

68. During the past decade almost 1 000 Africans have been held without trial for varying periods, some for as long as 200 days. The majority of these detainees have been released without being charged.

and frequently cited as an example of a territory on its way to full independence. If this is so, one is tempted to ask why it is that the past eight years have seen so little constitutional advancement in the status of the Transkei. Why is it that the legislative competence of the Legislative Assembly has not been increased in respect of matters not falling within the category of local government? Why is it that the number of elected members in the Legislative Assembly has not been increased if self-determination is the real aim, as the Government professes? Why is it that the harsh emergency regulations continue in force inhibiting genuine self-determination? If *de jure* independence, let alone *de facto* independence, for the Transkei is the Government's goal why is it proceeding at a snail's pace at a time when accelerated decolonization is demanded everywhere?

Since 1970 there has been an acceleration of the institutional development of the homelands. First came the Bantu Homelands Citizenship Act of 1970[69] which provides that every African who is not a citizen of a self-governing territory will become a 'citizen' of the territorial authority area to which he is residentially or culturally attached.[70] Then came the Bantu Homelands Constitution Act 21 of 1971 which empowers the Government to grant constitutions substantially similar to that of the Transkei, to territorial authorities after consultation with them. Although no provision is made for the granting of independence to homelands in this Act both the preamble to the Act and the White Paper[71] accompanying the Act, affirm the intention of the Government to lead the homelands to self-government and *independence.* To date several homeland legislative assemblies have been brought into operation under this Act by proclamation in the *Government Gazette.* These are the Tswana (1 May 1971), Ciskeian, Venda (1 June 1971), Matshangana, Lebowa (1 July 1971) and Basotho-Qwaqwa (1 October 1971) Legislative Assemblies.[72] Whereas the Legislative Assembly of the Transkei consists partly of elected members these Assemblies consist only of tribal and appointed members.

The preoccupation of the Government with its homelands constitution-building has left it little time for the more pressing problem of involving

69. Act 26 of 1970.

70. In international relations he will of course continue to have the status of a citizen of the Republic itself.

71. 1 of 1971.

72. Proclamations R 87 *Government Gazette* (*GG*) 3083 of 30 April 1971, R 118 and R 119 *GG* 3110 of 21 May 1971, R 148 *GG* 3163 of 25 June 1971, R 156 *GG* 3177 of 30 June 1971 and R 225 *GG* 3270 of 1 October 1971.

Africans resident in 'White areas', who constitute the majority of the African population,[73] in the political process. In theory it has done so by attaching each urban African to the political process in the homeland with which he is ethnically linked, but this is an exercise in metaphysics rather than practical politics. In a more practical vein provision has been made for the establishment of Urban Bantu Councils[74] in the White areas, but so far only twenty-three of these councils have constituted[75] and, in any event, the powers of such councils are limited to minor local matters and to the giving of advice to the White authorities.

The principle of separate, political development has also been applied to the Coloured and the Indian peoples, but here matters have been complicated by the absence of Coloured and Indian territorial homelands. The result is that Government legislative policy towards these two groups has been essentially negative. They have been denied participation in central, White political affairs and in return have been given partly- or non-representative councils with limited powers over their own peoples.

Government policy towards the political role of the Coloured people has been marked by indecision and vacillation. In the fifties the Government fought desperately to remove the Coloured voters in the Cape from the common electoral roll and to give them separate, White representation in the House of Assembly.[76] But in the sixties, when it appeared certain that the Coloured voters would elect members of the multi-racial Progressive Party to represent them in Parliament,[77] the Government withdrew this token representation[78] and in its place created a Coloured Persons Representative Council in 1968.[79] This Council, consisting of 40 elected and 20 nominated members to represent Coloured people throughout the Republic, has power to make laws affecting Coloureds (on a personality basis) on finance, local government, education, community

73. According to the latest census figures 53,5 per cent of the African population resides in 'White areas'. *A Survey of Race Relations in South Africa,* 1970, p. 134.

74. Urban Bantu Councils Act 79 of 1961.

75. *House of Assembly Debates,* vol. 30, col. 3600 (8 September, 1970).

76. See above p. 90.

77. In 1965 Coloured voters elected two Progressive Party candidates to represent them in the Cape Provincial Council. A similar result was anticipated in the General Election.

78. Separate Representation of Voters Amendment Act 50 of 1968.

79. Coloured Persons Representative Council Amendment Act 52 of 1968, read with Act 49 of 1964.

welfare and pensions, and rural settlements. No bill may be introduced, however, until it has been approved by the Minister of Coloured Affairs and the bill as passed must be approved by the White Cabinet. If it conflicts with an Act of Parliament it is invalid. Administrative functions are to be performed by an executive of five persons, four elected and one (the chairman) nominated by the Cabinet. In the first election in 1969, the Labour Party, which opposes the Government and separate development, won 26 of the 40 elected seats, but the Government then appointed members of the defeated pro-Government Federal Party to fill the nominated seats with the result that the party which won the election ended up as the opposition.[80] Mr Tom Swartz, leader of the Federal Party, was appointed chairman of the executive.

The Indian people have been similarly treated. In 1946 they were granted separate representation by three White Members of Parliament and two Senators in the central Parliament,[81] but, after this token representation had been rejected by the Indian people themselves, it was repealed by the National Party Government in 1948.[82] In 1968 a South African Indian Council was established[83] consisting of 25 Indian persons appointed by the Minister of Indian Affiers. The Council has advisory powers only and serves as a link between the Government and the Indian population. The Government has announced its intention of convenig this Council into a partly-elected one at a later date.[84]

Despite their exclusion from the franchise Non-Whites were permitted until 1968 to join political parties with a multi-racial aim, namely the Liberal Party and the Progressive Party. This enabled Non-Whites to participate indirectly in the only meaningful political process in the Republic by influencing the parliamentary policies of these parties. In 1968, however, this was brought to an end by the Prohibition of Political Interference Act[85] which prohibits racially mixed political parties. The Act distinguishes between the African, White, Coloured and Asian population groups and provides that no person belonging to one population group may be a member of a political party of which a person belonging to

80. For an account of this election, see *A Survey of Race Relations in South Africa, 1969*, pp. 5-8.

81. Asiatic Land Tenure and Indian Representation Act 28 of 1946.

82. Act 47 of 1948.

83. Act 31 of 1968.

84. *House of Assembly Debates,* vol. 22, cols. 1124-9 (26 February, 1968).

85. Act 51 of 1968.

another population group is a member, or address a meeting of persons of whom the majority belong to any other population group in order to further the interests of a political party. As a result of this legislation the Liberal Party voluntarily dissolved and the Progressive Party went White.

No picture of South African political life would be complete without mention of the, of necessity, extra-constitutional attempts of the disenfranchised majority to participate in the government of the country, and of the harsh, repressive measures taken by the Government to suppress these attempts.

In 1948 African popular political opinion was represented by the African National Congress (ANC). In the early fifties it sought to focus attention on the grievances of the African people by organizing a defiance campaign in which Africans were urged to peacefully defy certain discriminatory laws, such as the pass laws. This campaign was brought to an end by the combined operation of the Suppression of Communism Act of 1950[86] and the Criminal Law Amendment Act of 1953.[87] The former, which outlaws the Communist Party, makes it an offence to further the aims of 'communism' which, *inter alia,* includes any doctrine which 'aims at bringing about any political, industrial, social or economic change within the Republic by the promotion of disturbance or disorder, by unlawful acts or omissions'.[88] The latter makes it an offence punishable by a fine of R600 or three years imprisonment and/or a whipping to violate any law 'by way of protest or in support of any campaign against any law or in support of any campaign for the repeal or modification of any law'.[89]

In 1960 another defiance campaign sponsored by the ANC and the Pan-Africanist Congress (PAC), formed in 1959, resulted in the declaration of a state of emergency[90] after the police had fired on and killed demonstrators at Sharpeville. During this emergency both the ANC and the PAC were outlawed by means of the Unlawful Organizations Act.[91]

86. Act 44 of 1950.
87. Act 8 of 1953.
88. Section 1. The leaders of the ANC were convicted under this Act in ***R* v *Sisulu*** 1953 (3) SA 276 (AD) on the grounds that they had furthered the aims of communism by advocating a scheme aimed at bringing about political and social change by the abolition of laws differentiating between Whites and Non-Whites by means which included unlawful acts arising from the contravention of the pass laws.
89. Sections 1 and 2.
90. Under the Public Safety Act 3 of 1953.
91. Act 34 of 1960.

Since then it has been an offence punishable by one to ten years' imprisonment, for any person to become or continue to be a member of one of these bodies, to take part in any of their activities, or to perform any act calculated to further the achievements of any of their objects.[92] About 1 000 Africans, mostly from the Eastern Cape Province, have been imprisoned under this Act,[93] of whom many, on their release, have been 'banned' under the Suppression of Communism Act. The 'banning' provision of the latter Act permits the Minister of Justice to confine a person to a particular area (which may be a house or a magisterial district), to forbid him from publishing anything, to exclude him from certain forms of employment (for example teaching) and to prohibit him from communicating with more than one person at a time, when he is satisfied that such a person advocates the objects of communism or engages in activities which may further such objects.[94] No court of law may review such a decision.

Having been denied the right to open political association and expression outside the framework of the Government's separate development policy, many Africans have either gone underground or fled abroad to continue their struggle. In order to combat these activities the Government has introduced repressive security measures unknown to Western systems of jurisprudence. In 1963 the 90-day detention law[95] was introduced empowering a senior police officer to arrest and hold a person for 90 days for the purpose of interrogation in solitary confinement if he was suspected of having information relating to the commission of offences under the Suppression of Communism Act and the Unlawful Organizations Act. *Habeas Corpus* was expressly revoked in this instance. This measure remained in force for two years during which time 1 095 persons were held under its provisions of whom only half were later charged.[96] In 1967 the tradition of the 90-day detention law was reinstated by the Terrorism Act.[97] This statute provides for the punishment by death or

92. Sections 3 and 11 of Act 44 of 1950 read with section 2 of Act 34 of 1960.

93. This figure is arrived at by adding the estimated number of convictions provided by Muriel Horrell in *A Survey of Race Relations in South Africa* 1963, p. 53; 1964, p. 84; 1965, pp. 61, 67-68; 1966, p. 87; 1967, pp. 54-5; 1968, p. 57.

94. Section 10.

95. Section 17 of Act 37 of 1963. For an analysis of this law, see A.S. Mathews and R.C. Albino 'The Permanence of the Temporary – An Examination of the 90- and 180-day Detention Laws' (1966) 83 *South African Law Journal* 16.

96. *House of Assembly Debates*, vol. 13, col. 252 (29 January, 1965).

97. Act 83 of 1967.

imprisonment (not less than five years) of persons convicted of the crime of terrorism which is constituted, *inter alia,* by 'any act', committed 'with intent to endanger the maintenance of law and order', where the prosecution can prove that the act, *inter alia,* was likely 'to embarrass the administration of the affairs of the State'.[98] Section 6 permits a senior police officer to arrest without warrant any person whom he 'has reason to believe . . . is a terrorist or is withholding from the South African police any information relating to terrorists or to offences under this Act' and to detain him *indefinitely* for the purpose of interrogation. No person, other than an official of the State, may have access to such a detainee and 'no court of law shall pronounce upon the validity of any action taken under this section, or order the release of any detainee'. This statute, like the 90-day detention law, is non-racial in the sense that its operation is *de jure* not limited to a particular racial group. In practice, however, it has largely been used to suppress black political activity.

CONCLUSION

Apartheid is a creature of the law. Conceived in racial prejudice it is nurtured in the womb of Parliament and brought forth in legislative form. It is not merely declaratory of existing social convention, it is often constitutive of new discriminatory practices. The law is as indispensable to apartheid as is race prejudice itself. An understanding of the role of the law in South Africa is essential for an understanding of apartheid.

Basically the law fulfils four functions. First, it constructs a legal order based on racial discrimination and differentiation. Secondly, as has been shown above,[99] by legitimizing discriminatory practices, it neutralizes the immorality of such practices in the eyes of the majority of the White population who accept without question any rule which has been blessed by Parliament. Thirdly, those laws which institutionalize separate development provide a convenient façade for the outside world. The Promotion of Bantu Self-Government Act, the Transkei Constitution and the Bantu Homelands Constitution Act are useful for foreign consumption as they adopt the rhetoric of self-determination and self-government without disclosing the realities of South African life. Legal tinsel is used to conceal the fact that most of the African population lives outside the home-

98. Section 2.
99. See pp. 80 and 81.

lands and cannot in fact participate in the homelands political process; that the African people themselves have not been consulted about their future; and that self-determination inside or outside the homelands is meaningless while the harsh security laws remain in force. Fourthly, the drastic security laws, such as the Suppression of Communism Act, the Unlawful Organizations Act and the Terrorism Act, create a repressive atmosphere in which meaningful political debate and activity is stifled. They create a permanent emergency 'in which it is no longer possible to distinguish between the preservation of order and the preservation of the power of the ruling party and between opposition and subversion'.[100] Apartheid's legal order serves therefore to perpetuate the status quo – White supremacy.

The manner in which the legal process has been invoked to entrench racial discrimination does not promote respect for the law. Indeed, some might argue that some laws are so lacking in minimum moral content that they do not deserve the name 'law'.[101] While law, as a social process, may justifiably be used to promote even so daring a social experiment as separate development, those who do not distinguish completely between law and justice find it unfortunate that the law should be used as an instrument of repression and discrimination in the interests of a small, White oligarchy.

100. A.S. Mathews and R.C. Albino, 'The Permanence of the Temporary' (1966) 83 *South African Law Journal* 16 at 43.

101. Cf. Lon L. Fuller, 'Positivism and Fidelity to Law' (1958) 71 *Harvard Law Review* 630.

Petty Apartheid – the Tip of the Iceberg?

Dirk Richard

A former editor of Dagbreek en Sondagnuus, *once one of South Africa's larger circulation Sunday newspapers, Dirk Richard is widely respected for his advanced thinking on Afrikaans journalism and his open-mindedness regarding local political issues in general and apartheid in particular. After the amalgamation of the country's two Afrikaans Sunday papers in 1970, he was appointed Group Editor of Afrikaanse Pers, one of the top publishing concerns in Africa.*

To the outside world, and even to those who profess an interest in South African affairs, the distinction between small and big apartheid may appear confusing or a mere technicality or even completely incomprehensible. Apartheid is seen as a whole, a political policy which is generally condemned with none of its component parts to be commended. But a widespread and interesting controversy about small apartheid has arisen in South Africa. This is significant, especially when it is realized that the argument is going on mainly amongst Afrikaners, the authors of our colour policy of separation, the maligned White supremacists and so-called master race protagonists!

Some Afrikaners maintain that small apartheid is petty and must fail in the long run; others regard it as an integral and necessary part of our colour policy. The division, however, goes deeper than this. Those who favour the ultimate elimination of petty apartheid foresee and favour a new basis for White-Black relations. Those who back petty apartheid also resist wider contacts across the colour bar and would preserve rigid segregation as far as possible in all spheres of life. Many observers even believe that this could lead to a new political alignment in the Republic, that political parties can no longer divide on obsolete problems such as whether South Africa should belong to the British Commonwealth or not, as was the case in the thirties. What matters now, as the doyen of Afrikaans journalists, Willem van Heerden, clearly pointed out, are the future relations between Black and White states and their peoples.

The different viewpoints regarding petty apartheid could be just the visible tip of the iceberg lurking under the now placid waters of South African politics. A change in the political climate seems inevitable, but when and how this will come about is a matter of conjecture at this stage. Most would say, not soon. Both the governing National Party and opposing United Party accommodate members who, on the question of race relations, favour an exchange of team mates. Just as difficult as it would be to draw the borders between petty and big apartheid, so would it be to isolate the small, visible acts of segregation (such as separate entrances to railway stations and post offices) from the generally accepted and approved forms of segregation (or differentiation if you will).

The leading protagonists of a new approach to inter-racial communication are Afrikaans professors at the universities of South Africa, Potchefstroom, Pretoria and Stellenbosch. A number of Afrikaans newspaper journalists also favour a change in the rigid, dogmatic approach to colour relations. Even a few Nationalist politicians have sounded a subdued warning that South Africa cannot afford, or will not be allowed, to stay out of tune with the rest of the world indefinitely.

These men have declared war on forms of petty apartheid which they regard as blatant colour discrimination which cannot be defended before the world, or which they find difficult to reconcile with their own consciences or sense of justice. They cite a long list of examples:

> The initial refusal of a visa to a world famous Japanese jockey. This was hurriedly rectified when the consequences of the rash action were realized, but the Japanese then refused the invitation. And quite inconsistent with this was the approval of a Japanese swimming team to visit the Republic.
>
> The South African Indian golfer Papwa Sewgolum was on one occasion allowed to take part in a local championship, but on a later day he was refused permission. On the first occasion he had to receive his prize money in the rain outside a Durban club house.
>
> The Afrikaans writer Breyten Breytenbach, living in Paris with his Vietnamese wife, refused to visit his native country after a visa had been denied his wife on the grounds that she was Non-White. This

has so infuriated Breytenbach that he is now actively engaged in anti-South African activities in France.

The American Negro tennis player Arthur Ashe and the Coloured M.C.C. cricket player Basil D'Oliviera were forbidden to visit the Republic, but no official objection was raised to the inclusion of Maori and Polynesian players in the New Zealand rugby team which visited this country during 1970. The professors are asking openly what the reasons for the different treatment can be. Has a policy been evolved or conveniently adjusted to suit the needs of the moment?

An Indian who married a White English girl legally in Britain was prosecuted under the Immorality Act when they came to South Africa. This Act forbids sexual intercourse between Whites and Non-Whites.

A permit was refused a White symphony[1] orchestra to hold a concert in a Coloured township near Johannesburg. The soloist would have been a Coloured concert pianist who had just returned to his country after gaining the highest honours in London. (The term 'permit' is frowned upon more and more.) The basic principle of the Government's colour policy is separate but equal facilities. In this case, the academicians argue, there was no question of this principle being observed.

The treatment accorded to certain Chinese has caused much discussion. Objections were raised when Chinese played on a miniature golf course in Port Elizabeth, and the Chinese were barred from further participation. A Chinese scholar was not allowed to take part in a schools athletic competition, whilst another Chinese was banned from an examination room where White pupils were sitting.

It must be pointed out that these degrading exhibitions of petty apartheid were not due to government policy, but rather to local interpretation of the status of the Chinese in the country. The Government was quick to make amends and it is generally accepted that Chinese will not again be subjected to these embarrassing social indignities.

The intellectuals, however, resent a society where such events could have occurred. They also point to the apparent anomaly as regards the

1. Of the South African Broadcasting Corporation.

status of the Japanese in the country, who are classified as 'White' under the law.

The 'reformers' would like to see less of the visible signs of petty apartheid, such as the signboards 'Whites only' or 'Non-Whites only'. Are separate lifts still necessary for the successful implementation of our policy? The 'Whites only' signs are especially objectionable to them at international venues, like airports. They favour a few international hotels and restaurants where White and Non-White (including the native born) could meet and hold conferences.

The new thinkers can quote a host of further petty irritations, but these will suffice. They point out that changes are inevitable and will come about whether some Whites like them or not. Conditions have changed already. Before 1948 it was common practice to refer publicly to Indians and Africans as 'Coolies' and 'Kaffirs'. Today this would be regarded as an insult. Prominent Non-White visitors are accommodated in luxury class White hotels, which previously would have been hardly possible.

Without undue fuss or furore progress has been made in the public's attitude towards Non-White participation in international sporting teams visiting the Republic. While the presence of Maoris in the New Zealand rugby team caused quite a stir as recently as 1970, the visit in 1971 of the Australian Aboriginal tennisplayer Evonne Goolagong and French rugby star Roger Bourgarel (the darkest Non-White to appear with White teams in the country) passed without controversy.

So the evolution in human relations is making steady headway. To address an educated Non-White as 'Mister' is no longer an exception. To shake hands with them does not brand the White man automatically as a 'kafferboetie' (negrophile) as of old. The very fact that a frank discussion on petty apartheid has developed in Afrikaans society, is obvious proof of the need of a new approach to the delicate matter of human relations. Such protests would have been confined previously to the liberal journals of the very liberal, leftish organizations.

The academicians, journalists and other intellectuals argue that petty apartheid is not a principle, an integral part of the policy of separate development. Like apartheid as a whole, it is not in the elevated, untouchable sphere of principle. It is the political instrument whereby the National Party hopes to achieve its ideal of separate, independent nations living in peaceful and prosperous co-existence.

Petty apartheid is therefore a temporary measure which must ultimately disappear. In the transitional stage, until the goal of fully developed Black states has been achieved, it cannot be abandoned indiscriminately; rather, it must be retained to a large extent. This is to avoid racial friction, and it serves as a means of social and economic protection for the Black masses, which are less developed than their White counterparts.

These men are also careful to draw a clear line of demarcation between the forms and practices of petty apartheid which should be discarded and those that unavoidably must be retained. They are also aware that the elimination of certain lesser discriminatory measures could lead to more serious repercussions in racial friction, due to a White backlash. They also realize that their demand for a new and enlightened approach would not find favour with the man in the street. Even the politicians would not venture on such a ruinous path, and the large majority of the National Party caucus would back the view that small apartheid is a necessary part of the South African way of life which cannot be abandoned.

But there is a growing public demand for a more lenient and sympathetic application of apartheid measures. Care must be taken to avoid friction and personal affront as much as possible. The White man has little or no wish today to regard an African as a 'kaffir' or to treat him as such. The intellectuals see in this a healthy sign of advancement which must be improved upon. Their war against pettiness in policy application is directed not so much against physical measures as against an outdated form of colour prejudice – to judge all human beings and to base all policies and practices on the colour of a man's skin. It is wrong to remain blind to such matters as personal merit, civilization and intellectual prowess. Skin colour should not be the only factor in determining man's status and standing in life and cannot always be a basic principle of policy.

The crusaders for a new alignment in human relations are perhaps waging a mainly psychological campaign. They even solicit the support of the great Dr H.F. Verwoerd, who masterminded the whole concept of separate and independent states and nationhoods. Prime Minister Verwoerd himself foresaw the end of racial discrimination when he stated as far back as 1961 : 'As our policy has been developed and our cause stated more clearly, it must be clearly understood that when separation has been carried far enough, discrimination must be eliminated.' If the architect of grand apartheid prophesied the end of discrimination (which is the crux of petty apartheid), then the lesser mortals, the academicians and intellectuals who agree with this, must surely support the idea!

They point out the excellent example set by the present Prime Minister, Mr B.J. Vorster. While he adheres to the view that there is no difference between so-called petty apartheid or grand apartheid ('there is only apartheid and nothing else'), he added this careful qualification: 'The only question is whether certain acts and usages are not unnecessary for apartheid.' This is a view which the reformers heartily endorse. The Prime Minister has pledged himself to lead South Africa out of isolation into a changing world, and this embraces a policy of friendly co-existence with Black Africa. As benign and peaceful human or racial relations form a vital link in this development, Mr Vorster takes every opportunity of emphasizing this. When he, in his capacity as Chancellor of the University of Stellenbosch, gave the opening address at the beginning of 1971, he remarked:

'Having chosen separation myself, I will answer to you for it, but I want to impress on you strongly that there is one thing you must not do – you must not neglect a man's identity. No person, no matter what his race or his level of development, his background or his wealth, deserves to be looked down on. He is a creation of God, just like you . . . It is this quality of otherness which each accepts or respects in another person.'

The new thinkers place a high premium on human dignity. The Afrikaner in the street must be made aware of this. He must be enlightened as to which petty measures hurt the pride and self-respect of Non-White South Africans – pin-pricks which could be safely left behind without endangering major policy. Human relations will be of paramount importance in the whole scheme of things to come; it will determine the success of our future outward policy towards Africa, towards our own Non-White peoples, and it will bring disaster if mismanaged. This must be imprinted on people's minds. People must start at home and hammer at the built-in prejudice that every Non-White is an inferior being because he is not White. They must develop a constant alertness for petty forms of discrimination and social injustices which are no longer necessary in the bigger framework of separate development.

The great need is to keep the mind and the door open for inevitable future developments. If we succeed with our policy of separate development, South Africa will one day be a multi-national complex, with one White entity and at least eight autonomous African states. Our outward or African policy is one of friendship to all African states who wish to take our hand. In both these ideals we have made encouraging progress, but there is a growing demand for swifter advance, especially in the development of the Bantustans.

It will be impossible to create a White state totally isolated from its Black neighbours and Black friends further up the continent. There will be far greater communication than today. We will trade with each other, maintain diplomatic relations, confer on and discuss matters of mutual interest and cross the borders as tourists.

Will the future independent Black states inside our present borders and those outside be willing to channel all communication along diplomatic and trade lines, avoid sport and other contact so as not to disturb our segregated social pattern in South Africa? The intellectual pundits say 'no'. It is unavoidable that states which maintain friendly relations will also send their tennis and soccer teams to compete in South Africa. The black Transkeians, Basutos and Malawians will probably play against Black South African teams for as long as possible, but not for ever. Their sense of national pride will forbid segregated international contact.

It is quite clear that White South Africa will have to sacrifice some of its colour prejudices and practices if it wishes to survive on the Black Continent. Public opinion will, for instance, not tolerate a situation in which the Coloured and Indian populations (for whom no separate states are envisaged) are indefinitely denied privileges and amenities in their own country which they can enjoy elsewhere in the world.

Even the reformers do not envisage one multi-racial society for South Africa. They are fervent supporters of separate autonomous states. The White man cannot be expected to sacrifice his political power in his own country, just as the Black man cannot be denied just rights in his own territory. In the matter of political autonomy there is no difference between the viewpoints of those who advocate a new deal in racial relations and those who do not. This then is the position of the 'wind of change' men. They face a formidable barrier of resistance. What is the substance of this opposition?

Resistance to change is founded on the Afrikaner's inborn suspicion of pragmatism, liberalism and concessions on colour principles. Apartheid, which has today grown to the grander concept of separate development, is deeply ingrained in his national character and its roots go down to his earliest origins.

The Afrikaner has had a long struggle against foreign domination and attempts to destroy his identity. He would rather trek by ox and wagon into an unknown and hostile interior than tolerate British oppression. He would rather risk war with the mighty British Empire than yield to a foreign culture. Again, in 1912, it was the Afrikaner urge to preserve his identity that decided General Hertzog to break away from Botha's and Smuts' conciliation policy towards the British. Two decades later it was Malan who veered Afrikanerdom away from Hertzog's and Smuts' coalition venture. It meant many years in the political desert, but again Afrikanerdom in its exclusive, isolated form won.

Isolationism holds no fears for the Afrikaner mind. Facing a whole hostile outside world does not make him quiver. He is used to it. This resistance has made the Afrikaner what he is: strong, stubborn, self-confident, strong-willed, but wary of the changes that outsiders with their liberal ideas want to force on him. Especially as regards colour policy. He frowns upon the pragmatic, *laissez faire* approach of the English towards the Non-White peoples. His view that Smuts' indecisive, lackadaisical attitude towards the colour question would have led to the White man being swamped today, remains unchanged. The Afrikaner is a slow changer, but he has changed a lot – more than he cares to admit.

The prevalent feeling amongst a section of Afrikanerdom, is that his nation has come to another crucial point, to yet another of many cross-roads in its history where the *laager* must be closed again and dangerous, foreign influences resisted to the last man. How strong this section is, is unknown. The urgent appeals made to the Afrikaner for change, to adapt to a new way of life towards the Non-White peoples, to foresake the master-servant attitude and accept the Black and Coloured nations as equal partners in the future destiny of the African sub-continent, smells again of conciliation, dangerous concessions and the yielding of principles. A conservative reaction is always lurking below the surface to resist this liberalistic assault, to prevent the dogmatic, established forms of segregation being diluted further, even if it means going into isolation again and arousing the hatred of an angry world. To be branded as 'verkramp'[2] has become an honour in these conservative circles. (The Albert Hertzog[3]

2. For a definition and analysis of this concept, see W.J. de Klerk's chapter, *The Concepts 'Verkramp' and 'Verlig'*.

3. A former cabinet minister who clashed with the present Prime Minister, Mr Vorster, because of the former's ultra-rightist views. Dr Hertzog subsequently left the National Party to found the Herstigte Nasionale Party (HNP). The HNP is known for its fundamentally ultra-rightist views.

attempt to lead a conservative revolt was a dismal failure – a case it seems of a movement waiting for a leader.)

One has only to look at the attitude of the resisters towards petty apartheid to realize how deep-rooted this suspicion against change is. They maintain that small or petty apartheid must stay. It is impossible to draw a dividing line which will indicate where small apartheid ends and big apartheid begins. The one dovetails into the other. Small apartheid is the foundation of big apartheid. And 'small' integration will lead to 'big' integration.

The resisters speak a language which the ordinary man finds not only easier to understand but also involves him personally. This world, segregated at every station entrance and lift, is the one he knows, which has protected him through all his history, and which has assured him of his White, protected place in society. The reformers talk about strange, disturbing changes which must be made and it makes him uneasy. He has a vague feeling that these professors teach a doctrine which involves giving an inch and the Black man taking a mile.

The resisters argue along these lines: relaxation of colour restrictions in the White areas cannot be made subject to the establishment of independent Bantustans. While there are Non-Whites working and living in the White cities they will have to conform to the laws and practices of the host country, laws which include strict segregation measures. Even if the Black workers are fully-fledged citizens of their own independent countries, they will still be regarded as migrant labourers in the White country, without political rights and subject to the laws and practices of colour partition and discrimination, which can never be relaxed. In this respect the example of Italian workers in Switzerland and Germany is quoted.

Race and not the standard of civilization and education must decide. If one Non-White, however advanced, is accepted and integrated into the White society, how can the inevitable growing stream be curbed and full-scale integration stopped? A strong Black or White minority will never be absorbed peacefully into the ruling majority, and instances all over Africa and the world can be quoted. Resisters believe that once concessions have been granted, however insignificant at first, they will undoubtedly lead to other and bigger liberties. Social acceptance will lead to political equality and eventually to biological assimilation.

Apartheid, and petty apartheid, so these people argue, are founded on the desire of a nation to be a separate entity with its own language, culture and identity. Foreign elements which are foreign to a nation's character, however admirable in themselves, must never be absorbed. This includes the Bantu and his culture. Black and White must remain separate and equal, but nowhere must this rigid line be relaxed. Resisters declare that if petty apartheid disappeared altogether then big apartheid would become meaningless, superfluous and unnecessary. If White and Non-White in daily life were in all spheres acceptable to each other and were to mix freely it would be absurd to force them into separate states. They say that the restriction on freehold rights for the Bantu in White areas must remain. The Immorality Act must remain unchanged.

The resisters agree that South Africa's outward policy should be extended to more African states, but contact must remain limited to official diplomatic and trade channels. Mixed sport and social activities must be prevented at all costs. They argue that if Black Malawians and Transkeians were permitted to play soccer and tennis against White South Africans, nothing would prevent them and other Black men from sharing the same residential areas with Whites; children could hold multi-racial parties, play together and later on even marry. After a sporting event a mixed reception must follow, and the Zulu Mr Dingaan will dance with White Miss Smith.

'Do we want to go as far as this?' they ask. 'No. Political friendship and healthy interstate relations are one thing. Social contact and playing games are another.'

According to the ultra-rightists the ban on Ashe and D'Oliviera visiting South Africa was instituted because we play apart. The Maoris in the New Zealand team are acceptable, because they are fair-skinned. Black Maoris would have been another matter. The ultra-conservatives do not hesitate to draw the line to its extreme end (miscegenation) and the final picture makes the ordinary South African shudder. The die-hards accuse the reformers of vague thinking, of failing to present the ultimate outcome of their preaching.

The new thinkers again point an accusing finger at the no-change men for refusing to face realities. Do they wish to keep an educated Black man in an inferior position for ever? How can South Africa make Black friends outside her borders if she treats her own Black inhabitants, even the Black professors and doctors, as social pariahs? It is a colossal mistake to try and project an isolated, segregated Afrikaner society of the thirties into the colour-conscious world of the seventies.

The irony of the matter is that the ultra-liberals who subscribe to the Progressive Party policy of integration on the basis of merit, agree with the resisters that no difference can be made between small and big apartheid. Both are part and parcel of the same obnoxious business of segregation. The liberals wish the reformers every success – not because they support their limited targets, but because they believe that social and personal concessions, however small at first, could lead to larger cracks in the wall of apartheid.

The opponents of change chuckle at this and smile knowingly at their adversaries. Their attitude is: 'What did we tell you?'

How strong are the resisters? This would be hard to assess, but one thing is certain, South Africa will never go back to the anti-Goolagong and pre-Maori mentality. Whilst the National Party will always stand uncompromisingly on the matter of identity, the representative contacts within the multi-national society will increase. The pattern of a multinational society has already been created.

This then, briefly, is the substance of the debate on petty apartheid. Whether the different viewpoints will lead to stronger action and the re-drawing of party political lines, time alone will tell.

In the crucial five years ahead, the Prime Minister will be a key figure. It will be his challenge to keep the 'reformers' and the 'resisters' together within the broader framework of Afrikaner Nationalism. He has now served his 'apprenticeship' as premier. The first five years of his regime have in many respects been a trying time, during which he had to sever the super die-hards with their oxwagon mentality from the body of the National Party. He has cleared the scene of this dead wood and has emerged with a greatly enhanced reputation. Under his guidance South Africa has made remarkable progress with her African policy, and more South Africans than ever before place their faith in John Vorster to deal with the delicate and vital problem of human relations. For success or failure in this matter will determine whether the advocates of 'small' and 'big' apartheid will drift apart or follow side by side and differ loyally behind the banner of Vorster.

The Bantu Homelands

The Bantu Fatherlands and Separate Development

M. C. Botha

The Honourable Michiel Coenraad Botha, M.P., is South Africa's present Minister of Bantu Administration and Development, and of Bantu Education. He studied at the Universities of Stellenbosch, Pretoria and Cape Town. Mr Botha is today regarded as one of the very top men in the governing National Party hierarchy. He has written numerous articles on various aspects of South Africa's Bantu policy. A formidable parliamentarian, he is expected to play a vital role in shaping the political future of the Bantu nations.

Any consideration of the role of the Bantu fatherlands in implementing separate development must begin with the last two words: separate development. The fundamental questions to be examined are: Separate development of whom? And separate from whom? Development of individuals or of groups? If of groups, how have those who belong together been grouped together?

Over the years this policy has been referred to by a number of names: segregation, apartheid, autogenous, parallel, separate, independent or multi-national development, separate freedoms, and so on. In the course of time certain aspects of the policy have been given greater or less prominence than others, and understandably so, since this is a dynamic policy which keeps pace with the conditions and changing needs of the country.

The very existence of this policy testifies to the fundamental approach of its formulators to the population situation in South Africa and their recognition of the existing reality of a diversity of population groups.

The unmistakable reality which forces itself on the expert and the objective researcher, is that the population in South Africa consists of a number of identifiable, homogeneous groups which must in fact be recognized as peoples or nations – even if all of them are at varying stages of nationhood.

For many years in the past it was not clearly realized that within the Bantu race there are a number of separate nations, each with distinctive features and individual characteristics, differing strongly *inter se.* This is by no means unique, for in the same way Westerners consist of a number of separate nations, and elsewhere in Africa there is also a diversity of nations of the Negro race.

Thus the Bantu of South Africa comprise the Xhosas, Zulus, North and South Sothos, Tswanas, Swazis, Shangaans and Vendas. (The Native Territories in South West Africa will not be taken into account here.) The fact that, despite similarity of colour, there are separate nations, goes to show that multi-nationalism is based on dissimilarity between groups which are bound by special ties to form separate entities, and that colour is not the overriding differentiating criterion.

In the course of time the Whites developed a sense of homogeneity which grew stronger and stronger. The South African nationalism which had begun to develop in the previous century gained a more and more important place in the hearts of the Whites. It became the credo and central idea that gave impetus to political, cultural and religious movements. But this sense of homogeneity not only helped the Whites in South Africa to find themselves as an entity and to develop a sense of solidarity and kinship, but also to recognize and acknowledge as separate entities the other homogeneous and/or related units which differed radically from the Whites. This differentiation between the Whites and the various Non-White peoples in South Africa has been a recognized social custom since the earliest years of the history of our country. From this has developed the tradition of separateness of the various population groups which differ so markedly, and, on the strength of this, the policy of 'apartheid' was formulated as a political doctrine. For this reason, ever since it was formed nearly sixty years ago, the present governing party, the National Party, has advocated a policy of separation or differentiation between all the various peoples (often erroneously called races), each developing on its own, as the only reasonable, natural and acceptable policy to ensure the survival of the White nation as well as the Non-White nations. In its election manifesto before the 1948 general election this party stated: 'The Native reserves must become the true fatherlands of the Native.'

Over the years the various Bantu peoples have also developed a sense of national unity despite historical or traditional divisions into tribes, centred around chiefs with councils.

Implicit in the policy of separate development, therefore, is the separateness of nations. Any separation between individuals is a secondary or incidental aspect of the implementation of the policy which actually stems from the separateness of nations.

THE BANTU FATHERLANDS

The Bantu nations each have a part or parts of South Africa where their pioneers settled, mostly in the previous century. The regions where the ancestors of the present Bantu nations settled are the nuclei of their fatherlands.* These territories were recognized by the colonial administrations and republics of the previous century and at times adjusted by negotiation. Historically, this was how the fatherlands of the Bantu nations came into being. In 1913 these Bantu fatherlands were granted due recognition and reserved for the Bantu peoples by the Parliament of the unified South Africa, known as the Union. Subsequently, in 1936, provision was again made by legislation for the enlargement of the Bantu territories by 6,2 million hectares.

Unfortunately not all the territories of the Bantu nations are contiguous nor do they form solid geographic units. The reasons for this will not be gone into here. By acquiring new land and exchanging areas in the various fatherlands, the Government of the Republic is trying as far as possible to consolidate them into units. This is an exacting, time-consuming and difficult task because so many human, financial, physical and other considerations are involved. There may eventually also be Bantu fatherlands consisting of various scattered parts in South Africa, analogies of which are to be found in other fragmented countries.

The Bantu areas or homelands, as they are popularly known, are therefore the countries, or as they are referred to in the title, the fatherlands of the various Bantu nations. Especially recently, as a result of increasing development in nearly all spheres, these fatherlands are more and more becoming the spiritual and emotional homes of the members of these nations, even to those whose physical home happens to be outside these fatherlands. To them, as to those within the fatherlands, it is these fatherlands in which their national pride is rooted and which symbolize their national individuality.

It is of the utmost importance that these Bantu areas should be reserved,

* See map.

safeguarded and protected by law for the Bantu nations and their members. It is laid down by law that land ownership in these areas shall always vest in the Bantu, largely in the form of communal ownership. In terms of the policy of separate development, Whites – and other Non-Bantu – accordingly acquire no permanent rights, economic, political or any other, in these fatherlands. This prevents the Whites from infiltrating these areas and ousting the Bantu.

Without this protection of their territories, the Bantu might very easily have lost possession of their homelands through transfer of land to Non-Bantu. The sole right of the Bantu to their respective fatherlands is therefore upheld by policy, and the appearance or development image of each Bantu homeland is increasingly assuming the character of its particular nation.

The implementation of the policy of separate development has also necessitated the establishment of a special organization, with the necessary funds supplied by the Government of the Republic, to buy out White interests which were vested in the Bantu fatherlands, mostly in the Transkei, in the distant past, and to turn over these concerns to Bantu entrepreneurs.

It is a well-known fact that, as elsewhere in Africa, these fatherlands were not from the outset developed by the inhabitants to carry all their people. The reason for this is a subject in itself, and in any case extremely difficult to determine – something on which neither history nor science has as yet given a decisive answer.

One of the main objectives of the policy of separate or multi-national development is to develop the fatherlands of the various nations as much as possible in every sphere in order to raise their productivity and human carrying capacity. Such development embraces a diversified complex of human activities which have to be developed as a balanced whole. These activities, which are all given their rightful place in the programme of development of the Bantu fatherlands, are dealt with briefly below under some general categories.

AGRICULTURE

Historically, this industry, in the broadest sense of the word, was the first economic activity of the Bantu peoples. For many, many years and until quite recently, the Bantu practised agriculture in their homelands purely for subsistence purposes. But, especially in the past decade, they have now come to realize more and more that agriculture must also be practised for money and gain. However, there is still a need for greater progress, although much has already been achieved despite human limitations and natural problems in areas which up to a few decades ago were raw veld.

Capital investment to advance agriculture in the Bantu fatherlands must be credited almost exclusively to the Government of the Republic which, in the nine years up to 1969, spent an amount of at least R60 million on basic development in agriculture and forestry, an increase of nearly 150 per cent over that period. Undertakings and projects were launched in various new fields, including the extensive establishment of crops for fibre, forests, coffee and tea plantations, co-operative milk schemes, and citrus projects.

With the Bantu governments participating increasingly in all development in the fatherlands in recent years, there is every prospect of even greater progress in agriculture. The fact that agricultural planning of the whole of certain Bantu areas has been completed and that ancient prejudices against such planning are disappearing more and more rapidly, augurs well for the future.

LAND DEVELOPMENT

This embraces all physical development of the homelands such as roads, bridges, dams, towns, railways, fencing, soil conservation, etc. This provides each homeland with the necessary infrastructure, and there are already at least 40 000 kilometres of good roads, nearly 5 000 fair-sized dams, railways, telephone and radio services, etc. A major feature of the ten years up to 1970 was a phenomenal building programme under which 150 towns with about 100 000 houses were built in the Bantu homelands. These towns and houses, which become the personal property of the inhabitants, play an important role in giving great numbers of people from those homelands a sense of belonging to their own fatherland. These town-building programmes will be continued indefinitely.

SOCIAL DEVELOPMENT

This embraces every aspect of social development and service to be found in any normal community organization, such as school and university education, health services, welfare work (homes for the aged, care of the blind, etc.), the administration of justice, and so forth.

As it is not possible to go into each of these social aspects in detail, some general observations on the more important ones must suffice.

Like the other services, all these services are centred in the fatherland in that they have to be established as far as possible in them. In so far as some of the services, such as schools and hospitals, are required in White areas, they have to be instituted in conjunction with the main services in the fatherlands. All the social services have expanded considerably over the years with the result that they are becoming an ever stronger national centripetal force and are doing much to strengthen a sense of nationhood and patriotism.

The number of school-going children receiving all forms of non-university education rose from 351 900 (out of a Bantu population of 6,5 million, i.e. 5,4 per cent) in 1935 to 2,5 million (out of a Bantu population of 14,4 million, i.e. 17,7 per cent) in 1969, when a good 85 per cent of the Bantu children of school-going age were at school.

In 1960 two new universities for Bantu students were opened in addition to the one already functioning. These universities co-operate closely with all the other universities in South Africa in regard to academic work and the maintenance of standards. The number of students at the three universities combined rose from 481 in 1960 to 1 586 in 1969. There is also a medical school for Bantu students, while large numbers of Bantu students also take correspondence courses. In 1969 there were 3 300 Bantu graduates in South Africa, representing a wide range of professions.

As regards health, hospital and clinic services there are well co-ordinated facilities in all the Bantu fatherlands provided by the authorities and church bodies. At present there are nearly 80 larger and smaller hospitals in all the Bantu homelands, with nearly 26 500 beds and 510 doctors, whereas in 1962 the respective figures were 14 700 and 232.

Due attention is also being given to the spiritual and general human development of the Bantu peoples in their homelands. Apart from developmental activities which have a general formative value, there are a number of independent churches in all the homelands, and a great many of their spiritual workers are Bantu. Everything possible which makes for inner development is encouraged as regards attitudes and civilized patterns of expression such as attitude towards work, initiative, progress, and cultural enrichment. All this plays a part in unifying each nation round its own traditional heritage and ethos with a view to developing a sense of citizenship associated with each homeland or fatherland.

GENERAL ECONOMIC DEVELOPMENT

This aspect of development embraces a large area of widely ramified human activities. These may be summed up as including the promotion of commerce and industry, the mining of mineral deposits, capital formation and the mobilization of funds, in addition to agriculture, which has already been mentioned.

A fact that is all too easily lost sight of in this regard is that the inherent approach of the Bantu to money differs fundamentally from that of Westerners in whom materialistic motives of financial gain are deeply rooted – motives which were formerly almost completely absent in the Bantu. A direct result of the absence of a keen spirit of enterprise is, of course, lack of economic experience and insight.

It should be borne in mind that successful development depends mainly upon impersonal physical construction programmes (including infrastructure work), as well as on personal initiative, intellectual capacities and human qualities or relationships. Whereas it is relatively easy to provide the physical or impersonal programmes, it is by no means so easy when it comes to personal requirements because it takes infinitely more time, understanding, patience and training to cultivate them. As, in terms of the policy of multi-national development, processes of development must involve the members of the nations concerned – i.e. the Bantu crash programmes must of necessity be influenced by the human traits referred to above.

When designing and implementing an economic policy for the Bantu fatherlands, it was essential to bear in mind that, while each fatherland had to build up its own economic bulwark, there was economic interaction in the broader geographical context of the whole of South Africa.

The economic development of the Bantu homelands is a programme of action designed to serve the political ideals of the White Republic and the Bantu-speaking peoples themselves. Because the various Bantu nations as well as the Whites wish to maintain their separate social and political identities, the programme of providing opportunities for settlement and for the generation of income in the homelands constitutes the 'chassis' or the infrastructure upon which peaceful co-existence in Southern Africa is to be maintained. Proper settlement of people and growing job opportunities within daily travelling distance of their homes are, therefore, the twin objectives of this programme.

The achievement of these objectives is a matter of detailed planning since the normal market forces in South Africa obviously do not operate in this direction. The normal profit motive of the typical private entrepreneur in South Africa, as anywhere else in a capitalist society, does not take account of such socio-political objectives in its calculations and decisions on the location of industries and employment. The Government, as the agent of collective society, has the responsibility, and has received the mandate, to see to it that these major socio-political objectives of the peoples of South Africa are as well served as the striving for profit and overall material growth.

The present Nationalist regime is providing the administrative machinery and the economic instruments by which these objectives are being achieved without imperilling the economic growth potential of the peoples involved. It is obviously impossible to give a detailed account here of the various institutions and instruments by which the programme is being implemented. A broad outline of the system will have to suffice.

The twin objectives of the settlement of people and the creation of opportunities of making an income are to be achieved through every viable process which can be generated in these territories. The following are of strategic importance:

The building of new towns and the growth of existing towns in the Bantu homelands to accommodate the increasing Bantu population;

The decentralization of those economic processes which are mainly dependent upon Bantu labour from present growth points to new economic growth points inside the Bantu homelands or close to them in border industry areas;

The provision of rapid transport systems between these new towns and present economic centres in the Republic to carry workers who will continue to work in the Republic proper, but will live in their respective homelands;

The mobilization and training of Bantu labour for industrial, commercial and tertiary service occupations in the areas where such opportunities are opened up;

The activation of the citizens of the Bantu fatherlands to take over political, administrative and social responsibilities and initiative in carrying through the process of development to a truly Bantu objective.

CURRENT ECONOMIC TRENDS IN THE HOMELANDS

The economic trends in the homelands, as measured according to the conventions of the national accounting system of the United Nations Organization, show a close resemblance (except in the case of Tswanaland) as regards both total growth and the structure of the gross domestic product. While the growth rate was roughly 4 to 5 per cent per annum in real terms between 1960–1968, about one-half of the total activity in 1968 still took place outside the market sector on a subsistence basis. Of income in cash, roughly 40 per cent was generated in the government sector, and another 40 per cent in occupations controlled by Non-Bantu, while the remaining 20 per cent was accounted for by private activities among the Bantu themselves.

In Tswanaland, however, real income rose by an average of 7,7 per cent from 1960 to 1968, the actual increases having largely taken place since 1965 when the index (base year 1959/60) of real income rose from 109,7 in 1964/65 to 121,4, 154,8 and 176,6, respectively, in the succeeding years. This exceptional growth was due not only to good agricultural conditions, but in particular also to a doubling of the incomes derived from extensive mining activities (platinum and chromium). In addition, the most successful industrial decentralization scheme has been located in the vicinity of this territory, namely Rosslyn, where up to 1970 about 50 industrial enterprises have been located under the Government's 'border industry' scheme of industrial decentralization referred to above. These enterprises, including motor assembly plants, employ about 9 000 industrial workers, mostly living in the new towns established within the borders of the Tswana territory.

Furthermore, an industrial area within the borders of the Tswana territory has been established to accommodate industries with an employment capacity of about 8 000 workers. The site, which cost the Government of South Africa about R3 million, is not yet fully operational but all stands have already been reserved.

Tswanaland has benefited by its proximity to the economic activity in the Southern Transvaal. Greater efforts will have to be made to initiate similar expansion in the other homelands, although the Ciskei Xhosa may already have been brought to the threshold of such development by the decentralization of industrial activities to the East London region. In Lebowa, the homeland of the North Sotho nation, payable mineral deposits offer considerable opportunities for development, reducing the need to provide an economic stimulus through industrial decentralization. In Zululand, the industries in border industry areas within the Republic proper (the existing one at Hammarsdale and the new ones at Ladysmith and Richards Bay) are providing increasing employment for Zulus living in their homeland. With improved transport facilities, even Durban now has access to such sources of labour inside Zululand. Moreover, an industrial area, Sithebe, is being prepared in Zululand, near Zundumbili, to be ready for occupation in 1972. In the Transkei, the expansion of basic services at Butterworth has been completed to create industrial jobs for 9 000 workers.

In the course of the past decade three economic corporations were established to promote and undertake economic development in the Bantu fatherlands, namely the Bantu Investment Corporation, the Xhosa Development Corporation and the Bantu Mining Corporation, with a combined share capital of R43 million as at 31st March, 1971. Where there are not sufficient Bantu entrepreneurs to exploit all the economic potentialities, these corporations may step in in the interest of the Bantu homeland concerned or may enter into agreements with White entrepreneurs to undertake the development on an agency basis. The principle of the agency system is that the White entrepreneur may provide his capital and know-how, but in such a way that he will not acquire permanent rights for an indefinite time.

This system is applied in the fields of mining and industry, and in the last few years a steadily increasing number of contracts have been concluded. By the end of 1970 capital to the amount of R23 million had already been invested by private entrepreneurs in a short space of time in industries alone.

These references to industrial and mining operations already under way in most homelands are merely intended to illustrate that practical progress was made during the decade of the sixties. They can give no real indication of the overall impact which the programmes now being planned for implementation in the seventies are expected to have on economic and social progress in these homelands.

Although the acceleration of activities from the fifties to the sixties was somewhat sporadic, it is confidently expected that in the seventies not only will a more clearly defined structure of economic development emerge, but that the rate of such development will also be stepped up increasingly.

Since all the revenue from Bantu taxes has been earmarked for Bantu educational programmes, the South African Treasury has to bear the comparatively heavy financial burden of all developmental undertakings. While the total direct current and capital expenditure inside the Bantu homelands by Government institutions amounted to approximately R36,5 million in 1959/60, it increased by 211 per cent over seven years to about R113,4 million in 1967/68.

In view of the tremendous number of people involved, the total cost, in money, of this programme will of course be considerable, but it pales into insignificance when one considers that these programmes are providing the physical infrastructure for peaceful social and political co-existence in Southern Africa.

POLITICAL DEVELOPMENT

It is implicit in the policy of separate development that the governmental system and political development of the Bantu nations should be based on the traditional system of government of these peoples. The policy is also based on the premise that the urge for political self-realization is inherent in the Bantu peoples and that it should be encouraged to find positive expression.

Some of the earliest steps taken were to grant legal recognition to the traditional authority of the chiefs and tribes and to build up higher forms of government on that foundation. Thus, statutory provision was made for tribes and communities in a Bantu homeland to co-operate on a group basis in regional authorities, while all the regional authorities in turn could federate in a Territorial Authority which could exercise prescribed powers over the whole homeland.

This system found favour with the Bantu peoples because it was based on their traditional systems. The Transkei has already advanced to the stage where, in terms of a constitution of its own, it has had a Legislative Assembly since 1963, with a Cabinet and a number of administrative departments, to replace its former territorial authority. Its legislative assembly consists of traditional leaders, supplemented by elected representatives who are elected by all enfranchised citizens of the Transkei, inside as well as outside the Transkei.

In the meantime legislative provision has been made to enable all the other Bantu peoples and their territorial authorities to advance in the same way towards the status of legislative assemblies and self-governing territories, with their own administrations, cabinets, citizenship and symbols of nationhood, all associated with their homelands. The powers granted to the legislative assemblies with their executive councils or cabinets cover a wide range of matters.

The Government of the Republic of South Africa seconds experienced officials from its Public Service to the Bantu Governments because as yet there are not enough of their own citizens with the experience to run their public services. The seconded officials in the Transkei have decreased from 18,6 per cent of the total number in 1963 to 7,9 per cent in 1970.

It is of special interest to note that this constitutional system links citizens outside the homelands with their own people and with their homelands. This link is made possible by two political ties in particular. In the first place the Bantu Government has the right to appoint deputies in the White areas to maintain contact with their emigrant compatriots. For this purpose the deputies can appoint special councils and assistants. The other political tie is the vote which is given to those citizens of a homeland who are in White areas so that they can have a share in the government of their particular homeland. These measures afford striking evidence that tribal ties, which might become weakened by absence from the homeland, are not the only ties, but that national affinity and citizenship can also exercise a powerful binding force.

After it had long been customary for the White Government and its officials to administer the Bantu areas and to assume direct responsibility for all activities in these areas, the application of the policy of separate development put into operation an emancipating process. In terms of this process there must come forth from the ranks of each Bantu nation persons to serve in their respective homelands as political leaders, as officials in charge of the administration and as entrepreneurs to exploit economic prospects in order that the White element may be superseded in all these functions by Bantu persons. Thereafter the Whites will act as advisers and assistants, but only where such aid is required.

This approach, whereby the Bantu is increasingly activated to assume responsibilities and the Whites are reduced to the role of advisers, is creating a new relationship of interdependent independence between the White and the Bantu nations. As a result of this relationship the mutual knowledge and understanding which have, in the course of many years, grown steadily on the level of personal intercourse between White and Bantu, will also develop on the international level to a sound relationship between the people of the Republic and those of the Bantu homelands, which is essential for the inter-state relations which must inevitably follow.

It is in view of the attainment of such an end and national status for the Bantu homelands that the application of the policy of separate development is in essence the foundation of Bantu nations and the formation of their own countries for each of them.

Bantu homelands formed with such a content and character will cause their particular Bantu nations, and each individual member, thus supported by their national status, to feel inherently equal to other nations and states in the world, and more specifically also towards their former guardian state, the Republic of South Africa. In this way then the policy of separate development ensures for the Bantu nations and their fatherlands equality with the people of the Republic. Therefore the foundation of nations and the formation of their countries will be the most natural process whereby each member of such a Bantu nation can acquire his human and national self-esteem. The realization of this self-esteem, as well as the recognition thereof by the people of other nations, offers the best prospects for the elimination of offensive personal attitudes and increasing friction which are inevitable when heterogeneous individuals and nations live in an integrated society.

It has been said over and over again that the governments of each Bantu nation can develop to independence, a process for which there is no ready-made pattern, since the content of each nation's independence will depend on the agreement which will be entered into with it beforehand. In the same way there can be no timetable for political development because too much depends on the general programme of development of each nation and on indeterminable human factors and capacities. The political development of the Bantu fatherlands is not only significant to their citizens within and beyond their borders, but it also has important inter-state implications for the neighbouring states in Southern Africa.

It is foreseen that in the inter-nation relations between the various Bantu nations and the White nation there will be increasing mutual recognition and reciprocal aid which will lead to a natural and gradual advance towards the essential interdependence between nations, all of whom will eventually enjoy independent co-existence in the sub-continent. In such a constellation of independent nations without a central dominating authority over all of them, it is even possible that, in regard to specific matters, major or minor responsibilities may be entrusted to certain neighbouring nations in the interest of all.

The whole plan of development for each Bantu fatherland is aimed at strengthening and developing it as much as possible, because the fatherland is the geographical anchor or base of the Bantu nation concerned, where it can have its own seat of government and can flourish without being dominated by any other nation. In fact, the political strength of the policy of multi-national or separate development lies in the provision it makes for a national government for each nation by that nation. That is why, if this policy is implemented fully, there can be no question of a majority being governed by a minority or even of a minority nation being governed by a majority nation.

THE GUIDING HAND OF THE WHITE NATION

It should be understood that in regard to every aspect of development the fatherlands must be able to offer the optimum of everything that might reasonably be expected of a fatherland. The Government and the White nation of South Africa realize that the Bantu nations and their fatherlands have to be helped in this regard. Considerable assistance is being given in the form of money, manpower, expertise, services, and so on. Generally speaking, the view is advocated, pre-eminently by supporters of the Government of the Republic, that, since the White nation wants to hold what it has and to work out its destiny in its own way, the Bantu nations should also be allowed and helped to work out their destinies in their own particular ways.

From both experience and observation it would appear that the Bantu homelands have already become the fatherlands of the various nations, where, in consonance with the aims of the policy, peace and prosperity have been achieved for each of them. This acceptance will increase as the fatherlands more and more become territories which serve their specific nations, where their citizens can find fulfilment, and to which they can direct their pride and aspirations. The fatherlands will then be true national homes where the distinctive features and character of each nation will be preserved.

The development of all these elements to help each fatherland to come into its own in the best possible way, constitutes a great synthesis, and its realization – especially since there are a number of fatherlands – calls for a balancing or reconciliation of the following determinants or deciding factors:

The natural urge for self-realization;
The human capacities of the Bantu nations;
The means available, such as funds, manpower, etc.;
The public consent of the White nation;
The rapid march of time.

This is the challenge and the national task facing the White nation of South Africa for the coming decade: to help each Bantu nation to develop its territory into a true fatherland.

The Bantu Homelands and Cultural Heterogeneity

J. H. Coetzee

One of South Africa's most experienced anthropologists, Hennie Coetzee has many publications to his credit dealing with the social and cultural aspects of local ethnic groups. He is known for his objective approach to race relations and is widely accepted as one of the Afrikaners' top spokesmen on this subject. He is at present Professor of Anthropology at Potchefstroom University.

It is generally believed that the Republic of South Africa is the national home of the White descendants of both Dutch and British settlers with a sprinkling of other European nationalities; the Coloured population as the progeny of Whites, Hottentots and dark-skinned slaves; the offspring of indentured Indian labourers, and in the last instance a majority of Africans or Blacks. More correctly speaking this is only partly true, in the same sense that the British empire was inhabited by English, Scots, Irish, Welsh, Indians, Negroes, American Indians, Australian Aborigines, Maoris, Eskimos, etc.

In its unqualified generalization this assertion leads to a false impression, more so because of the prevailing idea that the Whites settled by means of land-hungry conquest and foul-dealing amongst the African tribes. Some people even believe that the Africans constituted one ethnically undifferentiated body politic distributed over the whole of South Africa, hence the reproach of a present policy of Balkanization of the country, by which is meant the artificial territorial division amongst artificially created ethnic groups in keeping with the imperialistic and colonialistic policy of divide and rule. Hence these territories are disdainfully called Bantustans, an appellation which is curiously enough never applied to countries such as Lesotho, Swaziland, Botswana, Zambia, Malawi or any other state in Africa.

As a matter of fact the creation or, more correctly, the recognition of the existence of Bantu fatherlands in South Africa differs in no sense from that of the countries of the different African peoples, all over the continent. They do, however, differ in their inception from those states and from the creation of the Balkan states in Europe in that in neither of these cases were the cultural, historical and traditional ethnic boundaries honoured to the same extent as is the case in the South African situation.

In this context the name *South Africa* is perhaps greatly misleading and confusing. The name has a geographical as well as a political meaning in the same way as we in South Africa have the custom of speaking of America, meaning popularly either the United States or the continent of North America. Geographical South Africa includes the geopolitical South Africa, more correctly and technically the Republic of South Africa (prior to 1961 the Union of South Africa) and, in addition to that, several other countries still under its jurisdiction although in the process of being prepared for ultimate political independence. These have an age-old existence.

Against this background of misunderstanding, false impressions and confusion I shall attempt to clarify in broad lines the situation as it developed in the course of three centuries. Here I shall draw attention to the existence of an ethnic plurality and diversity of African peoples arriving and making their home in this geographical area, each within its own carved-out boundaries and under its own political authority. To gain a true perspective it is necessary to stress the traditional fatherlands as well as the existence of socio-cultural and ethnic heterogeneity. I do not aim merely to provide a mass of detailed factual particulars and statistics. Figures change from year to year and space is relatively limited. Instead, I shall try to outline the past as a suitable background, the present policies and practice and the probable future.

Geographically South Africa is the culmination point of several ethnic migrations. At a time when the different groups of related Bantu tribes (correctly speaking, Bantu-speaking tribes) were moving southwards on more or less parallel paths from their places of origin in northern central Africa and reached the areas south of the Limpopo River, Europeans were settling at the southernmost point of the African continent and were slowly spreading northwards, either in a directly northern direction or more to the northeast or northwest.

Complicating the picture even further, neither the Bantu-speaking peoples nor the Europeans were the first or original inhabitants of the southern extremity of the 'dark continent'. Apart from the extinct peoples whose relics are being sought and studied by archaeologists, at the middle of the seventeenth century the region was inhabited by Bushmen and the Hottentot tribes. These are generally racially classified as Khoi-San (Khoi referring to the Hottentots and San to the Bushmen) to differentiate them from the Bantu tribes who belong to the Negroid race.

The Bushmen were nomadic hunters speaking a number of dialects of the Bushman language, quite distinct from other native languages. The Hottentots were pastoral nomads. Of the two, the Bushmen were quite probably the older settlers in the regions south of the Zambezi River. The Hottentots were later immigrants gradually moving southwards along the western seaboard a distance inland and later on eastwards from the Cape proper. Being pastoralists they were looking for the same pastures for their flocks of sheep and their herds of cattle that constituted the grazing fields for the herds of game the Bushmen were hunting and living on. Their consistent encroachment on the Bushmen hunting grounds brought conflict and strife amongst these apparently racially related but culturally totally different peoples. The Hottentots eventually applied the term 'murderer' to the Bushmen as a generic name.

Meanwhile the Bantu tribal groups, including Hereros, Ovambos, Sothos, Ngunis, Vendas, Tsongas, etc., practising cattlebreeding and agriculture, and speaking a vast number of related but foreign languages were slowly making their way to the south more or less in three streams. One went down the west coast, following in the track of the Hottentots. Another stream found its way through the central parts, which are separated from the western migration route by the Kalahari Desert. The peoples of Nguni origin betook themselves to the eastern portion of the southern part of the continent and moved further south along the east coast with the Drakensberg between them and the central stream.

The western Bantu migration consisting of the pastoral Herero and their pastoral-agricultural neighbours the Ovambo, following in the wake of the Khoi-Khoin, overtook their predecessors and became involved eventually in armed clashes with them in those parts of the country now known as South West Africa. The Nguni vanguard, consisting of various Xhosa tribes made contact with the north-eastward moving frontier tribes of the Hottentots. All these sections were practically flooding the hunting grounds of the Bushmen, who were soon fighting and being fought by them.

In the year 1652 the first Europeans arrived at False Bay with the intention of settling temporarily at the Cape. The original purpose of founding a refreshment station supplying the Dutch East India Company's merchant fleets with fresh water, vegetables and meat soon became a secondary consideration, losing its priority in favour of cattle breeding in the hinterland.

The history of the contact of the White expansion inland with the Bushmen hunters, the pastoral Hottentots and the Bantu in their movement southward is an unfortunate story of conflict. This tragedy cannot be explained realistically by ascribing everything to *mala fides,* unsatiable land hunger and wilful destructiveness on the part of the Whites. They were no more fallible than White settlers in the Americas, Australia or wherever Europeans or any other culturally more advanced people settled and met peoples of a less advanced culture. It was rather a question of misunderstanding as can be expected when peoples of totally different cultures and radically different sets of values and customs meet.

The Europeans came to South Africa, used to a system of private landholding. They were sedentary agriculturalists, accustomed to visual signs of ownership such as houses, barns, fields, etc. With most of the aboriginal inhabitants it was different. The Beachcombers, whom the Dutch settlers and other Europeans met at False Bay, had very little interest in landholding and even less in land usage. The Bushmen hunters and gatherers were without any livestock and unaccustomed to tilling the soil. They were living in caves or temporary huts. Hence there was no outward sign of landholding and ownership in Bushmen country. Notwithstanding this they did own land but in a communal sense. Land, that means hunting fields, belonged to the band. The boundaries – natural landmarks – were known to all members of the several adjoining bands. The hunters made their temporary living quarters at a distance from the water sources to prevent the game from becoming scared.

To the White stock breeders, unaccustomed to the ways of these peoples, these areas seemed to be no man's land. They settled close to the streams and pools to get water for household use, for their cattle and for their gardens. The game was scared off, especially because the farmers used fire-arms both for getting meat and in driving off the game from the pastures for their cattle. Retaliation on the part of the Bushmen was only natural. As the newcomers destroyed their source of subsistence, the Bushmen felt themselves justified in hunting the easily acquired 'tame game', the herds and flocks of the White farmers. In this way a chain reaction was started. The farmers on their part avenged themselves on the thieving and murdering Bushmen. The end was sure to come. Two irreconcilable ways of existence clashed and it should have been clear from the start which was to give way completely. Without any official annexation or act of government the Bushmen progressively lost their hunting grounds as they increasingly retreated to the marginal areas where the game also had fled. They pursued the diminishing herds of game, themselves becoming fewer and fewer in number, leaving their previous hunting grounds in the hands of Whites and other peoples who then used them for pastoral purposes.

This process of the Bushmen's being evacuated from their natural habitat was initiated by the coming of the pastorally better equipped and better armed peoples, the Hottentots and the Bantu, and was only accelerated by the advent of the Whites.

To a lesser extent the same story applies to the Hottentots. They were seasonal and purely pastoral nomads moving according to climatic conditions, making no gardens and removing their huts with them. Their ownership was nevertheless recognized by the earlier settlers. Alienation of land, however, caused misunderstanding. They, too, only knew a system of communal ownership with the tribal head as trustee for the tribe. Foreigners could – as with the Bantu – purchase land with the consent of the tribal chief. This purchase of land rather amounted to acquiring land usage from the tribe and this, according to the system, meant that those allowed on tribal land politically became subjects of the chief.

The Dutch East India Company bought land from the Hottentot chiefs living nearest to the settlement without having to comply with traditional political conditions. Before any serious conflicts arose the southern Hottentots were largely exterminated by a series of smallpox epidemics. The physical and cultural contacts with the Whites mysteriously but quickly disintegrated the Cape Hottentot tribes. The tribal groupings further to the north remained relatively intact and retained their lands as did the Nama, for example, who receded across the Orange River and settled in South West Africa. The Griquas settled in the north-western Cape Colony, then trekked to the Orange Free State and still later to the Eastern Cape, but lost more or less all their land in the process by selling individual titles to White farmers.

Their taking to cattle breeding coupled with some agricultural activity formed part of the reason for the northward movement of the growing

White population. Fresh grazing and water further inland increased their motivation to leave the Cape. This brought them in contact with the Bantu peoples of the Nguni group, who were moving in the opposite direction partly for the same reason as their White counterparts. In their case, however, they were being propelled from behind by intertribal wars and lured forward by the attraction of fresh pastures. The contact grew into conflict as the two parties, both intruders on the land settled by previous and older immigrants, were claiming portions of the country for their own settlement.

South of the Limpopo River, the territory usually referred to as South Africa, the following principal Bantu peoples made their geo-political homes. The Swazi, the Zulu and the Xhosa settled more or less along the east coast in Swaziland, Zululand (including the present province of Natal) and Xhosaland (the present Transkei and the Ciskei). The central regions of South Africa became the home of the Sotho tribes. The western group or Tswana took to the present Botswana and the north-western Transvaal. The Eastern Sotho came to live in Sekhukhuniland while some of the disintegrated and harassed Sotho tribes fled to the south where they found a refuge in the western foothills of the Drakensberg and the Maluti Mountains. Here the great Moshesh consolidated the refugees into the present Basuto nation in Lesotho. Except for the Basutos, the Sotho tribes, although culturally and biologically related and quite aware of these bonds, in reality never united as one nation. The different tribes maintained their socio-political independence. The tendency towards nationhood superceding tribalism is a new one. The first important step in that direction was the formation of the State of Botswana followed by the embryonic state of the Tswana who are now living on their tribal lands spread over the north-western parts of the Transvaal and the northern parts of the Cape Province.

In the northern parts of South West Africa, the Herero, a proud and purely pastoral people, consolidated their territories although they were more or less in constant strife with the Nama Hottentots. Their lands border on those of the matrilineal and primarily agricultural Ovambo and Okavango peoples. The Venda made their home between the Limpopo River and the Zoutpansberg with the Tsonga living to their east and extending into Mozambique.

Unlike the Bushmen, the Bantu tribes' way of living stressed their visible occupation and ownership of land. Towards the Bantu the Whites adopted a policy of barter and land purchase although there were problems concerning conflicting conceptions of private and communal landholding and the meaning of ownership and of a deed of sale. The best known examples of buying of land are the individual sale of titles by the Griqua and the sale of the Natal portion of Zululand by Supreme Chief Dingane of the Zulus to the emigrant Boers. Previously the depopulated northern part of the present province of the Orange Free State had been bartered from the Tswana chieftain Makwana. Payment was made in the form of goods, cattle, services rendered and protection tendered. The remuneration should be assessed in the light of the circumstances of the time. A small number of breeding cattle and the protection of a tribe were a coveted reward in the eyes of people totally impoverished and continually threatened by enemies from near and afar.

There were also cases of outright conquest. When the Zulu tyrant Mzilikazi was driven from the Western Transvaal by the Trekker leaders after he had militarily suppressed the Sotho peoples previously living there, the Whites considered themselves the new owners. The surviving sections of the disintegrated and dispersed Tswana tribes were allowed to return to their original settlements but under specific and strict conditions to maintain peace amongst themselves and with their new (White) neighbours.

The constant policy of all the regimes at the Cape Colony, whether that of the Dutch East India Company, the Batavian Republic or the first and second British occupations, was one of recognizing the right and fact of existence of the adjoining (Xhosa) political entities in their own territories. Cases of conflict were referred to as border wars, not as insurrections or rebellions, thus accepting the parallel existence of independent states. Neither military action nor appeasement, however, could persuade the Xhosa tribes to honour the existing boundaries and border agreements. Because of their attitude White authority was established over the Xhosa tribes for the sake of the safety and security of both parties. It was a last-resort policy reluctantly adopted, and maintained up to the 1950's. But even though the Cape government was forced to annex their territory by the British authorities, these lands were exclusively reserved for the Bantu natives. The only exceptions were the border areas of the annexed country where White settlement was promoted in an attempt to create buffer regions.

The policy of establishing White authority over Bantu tribes by force of necessity ultimately became the general pattern. Nowhere did customary intertribal warfare and plundering amongst the Bantu show any respect for borders. The authorities of the White political enclaves regarded it as their responsibility to protect the life and possessions of their subjects as well as those of the neighbouring Blacks. Their assuming authority over the Bantu tribes, reserving the land for the exclusive use of the Bantu, was primarily a way of keeping order and peace rather than of acquiring new territorial possessions.

Only a few exceptions can be cited as far as the reservation of land for the natives is concerned. The province of Queen Adelaide or British Kaffraria, more or less constituting the present Ciskei, was sliced into Black and White portions in an attempt to break the military power of the Xhosa and to create a military buffer strip. After the Zulu rebellion in Natal the same thing happened to Zululand. On the other hand, however, large portions of the southern part of the earlier Zululand, the part bought by the Boer emigrants from Dingane and conquered from them by the British, were settled by Zulus fleeing the tyranny of their rulers in Zululand proper. Eventually Bechuanaland was annexed late in the nineteenth century as part of Cecil John Rhodes' political objective of keeping Kruger's Transvaal Republic hemmed in while keeping an open road, the so-called missionaries' road, to the possessions of the British South Africa Company (the present Rhodesia and Zambia), and also to realize his dream of a British road from the Cape to Cairo.

In a few cases borders were moved to the detriment of the Bantu. The Cape-Xhosaland border was eventually changed from the Fish River to the Kei River and the Free State-Basutoland border to the Caledon River, deeper inland, for military expediency. Especially in the former case the Kei River as border could be more easily defended than the Fish River.

Such was, generally speaking, the way the different peoples, including the Whites, came to live where they are today. The first fact to be appreciated is that the Bantu peoples were immigrants to a country very sparsely inhabited by weaker and culturally less developed peoples, the Bushmen and Hottentots. By invasion, force and conquest they carved out countries or fatherlands from the southern region of the African continent and then came to blows with the Whites, who, immigrants like themselves, were seeking a home, according to their customs, by purchase of land through barter or service. Although in this process boundaries were altered, the care of the native lands was left in their hands.

The different native lands were for the first time legally scheduled and co-ordinated by the Land Act in 1913, shortly after the four colonies were united in the Union of South Africa. This was accompanied by an attempt to increase the extent of Bantu land, with the traditional homelands as nuclei. The administrative measures met with almost no success. In 1936 General Hertzog succeeded in passing the Native Land and Trust Act providing *inter alia* for the addition of 6,25 m hectares. This had to be provided partly from existing crown lands and the rest by purchase from the White owners. The general idea was to consolidate the existing dotted pattern of previous tribal lands. Before anything substantial could be done the Second World War interrupted the implementation of the scheme. The next attempt at doing this only followed after the National Party came into power in 1948.

The existence of traditional Bantu fatherlands for the different tribes formed the factual point of departure for a government policy of separate or parallel national development. The main objective was to achieve political independence for the Bantu peoples on the basis of their history as distinct ethno-political groups, with the maintenance of their traditional countries as a starting point. The next very important and imperative step was to develop these homelands so as to become fatherlands in the true sense of the word. In mapping out this course South Africa purposely aims at steering clear of the problematic and dangerous situations created in many newly independent African states. When they received their independence, these African states naturally clung to their traditional homes, but they shut their eyes to the problems which would arise by adhering to the artificial boundaries created by their previous colonial masters. This embraced two unsound political conditions. On the one hand ethnic entities were split up into minorities spread out over several countries, denying them the natural political aims of a nation as well as destroying their ethnic and national identity. On the other hand, culturally, ethnically, historically and racially unrelated peoples, or rather shreds of peoples, and tribes were accumulated forcibly in one state – a situation not unrelated to imperialism. For whatever political rights they may have been granted as individuals, their right of existence as peoples has been repudiated. Finally, they are not voluntarily subjects of those states.

DETERIORATION OF THE BANTU FATHERLANDS

Early in the twentieth century clear indications of grave deterioration in the homelands became visible. Soil erosion was becoming a general phenomenon; overstocking was a real problem while an impression of widespread pauperization was created. Secondary economic institutions were either totally lacking or were at their best only embryonic.

These negative conditions had their roots in the traditional Bantu economic system, which Americans would understand from their first-hand knowledge of the Indian reserves in the United States. Communal land holding, their stress on the quantity rather than the quality of their cattle, added to primitive methods of agriculture, were amongst the reasons for the above-mentioned situation. The Bantu were strongly, even antagonistically, averse to any curbing of the number of their cattle. Cattle were the best indication of a man's social and economic status; they were the most prized form of lobola or means of exchange in all marriage transactions, and the most highly valued sacrifices to the divine ancestors. Tilling of the soil was left to the womenfolk. Since neither fertilizing nor irrigation or a system of fallow land was practised, the land lost its productivity within a couple of seasons. The topography and sporadic rainfall combined with the absence of contour ploughing, increased the tempo of erosion. The population increase without diversification of economic activities and sources of income concentrated the whole economic burden on the inadequate system of agriculture to the detriment of gardens and pastures.

By tradition commerce and industry were almost non-existent in the Bantu economic system south of the Zambezi. They practised limited bartering of the basic necessities and home crafts. These activities or lack of activities were not conducive to the development of a modern infrastructure. They also did not ease or stimulate the necessary transition to a new economic system in a completely changed situation. What was needed was not merely a gradual adaptation but a revolution of economic and social structures.

The presence of the Europeans and the extension of their authority in geographical South Africa requires special attention in this connection. A rather ironical situation originated. In the first place the dilly-dallying border policy of the British regime in the Cape Colony was instrumental in causing the great inland migration of the Afrikaans-speaking population. This led to increased contact between White and Black and at the same time to the extension of White authority and land. The *pax Euro-*

peana that ensued, brought to an end the large-scale intertribal warfare and destruction of human lives and property. Previously, especially during the first decades of the nineteenth century, referred to by the Bantu as the *mfecane* or the period of travail, the great internecine wars, the migratory upheavals caused by Chaka, MaNtatise, Mzilikazi and a host of other leaders with their followers, caused the death of probably more than a million Bantu. Whole tribes such as the Leghoya were totally extinguished. Others were reduced to a mere shadow of what they had been. The country was depopulated. Large areas were left unoccupied.

The advent of the White man to the northern regions caused a new imbalance. Under conditions of peace, or rather, absence of war, the Bantu peoples experienced an unprecedented population increase. The modern term 'population explosion', is truly applicable to what happened from the second half of the last century. The Bantu like all rural peoples highly appreciate and value children. Coupled with a system of polygamy the result is self-evident. The population increased at a high rate and destroyed the natural balance between people and available land.

War, both as a check on population increase and as an economic enterprise, was becoming extinct. The pressure of the population on the land with the accompanying intensification of the struggle for existence did not have the effect of stimulating the invention of new productive systems and methods. Instead, the neighbouring White settlements provided an escape mechanism in the form of a system of labour export. Originally the Bantu hired themselves out as labourers to the White farmers; next, to the gold and diamond mining industries, and eventually they sought employment in the developing secondary industries and commercial concerns. In reality a vicious circle was created. The productive men and youths left their countries for employment and cash incomes in European areas. That left an abnormal ratio of old men, women and children in the homelands. Instead of productive self-sufficient fatherlands the homelands were little more than residential areas.

Viewed against the background of the traditional pattern of the Bantu economy, the absence of men from their homes did not, as is popularly believed, have the devastating economic influence usually ascribed to this practice. Traditionally the women tilled the fields and the younger boys tended the cattle. The men contributed to the economic activities mainly by warfare and hunting. Under the new circumstances the men started taking employment with the Whites. Even this step was taken reluctantly in certain circumstances. In Natal Indians were imported as indentured labourers for the simple reason that the Zulu men were unwilling to work on the sugar plantations because agricultural work was regarded as women's work. The negative influence of the Bantu men's absence from their homes was felt in a different direction. By finding a way of escape through taking part in the economic structure of a foreign nation outside their own country, the Bantu did not really need to improve and innovate their economic system. Of course, discovering progressive innovations through direct cultural contact and acculturation is the easier process and the shorter way. It is known to have happened all over the world where lesser and better developed countries have been in mutual contact. In the South African set-up very little feed-back to their own countries really took place. Instead of taking back their experience to their different countries of origin, improving and bettering their own national socio-economic institutions, the Bantu peoples migrated, temporarily in intention but permanently in practice, to the foreign country of the Whites leaving their own country poorer.

REHABILITATION OF THE BANTU HOMELANDS

One of the unfortunate results of this situation was that both Bantu and White tended to view the Bantu territories practically merely as labour reservoirs and to treat them accordingly. Since the unification of the four colonies, however, it dawned more and more clearly on the White political leaders that the existing situation could not be continued. One of the strong exponents of this line of thought was General Hertzog, leader of the opposition and Prime Minister of the Union from 1924 to 1939. His first steps were to enlarge the areas reserved as Bantu homelands. He was strongly motivated *inter alia* by the political concept of eventual restoration of Bantu independence and at the same time of safeguarding the political independence of the Whites. It was an increasingly difficult struggle. Apart from the internal political divisions, the effects of World War I, the economic depression, extensive droughts with dire effects on an economy leaning very heavily on the agricultural sector (the mining industry being the only important sector on the non-agricultural side), an alarming state of poverty amongst the rural, predominantly Afrikaans-speaking section of the population, and a consequent urban migratory movement in the hope of finding better living conditions, more serious obstacles were encountered. These were not yet overcome when World

War II ensued, absorbing all available manpower, attention, energy and capital needed for a comprehensive project of rehabilitation in the homelands.

White South Africa was itself only slowly and painfully emerging from relative poverty and an undifferentiated economic structure. The awareness of the undesirable conditions in these homelands found expression in and was stressed by several commissions of inquiry. In the light of existing circumstances such as depression, lack of capital, absence of industrial development apart from mining in the 'developed' regions of geographical South Africa, most of these findings were rather negative and pessimistic as far as the possibilities of a diversified economic structure were concerned.

Three directions of thought existed concerning the economic future of the Bantu ethno-national territories.

Any progressive and positive thinking and action had to cope in the first instance with the fruits of a previous *laissez faire* policy and overall neglect of these territories. This way of thinking had its roots in the approach to these areas as labour reservoirs. The poorer they were left, according to the more classical capitalistic thinking, the better, since that would act as a stimulus to their inhabitants to present themselves on the labour market at the lowest possible remuneration.

In liberalistic and leftist political circles pleas were expressed for development by discontinuing the traditional South African policy of separate Bantu and White territories. Economically speaking this line of approach, if implemented, should have led to a faster rate of development of the backward parts for the simple reason that Whites would have absorbed the land within a decade or two. With their skill, capital and better agricultural methods they would have created an improved infra-structure and would have raised the productivity, especially on the agricultural side, immensely. Socially and politically however, the Bantu peoples would by the same measures have been legitimately deprived of their lands and the fruit of development. A small minority would have remained in the ancestral lands, that had been sold to White foreigners, as farm labourers. The majority would have been practically forced to migrate to the towns and cities in the White areas at a time when neither adequate housing nor sufficient employment were available. That would have been the birth of a huge Black proletariat, culturally foreigners in the White man's cities and unaccustomed to an urban way of life; in short, totally unadjusted to an industrial environment.

A new approach was the acceptance of the existence of the national territories for the Bantu peoples and the demand that accelerated rehabilitation of their agricultural productivity and preparation for progressive industrial development should take place. Whereas the Bantu were instrumental, and still are, in building the White man's homeland, the *quid pro quo* from the side of White South Africa should consist in helping the Black nations in building and modernizing their own homelands.

This line of thought was accepted as official policy by the National Party government after 1948. Dr Verwoerd, initially as Minister of Native Affairs and later as Prime Minister, was the principal moving force. Actually it was a continuation of General Hertzog's ideas of the twenties and thirties, but with new drive and new perspectives. Two motives were combined, viz. the political and the economical. If the Bantu peoples were to become independent political entities, it was imperative that their territories should become economically viable and self-sufficient. At the same time it was hoped that in that way the Whites would be saved from being politically swamped by the hordes of Bantus rushing to the developing centres in the European area to seek employment.

Shortly after Dr Verwoerd took over as Minister of Native Affairs (later on renamed the Department of Bantu Administration and Development) the very important Tomlinson Commission (officially titled the 'Commission for the Socio-economical Development of the Bantu Territories within the Union of South Africa') was appointed and set to work. The main recommendation of this commission's report was that the agricultural sector of the Bantu economic system be developed as a primary activity and one in which the Bantu themselves could be immediately involved. But since these countries could not accommodate the whole of their *de jure* or their *de facto* populations as farmers (as no country in the world can), and since a large proportion of the *de facto* inhabitants had to be removed to take up urban residence and livelihoods, industrial development and a fully diversified economy were considered imperative. Several possibilities were mentioned as instrumental to the desired solutions.

The Tomlinson Commission was of the opinion, *inter alia,* that taking into account the lack of capital and technological know-how amongst the Bantu, the White man's capital, initiative and entrepreneurship should be used. In general terms it meant foreign investment and enterprise. The government, however, took a different stand and discarded this particular recommendation. Dr Verwoerd was exceedingly wary of and sensitive to any possible reproach of neo-colonialism or economic imperialism. His approach to a possible solution leaned heavily on state activity. Agricultural planning and rehabilitation were to be the responsibility of the agricultural branch of the Department of Bantu Administration and Development. The necessary finances and skill were to be supplied and canalized through state departments.

BORDER INDUSTRIES AND THE BANTU DEVELOPMENT CORPORATION

At a later stage Dr Verwoerd developed the concept of border industries as a means of reconciling the Bantu's need for employment and the labour needs of the expanding White industries. Entrepreneurs from the European area were to be encouraged to start new industrial plants or to move existing ones to the borders and to establish them on the European side of the borders. The Bantu would then be able to live on their side of the border while they were employed on the European side. These were to serve as new points of economic growth in the homelands. Dr Verwoerd strongly believed in the power of a natural feed-back of newly acquired economic and cultural skills. The money Bantu earned in the White territory could at least partly be spent in the Bantu residential area where smaller commercial enterprises and industries, such as dairies, butcheries, dry cleaners, general dealers, etc., would originate. The practice, however, did not come up to expectations. Instead of radiating economic activity inward into the Bantu homelands, the border industries caused a new concentration of population, luring the Bantu living inland to move closer to the borders.

Criticism of the concept and inception of the system of border industries gave rise to pleas for internal industrial and overall economic development of the Bantu territories, which would naturally involve the use of foreign, meaning White, capital, initiative and skill. This was a deviation from official policy. Earlier the border industry project was supplemented by the establishment of a general Bantu Investment Corporation (founded by an Act of Parliament in 1969) and eventually by separate development corporations for various Bantu territories. Capital was provided by Parliament from funds belonging to the Bantu Trust. The original share capital of R1 million was raised to more than R19 million in 1970. Industries and other undertakings are being established by the Corporation in trust for Bantu as part of the Corporation's policy of promoting the economic development of these territories and their inhabitants. In time these concerns will be transferred to qualified, experienced and competent Bantu businessmen. Necessary training is provided beforehand.

The Bantu Investment Corporation is responsible for the erection of the necessary shopping centres, garages and market premises in all Bantu townships for leasing to Bantu businessmen. The Corporation's building activities involve several million rands annually. The effect of the Corporation's activities in the building industry holds the following advantages for the homelands:

Practical training of trade-school qualified Bantu in trades such as plumbing, joinery, painting, masonry, and electrical wiring;

employment for Bantu in a labour intensive industry;

provision of shopping and office premises to Bantu at a reasonable rental with the prospect of their purchasing the shop and land on which it is situated as soon as it is possible for the Bantu to do so;

erection of shop buildings of good quality at reasonable cost;

consistent training of Bantu artisans to enable them to become independent contractors, by applying a policy whereby sub-contractors are in a position to learn to know and understand the duties and responsibilities of a building contractor under the guidance of the Corporation's supervisors.

A further function of the Corporation is to grant loans to Bantu businessmen. During the first ten years of its existence, the Corporation granted a total of approximately R6 million in the form of business loans to individuals and companies. A definite upward trend is noticeable in both the demand for and in the number of loans granted annually.

An important aspect of the Corporation's activities is to provide technical aid and advice to Bantu in their homelands. The Corporation undertakes the training of Bantu persons as employees, officials, managers or directors of industrial, commercial, financial and other business ventures.

Funds made available to Bantu in the form of loan capital must be invested productively, and to this end it is necessary that borrowers be given intensive training. During instructional visits, practical hints, aid and advice are offered in connection with all aspects of management. The Corporation employs White as well as Bantu personnel for this purpose. Major Bantu concerns are run by the Corporation as managers on behalf of Bantu companies. Managerial assistance is provided with a view to the training of Bantu personnel capable of assuming responsible management as soon as possible.

Mention must be made of the following activities of, and services rendered by the Corporation:

Previously the acquisition of essential commodities in the remote regions of the homelands created considerable problems for the local population. In order to alleviate the situation, the Corporation has established a large number of commercial undertakings in trust for the Bantu in the remoter parts of their countries. In these concerns Bantu clerks are trained to manage and control the undertakings once they have acquired the necessary business acumen. A number of wholesale concerns established by the Corporation in addition to the abovementioned, already render a comprehensive service to retailers in the various areas.

Bantu art and craft centres have also been established, and maintain a very favourable turnover. These centres are of great importance in creating outlets for Bantu artists in the homelands, in this way supplementing their earnings. Woodcraft, beadwork and pottery are the most important products marketed through the Corporation.

One of the latest ventures of the Corporation is the development of a holiday resort for Bantu on the South Coast of Natal and a nature reserve on a strip of virgin territory adjoining the Kruger National Park.

The Corporation's scheme for the mobilization of Bantu capital is in good progress. The number of savings banks increased to 23 and capital investment amounts to more than R4 million. Apart from the establishment of savings banks, which cater for savings bank accounts, fixed term and indefinite period investments, assistance in the financial field is also being rendered by the management of a property insurance company in terms of a management contract. During the financial year 1969-1970 an important step forward has been taken with the foundation of the Bureau for Economic Research on Bantu Development as an integral part of the Corporation. The Bureau has as its objective industrial economic studies and national economic research on behalf of the Department of Bantu Administration and Development, the different Bantu development corporations and the homeland authorities.

A new five-year plan, the capital requirements of which will amount to approximately R104 million, commenced on 1st April 1970. The object of this plan is to accelerate the economic development of the Bantu territories. Approximately R48 million will be allocated to industrial undertakings, R27 million to the concerns of the Corporation, R28 million to financing business and housing loans and one million rand to savings banks. It is envisaged that during this period employment opportunities will be created for 24 000 Bantu persons in the homelands.

THE ROLE OF THE AGENCY SYSTEM IN HOMELAND DEVELOPMENT

Although the establishment of the Bantu Investment Corporation and the different development corporations was hailed as a step in the right direction, it was felt at the same time that this was inadequate. The Government is unable to supply the gigantic amount of capital necessary for investment in the homelands were they to be developed to such an extent as to absorb their annual growth of available workers. This could be only the first objective, since to succeed in the political aspect of the development project, a homeland should also attract its population living and working in the adjoining White homeland. These are also the people who, by virtue of their experience and the skills they have acquired, can apply a new drive to the programme of national self-development. A project envisaging national development should also keep in mind the rise in the level of existence. These aims can only be reached by allowing private capital and initiative into the homelands. Decentralization of industry and economic activities should, according to this argument, be permitted over the borders into the heart of the Bantu territories and not only to the European side of the boundary. The Bantu Investment Corporation and its associates are valuable instruments and do excellent work as far as the Bantu entrepreneurs are concerned, but a far more comprehensive approach is imperative.

The next step in government policy, listening to the arguments of economists, industrialists, sociologists, etc., was the agency system. Although still wary of the danger of reproaches of economic colonialism, the government nevertheless conceded to the arguments in favour of private capital and skill. Capital from the non-state sector could henceforth be invested in Bantu areas under management of the investor acting as the agent of Bantu development. This at least provided a more elastic measure for development and opened a door for the necessary finances and managerial and technical know-how for promoting development in these territories at a much higher rate than could be expected from government involvement alone.

Since 1969 entrepreneurs were thus encouraged to promote industrial development in the Bantu homelands. Owing to the fact that Whites are not allowed to obtain ownership of fixed property in these Bantu territories – a measure meant to protect the Bantu – the Bantu Investment Corporation acting as trustee for the Bantu, makes available land and buildings against payment of a reasonable rental and encourages industrialists to establish their factories in the homelands for a period of time mutually agreed upon. It all depends on the Bantu authorities whether they are willing to grant extension of time or outright land ownership to these and other investors when the homelands receive their ultimate independence.

The White entrepreneur provides the equipment, machinery and working capital from his funds or funds provided by the Corporation on loan and undertakes to transfer his concern, after the agreed period has terminated, to the Corporation or to any Bantu company to be established.

Special benefits, such as tax concessions, low interest rates on loans, railway rebates, etc., are offered to the industrialist both in the border areas and in the Bantu homelands to encourage him to enter these fields and thereby to promote the economic development of the Bantu fatherlands. It is evident that concerns requiring large capital outlay, skilful management and highly technical abilities and promising considerable employment would specially qualify for these benefits and be doubly welcome.

Initially, four industrial growth points were planned for the first five years in co-operation with the relevant Bantu Territorial Authorities. The financial year 1969-1970 experienced the development of the first of these growth points, namely that near Hammanskraal, close to Pretoria. This point is being developed on behalf of the Tswana Territorial Authority at an approximate cost (as far as infra-structure is concerned) of R2,3 million. The project at Babalegi, as it is named, has progressed rapidly and the first industrialists moved in during September 1970. Roads are currently being tarred and power is available.

The interest shown by industrialists both in Babalegi and in Sitebe has been most encouraging especially since little interest was shown in this specific aspect of the economic development of the Bantu homelands in the past. Since the inception of negotiations in October 1969 approximately 70 concerns have been selected for Babalegi, 16 of which were already settled there before the end of the first financial year. A minimum of 8 000 Bantu can be employed in this industrial centre. On September 16, 1970. the Prime Minister made the following statement on the question of the establishment of industries in the homelands:

> 'If any industrialist establishes himself on the agency basis in a Black homeland and suffers any loss as a result of that homeland becoming independent and any political action on the part of the government of that Black homeland prior to the expiry of his contract, this government will indemnify him against such a loss.'

The Tomlinson Commission rightly concluded:

> 'The development of the human factor is a prerequisite for the whole of the development project. The Bantu should be enabled to take his place in all spheres of life in the homelands and to climb to the highest peaks.'

Parallel to the attempts at promoting economic development and modernization are those projects catering for human development. Apart from the phenomenal extension of schooling facilities and university education, stress is being laid on technical and vocational training. Qualified personnel are required for all the sectors of the expanding economy, for the public service, for the professions and in the technical, administrative, managerial, academic, etc. and other fields. An important part of this schooling for independence is provided by in-service training. Gaining ground is the concept of taking education and training in all its forms and aspects to the Bantu in his familiar environment instead of lifting him out of the milieu he is acquainted with to make use of educational amenities elsewhere.

THE FUTURE OF THE BANTU FATHERLANDS

The Government is being prodded from several sides to accelerate the pace of development and to adopt an even more open-door policy as far as investment and industrialization with the aid of outside capital and initiative is concerned. It is argued that agricultural planning and rehabilitation, notwithstanding its necessity, is a slow process, encountering many obstacles and even intensive resistance since changes in this field touch the very roots of Bantu tradition. Even in so far as successes can be documented, agricultural development represents only one sector of the economic spectrum and clearly is unable to carry the whole burden of economic welfare of the country and its people.

The quite considerable success in the field of agricultural progress dwindles in the light of the imperative need for a fast expanding labour intake. The only solution for the annually increasing supply of a new generation of workers can be sought in the field of industry and its associated areas of employment.

For successful and comprehensive social, cultural, political and economic development of the Bantu territories there are three prerequisites – they should be able to *house, feed and protect their inhabitants* adequately. The scattered portions of land, a condition inherited partly from the tribal past and partly from European influences, must be consolidated to form undivided units. The creation of a satisfactory infra-structure is impossible, economic viability is hampered and expedient administration is fettered under conditions of geographically divided and unlinked areas. Considerable progress has been made in this direction both by implementation of the provisions of the Bantu Land and Trust Act, the purchase of additional land, and the clearing up of Black and White spots by removing White communities surrounded by Bantu areas and Bantu enclaves within White areas. Undue publicity has been given to the removal of Black spots while the removal of Whites received no attention from the news media. The former contains an element of drama whereas the removal of Whites is a prosaic event – the owner sells his farm to the Bantu Trust, finds himself a new home and settles there. During the 1971 parliamentary session the Minister of Bantu Administration and Development promised an acceleration of the consolidation project.

Consolidation ought to be accompanied by expansion of the Bantu territories even beyond the additional areas to be purchased in terms of the Bantu Land and Trust Act. This is practical and possible on the same basis as provided by the existing act, viz. purchase of land by the Bantu Trust in such a way as to expand the present homeland territories to reach their natural boundaries. It is a false approach and an unrealistic idea, however, to think in terms of a division of geographical South Africa in proportion to the size of the population of each of its constituent peoples. Nowhere in the world does such an arrangement exist. The arguments developed on the thesis that only 13 per cent of the area of South Africa belongs to 80 per cent of the population (this represents the Bantu numbers) against 87 per cent in possession of the Whites (20 per cent of the population), are unrealistic and founded on false premises. It does not take into account the historical background nor does it reckon with unequal topographical, climatic or other natural conditions or with the qualitative contribution of the different sections of the population to the present structure. Only when viewed against the background of the greater geographical South Africa, including Botswana, Lesotho and Swaziland (even including Rhodesia, Zambia, Mozambique and Angola) does the picture come into perspective. Hence a challenge awaits those concerned, i.e. the prospective independent Bantu governments in Southern Africa, to decide on possible unification of their geographical and political areas of jurisdiction with those divided from them artificially, *vide* the Ovambo of South West Africa and Angola, Botswana and Transvaal Tswanaland, the Transkeian and Ciskeian Xhosaland. But also from a purely practical point of view, expansion of the national territories to make provision for natural boundaries, consolidating the area within the borders, providing serviceable harbours, etc., should receive consideration.

THE SYMBIOTIC RELATIONSHIP BETWEEN WHITE AND BANTU

Naturally, both consolidation and expansion means nothing at all if development is neglected. Everybody taking it seriously acknowledges the fact that, especially through the seven decades of the twentieth century, a symbiotic structure has developed – the Bantu territories supplied the unskilled and semi-skilled (and unofficially even a part of the skilled) labour force whilst the Whites provided the employment. This led to grave political implications which have to be solved. The choice of the past and of the present is in the direction of maintaining the existence of independent ethnic and national entities. South Africa is at least attempting to move towards the ideal of national separateness (not isolationism) in the political sphere. But this cannot deny the degree of integration or symbiosis that exists in the economic sphere. An abrupt ending of this situation would be fatal to all concerned. White South Africa cannot do without its Bantu workers, nor can the latter exist without the employment provided by their political and economic neighbour. It can, however, be expected that, steering a realistic and elastic course, the symbiotic structure will decrease in due course, in extent as well as in intensity, simply because it is the nature of all independent nations to work towards their own economic independence.

To grasp the full implication and extent of this thesis it is necessary to remember that the economic structure which caters for the needs of the more than twenty million people of geographical and multi-political South Africa, is mainly concentrated in the country officially belonging to more or less five million of the population. Apart from its political importance, voices are also raised against the economic, social and other dangers of overcentralization, such as strategic dangers, pollution, health, water supplies and social accumulation. The economic development of the Bantu territories, with the principal view of developing real fatherlands for their inhabitants on a basis of ethnic relationship can for other reasons, too, easily and logically be harnessed to a sound policy of socio-economic decentralization.

It cannot be denied that the ultimate ideal of homeland development is still very near to its starting point and a long distance from its final goal. Neither can one deny that progress is slow, almost disappointingly slow. The realist, however, does not become disheartened. Taking into consideration the great handicaps the venture started with, human unwillingness to accept change, the short period for which the project has actually been in progress and the symptoms of increasing momentum, one again becomes encouraged. South Africa has accepted the challenge and is determined to work towards the goal set for the future of this country. At this juncture it seems less important to take account of where we stand in the sense of real practical achievements but immensely important to see in what direction we are moving . . . and that we *are moving.*

Hazards of the Homeland Policy

Gideon Jacobs

Gideon Francois Jacobs (O.B.E.) is a senior United Party M.P. and one of its chief spokesmen on labour matters and race relations. He holds a Ph.D. from Pretoria University and is a personnel consultant by profession. Dr Jacobs has a distinguished World War II record and is now establishing himself as a brilliant writer and formidable Parliamentary debater.

From the first occupation of the Cape by the Dutch East Indies Company in 1652 until 1847 it was the official policy and declared aim of all Cape Governments, both Dutch and British, to contain the White settlement and to keep the races apart. With this end in view the Dutch Governors issued stern edicts prohibiting the colonists from moving further inland whilst the British, when they occupied the Cape, tried to enforce an inviolable frontier by means of treaties with African tribal chiefs. However, all efforts to keep the races apart failed because the colonists were continually seeking more land and labour for their farms and there was a mutual desire to trade.

After the Great Trek and the Kaffir War of 1846 the long sustained attempt to maintain territorial separation in the Cape ended and was replaced by a policy of ruling Black and White as inhabitants of the same country. In 1854 Sir George Grey, the British High Commissioner and Governor of the Cape, initiated a policy of gradual political and economic integration which persisted in the Cape until the Union of South Africa was formed in 1910. In pursuance of his policy Grey encouraged White farmers to settle in British Kaffraria (Xhosa territory). He rejected the idea of large African reserves in favour of a policy of intermixed settlement of Black and White because by this policy a concerted uprising of Xhosa tribesmen could be prevented, White settlers could obtain labour and it was hoped that the Xhosa would acquire habits of work and more progressive methods of farming and thereby learn the customs of civilized living.

At the time of the annexation of Natal the African population was sparse because the Zulu wars had decimated and dispersed the weaker tribes. When White rule had been established and peaceful conditions restored many Africans returned and a large number of small reserves was established for their occupation. This later found expression in the 'grid-iron' plan, a deliberate policy of keeping African reserves scattered by interspersing White colonists between them. Because there was at the outset adequate land for them the Africans saw no need to leave their reserves and to work in the White economy. This resulted in an acute labour shortage and to overcome this situation indentured Indian labourers were brought into the colony.

In the Orange Free State and the Transvaal the first Boer settlers had to fight desperate battles for mere survival. For reasons of security they broke up the larger tribes and settled many of them in numerous small reserves which President Kruger considered should not be larger than 2 400 hectares in extent. Despite Boer desire for separation many Africans were drawn into the White economy as farm workers and, after the discovery of gold on the Witwatersrand, as workers in the mines.

DELIMITING THE AFRICAN TRIBAL TERRITORIES

The territorial conquests of the Whites resulted in land, capital and entrepreneurship being relatively abundant but labour scarce in White areas; in African areas labour was abundant but the essential factors for economic development were non-existent. There arose, therefore, pressure on both sides for labour to migrate to the White areas. The great cultural gap between themselves and the Africans, added to the fears engendered by a century of conflict, made the Whites anxious to keep the African tribes as far away as possible; on the other hand the need for workers on farms, in the mines and in industry made it desirable to have them close on hand. Thus, when tribal reserves were adequate to support their population in the traditional manner, it was necessary to attract African labour to White areas by recruitment agencies or by imposing money taxes, the payment of which necessitated acceptance of wage-earning employment. Later, however, when the reserves became inadequate through natural increase of the population, legislation was introduced to restrict the right of entry to White areas and to limit African employment opportunities in these areas. This remains the situation even today.

By the end of the nineteenth century White administration and control had been extended throughout Southern Africa; nevertheless, considerable areas remained in African tribal occupation in the Transvaal, Natal and the Cape Colony. The Land Act of 1913 introduced uniformity of tenure by making a schedule of all existing land in African occupation, then amounting to 9 170 000 hectares, and providing that no non-African might acquire land within any scheduled area.

In 1932 a Native Economic Commission presided over by Dr J.E. Holloway reported that, 'It is essential that no time should be lost in developing the Reserves and in reducing the present pressure on land by making available more areas for Native occupation.' General Hertzog was Prime Minister at the time and he set himself the task of obtaining legislative sanction for the segregation policy which he had first propounded nearly a quarter of a century earlier. As far as the Reserves were concerned this policy resulted in the Native Trust and Land Act of 1936 which released a further 5 800 000 hectares of land to be purchased for African occupation.

THE GOVERNMENT'S BANTU POLICY

Towards the end of 1947 the National Party, with the next general election in view, issued a pamphlet in which it stated its African policy in the following terms:

'In general terms our policy envisages segregating the most important ethnic groups and subgroups in their own areas where every group will be enabled to develop into a self-sufficient unit.

'We endorse the general principle of territorial segregation of the Bantu and the Whites . . .

'The reserves should be the national home of the Bantu. There their educational institutions should be situated and there social services should be provided instead of the present practice of providing them in urban areas . . .'

After the National Party gained power in 1948 the divergent views of White opinion in South Africa on African policy were given expression in two reports known as the *Fagan Report* and the *Tomlinson Report.*

The Commission appointed under the chairmanship of Mr Justice Fagan by General Smuts before he lost power in 1948 insisted that any colour policy ought to be based on the assumption that there would eventually be a multi-racial society in South Africa in which both Whites and Non-Whites must have a permanent place. Having discussed the difficulties which would stand in the way of total segregation and of a policy which would allow no racial discrimination the report stated, 'Only a third policy remains: the policy which recognizes that European and Native communities scattered throughout the country as they are to-day will permanently continue to exist side by side economically intertwined and should therefore be accepted as permanent and as being part of a big machine: but at the same time there are differences between them to which legislation has to pay due regard and which in administrative affairs make necessary a measure of separation with machinery for consultation on matters of joint concern. We take it, too, that the best development is an evolutionary one and not a revolutionary one . . . We believe that the measures rendered necessary by the new approach should be introduced by way of a gradual change of direction; that we must show respect for existing institutions, for their historical background and for the mentality which is linked to them and should, where we find it possible, rather build on them than try to overturn them.'

THE TOMLINSON REPORT

When the National Party assumed office in 1948 it wasted no time in trying to give effect to the 'apartheid' policies outlined in its pre-election manifesto. To recommend on how its Native policy should be implemented it set up a Commission under the chairmanship of Professor Tomlinson, whose report became available in 1955. The composition and terms of reference of the Commission made its findings in favour of the Government's 'apartheid' or separate development policy a foregone conclusion. Not surprisingly the Commission found that separate development was essential for the maintenance of White political control but it based its recommendations on the erroneous possibility of incorporating the three (British) High Commission Territories (Swaziland, Basutoland and Bechuanaland) into the Union. It reported that the only way out of the White dilemma lay in the consolidation of the African Reserves and their sustained development on a large scale and with the greatest possible speed.

The Government issued a White Paper on the Tomlinson Report in which it stated: 'The Government welcomes the unequivocal rejection of the policy of integration and of any theories of a middle course as well as the justification of the Government's policy of Apartheid (Separate Development) as gradually and purposefully applied. It also welcomes the endorsement of the Government's repeatedly expressed standpoint that sufficiently rapid progress will have been made and further advancement of the progress of separation guaranteed; in other words, that security would be assured for White civilization and opportunities created for both racial groups in all spheres if, after a period of fifty years, an approximately equal proportion of Whites and Bantu had been reached in European Territory.'

THE VISION OF INDEPENDENT HOMELANDS

It should be noted that until this time, whilst various attempts had been made to set aside certain areas of ground for the exclusive development of specific ethnic groups and for establishing self-governing areas, no political leader had advocated the creation of independent African states as a solution to the race problem in South Africa. This point was also clearly made in 1951 by Dr Verwoerd.

Speaking in the Senate he said:

'Now the Hon. Senator wants to know whether the series of self-governing areas would be Sovereign. The answer is obvious . . . How could small scattered states arise? The areas will be economically and otherwise dependent on the Union. It stands to reason that when we say that the Protectorates should be incorporated in South Africa and, at the same time talk about the Natives' rights of self-government in those areas, we cannot mean by that to cut large slices out of South Africa and turn them into independent states.

'. . . if they would only look at a map of South Africa they would see that it is a completely impossible and impracticable interpretation of self-government in their own areas. Self-government within one's own area is something entirely different from saying that South Africa is to be divided into a series of states.' (*Senate Debates,* 1951, Vol. 2, Col. 2893.)

It was not until 1959, when the Promotion of Bantu Self-Government Bill was launched through Parliament, that Dr Verwoerd admitted that he had abandoned the position that he had previously adopted. The preamble to this Bill made it clear that the Government regarded the Africans as a number of separate national units on the basis of language and culture. The Bill therefore contemplated the creation of eight main national homelands in which the Africans would be able to develop to their full capacity as independent communities. Those in the White areas, even if they had been born there and lived there all their lives, would not be regarded as permanent residents and would remain citizens of one of these African areas.

Since then the Transkei has been granted partial self-government and territorial authorities have been established in other African areas.

During its 1968 Session the Transkeian Legislative Assembly passed a motion that the Republican Government be approached to do everything in its power to prepare the Transkei for independence in the shortest possible time. A reply was given by the Minister of Bantu Administration and Development in the House of Assembly on 6th April, 1968; his remarks he said were directed at all the peoples of South Africa and not only to those of the Transkei. The road to independence, he indicated, was a long and difficult one. Before any people could aspire to it certain prerequisites had to be fulfilled:

> Considerable administrative experience in management and control of government departments;
>
> Deep-rooted reliability in all actions particularly in the control of finance and budgeting;
>
> Integrity of purpose in public affairs from the highest to the lowest official;
>
> A democratic way of life and sense of complete responsibility;
>
> The control and management of all fields of administration by its own citizens and not on a large scale by citizens of another country because there were not enough local men qualified to do the work;
>
> Economic development and provision of jobs for its own people by its own government;
>
> A firm desire for peaceful existence. A nation that wished to govern itself independently must show by word and deed that it was prepared to live in peace with its own people and with other peoples and nations, especially its neighbours.

If these prerequisites for independence were applied no homeland would ever become independent and few nations in the world which today are independent would be judged qualified for it. Despite this attitude recent pronouncements by the Prime Minister, Mr Vorster, make it clear that the Government wishes to accelerate the process of independence whether or not the homelands are consolidated or viable or equipped to meet the demands of independence. This therefore signifies another important change of approach.

THE HOMELAND GAMBLE

The word 'hazard' is derived from the Spanish word 'azar' which means an unlucky throw of the dice. Judged against the above background this very aptly describes the policy on which the Government has staked the future of the South African Republic and all its citizens. Certain aspects need further emphasis.

It is extremely difficult to obtain accurate, reliable, up to date and meaningful statistics regarding the areas or the *de facto* populations of the African Reserves.

Preliminary figures for the census conducted in May 1970 do not indicate the numbers of people actually resident in the homelands which constitute 12,59 per cent of the total area of the Republic, and, as can be seen on the map on pages . . . ., consist of more than 80 separate pieces of land. Moreover the Government has not yet bought all the land earmarked in 1936 for African occupation; thus after some 35 years the first essential aspect of the homelands policy has not been implemented.

Much of the land in the homelands is mountainous and much of what remains is badly eroded. Throughout all the homelands not more than ten per cent of those engaged in subsistence farming earn more than R120 a year and over forty per cent less than R40 a year.

Notwithstanding consistent prodding from official quarters, Africans in the homelands have failed to adapt their tribal economy to the changed circumstances of relative land scarcity; they have failed to appreciate that the system of communal land tenure and the demands of sound farming techniques are incompatible. The custom of 'lobola' has lead to an excess of inferior and unproductive cattle and over-grazing. The ploughing of steep slopes, repeated monoculture with maize and inadequate care for soil fertility have caused soil erosion on a large scale and a further decline in productivity. Agriculturally the homelands could, therefore, only sustain a portion of their existing population and improvement in this regard must be seen as a very long-term proposition.

The Tomlinson Commission felt that agricultural rehabilitation could not take place in isolation and stressed that a precondition for agricultural development was general economic development to provide employment in occupations other than farming so as to relieve the pressure of population on the land and to enable family farming units to be economic and not less than 40 hectares in extent. The Commission accordingly proposed that about half the existing Bantu population be taken off the land and that 20 000 employment opportunities be created annually in secondary industry and 30 000 annually in tertiary industry.

Dr Verwoerd, however, rejected many of these recommendations because he considered that they would accelerate the breakdown of the tribal system. He also refused to permit industrial development of the homelands by private White capital and entrepeneurs, although without such assistance economic progress would continue to be negligible.

It has now also become clear that the Tomlinson Commission had greatly underestimated the job opportunities which would have to be created. Latest estimates indicate a much more formidable task. Professor J.L. Sadie has calculated that 181 000 new jobs will have to be provided in the homelands each year if the African population in the White areas is to be reduced by 5 per cent per year. Dr A.S. Jacobs, former economic advisor to the Prime Minister, has estimated that by the end of the century 5 800 000 jobs will have to be provided in the homelands and border areas (i.e. 193 000 a year) if 70 per cent of the natural increase in the total African population is to be absorbed in these areas. Against figures of this magnitude the failure of the Government to meet the challenge of its own policy is woefully apparent. There is still practically no industrialization of consequence in the homelands themselves and in 1968 the permanent commission for the location of industry reported that about 5 000 employment opportunities had in fact been created annually for Africans in secondary industry in border areas and that in time this figure should rise to 9 000 annually.

Success of the African homelands policy is undoubtedly related to a massive increase in the economic carrying capacity of these areas but industrialization on any significant scale cannot be attained without active infusion of private White capital and entrepreneurship. Whilst the Government has established several public utilities in the form of Development Corporations for this purpose and has recently agreed to permit White capital into these areas on an 'agency' basis, results are predictably disappointing. The bureaucratic mind is not one that is normally attuned to risk-taking and the 'agency' plan has engendered little enthusiasm.

Government reluctance to stimulate joint enterprises inside the homelands is given cogency when viewed against the background of future independence of these areas. Not unnaturally there is the fear of economic vulnerability and of major capital losses if these areas, after they have become independent, turn hostile to South Africa. The basic dilemma of the Government is that economic viability is a prerequisite for independence – but independence might seriously jeopardize the viability of the South African economy as a whole.

THE BORDER AREAS SCHEME

As a compromise arrangement the Government has in recent years concentrated on a new plan – the border areas scheme. The basic idea is that industries should be established just outside the borders of the homelands and inside the White areas, where they will be operated under White control.

Industrialists are offered impressive inducements to move to these areas whilst Africans, who constitute the bulk of the work force, would be required to commute daily or weekly from their homes to their places of work. Insignificant progress has, however, been made with this scheme except where new industrial areas are merely extensions of existing economic complexes and the Transkei, the most advanced of the homelands, has not got a single border industry of any size. Lack of infrastructure makes development of this kind costly and few social benefits would accrue to the African workers unless these industries were strung out like a string of beads all along the borders of the homelands, a clear economic absurdity.

The border areas plan would seem to hold out few advantages to the homelands. Whilst new job opportunities could admittedly be created in this manner, little wealth would be brought to the homelands as a considerable portion of the workers' earnings would be spent in the White areas and all company taxes would accrue to the central Government. Black workers would continue to operate as migrants in White-controlled industries in which they are given very limited opportunities for occupational advancement. These border industries would have the effect of draining off the limited number of Africans who have acquired technical skills, thereby further retarding homeland development. In this sense border areas constitute the very antithesis of establishing separate states for the Africans.

Finally, the border areas scheme also raises serious strategic questions, as no nation deliberately sites its industries next to the borders of foreign states. The reverse obtains in Russia where satellite states are forced to site their industries near the Russian border in order to increase their vulnerability.

AFRICAN WORKERS IN WHITE AREAS

At present there is thus no evidence that the homelands will ever drain Africans away from the industrial White areas. On the contrary these areas will have to continue to absorb the surplus homeland Africans who cannot be given jobs in their own or border areas. The number of Africans employed in White areas, instead of declining, as is required by Government policy, will continue to grow. This process will be accelerated by the vastly increased rate of absorption of African workers dictated by the requirements of the White economy itself. Presently Africans constitute nearly 90 per cent of the labour force in mining, 80 per cent in agriculture and nearly 70 per cent in manufacturing industry. In practice, economic growth in South Africa is primarily dependent on moving workers from areas of low productivity like the homelands to areas of relatively high productivity like manufacturing industry in the White areas. South Africa has 1,3 million factory workers at the present. At an annual growth rate of 5½ per cent in GNP, 4 million factory workers would be needed at the end of this century. On present indications more than 80 per cent of them would have to be African.

Africans not only constitute the bulk of the workers in the White economy but they are increasingly being drawn into more skilled occupations. This process will inevitably continue as a modern industrial economy requires at least 10 per cent of its total population for higher skilled tasks. With only 35 per cent of the 3,7 million Whites economically active they could at best fill only a portion of the jobs that exist in these grades. Each passing year makes the South African economy more dependent on the employment of trained and skilled Africans; the homelands policy therefore places the Whites in the ridiculous situation of striving for a goal whose actual attainment could bring about their own economic downfall.

The argument that Africans, whilst remaining citizens of foreign states could continue to supply the bulk of the manpower for the White economy, is demonstrably untenable. It means perpetuation of the migratory system which has been vigorously condemned by all South African churches and even by supporters of the Government.

DANGERS POSED BY HOMELANDS

The migratory system introduced long ago as a matter of necessity will be greatly expanded if and as the homelands settlement plan gathers momentum. It is a system that leads to massive economic wastage and many social evils. Apart from the loss of time in travelling to and fro from place of work, the intermittent character of employment makes specialization extremely difficult. Migrant labourers tend to become birds of passage; they have no incentive to excel, to acquire skills or to make a permanent career for themselves with a particular organization. The constant turnover of labour inhibits advancement of the workers themselves and has a very adverse influence on productivity and on the efficiency of the economy of the country as a whole.

In the meantime, the women are left in the homelands living lonely lives with responsibilities for which they are not equipped and with their children growing up without adequate discipline and deprived of full parental guidance. The men, on the other hand, are forced to live for long periods under unnatural conditions which give rise to crime, homosexuality, drunkenness and other social aberrations. Whilst the migratory labour system cannot suddenly be abolished it should be accepted for what it is – an evil canker at the heart of our whole society, wasteful of labour, destructive of ambition and a symptom of our fundamental failure to create a progressive and coherent economic society.

With three-quarters of the work force citizens of foreign independent states, immense industrial relations problems could also arise. African workers are presently not organized into trade unions because they are not defined as employees in the Industrial Conciliation Act. There would, however, be no way of preventing separate unions being formed in the independent homelands themselves. This could lead to chaotic collective bargaining conditions. Workers' claims would be turned into demands by foreign Governments, minor problems at work could become international incidents and the economy as a whole could be made extremely vulnerable.

The problems associated with dynamic implementation of the homelands policy are truly immense. Achievement of complete separation in every field, social, economic, political and territorial, as required by this policy, would mean forcing several million Africans out of the White industrial complexes, removing several millions of Africans in the Reserves from the land, developing industries in or on their borders to provide them with an adequate livelihood, re-allocating the use of some 15,5 million hectares of land and at the same time perpetuating the tribal system which has proved itself to be totally incapable of adaptation to the demands of a money economy.

In view of the insurmountable demographic and economic problems the Government has contented itself by creating an elaborate political facade for the homelands. Legislative Councils have been introduced, Chief Ministers appointed and national anthems and flags provided for in the legislation. The constitutional framework is impressive and there are many political trappings but there is complete absence of a viable economic base. Little progress has been made with the consolidation of the various territories. In some cases they consist of several dozen disconnected areas making effective administration a sheer impossibility. The effect of this is best illustrated by driving from Eshowe, the capital of Zululand, to Durban, a distance of some 160 kilometres. In that short distance you would travel in and out, crossing between the White and Black areas some twelve times. If by any stretch of the imagination these areas were to become part of an independent state(s) it could mean passing through immigration and customs formalities many times over a distance of 160 kilometres. Decisions of homeland legislatures furthermore remain subject to approval by the central government on all but very minor local issues. Education and training is inadequate to prepare them to meet their new obligations with success whilst there is a totally inadequate allocation of the vast funds essential for rapid development. African political aspirations have been awakened, feelings of nationalism have been stimulated, grandiose promises made, but few of the major objectives have been attained and the ideal of complete separation has become increasingly remote.

DANGERS POSED BY GOVERNMENT COMMITMENT TO BANTUSTAN INDEPENDENCE

Undeterred by this the Government continues to state its ideals with gathering vigour, the lack of real achievement being increasingly camouflaged by a new kind of political mumbo-jumbo. In a recent radio broadcast the Minister of Bantu Administration and Development talked about preparing ' . . . for the indispensable interdependence among the nations of South Africa which will ultimately be involved in independent coexistence.' He failed to indicate that less than R50 million a year is spent on the development of the homelands which is less than the annual budget of a middle-sized city in South Africa.

Even the ultimate destiny of the homelands now seems to be in question. The Minister concerned recently talked about 'possible ultimate independence' thereby raising grave doubts about the future sovereign independence of these areas. On a simple issue such as the establishment of alliances with Communist countries by the independent homelands there is also a marked divergence of view on the Government side. Two Cabinet Ministers have in the last year indicated that this would be acceptable to South Africa but the Minister of Defence stated emphatically that it was completely out of the question and would not be permitted. Independence cannot be conditional and restrictions of this kind would surely serve to exacerbate relations between Whites and Africans even further.

Certainly the Government has so far shied away from the strategic implications of independent homelands. Experience elsewhere has shown that impoverished satellite states easily become nuclei of discontentment and constitute fertile ground for subversive activities of agitators and foreign political adventurers. Several of the homelands, unlike the ex-Protectorates, occupy a most important strategic position in South Africa. They straddle some of the major communications systems, control important water resources and have direct access to the sea. South Africa could not afford the establishment of several 'Cubas' inside its own border and must of necessity take steps to prevent hostile powers from gaining this kind of foothold.

Whilst no African state or combination of states could mount an invasion of South Africa with any chance of success, the security danger which has to be guarded against is primarily that of infiltration by trained terrorists and agitators. Such actions could be successfully countered only if the African population actively assisted the military forces of South Africa in their counter-operations. Guerilla operations elsewhere in Africa and in Asia have also demonstrated that success in unconventional warfare depends on the availability of a secure base in neutral territory: the possibility that independent homelands could be coerced by powerful states into this role cannot be ruled out and any retaliation by South Africa would trigger off a major conflict.

It is not surprising therefore that the Transkei, the shop window of this policy, is even today in a declared 'state of emergency' under proclamation 400, in which even the right to hold public meetings is curtailed. Its only potential sea port, Port St Johns, is zoned as a 'White' area.

The homelands, however, constitute only one, and not the most important facet at that, of the whole range of problems arising from the fact that Whites and Africans must by the accidents of history live intermingled in one country. It is a form of escapism to believe that it will ever be possible to concentrate the vast majority of the Africans in their poverty-ridden and under-developed homelands. It is equally unrealistic to believe that the large numbers who are permanently domiciled in the White area, who have severed all connection with tribalism and their homelands of origin, and who represent the most advanced and educated segment of the African population, will be willing for all time to forego any say in the manner of Government in the area in which they live and work. On the contrary, depriving them of meaningful political participation and the right of freehold title to the homes they occupy creates the classical background for increasing unrest. 'A landless, rootless, voiceless proletariat', the Communists claim, 'constitutes the spearhead of the revolution.'

Developments in South Africa over the last quarter of a century have thus fully vindicated the conclusions reached many years ago by the Fagan Commission. They have also shown that the objectives set by the Tomlinson Commission are unattainable or rather that the Government has failed to implement even the minimum requirements of this plan, thus destroying whatever merits it might have had.

In trying to persuade the White population that this policy provides a solution for African numerical superiority and an avenue of escape from their racial fears, the Government has been forced to create an elaborate political myth, in which flights of fancy have been substituted for reality. The concept of the 'right of self-determination in their own areas' has been used to provide justification for perpetuating a pernicious system of outmoded discrimination in the rest of the country. The Africans' right of occupational advancement in the areas in which jobs exist has been restricted by claiming that the 'sky is the limit' in areas where jobs do not exist. Opportunities for political expression in the places in which they live have been replaced by granting illusory rights in territories where they do not live. More and more political fiction is necessary to obscure the reality of the South African situation and sustain the apartheid myth.

BALKANIZATION NOT FEASIBLE

Not unnaturally the bulk of the detribalized, educated Africans in White South Africa reject the homelands plan outright. The probable reactions of the African leaders in the homelands themselves, once they have been entrusted with the responsibilities and powers conferred by independence, remain as unpredictable as human nature itself. At the present time they tend to express overt support for the Government's approach but they are increasingly using their positions as a starting point from which to bargain for further concessions. Already they are clamouring for more land, greater financial assistance and increased legislative and executive powers; further demands are being formulated to include privileges for the Africans living and working in South Africa itself. History shows that minorities invariably create interstate problems but in South Africa 'minority' problems on an unheard of scale are being deliberately created.

More and more Whites are also beginning to have doubts about the feasibility of this policy; the prospect of dismemberment and 'Balkanization' of South Africa is being viewed with increasing disenchantment and concern. The desirability of a form of neo-colonialism, abandoned twenty years ago by the European powers, is being seriously questioned. The insight and driving power to provide the necessary impetus to the plan is lacking; the belief is therefore growing that it was started too late, that there is too little land, too little money, too litle time and too little determination to make this policy work. Perceptive White South Africans can perceive the grand design crumbling and the Verwoerdian new vision fading into the background.

This feeling is succinctly summarized in a recent leading article in *Die Burger,* the Government's mouthpiece in the Cape. 'The Nationalist plan, theoretically acceptable but in practice tremendously difficult in its implementation, has to deal with a problem of disbelief, inside as well as outside the country. People ask not so much whether it is right or wrong in principle but whether we are in earnest. They do not believe that what is said can be done, or will be done.'

The outside world cannot understand why 87 per cent of the land area is reserved for Whites and only 13 per cent for the Africans who constitute almost three-quarters of the population. They note the outward manifestations of discrimination, and how the aspirations of Africans to be treated as human beings are being thwarted. They support the African desire for a better way of life and a greater share in the benefits which modern science and invention place within the reach of all humanity. Against this background of hostility to the existing system the positive steps taken by the Government to improve the lot of the African are ignored and international antagonism is gathering new momentum. Increasing isolation resulting in trade and arms boycotts and mounting pressure from certain countries for the use of force have become a feature of the situation confronting South Africa and will greatly influence the future pattern of race relations.

A WORKABLE PLAN FOR THE FUTURE

Before it is too late South Africans themselves will have to come to terms with the reality of their situation. Valuable time has been lost during the last twenty years in trying to define various forms of political Utopia that could, on paper at least, meet the aspirations of the Africans. Concurrently there has been an almost pathological emphasis on franchise rights and ultimate goals. What is desperately needed today is a workable plan for the immediate future – not a vision based on reaching the end of a political rainbow. This plan must of necessity embrace the following features:

Firstly, recognition of the fact that South Africa is a pluralistic society consisting of many different communities at different stages of development which imposes the fundamental task of creating conditions conducive to the future peaceful co-existence of these communities.

Secondly, neither the doctrine of forced separation nor that of forced integration will achieve this objective. The absence of racial strife in the past has been due to the fact that South Africa has, until recently, been relatively free from racial dogma.

Thirdly, the standard of civilization already attained must be extended for the benefit of White as well as Black. The root causes of Communism, such as ignorance and denial of fundamental human rights, must be combated and the basic tenets of the democratic way of life, such as respect for the rights and dignity of the individual and observance of the rule of law, must be vigorously safeguarded.

Fourthly, in cultural and social affairs there should continue to be a measure of separation because it is desired by the majority of the Blacks as well as the Whites. Separation could in any case help to eliminate some of the points of friction but forced separation merely for the sake of separation achieves the opposite effect.

Fifthly, in economic affairs there will be growing interdependence and any policy aimed at placing an artificial ceiling upon the occupational development of the African is certain to disrupt racial harmony and economic progress.

Sixthly, there must be a growing degree of decentralization in decision-making in the political sphere and here the homelands should play an important role. They should be seen as economically depressed areas and vigorously developed with the assistance of private White capital and enterprise. The interests of the indigenous populations should, however, be entrenched as far as new enterprises are concerned both with regard to ownership of land and share equities. Facilities for education and training also need to be greatly expanded.

The maximum degree of self-government under freely elected legislative bodies should be the aim for the homelands. Present Government policy is directed towards sovereign independence of these areas with secession from South Africa as an inevitability; the interests of the homelands would, however, best be served by political accommodation in a greater South African Federation. Group interests make decentralization of political activity desirable – but common interests emphasize overwhelmingly the need for co-ordination and central direction.

In South Africa there are many factors that tend to separate the races, but there are as many that bind them together. Whilst deep prejudices exist on the one hand, on the other hand an immense reservoir of goodwill has been built up over many years. What is urgently needed is a return to the empirical approach, the middle road based on the creation of a new political climate within which the leaders of the various races could, in consultation with one another, work constructively towards the common ideal – the betterment of our society.

The Economic Philosophy of Homeland Development

J. A. Lombard

Professor Jan Lombard is Head of the Department of Economics at the University of Pretoria. He studied at the University of Pretoria and the London School of Economics. An authority on the economic problems of Southern Africa's developing peoples, he is currently, in his capacity as a member of the Bantu Affairs Commission, intimately involved in blueprinting the economic development of the Bantu Homelands.

The benefits for both Black and White to be derived from the development of the Bantu homelands in South Africa constitute a kaleidoscope of material and immaterial gains, some of which are expected to be realized over relatively long periods. These benefits are difficult to express in terms of a single money figure, particularly over the short term. Both the Black and the White communities tend to base their support for the policy of separate development on the benefits to be derived from increasing settlement of Bantu in their own areas, despite the costs directly and indirectly required to implement this settlement. These attitudes are not 'heroic' but are not necessarily purely materialistic. Resistance by Whites against settling Bantu in their own homelands may have arisen from purely short term personal material considerations, but they may also have arisen from 'higher' value systems which take into account less personal and more general sacrifices of other objectives of the South African communities.

Analogous situations arise elsewhere in the world wherever national communities embark upon policies of international assistance. Possibly the most spectacular example of a gigantic effort by one national community to devote a large percentage of its resources to the reconstruction of the social system of other communities, was the Marshall Plan organized by the United States Government and nation shortly after World

War II in order to step up the process of European economic recovery. Was this idea of General Marshall's an emotional reaction to the plight of the Europeans? On the contrary, the economic and consequent political weakness of Europe was only driven home to the United States administration when the British Government revealed that it would not be able to continue to provide aid to Greece beyond the end of March, 1947. The threat of Greek political collapse convinced the Truman administration that not only was aid needed for those countries directly or indirectly threatened by Communism, but also that Western Europe had to be saved from complete economic collapse. The history of the events preceding General Marshall's famous speech on 5th June, 1947, at Harvard, indicates that his plan was the outcome of a very rational weighing up of costs and broad benefits to the American community.

The political economy of developing the Bantu homelands in South Africa did not originate in a similarly spectacular fashion. The basic ideas of this policy existed in South Africa even before the Union of South Africa was formed, and were mainly conceived in political and social terms.

Shortly after Union, General Smuts, for example, as a member of the Imperial War Cabinet in London formulated his policy of segregation in terms of constitutional matters rather than in terms of economic development programmes. South African thinking in this connection expanded to reach the economic horizons after the well-known Tomlinson Report appeared in the late fifties and started taking shape in specific programmes only during the past decade. Even now the White community of the Republic of South Africa has not constructed a definite framework for Bantu homeland development. For this reason foreign observers find it very difficult to make up their minds whether the idea is a 'pipe dream' or a 'determined effort by the peoples of South Africa to lay the foundations for peaceful co-existence in the sub-continent'.

It is my belief that the peoples of South Africa, both White and Black, can and will bring about the structural economic changes required for the establishment of respectable and respected Bantu national states in South Africa, provided that the people can clearly see ahead, not necessarily into the ultimate future, but along a path which will lead to the cultivation of the dignity of man. For this end we need, among many other things, to construct a framework outlining our objectives, our means and how these should be applied to achieve our ends, as well as evolve a technique of evaluating the effectiveness and efficiency of the means employed.

THE MEANING OF DYNAMIC PLANNING

There are important differences between a plan and the process of planning. A development plan is merely a product of the process of development planning. It may, in fact, not even be the most important product of the planning process. Equally, if not more valuable than the particular documents usually thought of as 'plan', is the meeting of the minds of people actively concerned with the decisions and activities involved in development, but most important of all is the knowledge gained in the process of planning of the process of development – that is, the planners recognize that they are planning with imperfect knowledge of the development process in their particular community and that they are really 'test driving' a new model rather than racing along in a standard model.

At the same time, planning which does not, *inter alia,* result in some set strategy for a particular period, is somewhat like a banquet without food.

Probably the most important, humbling fact about planning the development of any homeland is our imperfect knowledge about the way in which this development will take root and grow. We cannot plan on the basis of a 'general theory' of development. Thus even the planning process itself must be dynamic. What is planned in 1973 will depend, not only on the results expected in 1974 or thereafter, but also on experience gained in 1972! Thus planning moves forward towards expectations on the basis of experience; the specific technical targets as well as the particular activity programmes adopted may be expected to alter in time as increasing knowledge is gained of costs and benefits within the broad limits of the long-term perspectives set.

Essential in such a process of dynamic planning – i.e. test driving our development model – is regular and up-to-date information about performance upon which periodic revaluations and new strategic decisions can be based.

The essential elements of the planning process may therefore be itemized under the following planning stages:

(a) the structuring of the development process to be planned;

(b) the analysis of the effectiveness and efficiency of the activities involved in the overall development process;

(c) the design and administration of the system of control over the performances achieved under the programmes to be decided upon.

Because of the need for *dynamic* planning, the information gained from the control system should form the basis of :

(d) the reassessment of programme performances in terms of the comprehensive perspectives of the policy; and

(e) the setting of new targets for existing programmes or the introduction of entirely new programmes in addition to, or as replacements of existing programmes in the light of effectiveness and efficiency.

It should be realized that the creation of development opportunities in the several Bantu homelands has been greatly increased during the past decade. Thus the amount of money channelled into this process by the South African Treasury through the South African Bantu Trust Fund has increased from less than R10 million in 1960 to approximately R200 million in 1971. The structuring of the planning process, therefore, does not start from scratch. What is needed is an interpretation of the current flow of activity according to a more systematic framework of evaluation. In particular, the current activities have to be identified in programmes with technically fairly homogeneous outputs, while these technically defined programmes should be further grouped under broad categories or dimensions of politically homogeneous ideas of what development means. Thus a framework begins to arise according to which technical outputs and their costs can be politically evaluated. (The format of the classification should obviously show the position for each Bantu homeland separately.)

Several levels of planning structure can be conceived and have been employed the world over where development planning is being practised. Judging by the experience of the International Bank for Reconstruction and Development, commonly known as the 'World Bank' [1], the scope of national development planning at any time can and does range from the limited and piecemeal, project by project approach found in mixed economies in early phases of development to the comprehensive, centralized planning found in socialized economies.

The formulation of public investment projects unrelated to each other or to a unifying concept has serious shortcomings. Except for being listed in the budget, often with omissions, these projects may never appear in a

1. See Albert Waterson, *Development Planning, Lessons of Experience,* Johns Hopkins Press, 1965.

single document: according to Waterson this approach is characteristic of governments without a clearly defined development philosophy or a long-term outlook. 'An effort is not made to establish priorities for projects on the basis of uniform economic, technical and administrative criteria, or to evaluate the feasibility of the programme as a whole in relation to available funds, raw materials and other supplies, technicians, skilled manpower and management . . . The project by project approach frequently results in the frittering away of public investment resources on too many small, unrelated projects or on a few unduly large ones.'

Advocates of comprehensive planning, on the other hand, 'do not seem to understand that in most less developed countries the basic weakness is not the absence of a comprehensive approach to development planning, but the shortage of soundly conceived projects'.

In between these two extremes lies the so-called 'integrated public investment planning'. According to Waterson 'those who would bypass integrated public investment planning and make a great leap forward with comprehensive planning are not likely to arrive at their destination sooner. It may well take them longer. Experience in Latin America and elsewhere shows that if planners attempt too much by insisting on comprehensive planning, the preparatory stage is likely to go on indefinitely without tangible results.'

Development planning of the Bantu homelands could, therefore, be approached most practically by means of a systematic classification of the rapidly rising development expenditure through the South African Bantu Trust Fund according to the functional purpose of this expenditure, as will be done in the next section.

Planners will, in practice, do their work in terms of three different time scales, namely, 1. the long-term, broad political perspectives of what the development of the several homelands should comprise of; 2. the shorter specific programme targets serving these broad objectives where the time span would be largely determined, on the one hand by the degree of certainty or uncertainty about the particular need to be catered for such as the construction of a town, a road, an irrigation project, or simply fencing agricultural land, and, on the other hand, the time technically required to construct such towns, dams, fencing, etc.; 3. annual budgetary decisions upon which all projects requiring finance depend for their continuation.

Experience indicates that the planning process should not necessarily be completely integrated with the normal annual cycle of the budgetary procedure. Planning without the support of budgetary decisions is, of course, of very little practical meaning, but the full timetable of officials concerned with drawing up the kind of details required by Parliaments for appropriation of funds, seriously limits the depth to which planning analysis would aspire.

In this connection the planners of the Transkei Government and the seven other emerging Bantu Governments in South Africa will have to recognize the fact that the authority and responsibility for development processes is shifting from Pretoria to the several Bantu homeland capitals. As the other Bantu authorities proceed towards administrative and political independence similar to that of the Transkei Government, the South African Parliament will allocate its financial assistance to these territories directly and separtely (according to predetermined formulae), rather than through the central channel of the South African Bantu Trust Fund. The only exception will be the allocation of additional funds beyond the agreed limit. These authorities will thus be treated financially in exactly the same way as the Transkei Government has been dealt with since its establishment. The consequences for the planning process of this financial system are clearly that public investment planning will be very largely decentralized to the homeland capitals, which will require a great deal more co-ordination between these capitals and Pretoria. The system of planning will accordingly very rapidly change in nature from that of centralized planning of regions within one political unit, to a system of international economic co-operation.

To a much larger extent than previously, the nature and the tempo of development in the homelands will depend upon the Bantu authorities and Bantu peoples themselves. Such a situation is obviously desirable because the Bantu become the subjects – or decision makers – of their own destiny rather than the objects of the planning decisions of the Whites. On the other hand, we still have to learn by experience whether this increasing decentralization of authority and initiative will accelerate or slow down the pace of actual development. In practice the central department of Bantu Administration and Development would still be very directly concerned with both the pattern and the tempo of activities in the homelands because of the responsibility of this department for the resettlement of people out of the White areas into their own and the co-ordination with the central government's policy of industrial decentralization. At the same time, it is expected that, as in the case of the Transkei, the several Bantu authorities will for a very long time still be in need of 'additional appropriations' above the statutory appropriations agreed upon. These additional appropriations would provide the central department with a practical instrument for controlling the incremental pattern of expenditure and planning in these areas.

THE ECONOMIC STRUCTURE OF THE CURRENT DEVELOPMENT PROCESS

Viewed in terms of the conventional classification of the so-called 'national accounts', the economic structures of the several Bantu homelands appear very similar. The average rate of growth in the real gross national product of each of these territories between 1959/60 and 1967/68 was 4 per cent per annum, except in the case of Tswanaland which grew at an average rate of 7,7 per cent, and Witsieshoek which, at a rate of 2,2 per cent did not grow very much. In all cases the contribution to the GDP of the 'subsistence sector' was still very large, but declining, particularly in the Ciskei where this percentage declined from about 40 per cent at the beginning of the period to about 35 per cent at the end of it. Next to agriculture and forestry the most important contributors to the gross national product were the public administration's education and health services. Trading activities were, furthermore, much more important than industrial activities, although both were relatively unimportant. The percentage contributions of each type of economic activity to the gross national product of the several homelands are shown in the table.

Another important aspect of the structure of the economies in these territories are the sources of the income of the Bantu populations themselves. Thus of the almost R70 million produced in the Transkei during 1966/67 only about R54,5 million accrued to the Bantu themselves, the difference having been earned in these territories by non-Bantu residents. In addition, the income of the migrant labourers from the Transkei during the same year amounted to approximately R76 million, or more than what was actually generated within the territory by the Bantu. This pattern was typical of all the other Bantu homelands except that, particularly in Zululand and Tswanaland, fairly substantial flows of income accrued to workers who lived in their own territories but worked in border industries.

As was said before, the most dynamic element of the development process in the several homelands at the moment is public expenditure. In

TABLE 1: The Percentage Contribution of each type of economic activity to the Gross Domestic Product of the several Bantu homelands, 1959/60–1967/68.

Industrial sector	*Transkei*		*Ciskei*		*Zululand*		*North-eastern Transvaal homelands*		*Tswana-land*		*Witsies-hoek (South Sotho)*		*All Bantu homelands*	
	A[1]	*B*[2]	*A*[1]	*B*[2]	*A*[1]	*B*[2]	*A*[1]	*B*[2]	*A*[1]	*B*[2]	*A*[1]	*B*[2]	*A*[1]	*B*[2]
1. Agriculture, forestry and fishery	44,7	42,3	29,1	20,4	41,2	34,2	41,1	31,4	34,6	35,9	22,1	23,1	40,9	35,8
2. Mining and quarrying	—	—	—	—	7,6	8,3	11,7	11,7	14,5	13,8	—	—	5,7	6,3
3. Manufacturing, construction and electricity supply	5,9	5,6	4,1	3,4	5,3	4,2	3,6	3,1	3,1	2,6	3,4	3,0	4,9	4,2
4. Commerce and accommodation and catering services	10,9	11,5	6,0	6,4	5,2	5,9	6,2	5,7	5,2	5,1	10,3	10,3	7,6	7,8
5. Transport and communication	2,0	3,0	9,0	12,4	3,2	4,4	1,9	3,6	4,9	5,1	1,2	1,6	3,1	4,4
6. Fixed property, financial and business services	2,5	2,2	1,4	3,4	2,1	2,3	1,1	1,7	1,0	1,9	0,7	0,8	1,7	2,2
7. Community, social and personal services:														
a. Public administration	7,0	10,5	10,2	15,5	6,1	9,2	5,5	12,7	5,3	9,6	10,9	18,9	6,6	10,8
b. Educational services	8,1	7,6	18,1	17,6	10,0	9,4	8,3	10,6	13,9	12,0	27,1	16,9	9,9	9,9
c. Health services	2,5	3,0	5,0	6,5	3,4	8,4	3,9	6,9	3,0	5,1	10,8	14,5	3,3	5,7
d. Religious, charity and personal services	0,3	0,5	0,2	0,3	0,2	0,4	0,3	0,5	0,2	0,4	1,0	1,0	0,3	0,4
e. Personal services[1]	16,1	13,8	17,3	13,8	17,0	13,2	16,4	12,1	14,4	8,7	12,4	10,0	16,3	12,9
TOTAL	100,0	100,0	100,0	100,0	100,0	100,0	100,0	100,0	100,0	100,0	100,0	100,0	100,0	100,0

A^1 = the average of the figures for 1959/60 and 1960/61.
B^2 = the average of the figures for 1966/67 and 1967/68. (In the case of the Transkei B^2 is the average of the figures for 1965/66 and 1966/67. The figures for the year 1966/67 are included under B^2 in the case of the total for all the Bantu homelands).
(The average figure for the first and last two years was used to exclude the effects of the large fluctuation in the contribution of the agricultural sector from one year to another. This is necessary in the case of the Bantu homelands because of the relatively large contribution of the agricultural sector to the gross domestic product.)
1. Services rendered within the family unit and/or community such as funeral services, hairdressing, medical services, judicature, transport services, storage, recreation and personal care.

the Transkei, for example, current expenditure by all public authorities increased from about R10 million in 1960/61 to over R18 million six years later. Spending authority was transferred to the Transkeian Government very rapidly, from about 5 per cent at the beginning of the period to about 63 per cent at the end of it. Even more striking increases were registered in the annual fixed capital formation which amounted to less than R2 million in 1961 as compared to more than R8 million in 1966/67 with a similar shift in the spending authority from the central government to the Transkei Government.

A functional breakdown of the capital formation indicates that the bulk of the expenditure was confined to improvements in agriculture (R3,2 million), roads and bridges (R1,2 million) and trade (R2,1 million), including the cost of taking over White trading stations. In the Ciskei, current expenditure more than doubled since 1959/60 to R7,6 million in 1967/68 of which almost 30 per cent was spent on education, 17 per cent on health services, 15 per cent on general administration and 12 per cent on social security. With regard to capital formation which increased very strikingly by a factor of 12 during the period, no less than 37,5 per cent was devoted to housing and township development in 1967/68, while an additional 27,4 per cent was invested on the purchase of land and buildings. In the case of Zululand current expenditure increased by 150 per cent with similar emphasis on health (29%), education (22,8%), social security (17,7%) and general administration (10%). Fixed capital formation increased from R1 million to slightly under R20 million in 1965/66 and dropped to R10 million in 1967/68. Of these amounts more than one half was devoted to the building of new towns, whereas 13,5 per cent was devoted to the purchase of land and buildings. In the northern Bantu territories, for which separate accounts are not available, similar patterns of increase in current expenditure, emphasis on education, health and social security, and rather striking increases in fixed capital formation appeared from the available statistics.

Finally in Tswanaland, the most rapidly growing Bantu homeland, the available figures show very similar tendencies, but in this case the current (1970) pattern of expenditure, particularly with regard to industry, mining and urbanization, must have changed beyond recognition as compared to the situation before 1967/68. In fact, for the territories as a whole the total figure for gross fixed capital formation of R41 million during 1967/68 may have been doubled by 1971/72 while the emphasis on housing, industry and commerce may also have been considerably strengthened.

These figures and their underlying supporting statistics suggest that, at least up to 1967/68, most of the homelands were not supported by a market economy capable of generating rapid growth endogenously and that the main vehicle of market activity (gradually eroding the importance of the subsistence sector) was expenditure by the authorities on the creation of social infra-structure such as towns, educational and health facilities as well as social security programmes, with some notable emphasis on agricultural improvements in the Transkei, some important mining activities in the northern territories, and significant contributions to income from employment in border industries in Zululand and Tswanaland. In all cases the gross income from migrant labour exceeded that derived from the gross domestic product. Since 1967 a number of structural improvements have probably taken place, such as, for example, in the Ciskei where the border area activities near East London and King William's Town have greatly contributed towards the growth of the very large industrial urban complex in the town of Mdanzani. Likewise in Tswanaland the rapid development of the Rosslyn border area and the Babelegi homeland industrial area (about 32 kilometres to the north) are introducing incisive structural changes into the Tswanaland socio-economic system.

The homelands are therefore still to be considered as economically dependant systems although with fairly advanced social infrastructures. There can be no doubt that whereas their economic dependence on outside forces may not compare favourably with the situation in other African territories, their educational and health facilities must be unequalled in Africa, while the rate at which townships are being established, with either fully fledged or at least rudimentary services, would bear most comparisons. Such comparisons in the international 'ranking game' are, however, of very little, if any, use to the planner interested in functional progress. Evaluated in terms of its own development requirements, each of these homelands needs a broader employment base in relation to the social overhead system. Like many other African territories and economies in the underdeveloped world, it will take a very long time before the homeland economies will be able to provide employment opportunities of sufficient growth elasticity from within.

In this respect the most favourable opportunities to do so exist in agriculture. Nearly one half of the agriculturally most productive areas of South Africa, as far as climate and soil combinations are concerned, lie within the borders of the homelands. In the Transkei alone the productive exploitation of the 1,1 million hectares available could produce an output of R200 million, which is more than 300 per cent higher than the total gross national product of that territory at the moment. The reasons why this potential does not materialize do not lie in the climate and the soil, but in the institutional framework under which agricultural activities are at present functioning. Structural changes in this institutional framework, necessary as they are, will require supporting programmes ranging from the difficult matter of changing existing customs and traditions, to the introduction of modern credit facilities and the absorption of the surplus rural population in new urban concentrations where alternative bases of income have to be organized, possibly financed from the new income generated by agriculture. Whatever is done, it is clear that the programmes for agricultural change will have to be closely integrated with the rest of the public investment programmes.

THE MEANING OF DEVELOPMENT

How should, or could the expenditure of scarce resources in the Bantu homelands be evaluated?

Let us assume for the purposes of planning that this evaluation should proceed in terms of the value judgements of the present Government of the South African Republic, which has in fact been responsible for the pattern of activity in these areas during the past two decades. It is clear that during the fifties the main object of the administration was administration, but that during the sixties the expenditure through the South African Bantu Trust Fund rose very rapidly, partly due to the increasing costs of decentralization of the administration in the hands of the several separate Bantu Territorial authorities, but partly also as a result of larger development activities in these areas. During the sixties, therefore, the idea of development became practical policy. Furthermore, the stated policy intentions are that the decade of the seventies should contain the real development effort. Development planning must consequently now take the place of administration in the imagination of the public and the civil servants concerned.

Judging by the nature of the South African Bantu Trust activities financed in the fiscal year 1971/72, the first step into the development decade, the Trustee (in practice the Minister of Bantu Administration and Development) with the concurrence of the Bantu Affairs Commission, conceives the idea of development in terms of about five major dimensions, identifiable from the budget as follows:

The purchase of land for homeland consolidation;
The settlement of Bantu in their respective homelands;
The creation of income and employment opportunities for these settlers;
The activation of the human potential of these communities;
General development overhead serving the above four identifiable objectives collectively.

From the point of view of economics this conception of the major dimensions of development is quite acceptable in principle – as a more specific set of qualitative identifications of what is desired. In pursuing these broad objectives through the expenditure of scarce resources, however, the problem of economic planning arises mainly in the following manner: money, representing scarce resources, is involved in the pursuance of the above-mentioned objectives to the extent of at least R200 million per annum spent on administration and development in the various homelands. These funds have to be raised from sources among the Bantu themselves or by means of grants and loans from the South African Treasury through the South African Bantu Trust Fund.

The South African Treasury and Cabinet are not in a position to allocate an unlimited amount of money for the financially unlimited pursuance of each development objective in its own right. *A problem of choice, of the determination of priorities, necessarily arises.*

The only rational way in which this problem of priorities can be approached is through determining the relative effectiveness of the many activity programmes serving the several objectives of developing the areas and their peoples. The question that arises is what is meant by *effectiveness* in this context?

One commonly employed approach in the practice of public finance is simply to maintain the existing distribution of funds, assuming that the total to be distributed is extraneously determined. Unfortunately, such an approach is without meaning for the problem of financing a process of structural change in an emergent economy.

There is no escape (in this process of choosing priorities) from the need to work out and apply a fairly comprehensive *philosophy of development,* which is sufficiently clear cut, to the phases of the planning perspective and its specific programme targets, and in terms of which the effectiveness of these specific targets could be evaluated for purposes of decision-making at the highest policy level.

The kind of philosophy required would enable the decision-maker to evaluate all costly targets in terms of a single norm or, more practically, a single set of norms which the decision-maker can in his own mind relate to one another in a consistent manner. If such a development philosophy does not yet exist because knowledge is lacking about how such a development process in the particular circumstances in South Africa would take place, the first requisite for gathering this knowledge by experience as rapidly as possible would be to organize a regular flow of systematic information about programme performances in real terms.

Essential to building up a set of value-judgements about the various programmes in operation, is an answer to the question : What performance is expected of each programme? Is it, for example, sufficient to find out how many hectares of land are being bought for the Zulu nation in pursuance of the general objective of consolidating the Zulu homeland? Is it sufficient to record how many residential units are being created in the Ciskei towns in pursuance of the objective of urban settlement of the Ciskei Xhosa? Is it meaningful to record how many children of various ages are accommodated in the schools in Tswanaland in pursuance of the objective of developing the human potential, and so on?

Obviously every single programme is in fact a sub-system with its own set of characteristics which can only be measured properly by means of a complex set of data. For a comprehensive impression of the development process, one or two cardinal indices of performance for each programme may be sufficient, but for purposes of analysis, more in-depth data will also be needed. What data? Since gathering statistics can become a waste of time and money, the managers of the various programmes should have a clear idea of those characteristics of their activities which have important development value.

Whatever activity targets are pursued under the heading of land, settlement, income and human potential in the respective Bantu homelands, one universal requisite has to be imposed on all investment programmes. This requisite is very Western in origin, namely the *dynamics of economic growth.*

The principle may be stated as follows: In so far as the objectives of a society require the application of scarce resources, the perspectives of that society can only grow realistically to the extent that the activities serving these objectives are reproductive in the sense that the achievement of the objectives leads to an expansion of the resource base of the society. If these objectives are such that they consume scarce resources without reproduction, without a return flow, a resource multiplier, the society in question cannot escape the vicious circle of poverty.

This economic aspect of the philosophy of development is admittedly an 'intermediate' consideration. Resource reproductivity is not a 'final' end such as land possession, social settlement, material welfare or human dignity, but it is unfortunately the dominant cultural discipline of society. Without this *cultural* planning discipline, the *natural* survival of the species is governed by a stark balance between high mortality and fertility.

The ways in which each public expenditure programme lead to such flows of scarce resources differ greatly from one another in nature and over time. Thus the investment in the projected tea plantation in Vendaland would be aimed at creating employment, but it could provide some direct savings from income for reinvestment within a relatively short time. Investment in building a new capital city for Lebowa, on the other hand, while creating employment in construction, would not directly create employment after its completion. Its power to stimulate the generation of scarce resources for further growth, however, arises from the great variety of reproductive activities stimulated by large urban nodes. The economic reproductivity of cities may be very indirect, roundabout and not necessarily realized over short periods, but they are usually very large.

Consequently each programme evaluation would require system information of a kind tailored to the nature of the programme. In each case, its resource reproductivity, whether long or short term, direct or indirect, should be one aspect of development effectiveness added to its effectiveness in terms of the objective it was basically conceived to serve.

The Economic problems of the Homelands

Sheila van der Horst

One of South Africa's best known economists, Sheila Terreblanche van der Horst has written several outstanding works on local race relations. She studied at Cape Town University and holds a Ph.D. from the London School of Economics. She is at present Associate Professor in the Department of Economics at Cape Town University and is also President of the South African Institute of Race Relations.

The economic problems of the African 'homelands' lie both within these areas and also outside them in the rest of the Republic. Their *complete* political independence is problematical and lies in the future. Meanwhile they constitute economically backward regions with many of the same problems as the poverty-stricken less developed members of the third world. The homelands derive certain advantages from their proximity to the industrial areas of the Republic. There are, however, counterbalancing disadvantages arising from the competition of these relatively highly developed areas in attracting capital and labour and from the political control of the Republic with its varied vested interest groups. In comparison with the industrialized areas, the homelands have little to offer in the way either of a market for goods or a supply of raw materials for industry. Their chief present economic importance is as a source of relatively unskilled labour : their problem to provide a livelihood for their inhabitants.

The Republic of South Africa is often described as a dual economy. In some regards this is an apt description but the Republic differs from the typical dual economy in several ways. Instead of there being enclaves of modern industry, and, perhaps, plantation type agriculture in a generally undeveloped countryside, not only is virtually all mining and manufacturing in the modern sector but more than eighty per cent of the farm land is also in the modern sector. The homelands, when certain additional planned purchases of land are made, will comprise between thirteen and fourteen per cent of the surface area of the Republic. At the 1970 census just less than seven million Africans,[1] 27 per cent of the total population, were enumerated in the homelands, and of these seven million no less than four million were females. This brings out the second singular characteristic of the homelands, the fact that their economies are dominated by labour migration and the absence of half or more of their adult population who work in the mines, factories, shops, railways and, as domestic servants, in the homes of the Whites in the modern sector.

It is misleading to speak of the homelands as though they were all alike, for they comprise not only land of very varying potential but also towns, or perhaps it would be better to say, areas of settlement, of different economic function, which vary from administrative centres to the dormitory suburbs of relatively old, or new, border industrial areas; the 'resettlement' towns and villages housing the wives, children and parents of migrant workers, widows and others who have no claim to land and are not permitted to live in the major part of the Republic allocated by law to the Whites.

Most areas are not homogeneous and several are linguistically and ethnically mixed. Whereas the homeland of some groups, notably the Xhosa of the Transkei, is a large area, 43 200 square kilometres, of contiguous land, that of the Zulus in Natal, comprising 31 500 square kilometres, is scattered in no less than 29 separate areas, the Xhosa of the Ciskei in 17, and the Tswana of the Western Transvaal, Northern Cape Province and the Orange Free State, in 19 areas.

Some areas, notably those of the Tswana in the Western Transvaal and Northern Cape and those of the Northern Sotho in the Northern Transvaal have mineral resources of platinum, chrome, vanadium, asbestos, iron ore and limestone, some of which are already being mined. Some other areas are potentially well situated for agriculture and forestry. Thirty-three per cent of the total has a temperate rainy climate, 76 per cent receives more than 508 millimetres of rain a year; but the remaining 24 per cent is barren, mountainous or arid land with little potential for agricultural development.

In 1960 density of population, excluding migrant workers, varied from a little over 62 per square kilometre in the Transkei, Ciskei and Natal

1. 6 998 234.

(where the rainfall is good, being for the most part from 635 to 1016 millimetres per annum) to 37 persons per square kilometre in the north-eastern Transvaal and 21 persons per square kilometre in the arid Tswana areas of the Western Transvaal. For the Republic as a whole, including the industrial centres, the average density of population was 21 per square kilometre.[2]

With such heterogeneity it is difficult to generalize, but the history of the creation of the homelands, which used to be known as Native Reserves, gives a clue as to their condition. They were areas which were left in African occupation during the nineteenth century when the Whites took over possession and control of much of the land which now constitutes the Republic. The districts left to the Africans tended to be more remote and to be skirted by the railway system, the main lines of which connected the diamond and gold fields to the ports, with subsidiary lines designed to assist White agricultural development.

White settlement had begun around the ports of the Cape Colony and Natal and fanned out in the Orange Free State and across the Vaal River into the present Transvaal. In Natal, for reasons both of military security and to provide labour for the White farmer settlers, much of the land allotted to Africans was deliberately broken up into small reservations scattered throughout the colony. In the Cape Colony, the Transvaal and the Orange Free State, the Native Reserves were, for the most part, on the fringes of the areas of White settlement. In addition to the land formally reserved for Africans many farms in White ownership were in fact occupied by Africans. Indeed, in the Transvaal farms in some areas were known as 'labour farms', for they were not farmed but served as reservoirs of labour.

In 1913 an attempt was made to stabilize and clarify the position in regard to the ownership and occupation of land. The purchase of land by Africans was prohibited outside areas enumerated in a schedule to the Natives Land Act[3] and 'released areas' designated for addition to the

2. J.J. Stadler, 'Economic and Demographic Characteristics of the South African Bantu Areas', *Agrekon,* Vol. 9, No. 1, Jan. 1970, Department of Agricultural Economics and Marketing, Table 4.

3. This Act, No. 27 of 1913, was declared *ultra vires* in the Cape Province as its application would have prevented Africans acquiring parliamentary franchise qualifications. It was not until 1936 that the Natives Trust and Land Act prevented Africans from buying land in the Cape Province.

'scheduled areas'. This land, amounting to 13,6 per cent of the Republic, constitutes the present 'homelands'.

As early as 1865 the African Reserves within the Cape Colony were inadequate to support their indigenous inhabitants and Africans went out to work as shepherds, farm labourers, road builders and in other fields,[4] After the discovery of diamonds and gold and the quickening of economic life which followed, African labour was in greater demand and by the end of the century 97 000 Africans were employed on the gold mines of the Witwatersrand. As is the case today they were drawn from all over the present Republic, including the homelands, and from beyond its frontiers.

CAUSES AND EFFECT OF LABOUR MIGRATION

This fact of labour migration has been the dominating feature of the economy of the homelands. It is a long established one. Moreover, it has certain peculiar characteristics. In the early years of mining, the Africans going to the mines were only prepared to work for short periods of three to six months. The system of temporary migration of men grew up to meet the needs of the mining industry in the late nineteenth and early twentieth century and has continued to this day. To some extent this system became incorporated in the culture of the Africans, and now a period on the mines serves as an initiation into manhood. Other industries, also, used migrant labour but in most the system was not formalized to the same extent as upon the mines and in closely associated industries. The system has had important repercussions. For the African areas, instead of extruding their surplus population by permanent emigration, have continued to be the base for migrant labourers, working intermittently, nowadays usually for periods of one or more years, in the modern sector of the economy. Throughout the Republic almost every occupation of lower grade and status is performed by Africans, many of whom are from the homelands. There has been considerable permanent migration in addition to the temporary. Other chapters of this book discuss the more permanently urbanized Africans.

From the point of view of the homelands the situation is that for a generation and more there have been few adult males who have not worked outside their borders and many spend the greater part of their working lives away from their rural homes. Ever-tightening restrictions

4. S.T. van der Horst, *Native Labour in South Africa,* O.U.P., 1942, pp. 24-35.

on permanent migration, on the movement of women to join their men and on the presence of women in the towns have retarded the more permanent movement to the growing towns and industries of the Republic. This development undoubtedly would have taken place as a result, on the one hand, of increasing familiarity with industrial work and town life; and, on the other hand, of the increasing poverty of the homelands where population has increased without any corresponding improvement in agricultural techniques or significant industrial development.

The predominant cause of this labour migration is the poverty of the homelands. Their total product in 1966/67 was estimated to be 1,9 per cent that of the Republic. Output per head averaged R34, one eighteenth of that in the remainder of the Republic where at that time output per head averaged R611.[5] The average cash[6] wages of African men in urban areas ranged from R183 per annum on the gold mines to R498 in manufacturing industry.[7] Surveys of income and expenditure have shown that the family income of Africans in the larger towns averages between R643 and R714, which is three to four times the average homeland income, even when the latter is supplemented by one-fifth of the migrant workers' earnings, the proportion they are estimated to send home.

Drained of men the reservations have stagnated. The more enterprising Africans have left, for there has been little chance of economic, or social, advance within them. The increasing population has been sustained in spite of the stagnation because the income from the very inefficient peasant farming carried on has been supplemented from the earnings of migrant workers. The traditional system of 'one man, one lot', or rather one wife one arable allotment, has remained basically unchanged. Apart from the introduction of the ox- and cow-drawn iron plough there has been little improvement in agricultural techniques. At the same time the increase of population, in an area already restricted by White conquest and encroachment, has meant that many men do not receive arable allotments for their wives and, until a period of nearly seven year's exceptionally severe drought (1963-1970) reduced the number of cattle, the communal grazing land had become over-grazed and much of both arable and grazing

5. Calculations based on the figures of national product in J.J. Stadler, 'Economic and Demographic Characteristics of the South African Bantu Areas', *op. cit.*, pp. 25 and 26, Tables 9 and 11 and population statistics, *South African Statistics*, 1968, A 11.

6. African mine workers are housed in barracks and on most gold and coal mines food is provided, and some other services, in addition to the cash wages.

7 *Quarterly Bulletin of Statistics*, Department of Statistics, Pretoria, June, 1970.

land badly eroded. The stagnation and economic deterioration of the Reserves has long been recognized as a basic cause of African poverty.

Forty years ago an official Commission reported: 'We have now throughout the Reserves a state of affairs in which, with few exceptions, the carrying capacity of the soil for both human beings and animals is definitely on the downgrade; a state of affairs which, unless soon remedied, will within one or at the outside two decades create in the Union an appalling problem of Native poverty.'[8] The White Paper on Land Policy under the Native Land and Trust Act, 1936, said: 'Speaking generally, it is notorious that the existing Native locations and Reserves are congested, denuded, overstocked, eroded, and for the most part, in a deplorable condition.'

PLANS FOR THE REHABILITATION OF THE HOMELANDS

The Tomlinson Commission, appointed four years after the present governing party came to power, 'to conduct an exhaustive inquiry into and report on a comprehensive scheme for the rehabilitation of the Native areas with a view to developing within them a social structure in keeping with the culture of the Native and based on effective socio-economic planning' was the architect of the policy of apartheid or separate development.[9]

Economically, the primary purpose was to overcome the impoverishment of the reserves and to reverse the outward flow of man- and woman-power. The development it recommended was to be diversified by encouraging the growth of local industries, but agriculture was regarded as the keystone. 'The first essential,' the Commissioners wrote, 'is the development of a true Bantu farming class, settled on farm units which will ensure the full means of existence to each family, and in the second place, it is necessary to develop a true urban population. This in turn implies the necessity of large-scale urban development . . . which can provide the means of existence to the surplus agricultural population, as well as for the further increase of population within, and also partially outside, the Bantu area.'[10]

8. Native Economic Commission, 1930-32, U.G. 22, 1932, para. 69.

9. Official *Summary of the Report of the Commission for the Socio-Economic Development of the Bantu Areas within the Union of South Africa,* U.G. 61, 1955. Subsequently quoted as Tomlinson Commission.

10. Tomlinson Commission, *op. cit.,* p. 208, para. (v).

The Commission estimated that if the land were allocated to families in economic units, the agricultural land could provide a living for 307 000 families which was about half the 1951 population of the Reserves. The income per family which could be produced from an 'economic unit' was estimated to be R120 per annum, at prices then current and with the prevailing methods of agriculture. The Commissioners considered that double that amount could be attained if improved agricultural techniques were adopted.

It has since been widely recognized that the income from peasant farming which the Tomlinson Commission set as a standard was unrealistically low if it were to hold African peasants on the land. For, if the hurdle of 'influx control' could be overcome,[11] much higher incomes could be earned in town. In 1956 when the Commission reported, the average earnings of Africans working in manufacturing industry were R300 a year and, although costs are higher in town, more than one member of a family may be able to bring in a cash income.

The Commission recommended the modification of the system of land tenure in order to enable the more successful and enterprising to acquire more land and to bring to an end the deadening system of 'one man, one lot'. According to the tribal system use of arable land was the right of every married man, together with grazing on communal land for the much prized, culturally and religiously significant cattle. Tending the fields has traditionally been woman's work and it is this division of work which permitted the migrant labour system to develop so extensively without completely disrupting the rural economy. The meagre and diminishing income per head of population has been supplemented and made tolerable by the remittances of migrant workers. Agriculture has languished to a sub-subsistence level and cannot be improved without radical changes.

It has been estimated that *earnings* of migrant workers temporarily absent from the homelands (not the remittances, estimated to be one fifth of earnings) are greater than the value of the gross output from all sources.[12]

The Government rejected three of the major recommendations of the Tomlinson Commission, namely the introduction of a modified form of individual tenure and the sale of arable agricultural land to the peasant

11. Restrictions on the movement of Africans into town are described in the Chapters by Hellman, Mervis and Dugard.

12. J.J. Stadler, 'Economic and Demographic Characteristics of the South African Bantu Areas', *Agrekon, op. cit.*, p. 26, Table 10.

farmers (designed to establish full-time African peasant farmers); the use of private White entrepreneurship and capital to develop manufacturing; and the scale of financial assistance and expenditure.

For agriculture it provided instead for a speeding up of 'land stabilization' on lines improved from the old 'betterment areas', begun in the thirties.

For industrial development the Nationalist Government placed its faith in the encouragement of industry in officially 'White' areas close enough to the homelands to enable African labour to commute daily or, in some cases, weekly from 'homeland' towns or suburbs. The scale of spending was also reduced below that recommended by the Tomlinson Commission although subsequently it has been stepped up to approximately the level recommended.

1. *Agricultural Progress*

It has been reported that over half the agricultural land has been planned, that is to say divided into arable allotments and grazing camps. Where necessary contour ridges have been made and planted with grass. Grazing camps have been fenced and the traditional rondavels or square single-roomed dwellings grouped into larger clusters in order to make more effective use of the agricultural land. Moreover, the Africans are reported to be more willing than in the thirties to participate in the planning, although in some districts, such as Eastern Pondoland, there has been resistance to such innovations. In some districts, notably in the Ciskei, where rotational grazing has been practised, it is reported that the pasturage has improved and recovered in spite of severe drought.[13]

One difficulty that has arisen is that, in order to accommodate the population on the land, arable allotments for the most part fall far short even of the Tomlinson Commission's recommendations, many Africans receiving a half, a third, or even a quarter of the already inadequate 'economic unit'. Consequently, the migrant labour system continues to supplement sub-subsistence agriculture and there appears little basis for the development of a self-supporting peasantry, if the creation of such an economic group is a feasible proposition in the late twentieth century.

Irrigation farming, too, has not so far given much promise of success. On the irrigation settlements where intensive agriculture is practicable,

13. *Report of the Department of Bantu Administration and Development for the period 1st Jan., 1968 to 31st Dec. 1968*, p. 5.

very few have shown the industry and enterprise required to make a good living. For the most part the 15 000 hectares already under irrigation are not used to their full potential. This is because of lack of knowledge as well as lack of industry and application. Studies of irrigation settlements have shown that there is no correlation between formal schooling and successful cultivation.[14] However, previous experience on White-owned farms was correlated with better farming. There are estimated to be 53 379 hectares of potentially irrigable land in the homelands which, on the basis of the standard size of irrigable allotment of 1,3 hectares, might provide a livelihood for 42 000 families. However, so far it has proved difficult to select allotment holders, because of the claims to land of those in occupation before schemes were established. Agricultural extension officers are too few. In many areas marketing facilities are poor, especially for perishable crops. In any case the amount of suitable land available means that such settlements can only cater for a small number; although successful farming might raise the status and improve the image of farming.

The only form of agricultural production which appears to be a commercial success at present is that carried out under the close supervision of White officials on large farms owned by the Bantu Trust. Such farms are producing *phormium tenax* (a fibre used for making bags), tea and are also being used as nursery gardens and experimental stations. Forestry plantations operated under the supervision and control of the Republic's Department of Forestry are also commercially successful and provide one of the homelands' main commercial products and exports.

The improvement of peasant agriculture to a standard sufficient to provide an acceptable level of income has so far proved an intractable problem in many of the less developed countries. In Southern Africa the problem is particularly difficult as there is no tradition of intensive cultivation. In the African areas of the Republic this problem has been intensified because virtually no cash crops have been developed.

The homelands still produce virtually only one crop – maize – and the yield of this crop is very low, averaging one fifth to one third the average for the rest of the Republic. This low yield is not because the land is basically unsuitable for agriculture. On the contrary, the homelands include areas with a higher than average rainfall and good agricultural

14. J.J.S. Weidemann, *Die Ekonomie van Ontwikkelingsbeleid in die Suid-Afrikaanse Agtergeblewe Gebiede met spesiale verwysing na Bantoebesproeiing*, pp. 263-267, unpublished D.Comm. thesis, University of Pretoria.

potential, yet, despite the concentration on maize production, the homelands do not produce sufficient to meet their own requirements and normally import about half their consumption.

The system of one man, one lot is inimical to technical advance because the individual arable allotments are unfenced and may even, where the country is hilly, run across the contour banks. It is customary to turn the cattle in to graze when the staple crop is reaped, which precludes winter cropping and limits advance to the pace of the slowest.

The chief exports of the homelands continue to be hides, skins, wool, forestry products, *and labour.* The people have learned to look outward to the industrial economy to increase their incomes. Indeed, Rutman,[15] in a study of the Transkei, has shown that this is a rational economic decision given the prices of the staple crops, the amount of land available and the wages outside. Considerably higher incomes than could be earned by full-time farming can be secured even by the lowly paid mine labourers, who go out to work to supplement what is raised on the limited farming allotments of 2,6 to 4 hectares of arable land.

The physical replanning of the land and division into fenced grazing camps, planting of grass stuffs and contour ploughing is not sufficient to transform agriculture. Board has shown that there is no significant difference between replanned or 'stabilized' areas and unrehabilitated areas in regard to agricultural practices, productivity and the retention of men on the land.[16]

Despite the progress with replanning the agricultural land in the Reserves and the arrest of soil erosion, little progress has been made in developing a full-time farming community. Nor do the prospects for the future look bright.

In 1970 Dr Leistner, a not unfriendly critic of official policies, in a realistical appraisal of 'the role of the non-White population groups in the South African economy' wrote, 'one may conclude that despite all efforts and despite great expenditures, Bantu agriculture in general is stagnating.'[17]

15. G.L. Rutman, 'The Transkei: An Experiment in Economic Separation', *South African Journal of Economics,* Vol. 36, No. 1, March 1968.

16. C. Board, 'The Rehabilitation Programme in the Bantu Areas and its effect on the Agricultural Life of the Bantu in the Eastern Cape', *S.A. Journal of Economics,* Vol. 32, No. 1, March 1964.

17. *Mercurius,* No. 11, September, 1970, Journal of the Department of Economics, University of South Africa, Pretoria, p. 16.

Mr L.A. Pepler, Chief Planning Officer of the Department of Bantu Administration and Development, said in 1970 '. . . a genuine farming class practising progressive agriculture has been the exception and not the rule. As a consequence the Bantu pattern of farming has been characterized by wrong use of land, inefficient methods of cultivation and animal husbandry practices, deteriorating soil fertility, soil erosion, low yields and a generally low standard of living. To remedy these adverse conditions and the resultant consequences, the basic causes had, *and still have* to be eradicated.'[18]

It will be interesting to see whether the homelands, as they achieve a measure of self-government, introduce reform of the system of land tenure which appears a basic, but not a *sufficient* condition for significant agricultural progress.

The Chief Minister of the Transkei, Chief Kaiser Matanzima, broached this subject in his policy speech to the Transkeian Legislative Assembly in 1970. After quoting Professor Hobart Houghton's statement that the Transkei should not rely on the windfall of mineral discoveries to break the 'vicious circle of poverty' in which it was enmeshed, the Chief said: 'If we all agree that agricultural production is to be the base or launching pad for accelerated economic development in the Transkei then a number of very pertinent questions come to mind – questions which we shall have to face sooner or later, such as the following for instance:

'Can we still afford the luxury of dishing out valuable agricultural land to people who in many cases are too old, lazy or lethargic to work such lands profitably or should lands be given only to those who are physically able and willing to work such lands properly?

'If individual farming is not suitable to our temperament and aptitudes, should we not go over to corporate or communal farming and working of our lands?

'If diversification is necessary in our farming should we not compel farmers to diversify as is done in many countries?

'If mechanization is essential to step up production should we not consider ways and means to foster mechanization?

'Our schemes and attitudes up to the present seem to have shown little results as far as increased production is concerned. If we acknowledge this

18. My italics. Speech at 40th Annual Council Meeting of the South African Institute of Race Relations. Published R4/70, South African Institute of Race Relations, Johannesburg, 1970.

to be the case, then we should not be dogmatic but should be prepared to re-examine our agricultural policies, priorities and methods of the past in order to change this stagnant – and sometimes even deteriorating – situation. The wealth of the Transkei lies in agriculture but this wealth must be exploited and we cannot allow it to lie dormant for ever.'

There was no discussion of the Chief Minister's statement.

Although beneficial occupation is a condition of holding land it has proved difficult to enforce. On the irrigation settlements the presence of the allotment holder is a condition of tenure but this also has proved difficult to implement and indeed it appears unreasonable to insist that the allotment holder should be present in off-seasons.

There are two important underlying reasons why a significant alteration of the conditions of land tenure is likely to be difficult, however desirable it may be for agricultural progress. One is the lack of security of the African population which causes them to cling to customary rights to land, although they may be reluctant to entrust their main livelihood to agriculture. The other is that chiefs and tribal authorities, who occupy a dominant position in the constitutional system of the homelands, draw their authority from their power over the allotment of land and they are likely to be loath to surrender such power to market forces. Indeed, it was the fact that the buying and selling of land would encroach upon the power of the chiefs that led the Republican Government to reject the Tomlinson Commission's recommendations in this respect.

One attempt to reduce customary claims to land is being made. Those who buy or occupy a site in the new dormitory towns housing Africans employed in border (or homeland?) industries are required to renounce claims to land in tribal or Trust areas. The reduction of claims to land for this reason thus depends upon the growth of industry.

The only hope of modernizing agriculture in the homelands lies in finding alternative permanent, not merely intermittent, employment for more than half the population.

What then of the other side of the picture, the growth of industry to provide an alternative livelihood?

2. *Industry*

The Tomlinson Commission recommended encouraging industrialization in the Reserves, given certain safeguards. This was not a new idea. As early as 1936 the official Board of Trade and Industries had considered the encouragement of industry as a means of ameliorating the poverty of the Reserves. Significantly it restricted its recommendations to industries which would not be competitive with those in other areas. In 1946, that is before the advent of the National Party Government, a textile plant had been established in the Ciskei by the official Industrial Development Corporation in partnership with a British firm. Official encouragement of manufacturing industry in the poverty-stricken Reserves was thus not a new phenomenon when the Nationalist Government came to power in 1948.

In 1956, the Government rejected the Tomlinson Commission's recommendation that White industrialists should be encouraged to establish industries within the Reserves or homelands on the ground that this would create new areas of racially mixed population. The official statement of policy reads: 'The Government regards the development of industries owned by Europeans but requiring large numbers of native labourers in suitable European areas near Bantu territory *as of the utmost importance for the sound socio-economic development of the Bantu areas* and intends to take the necessary steps gradually to create the desired conditions for attracting industries to such areas.' [19]

And so the border areas policy was substituted for that of industrial development within the Reserves. It is not a policy of genuine separate development. For the industrial areas, the sinews of the economy, remain under White control and the Africans become daily or weekly commuters from neighbouring homelands. In one case, e.g. Mandantsane, some 19 kilometres from East London, a 'homeland' has been created from land previously in White ownership to provide a dormitory town for the workers in East London 'border area factories'; in another, what had been regarded as a 'Black spot', i.e. an area in African ownership surrounded by White-owned land, was permitted to remain and the adjoining area was designated a border area after the working of copper and phosphate deposits was found to be economic.

Many 'border areas' have advantages over the homelands as industrial centres because they tend to be nearer the larger towns and established industrial areas, to have better transport facilities and to be nearer the main power networks. Nevertheless, despite the rapid growth of manu-

19. Memorandum: Government decisions on the recommendations of the Commission for the Socio-economic development of the Bantu areas within the Union of South Africa, W.P.F., 1956.

facturing industry during the years when special inducements and concessions have been in operation, the growth of industry in most of these areas has been slow. In two areas, Rosslyn, 19 to 23 kilometres north-west of Pretoria, and in Hammarsdale, near the Durban-Pinetown industrial complex, there has been fairly rapid growth of factories and special inducements to the establishment of factories have been terminated.

The Tomlinson Commission had recommended that industrialists should be encouraged to establish factories in the Reserves but that they should not be compelled to do so by a system of licensing. At first Government spokesmen, including the Prime Minister, adopted the same attitude in regard to the 'border areas'. The official memorandum on the Tomlinson Report stated : 'Throughout, the policy of industrial development will be implemented with due regard to the interests of established industries and employees in European areas, and for this reason its application will be effected in the closest co-operation with organizations and departments concerned.' [20]

Inducements, including subsidized power and water, reduced railway rates, tax allowances, the advance of money at low interest rates, preference in the award of official contracts, exemption from or reduced statutory minimum wage rates have been permitted to individually approved concerns which industrialists wished to establish or extend in border areas. The policy, however, has not made the headway desired. In the first ten years after it was introduced, according to official reports, the increase in the number of Africans employed in border areas was 68 500, an average of less than 7 000 a year.[21] Nor was all this increase a result of the policy. Bell has argued cogently that a part of the increase in employment should be attributed to the general growth of industry throughout the economy and that the extra growth due to the special incentives was not more than 3 000 Africans a year during this period.[22]

Disappointed with the progress of these areas and alarmed by the continued growth of industry in the four main industrial areas, the Government passed the Physical Planning Act in 1967 in terms of which no factory may be established or expanded in specified areas without official approval if this involves the employment of a single additional African

20. Memorandum, W.P.F., 1956, *op. cit.*, para. 11.

21. Permanent Committee for the Location of Industry, Report for 1970.

22. R.T. Bell, *Government Policy and Industrial Location in South Africa*, unpublished Ph.D. thesis, Rhodes University, 1968.

worker. This Act has been applied to most of the major towns which are not in border areas or in Natal. In addition, in 1968 the Government increased the inducements offered.[23]

During the first two years of the operation of the Physical Planning Act the refusal of applications for exemption from its provisions denied opportunities of employment outside the border areas to 27 468 African employees.[24] This does not necessarily mean that this employment was diverted to the border areas.

In 1969 the Government, now under the more pragmatic leadership of Mr Vorster, reversed its position in regard to the use of private 'White' capital and entrepreneurship to develop industry within the homelands. The Prime Minister announced that 'White enterprise and capital might be admitted to the homelands on an "agency" basis, individual agencies being allowed a prospective life of twenty-five to, in the case of mining concerns, fifty years.' Later, it was announced, that all 'border area' concessions and subsidies would be available within the homelands, and some additional concessions have also been offered. In 1971 a new type of assistance in the form of a direct subsidy based on the 'cost disadvantage' of the area was announced as an alternative to the concessions already operating. In addition, the application of the Republic's industrial legislation controlling wage-rates and other conditions of work no longer applies to Africans within the homelands.[25]

Industrialists thus have a much freer hand in the employment of labour; on the other hand, they are required to sign an undertaking to transfer the ownership of their concerns to the official Bantu Industrial Development Corporation or any company that may be established for the purpose after a stated period at an agreed valuation.[26]

Despite the special concessions and subsidies offered to industrialists, it is very doubtful whether the homelands offer any general significant promise to the White entrepreneur. It would seem likely that the direct subsidies will have to be very high to compensate for the direct cost disadvantages, in addition to the economic and political uncertainties and the dislike of White executives, artisans – and their wives – to isolating them-

23. Permanent Committee for the Location of Industry, Report for 1968.

24. *Hansard* 1, Col. 119, 1970, *Hansard* 2, Col. 605, 1970. Quoted in *Survey of Race Relations in South Africa, 1970,* p. 86.

25. White Paper on the Decentralization of Industries, para. (xv), Department of Industries, 1971.

26. M. Horrell, *Survey of Race Relations in South Africa, 1970,* p. 140.

selves in the more remote areas. Where homelands are near existing industrial concentrations, as in parts of Natal and the Transvaal, the prospects of industrial development are more favourable. With few exceptions the enterprises so far begun are very small-scale concerns. Thus of eleven agreements entered into on the agency basis in 1970 it was anticipated that one (a grain bag factory at Butterworth) would eventually employ 800 Africans but the other ten would eventually employ only 880.[27]

Although freer use of labour and wage rates below the minima laid down by collective bargaining and statutory regulation are the chief advantages ostensibly offered industrialists to site their factories in the homelands, this freedom may be on paper only. Many of the barriers to the industrial advancement of Africans in the Republic have been imposed by trade union policy and practice. Perhaps, most important of all has been the closed shop agreement combined with the trade union practice, re-enforced by law, excluding Africans from many trades traditionally practised by skilled artisans. Even if the legal sanction were withdrawn, in most industries trade union policy would most probably remain. This has been clearly demonstrated by the resistance of the powerful White mine workers unions to the lifting of the statutory colour-bar in a mine established within an African homeland in the Transvaal. The eventual 'compromise' whereby the unions agreed to the advancement to jobs previously closed to them of members of the tribal group concerned, the Tswana, is no meaningful concession because few Tswana are employed on the mine, and, of those employed, most work above ground.

Trade unions, like employers, have been very suspicious of the border areas policy, for they fear the undermining of wages. Thus were either the border areas or the homelands to achieve significant success as a result of their chief advantage[28] relatively large supplies of labour and consequent wage advantage, there is likely to be strong political reaction both from organized labour and from employers in the established industrial areas.

27. *Hansard* 3, Col. 998, 1970 and *Hansard* 4, Col. 1452, 1970. Quoted in *Race Relations Survey,* 1970, p. 158.

28. 'The comparatively low cost of labour was the only advantage Border Industry had to compensate for numerous disadvantages suffered', Chairman of the Permanent Committee, *Star,* 1/11/65, quoted in the *Industrial Development of the Border Areas of South Africa,* issued by the Trade Union Council of South Africa, Johannesburg, April 1966.

In 1966 the Trade Union Council of South Africa, the largest federation of unions representing over 150 000 employees,[29] issued a 'fact paper' on industrial development in the border areas. When discussing wages this report stated: 'Perhaps one way of ensuring that the Industrial Conciliation Act [the act which provides the statutory framework for collective bargaining] is extended to cover the border factories would be to play a waiting game, based on the experience of the clothing industry. The low-wage advantage for the factories in the uncontrolled areas soon brought complaints by employers of the undercutting of prices in the common market. The Minister of Labour stated that the relevant Industrial Council Agreement would be applied to any area, if the Industrial Council made representations which appeared justified. If industrialists find that they are losing business, they will exert pressure to remedy the situation.'[30] This appears a realistic assessment.

Although the border areas policy caused uneasiness from the outset, it was not until the prohibitions of the Physical Planning Act really began to bite that industrialists felt the sting of the policy. The Physical Planning Act has been widely blamed for the fall in private investment in fixed capital which occurred in 1968 and 1969. Although it is inevitably difficult to pinpoint causes of recession, there is no doubt of the widespread and strong opposition of industrialists to this act. There have been many calculations of the number of jobs 'required' in or near the homelands. None of the more recent envisage an actual reduction of the number of Africans in the areas allocated to Whites. The most ambitious objective appears to be an absorption of half of the natural increase of the 'White' areas.[31]

EMPLOYMENT TARGET FOR THE HOMELANDS

Dr Riekert, Economic Advisor to the Prime Minister, in 1970 considered that, on the more conservative assumption that the absolute number of temporary migrants from the homelands remained the same (in 1960 some 704 000 men and 150 000 women), 17 per cent of new industrial development, including construction, would have to be channeled to the

29. M. Horrell, *South Africa's Workers,* South African Institute of Race Relations, Johannesburg, 1969, p. 146.

30. Trade Union Council of South Africa, *The Industrial Development of the Border Areas of South Africa,* Johannesburg, 1966, pp. 67-68.

31. Leistner, *op. cit.,* p. 24, Table 4.

homelands and border areas. The total number of new jobs provided would have to be 36 000, of which he estimated 21 000 would be in agriculture, mining and services and 15 000 in manufacturing and construction. This he considered a feasible target.[32] This projection makes no provision for the absorption in the homelands of the natural increase of Africans now in the towns nor for those on White farms who are displaced either by deliberate policy, as in Natal, or because employment in agriculture is not expanding or likely to expand *pari passu* with the growth of population. Chief Gatsha Buthelezi has estimated that 400 000 Africans will be evicted from farms in Natal if the present policy is implemented.[33]

A more ambitious target is that half the natural increase of the African population living outside the homelands, should be absorbed into homeland and border employment. This would imply at least 65 000 new jobs per annum in the decade 1970-1980 of which two thirds should be in Natal and the Ciskei and Transkei.[34] If we accept Dr Riekert's estimated proportions, 27 000 of these jobs should be in manufacturing and construction. To put these figures in perspective, in 1960, before the introduction of the border areas policy, a total of 76 000 persons of whom 55 000 were Africans, were employed in manufacturing and construction within the homelands or in areas which could qualify as border areas[35] and the average annual increase in employment in manufacturing and construction in these areas in the period 1960-1970 has been less than 7 000 Africans.[36] But even if the policy of diverting industrial development to the border areas and homelands achieves the most optimistic goals of its proponents, which is unlikely, Africans in the 'White' areas would approximately equal the Whites in number. So we are back to the original argument of the Tomlinson Commission and Dr Verwoerd

32. P.J. Riekert, 'The Economy of the Republic of South Africa, with special reference to Homeland and Border Industrial Development and the Economies of Southern Africa', Address at the 40th Annual Council Meeting of the South African Institute of Race Relations, January, 1970, R.R. 19/197, republished in *Mercurius, op. cit.*, June, 1970, p. 13.

33. *Sunday Times,* April 18th, 1971.

34. Based on estimates of Prof. H.J.J. Reynders in an address given at the Sabra conference, September 1970, and published in *Jaarboek van die Suid-Afrikaanse Buro vir Rasse-aangeleenthede,* Nr. 6, 1970, p. 72. The unexpected increase in the African population enumerated in the 1970 census indicates that these figures should be revised upwards.

35. Permanent Committee for the Location of Industry, Report for 1968.

36. Permanent Committee for the Location of Industry, Report for 1970.

when he addressed the legislature on the subject in 1956.[37] The policy of apartheid or separate development was not and is not designed as one of complete separation but is only a means to maintain a balance in the 'White' areas; to prevent further migration from the homelands; and to prevent the White areas being 'swamped'. There is no suggestion that the White areas should have no African population or African workers, only that these be limited in number, and as far as possible temporary migrants.[38]

HOMELAND BACKWARDNESS PRECLUDES TOTAL APARTHEID

Those who believe that the protagonists of separate development contemplate complete separation of the different racial groups in different states are deluding themselves and will be disillusioned. Moreover, the slow economic development of the homelands is likely to be equally disillusioning to Africans hoping for real independence.

The homelands are not only agriculturally backward and virtually devoid of manufacturing industry, they also lack a sufficiently educated population to provide administrative, professional and technical services. Although it is estimated that over eighty per cent of the children now attend school, many do so for very short periods and never become fully literate, for which four years schooling is considered a minimum. In 1970 in the Transkei, with a population of 1 734 116 (excluding temporary migrant workers) there were only 450 children in the final year of school. Five years earlier there had only been 200.[39] Most of the senior officials and technical officers continue to be White, although the number of Whites in the administration has been reduced and there are now three African magistrates.

The homelands also lack artisans, for trade union practice, sanctioned by law, has prevented Africans from being apprenticed in the skilled trades even in the homelands. In the Transkei, the largest and most politically advanced area, in 1971 a total of 25 Africans were apprenticed (in the motor trade), the trade union ban having at last been breached in the homelands. Since 1951 the building industry has been an exception to this general trade union ban on the training of Africans for its skilled trades. In this industry under a special Act of Parliament Africans have

37. *Hansard,* 1956, Col. 5295 *et seq.*
38. *Hansard,* 1962, Vol. 2, Col. 91.
39. *Transkei Annual,* 1971, p. 43.

been trained for artisan work, but only for employment in their own areas and townships.

The tendency has been for the better educated Africans to come from, or make their way to, the larger urban areas. The Government is trying to reverse this by restricting opportunities for African businessmen even in the African dormitory townships of such areas, unless the latter are also homelands.

Critics of the policy of curbing the further growth of the major industrial centres and encouraging industrial development in the border areas and homelands argue with validity that not only will the rate of economic growth be retarded but that the only result will be to substitute the border areas as centres of economic integration.

It is most unlikely that even with the increased incentives to White industrialists, the homelands will become economically viable in the foreseeable future. So far there have been few 'spillover' effects from the border industries into nearby homelands; indeed, the tendency has rather been for Africans living in homeland dormitory towns to shop in nearby White commercial centres.[40] To create economically viable homelands the border areas would have to be incorporated in them. There are some protagonists of separate development who would advocate such an outcome but there is little doubt that the White electorate in those areas would oppose it and that they would be supported by many Whites in the rest of the Republic, for there is a very genuine fear among Whites of the creation of really independent Black states within or adjacent to the Republic.

Without geographical consolidation and the incorporation of the border industrial areas, the policy of separate development is likely to be essentially one of limited powers of local government behind a facade of political rights in areas which are essentially labour reserves. The current official slogan of political independence and economic inter-dependence masks the actuality of both political and economic dependence.

40. See Leistner, *op. cit.*, p. 14.

Independence for the Zulus
Gatsha Buthelezi

Chief M. G. Buthelezi is the Chief Executive Officer of the Zulu Legislative Assembly, the embryo Zulu Parliament. An outspoken critic of certain aspects of separate development, he is determined to lead the Zulu people to greater political freedom within the framework of the White Government's policy of separate political development. He is uncompromisingly opposed to doctrinaire 'colour' apartheid and is a staunch advocate of the equal opportunities doctrine. Chief Buthelezi recently visited the United States and Britain as a guest of the two Governments concerned.

Ever since the Zulus were defeated by the British army in 1879 they have not enjoyed any self-determination whatsoever. We know that such empire-builders as Sir Bartle Frere set out 'to break the Zulu power once and for all' and the Zulus found themselves embroiled in a war which they were deliberately and purposely provoked into. The conquerors then applied the old and well-known technique of *divide et impera* and destroyed the Zulu kingdom. King Cetshwayo and his son King Dinuzulu had to bear the brunt of the war and the Zulu nation as they had known it was destroyed almost beyond recognition.

Since that period the Zulus have been subjects of various White Governments in South Africa. They lost all the self-determination they enjoyed before and found themselves not much more than cogs in the big wheel of White domination. King Cetshwayo returned from pleading his case with Queen Victoria to a Zululand split from top to bottom. Certain Zulu chiefs were invited by the British authorities to defy him and to rule as autonomous rulers and not as before under his reign. Their rule led to chaos in Zululand and when King Dinuzulu succeeded his father, he walked into an impossible situation. As a result of this he was involved in a war with one of the autonomous chiefs, Chief Zibhebu, and for this King Cetshwayo was banished to St Helena. When he was eventually allowed to return in about 1897, his arm was twisted by the Natal British Authorities to sign an annexation of Zululand as part of Natal. This was made a condition for his return.

After this everything was decided for the Zulus and a poll tax was imposed on them which resulted in the Bambatha Rebellion of 1905-6. King Dinuzulu's implication in the Rebellion resulted in his being banished for the second time.

In 1910 Whites of the four provinces formed the Union of the four provinces, known as the Union of South Africa. This they did without consulting Blacks in any way. Here we see former enemies, the Boers and the Britons, uniting in order, amongst other things, to have a uniform Native policy. In other words they were uniting on the basis of their colour and were seeking a better control of Blacks. Thus the Zulus found themselves new subjects of the Union of South Africa.

A Zulu barrister, Dr P. ka I Seme, who was married to King Dinuzulu's eldest daughter Princess Harriet, inspired African leaders to form the African National Congress in 1912. Blacks of various ethnic groups learnt the lesson of sinking their differences and sought a unity such as the former White enemies had found, on the basis of their colour. They attempted to voice Black grievances and even sent delegations to England and Europe, all to no avail.

In 1931, when by the Statute of Westminster, Great Britain gave the Union of South Africa autonomy, the Black majority was again not even consulted. This resulted in a lot of resentment.

In 1936 General Hertzog passed his famous Bills. Important amongst these was the Land Act under which Blacks were promised a certain quota of land. Another was the Native Representation Act under which Blacks, including Zulus, through a College system, elected certain Whites to represent them in the Senate, and in the Cape also in the House of Assembly. Furthermore, Blacks elected other Blacks to represent them on the Native Representative Council in Pretoria. African leaders were far from satisfied with this token representation but agreed to make full use of these bodies in order to voice their aspirations. All these things were imposed by a White minority on the Black majority. In 1946 members of the Native Representative Council decided to pass a resolution requesting repeal of all discriminatory legislation and decided not to function until this was done. The following was their unanimous resolution: 'This Council, having since its inception brought to the notice of the Government the reactionary character of the Union Native Policy of Segregation in all its ramifications, deprecates the Government's post-war continuation of a policy of Fascism which is the antithesis and negation of the Charter. The Council therefore in protest against this breach of faith towards the African people in particular and the cause of world freedom in general, calls upon the Government forthwith to abolish all discriminatory legislation affecting Non-Europeans in this country.' The members of the Native Representative Council included the then Acting Paramount Chief of the Zulus Mshipeni kaDinuzulu. Attempts by the Prime Minister, General Smuts, to resolve this matter failed in May 1947 when he held discussions with the Acting Paramount Chief of the Zulus, Mshiyeni kaDinuzulu, and five other councillors. In 1948 the present National Party Government came into power on the policy of apartheid, now commonly called separate development. The 1936 Representation Act was then superceded by the Bantu Authorities Act of 1951 and the Promotion of Self-Government Act of 1959.

The Zulus were told that the Bantu Authorities Act was optional. There began a campaign of wooing individual chiefs and tribes to 'accept' the Bantu Authorities Act. As this campaign was not meeting with much success, our late *Ingonyama,* King Cyprian, was placed under tremendous pressure to round up the chiefs and make them accept the Act. Here and there a chief and his tribe 'accepted', while other chiefs and their tribes hesitated in spite of the tremendous pressures. The Paramount Chief of the Zulus, *Ingonyama* Cyprian Bhekuzulu then convened a conference of chiefs in order to urge them 'to think quickly on this issue and accept'. The chiefs replied by an almost unanimous resolution not to accept, but requested that the matter be put to the Zulus by a referendum. This was never done.

In the late sixties the tune changed completely and we were then told that we were not supposed 'to accept' but were merely being consulted, and consultation did not mean we had to give consent. It was made clear that, as in the past, we had no option, and consequently complied with the law.

The Paramount Chief went to Pretoria in August 1968 to request the establishment of a Zulu Territorial Authority. By this time many tribes and districts had complied with the law and had Tribal and Regional Authorities respectively. On the 11th June, 1970, the Zulu Territorial Authority was inaugurated by the Hon. Mr M.C. Botha, Minister of Bantu Administration and Development. Under this policy it is proposed to set up a Zulu nation from the ashes of the one that was deliberately destroyed by the White conquerors. It has been promised that under this policy we will be given ethnic self-determination and self-realization, although Africans had also decided, after the Boers and Britons had united on the basis of colour, to speak through Congress as Blacks and not as separate entities. Political organizations as well as many Africans were opposed to ethnic self-determination because to them it smacked of the old *divide et impera,* the more so since Whites are not ethnically divided into Boer nation, British nation, German nation or Jewish nation. The African political organizations became more militant and attempted to resist the self-determination and ethnic self-determination offered to them in this Santa Claus fashion. For this and other reasons they were banned. After this more and more Blacks, including Zulus, decided to co-operate despite reservations on the philosophy behind the apartheid experiment, because they realized that they had to as subjects of White South Africa. The Zulus consider it unique in the history of the human race that freedom can be offered voluntarily to a people by a metropolitan power, such as White South Africa is vis-à-vis Black South Africa.

We realize that as a people we are under-developed and that this goes for all Blacks. Despite our reservations we are co-operating in the hope that the development we are promised may mean an improvement in our plight. The condition under which we offer our co-operation is that the Zulu homeland be consolidated and increased in order that it will be a meaningful homeland for four-and-a-quarter million Zulus. We have been promised by the Hon. The Prime Minister that additional land is going to be added to the Zulu homeland. But we are not very encouraged by the fact that what was promised as long ago as 1936 has not yet been fully delivered to Blacks. Moreover, the Hon. The Prime Minister has stated in Parliament and to us that once what was promised to us in 1936 has been delivered, no more land will be added on to the Zulu homelands. This we find perturbing since the quota promised under the 1936 Act is not adequate to satisfy our land requirements. Furthermore we do not think that it is morally justifiable to expect us to be satisfied with what was promised under the 1936 Land Act by General Hertzog, long before present policies of creating Black States within South Africa were even contemplated, and long before we had the present population to accommodate.

From about April 1972 the present Zulu Territorial Authority will probably become a Legislative Assembly under the Homelands Constitution Act of 1971. This will mean that we shall have departments in full operation under each one of the six members of the Executive or Legislative Councillors. (See Editor's Note, next page.)

Some members of the Legislative Assembly will be elected by Regional Authorities in the various districts of the Zulu homeland. Some will be elected by all Zulu voters from the age of 18 from amongst Zulu candidates in both Urban and Rural Areas.

The Constitution is now under consideration. The Executive Committee have already made certain amendments. A move to vest the Zulu king with certain powers including the appointment of the Chief Councillor or 'Prime Minister' were rejected in toto by the Executive Committee. Zulus love and revere their king and it is unthinkable that he should be given executive powers which will mean inevitable involvement in politics. Ideological differences can result in extremely mundane exchanges which would tarnish the royal image. The late king of the Zulus, Cyprian Bhekuzulu ka Solomon was himself against the idea of being involved in politics as he realized that that was the surest way of destroying the monarchy. The members of the present Assembly of the Territorial Authority at a session convened to consider the present regulations under which the Territorial Authority operates, also rejected the idea of involving the king in politics. If the South African Government imposes the provisions vesting the king with such powers as was hinted at by the Hon. the Minister of Bantu Administration at the king's installation, this will be clear evidence that 'self-government' under the Government's policy of separate development is a big fraud, as some people already suspect. The four and a quarter million Zulus are watching with great interest to see whether in order to exercise control over the 'Zulu Government' the South African Government will risk exposing its policy as such a fraud. It seems too high a price to pay and we can only hope that wiser counsels will prevail in the interests of their own policy. This will be the test of whether the criticisms of this policy as 'institutionalized racism' are valid or not. The stage is set and we are all ready to watch the drama.

We feel that if this policy offers us a share of the wealth of South Africa by ensuring equal pay for equal work, for instance, we may think that, despite our reservations, it has something to commend it. We feel that if it must give us any meaningful self-determination and real development, then, in the same way as Whites, we must have free and compulsory education. This is urgent because, faced as we are with a population explosion, any gospel on family planning will not bring results so long as our people are illiterate and their minds are not sufficiently trained to understand the meaning of such teachings.

We feel that the policy will be meaningless if it does not offer us full human dignity and full human rights, including the freedom of movement enjoyed by people of other racial groups. We feel that, wherever possible, the Zulu homeland must be fully developed to enable us to take part fully in the industrial development of South Africa. This means a decentralization of industries and an amelioration of the vagaries of the migratory labour system which has destroyed both the fabric of our society and the moral fibre of our people.

We feel that self-determination must not be a cover for continued White domination, and the less we feel White control and determine our own future, and that of our children, the more can this policy make any sense.

We feel that it is urgent in the interests of South Africa, particularly when Blacks in other parts of Africa are ruling themselves and in view of international pressure on South Africa, that this policy must not merely be declared feasible but must appear feasible not only to its architects but to all and sundry.

We expect and will not be satisfied with anything less than full freedom, so well set out by President Roosevelt of America in 1941 when he said: 'The first is freedom of speech and expression, the second freedom of every person to worship God in his own way, the third the freedom from want and the fourth is the freedom from fear.' The fifth freedom, added by a great South African Afrikaner leader, is freedom from prejudice.

These are Zulu expectations under this policy, and should it fall short of these within the next decade, separate development will be dismissed in the words of its critics as sheer 'institutionalized racism' or, as other critics call it, 'a gloss on racism'.

Editor's Note: The Kwazulu Legislative Assembly officially came into being on 1 April 1972. The Assembly will consist of 75 nominated and 55 elected members. King Goodwill Zwelithini will be a constitutional monarch with no political powers.

White Alternatives to Apartheid

The United Party's Policy of Race Federation

Sir De Villiers Graaff

Sir De Villiers Graaff (Bart) M.B.E., M.P., is the leader of the official (United Party) Opposition in South Africa. He studied at the Universities of Cape Town and Oxford and holds an honorary LL.D. from the Rhodes University. Sir De Villiers is a highly respected and popular public figure and widely recognized as one of the true gentlemen of South African politics.

History and the need for national survival have woven a golden thread of unity into the fabric of South Africa. The United Party's basic aim is to maintain and strengthen that thread to give cohesion and meaning to as varied and colourful a tapestry of peoples, colours, languages and cultures as is to be found anywhere else on earth. This concept of unity is fundamental to an understanding of our party's policy of race federation.

A brief introductory summary of the policy is given below to serve as a background to the subsequent discussion on the general approach and basic principles. Details are supplied later:

1. Under a United Party Government South Africa will maintain its geographic unity.
2. This Government will be exercised, as at present, through a Central Parliament with certain added features in regard to its composition.
3. Each population or racial group will be granted a considerable amount of local autonomy in its domestic affairs through its own communal council. These councils are seen as a natural development of representative institutions whose foundations were laid down at various stages of the country's history. They will be shorn of the unnecessary ideological trappings which characterize present Government institutions.
4. Some communal councils will have jurisdiction over a defined geo-

graphical area, as do provincial councils and territorial or regional authorities. Others, akin to representative bodies for the Coloured or Indian population, will exercise local jurisdiction over members of a group, irrespective of where they live. Some communal councils may conceivably have partly an ethnic and partly a geographic content.

5. New constitutional provisions will ensure unbroken consultation and co-operation between the councils and the central authority.

HISTORICAL BACKGROUND

In order to appreciate this policy, which is one of evolution and not revolution, the historical background of South Africa and the United Party must first be considered.

Since the time the Dutch settled in the Cape in 1652 certain developments tended to go counter to the evolution of a single unified country in Southern Africa. Dissatisfaction with the Dutch East India Company rule led to the formation of short-lived breakaway republics in the Cape. The Great Trek to the North which started in 1834, and holds a place in South African history and legend parallel to the conquest of the West in America, resulted in the establishment of republics in the present areas of Transvaal, the Orange Free State and Northern Natal. The British colonies in the Cape and Natal, though tied to Whitehall, were separate entities, while in the Eastern Cape the Kei and Fish Rivers formed the shifting border of an embryo Bantustan.

Wars and skirmishes broke out between Black and White, republicans and colonials, and Dutch and English, the latter culminating in the Anglo-Boer War of 1899-1902.

Yet the thread of unity in the end proved the stronger. The centripetal forces in South Africa's history were and still are more powerful than the centrifugal. Wise statesmanship in South Africa, assisted by a Liberal Government in London, led to the amalgamation of the four original colonies into the Union of South Africa in 1910 with General Louis Botha as the first Prime Minister.

This Union was not a unitary state since the four provinces maintained a considerable deal of autonomy mainly in regard to education and hospitals. Neither was it a federation in the accepted sense, namely that sovereignty remained vested in the four constituent provinces. Since 1910 tribal institutions have been developed with their own rights and privileges, while in certain areas Native Law is recognized side-by-side with official

Roman-Dutch Law. Franchise qualifications until recently differed substantially from province to province.

I mention this 'diversity in unity' to emphasize a fact sometimes lost sight of by viewers of the South African scene, namely, that the traditional definitions of political science such as 'union', 'federation', 'confederation', 'suffrage', 'democracy', 'autocracy', 'self-government', 'autonomy', 'sovereignty', 'liberalism', and many of a similar nature, cannot be applied without qualification to multi-racial or multi-national states nor, for that matter, to many of the present emergent states in Africa.

Sometimes new constitutional ideas demand a revised vocabulary. General Smuts originated the felicitous phrase 'Commonwealth of Nations' to describe the dominions of the British Empire which had attained the status of full self-governing bodies. 'Race Federation' is also a new term, and it has a connotation differing in several respects from the traditional one associated with federalism.

A tyranny of words has contributed its share to confusion and aridity in much of the political debate in South Africa. Discussions involving often-used expressions such as 'apartheid', 'integration', 'separate development', 'White leadership', 'parallel development', 'multi-racial', 'multi-national', 'merit not equality' and 'segregation' can be meaningless and frustrating when the disputants cannot agree on the definition of their terms.

SMUTS AND HOLISM

After Union in 1910 division arose between the leaders of the new state, giving rise to parties with largely separatist tendencies. Once again, however, the forces that bind proved more powerful than those that divide, and in 1932 the South African Party of General Smuts and the greater part of the National Party led by General Hertzog came together to form the United or, to give it its full name, the United South African National Party.

Apart from being a distinguished statesman and scientist General Smuts was that rare being – an original thinker. His book *Holism and Evolution* is a major contribution to twentieth century philosophy. Holism teaches that the whole can be greater than the sum total of its constituent parts; that, for instance, a United States of America is greater than the mere aggregate of its forty-eight (now fifty) states, and that a united South Africa contains a new dimension not found separately in its original constituent colonies and republics. The United Party believes that this concept of a greater ῤλος would be lost forever if the Republic of South Africa were to be divided into up to nine separate Black and White states as envisaged in the policy of the Party of Dr Verwoerd and Mr Vorster. All South Africa would be the poorer for it.

In his famous Inaugural Address, President Lincoln stated his belief that the central idea of secession was the essence of anarchy. We find it almost incomprehensible that a Government, such as the present one in South Africa, can actually encourage similar secession. Abraham Lincoln's noble words in his Inaugural carry a message for South Africa in these troubled times:

> 'Physically speaking, we cannot separate. We cannot remove our respective sections from each other, nor build an impassable wall between them . . . Can aliens make treaties easier than friends can make laws? Can treaties be more faithfully enforced between aliens than laws can among friends?'

For the United Party, as for President Lincoln, the word 'unity' is much more than a political formula – it is part of our way of life. South Africa contains peoples of many races, languages and cultures, but it is one country within a single enclosed border and with all its citizens bound to it by a single loyalty.

The richness and variety of this multi-racial, multi-national, multilingual country with its 15 million Blacks divided into at least ten ethnic groups, $3\frac{3}{4}$ million persons of European descent, two million Coloured and Eurasians and 600 000 Asians offer a real challenge in human relations and in original political approaches to those who seek to guide its destiny.

In many ways South Africa is a microcosm of the greater world and even if the United Party's modest claim that it can, conceivably, offer a new approach or a fresh point of view to those on the larger scene, should prove too sanguine, it will at least not be denied that Pliny was looking further than he ever realized, both in time and distance, when he declared: *'Ex Africa semper aliquid novi.'*

SEEKING BALANCED ADJUSTMENT

The United Party, having agreed to espouse a policy of 'unity in diversity', and to eschew the tyranny of words, next had to consider the proper approach to what is called the Colour problem.

Here too, there is a semantic trap. This 'problem' is by no means a problem in the mathematical sense which, once a solution is found, simply disappears. There is no easy answer. Once a race federation (or the Nationalist alternative of eight 'Bantustans' – independent Black States – cut out of the present borders) is established, new developments and new situations will face the generations and Parliaments of that era. Instead, therefore, of speaking of a Colour problem (or a White problem, as some prefer to call it) the correct view is to regard race relations in South Africa as a continuous challenge to find a balanced adjustment between population groups, in a society that is dynamic and expanding.

This approach of seeking a balanced adjustment implies a rejection and distrust of final solutions. It is essentially pragmatic and based on common sense and tolerance rather than ideological orthodoxy. Such a policy leaves room for experimentation, for trying out and developing new approaches, and allowing consideration to be given within its framework to different stages of development between population groups, and often within the groups themselves.

The United Party accepts that politics is the art of the possible. It looks at facts as they are, and not as it would like them to be.

Democracy with its most important manifestation, parliamentary democracy, is basic to our Party's policy. Here, again, terms have to be defined. Democracy involves the recognition of a significant proportion of what has come to be known as basic human rights. Most countries disagree as to their extent. Those accepted by the United Party include the recognition of the inherent dignity of the individual, equality before impartial courts of law, the rejection of restrospective legislation, the right to freedom of the press, thought, conscience and belief, and the right to social services involving education, health and old age benefits.

While universal suffrage is at present accepted as a basic human right in most Western states, this has only been the case for a very small fraction of the 25 centuries separating the modern world from ancient Athens, who invented the system, gave it a name and laid down its first principles. Universal suffrage was not one of them, and was never even considered.

The United Party is opposed to universal suffrage precisely because it desires to safeguard the human rights, mentioned above, for all. This is not as paradoxical as it may appear, when set against the experience of most of the newly-emergent Black States in Africa where universal suffrage granted to an unsophisticated electorate has led, in the vast majority of cases, to the overthrow of the Government by revolution, followed by one-man or one-party rule with very little if any human rights left at all.

Black majority rule in South Africa which will inevitably result from universal suffrage, or from suffrage based on low franchise qualifications, will bring with it most elements leading to revolution and disaster.

At the same time, a right to a voice, direct or delegated, in the central legislature, as well as the right to be consulted on issues affecting their special interests should be provided for persons at present disenfranchised, and who have certain defined basic qualifications in regard to education, income and property. The United Party's policy makes such provision.

THE PARTY AND PLURALISM

'Political pluralism' is a fairly recent term in political science. Its definition includes systems of government in which, owing to a wide divergence of civilization, education and culture amongst different groups within a state, a plurality of political institutions may be established to cater for each group's special needs and to protect its rights. Political scientists agree that pluralism and democracy are not incompatible. The United Party believes its race federation policy to be such a form of political pluralism.

Perhaps political pluralism is not such a new concept, after all. The writer came across the following in Aristotle's *Politics* (Jowett's version):

'Unity there should be, both of the family and the state, but in some respects only. For there is a point at which a state may attain such a degree of unity as to be no longer a state, or at which, without actually ceasing to exist, it will become an inferior state, like harmony passing into unison, or rhythm which has been reduced to a single foot. The state, as I was saying, is a plurality, which should be united, and made into a community by education.'

The context aside, this is not an unacceptable description of the United Party's approach of 'diversity in unity'.

Our policy recognizes the realities of South Africa. These are that the economic interdependence of the races is essential to continued survival and growth; that the country has a permanent urban African, Coloured and Indian population becoming progressively more detribalized; that the growth of a responsible Non-White middle class is essential to national stability; that the Non-White population of South Africa enjoys a higher standard of living, income, education and social services than that in any other country in Africa, and that Communism and intolerant Black Nationalism can present special dangers in a plural society.

The United Party further accepts that the basic human rights mentioned earlier can best be maintained through the enlightened leadership and guidance of the White group, in the interests of all races. This is not based on real or spurious claims to superiority on the grounds of colour alone, but on the fact that this group introduced and developed Western civilization, religion, education, medicine, technocracy, industrial development, commerce, modern agriculture and management know-how in a country which was still at a relatively primitive stage of development. Without the group's initiative, capital and leadership, South Africa would not have become, and cannot remain a modern industrial state.

Unstinted recognition should, however, also be given to the Blacks who contributed their labour, very largely unskilled, which was an essential factor in the growth of our mines, agriculture and industries.

The United Party is an enlightened and practical organization inclined to look askance at strange new ideologies and untested ideas. As a result it is not a party with a messianic urge to lay down irreversible blueprints on racial policies for several generations to come.

It realizes only too well that Governments are in time replaced by Oppositions who have a regrettable tendency to reverse their predecessors' policies.

We set great store by one of the fundamental principles of parliamentary democracy which declares that one Parliament cannot bind its successor. Accordingly we have, in formulating our policy, divided the execution thereof in practice by future United Party Governments into several phases of which only the initial ones are presented in any considerable detail. Subsequent phases convey a general outline or guide to future administrations in the knowledge that they may well alter the policy significantly, as indeed they will have every right to do. Some of these phases overlap and run parallel, while policies which may fall under the first phase for one race group may well only be executed in a subsequent phase in respect of another group. There can be no rigidity in dealing with problems involving human relations.

THE THREE PHASES

The United Party is the only conceivable alternative Government in South Africa. Other parties, groups and individuals may speculate about the future with the best of intentions – and their views will always be welcome – but only the United Party can put an alternative policy into practice.

The three phases in which the policy will be applied can be compared to the steps taken by an entrepreneur asked by the shareholders to take over the control of an outmoded and near bankrupt business.

His first concern will be to install new top management, raise finance, get the books in order, replace outmoded stock and perhaps even hold a clearance sale. That is the first phase.

Next the entrepreneur will concern himself with rebuilding, renovation and expansion. New staff will be trained, modern methods introduced, profitable contracts negotiated and fresh markets sought. This is the second phase.

In the third phase the new enterprise is seen as an integrated whole with its own individual character and image. It is all set for a future of growth and prosperity under its new management with new methods and new ideas.

These then, are the three phases – the first: repairing; the second: rebuilding; the third: forging ahead.

REVIEW OF LAWS IN THE FIRST PHASE

During the vital first phase, which we shall initiate immediately on the return of the United Party to power, we shall review all laws which discriminate without rhyme or reason, offend the rule of law or detract from the dignity of the individual in order to determine which laws should be amended or repealed.

Amongst these are the following:

The various so-called Bantustan measures, aimed at fragmenting South Africa into independent states. An intricate series of Acts have been passed, and Proclamations issued, by the Nationalist Government to facilitate the granting of complete independent sovereignty to up to eight Black states, to be carved out of the present borders of South Africa. That such a transition may not be as peaceful or acceptable to the Blacks as the Government hopes, is shown by the fact that an Emergency Regulation, under which certain basic human rights are suspended, has been applied to the Transkei, intended as the show-piece of the Bantustan policy. At the same time this policy of deliberate secessionism has encouraged the emergence of a narrow type of Black nationalism, in many ways akin to the Black Power movement in the United States.

The United Party has consistently fought against this Bantustan policy, both inside and outside Parliament. In this too, it has adhered to its fundamental belief in unity in diversity. The creation of an alternative structure for South Africa, which will recognize that unity, but make provision for wide degrees of differences in history, culture, standards of civilization, training in administration and education between the different races, we call 'race federation'.

It will therefore be essential to review all the Bantustan measures with a view to repealing those that are unacceptable, amending others to fit in with our policy, and maintaining those which have a sound basis in practical as distinct from ideological development. Continuity between successive administrations is an essential feature of parliamentary democracy and the new United Party Government, in recognizing this, will proceed along the road of evolution, not revolution.

The Physical Planning Act under which the Government can dictate to industries where they should move to and what Black labour they may employ. The number of potential Black employees affected by the Government's refusal of applications to employ them totalled 30 217 up to the middle of 1970.

The Security Laws to the extent that they infringe the rule of law without contributing anything to the safety of the state. Emergency Regulation No. 400 for instance, still applies to the Transkei, supposed to be the showcase of the Bantustan policy.

The Acts controlling Blacks in urban areas: The latest report of the Commissioner of the S.A. Police shows that 623 077 Non-Whites were prosecuted in 1968/70 for infringement of so-called Pass Laws, the laws controlling their movements. This is 26 per cent of the prosecutions of persons of all races, for all offences. In one year more than 40 000 Blacks were sent back to the Reserves – to such an extent that the Transkei Legislative Assembly had to plead with the Government to stop sending them back until employment and housing were made available.

The Population Registration Act, which attempts to classify every inhabitant according to race. It has caused great hardship in borderline cases, and the United Party has promised a radical review of the law.

The Immorality Act, which prohibits marriage and sexual relations across the colour line. An alarming number of persons charged under this Act have committed suicide. The United Party has undertaken to have the application of the Act reviewed by an independent top-level commission of experts in sociology, psychology, medicine, religion and law.

The Group Areas Act, which provides for the removal of persons to predetermined areas set aside for occupation by a particular race. According to the latest figures (17.2.1970), 69 000 Coloureds, 38 000 Indians, 1 300 Whites and unspecified thousands of Blacks had already been deemed 'disqualified' to remain in their original homes. Of these about half had been resettled.

The Industrial Conciliation Act, particularly insofar as its job reservation clauses have proved abortive and have slowed down the economy.

Acts involving the development of *industries on the borders of the Reserves,* insofar as they vitiate development planned on sound economic lines.

Measures affecting Education, Health and Social Welfare: Tuberculosis and deficiency diseases such as pellagra, kwashiorkor and scurvy are still widespread amongst Non-Whites. There is a shortage of doctors, nurses and para-medical personnel. Schools are overcrowded and staff inadequate. Social welfare payments are not keeping pace with inflated living costs. All these matters will receive prompt attention.

A major task of the new United Party Government during the first phase of putting its policy into practice, will be to establish the basis for a significant and effective dialogue between the races by improving the machinery for consultation with the Non-White people. This will be done even before establishing the communal councils. Many existing organizations will be adapted to this purpose as an interim measure. These bodies include Urban Bantu Councils, Authorities in the Reserves and the Councils representing Coloureds and Indians.

Immediate steps, even before the legislative programme for the first Parliamentary Session has been worked out, will be taken to consult with representatives of labour and management to break the labour bottleneck, increase production, get the economy moving and to make full use of all available human resources.

Active steps to improve South Africa's image abroad, based on expounding the measures envisaged in the race federation policy, will receive urgent attention. The harm done to South Africa's international relations in diplomacy, defence, commerce and sport will receive urgent attention.

PLANNING IN THE SECOND PHASE

The first phase, as outlined above, will demand a great proportion of the attention and energies of the new United Party Government during the first months.

This period will be followed immediately by the second phase when the Acts which have been reviewed during the first phase will be amended or repealed, while the Black areas or Reserves will be brought into closer association with the rest of the country and communal councils will be established. As in the analogy of the business enterprise mentioned earlier, the period of making repairs is now superseded by the phase of reconstruction and rebuilding.

The Acts affecting urban development, physical planning, labour and the development of natural resources, will be amended to ensure that existing and planned industries are supplied with their rightful labour needs. It will provide for planned decentralization of industry where economic, strategic or social reasons (such as the development of backward areas) demand it.

Other important developments in this, the second phase, which affect the Black areas, the urban worker, the growth of the economy and political representation, are outlined in the pages which follow.

Developing the Bantu areas: The laws affecting the Black areas will be amended to make it possible for the Reserves to share in the growth of the rest of South Africa. The continual association of these Black areas with and within South Africa will be ensured through the necessary statutory measures, without, however, derogating from their existing rights of self-administration on the elective principle in regard to local matters.

The first communal councils will be established in areas which already form a natural geographical unity (no forced consolidation of borders will be necessary under race federation) and where elective administrative bodies for the purpose of self-rule have been developed. The Transkei could well be one of the first areas to have such a communal council.

Should a Black area already have achieved full independence through the transfer to its Government of sovereignty under International Law, such independence will naturally be recognized, but all efforts will be made to persuade the country to renew and strengthen its ties with the Republic in some form of confederation or association which will be economic or political, or both. Problems may arise too, in respect of areas promised independence, prepared for it and anxiously and determinedly seeking it.

Here the undertakings of former governments may have to be honoured though only after persuasion and negotiation have failed to maintain economic and/or political ties of the kind outlined above.

In the second phase, effective measures will also be taken to develop the economy of the Black areas or Reserves through soil conservation, improved agricultural methods, changes in the system of land tenure and the building of an infra-structure for industrial development. Such development will be encouraged with the aid of capital, skill and know-how from established private and state enterprise in the existing industrial areas. Legal safeguards will prevent the exploitation of Black labour, and the Blacks could in time become major shareholders, managers and even owners of those industries. The Blacks' age-old rights to the land in the Reserves will be protected from alienation – proprietary rights in the land will remain in the hands of the Black people.

This plan for development of the Black areas is, incidentally one of the many instances under race federation where differentiation between the races need not mean discrimination against a group – unless it be against the White group, in this case.

The urban worker : In urban areas a measure of labour regulation will continue to protect the wages and living standards of the established Black work force against unfair competition from unrestricted cheap labour from the reserves. Such regulation will, at the same time avoid the evils attending overcrowding, shortage of accommodation and schools, and inadequate health and sanitation services which history and experience have shown can result from an unrestricted inflow of low-paid workers – whether in Johannesburg or Vereeniging, Buenos Aires or Calcutta.

Where work in industry, commerce or domestic service, together with accommodation in the urban Bantu townships, are both available, labourers will be helped to take up such employment. Labour bureaux will exist to guide and advise Blacks seeking employment, also in the Reserves.

Prison sentences for purely technical offences will be avoided. Black people with certain qualifications, such as owners of immovable property, chiefs and headmen, ministers of religion, teachers, lawyers, doctors and clerks with certain educational standards will be exempted from the regulations.

The growth of a stable and responsible middle-class amongst the settled urban Black population will be encouraged by making it possible for those having the means as well as security of employment, to gain freehold title to their homes in the Black townships – a right at present denied them.

Measures at present keeping husbands and wives apart and breaking up families will be altered to encourage a stable family life. Every person, however humble and of whatever race, will be entitled to some fit place where he can go and which he can call his home.

The law-abiding Black people are the biggest victims of crimes committed by Blacks themselves. Radical measures will be taken to combat lawlessness, including the expert training of more Black police and the introduction of the latest scientific aids in crime detection and prevention. Social evils leading to crime – vagrancy, drug-taking, slum conditions and wages below the breadline – will be combated in the townships through housing development, better educational, health, social and recreational services, and fuller opportunities for the training of unskilled workers. The severe restrictions on the development of even modest industrial and commercial undertaking by Blacks in the townships will be altered to make the rise of a Black entrepreneural class possible.

Economic growth : During this and subsequent phases we shall do everything possible to ensure a substantial rate of economic growth. Prosperity and security are indispensable to racial peace. New avenues of economic development will be opened for Non-Whites in their own communities and areas.

A Manpower Training Act will be passed to provide accelerated industrial training, while a planned programme, in consultation with labour unions and organized industry and commerce, will be inaugurated to introduce a larger number of Non-Whites into tasks requiring a greater measure of training and skill. The rate for the job will be applied at realistic wage levels, protecting established workers against unfair competition.

Greater progress will be made in regard to housing, health and education. Our aim is to double the total amount spent on education for all groups within a reasonable period. (At present South Africa spends less than four per cent of her Gross National Product on education). Television which, incredible as it may sound, South Africa still lacks, will not only provide news and entertainment, but will become a powerful supplementary aid to education.

While most of the positive measures outlined above refer to the Black population, they will of course also apply, with the necessary adaptations, to the Coloured and Indian population groups where they are subjected to comparable disabilities.

Political representation: During this second phase, legislation will also be passed to provide for the representation of the Non-White groups in the Central Parliament. These M.P.'s will be freely elected on a separate roll for each group, with stated franchise qualifications. The envisaged representation is:

For the Coloureds, 6 M.P.'s and 2 Senators, who may be White or Coloured.
For the Indians, 2 M.P.'s and 1 Senator who will be White.
For the Bantu, 8 M.P.'s and 2 Senators, who will be White.

This parliamentary representation will not be altered without the approval of a decisive majority, such as two-thirds of the existing White electorate at a general election or a special referendum.

This system will ensure that Non-White persons with a certain standard of civilization and education will not be denied a voice in Parliament, while the rights of minorities will at the same time be protected. During this second period the voters rolls will be prepared and the elections for the additional representatives held. We now consider the third phase of our race federation policy.

THE THIRD PHASE

In our previous analogy of a business undertaking, the period of rebuilding was followed by a third period of expansion and growth. Similarly, the third phase of the race federation policy now follows the second phase of reconstruction. The system receives its finishing touches and will be working smoothly as an integral whole within the framework of a Central Government in which all races will have a right to be heard, supplemented by a nation-wide system of communal councils.

The Central Government will exercise general control over the affairs of the Republic and will specifically control such matters as central finance, defence, foreign policy, international trade agreements, communications and similar subjects generally reserved for central legislatures under a federal system.

Subject to the overriding consideration of the safety of the state the several population groups will each have the widest possible measure of local self-government, especially in matters such as education, local government, cultural affairs and public health.

Communal councils will by this time have been established, not only for defined geographical areas such as the provinces and the larger Black areas, but also for smaller areas grouped together, and for population groups not living in a defined geographical area.

These latter groups will include the Coloureds and Indians (who already have their own communal councils in embryo) as well as the Blacks permanently settled in urban or rural areas.

The latter will be scattered over a wide area and a communal council will probably be established for them in each province to see to their educational, health and local affairs. They will be closely associated with existing Black urban councils.

The name 'Communal Council' need not be strictly adhered to. South Africa has a rich variety of names for subordinate bodies – such as 'provincial councils', 'territorial authorities', 'assemblies', 'Bungas', 'representative councils', etc., anyone of which may be found suitable for a particular body.

Constitutional provisions for liaison between the councils and the Central Government, or between two or more councils amongst themselves in regard to matters of common concern, will also have been enacted, and the system will be working in practice. The country can now advance along the road of race federation.

Fetters will have been cast from the economy, manpower will be progressively more productive and the country will be poised for a spectacular period of growth. All groups will be bound by a common loyalty to South Africa, without losing their identity or having their language and cultural rights affected.

All areas of the country will be developed to produce the wealth whereby social welfare, education, health, research and the constructive enjoyment of leisure can be promoted.

South Africa will enter a period of dynamic advance. No Government can stand still and the citizens of the race federation will find great new challenges facing them – such as preserving the ecological balance of the environment, trebling the country's water supplies, extending the span of human life through the conquest of disease, controlling the population explosion, applying atomic energy for peaceful development, growing food by revolutionary new processes, initiating greater economic and scientific co-operation between the peoples of Southern Africa, creating expanding markets for the country's goods and transforming South Africa into a major industrial state able to play a significant role on the world stage.

South Africa will face these tasks united in its broad aims, strengthened by the disappearance of the mutually destructive racial confrontations of the past, and determined to uphold justice for all its peoples.

Race federation will have played, and continue to play, a major role in these achievements.

In politics, unlike mathematics, there are no final solutions. Problems are not solved and made to disappear by a parliamentary *quod erat demonstrandum.*

Neither does a blueprint exist elsewhere which can be applied successfully to a country such as South Africa with its many population groups with their great diversity in history, culture and civilized values as well as their different ceilings of achievement in different callings and spheres of economic and political activity.

Forced integration is as unacceptable to us as forced secessionism. In our view the 'busing' of children to meet racial quotas in U.S.A. schools and the forcing of American universities to admit new students on a basis of racial percentages, is an unwarranted emphasis on race at the expense of merit. On the other hand, the secessionist policies of the South African Nationalists are far too close for comfort to an ideological mania *in extremis.*

We believe there is merit in the Golden Mean, and that common sense should count in politics. It is this common sense which commands us to ensure that government in South Africa shall remain in civilized hands, now and in the future, and persuades us, as far as it is given us by Providence to see into that future, that such civilized rule can only be maintained through White leadership and justice.

We do not wish to lay down the law for future generations – that way lies authoritarianism and the police state. We do see it as our duty, however, to lay the foundation for future security and racial co-operation on which we hope future generations can build with profit.

If our race federation policy can achieve this, as I believe it must if we want to survive, the United Party will have done a great service to the Republic.

The Progressive Party's Programme for a multi-racial South Africa

Helen Suzman

Mrs Suzman is the M.P. for Houghton, Johannesburg and the Progressive Party's sole representative in the Assembly — one of the only two women members in the House. One of South Africa's most astute Parliamentarians, Helen Suzman is respected in all walks of life for her unstinted dedication to the Progressive Party's policy of multi-racialism. She is unquestionably one of the most hardworking M.P.'s and her courageous and indefatigable one-woman battle in the Assembly has earned her praise from both Government and Opposition ranks.

The Progressive Party bases its policy on two fundamentals. The one is a fact, the other a philosophy. The fact is that South Africa is one multi-racial country – its citizens are Black and White and Brown.[1] This is so today, it will be so tomorrow and for as far as one can see into the future. For each is dependent on the other. Our farms, our factories, our mines, our homes, our present prosperity, our future progress – all require the united effort of all our citizens.

Central to the philosophy is the concept that in any society, it is the individual human being that is of paramount importance. It is the individual citizen's rights, freedoms, welfare, prosperity and happiness that the society should cherish and the State should serve.

This means that there must be equality before the law. It means that there must be unremitting effort to ensure equal opportunity for the individual to develop his ability and talents, and equal opportunity for their

1. The term 'Black' as used henceforth in this chapter denotes all racial groups other than the White group.

use and expression. Merit, and not colour, must be the yardstick by which the worth of the individual is judged.

Translating fact and philosophy into policy has resulted in the acceptance of principles very different from those traditionally applied in South Africa. It entails the rejection of race discrimination in every aspect of life – political, social, economic – an extension of rights and responsibilities to Africans, Coloured people and Asians, while affording protection to minority groups and ensuring the continuation and expansion of a modern industrial society in South Africa.

THE POLITICAL PROGRAMME

To these ends, the Progressive Party proposes a qualified franchise for every citizen over the age of 18 years who has –

passed Standard VIII;

or who has passed Standard VI and either –

had an income of R600 per year for 2 consecutive years; or has occupied property worth R1 000 for 2 consecutive years;

or who owns unencumbered property to the value of R1 000, and is literate.

A married person may claim the economic, but not the educational qualifications of the husband or wife; and any person who has at any time been a voter for the House of Assembly will be entitled to the ordinary franchise. The financial qualifications will be adjusted to meet proved fluctuations in the value of money. Any qualified voter will have the right to stand for election to Parliament.

So far, we have dealt with the ordinary voters roll, which will list the fully qualified voters of all races. However, the Progressive Party believes it is also very desirable – until such time as educational and economic progress shall have enabled the whole, or nearly the whole, of the adult population to qualify for the vote – that unqualified people should also have a voice in Parliament.

Initially, therefore, 10 per cent of the seats in Parliament will be set aside for the representatives of South Africans who cannot qualify for the ordinary vote, but who are 18 years old and literate. Once their number diminishes below 20 per cent of the total of those entitled to vote, the number of seats will be reduced proportionally. Ultimately, when South Africa has reached an overall level of development comparable with that of Western countries generally, this 'special voters roll' will disappear.

The Progressive Party has designed a Senate plan which will protect minority groups by having a Senate so elected that it will ensure multi-racial government and prevent the passage of legislation likely to discriminate against or detrimentally affect the interests of a particular racial group.

Firstly, the Senate will be powerful. Its assent will be needed for the passage into law of any measure other than a money bill, i.e. it will be able to block any other law passed by the Assembly. Secondly, the Senate, because of its importance, will be directly elected in special constituencies by the voters on the ordinary roll – i.e. the fully qualified voters.

The elected candidate will be required to have secured at least one-fifth of the votes cast by the members of each racial community represented on the voters roll of the constituency: and if no candidate achieves this, then he who had the best 'spread' of votes would be elected.

This is a simple, but very far-reaching measure. It means, in effect, that no Senator will be elected who does not appeal effectively to voters of all racial groups. The Senate will, therefore, be bound to block any legislation which is offensive to any particular group. It also means that no party which does not appeal to all races can win a majority in the Senate. Without a majority in the Senate it will be very difficult (though not quite impossible) to govern; and it is hard to envisage any party gaining a Senate majority unless its membership, or at least its list of candidates, included people of all racial groups. And, of course, no party could in practice be multi-racial for purposes of the Senate but not the Assembly.

It is necessary, perhaps, to answer the contention that the Senate plan requires voters rolls based on race and that therefore this entails acceptance of the communal franchise and even of racial discrimination.

It should be noted that under Progressive Party policy colour in itself neither confers privileges nor does it incur disabilities, as is the case in South Africa today. Registration on a particular racial roll for the purpose of electing a Senator will be purely and simply to ensure that sufficient voters of each racial group approve the choice of the common roll majority – it is a protective mechanism and nothing else.

The individual, registering on the communal voters roll, will indicate his racial group himself. The present Population Registration Act will be repealed; and with it, the whole repugnant network of regulations providing for classification and reclassification, for appeals and third-party objections, which lend themselves to blackmail and other forms of abuse, causing incalculable human suffering.

No disadvantages will flow from proclaiming one's race for the purpose of Senate elections. On the contrary, the voter will be protecting his own interests by giving himself the power to block the election of someone he considers hostile to his own racial group. This electoral procedure is designed to ensure that the successful candidate for the Senate will have at least a minimum measure of multi-racial support, as a condition precedent to his election.

A Bill of Rights will protect the rights of the individual. It will guarantee to every South African such basic rights as freedom of speech, worship and assembly, freedom from arbitrary arrest, the right of access to the courts and the equal protection of the law. The franchise qualifications, the senate plan and the Bill of Rights will all be entrenched in a rigid constitution. Constitutional amendments will require the assent of each of the major racial communities, expressed at referenda of their ordinary roll voters.

It is considered that these inter-dependent measures will provide protection for the rights of each community and for those of each individual.

The task of enforcing the provisions of the constitution will fall upon the courts. Whenever Parliament, or any other body or individual, acts in such a way as to infringe basic rights, it will be for the courts to pronounce this action null and void. That is why the Progressive Party has undertaken to ensure the maintenance in South Africa of an independent and learned judiciary, impartial justice and the rule of law.

The Progressive Party is firmly wedded to the rule of law. Thus, equality before the law, access to the courts of law, the right of defence and *habeas corpus* are basic to our policy.

All laws that conflict with these basic principles will be repealed. Bannings and restrictions on persons by ministerial edicts and detentions without trial will disappear from the South African scene. Such measures would in any case be redundant in a country governed by consent. Apartheid and the rule of law are incompatible. A multi-racial government elected on a broad common roll, in a South Africa in which all legal discrimination based on race or colour has been eliminated, will be able to rely on the normal legal procedures used by all democratic countries.

The overall political plan embodies a geographic federation consisting of several states or provinces, where the rights and powers of the provinces will be widened and entrenched, so that they may be safeguarded from central interference in their own affairs. The Party does not consider present provincial boundaries as necessarily permanent. We believe that it might be advantageous, with the consent of the people concerned, to modify existing provincial boundaries. In particular, certain of the former African Reserves, now called homelands, might opt for this form of provincial autonomy. In areas such as these, the populations of which are overwhelmingly African, millions of Africans would have the opportunity to govern themselves in matters affecting their daily lives, without the rights and freedoms of those living in the rest of the country being affected in any way, and without any question arising of the partition of the country into exclusive Black and White areas.

This policy obviously provides for the future incorporation of any self-governing state (or indeed, independent Bantustan, should one exist), into the Republic of South Africa, should it so desire, after the Progressive Party has assumed power.

The Progressive Party federal plan envisages the provincial governments exercising considerably wider powers than those presently held. Taxation powers will be extended. Also, for example, technical and vocational training would be administered by the provinces, which would also have the power to legislate for the establishment and subsidization of universities. The provinces would again be responsible for all primary and secondary education, which means that the education of Africans will be restored to the provinces. Each provincial government would control its own public service for the administration of the departments of government that fall within its competence.

The primary responsibility for law and order, and hence for controlling the police, should be discharged by the provinces. It is our contention that a centralized police force, organized on semi-military lines, lends itself to being used as a means of political oppression and hence can represent a threat to freedom.

We accept, however, that the Federal Government should be responsible for the internal security of the country as a whole, and should maintain its own security service to supplement the efforts of the provincial police forces.

The powers handed over to the provinces would be constitutionally entrenched against any interference by the Federal Government.

The form of provincial government under the Progressive Party plan would be that of responsible government administered by a council of ministers, headed by a prime minister. The provincial legislatures would be a replica of the Federal Parliament. They would be bi-cameral, each consisting of a lower house, or Legislative Assembly and an upper house or Legislative Council. The methods of election for the provincial legislatures would be exactly the same as those applying to the Federal Parliament, the same qualifications would be laid down, and the Bill of Rights would also be binding on the provincial legislatures.

The Progressive Party realizes that sooner or later Whites will be outnumbered by Africans, Coloured people and Asians on the common voters roll. We do not, however, consider that this will mean an all-Black Parliament.

We believe that once South Africans are freed from the strait-jacket of colour, which now irrevocably determines the life chances of every individual, people will – in the pursuit of their own interests – cohere on the basis of common objectives, which will cut across racial and ethnic affiliations. This will bring about co-operation and continuing inter-action on a multi-racial basis, with the forces normally operative in political life bringing to the fore people of the necessary drive and ability. We do not believe that any one group commands a monopoly of people of this quality, nor do we believe that, given free play for merit, any group will be prevented from participating to the fullest extent of its proven ability. We are convinced that the outcome will be a multi-racial parliament, and that the rights of minorities will be adequately protected by the constitution.

The alternative is the denial of all meaningful rights to Blacks in the legislative body that passes all the laws that regulate their lives from the cradle to the grave, as advocated by both the National and United Parties. This is completely unacceptable to us, both in principle and because it is in the long run untenable, fraught with the menace of the utter disruption of the South African polity.

There are those, more radical than we are, who heap scorn on the idea of a qualified franchise, which they regard as a mechanism to perpetuate White political control. In reply to such critics, we can only stress that the opportunity to obtain the qualifications for the franchise will be open to all under Progressive Party policy, since free and compulsory education for children of all races, up to the end of primary school at least, is part and parcel of Progressive proposals; and the removal of all restrictions on earning capacity is likewise included in our policy. We frankly concede that any franchise qualifications which are administratively feasible must to some extent be arbitrary. But we claim with confidence that educational and economic criteria are those best suited to serve as a measure of modernization. The criteria we suggest are based on the recognition that the maintenance of a modern industrial economy in South Africa and its effective administration, is dependent on people who have the requisite training and know-how. And these abilities, through no fault of their own, the vast majority of Blacks have not yet had the opportunity to acquire.

At present only White children are afforded free and compulsory education. Asian and Coloured children enjoy free education, but it is not compulsory except for Coloured children in three or four localities. Some 80 per cent of African children of school-going age are at school, but 75 per cent of them have left school by the end of Standard 2. Of Coloured schoolchildren 62,2 per cent and of Asian schoolchildren 42,5 per cent go no further than Standard 2 – barely functionally literate. Only 0,11 per cent of enrolled African schoolchildren reach Standard 10, and only 0,38 per cent of Coloured schoolchildren and 1,57 per cent of Indian schoolchildren.

THE SOCIO-ECONOMIC PROGRAMME

The Progressive Party has unequivocally opted for the removal of all restrictions on mobility that presently so drastically affect the family life of Africans and their ability to sell their labour in the best market. This means the end of the pass laws and influx control which restrict the right of freedom of movement of Africans from town to town or country to town. The pass laws have over the years been *the* greatest source of racial friction in South Africa. They have resulted in the prosecution of millions of Africans – over 600 000 last year alone – for the 'crime' of seeking work or of being in a 'White' area without permission. They have turned law-abiding people into statutory criminals, they were the detonators at Sharpeville, and they have cost South Africa inestimable hostility and have caused the erosion of harmonious race relations. Influx control cannot be implemented without pass laws. It has resulted in countless Africans being condemned to lives of grinding poverty in the rural areas, on White farms and in the Bantustans.

Africans are no different from other citizens who wish to move to the urban areas in order to improve their economic position. They can be guided to those areas where their labour is required, through the operation of voluntary labour bureaux, but the Progressive Party rejects completely the concept that they should be rendered immobile – 'once a farm labourer, always a farm labourer', as the Deputy Minister of Bantu Administration and Development put it recently – doomed to a life that can never be improved.

The Progressive Party rejects too the concept that Africans presently in the Bantustans, which offer hardly any employment opportunities outside of subsistence agriculture, shall be forever condemned to the life of a migratory worker, a contract worker who may himself take a job in a city but whose family must remain behind in a Bantustan – his wife deprived of the comfort of a husband and his children deprived of the love and discipline of a father, except for one month in every working year of his life. The migratory labour system not only undermines the whole fabric of African family life, it also brings other serious repercussions in its wake.

The rate of illegitimate births in the homelands has risen steeply. In the urban African townships it has reached very high proportions, more than 50 per cent of recorded births in some places. In the Western Province of the Cape, where the system is most intensively applied, miscegenation between African men and Coloured women is resulting in the birth of hundreds of illegitimate babies. All these children, often uncared for, as their mothers have to work to support them, are posing considerable social problems. Juvenile delinquency and crime are on the increase. Moreover, sociologists warn that restless, rootless masses of men separated from their families are the least responsible members of a community. The families in the homelands are often deserted as the migratory workers in the cities 'take up' with other women.

Economists have pointed out that the migratory labour system is costly and inefficient, that it is impossible to train men on the move, and that a modern industrial society requires a stable labour force of ever-more semi-skilled and skilled workers.

The Progressive Party is unequivocally opposed to the evil system of migratory labour – we aim to bring into being a stable rural African population and a permanently urbanized African population based on family life.

Critics of the Progressive Party have voiced strong objections to the removal of pass laws and influx control – it will lead, the objectors say, to an overwhelming movement of Africans from country to town with all the attendant social evils of overcrowding, of shanty towns and unemployment. But if it is really believed that the pass laws are effective, why the huge numbers who are arrested and convicted under these laws? For every one arrested, several have not been apprehended. It is surely better that these people be allowed legal residence in the White areas, permitted to sell their labour in the best market, than having them ever on the run from the police, or exploited in illegal employment at very low wages. Most important of all, the right to live a proper, secure family life is basic to any decent society.

There will obviously be some transitional difficulties with regard to urbanization – they are not insuperable. Houses can be built. Employment opportunities can be greatly increased. Sending hundreds of thousands of Africans to gaol every year for statutory pass offences, or leaving them to starve in the Bantustans, is in any case no solution of what is basically the problem of under-development and unemployment.

Economic development of the Bantustans – to which the Progressive Party is committed – will to some extent check the rural to urban influx. So, too, will the payment of a reasonable cash wage by White farmers employing African labourers. (The average wage was R83 per annum, plus wages in kind such as rations and use of land, according to the latest available agricultural census, 1964.) But the urbanization of the Africans is an inevitable consequence of the industrialization of South Africa.

The economic policy of the Progressive Party is based on the operation of the free enterprise system, together with recognition of the responsibility of the Government to use fiscal and monetary measures to regulate the rate of growth. We hold it to be the business of government to steer the economy between the twin dangers of inflation and deflation. Government responsibility also includes the provision of those essential services that private enterprise is unable to provide for the infrastructure of the economy.

The Progressive Party is strongly opposed, however, to the powers taken by the present Government to 'persuade' industry to move to the borders of the Bantustans for ideological reasons. Decentralization on an economic basis is one thing: decentralization to prevent more Africans from leaving the Bantustans to seek work is another. Thus the Physical Planning Act of 1967, which had as its main objective the granting of powers to the Minister of Planning to grant or refuse permits to entrepreneurs to expand or establish factories in existing White industrial areas, the decision to be based on the number of Africans to be employed, would be scrapped. So, too, the restrictions on the development of the Western Province of the Cape by attempts to reduce the number of Africans presently employed in that area in a vain effort to replace them with Coloured labour.

Job reservation, whereby the Minister may reserve certain occupations for the different racial groups would be dropped from the Industrial Conciliation Act. This provision is presently largely inoperable, many exemptions having been granted simply because there are not enough White hands to do the jobs reserved for them. It is estimated that only about three per cent of industrial occupations are affected by job reservation. Nevertheless, the Physical Planning Act and the job reservation provisions inhibit industrial development by engendering uncertainty among industrialists regarding future utilization of Black labour.

Far more potent in hindering the full use of manpower, however, are trade union restrictions and the conventional colour bar which restrict the acquisition of skill by and employment of African, Coloured and Asian workers. Africans are by law prohibited from belonging to registered trade unions. Thus, not only are the benefits of collective bargaining denied to them, but all closed-shop occupations are closed to them. Moreover, very few vocational training institutions operate for Africans. As at mid-1969, only 2 149 Africans were at vocational training schools.

Coloured people and Asians may belong to registered trade unions. Relatively few, however, are accepted as apprentices by the craft unions, except in the building and furniture trades. In 1969, of a total of 1 391 newly registered apprentices in the building industry, 54 per cent were Coloured and 5 per cent were Asians. In the furniture industry, out of 396 apprentices, 78 per cent were Coloured and 13 per cent Asian. But in the engineering trades, of 2 384 apprentices, only 3 per cent were Coloured and $\frac{1}{2}$ per cent Asian, and in the motor trade, of 1 702 apprentices, only 4,5 per cent were Coloured and 1,8 per cent Asian. In Government undertakings, only 6 apprentices were Black.[2]

It is in the semi-skilled machine operative jobs that Black workers have made the most headway – often against great opposition from White workers. The present crippling shortage of skilled and semi-skilled manpower is entirely artificial. It has developed because of the traditional South African pattern of considering skilled and semi-skilled work as the sole prerogative of the White man, while unskilled work is left to the Blacks, more particularly the African workers.

The economy of South Africa has become increasingly dependent on Black workers. At the end of 1970, the ratio between Black and White workers in the six major industrial sectors was nearly 5 to 1.

2. S. van der Horst, *Presidential Address, 1971*, S.A. Institute of Race Relations.

In mining and quarrying, it was more than 10 to 1; in manufacturing, 4 to 1; in construction 6 to 1. Agriculture is almost entirely dependent on African and Coloured labour. With the enormous expansion of manufacturing industry since World War II, the demand for skilled and semi-skilled workers has increased proportionately. Since the four million Whites are almost the entire source of skilled labour required to service the needs of 21 million people, wages have shot up, greatly increasing the costs of production and leading to serious inflation. Reluctantly, the craft unions have surrendered some jobs, through a process of fragmentation, permitting them to be taken over, at lower wages than previously, by Blacks. The process is known as 'de-skilling'. The jobs remaining in White hands usually carry an even higher wage after fragmentation.

Piecemeal, *ad hoc* ways of dealing with the country's most serious economic problem are clearly inadequate. Already industry and commerce are short of some 100 000 skilled workers. Only a determined and forthright change of policy will overcome the manpower shortage. The Progressive Party's policy is to abolish all statutory job reservation, as well as the conventional industrial colour bar. The Mines and Works Act of 1911, which precludes Black workers from all but unskilled work on the mines, will go, as well as the Native Building Workers' Act, which prohibits Africans from doing skilled building work in 'White' areas. We plan to educate and train Blacks for all semi-skilled and skilled jobs in industry and commerce. The rate for the job will be maintained to prevent undercutting of wages by employers hiring Black workers. It is planned to introduce minimum wages for all occupations, based on the regional cost of living. Trade union rights – basic to all modern industrial societies – will be extended to include all workers. Collective bargaining will thereafter reduce the inordinate disparity between unskilled and skilled wage levels that exists in South Africa, and which, unlike the pattern in most developing, industrial countries, has increased over the years.

The differential between skilled and unskilled wage rates in South Africa corresponds to 'White' wages and 'Non-White' wages. In 1945/6, average African earnings in manufacturing and construction were 25 per cent of those of Whites, average Coloured earnings were 42 per cent and Asian earnings 40 per cent of White. In 1970, African earnings in these industries were 17 per cent of White earnings, and Coloured and Asian, 26 per cent of White.[3] During the 12-month period ending September

3. *Ibid*, p. 13.

1970, the average wage of African workers in construction increased by R1 to R48 per month, while that of White workers increased by R25 to R319. During the same period the average wage of African workers in manufacturing rose by R3 to R52 per month while that of White workers increased by R27 to R300. In the gold mines the average earnings of White workers in 1948 were twelve times as much as the average cash earnings of Africans; by 1968 they were more than 17 times as much.[4]

The conventional colour bar will be combated by measures to prevent racial discrimination in the labour market. All efforts will be bent to re-educate White workers, long indoctrinated with the fear of Black competition, to the concept of an expanding economy wherein the widening of employment opportunities for the vast mass of unskilled Black workers will not be a threat to their own livelihood. On the contrary, this will result in greater productivity, an immensely bigger internal market, lower unit costs of production, all of which can only redound to the advantage of all workers, since the demand for goods and services of all kinds will increase too.

The 'traditional' different salary structures for the various races in State services – such as teachers, nurses, doctors, university staff – will be abolished. Until recently, a White, trained nurse earned twice as much as her Coloured or Asian colleague and nearly three times as much as an African trained nurse. A Coloured or Asian doctor earned three quarters, and an African doctor five eights of the salary of a White doctor. While a White professor at an 'ethnic' university could earn up to R8 700 per annum, a Coloured or Asian professor at the same university reached top salary level at R6 240, and an African professor at R5 520. Recent salary increases have increased the disparity of earnings between these professional employees of the State.

The Progressive Party considers discrimination in salary scales for services that require precisely the same training, qualifications and work, to be totally indefensible.

The implementation of the Party's economic and labour policies will stimulate economic growth, increase national income and eliminate the current high administrative costs involved in implementing racially discriminative legislation. We envisage the financing of a steadily expanding programme of pensions, health and welfare services, based on a national

4. F. Wilson, *Labour on the South African Gold Mines, 1936-1969,* Cambridge University Press, 1972.

contributory social security scheme, without the imposition of a means test. Need, and not colour, will be the criterion in the provision of social services from public funds. The gross disparity regarding pensions, disability grants, family allowances and other benefits presently provided by the State to the different racial groups, will be eliminated. (Maximum monthly social pensions at present granted to White persons are R38, for Coloured and Asian people about R18, and for Africans a little more than R5.)

With the goal of the elimination of racial discrimination in South Africa firmly set, the hostility of the African States would also subside. South Africa could assume her rightful place as the industrial workshop of the continent of Africa. Threats of boycotts would no longer harass exporters and our overseas markets would expand. The gradual decline in gold production necessitates a more important role being played by manufactured products as an earner of foreign exchange. This would be greatly assisted by the radical change in South Africa's racial policy as proposed by the Progressive Party. All in all, South Africa could look forward to an era of international co-operation, and of expansion and prosperity greater than ever before, for all our people.

NEITHER COMPULSORY SEGREGATION NOR COMPULSORY INTEGRATION

The Progressive Party believes that each citizen should be free to associate with whom he wishes, provided that he does not exercise his freedom in such a way as to interfere with that of others. The Progressive Party is opposed to compulsory segregation just as it is opposed to compulsory integration. It follows that the mass of legislation, which makes segregation compulsory, would be repealed. Social relationships should not be regulated by compulsion. They are best regulated by conventions of society and the attitude of individuals. Thus, the Progressive Party will repeal the Prohibition of Mixed Marriages Act and Section 16 of the Immorality Act, the section which makes sex relations between White and Black a criminal offence.

University autonomy will be restored and academic freedom to determine who shall be taught, what shall be taught and who shall teach will be decided by the universities. In principle, the Progressive Party is wholeheartedly in favour of multi-racial universities, believing it to be in the best interests of South Africa for our young people to associate with each other across the colour line.

The same holds good for sport. In principle we are in favour of multi-racial sport and of mixed teams chosen entirely on merit, representing South Africa at international events.

The Progressive Party wants non-segregated schools to be established in those areas where the integrated communities demand them. Segregated schools will continue to function as long as the communities demand them. And the same holds good for other public amenities and for residential areas. Integration will not be forced on communities: but no legislation will be valid that prohibits voluntary integration, such as the Group Areas Act and the Separate Amenities Act.

Considerable differences of opinion were voiced within the Party concerning some of the aspects of policy at the time when they were discussed and adopted. To expect unanimity on questions relating to the complex area of prejudice, its containment and resolution, would indeed be demanding the impossible, a position not yet attained in any country with a heterogeneous population. These differences have not been entirely resolved but members have reached a compromise on these currently thorny questions.

It is clear from the experience of other countries engaged in the endeavour to effect a just accommodation of differing racial groups, that racial prejudice may persist even when legal discrimination has been eliminated. But the law itself is educative and it has also been shown that when people engage in desegregated activities, this form of inter-action in pursuit of common ends acts as a solvent of prejudice. Recent research in South Africa suggests a close correlation between prejudice and social conformity, and that when social patterns change, intolerance decreases.

The trouble is that the present dispensation prevents White South Africans, who adjust without difficulty to integrated travel, accommodation and entertainment when they go abroad, from participating in desegregated activities in South Africa. The Government has made segregation an end in itself. Even voluntary welfare committees were by Government decree compelled to divide into separate racial compartments. Not only is segregation rigidly enforced, but racial intolerance is strengthened by inflaming White fears of swamping by the Black majority. The African man is stereotyped as the traditionalist of tribal society who poses a threat to what is called 'White' civilization, while the extent of cultural change brought about by the processes of modernization is played down.

South Africans have been conditioned to a stark 'either-or' approach instead of an appreciation of the gradualness of the processes of change. In regard to residence, for instance, the alternatives are represented as a choice between the manicured lawns of the most affluent White suburbs or submergence in environs as bleak as those of the poorest Black community. It is overlooked – or conveniently forgotten – that people everywhere associate in groups with common interests and that they voluntarily cluster in different areas on the basis of income, occupation and also frequently of ethnic, national and religious affiliation. The White worker is encouraged to regard the Black worker as a rival threatening his own job. It is the caricature of integration, as presented by the advocates of the status quo, that keeps White South Africa captive to its fears and intolerance. The Progressive Party is convinced that once new social patterns of integrated activities, pioneered in the first instance by people of liberal view, are brought into being, integrated schools, residential areas and public amenities will no longer be the contentious issues they are today; for the whole climate of opinion will have changed in South Africa.

The Progressive Party does not claim to have all the answers to the South African racial problem. It does, however, lay claim to a direction of policy which is in keeping with the thinking of the Western world, and which will ensure a more just society in South Africa. Neither of the two major political parties, the National Party or the United Party, can make such a claim. Both are bent on maintaining the status quo of White supremacy – the Government party in what it calls the 'White' Republic, i.e. those parts of the country which exclude the African areas, and the United Party over the entire Republic.

The National Party's concept of separate development has, in theory, an ethical background. It offers the Africans political rights in self-governing, and possibly even ultimately independent states. At present these areas have at best local government powers, are almost entirely dependent financially on the White Republican Government, and can pass no law unless approved by the White Republican Government. In exchange, those Africans living in the 'White' Republic are considered as temporary sojourners only, with no political rights whatsoever. The Progressive Party rejects this concept as being completely unrealistic. The Bantustans or homelands which constitute some 13 per cent of the land area of the Republic, consist of over 81 fragmented areas, only one of which, the Transkei, is a large continuous area. They are not economically viable, nor can they become so. Many years of striving after separate development has left South Africa virtually in the same demographic situation as before – there are many more Africans living in the 'White' areas than the Bantustans – some eight million in the cities and on the 'White' farms, as against under seven million in the homelands. Hundreds of thousands of Africans were born in the White areas, and have never set foot in the homelands, where employment opportunities can never hope to compete with those offered in the White industrial areas. It is palpably absurd to expect these Africans to accept forever, political rights where they do not live, as a *quid pro quo* for the deprivation of rights where they do live, where very many of them were born and where they will die. The physical presence of millions of Africans in 'White' South Africa is a fact, an ineluctable fact, now and in the future. It should be accepted as such, not veiled by the myth of separate development.

WEAKNESSES IN NATIONAL AND UNITED PARTY POLICIES

The National Party's policy towards the two million Coloured people and the half million Asians is equivocal to say the least. Their paths towards separate development do not lead to any homelands, only to separate residential and trading areas inside the 'White' Republic, areas into which thousands of families have been moved through the instrument of the Group Areas Act. This uprooting of settled communities has led to bitter resentment among the people concerned. The Coloured people of the Cape Province were deprived first of their common roll franchise, and more recently of their tiny communal, White representation in the Republican Parliament. In its place came the Coloured Persons Representative Council, consisting of Coloured members elected on a common roll, on a universal suffrage basis throughout the country, and of Government-nominated members. It, too, exercises limited functions of local government, is entirely dependent financially on the White Parliament, and may pass laws only with the approval of that Parliament.

The Asians, who never enjoyed any franchise, have only a nominated council with no legislative powers whatsoever. Asians and Coloured people, despite separate development, remain irrevocably part and parcel of multi-racial South Africa, economically and socially, and they should be so politically too.

The United Party, while accepting the fact of one multi-racial Republic, does not accept the consequences thereof. It is wedded to 'White leadership', and its proposals for communal franchise on a very limited basis in a 'Race Federation' for Africans, Coloured people and Asians, are designed to preserve White supremacy over the entire Republic, Bantustans included. It will give the different racial groups certain powers of local government in their own residential areas. But the political power structure of the Central Government will remain firmly in White hands, with eight elected White representatives for the Africans in the House of Assembly, and two in the Senate, six elected representatives for the Coloured people (who may be Coloured) in the House and two in the Senate, and two elected White representatives in the House and one in the Senate for the Asians. Its economic policy is equivocal, for while condemning job reservation on the one hand, it pronounces its adherence to and maintenance of the traditional industrial colour bar on the other. It supports in principle all the cornerstones of apartheid – separate amenities, the Group Areas Act, influx control and the pass laws, though it says it will administer such measures more leniently.

Neither the National Party nor the United Party will in fact be able to govern without measures that infringe the rule of law, for the political systems they adhere to exclude the vast majority of the population from any meaningful say in the laws that control their lives.

The Progressive Party is well aware of the difficult task it has to convince the White electorate of the soundness of its policies. The most telling factor is the intense fear of handing any meaningful political say to Blacks. Events in the rest of Africa over the past two decades have strengthened this fear.

The fact that there are significant differences between South Africa and the other states in Africa is ignored. The Progressive Party must emphasize over and over again that South Africa is the only state in Africa where there is (or ever was) a large permanently settled White population. That Whites are indispensable for the continued development of South Africa's resources is accepted by the overwhelming majority of the Black people. Black leaders, before their political movements were banned and it was still possible for them to speak out, demanded equal opportunities for participation with Whites, not their expulsion. There is, even at this late stage, reason to believe that the Black majority is prepared to negotiate reasonable adjustments. The 'give them a finger and they take an arm' argument just does not hold for South Africa. Secondly, the Africans in the Republic are educationally more advanced, more industrialized and urbanized than are Africans elsewhere. The Africans in

South Africa are well aware of the advantages a modern industrial economy can confer. They have clearly expressed their commitment to further economic development.

And thirdly, South Africa, unlike most other states in Africa, has the material resources to maintain and improve the standard of living of all her inhabitants. Poverty, surely, has been the greatest ally of instability in Africa.

Despite the difficulties in convincing the White electorate of the urgent need to make the necessary adjustments, from a position of strength, the Progressive Party has every intention of continuing on its chosen path. It already represents a considerable body of enlightened opinion in South Africa. It has every hope that changing circumstances and economic pressures inside South Africa will enhance its chances of returning more representatives to our public forums in the future. To the Africans, Coloured people and Asians living in the Republic of South Africa, acceptance by the White electorate of the policy of the Progressive Party certainly would present the most hopeful augury of peaceful change in South Africa.

The Case for a Common Society in South Africa

Alan Paton and A. S. Mathews

Alan Paton is one of South Africa's best-known authors. His book, Cry the Beloved Country, *has won him international acclaim. For many years leader of the South African Liberal Party, he is still adamant in his opposition to the Government's race policies. Mr Paton has travelled widely abroad and has written numerous articles on South African issues. Doctor Mathews shares many of Mr Paton's views. A brilliant legal academician, he is at present Professor and Head of the Department of Law at the University of Natal, Durban.*

In this paper[1] attention will be directed first towards the meaning of the expression 'common society'. Thereafter the obstacles to the achievement of a common society in South Africa will be examined. Finally, the problem of transition from the present political arrangements to those of the common society will receive attention.

THE MEANING OF THE EXPRESSION 'COMMON SOCIETY'

In the first place advocates of the common society see South Africa as a single political unit, both now and in the future. The starting-point of the solution of South Africa's problems, particularly the problems produced by the racial diversity of its people, is the acceptance of the fact that the racial groups in South Africa are irrevocably bound up in a common destiny which cannot now be undone. The population distribution and

1. Presented at a meeting of the Political Commission of SPRO-CAS (Study Project on Christianity in an Apartheid Society). This project was initiated by, and organized under the aegis of the South African Council of Churches and the Christian Institute of Southern Africa. SPRO-CAS was launched in 1970 with a view to analysing apartheid in terms of Christian principles and formulating recommendations aimed at the creation of a non-apartheid social order in South Africa.

the involvement of all races in a single dynamic economy are the two main factors which have combined to produce this irreversible common destiny. Though small fragments of the territory of South Africa may break off and become independent (as envisaged under the policy of separate development) the essentially unitary nature of the community will remain unaffected. While supporters of separate development declare that the correct response to diversity is the creation of separate, independent and (presumably) racially homogeneous states, the advocates of the common society argue that it is unrealistic in South Africa to seek answers to the problem of diversity in anything but a single political jurisdiction.

Supporters of the common society believe that the political arrangements within that single jurisdiction must be of a kind which is commonly labelled 'liberal-democratic'. What precisely is meant by government in the liberal-democratic tradition? Such a society (which may be called a free society) may be looked at in two ways: It may be characterized by the *processes* of government operative within it or by the *ends* (or ideals) towards which government is directed. While the procedural and substantive features of the free society are obviously related and interdependent, separate consideration of each will facilitate the task of spelling out more precisely the meaning of a liberal-democracy or free society.

Considering first the methods of government in a free society, the following characteristics stand out: Representative institutions, individual and civil liberties, constitutionalism, division and decentralization of powers, pluralism and piecemeal planning. Each of these features requires a brief elaboration.

Representative Institutions. The principle of government by consent is realized in the free society by a system providing for the free election of representatives within a democratic framework which makes it probable that there will be a regular change of government – a feature which is central in any conception of a free society. The fact that many people today feel alienated even where representative institutions are operative does not require the abandonment of such institutions. The answer to the problem of alienation seems to lie in a wider devolution of power and in the participation in the development of power centres other than the state (see below under pluralism). The latter activity should not be seen as a substitute for representative government in its present form but rather as complementary to it.

Personal and Civil Liberties. Representative institutions would be pointless unless supported by a system of personal and civil liberties enabling the people to acquire information, to debate the virtues and vices of candidates and policies and to organize freely for the advancement of their views. Individual and civil liberties are therefore as much essential instruments for the operation of representative government as they are claims of the individual citizen.

Constitutionalism. The principle of constitutionalism implies that governments are accountable to the people and that they are therefore subject to a series of restraints to ensure that power is not abused. Constitutionalism incorporates the notion of the Rule of Law which is one of the most important principles of restraint upon government in the Western world. The Rule of Law subjects the government itself to law and to independent check on its actions by the judicial arm.

Division and Decentralization of Power. In free societies power is divided among various arms of government each of which, to a greater or lesser extent, functions as a check upon the others. Though it is now fashionable to criticize the doctrine of the separation of powers on the ground that no function inherently belongs to any one branch of government, it nevertheless remains a vital feature of government in the liberal-democratic tradition.[2] The existence of a separate and independent judiciary is of special importance. The distribution of power between different levels of government – national, regional and local – is another method of avoiding that concentration of power which is a feature of authoritarian or totalitarian regimes.

Pluralism. In the free society institutional orders other than the state are recognized and are accorded a certain measure of independence and autonomy. Whereas under totalitarianism independent groups barely exist (or if they do are merely instruments of the ruling party), in open societies a variety of interest groups enrich the social life and act as countervailing forms of power. The pluralism which is a feature of the free society incorporates a measure of freedom for groups with economic or business interests. It follows that full-scale socialism is not compatible with that kind of society.

Piecemeal Planning. Because it is committed to recognize groups other than the state and also respect the interests of the individual (see below), the free society must implement its social programmes by *ad hoc* planning.

2. See, for example, M.J.C. Vile in *Constitutionalism and the Separation of Powers*, Oxford, 1967.

In other words, the implementation of policy will follow the empiricist tradition in terms of which programmes are submitted to the people for debate and criticism and are put to the test of actual experience. This contrasts with totalitarian utopian planning in which the validity of plans is decided *a priori* and individual and group interests overridden.

Turning from the methods of government in the liberal-democratic tradition, we now focus briefly on the goals of such societies. These may be discussed under the headings of negative freedom, positive freedom and equality.

Negative and Positive Freedom. The recognition of individual freedom in Western democracies is an acceptance of the individual's claim to be free in two senses – in the negative sense (freedom from) and in the positive sense (freedom to). A person enjoys negative freedom when he is free to do as he pleases within a certain area. Within the confines of the laws' restrictions the individual has the right to act without interference or coercion. Negative freedom is a vital aspect of liberty; Justice Brandeis[3] has described it as 'the right to be left alone – the most comprehensive of rights and the right most valued by civilized man'. In constitutional terms negative liberty takes the form of the fundamental freedoms – the freedoms of the person and of conscience, expression and association. If these freedoms are to be effective they should be guaranteed by the law. They have been strengthened in liberal legal systems by the principle that a man may do everything that the law does not forbid – hence negative freedom is sometimes called juridical freedom.

Positive freedom implies the power or ability to play a determinative role in shaping the conditions in which one lives. In the political sense, this means that a man is free when he can influence 'the aims and methods of political power'. Positive freedom is institutionalized in Western democracies in the form of representative government. Though representative institutions in their present form are in need of much improvement so as to involve citizens more meaningfully in political decision-making, they are an essential part of what we mean by the free society and cannot be dispensed with.

Since positive freedom implies the power to determine (to a greater or lesser extent) the destiny of others, the two freedoms appear to be in conflict. Positive political power may be used to limit or destroy negative

3. *Olmestead v. United States,* 277 U.S. 438 (1928) at 478.

liberty. However, they are not necessarily in conflict. Positive freedom can equally be used to preserve negative liberty; in fact, negative liberty will very likely be lost unless the citizens actively involve themselves in politics to preserve it. Thus Neumann[4] has said:

> 'Whether or not one believes political power is alien to man, it determines his life to an ever increasing extent; thus the need for participation in its formation is imperative even for those who prefer the cultivation of individual contemplation.'

Moreover, it is only in their extreme application that positive and negative freedom seem to be opposites. In the free society they are balanced against each other and each is permitted a certain measure of recognition.

Equality. There is no doubt that equality is an ideal of the free society but there is much confusion as to what it means. At the outset it must be stated that equality is not meant to be a 'description of fact' but rather a 'prescription or policy of treating men'.[5] Secondly, it is not a policy which demands that men be treated equally in all respects. What is a basic principle in liberal-democracies is that all are entitled to identical treatment in respect of political rights, personal and civil liberties and the impartial administration of justice. Distinctions based on race, religion, sex or creed are not permitted to determine the grant or refusal of such rights. However, the principle of equality is usually carried beyond this limited demand to incorporate a claim for social and economic equality.

It is at this point that the real difficulties begin because a policy of enforcing equality will inevitably limit freedom – 'The passion for equality made vain the hope for freedom.' The only solution to this dilemma is to recognize that equality, like the other values or goals of the free society, has to be balanced against other ends; it must be pursued with a certain amount of restraint and respect for other fundamentals. Where the balance is struck cannot be stated with mathematical precision. However, it should be stated that at the very least all are entitled in a free society to the necessities of life without which other claims would be meaningless.

The Common Society Defined. By way of summary we may therefore

4. F. Neumann: *The Democratic and the Authoritarian State,* Free Press, New York, 1966, p. 185.

5. Sidney Hook: *Political Power and Personal Freedom,* Criterion Books, New York, 1959, p. 38.

define the common society as a single political unit in which there is personal and political liberty and in which power is divided and decentralized and subjected to the Rule of Law.

THE OBSTACLES IN SOUTH AFRICA TO THE ACHIEVEMENT OF A LIBERAL-DEMOCRACY

All that has been attempted up to this point is the clarification of the common society approach. Whether the common society can realistically be advocated in South Africa is another matter. Advocates of the common society have not on the whole undertaken a hard-headed appraisal of the viability of free institutions in the South African context. An appraisal of that kind would have to recognize the following serious obstacles to the proper functioning of democratic institutions:

(a) The racial diversity in the Republic. Mill thought that representative institutions can only work where state boundaries coincide with national boundaries. Though racial and religious differences have not always prevented the operation of free institutions (Switzerland, Canada) it is not clear whether there is at present sufficient unity in South Africa to ensure that democratic procedures will be allowed to function. Another paper has shown that the mere introduction of the whole panoply of democratic liberties and constitutional guarantees is in itself no guarantee that there will be sufficient unity and loyalty to preserve them against the pressures of sectional interest.

(b) Over and above the racial distinctions, there are vast differences in the educational, economic and social levels of the various race groups. These distinctions, which run along racial lines, make the racial diversity a more dangerous and explosive factor.

(c) The common society lacks adequate support among the various groups that make up the population. Though there is a strong liberal tradition in the country, it is at present muted. The great majority of the White population prefers to maintain the present system of domination even if for some it is to be tempered by the limited concessions inherent in the Bantustan policy. The attitude of the Non-Whites to the common society is not really known.

The factors set out in (a), (b) and (c) above are all related. For instance, social and economic inequality exacerbates racial hostility and suspicion.

This in turn hardens the feelings of all groups towards the common society. The key to removal of the obstacles appears to lie in the second factor (b). The removal of economic and social inequality will lessen fear and suspicion which in turn is likely to strengthen support for the common society.

While the common society programme has to overcome the obstacles described above, it is insufficiently recognized that there are a number of favourable factors. The chief of these is a highly developed economy which is not only a stabilizing factor in itself but which can also generate other conditions upon which free institutions depend. Some of the other prerequisites which can be created are a strong middle class amongst all groups, mass education and a healthy pluralism incorporating the growth of interest groups which *cut across colour lines.* Under present policies the possibilities which the economy promises for creating the foundations of a stable common society are being squandered. In fact, the policy of apartheid is destroying forces favourable to the common society and thereby *creating* its own justification.

THE TRANSITION FROM APARTHEID TO THE COMMON SOCIETY

The assumption of many advocates of the common society was that it could be legislated into existence. It must now be frankly recognized that the institutions of the open society will not flourish unless the social conditions are favourable and that South Africa faces the mammoth task of creating the necessary social foundation for democratic institutions. Advocates of the common society would be more realistic if they accepted the following propositions as the basis of their attitude to bringing about change:

1. That initially economic and social change is more important than the extension of political rights. Political change should come as a consequence of enhanced economic and social status. As Emerson has said, there should be a coincidence between the rise of new elements to social power and access to the ballot box.
2. That the aim of the common society programme is not to produce a cultural melting pot. Some provision ought to be made for separate cultural evolution for those who desire it. This might include the right of cultural groups to control education, at least at the primary and secondary levels. A loose federal structure in which cultural groups could enjoy a large measure of local autonomy also seems desirable.

3. That in a period of change there will have to be a judicious mixture of liberalization and control. In other words, personal and civil liberties and the Rule of Law can receive only qualified recognition whilst power shifts are taking place. Measures of control which would offend the liberal tradition in fully democratic societies will also certainly be necessary as temporary expedients. Instead of demanding the full panoply of civil liberties and the Rule of Law, advocates of the common society should rather work for their gradual implementation as conditions become more favourable.

4. That Bantustan policy is a 'fact of life' at present and should (on its positive side) be accepted as a policy which might facilitate evolution towards democratic institutions. Its chief value appears to lie in its potential for lessening White fears and satisfying *some* Black aspirations. This potential of the policy for bringing about a more relaxed relationship between the races should be exploited because in such an atmosphere concessions to Non-Whites in the 'White' areas could come about. Separate Black institutions will also be useful as countervailing forms of power capable of wringing concessions from the present controllers of government in South Africa. It follows from what has already been said that the emphasis should initially be upon economic and social concessions to Non-Whites which, if granted, will prepare the ground for political changes.

The foregoing propositions have little relevance in a country where the government is determined not to liberalize policy. In other words, there seems little point in discussing the problems of transition when all the power and resources of government are being employed to stop it from happening. Nevertheless, it may be useful to discuss the movement towards a common society for two reasons: Firstly, it should be kept alive as a viable option when change is eventually forced upon society. Secondly, a more realistically argued case for the common society may provoke some change in attitudes which are at present fixed and rigid.

Race Relations and the South African Economy

Non-Whites in the South African Economy

G. M. E. Leistner

The author is widely known for his authoritative publications on economic development in Sub-Saharan Africa in general and on South Africa in particular. Born in Leipzig, Germany, the son of a missionary, Professor Leistner has studied at the Universities of South Africa, Pretoria and Stellenbosch. He is at present attached to the Department of Economics at the University of South Africa, and is an expert on race relations in the economic context.

Economic factors are exercising a crucial – perhaps even a critical – influence in the interplay of forces shaping South Africa's destiny. The following exposition focuses on those aspects of the economy where the ethnic heterogeneity of the population is particularly noticeable. Our somewhat single-minded concern with the economic dimension of what is in fact a multi-dimensional complex may help to show that South African realities entail far more than the search for a just and stable political order.

SOUTH AFRICA'S ECONOMIC AND DEMOGRAPHIC STRUCTURE

1. *Economic Structure*

Of the 44 independent states in Africa only the Republic of South Africa disposes of a modern and industrially diversified economy. The South African population amounts to less than six per cent of that of total Africa, but it accounts for about one quarter of the total Gross National Product, 90 per cent of the steel and 63 per cent of the electricity produced in Africa. Whereas in the rest of Africa the real income per head of the population increases annually by only 1,1 per cent and is even decreasing in many countries,[1] South Africa shows a growth rate of 3,5 per cent.[2]

In view of these and similar facts it is understandable that South Africa's problems of development policy are often judged by criteria which are appropriate to the highly industrialized countries of Western Europe or North America. However, anyone familiar with the development problems of pre-industrial and infant-industrial countries, recognizes in the South African situation the socio-economic *dualism* characteristic of the early stages of modern economic development.

Development policies in poor countries seek to eliminate as rapidly as possible the traditional sector in favour of the modern sector. The entire structure of social and economic life is to be modernized. However, the elimination of dualism constitutes a substantially more difficult problem than the mere extension of markets, the achievement of higher savings and investment ratios, industrialization and the like. Economic activities depend on human factors – psychological, cultural, religious, etc. – which cannot be manipulated or replaced at will.

Despite South Africa's high overall level of development it has not yet eliminated this dualism as far as the Bantu are concerned. Geographically, the greater part of the Republic is being used in accordance with modern economic and technological practices. Only about 12 per cent of the total surface area is occupied by the Bantu areas, the agricultural economy whereof is mainly directed at self-sufficiency. Economically the Bantu population largely has been drawn into modern production by wage labour. A substantial number of Bantus are orientated towards modern Western consumer habits, especially in the towns. The majority is still strongly influenced by social views and behaviour patterns dating from pre-industrial eras and conflicting with the claims of the modern market economy. So far only a few have truly abandoned traditional religious and other social concepts and values and replaced them by Western norms. This explains why, with very few exceptions, Bantu play no creative and dynamic role in modern economic activities and technology. If one compares the economic achievements of South African Indians and Coloureds with those of our Bantu, there can be little doubt that cultural rather than political factors must be primarily responsible

1. See United Nations Economic Commission for Africa, *A Survey of Economic Conditions in Africa, 1967,* New York 1969. (Sales No. E.68.II.K4) pp. 1-17.

2. The Gross Domestic Product at constant prices rose by 5,84 per cent annually, between 1960 and 1968, the population by 2,34 per cent p.a.

for the latter group's relatively passive role. Several figures quoted below illustrate this point.

The modern economic history of South Africa began about one hundred years ago with the discovery of diamonds and gold. An important manufacturing industry did not originate before the nineteen thirties and it experienced its real growth during the Second World War and especially thereafter. In 1911 manufacturing and construction accounted for only 5,6 per cent of the Gross Domestic Product (GDP), compared with a contribution from the mining sector of 27,6 per cent and agriculture's 21,0 per cent. In 1969 the contribution of manufacturing and construction to the GDP amounted to 29,8 per cent, whereas mining and agriculture had fallen to 11,7 per cent and 10,0 per cent respectively.[3]

Even though mining and agriculture have declined in relative importance, they are still of crucial importance. In 1967 and 1968 exports of agricultural products and minerals amounted to approximately 70 per cent of the total export of goods, gold included. Manufactured products account only for the remaining 30 per cent of total exports.

What is more, our manufacturing industry needs more foreign exchange to pay for imports of materials, machinery, spares, etc., as well as in respect of licence fees and patent rights, than it provides through exports. Gold mining, on the other hand, is a substantial net contributor of foreign exchange and helps to shield South Africa from balance of payments crises similar to those experienced by almost all young industrial countries.

Hence it is a vital question for how long gold output can be maintained at its present level of around 30 million troy ounces a year. According to expert estimates, production will have virtually ceased by the end of the century, but new discoveries as well as the industry's ceaseless search for cost-saving technological improvements may yet put the pessimists in the wrong, as so often before in the history of South African mining. Eventually other mining products such as chromium, vanadium, tungsten, iron ore, tantalite and platinum, processed as far as possible, are bound to take over the role of gold. Nevertheless, it is a major aim of South African economic policy to restrain price and wage increases to the greatest possible extent because every rise in production costs reduces the amount of auri-

3. Figures for 1969 are based on provisional estimates by the S.A. Reserve Bank; see S.A. Reserve Bank, *Quarterly Bulletin*, June 1971, p. 5-68. Figures for 1911, see Republic of South Africa, Department of Statistics, *Statistical News Release* No. P.12, 19 March, 1969.

ferous ore which can be profitably mined. Put in another way, wage and other cost increases that are not compensated for by higher productivity shorten the life of the gold mines and are thus detrimental to the national economy.

It is to be expected that for a considerable time to come mining and agriculture will play a vital role in the South African economy. But already at the present time, and even more so in the future, the population increase of the Republic must be absorbed into manufacturing and the service industries. The growth of manufacturing in a market economy leads to an appropriate development of the necessary service establishments more or less automatically. Industrial development, on the other hand, may be compared to a plant which needs the right climate, suitable soil and good care if it is to flourish. This is illustrated by experience in all less-developed countries, and South Africa's industrialization is by no means due to windfalls, but is largely the result of a sound and far-sighted economic policy.

The future development of the South African factory industry will increasingly have to contend with two impediments, that is, firstly, the relatively small domestic market and, secondly, the shortage of skilled labour. The two resulting tasks, i.e. the widening of markets and greater integration of the Bantu into the market economy, are closely interdependent.

The rapid development of modern technology, together with the world-wide integration of trade, necessitates ever larger, highly mechanized or even automated production plants, whose establishment requires ever heavier capital investments but which lower production costs per unit relatively or absolutely. Enterprises which do not attain a substantial minimum output are unable to compete. In many respects South Africa's domestic market is too small to enable local industry to produce and sell such large quantities as would be required to compete at world prices.

It is true that the population of the Republic numbers about 22 million, but the Bantu's purchasing power is relatively small and, if one takes the purchasing power of White South Africans as a yardstick, these 22 million are equal to only six million Whites. If the manufacturing industry is to produce more cheaply under these circumstances, its sales abroad must be expanded accordingly. Failing this, it must be protected in the home market by high import tariffs. At present this is largely the situation of

South African industry, with the exception of a few highly successful exporting enterprises.

However, protective tariffs tend to foster inefficiency, and inefficiency means that the national product does not grow as fast as it could. If the protective tariffs were simply to be abolished, many enterprises would be forced to close down and dismiss their employees. Hence the central issue is how to make industry competitive by expanding local as well as foreign markets. The home market can grow chiefly through an increase in the purchasing power of the Bantu. Their purchasing power, in turn, is influenced decisively by the efficient use of Bantu labour, and the lower production costs are, the better are the prospects for opening up markets abroad. In brief, rational use of the as yet insufficiently used productive potential of the Bantu is an essential prerequisite for future economic progress.

2. *Demographic Structure*

According to the census taken in 1970, the population of the Republic numbered 21,4 million. Of these, about one-sixth were Whites, one-tenth Coloureds, three per cent Asiatics and no less than 70 per cent Bantu. The comparative figures presented in Table 1[4] show that these ratios have changed but little during the past seven decades. At the beginning of the century the total population was 5,2 million, i.e. only little more than one-quarter of the present 22 million.

There are, however, signs that in the coming decades the ratio will become increasingly unfavourable for the Whites. Whereas in 1969, for instance, the average birth rate of Whites was 24,0 per 1000 of the group, the corresponding figure for Coloureds was 41,0 and for Asiatics 37,8 per 1000. Taking death rates into consideration, the annual natural growth rates are the following : Whites 1,53 per cent, Coloureds 2,64 per cent and Asiatics 3,06 per cent.[5] A growth rate of 2,6 per cent annually may seem low. However, a population growing by 2,5 per cent annually doubles itself in about 28 years; with a growth rate of 3 per cent only 23 years are needed.

Thus far growth rates for the Bantu population have not been calcu-

4. Tables 1-12 appear at the end of this chapter.

5. Official information quoted in *Survey of Race Relations in South Africa, 1970,* compiled by M. Horrell, Johannesburg, South African Institute of Race Relations, 1971, p. 25.

lated reliably. Census figures indicate a rate of 3,37 per cent. About 18 years ago the Tomlinson Commission estimated the South African Bantu population at 21,4 million in the year 2000. The current official forecast is nearly 28 million (see Table 3). On the basis of present indications one may assume, however, that in 30 years time there will be about 40 million Bantu in the Republic, and even higher figures are being mentioned.

Amongst others, this rapid growth is responsible for a relatively high percentage of young persons in the total population and a corresponding share of economically unproductive people who must be fed, clothed, cared for and above all educated by a relatively small number of economically active people. Although beneficial for some branches of industry, a situation like this burdens the national economy (and this in fact is one of the biggest problems of many less-developed countries).

Concurrently with the industrialization of South Africa a rapid urbanization of all population groups took place. Looking at Table 2, it is interesting to note that the number of urban dwellers has more than doubled during the two post-war decades and that in 1970 already about one-third of all Bantu dwelt in urban areas. In view of present tendencies it is clear that in future the Bantu will have to become urban dwellers at an even more rapid rate. The question is only what percentage will be in towns in their homelands.

THE NON-WHITE POPULATION GROUPS IN THE ECONOMY

1. *Labour*

At the end of 1969 about 7,15 million South Africans belonged to the economically active age groups of 15 years and over. Details were as follows:

Whites	1 438 000
Coloureds	692 000
Asiatics	157 000
Bantu	4 860 000
Total	7 147 000

The latest available sectoral division of the total economically active population is that for 1960 when 16,8 per cent were employed in the secondary sector and 34,5 per cent in the tertiary sector. But whereas in highly developed countries only about 5 to 10 per cent of the economically active population is occupied in agriculture, the figure for South Africa was about 30 per cent in 1960. If, however, the Bantu population is excluded, the percentage falls to 9,4. On the other hand about 37 per cent of all Bantu were occupied in agriculture, partly in Bantu homelands and partly on White-owned farms.

Here the dualism mentioned earlier shows itself clearly. Whereas practically all the Whites, Coloureds and Asiatics are employed in the market economy, a substantial percentage of the Bantu still remain in the subsistence economy (in which also an appreciable portion of Bantu living on White farms must be included). The percentage of 37 in agriculture indicates the relative economic backwardness of the Bantu vis-à-vis the other population groups. At the same time, however, it also underlines the extent to which South African Bantu are ahead of the inhabitants of the rest of Africa where 80 per cent and more of the total population depend on field and animal husbandry.

The Bantu's economic development must, to a considerable extent, entail a departure from agriculture and their absorption into the secondary and tertiary sectors. The report of the Tomlinson Commission (published in 1955) states that about 300 000 families, i.e. more than 40 per cent of the inhabitants of Bantu homelands, would have to leave agriculture and move into towns.[6] No substantial increase in employment is to be expected in mining, rather a decrease, and modernization of White farms necessarily implies a saving of labour. This underlines the importance of a growing secondary sector for healthy economic (and hence also social and political) development.

As the figures in Table 5 show, the numbers of Bantu workers in secondary industry have risen after World War II from 182 000 to 609 000, i.e. more than threefold; in construction the increase was eightfold (from 26 000 to 237 000). Between 1960 and 1970, the level of Bantu employment in the secondary sector increased by more than 90 per cent. During the period 1960-1969 there was an increase of 56 per cent in central government service, where no less than one half of all employees are Bantu. Everywhere (provincial administrations excepted) the relative share of Whites is receding in favour of Non-Whites. This is especially noticeable in

6. Union of South Africa, *Summary of the Report of the Commission for the socio-economic development of the Bantu areas within the Union of South Africa* (the Tomlinson Commission), Pretoria, Government Printer, 1955 (U.G. 61/1955), p. 145. par. 5 and p. 49, Table 2.

manufacturing where Whites decreased from about one-third of all employees at the end of the war to one-fourth in 1969. In individual branches of industry, such as textiles, the changes are still more striking.

Few useful figures exist in respect of the distribution according to occupational groups. The 1960 census is the latest source from which a reasonably complete picture emerges. The percentage of persons in the group 'professional, technical and managerial' was the following (expressed as percentages of economically active persons in the respective groups): Whites 18,5 per cent, Coloureds 3,7 per cent, Asiatics 13,2 per cent, Bantu 1,7 per cent, total population 5,5 per cent.[7] The 205 000 persons in the category of 'professional, technical and related' in 1960 were distributed as follows: 67,1 per cent Whites, 6,8 per cent Coloureds, 2,4 per cent Asiatics and 23,6 per cent Bantu.

Whites fill the greater part of the more responsible posts in business, administration, health services, etc. However, as the above-quoted figures show, it is quite erroneous to believe that the other population groups comprise only unskilled or semi-skilled labourers. Those enumerated in the 1960 census as 'labourer', i.e. unskilled worker, represented the following percentages of all economically active males in the respective population groups: Asiatics 29,8 per cent, Coloureds 53,6 per cent, Bantu 67,4 per cent, Whites 15,6 per cent.

Even these percentages do not give an exact picture, for in fact very many persons described as 'labourer' perform activities which require appreciable experience, skill and responsibility. This applies above all to manufacturing where the shortage of skilled labour increasingly necessitates the 'splitting' of certain operations. These may then be performed by, say, three semi-skilled persons instead of one skilled worker. Thus one finds that, in practice, official policies and regulations are often ignored; and apart from this, any classification according to degrees of skill is very difficult. This should be borne in mind in interpreting the published figures concerning the occupational pattern of the Bantu.

The wage structure, especially the appreciable differences between the average incomes of Whites and Bantu, are often quoted as a typical example of racial discrimination. A few figures on average earnings in 1969 are shown in Table 7. These figures are unsatisfactory because they are averages which hide a wide range of actual individual earnings in respect of

7. See Muriel Horrell (comp.), *Survey of Race Relations in South Africa, 1969*, Johannesburg, South African Institute of Race Relations, 1970, pp. 86-87.

each of the four main population groups. It appears that, roughly, Coloureds and Asiatics earn on the average two or three times as much as Bantu. The ratio of Bantu to White is about one to five.

Although the average cash earnings of Bantu in the secondary sector have risen by about 85 per cent during the past 10 to 15 years, the ratio of one to five mentioned above has not changed. According to some calculations, the real income of Bantu (i.e. income after elimination of increases in the general price level) has risen more slowly than that of Whites during recent years. One also has to bear in mind that even at equal rates of growth, say two per cent annually, the absolute difference must become ever larger when growth is based on unequal initial earnings.[8]

In this regard one has to appreciate the important role played by the supply of and demand for labour and – closely connected herewith – the productivity of labour in determining wages. Bantu labour, local as well as foreign, presents a practically unlimited supply. This is a situation which typically exists in less-developed countries and entails the availability of unlimited numbers of unskilled labourers at wage rates at about the same level as the value of income in kind earned by workers in the subsistence sector. When over and above that the subsistence sector is experiencing heavy population pressure, workers tend to offer their services at any wage that ensures physical survival. Faced by an abundant supply of unskilled labour, the employer has little incentive to use this production factor efficiently. This means low productivity and correspondingly low pay. The situation would change dramatically if all of a sudden the number of unskilled Bantu workers were to decrease substantially.

This, however, is only a partial explanation of the relatively low level of Bantu wages. It is illuminating to imagine what would happen if the majority of the available Bantu workers were not only well qualified professionally and educationally but also had the same will to work and the

8. Some comparative figures may help to put the ratios mentioned in the text into better perspective. The average earnings of Whites bore the following ratio to those of Blacks:

Country	*Year*	*Manufacturing*	*Construction*
South Africa	1965/66	5,3:1	5,6:1
Ghana	1963	10,4:1	12,3:1
Rhodesia	1965	6,9:1	8,4:1
Uganda	1964	7,1:1	8,8:1
Zambia	1965	6,4:1	10,9:1

(*Compiled from various sources*)

same attitude towards material progress as the majority of West European or North American workers. Employers would face an entirely different situation, for with an almost unlimited supply of such labour the national product would rise so fast that Bantu earnings would soon approach those of Whites. (The development of the Japanese labour market comes to mind in this regard.)

Explanations such as the foregoing are commonly countered by the argument that it is government policy which prevents the Bantu from obtaining the professional and other knowledge which would raise their productivity. If there were actually no schools, universities, technical colleges and other training institutions for the Bantu this argument would be more plausible. However, even the few facts on education quoted below, indicate that discrimination cannot possibly be a sufficient explanation for the relative economic backwardness of the Bantu. Decisive impediments such as the Bantu's traditional religious and other concepts can merely be mentioned, but cannot be appropriately dealt with here.

Finally, the fact that there are appreciable differences between the average earnings of Bantu on the one hand and those of Coloureds and Asiatics on the other, shows clearly that an explanation of Bantu-White differentials in terms of racial discrimination cannot be adequate.

Like in many African and other countries, large numbers of the male population intermittently perform wage labour in the towns, on the mines or in plantations for a shorter or longer period and subsequently return to their homelands. Many, however, leave their homeland permanently or at least for as long as they are able to work. Many girls and women migrate to the towns as well, mostly with the intention of remaining there. Without the money remitted to them by migratory labourers, the Bantu homelands could only sustain a fraction of their present population. There are no exact figures concerning the number of migratory labourers. According to the estimates shown in Table 4 about 700 000 men and 150 000 women were temporarily absent from the Bantu areas in 1960. Bearing in mind that the people present in the Bantu areas at any given time include large numbers of migratory workers on 'home leave', one may assume that at least one million South African Bantu are migrants.

Apart from the indigenous Bantu, 600 000 or more workers from Lesotho, Botswana, Swaziland, Malawi, Mozambique, etc., are employed here at any given time. For the year 1964/65 their total earnings were estimated at R133,4 million, of which about R24 million was transferred to the countries of origin.[9] For these countries this is a factor of decisive importance. It must be realized, though, that the presence of the foreign Bantu contributes substantially towards keeping 'unlimited' the supply of unskilled labour, and thus exerts a downward pressure on the earnings of South African Bantu.

2. *Entrepreneurs*

Among the roughly 12 000 Bantu entrepreneurs only a few have scored notable success in commerce and hardly any in manufacturing. Most of them are small dealers, owners of restaurants and bottle-stores, bakers, butchers, etc. However, there are a considerable number of successful cartage firms, undertakers and insurance agencies. A few have founded large sales and service organizations with supermarkets, filling stations, cinemas, washeries and so on. No major factories are as yet owned by Bantu. The cane furniture manufacturing establishment of Mr Habakuk Shikwane near Pretoria is a promising start and, given appropriate assistance, many of the existing small firms may grow in a similar fashion.

665 Asiatics were enumerated as working proprietors of factories and workshops in 1961/62. Of these, 433 were manufacturing textiles, clothing and footwear and 86 were producing furniture. Above all, Asiatics play an important role in commerce. In 1960/61 they owned 6 908 or 20,2 per cent of all retail establishments in the country, and 304 or 3,5 per cent of all wholesale businesses, excluding limited liability companies.

Strikingly few Coloureds are to be found in business. In 1960/61 only 894 retail shops, mostly of small size, were owned by Coloureds.

3. *Total income, purchasing power, etc.*

The official figures in respect of South Africa's national accounts are not subdivided according to population groups so that one has to rely on unofficial estimates. Professor J.J. Stadler of the University of Pretoria has calculated the Bantu's gross national product at R1 343 million, i.e. R112 per head, for the year 1966/67. This is equal to about one quarter of the average for the whole of South Africa in that year, viz. R434. The Bantu's national income per head can be put at about R164 in 1969.

Estimates of purchasing power have a greater practical value, and a

9. See G.M.E. Leistner, 'Foreign Bantu Workers in South Africa, their present position in the economy', *South African Journal of Economics,* volume 35, No. 1, March, 1967, pp. 30-56.

compilation of estimates for the years 1959/60, 1962 and 1967/68 is presented in Table 12. It would be wrong to base far-reaching conclusions on these figures which have been calculated by diverse methods. It is remarkable, though, that the average purchasing power of Whites, Coloureds and Asiatics in these years has risen more than that of the Bantu. In fact, this tendency had to be expected because of the relatively large numerical growth of the Bantu as compared with the other population groups which generally are better qualified professionally and, thanks to their whole background, can hold their own in modern economic life more readily than the Bantu.

No less significant than these global estimates are concrete data provided by market research based on scientific methods. These investigations also show that on the whole the material position of the Bantu compares unfavourably with that of the other population groups. On the other hand they clearly illustrate how above all the urban Bantu are adapting to normal Western consumer patterns. Investigations in 1968 showed that 65 per cent of adult urban Bantu consumed chocolate and other sweets, 78 per cent soft drinks, 42 per cent cigarettes, 42 per cent 'European' beer, 25 per cent brandy, 81 per cent headache pills and 28 per cent deodorants. More than half the urban Bantu women used cosmetics, e.g. 31,1 per cent face cream, 22,0 per cent body talcum powder, 15,8 per cent hand lotion, 15,0 per cent lipstick, etc.; 45,7 per cent of urban Bantu households consumed instant coffee, 37,8 per cent tinned fruit, 32,3 per cent soup powder, 93,3 per cent soap and other cleansing materials, 78,4 per cent tinned or dried milk, 64,8 per cent skin bleaching creams.

Of the approximately 1,23 million private motor-cars registered in December 1967, 96 000 (that is 7,8 per cent) belonged to Bantu, 46 000 (3,7 per cent) to Coloureds, 38 000 (3,1 per cent) to Asiatics.[10] About 60 per cent of all accounts with Barclays Bank are held by Non-Whites.

Despite the considerable progress made in recent years, there still exist distinct differences in the average levels of living of Whites and Non-

10. Figures quoted from W. Langschmidt, 'Some characteristics of the urban Bantu market', in *The Urban Bantu Market – understanding its complexities and developing its potential,* Johannesburg, National Development and Management Foundation of South Africa, (NDMF), 1969, pp. 11-31. Those who wish to inform themselves further are referred to an earlier publication by the NDMF, viz. *Planning for the Bantu Market,* Johannesburg, 1966, as well as to the publications of the Bureau of Market Research, University of South Africa, Pretoria.

Whites, notably Bantu. Even though the *relative* differences can change only gradually, it is nonetheless highly significant that the standard of living in *absolute* terms is rising continuously among all population groups. Some time ago an American political scientist pointed out that the South African economy is growing even more rapidly than the expectations of the various population groups, all of which are sharing in this growth. In this way, potential political tensions are being reduced to a tolerable minimum. To quote,

> 'To summarize the arguments, a beginning can be made with the phenomenal ability of the South African economy to outstrip "the revolution of rising expectations". Economic advance has tended to reduce political tension to a point at which it can be managed.'[11]

Table 8 illustrates how the earnings of all population groups have improved over the past decade. To mention but one example: Whereas in 1960/61 there were only 70 Coloureds with taxable annual incomes between R4 000 and R10 000, this figure had risen sixfold by 1966/67, when it was 424.

4. *Border area development*

The concept of border areas was introduced by the Tomlinson Commission which advocated industrial development in certain regions adjoining Bantu homelands. The Commission's definition of a border area, which is still valid, reads as follows:

> 'By a border area is to be understood one where development takes place in a European area situated so closely to the Bantu Areas, that families of Bantu employees engaged in that development, can be established in the Bantu Area in such a way that the employees can lead a full family life.'[12]

Apart from the fact that such development would contribute towards a wider dispersal of economic activities – concentrated as they are in a few

11. E. Feit, 'Conflict and Cohesion in South Africa. A theoretical analysis of the policy of "separate development" and its implications', *Economic Development and Cultural Change* (Chicago), volume 14, No. 4, July, 1966, p. 495.

12. Summary of the Tomlinson Report, p. 140.

industrial areas – the Commission saw in it a means of creating employment and imparting skills in the immediate vicinity of the Bantu homelands, much more rapidly than could be achieved by projects *within* the Bantu areas. To the extent that employment opportunities are created in border industries, fewer Bantu have to go to the cities as migratory workers and experience all the social disadvantages this entails.

Since 1963/64, that is about eight years after the publication of the Tomlinson Report, this programme has been actively pursued. Until the end of 1970 about 69 000 new employment opportunities for Bantu and a further 18 000 for other population groups had been created. The investments for this purpose have been estimated at R429 million in the aggregate and at over R6 000 per Bantu employed (see Table 11). So far the Tomlinson Commission's expectation that border area development would canalize increased purchasing power into the Bantu homelands, has not been fulfilled. The Bantu prefer to buy in the centre of Pretoria or Durban rather than in Ga-Rankuwa or Umlazi.

Industrial growth in the border areas of Rosslyn and Hammarsdale is generally considered highly satisfactory. In some areas farther removed from the principal economic centres, such as Brits, Rustenburg, Pietersburg and Ladysmith (Natal), development is proceeding at a reasonable pace. However, there are signs that the more successful border area development is, the smaller is the prospect for rapid industrial progress within the Bantu homelands. Three factors, in particular, may adversely affect the prospects for industrial development inside the Bantu areas. Firstly, White investors may be deterred by the uncertainty as to what course events will take once full political independence has been granted to the homelands. Secondly, it is very difficult to persuade leading personnel such as engineers, chemists, artisans, etc., to settle in relatively little developed regions. Thirdly, the establishment of factories far away from suppliers of spare parts, from repair facilities and other specialized services, poses considerable difficulties. By offering tax concessions, low-cost loans, railage rebates, tender preferences, etc., the Government seeks to provide incentives sufficiently attractive to overcome these difficulties. Following the report of an inter-departmental committee that recorded numerous complaints about administrative obstacles facing firms interested in moving, the Government announced yet further concessions in June, 1971.

5. *Development of the Bantu homelands*

The Gross Domestic Product (GDP) of the Bantu homelands has been estimated at R160 million for the year 1966/67, i.e. less than two per cent of the GDP of the Republic. Since 1946/47 when the GDP of these areas amounted to R79 million, an annual growth rate of 3,5 per cent has been realized. During the period 1960/61 to 1966/67, the annual rate was substantially higher, viz. 5,14 per cent, and the Economic Adviser to the Prime Minister has expressed the opinion that during the seventies (1970-79), the growth rate would be substantially higher.[13]

The average income per head in the Bantu homelands has been estimated at R75 in the year 1966/67, of which about 60 per cent represented earnings outside the homelands.[14] Economically these areas are rather backward compared with the rest of the Republic. However, the economy of South Africa as a whole is experiencing persistently high growth rates, and consequently the resources that can be applied to promoting the development of the Bantu areas increase correspondingly. The problem of narrowing the gap vis-à-vis the rest of the economy is thus rendered less formidable. In the above-quoted paper, the Economic Adviser stressed that political stability is the first and foremost condition for economic development and that the Government has thus, in its planning, given preference to progress in the fields of politics, administration and education as distinct from purely economic advance.

Under the first five-year plan for the Bantu homelands which ended in 1965, R114 million was spent. For the period 1966 to 1971, R490 million was provided which comprised, *inter alia,* the following items: education, R163 million; agriculture and other physical development, R162 million; social development, R58 million; purchase of land and capital requirements, R50 million; economic development, R39 million.

The Bantu Investment Corporation (B.I.C.) and other similar development bodies play an active role in establishing and/or promoting agricultural, processing, trading and other projects. Apart from initiating new ventures itself, the B.I.C. also encourages Bantu enterprise by means of loans, training and expert advice. Furthermore, it actively attracts and

13. P.J. Riekert, 'The economy of South Africa, with special reference to homeland and border area development and the economies of Southern Africa', Address at the Annual General Meeting of the S.A. Institute of Race Relations, Cape Town, 28 February, 1970, in *Mercurius* (University of South Africa, Department of Economics) No. 10, June, 1970, p. 7.

14. See *S.A. Financial Gazette,* Johannesburg, 7 November, 1969, p. 11.

mobilizes the Bantu's savings. The B.I.C. is of special importance because of its function as an intermediary for White entrepreneurs intending to establish factories, mines and other ventures in Bantu areas where even more favourable conditions are being offered than in respect of border areas.

Until a few years ago the economic development of the Bantu homelands had been concerned mainly with agriculture. In the first place, measures were taken to combat soil erosion which was spreading ominously. Once the position had been stabilized, more attention could be given to the modernization of crop and animal husbandry. At present about 60 per cent of the surface area of the Bantu homelands has already been planned, including the consolidation of scattered holdings, concentration of many separate hut groups into large settlements, fencing of catchment areas, etc. However, despite all efforts and despite great expenditure, Bantu agriculture in general is stagnating. On the other hand an increasing number of Bantu are becoming farmers – 'cultivators' of the soil – in the proper sense of the word. New employment opportunities outside agriculture have yet to be created on a major scale.

6. *Government expenditure in respect of Non-Whites*

Having regard to the differences in the average productivity, and hence the earnings, of the four main population groups, the question has to be asked what is being done to raise the Non-Whites' productivity. In this respect, education and vocational training as well as health and nutrition, that is, measures on which the Government can exercise a strong influence, are of special importance. A factor that is frequently overlooked is the significance of family, friends, church congregation and other social groups in which the individual moves, for his attitude towards steadiness, punctuality and care in his work – factors which profoundly influence productivity.

At present, where development policy pays so much attention to the amount of expenditure for education, training, health, housing and other social ends, one should recall from time to time that real progress is not in the first place dependent on the quantity or even the quality of these social expenditures. What is decisive is the will of the individual to get ahead.

In South Africa, there is much criticism of the appreciable difference between government expenditure on the education of Whites and Non-

Whites. Thus it has been calculated that government expenditure per pupil was as follows:[15]

	Primary pupils	*Secondary pupils*
Whites (Transvaal) (1968/69)	R189,00	R248,00
Asiatics (1968/69)	R58,00	R89,00
Bantu (excluding Transkei) (1968/69)	R13,55	R55,00
Bantu (excluding Transkei (1969/70)	R14,00	R79,30
Bantu (Transkei) (1969/70)	R13,89	R83,38

It is an open question how far these figures are truly comparable. In the case of Asiatics, for example, the figure excludes capital expenditure, whereas it is apparently included in the figures for Whites.

Table 10 illustrates the very substantial expansion of Bantu education during the past 25 years. Between 1945 and 1970 the number of pupils increased almost fivefold; the number of teachers rose more than threefold, and that of schools far more than doubled. In 1970 nearly ten times as many children attended secondary schools as at the end of World War II. Whereas in 1945 only 7,6 per cent of the total Bantu population was at school, the percentage had risen to 18,2 per cent in 1970. Each year the number of Bantu children at school increases by approximately eight per cent.

At present it is simply not possible to equalize *per capita* spending in respect of all population groups – after all, South Africa disposes only of limited means. Thus the Secretary for Bantu Education has pointed out that if the unit costs currently applicable to Whites were to be applied to the Bantu educational system, the cost of the latter would amount to about R400 million a year[16] – an amount roughly equal to the Republic's Exchequer Account's deficit on current account in 1969/70. From an egalitarian point of view it might satisfy some if the standard of White schools were to be lowered in order to spend more on other population groups. However, a solution should be sought in raising the Non-White groups' productivity, and hence their contribution to revenue, rather than in a redistribution which would merely lower overall standards and economic growth for the country as a whole.

As Table 9 shows, the Bantu population contributes through direct and indirect taxation only about 18 per cent of the annual amount spent

15. *A Survey of Race Relations, 1970, op. cit.*, p. 205/6, 227 and 231.
16. *Op. cit.*, p. 206.

by the government on their education, health, housing, etc. Against this it can be held that in every state the more well-to-do are taxed in favour of the less privileged groups, and that the White taxpayers simply should accept a heavier burden. The question as to what extent this would be politically and economically feasible cannot be pursued here.

7. *Psychological Aspects*

Finally, an issue which in all likelihood represents the central problem of Bantu development, can merely be mentioned here. That is the question in how far the socio-cultural inheritance of the Bantu is compatible with the demands of modern economic life. It is a fact that the gap between Bantu culture and the Western way of life is enormous. Furthermore, it is also known that both spheres can be fused to a certain extent. However, it remains to be seen whether, and how, Bantu peoples can be bearers of, or create, a dynamic economic order that is characterized by technological progress.

PROBLEMS OF FUTURE ECONOMIC DEVELOPMENT

The problems of future economic development can be summarized in one sentence : How can South Africa provide full employment and rising real incomes for its fast growing Non-White population and, at the same time, forestall social and political conflicts that would hamper economic development in the long run?

Above all one must realize that at the present stage of development of the South African economy, it is simply not possible to attain both full employment and a high growth rate of income for the Bantu. There are two reasons. Firstly, there is the fact that the Bantu peoples of South Africa and neighbouring countries increase so fast that they present a practically unlimited supply of unskilled labour. Secondly – and this reason is closely interrelated with the first – the economy needs skilled manpower as a prerequisite for the employment of unskilled workers.

From this, three essential requirements follow : firstly, a slower rate of population growth among the Bantu; secondly, measures for raising the level of Bantu education and productivity generally, and thirdly, the promotion of economic development and especially the creation of employment opportunities in neighbouring countries.

As regards a decline in the population growth rate, family planning probably results from rather than precedes economic development. This means that when the poorer population groups advance materially, they will be more inclined to limit the number of their children than under the traditional economic and social order.

Rising individual productivity is dependent mainly on two factors – firstly, on the Bantu workers' attitude, which in its turn is determined to a large extent by the social 'climate' of their respective communities, and secondly, on the quality of the organization in the establishment where the labour is being performed. To the extent that labour becomes scarcer, businessmen will endeavour to use it more efficiently.

The opinion is frequently expressed that official minimum wages are the only way to ensure a higher level of living for the large majority of unskilled workers. In practice only a limited number would benefit whereas many more would lose their work because the increased cost of labour would compel businessmen to calculate their labour requirements more carefully. It is possible that this may lead to higher profits and hence, eventually, to an increased demand for labour. This, however, is by no means certain; for it is equally possible that businessmen might resort to more capital-intensive methods of production.

This matter can be argued at length, but wage increases prescribed by the State are a dubious means of promoting economic growth. I have already indicated why it is important for gold mining and also for secondary industry to keep their production costs as low as possible. In this respect wages play an important role.

A few remarks can still be made about the geographical distribution of employment.

At the time of the 1960 census 4,12 million Bantu, i.e. about 40 per cent of the indigenous South African Bantu, were counted in their homelands. Of the other 60 per cent more than half were in urban areas, and the rest on farms (see Table 4). Whereas at present about four million Bantu men are in the economically active age groups, this figure will have risen to approximately 10 million in the year 2000. This means that on the average 200 000 new male workers will be looking for work every year as compared with approximately 120 000 at the present time. Moreover, Bantu women are seeking entry into the labour market at a rapidly rising rate and have not even been considered here.

Assuming that it were possible to provide about 500 000 jobs for men and 200 000 for women in the homelands up to the year 2000 as well as a further one million jobs for males and 400 000 for females in border areas, there would still remain about 4,5 million men alone who would have to look for work in the existing major mining and manufacturing centres, not to mention the women. By way of comparison, it can be mentioned that in 1960 only about 2,0 million adult Bantu males were counted in urban areas.

It is difficult to visualize the implications of these admittedly hazardous estimates together with the more reliable projections of the total Bantu population. According to the figures in Table 4 there will be about 40 million Bantu in South Africa by the turn of the century of whom ten per cent may be living in non-Bantu rural areas and one-quarter in Bantu homelands. That would leave almost 26 million in the present urban complexes – a figure well in excess of the Tomlinson Commission's most pessimistic forecast, that is 15 million.[17] It should be added, though, that a major portion of these 26 million might be living in homeland towns close to the present metropolitan areas. Economically they would be part of these metropolitan complexes, regardless of where they sleep at night. Whereas in 1967 the numerical ratio of Whites to Bantu in urban areas was 1 to 1,4, it may well be 1 to 5 three decades hence.

In all probability the future growth of the South African economy will be sufficiently vigorous to absorb the domestic population increase. The shortage of skilled labour which has become a bottleneck during recent years is inducing more and more enterprises – also in the public sector – to let Bantu and Coloureds perform work that had hitherto been reserved for Whites. This tendency will become more pronounced as the years go by.

Among the major issues that are bound to demand more attention are Bantu labour organizations, the influence of homeland authorities on labour conditions, care for the aged, housing, local administration, and the position of foreign Bantu. The purpose of the above exposition was not to make forecasts, much less to suggest a programme for the future, but rather to contribute towards a better understanding of present problems and tendencies.

It should have become clear that even though a great deal remains to be done to raise the productivity of the Non-White groups, notably the Bantu, very considerable progress is being made by all groups. The phenomenal economic upsurge of the past two decades has brought the various

17. See *Summary of the Tomlinson Report,* p. 29, par. 32.

population groups ever closer together spatially and has made them more dependent upon each other. In the decades to come this development will necessarily accelerate.

TABLE 1: The Population of South Africa, 1904-1970

	1904	1921	1963	1946	1951	1960	1970
Number (in thousands)							
Whites	1 117,2	1 521,3	2 003,2	2 372,0	2 641,7	3 080,2	3 750,7
Coloureds a)	445,0	545,2	769,2	928,1	1 103,0	1 509,1	2 018,5
Asiatics b)	122,3	163,6	219,7	285,3	366,7	477,0	620,4
Bantu	3 490,3	4 697,3	6 595,6	7 830,6	8 560,1	10 927,0	15 057,6
TOTAL	5 174,8	6 927,4	9 587,9	11 415,9	12 671,5	15 994,2	21 447,2
Per cent							
Whites	21,6	22,0	20,9	20,8	20,9	19,3	17,5
Coloureds	8,6	7,9	8,0	8,1	8,7	9,4	9,4
Asiatics	2,4	2,4	2,3	2,5	2,9	3,0	2,9
Bantu	67,5	67,8	68,8	68,6	67,6	68,3	70,2
TOTAL	100,0	100,0	100,0	100,0	100,0	100,0	100,0

Sources:
Republic of South Africa, Department of Statistics, *South African Statistics 1968* and *Statistical News Release.*
Notes:
a) In South Africa, Coloureds are people of mixed racial origin, e.g. mulattoes in contrast to Europe where all Non-White people are commonly referred to as Coloureds.
b) People originating from India and Pakistan as well as a few Chinese.

TABLE 2: Urban Population, 1904-1970

	1904	1921	1963	1946	1951	1960	1970 (estimates)
Number (in thousands)							
Whites	599	908	1 367	1 793	2 089	2 575	3 258
Coloureds	219	286	446	580	731	1 031	1 494
Asiatics	44	99	153	208	285	397	539
Bantu	361	658	1 252	1 902	2 391	3 471	4 989
TOTAL	1 222	1 950	3 218	4 482	5 494	7 474	10 280

(continued on page 276)

Table 2: Urban Population, 1904-1970 (continued)

	1904	1921	1963	1946	1951	1960	1970 (estimates)
Urban population expressed as a percentage of the respective group							
Whites	53,6	59,7	68,2	75,6	79,1	83,6	86,8
Coloureds	49,2	52,4	58,0	62,5	66,2	68,3	74,0
Asiatics	36,5	60,4	69,5	72,8	77,6	83,2	86,8
Bantu	10,4	14,0	19,0	24,3	27,9	31,8	33,1
TOTAL	23,6	28,2	33,6	39,3	43,4	46,7	47,9

Sources:
1904-1960: Republic of South Africa, Bureau of Statistics, *Statistical Year Book, 1966,* A-22 and A-24; *Statistical News Release,* p. 11, No. 63, August 10, 1971.

TABLE 3: Prospective Population Growth, 1970–2000[1] (official estimates)

Population group	*Estimate*	*1960 census*	*1970*	*1980*	*1990*	*2000*
Number (in thousands)						
Whites	H[2]	3 080	3 808	4 704	5 747	7 033
	L		3 736	4 420	5 152	5 948
Coloureds	H	1 509	2 055	2 851	4 039	5 831
	L		2 026	2 687	3 542	4 606
Asiatics	H	477	598	759	944	1 159
	L		596	750	918	1 103
Bantu	H	10 928	13 721	17 393	22 048	27 949
	L		13 521	16 644	20 489	25 222
TOTAL	H	15 994	20 181	25 708	32 778	41 972
	L		19 878	24 501	30 101	36 879
Per cent						
Whites	H	19,3	18,9	18,3	17,5	16,7
	L		18,8	18,0	17,1	16,1
Coloureds	H	9,4	10,1	11,1	12,3	13,9
	L		10,2	11,0	11,8	12,5
Asiatics	H	3,0	3,0	3,0	2,9	2,9
	L		3,0	3,1	3,0	3,0
Bantu	H	68,3	68,0	67,6	67,3	66,5
	L		68,0	67,9	68,1	68,4
TOTAL	H	100,0	100,0	100,0	100,0	100,0
	L		100,0	100,0	100,0	100,0

Sources:
Republic of South Africa, Bureau of Statistics, *South African Statistics 1968;* A–12.
Notes:
1) These estimates were compiled prior to the 1970 population census, and have not yet been revised. From the preliminary results of the latter census it is, however, clear that at least the estimates concerning the Bantu are too low (see text).
2) H = high estimate, L = low estimate.

TABLE 4: Estimates in respect of the Geographical Distribution of the Bantu Population, 1960 and 2000

Number (in thousands)

Area and type of population	*1960* Male			*2000*[2] Male		
	Male	*Female*	*Total*	*Male*	*Female*	*Total*
Urban areas[1]						
Temporarily resident	825	200	1 025	13 125	12 755	25 880
Permanently resident	1 198	1 248	2 446			
Total present	2 023*	1 448*	3 471*	13 125[3]	12 755[3]	25 880[3]
Bantu areas						
Present	1 732*	2 338*	4 120*	4 208	5 792	10 000
Absent	704	150	854			
Total population	2 436	2 538	4 974	4 208	5 792	10 000
Other, mainly rural areas[1]						
Temporarily resident	246	131	377	2 200	1 800	4 000
Permanently resident	1 511	1 449	2 960			
Total present	1 757*	1 580*	3 337*	2 200	1 800	4 000
Total Bantu population	5 512*	5 416*	10 928*	19 533	20 347	39 880

Notes:
1) The terms "temporarily resident" and "permanently resident" are used here in a purely demographic sense (distribution according to age and sex) and do not take into account sociological or legal aspects.
2) An annual growth rate of 3,3 per cent is assumed for the period 1970–2000. Further, it is assumed that the number of foreign Bantu remains at the level of 1960.
3) The inhabitants of towns like Ga-Rankuwa, Mabopane, Umlazi, etc., are included, which, even though located in Bantu areas, are in fact part of the economic spheres of cities like Pretoria, Durban, etc.
General:
Figures marked by an asterisk * have been taken from official reports. All other figures are estimated by the author.

TABLE 5: Employment in the Principal Sectors of the Economy (thousands)

Sector	*Year*	*Whites*	*Coloureds*	*Asiatics*	*Bantu*	*Total*
Agriculture[1]	June 1964	12,9	172,3	7,6	1 060,9	1 253,7
Mining[2]	1945	51,6	1,8	0,6	419,0	473,0
	1950	55,9	2,5	0,7	444,2	503,3
	1955	65,3	3,1	0,5	471,0	539,9
	1960	67,7	3,9	0,5	547,9	620,1
	1965	65,8	5,2	0,7	556,6	628,3
	1969	61,1		546,6		607,7
	March 1970	60,0		561,5		621,5
	March 1971	61,8	6,4	0,6	592,8	661,5
Manufacturing [3] [4]	1945/46	119,0	53,0	16,9	181,7	370,7
	1950/51	159,5	75,5	19,5	269,7	524,0
	1955/56	158,8	86,7	26,7	338,5	610,7
	1960/61	175,6	96,9	31,6	353,0	657,1
	1965	233,9	150,1	50,9	494,6	929,5
	1969	269,9	180,3	67,7	581,4	1 099,4
	March 1970	278,1	194,8	73,3	609,1	1 155,4
Construction [3] [4]	1945/46	10,2	3,9	0,1	25,8	39,9
	1950/51	22,0	9,3	0,3	60,2	91,8
	1955/56	28,8	12,8	0,8	77,8	120,2
	1960/61	28,5	18,1	0,7	83,5	130,8
	1965	36,6	21,5	1,1	122,3	181,5
	1969	54,5	41,6	3,8	215,0	314,9
	March 1970	58,9	44,1	4,2	237,4	344,6
South African Railways and Harbours[5]	1945	85,7	8,4	0,6	55,1	149,9
	1950	103,4	9,7	0,7	74,2	188,0
	1955	103,7	10,8	0,6	95,2	210,3
	1960	110,0	9,7	0,6	97,7	218,0
	1969	115,1	13,7	1,0	94,8	224,6
	1970	110,0	14,1	1,2	96,4	222,7
	1971	112,8	14,4	1,3	97,7	226,2
Central government[5]	1960	103,7	9,9	0,6	105,5	219,7
	1965	122,7	24,3	1,5	119,2	267,7
	1969	130,0	31,8	7,4	164,2	333,4
Provincial authorities[5]	1960	63,7	14,2	4,5	56,7	139,1
	1965	72,4	7,6	6,5	66,6	153,2
	1969	88,7	11,4	2,2	72,9	175,2
	1970	91,8	12,2	2,3	76,0	182,3

(continued on page 279)

Table 5: Employment in the Principal Sector of the Economy (thousands) (continued)

Sector	*Year*	*Whites*	*Coloureds*	*Asiatics*	*Bantu*	*Total*
Local authorities[5]	1960	38,4	14,8	2,3	95,9	151,5
	1965	40,8	15,3	3,0	103,7	162,8
	1969	44,5	17,5	3,5	110,4	175,9
	1970	44,3	18,2	3,7	110,7	176,8
Wholesale trade[6]	1967	70,9	16,4	7,0	71,5	165,8
	1969	74,2	17,9	8,3	77,8	178,2
	March 1971	76,2	18,7	9,1	80,0	184,0
Retail trade[6]	1967	110,4	25,7	14,9	98,6	249,6
	1969	115,4	28,3	15,3	104,5	263,4
	March 1971	118,9	30,0	16,0	108,4	273,3

Sources:
Republic of South Africa, Department of Statistics, *Statistical Yearbook, South African Statistics 1968, Bulletin of Statistics* and *Statistical News Release.*
Notes:
1) Domestic servants on farms included.
2) Unless otherwise indicated the figures refer to the daily average in the respective years.
3) Only private firms.
4) Data for the years 1945/46, 1950/51 and 1955/56: yearly average; 1960/61 and 1969: position end of September; 1965: position end of June; March 1969: position end of month.
5) Position as per 31 March of the year shown.
6) 1967 and 1969: annual average; March 1971: end of the month.

TABLE 6: Employment in the Principal Sectors of the Economy (percentage distribution)

Sector	*Year*	*White*	*Coloureds*	*Asiatics*	*Bantu*	*Total*
Agriculture	June 1964	1,0	13,7	0,6	84,6	100,0
Mining	1945	10,9	0,4	0,1	88,6	100,0
	1950	11,1	0,5	0,1	88,3	100,0
	1955	12,1	0,6	0,1	87,2	100,0
	1960	10,9	0,6	0,1	88,4	100,0
	1965	10,5	0,8	0,1	88,6	100,0
	1969	10,1		89,9		100,0
	March 1970	9,7		90,3		100,0
	March 1971	9,3	1,0	0,1	89,6	100,0

(continued on page 280)

Table 6: Employment in the Principal Sectors of the Economy (percentage distribution) (continued)

Sector	*Year*	*Whites*	*Coloureds*	*Asiatics*	*Bantu*	*Total*
Manufacturing	1945/46	32,1	14,3	4,6	49,0	100,0
	1950/51	30,4	14,4	3,7	51,5	100,0
	1955/56	26,0	14,2	4,4	55,4	100,0
	1960/61	26,7	14,7	4,8	53,7	100,0
	1965	25,1	16,1	5,5	53,2	100,0
	1969	24,6	16,4	6,2	52,9	100,0
	March 1970	24,1	16,9	6,3	52,7	100,0
Construction	1945/46	25,5	9,7	0,2	64,6	100,0
	1950/51	23,9	10,2	0,3	65,6	100,0
	1955/56	24,0	10,6	0,7	64,7	100,0
	1960/61	21,8	13,8	0,5	63,8	100,0
	1965	20,2	11,8	0,6	67,4	100,0
	1969	17,3	13,2	1,2	68,3	100,0
	March 1970	17,1	12,8	1,2	68,9	100,0
South African Railways	1945	57,2	5,6	0,4	36,8	100,0
	1950	55,0	5,2	0,3	39,5	100,0
	1955	49,3	5,1	0,3	45,3	100,0
	1960	50,4	4,5	0,3	44,8	100,0
	1969	51,2	6,1	0,4	42,2	100,0
	1970	49,8	6,3	0,5	43,3	100,0
	1971	49,9	6,4	0,6	43,2	100,0
Central government	1960	47,2	4,5	0,3	48,0	100,0
	1965	45,8	9,1	0,6	44,5	100,0
	1969	39,0	9,5	2,2	49,3	100,0
Provincial authorities	1960	45,8	10,2	3,2	40,8	100,0
	1965	47,3	5,0	4,2	43,5	100,0
	1969	50,6	6,5	1,3	41,6	100,0
	1970	50,4	6,7	1,3	41,7	100,0
Local authorities	1960	25,3	9,8	1,5	63,3	100,0
	1965	25,1	9,4	1,8	63,7	100,0
	1969	25,3	9,9	2,0	62,8	100,0
	1970	25,1	10,3	2,1	62,6	100,0
Wholesale trade	1967	42,8	9,9	4,2	43,1	100,0
	1969	41,6	10,0	4,7	43,7	100,0
	March 1971	41,4	10,2	4,9	43,5	100,0
Retail trade	1967	44,2	10,3	6,0	39,5	100,0
	1969	43,8	10,7	5,8	39,7	100,0
	March 1971	43,5	11,0	5,8	39,7	100,0

Sources and notes: See Table 5.

TABLE 7: Average monthly earnings in various sectors, 1969

Sector	*Month resp. monthly average*	*Whites*	*Coloureds*	*Asiatics*	*Bantu*	*Bantu earnings related to earnings of other population groups (Bantu = 1,0)* Whites	Coloureds	Asiatics
Mining	October	325,6	72,5	52,0	17,5	18,6	4,1	3,0
Manufacturing	October	276,5	69,2	74,3	49,8	5,5	1,4	1,5
Construction	October	303,9	109,2	140,3	46,5	6,5	2,3	3,0
Railways & Harbours	March	247,2	—	47,1	—	—	—	—
Central government	January March	211,3	100,3	127,0	36,1	5,8	2,8	3,5
Provincial authorities	January March	198,1	49,2	66,9	31,9	6,2	1,5	2,1
Municipalities	January March	230,2	70,9	48,9	38,0	6,1	1,9	1,3
Wholesale trade	July September	251,9	67,8	100,4	49,1	5,1	1,4	2,0
Retail trade	July September	134,7	53,8	83,7	39,3	3,4	1,4	2,1

Sources: See Table 5.

TABLE 8: Persons in Higher Income groups 1960/61 and 1964/65 to 1966/67

Population group	*Fiscal year*	*Taxable annual income* R4 000 – 9 999	*R10 000 – 19 999*	*R20 000 and more*	*Total R4 000 and more*
Whites	1960/61	69 383	6 865	946	77 194
	1964/65	110 854	11 500	2 268	124 622
	1965/66	136 274	13 676	2 738	152 688
	1966/67	174 212	15 323	3 106	192 641
Coloureds	1960/61	70	2	—	72
	1964/65	182	5	2	189
	1965/66	270	14	2	286
	1966/67	424	21	—	445
Asiatics	1960/61	905	70	—	975
	1964/65	1 658	121	6	1 785
	1965/66	1 921	152	4	2 077
	1966/67	2 258	167	6	2 431

(continued on page 282)

Table 8: Persons in Higher Income groups 1960/61 and 1964/65 to 1966/67 (continued)

Population group	*Fiscal year*	*Taxable annual income* *R4 000 – 9 999*	*R10 000 – 19 999*	*R20 000 and more*	*Total R4 000 and more*
Bantu	1960/61	38	2	—	40
	1964/65	108	7	1	116
	1965/66	119	4	2	125
	1966/67	152	11	1	164
Total	1960/61	70 396	6 939	946	78 281
	1964/65	112 802	11 633	2 277	126 712
	1965/66	138 584	13 846	2 746	155 176
	1966/67	177 046	15 522	3 113	195 681

Sources:
Republic of South Africa, Department of Inland Revenue:
1960/61: *Annual Report 1959/61* (R.P. 28/1961),
1964/65: *Annual Report 1963/65* (R.P. 50/1966),
1965/66: *Annual Report 1965/66* (R.P. 73/1967),
1966/67: *Annual Report 1966/67* (R.P. 76/1968).

TABLE 9: Direct Expenditure by the Authorities in respect of the Bantu Population, and Taxes Contributed by the Bantu[1)]

	1929/30	*1946/47*	*1955/57*	*1964/65*
Direct expenditure[1)] (million rand)	4,3	30,4	125,2	215,2
Taxes paid by Bantu (million rand)	6,5	13,4	22,5	38,0
whereof: direct taxes	3,0	4,5	7,6	9,5
indirect taxes	3,5	8,9	14,9	28,5
Tax payments as % of direct expenditure	151,2	44,1	18,0	17,7

Source:
Bulletin of the Africa Institute (Pretoria), vol. VIII, No. 6, July, 1968, p. 175.
Note:
1) More detailed figures are shown in the original source.

TABLE 10: Figures on Bantu Education, 1945–1970[1]

	1945[2]	*1955*	*1960*	*1965*	*1967*	*1969*	*1970*
Schools	4 373	5 801	7 718	8 810	9 258	9 843	10 125
Pupils:							
Lower Primary	444 924	731 170	1 092 469	1 399 535	1 594 740	1 781 749	1 884 900
Higher Primary	128 867	239 069	359 777	484 455	552 655	653 671	730 061
Secondary	12 625	34 983	47 598	66 568	86 109	106 945	122 489
Training of teachers	5 382	5 899	4 292	4 548	5 607	7 052	7 548
Vocational and technical training	—	2 237	1 734	2 730	2 366	3 390	3 637
Not indicated	2 167	552	164	—	—	—	—
TOTAL	587 586	1 013 910	1 506 034	1 957 836	2 241 477	2 552 807	2 748 635
Teaching staff	13 900	21 974	27 767	34 810	38 403	43 638	45 953
Pupils as a % of total Bantu population[3]	7,60	10,59	14,10	16,07	17,58	17,50	18,25
Pupils in secondary schools as % of all pupils in lower and higher primary and in secondary schools	2,15	3,46	3,17	3,41	3,86	4,22	4,47

Sources:
Republic of South Africa, Department of Bantu Education, *Annual Report 1967* (R.P. 44/1969), Tables XXXIV A and XXXIV B; *Statistical Yearbook 1964*, E-5 and E-26; *Bantu Education Journal* (various issues).

Notes:
1) Transkei included.
2) Number of pupils, excluding 'Total', are only comparable to a limited extent with those for later years.
3) Figures for 1969 and 1970 are based on results of 1970 population census and are not strictly comparable with earlier ones. The difference, however, is not important.

TABLE 11 : Development of the Border Areas[1)]

	1960	*1965*	*1966*	*1967*	*1968*	*1969*	*1970[2)]*
Employment (in thousands)	76	128	133	138	145	176	163
of which Bantu (in thousands)	55	91	99	104	109	136	124
Estimate private investments (million rand)	—	177	221	296	314	400	429

Source:
Republic of South Africa, Permanent Committee for the Location of Industry, *Annual Reports.*
Notes:
1) Excluding Durban-Pinetown area.
2) Whereas figures for the years 1965 to 1969 refer to new projects approved by the Permanent Committee, the 1970 figures show projects *actually* established or shortly to be established.

TABLE 12 : Estimates of purchasing power of various population groups 1959/60, 1962 and 1967/68[1)]

	1959/60			*1962*	*1967/68*		
	Total		*Per capita*	*Per capita*	*Total*		*Per capita*
	Mill. R	*%*	*R*	*R*	*Mill. R*	*%*	*R*
Whites	2 587,6	69,3	837,8	782	4 134	73,4	1 141
Coloureds	212,1	5,7	140,5	120	306	5,4	165
Asiatics	73,8	2,0	154,7	139	136	2,4	233
Bantu	857,5	23,0	78,5	62	1 063	18,8	82
TOTAL	3 731,0	100,0	—	—	5 648	100,0	—

Sources:
1959/60: P.A. Nel, *Metodes vir die berekening van markpotensiale vir verbruiksgoedere en die ontwikkeling van regionale algemene markpotensiale.* Unpublished D.Com. dissertation, University of South Africa, Pretoria, 1968, pp. 360-369.

Other years: W. Langschmidt, 'Some Characteristics of the Bantu Market,' in: *The Urban Bantu Market – Understanding its Complexities and Developing its Potential,* Johannesburg, National Development and Management Foundation of South Africa, 1969, pp. 12, 19 and 31.

Note:
1) If the Bantu's *per capita* purchasing power is taken as equal to 1,00 the following ratios result:

Year	*Whites*	*Coloureds*	*Asiatics*
1959/60	10,67	1,79	1,97
1962	12,61	1,94	2,24
1967/68	13,91	2,01	2,84

Apartheid Idealism versus Economic Reality

D. Hobart Houghton

An eminent economist, Professor Hobart Houghton is an authority on economic development in South Africa's Bantu homelands. He is at present Director of the Institute of Social and Economic Research at Rhodes University, Grahamstown, and a member of the Prime Minister's Economic Advisory Council.

In 1890 the distinguished Cambridge economist, Alfred Marshall, wrote that

> 'the two great forming agencies of the world's history have been the religious and the economic . . . religious motives are more intense than economic; but their direct action seldom extends over so large a part of life. For the business by which a person earns his livelihood generally fills his thoughts during by far the greater part of those hours in which his mind is at its best; during these his character is being formed by the way in which he uses his faculties in his work, by his thoughts and the feelings which it suggests and by his relations with his associates in his work, his employers and employees'.

If we substitute the modern word *ideological* for *religious,* Marshall's words have as much relevance for the world of today as they had when they were written eighty years ago.

In Southern Africa the way of life of the people, Black, White and Brown, has been transformed by the industrial revolution that has taken place during the last hundred years. A century ago South Africans of all races were largely engaged in farming, and the general standard of living was low. As a result of the great mineral discoveries all this has been changed, and it is now a diversified industrial economy. The impact of this transformation has been greatest upon the indigenous African people for it has necessitated a greater change from traditional semi-nomadic stock farming to an industrial society, requiring from them flexibility of mental attitudes and social habits. That this has been so successfully achieved indicates qualities of adaptation and willingness to absorb new ideas on the part of the African people that have not always been found when a more technically advanced society makes its impact upon a primitive traditional community.

In this process of transformation the gold fields of the Witwatersrand have probably had a more profound influence than all the devoted services of missionaries and teachers, the administrative efforts of civil servants or military conquests. These various influences may be interrelated as components of the general civilizing process, but it was through the gold mines that there passed that endless stream of African workers in their hundreds of thousands a year. This has continued for almost a century, and millions of Africans have worked in the mines, shoulder to shoulder with traditional tribal enemies. Here too they made their first contact with White miners, were introduced to regular work and precision in labour management, and to the marvels of modern engineering enabling them to work a rock face 3 000 metres below the surface. Here it was that many first made their acquaintance with modern medicine and hygiene, and made their first elementary contact with an urban society. They were drawn from all parts of Southern Africa and they came as contract workers. On the conclusion of their stint they returned home, bringing their earnings, their purchases of exotic goods and their newly acquired experience with them, and soon even the most isolated African homestead was affected by the new ideas. Today there are 606 000 Black and 63 000 White men at work in the mines and this great vortex is still drawing men in their thousands.

The mining industry stimulated other economic development, and in the nineteen twenties the third main sector of the modern economy – manufacturing – began to forge ahead. There was at that time great poverty, particularly among Whites who had been forced off the land by the instability of world agricultural prices after World War I, and the 'poor White problem' (as it was then called) dominated the political and economic scene. The government embarked upon a policy of fostering manufacturing in order, primarily, to provide employment for the poor Whites. The growth of manufacturing industry was, however, so rapid that soon it had absorbed all the available White labour, and Coloureds, Indians and Africans entered the factories in ever increasing numbers. The economy, which in the eighteen seventies had been based almost solely upon farming, had, a century later, become a well-balanced diversified structure, and people of all races had been drawn out of subsistence farming into the expanding industrial sectors.

In 1970 the total number of all races and both sexes employed in the economy of the Republic was a little over seven million, distributed as shown in the table below.

		All races	*Whites*	*Africans*	*Coloured & Asian*
		(in thousands)			
1	Mining	676	63	606	7
2	Manufacturing and construction	1 539	336	882	321
3	Wholesale and retail trade	452	193	187	72
4	Transport and communications	279	149	110	20
5	Public authorities	649	238	336	75
6	Other services	1 465	301	990	174
7	Agriculture, forestry and fishing	1 980	115	1 680	185
	Totals	7 040	1 395	4 791	854

(Items 1 to 5 are the actual employment figures in September, 1970, as released by the Department of Statistics. Item 4 includes only those employed by the South African Railways and Harbours and the Post Office, and excludes those employed in private transport undertakings who are placed under 'other services'. Items 6 and 7 are estimates.)

Practically all employment shown in this table arises within the so-called 'White' area of the Republic, except for the activity of some 440 000 African peasants and a small, though growing, number of traders and small-scale industrialists and civil servants in the Bantu homelands. This latter group, both in number and in the value of their productive output, is at present relatively insignificant. It is difficult to give a precise numerical figure for the number of African peasant farmers because one and the same person may in the course of a year be both an industrial worker and a peasant farmer as a result of the migratory labour system. However, if we deduct 440 000 from the figure of employment in agriculture we are left with a fairly accurate picture of the composition of the labour force in the national economy excluding the Bantu homeland areas.

This table, if so amended, clearly reveals the very great dependence of the whole national economy upon the African worker. Africans constitute 90 per cent of the labour force in mining; 58 per cent in manufacturing; 42 per cent in trade; 39 per cent in transport; 52 per cent in the public service; 67 per cent in other service activities and 80 per cent in agriculture; and in the aggregate they account for no less than 65 per cent of the total labour force of the 'White' economy.

In the light of these figures any talk of complete territorial apartheid or separate economic development in the foreseeable future is sheer fantasy because it would inevitably cause the utter destruction of the national economy and mean that over four million African workers would lose their jobs, not to mention the disaster this would bring to the other races in the country. This is certainly not the policy of the government, and no government of South Africa could seriously contemplate such a course. Nevertheless, the ideal of separate development for the different races may act as a will-o'-the-wisp and divert attention from the basic economic realities.

APARTHEID IDEALISM AND ECONOMIC REALISM

The ideal of separate development, and the meaning to be attached to it in practice, have been discussed by other contributors to this volume in particular by Dr C.P. Mulder (page 49) and Mr M.C. Botha (page 113). It is widely recognized that the present political and social structure of the Republic does not meet the legitimate aspirations of the African people. Although they represent almost 70 per cent of the population, they are denied political representation; and, in spite of the large number employed, relatively few have risen above the level of unskilled and semi-skilled workers. The phenomenal growth of the South African economy, and the rising standard of living it has provided for people of all races, is largely due to the initiative and drive of the relatively small number of White people who have made their homes here and lived for many generations in South Africa. The vast majority of this White group sincerely believes that to adopt a more democratic political constitution involving universal franchise, which would transfer political control to the Black majority, would place the prosperity of the whole country in jeopardy.

This fear must be clearly and unambiguously stated. For the majority of thinking White people it is not a simple case of race prejudice or a belief in the inherent superiority of a White skin. Most would agree that there are individual Africans of outstanding merit every whit as competent as any White. They believe, however, that a dynamic modern industrial society requires policy to be directed by people possessed of certain relatively rare qualities of leadership, enterprise and initiative, and that these qualities, despite the proved adaptability of Africans, are more abundant among White South Africans than among Black, because of the latter's cultural history and social institutions. The selective recruitment of individual Africans into the ruling class, which was the essential feature of the Cape franchise before Union, has been abandoned. The concept of equal rights in a common society has been rejected for fear that it must inevitably lead to Black dominance; and the recent history of newly independent nations in Africa has done nothing to alleviate this fear.

The idea of separate racial development has been advanced as an alternative to meet what are generally recognized as legitimate and reasonable demands of the African peoples for a say in their political and economic development. The aim is to provide for each of the eight major African groups a territory where they can enjoy a progressive measure of self-government and where individuals can advance economically without the inhibiting restrictions at present placed upon them in the White-dominated society of the Republic. The first of the Bantu homelands (as they are called) was the Transkei, where a territory of 36 700 square kilometres (comparable in size to Holland, Belgium, Switzerland or Denmark) inhabited by one and three-quarter million Xhosa-speaking people, has been given a considerable measure of self-government with its own parliament and civil administration. Other similar homelands are expected to be granted a measure of self-government in the near future. In these areas the African people will each have their own language and be able to manage their own affairs, and individuals can aspire to the highest posts in the land. It is envisaged that at some future date these territories will be granted full sovereign independence and will become similar in status to Lesotho, Swaziland and Botswana.

This ideal of the building up of separate independent states for each of the major African groups attracts many South Africans, both Black and White; but it raises many important problems which can conveniently be grouped under three heads. Firstly, there are the difficulties concerned with the transformation of these African areas into progressive modern societies with viable economic structures of their own. Secondly, the relationships, particularly the economic relationships, between these states (including already independent neighbouring countries) and what remains of the Republic of South Africa must be considered. Thirdly, there is the status of the many millions of Africans, who are never likely to be accommodated in an independent state, but will remain permanent dwellers within the Republic. These three problem areas will be considered in turn, but before doing so something must be said about industrial location in South Africa.

Economic development during the last century has been extremely rapid and a vast mining industry and a considerable manufacturing industry has arisen in a land that formerly was almost wholly devoted to farming. The modern industrial activity is, however, concentrated in four relatively small areas, and the rest of the country has been mainly untouched by the industrial revolution. These areas are the Southern Transvaal surrounding the Witwatersrand gold fields, and the ports of Durban, Cape Town, and Port Elizabeth with their immediate hinterlands. These four areas together account for 80 per cent of the industrial output of the whole country.

THE BANTU HOMELANDS AND ECONOMIC DISPERSAL

The government regarded this state of affairs as unhealthy and, since 1960, has adopted policies designed to secure a wider geographical distribution of manufacturing activity. These measures include the offer of various incentives to industrialists setting up factories in approved areas and, under the Physical Planning Act, the imposition of restraints on industrial expansion in certain metropolitan areas. While strong arguments in favour of a policy of industrial dispersal may be advanced, based on the diseconomies of further expansion in the Southern Transvaal arising from traffic congestion, housing, pollution and above all the inadequacy of the water supply to support further growth, industrial dispersal also presents disadvantages. The pull of the market provided by the vast concentration of wealth and population in the Southern Transvaal naturally attracts the manufacturer. If he is forced to go elsewhere it will presumably be to a less advantageous location and he will require to be compensated for this loss of locational advantage. This compensation is naturally a burden upon the community as a whole, and there is controversy as to whether it is to be regarded as a temporary phenomenon, which will disappear as new manufacturing complexes develop to maturity, or whether it will be a permanent burden on the country's productive capacity.

When consideration is given to industrial dispersal, attention is naturally directed towards the Bantu homeland areas. According to the latest census (1970) these areas have an African population of about seven million as against the eight million in the 'White' areas, as shown in the table below.

Population of the Republic (1970)

Whites	3 750 716
Coloured	2 018 533
Asian	620 422
Bantu	15 057 559
	of whom 6 998 234 are in the homelands
Total all races	21 447 230

Moreover these homelands have been very little affected by the industrial development of the country except for the exodus of migrant workers from them to the industrial centres. The standard of living is low in relation to other parts of the Republic, and comparable with that prevailing in many other countries in Africa. Their subsistence is derived from peasant traditional-type farming with a heavy emphasis on cattle as part of their cultural heritage. Arable farming is largely a monoculture of maize, and productivity is very low. Like the neighbouring independent states of Botswana, Lesotho and Swaziland their low domestic product is augmented by the remittances of migrant workers who go out from their villages to earn in the industrial centres of the Republic sufficient to enable the family at home to continue to survive. Overstocking of the grazing and bad methods of arable farming are destroying the productive capacity of the land with the result that the two main exports of the Bantu areas are labour and soil : The former goes to the Southern Transvaal, and the latter is washed into the Indian ocean. There is urgent need for the transformation of traditional farming into a more scientific and productive agriculture but little has been achieved in the past by the devoted service of agricultural officers. Perhaps the energy released by the granting of independence may enable the new African governments to achieve greater success than in the past.

The Tomlinson Commission came to the conclusion that a pre-condition for any effective rehabilitation of agriculture in the Bantu areas was the removal of at least half the population from the land and their redeployment as workers in industry and tertiary economic activities. There is thus a strong *prima facie* case for looking towards the Bantu homelands in any policy of industrial dispersal on the principle of bringing the factories to the people who need new employment opportunities. Unfortunately, as experience in many parts of the world has shown, the task of industrializing a primitive and economically backward peope is beset with many difficulties. The essential infrastructure for a modern industry is almost wholly lacking in most of the Bantu areas and the cost of providing it would strain the capital resources of the Republic to the point that might inihibit the overall growth of the economy. Moreover, the Bantu areas are generally far removed from the main markets of the country, and at present the people in the homelands are too poor to constitute an effective local demand. The locational disadvantage of a site deep in the homelands would discourage all but the most intrepid entrepreneur.

While continuing to give support to the idea of industrial development in the homelands, the Government has embarked upon a compromise solution in its policy of 'border industries'. This is a policy of encouraging the establishment of factories in the 'White' areas on the periphery of the Bantu areas. Here much of the necessary infrastructure is aready available, particularly in the areas which lie along the main railway lines from Durban to the Witwatersrand and from East London to the Witwatersrand. These railways run for hundreds of kilometres in close proximity to Bantu areas, and they have the locational advantage of direct rail links with both the Southern Transvaal and a port. This policy has met with a fair measure of success since its inception in 1960 and claims to have provided, during the last ten years, new employment opportunities for 100 000 persons, of whom 80 000 are Africans, at an investment outlay of R400 million. This industrial development has not been paralleled in the Bantu homelands, and there are those who argue that the greater advantages of the border areas impede development in the homelands. This is indeed not surprising, and a hard look at the situation indicates that large-scale industrialization within the homelands would be a fantastically costly business.

With the granting of political autonomy to the homelands the status of these border area industries presents serious problems. They will draw their labour from the homelands and are likely to be major generators of income; but, being situated in the 'White' areas, they will be subject to taxation by the Republic and will not therefore assist in providing revenue for the struggling governments of the new African states. The migrant workers from the homelands commuting to border areas will, it is true, not have to travel as far as when they went to the older metropolitan centres, but they will spend some portion of their earnings in the 'White' areas, and thus deplete the already meagre income flow of the homelands. Thus they will be much less effective in promoting the economic progress of the new states than industries within their borders.

THE ECONOMIC INTERDEPENDENCE OF SOUTH AFRICA'S PEOPLES

This raises the whole matter of the future relationships between the Republic and the proposed new states. If they eventually attain complete political independence they will rank with Botswana, Lesotho and Swaziland; but all these states, old and new, are heavily dependent upon the economy of the Republic. Does separate development mean the Balkanization of Southern Africa, or is it possible, as Dr Verwoerd once suggested, to combine separate geographical and political development with economic co-operation?

If one reads the history of the events leading up to the Union of South Africa in 1910 one is impressed by the forward-looking vision of the leaders of that time, and their faith in the benefits to flow from 'closer union' (as it was then referred to) – *ex unitate vires* was their motto – a faith that has been abundantly vindicated by the subsequent expansion of the South African economy. Whether they advocated union or federation those architects of modern South Africa sought *aggregation* not *separation,* some even hoping to include Rhodesia and the High Commission Territories in the greater South Africa. To those who created the Union, *separation* and *development* seemed incompatible.

The vast majority of those who today advocate separate development for the various African groups do not intend the establishment of small isolated units cut off from the benefits of trade and economic relations with the rest of South Africa and the world. The benefits that flow from co-operation and free economic interchange over a wide area have been accepted since the days of Adam Smith. Moreover, how can more backward areas be assisted save by contact with the more advanced? 'The White man's burden' cannot simply be dropped by the granting of independence because, as Dr Anton Rupert, a prominent Afrikaner financier, has so rightly said, 'If the Basutho starve, we shall live in fear'. Therefore earnest attention must be given to the ways in which the various nations of Southern Africa can work together to maintain and enlarge the prosperity at present enjoyed, and to ensure a more equitable distribution of the product of their common effort. At present the Bantu homelands are part of the Republic, and Botswana, Lesotho and Swaziland have remained within the South African Customs Union, and have a common currency and banking system with the Republic. It is essential that these links be preserved, and if possible extended, to facilitate investment and the development of the less advanced areas. Careful thought should be given to how best to ensure a Common Market or Co-prosperity Sphere for Southern Africa.

Even if the policy of developing the Bantu homelands is outstandingly successful, large numbers of Africans are likely to remain within the Republic. There is fortunately little prospect of any large reverse flow of Africans to the homelands from the metropolitan centres because the South African economy is basically dependent upon their labour. The figures given earlier make this abundantly clear. According to the 1970 census there were approximately eight million Africans in the 'White' areas and four-and-a-half million were economically employed, and by the end of this century both these figures will be more than doubled. The question therefore arises what their status is to be. At present most of the skilled workers in mines and industry are White, and their position has been entrenched by a strong legislative and customary colour bar. The White workers are opposed to any vertical advancement of Africans that might endanger their position as skilled workers, and an earlier attempt to modify the colour bar led to the Rand Rebellion of 1922. Although this happened half a centry ago the memory of it is ever present in the minds of politicians and employers.

The rapid expansion of the economy, particularly during the last decade when the real gross domestic product (at 1958 prices) rose from R5 139 million in 1960 to R8 768 million in 1969 (an increase of 70 per cent in ten years), has led to an acute shortage of skilled manpower. The dilemma is illustrated by the fact that in the Economic Development Programme (1965-70) a 5½ per cent growth rate was expected to expand the demand for skilled labour between 1965-70 by 200 000, but the White labour force was only expected to grow by 155 000. The shortfall of 45 000 skilled workers could only be met by increased productivity, immigration or greater use of Non-White labour in skilled occupations. The gross national product has continued to expand and the conclusion is that all three of the above possibilities have been operative. Although difficult to quantify, it is widely accepted that there has been considerable upward movement of Non-Whites and that many are now employed in jobs formerly performed by White persons. It is becoming increasingly clear to all that the continuing economic progress of the country requires a more rational deployment of South Africa's human resources, irrespective of race, if its great potential is to be realized. Despite continuing pressure from the major employers' organizations the Government has shown little sympathy for repeal of restrictive colour bar legislation. This is perhaps explained by a recent statement by the Prime Minister who said that while we must recognize economic realities we must also recognize political realities. Nevertheless, if organized White labour successfully continues to oppose relaxation of restrictive measures that prevent full utilization of our human resources it will be a major tragedy for South Africa; and it makes a mockery of the belief that White rule is most likely to promote the economic progress of the country.

MORE DEVELOPMENT AND LESS SEPARATENESS

The policy of development of the poverty-stricken Bantu areas is excellent in itself, provided that it does not impede the general economic growth of the country. The real danger of the policy of Bantu homelands is that it may split up the economy into different compartments, and that too much attention will be given to the development of the homelands and too little to the utilization of African labour in the Republic itself. The mines and factories of the Republic are still, and are likely to remain for the forseeable future, the main generators of wealth and employment in Southern Africa, and the homelands and adjacent African states will remain dependent upon the prosperity of the Republic. The population of the Republic is fast-growing, and rose from 16 million in 1960 to 21½ million in 1970, and every year there are half-a-million new South Africans to be fed, clothed and housed, and eventually to be given employment. These people will exist, irrespective of whether they are deemed to be citizens of the Republic or of one of the homelands, and their human needs should be met. Hence the urgent and imperative need to maintain a high rate of economic growth. South Africa has been fortunate in maintaining over the last 40 years a growth rate substantially above that of population increase enabling a rising real per capita income. The continuation of this is essential if internal peace and stability are to be preserved and rising expectations of the population as a whole are to be satisfied. This in turn necessitates the optimum utilization of natural and human resources.

If Africans, who constitute so large a part of the labour force of the Republic (excluding the Bantu homelands), are to make their effective contribution, opportunities for vertical advance in employment combined with better education and technical training are essential. Moreover, housing, a stable social environment where normal family life can be achieved, and a sense of security and belonging to the community are essential in a modern industrial society which increasingly is demanding skilled rather than unskilled labour. The policy of separate development would seem to necessitate the continuance of the migratory labour system, and this system is destructive of normal family life and the building up of a stable community at the place of employment. It breeds social and economic instability in the labour force, which impedes the evolution in workers of a lasting commitment to an industrial society and an incentive to improve their skills and productivity.

As stated by Marshall in the quotation at the beginning of this article, the place and conditions under which men work largely determine the course of history. The granting of rights in some far off homeland is no substitute for participation in the decision-making about their wages, conditions of work and their social environment in the place where they work. The real problem is to find some method, acceptable to all, by which the Africans remaining within the Republic can be effectively integrated into a common society without constituting a threat to the other minority groups.

Separate development of African homelands has many attractive features, but the greater the emphasis on *development* and the less on *separate* the more likely is it to succeed. Moreover homeland development, while it may be a useful method of training in political and economic responsibility, cannot be regarded as a final solution to the problems of living together in the multi-racial society which the Republic is at present, and which it is likely to remain.

Race and Labour Relations

J. A. Grobbelaar

James Arthur Grobbelaar is the General Secretary of the Trade Union Council of South Africa. A recognized authority on labour relations, the author is widely known for his stringent criticism of the South African Government's policy of apartheid.

Any assessment of racial attitudes as they affect labour relationships and the broader field of human relationships, demands, of necessity, that a glance should be taken at the development of South Africa's industrial legislation. The original legislative procedures were designed to offer protection to both employers and employees, and were meant to serve as the medium for resolving conflict and dispute in the labour field.

This early legislation expressed the traditional attitudes of the time, and was based upon the unwritten laws which have always functioned in South Africa. These unwritten laws were in turn based upon deep racial prejudices. Unfortunately, there has been a tendency to accentuate these very definite racial prejudices through successive forms of industrial legislation.

An equally important factor which influenced this legislation was the natural desire of the 'haves' to retain their privileges, particularly if cognizance is taken of the fact that the early White settlers in South Africa had a premium on industrial and economic abilities, which they had developed in the more sophisticated environment and advanced form of civilization which they had recently left. It must also be accepted that the White settlers' culture was several hundred years ahead of that of the indigenous population. This greater degree of knowledge and ability, taken with a relatively high degree of civilization, when brought into contact with that of the Bantu peoples of the time, automatcially established a master/servant relationship.

It can also hardly be argued that this original legislation was not suitable for the age, the place, and the population, in the situation as it existed at that time.

An analysis of South Africa's more important measures of industrial legislation will highlight its special characteristics, and to some extent, will pin-point its weaknesses, having regard to the present-day requirements of a modern industrial state.

The Cape Masters' and Servants' Law of 1865 is generally looked upon as the forerunner of our industrial legislation. It clearly defined in quasi-legal terms the obligation of the servant to the master and vice versa, and a strong paternalistic philosophy was its most salient feature.

The introduction of the Mines and Works Act in 1911, which basically sought to prohibit the entry of Non-Whites into those occupations that were the prerogative of the skilled and trained White immigrants, was the first legislative manifestation of racial discrimination. The Act came into being following upon the demands of White miners that the skilled positions be reserved only for them. It prohibited Non-Whites from obtaining a blasting certificate, and also established the original ratio of Bantu workers that a White miner could supervise.

Successive amendments to the Act have tended to more directly entrench the principles of out-right racial discrimination. Specific occupations in the mining industry have been reserved for the White racial group, and although some relaxation has taken place (due to economic pressures), there is still a general tendency for nearly all forms of skilled work in this industry to remain the sole prerogative of the White workers.

The long-standing migratory labour contract system for Bantu workers, and the policy of the mining companies to employ tribalized Bantu for all of the more menial occupations, has also assisted in perpetuating the discriminatory pattern. By far the greater proportion of these contract workers are foreign Bantu, and consequently they have no lasting stake in the industry, thereby ensuring that any avenues for improved conditions or better job opportunities are closed to them.

The introduction of South Africa's premier industrial legislative measure, the Industrial Conciliation Act of 1924, had as its purpose the setting up of the necessary machinery for determining the conditions of employment, through the medium of consultation between management and the trade unions. The Act legalized the principles of arbitration and collective bargaining for Whites and Coloureds, but it specifically excluded (by means of the definition of 'employee') all Bantu workers from its provisions. The later amendments to the Act in 1956, further reinforced the principles and exclusiveness of the original Act, and further entrenched the position of the White workers, through the inclusion of the controversial Section 77 – the 'Job Reservation' Clause.

The creation of the Industrial Tribunal, introduced in these 1956 amendments to the Act, whose main function is to reserve specific occupations for members of a particular racial group, has largely ensured that the existing privileged position of the White workers will be a constant feature of South Africa's industrial scene.

Other amendments to the Act, at this time, provided for the splitting of racially mixed trade unions, and also prevented any new mixed unions consisting of White and Coloured members from becoming established from that time onwards. It is only when the total membership of a racially pure union is too small to function effectively, that a mixed union can now be brought into being. It is perhaps significant to note that since 1956 not one further mixed union has been registered!

THE BANTU WORKER IN INDUSTRY

It can thus easily be seen that the position of the Bantu worker in industry was therefore, both directly, and through inference, relegated to a special and separate category. The Act and its subsequent amendments has ensured that the normally accepted forms of industrial and labour institutions, whilst deemed suitable for the Whites and Coloureds, are clearly not meant to apply to the Bantu workers.

The Wage Act introduced in 1925, which established the Wage Board, whose function is that of determining conditions of employment for workers in the industries where they are not sufficiently organized to be able to engage in the practice of collective bargaining, is remarkable for the degree of its unquestioned acceptance of a philosophy of paternalism. The Wage Board is statutorily empowered to determine the basic minimum conditions of employment, and entrusted with the task of looking after the interests of those who are not able to do so through their own endeavours.

The practice of the Act has resulted in the paternal figure of officialdom largely determining the conditions of employment of most Bantu workers. Even in those industries which have effective White and Coloured trade unions, which choose to bargain on behalf of the Bantu workers in their industries, the Board is able to exercise and exert its influence in determining the employment conditions of the Bantu workers, since it establishes the criteria of employment for the unorganized, and thereby furnishes guidelines for employers, who willingly adhere to the Board's standards!

The Apprenticeship Act of 1922, with its many succeeding amendments, established the criteria for becoming a skilled worker. The minimum educational requirements for admission to an apprenticeship, and the required agreement by the parties on apprenticeship committees (which consist of equal employer and trade union representation in the industry concerned) for granting an apprenticeship, whilst desirable controls in themselves, have also been a very effective means of debarring the Bantu from gaining apprenticeships, since the Bantu has no trade union!

The Act has no specific colour bar as such, but the success of curtailing the entry of Bantu into the skilled occupations, in this indirect manner, has been most effective.

The introduction of the Unemployment Insurance Act of 1948, and the Workmen's Compensation Act of 1934, both of which apply to all races, are still nonetheless reasonably effective measures for perpetuating discriminatory practices. Although they are good social welfare measures, they either exclude Bantu workers from their provisions, if these workers earn below a certain minimum income, or alternatively, they limit the amount of benefit which a Bantu can obtain.

It can be argued that these limitations and restrictions are an economic necessity, but nonetheless both the Acts as they presently stand, also perpetuate the practice of discrimination, to a greater or lesser degree.

The Bantu Labour (Settlement of Disputes) Act, originally introduced in 1953, under the title of the Native Labour Act, very definitely emphasizes the policy of discrimination and differentiation between the races. The Act is applicable only to the Bantu workers, and is quite blatantly paternalistic in its underlying philosophy.

The mantle of protecting and representing the interests of the Bantu worker falls squarely upon the shoulders of Government, which is in direct contradiction with the philosophy inherent in the Industrial Conciliation Act, with its provisions giving White and Coloured workers the right to determine their own destiny. It is also in direct contradiction with the philosophy of self-government in industry, as epitomized in the Industrial Conciliation Act. It also specifically prohibits strikes and lockouts amongst the Bantu workers, and provides the Bantu with a type of institutional or organizational structure which is devoid of any real force or power.

The system of Works Committees which it allows for, can only function with the blessing, and under the direct supervision and control of either management, or the Department of Labour. The normal workers' rights, such as freedom of association, recognition of collective bargaining practices, and workers' actions on any collective basis, are all specifically denied through the rigid provisions existing in this Act.

The defined functions of the institutions permissible in the Act, namely, the Central Bantu Labour Board, and the Bantu Labour Committees, which will supposedly settle, in an equitable manner, all possible disputes between labour and management, are based upon the reasoning that 'big brother knows best'. The Act's provisions also very clearly emphasize that there is no intention on the part of the authorities to officially recognize that trade union action for Bantu workers is a desirable development.

With this background, and brief summary of our industrial legislation as it has developed over the years, it must be accepted that the Government (and quite obviously the majority of the White electorate) are determined, at this stage, firstly to retain a privileged position for the White workers, and to a lesser extent a privileged position for the Coloureds, and, secondly, to continue with a system which, either directly or indirectly, exercises full control over the utilization of Bantu labour.

It is obvious that the Bantu worker is looked upon as being the responsibility of the privileged White group, which has adopted the paternalistic attitude of knowing what is best for him. Conversely, it can be opined that these restrictions and limitations on the utilization of the Bantu worker, whilst they might have been desirable instruments in the past, are an anachronism in a modern industrial society.

The entrenchment of these blatant privileges in our industrial legislation are also fatal flaws, since they are based on the faulty assumption that the Bantu workers will continue to remain docile and contented. They presuppose that the Bantu have no real ambitions to aspire to more skilled work, and to hold down better occupations with their commensurate rewards. They also tend to propagate the myth that the majority of the work force has no desire to have any say in its own destiny.

On the other side of the coin, again, it could be argued that the Bantu workers are, in the main, not in a position at this stage, to regulate their own affairs in a manner which conforms to the sophisticated standards of the Whites in South Africa, *but* the negative and rigid nature of our industrial legislation guarantees that they will never be able to measure up to these standards, since no provisions exist whereby they can be lifted up to the levels and norms of our White society! The maintenance of differential practices in our laws, and the retention of discriminatory provisions which ensure that a gap between the privileged and under-privileged will remain, are also going to ensure that racial prejudices are going to be perpetuated.

In some respects, and in contradiction to normal world developments, there has been a widening of the already considerable income gap between various occupations in South Africa. This is generating a sense of frustration and bitterness which, if unchecked, must ultimately lead to a revolt and the destruction of the reasonably good industrial relationships which presently exist. It should be recognized that no situation remains static, and that the inevitability of change also demands change in the mediums which govern our industrial behavioural patterns.

RACE ATTITUDES IN THE TRADE UNION MOVEMENT

Having looked at the anachronistic character of our industrial laws, which over-accentuate racial differences and provide for discrimination, it is now necessary to look at race attitudes within the trade union movement itself, since the trade unions wield considerable authority and to some extent mirror public attitudes. To attempt to define, in general terms, race attitudes in the trade union movement is a task worthy of Solomon, but is vital for the purpose of this study.

The movement in South Africa is deeply divided on its approach to racial issues, and also unduly influenced by the prevailing racial prejudices so prevalent throughout the country. Attitudes fall within a broad spectrum which ranges from a belief that absolutely no discrimination or differentiation should exist, to that of an outright view that all Non-Whites should forever be classed as inferior, and deserving of absolutely no improvement. This deep division in the movement on these fundamental principles, which in the main are based upon the fear that the White's position will be eroded through any mass influx of the Non-White majority into the more skilled occupations held by the Whites, coupled with a fear that there will be a lowering of standards, has also been largely responsible for the decision by many White worker organizations to resist any form of labour integration and advancement for Non-Whites. This attitude is, of course, in complete contradiction to the generally accepted world standards of equal opportunity, and participation for all, irrespective of race, colour or creed.

Fortunately, not all of the White trade unions and their members have subscribed to this philosophy of fear, which is so prevalent in South Africa.

From the recorded start of trade unionism in South Africa, a number of organizations have pursued policies which conform, in the main, to those of the outside world's trade union movements. Trade union development therefore requires to be explained, and a brief historical review becomes necessary in order to enable certain conclusions to be drawn.

Prior to 1926, fairly wide national co-ordination and a healthy measure of solidarity existed in the trade union movement, largely due to the fact that the trade unions in existence right up to this time were craft unions, and were thus able to dominate the scene. As craft unions, their memberships were also solely made up from the White racial group but with the emergence of the first industrial unions, which consisted of members of other racial groups, divisions within the working class movement soon became apparent.

Nonetheless, 1926 saw the establishment of the Trades and Labour Council, which had as its aim a policy of open membership, regardless of race, for trade unions. Noteworthy achievements towards national unity, and for a composite force of all workers' organizations, characterized the activities of this body. Activities were confined mainly to the Transvaal, since it was only in this province that there were any industrial unions of real stature. In the Cape Province, the Cape Federation of Trades remained independent, as a predominantly craft union type of organization. The Trades and Labour Council continued in existence for nearly 30 years, but an early result of the coming into power of the Nationalist Government, in 1948, was the fierce criticism levelled by the then Minister of Labour against the organization for its multi-racial policy. At that time the organization had a membership of more than 200 000 persons, which included a number of avowedly Communistic and leftist unionists.

Many of the more moderate unions had been unhappy for some time about their affiliation to the Council because of this Communistic influence, and some of the more rigid Afrikaner-orientated unions were also more than eager to break away.

This latter group soon did so, and they were quickly followed by a group of the more moderate unions, which were sufficient in numbers to challenge the position of the Trades and Labour Council. The small group of unions remaining were now faced with a situation whereby the leftist elements were in the majority. It only needed the Minister of Labour, in 1954, to indicate that it was his intention to amend the Industrial Conciliation Act, with measures aimed at encouraging the mixed White and

Non-White unions to split up on a racial basis, and also to reserve particular jobs for certain racial groups, to ensure the demise of the Trades and Labour Council becoming a fact. Thus by 1954, the movement found itself split into no less than five different co-ordinating bodies.

They were:

1. The Federal Consultative Council of South African Railways and Harbours Staff Associations (State employees) who were mainly right-wing orientated.
2. The Co-ordinating Council of South African Trade Unions, which consisted of White industrial unions, completely Afrikaner-orientated, and ultra right-wing in attitude.
3. The middle of the road South African Federation of Trade Unions, consisting mainly of artisan and skilled workers' unions, which had no definite attitudes.
4. The Trades and Labour Council, which had been reduced to a few artisan and industrial unions (as well as three Bantu unions), and which was left-wing in attitude.
5. The Western Province Federation of Labour Unions, consisting of both artisan and industrial unions, with mixed membership, and generally following policies of moderation.

Trade union concern over the Government's proposed amendments to the Industrial Conciliation Act led to the formation of a Unity Committee in 1954, so that a united front could be presented to the proposals. The biggest tasks facing the Committee were to attempt to submerge past differences; to compromise on the fundamental questions of racial attitudes; and thereby again weld the worker movements into a single organization.

The Unity Committee arranged a conference, which was attended by delegates from some 73 trade unions, representing some 230 000 workers. Although the conference was a failure in that the unions were unable to achieve broad agreement on these fundamental questions, and also failed in their attempts to influence the Minister of Labour to withdraw the proposed legislation, steps were nevertheless taken to draft a constitution for a new co-ordinating body, which would provide a home for most of the unions in South Africa.

At a conference several months later, delegates from some 61 trade unions formed the Trade Union Council of South Africa (TUCSA). The new co-ordinating body stated in its policy resolution that 'whilst accepting that the true principles of trade unionism require unity of all workers, the factual position is that, in order to obtain the broadest possible unity, it is necessary to confine membership to registered unions'. Thus automatically, the Bantu workers were excluded from membership, although the Coloured and Indian workers were welcome to join, and played an active part in the affairs of the new body from the day of its inception.

However, both the Railways Consultative Council and the Co-ordinating Council of South African Trade Unions elected to remain outside of the new body, and even elements of the S.A. Federation of Trade Unions decided not to become members of the organization. The remaining unions in the now almost defunct Trades and Labour Council also decided to remain outside, and shortly afterwards they formed the South African Congress of Trade Unions, which consisted largely of Bantu-member trade unions. These latter organizations soon fell increasingly under Communist influence.

TUCSA AND THE NON-WHITE WORKER

The TUCSA trade unions were fully aware of the imperative need for Bantu trade unions, if the standards of South Africa's workers, on purely economic levels, were to be protected. They saw very clearly, right from the beginning, that prosperity was indivisible, and that unless Bantu wages and living standards were improved dramatically, the domestic market for the country's swiftly developing programme of industry would remain small, and all workers would suffer. Moreover, unorganized Bantu labour could be exploited as cheap labour, which in turn would prove to be fatal for the more highly skilled White workers. It must be recognized that their pre-occupation with the need for trade unions for Non-Whites has always been governed more by the need for self-protection in the economic field, rather than by moral considerations.

Over the last sixteen years TUCSA has continued, through strenuous and varied activities, in its attempt to create a climate which would lead to the acceptance of these basic truths by the Government and the general public, but it has not yet succeeded, even though the forces of evolution are on its side. This policy has led to crisis after crisis facing the organization, and on several occasions it has been on the point of breaking up and dissolving.

As an experimental institution of multi-racialism (and its actual motives are not relevant) it continues to face opposition and disruptive attacks from not only the Government, but also from those trade unions outside of its ranks. It is also criticized by all types of racially inclined groups and power cliques, and at times it is at odds even with those in its own ranks. Nevertheless, it has persevered, and a significant measure of success has been achieved in the complex field of racial co-operation.

The proof lies in the fact that its present membership consists of some 76 White, mixed, and Coloured trade unions with nearly 200 000 individual worker members, of which total approximately fifty per cent are Coloureds and Indians. Although the Bantu racial group is not included in this membership, TUCSA is continuing to act on its behalf, and pursues its economic and social aspirations in every possible way it can. It continues constantly to call for recognition for the Bantu worker; for public acceptance of the fact that the Bantu is entitled to representation and must be allowed to achieve his aspirations and desires, through the creation of job opportunities; for changes in the existing social and industrial patterns; and to maintain that the Bantu must have a say in determining his own destiny.

As an organization TUCSA has been tempered through the hard battles which it has had to fight on all fronts. Its lack of sympathy with most of the racial policies of the present Government, and many of those unions which are not affiliated, bring it into constant conflict with them. It must be recognized that hostility from these elements, because of TUCSA's clearly stated stand on the question of the Non-White worker, has exposed the organization to the charge of being liberal, and to be called 'liberal' today in South Africa is equivalent to being classed as 'communistic' or, at best, as a 'fellow traveller'.

Racial attitudes which prevail within the organization itself, rooted as they are in the country's history, also impose a certain amount of caution on TUCSA's leadership. Although the policies of the organization are based firmly on economics and aim at obtaining the best possible conditions for all workers as well as at alleviating racial distrust and friction, the existing climate in South Africa, in which people are inclined to think emotionally rather than rationally, creates opportunities for the ill-disposed to label TUCSA's sound economic and moderate approaches as subversive.

This prevailing climate inhibits the leadership of TUCSA (as well as the desires of members) as do the restrictive policies that have been formulated by the authorities. These factors, coupled with the need to do whatever practical work it can within the confines set for it by the extremists, has led to TUCSA's taking some contradictory actions. Consequent misunderstanding of its motives has resulted. These enormous pressures have nearly broken the organization on several occasions, but it is nevertheless withstanding them, and attempting, through practical and pragmatic actions, to fulfil its destiny.

The other organizations in opposition to TUCSA have not met with a great deal of success. The S.A. Confederation of Labour, which consists of the Railway trade unions, the ultra right-wing Co-ordinating Council of South African Trade Unions, and elements of the more moderate South African Federation of Labour, has never succeeded in functioning as a very effective and representative body of trade unions, since the date of its inception.

Its main purpose until recently seemed to be that of criticizing and attacking TUCSA, and rubber-stamping any measures proposed by the Government, of whatever nature. It has also faced a number of crises recently, generated by conflicting attitudes within the organization. The more extremist right-wing groups are likely to 'hive off' from the organization, since their rigid policies do not allow them to adapt to changing circumstances. This adherence to past practices is, amazingly enough, also bringing them into conflict with the authorities. An almost continuous state of dispute now appears to be the order of the day between the ultra right-wing groups and the more moderate elements, since the latter appear to be recognizing the need for change, and are also once more reverting to the international concepts of fundamental trade unionism. Recent actions by this more moderate group in questioning Government policies, and stating attitudes on various matters, tend to express a growing disillusionment with the authorities' programmes.

The organization has also become a declining force, both in terms of membership and spread of representation, since its membership is confined to Whites only. It is significant that the fastest growing group of trade unions are those which have Coloured and Indian membership, and the inference is therefore obvious.

On the other side of the coin, the South African Congress of Trade Unions, S.A.C.T.U., (which catered principally for Bantu workers) fell foul of the Government a number of years ago. Its Communistic philosophy quickly resulted in the Government's either removing or restricting its leaders. These actions, the apparent present apathy of the Bantu workers towards the Western world's form of trade unionism, and the restrictive legislation which presents so many difficulties in forming Bantu trade unions, has made this organization virtually disappear from the labour scene in South Africa. Nevertheless, its 'government and organization in exile' is much more effective here than any other organization. Its nuisance value overseas, however, is not going to achieve the formation of a democratic trade union movement in the Republic, so its real worth in furthering this ideal is questionable.

Another Bantu organization which emerged several years ago is the Federation of Free African Trade Unions of South Africa (F.O.F.A.T.U. S.A.). It also had but a short life, and some blame must be laid at TUCSA's door for this. Although it was created by TUCSA in order to establish a home for the Bantu unions which were not eligible for membership, TUCSA's decision in 1962 to admit Bantu trade unions to membership was mainly responsible for the organization's dissolution.

The increasing pressures placed on TUCSA after this decision in 1962, finally led the organization once again to restrict its membership to Whites, Coloured and Indians from 1969, leaving Bantu workers without any form of national co-ordinating body. With the exception of one or two unions, the Bantu are today almost completely unorganized, and no form of co-ordinating body presently exists for them.

RACIAL COMPOSITION OF THE LABOUR FORCE

Having explained the situation concerning existing labour legislation, and the differing racial attitudes in the labour movement itself, it is also necessary to look at the present composition of the labour force, with reference to the changing employment patterns and racial ratios.

The rapid escalation of South Africa's expanding industrial economy over the last decade has drawn in, to an ever increasing and accelerating degree, large numbers of Bantu workers. In all sectors of industry and commerce it has given them job opportunities which were either directly or indirectly closed to them until a few short years ago. At the moment the Non-Whites employed in all sectors (with the exclusion of agriculture) constitute 74 per cent of the total work force. A study of the situation shows that in 1960 the total number of Whites employed was 987 000 while Non-Whites totalled 2 561 000. The number of Whites presently employed is 1 283 000, and the number of Non-Whites in employment has shown a dramatic upsurge to 3 733 000! This remarkable change has taken place in the short span of ten years! Simple comparisons show that three out of every four workers are Non-White, and the increase in the number of Non-White workers over the past decade is, in itself, almost equal to the entire total of Whites presently employed!

It must be quite obvious that this dramatic process of labour integration is going to speed up further in future in order to meet the insatiable demands of our expanding industrial economy. It is clear, too, that South Africa will become ever more absolutely and irrevocably dependent on Non-White labour for its economic survival. It is also particularly significant that this process of labour integration has taken place despite tremendous efforts on the part of the Government to prevent it.

The Government's subsidiary measures of legislation (and administrative practices) which profoundly influence the labour situation in South Africa, such as the Influx Control Laws, the Physical Planning and Utilization of Resources Act, the Border Industrial and Bantu Homeland Industrial projects, stepped up immigration drives in Europe, and the introduction of automation wherever possible, have all not succeeded in curtailing the entry of Non-Whites into the established industrial metropolitan areas, and the labour force as such.

It is equally obvious that this increasing labour integration is already so deep-rooted, and of such magnitude, that virtually nothing can be done to reverse or eliminate it. The fact of the matter is that South Africa has virtually run out of White hands to do the work. The inexorable forces of economics demand that whatever labour is available must be used, and will be, despite any ideologically based restrictions, or attempts at curtailment.

The traditional policy of reserving certain jobs for Whites only has been completely eroded. Scarcely a day passes that further inroads do not take place, and constant attacks are being made upon the preserves of White-held occupations. Because so much Non-White labour is available at cheaper rates than the standards laid down for the White working force, there is a constant tendency, on the part of profit-orientated employers, to speed up this process of erosion. Circumvention of the labour laws, of existing practices, and of traditional attitudes, have therefore become a constant feature in this process of erosion.

Although Government spokesmen continue to hold the view that this process will be halted, firstly, and then reversed, it is unlikely that this can happen, since economic reasoning runs counter to such an argument. The most that the Government can hope to achieve, even with measures of unreasonable magnitude, is a braking effect, which will not be particularly significant in changing the inevitable end result.

The strong attempts being made to at least slow down the process, are based mainly on a too sensitive attitude towards change. The Government far too rigidly holds to outmoded conservative philosophies of the past to counter the challenges of a changing environment and circumstances. It is blind to the necessity for change, and reluctant to face up to the realities of the present situation. Particularly disturbing are the constant references made to the racial friction which must result if the process of labour integration continues, and yet, what are the facts of the matter?

Despite all these gloomy prophecies, the enormous influx of Non-White labour into traditional White jobs has not led to any significant increase in racial tension or friction. Any study of legal and criminal records will show that the number of racially prejudiced assault cases in work places has declined rather than increased in recent years. It can be readily conceded that because those concerned with the administration of justice view assaults in the working environment as being extremely serious, punishment meted out for these offences is so severe that it has deterred workers of any race from assaulting persons of any other racial group. But this is as it should be. It is vitally necessary to continue to impose these severe penalties on those who, through irresponsible action, could generate serious racial conflict in a place of work.

The goodwill and common sense attitudes of the workers themselves to racial issues directly contradict the views expressed by so many of our more flamboyant, extremist politicians. These so-called experts in the field of labour relations are not in a position to judge what the racial attitudes of the workers are, since they have never themselves been in the environmental work situations of the country's factories and other places of employment!

A contradiction is apparent when political protagonists expound on the soundness of South Africa's industrial legislation. The protagonists ignore the vast influx of Non-White labour into all sectors of commerce and industry, which takes place despite the restrictive procedures enforced by law and without noticeable racial friction during the process. Instead they claim that the lack of racial friction in industry is a result of the Government's restrictions on the use of Non-White labour!

The workers of South Africa, irrespective of race, colour or creed, are generally the same as workers anywhere else, in that they cannot afford the luxury of spending time at work generating racial friction. Their common objective of producing results at work generally prevents time being wasted on questioning any job activity on the part of a worker of another racial group. Anybody who has been actively engaged in the work environment knows that race becomes important only when the factory hooter blows for stopping the day's work. Social segregation then takes place, as distinct from the labour integration which exists during the working hours.

RESTRICTIVE LABOUR PRACTICES AS A CAUSE OF RACIAL FRICTION

South Africa's restrictive labour practices and legislation, coupled with irresponsible political antics, will be the major factor for generating racial friction. Hardline racial attitudes by some worker groups and labour organizations are established solely through following the lead set for them by irresponsible politicians. Our integrated labour force is, up to the present time, not displaying frightening signs of immediate racial conflict in the place of work itself.

It is outside the environment of the work place, and beyond the practice of work, that our concern for racial harmony must be focused. The responsibility for this lies squarely on the shoulders of Government, the leaders of commerce and industry, trade unionists, and all other opinion-makers and men of conscience. It must be remembered that our original industrial legislation was only introduced as a result of serious industrial unrest during 1922, which was confined to the White workers. There is no guarantee that further industrial unrest will not result if the Non-White workers are not also given more of a say in determining their own destiny, and a more equitable share in the rewards for work. It is unrealistic to expect any work force in a modern industrial society not to demand improved conditions. The Non-White workers in South Africa, who are becoming our industrial proletariat, who are the muscle and sinew of our production processes, are going to demand the removal of existing discriminatory practices.

It is a myth to believe that these workers will continue to remain docile, contented, and silent, particularly since their newly developing skills are making them ever more sophisticated. It is also unreasonable to expect that a less privileged class shall develop these skills, become more sophisticated, produce the major portion of the work, and yet have no desire to challenge the authority of the more privileged class. The mass of the working poor are also the mass of the racially under-privileged. This makes it vitally necessary to ensure that progressive removal of discrimination (particularly in the work place) becomes a fact. Non-White economic and status advances are essential if a political explosion is to be averted. Steps for improvement can be instituted without generating White reaction, or racial friction, if these steps are taken in a constructive, responsible, and orderly fashion.

Those who have the future of South Africa at heart should take advantage of the tremendous goodwill which still exists amongst the vast proportion of people of all racial groups in the labour force, and build on this rather than continue with policies which attempt to prescribe solutions of disengagement and abdication for situations, which are in themselves already irreversible.

The Urban African

Urban Bantu Policy
P. G. J. Koornhof

As Deputy Minister of Bantu Administration and Education, the author (who holds a doctorate from Oxford) is intimately involved in the application of the South African Government's Bantu policy. He is particularly concerned with the socio-political implications of Black urbanization.

The decade of the sixties will be known to future generations as the period when the Continent of Africa emerged from its somnolence into the twentieth century. Rising expectations on the part of its teeming millions came in the wake of the political emancipation of the largest part of Africa during this period. Falling infant mortality, declining death rates and a fertility which is estimated to be among the highest of the world's major regions caused a population explosion of unknown dimensions, particularly among the peoples of Black Africa. With their subsistence economy and often primitive agriculture, the rural areas could not cope with the surplus population brought about by the excessive growth of recent years. Large numbers of people were therefore forced to seek refuge in the towns and cities. Urbanization in the form that we have it in Western Europe and in South Africa is unknown in Black Africa. As a result of the factors mentioned above, however, urbanization is at present taking place at a rate calculated to be twice that of the average population growth rate.

Although different in many essential aspects from that prevailing in the rest of Africa, the position in South Africa has not remained unaffected by the pressures of population and spiralling economic and industrial growth.

The South African situation is a complex one with many facets. The country is inhabited by a diversity of peoples of varying backgrounds, cultures, traditions and skin pigmentation. On closer scrutiny we find that the White inhabitants, although divisible into two language groups, Afrikaans and English, have much in common as regard traditions, origin, cultural and religious background, social behaviour and in their level of economic development, measured in accordance with Western standards.

A large measure of inter-marriage has taken place and they are living and working together as a nation, largely bound together by a common weal.

When we look at the Black inhabitants we find that they speak no less than eight different languages with many variations, have as many different customs and cultural systems and are grouped together in their traditional homelands according to their respective cultural systems. We find, where they have not been Westernized, that they dress differently, have different marriage rites, different civil laws and customs, different political and government systems and have reached various stages of economic development. Because of these differences we cannot speak of one Bantu or African nation but must identify eight different Bantu nations, namely the Xhosa, Zulu, Swazi, North Sotho, South Sotho, Batswana, Bavenda and Matshangana.

At the turn of the century large parts of South Africa were inhabited almost exclusively by Whites in the White homeland, with a Western money economy system. On the other hand the eight traditional Bantu homelands, settled by the various Bantu nations in most cases since their forebears migrated from the Great Lakes of Central Africa, were inhabited virtually exclusively by Black people, accustomed only to a subsistence economy.

The position changed markedly with the rapid transition in South Africa from an agricultural to a mining and, finally, to a modern industrial economy. Tens of thousands of Black people were drawn into the White areas. They came at first as individuals, and for short periods, to sell their labour for the cash required for the upkeep of their families in the homelands.

CAUSES OF URBANIZATION

The reasons for the drift of Black men into the White areas are obvious. The White man with his advanced knowledge and varied skills, his drive to make his mark in life, made the best of the natural resources he found at his disposal. In so doing he created surroundings which became attractive also to many members of the Black populations. New avenues of making a living were opened to them and in time they developed a taste for the same things that are appreciated and striven for by the White man, things that are not found in the Bantu homelands. The White man made things more attractive by providing the newly arrived Bantu with housing in the White area, by giving him health services and, above all, education and the principles of Christianity.

This situation arose in spite of the natural resources and opportunities for development that exist in the homelands, which have some of the best agricultural land available in South Africa. Of the total area, 76 per cent has a rainfall of more than 500 mm per year. The Transkei, for instance, covering 4 per cent of the total area of the Republic, has 635 mm of rain per annum. It has been calculated that the dry land production potential of the homelands could provide in the food requirements of 24,6 million people. The Bantu own 40 per cent of all the cattle in the Republic. According to another analysis 200 hectares of land in the Bantu areas are worth about 300 hectares in the White areas. And yet, in spite of these advantages, the contribution of the Bantu homelands to the total agricultural production of the Republic is very small.

In mining we find a similar situation. Although some of the Bantu homelands are rich in minerals, the local populations have, through lack of know-how, capital and managerial talent, been unable to exploit these resources. Even after White entrepreneurs were allowed, with the consent of the owners and inhabitants of the land, to start mining operations, the local population failed to take advantage of the opportunities offered. For instance, a survey conducted three or four years ago found that of over 25 000 Bantu employed at certain mines in a particular homeland, only 800 were natives of that homeland.

In commerce the situation was, until recently, not very different. Up to a few years ago the distributive trade in the homelands was largely in the hands of Whites.

These brief sketches of the economic situation in the homelands are given to illustrate that although the homelands have certain comparative economic advantages over the White areas, they have failed to keep up with development in the White areas. The inevitable result has been a constant outflow of their Bantu inhabitants to the more developed White areas. As agricultural output rose, as new mines were opened in the Orange Free State and elsewhere and as the wheels of industry kept turning faster and faster, more and more Bantu moved into White South Africa and, more specifically, into its burgeoning towns and cities. The extent of this migration can be gauged by the fact that, according to the 1970 census figures, of the slightly more than 15 000 000 Black people, 7 376 000 are living in the White areas. (This figure does not include Bantu from outside South Africa's borders.) This also means that approximately 51 per cent of all the Bantu are still living in the homelands.

In the years immediately following World War II the 'urban explosion' of Bantu in South Africa's main industrial centres – the Witwatersrand, the Durban-Pinetown, Port Elizabeth-Uitenhage and the Cape Peninsula complexes – created a critical, even dangerous, situation. There was a desperate shortage of accommodation. A survey made for Dr H.F. Verwoerd, when he became responsible for Bantu affairs in 1950, showed that there was an immediate shortage of 167 000 houses. In the slums and shanty-towns that had sprung up haphazardly during and immediately after the war years, over-crowding and insanitary conditions became hazards to public health. Crime was rife and the general disenchantment provided a fertile field for Communist agents and agitators.

Since that time the problems connected with the Bantu in the urban areas have been tackled with great drive and determination. The entry of migrant workers, more often than not accompanied by large families and even distant dependants, was made subject to influx control measures. A labour bureau system was introduced to establish a ready link between work-seeker and employer.

Housing and slum clearance projects were tackled with the energy and urgency normally manifested in times of national emergency. The results were rather remarkable. The ugly slums are now only an unpleasant memory. In the twenty-year period from 1950 to 1970, 315 738 Bantu houses were built in South Africa's urban areas. This is the equivalent of some 25 new cities with a population of 100 000 each. The cost was tremendous. Direct expenditure amounted to R166 569 054 while the total spent on this housing effort in White urban areas was probably in the vicinity of R400 000 000, if subsidiary services, roads and railways are taken into account.

An equally large amount of energy and money went into the provision of educational facilities, health services and social and recreational amenities. Without going into too much detail, the position in regard to Bantu education can be mentioned as an illustration. Even though overall policy in respect of Bantu education is centred around the homelands concept, there are today no fewer than 1 114 000 Bantu children (out of a total of 2 841 000 for the whole country, including the homelands) attending 4 836 Bantu schools in the White areas. This, incidentally, is considerably more than the 827 000 White children who are at school in the White areas.

There are quite a few Bantu millionaires in the White areas, and in

Soweto, a Bantu township near Johannesburg, there are thirty thousand Bantu-owned motor cars.

Faced with a situation where large numbers of residents of the relatively underdeveloped Bantu areas are continually attempting to enter the White urban areas, the White man sees his future endangered by the preponderance of numbers and by unrestricted competition. He has not shirked his responsibility of providing the money and the means needed to create decent living conditions for those Bantu who can be legally and productively accommodated in the White urban areas. He regards it, nonetheless, as his natural right to take steps to safeguard his position. While the White man, for instance, does not begrudge the Black man his right to exercise his political ambitions in his own homeland, he is not prepared to share it with him in the White areas. From a social point of view situations abound in other parts of the world where friction, hatred and strife are the result of people of different cultures being compelled to share the same society.

The urbanization process in South Africa and the Government's policy in respect of the urban Bantu can only be understood when seen against the background sketched in the preceding pages.

IS THE URBAN BANTU POPULATION IN THE WHITE HOMELAND PERMANENT?

The Tomlinson Commission[1] pointed out that when endeavouring to determine the number of Bantu 'permanently' settled in White urban areas, the interpretation of the term 'permanent' presents many difficulties and that a number of degrees of 'permanency' can be distinguished.

As far back as 1922 the Stallard Commission[2] reported as follows:

'We consider that the history of the races, especially having regard to South African history, shows that the co-mingling of Black and White is undesirable. The Native [Bantu] should only be allowed to enter urban areas, which are essentially the White man's creation, when he is willing to enter and to minister to the needs of the White man and should depart therefrom when he ceases so to minister.'

In 1935 a Departmental Committee[3] was appointed to inquire into the question of the residence of Bantu persons in urban areas of the White

1. Commission for the Socio-Economic Development of the Bantu Areas in the Union of S.A. (1956).

2. Transvaal Local Government Commission (TP 1-1922).

3. Young-Barrett Committee.

homeland and to make recommendations regarding the introduction of legislation concerning:

> the principles of limiting the number of Natives in White urban areas to the labour requirements of such urban areas;
> provision for controlling the entry of Natives into White urban areas; and
> the withdrawal of superfluous Natives from the White urban areas.

In the four colonies which became the Union in 1910, local authorities were given a free hand in controlling Natives within their areas of jurisdiction.

In the Cape Colony, statutes constituting the municipalities contained provisions for the control and management of locations (i.e. Bantu residential areas) by way of regulation which enforced the residence of Natives in locations.[4]

Following the discovery of diamonds in Griqualand West and the resultant influx of Natives to the diggings, a proclamation[5] was issued providing for registration of service contracts.

In Natal town councils were given power[6] to establish locations within which Natives could be compelled to live.

In the Transvaal, municipalities could also establish locations where Natives had to live.[7] The central government of the Transvaal, however, retained control of (i) the curfew; and (ii) provision for the carrying of passes and the registration of servants.[8]

In the Orange Free State the legislation for the control and management of locations did not distinguish between Native (i.e. Bantu) and Coloured (i.e. of mixed origin) persons. All Non-Whites were designated 'Coloureds' and local authorities could compel all persons so classified to

4. The enabling authority was the Public Health Act, 1897, which provides for the right to regulate the use of Native locations and for the maintenance therein of good order, cleanliness and sanitation and the prevention of over-crowding and unsuitable huts and dwellings.

5. Griqualand Proclamation 14 of 1872.

6. Act 2 of 1904.

7. By different Ordinances.

8. Urban Areas Passes Act 18 of 1908.

live in locations. Local authorities could make regulations for the registration of servants.

INFLUX CONTROL MEASURES

These diverse measures were summarized as follows by the Department of Native Affairs (now known as the Department of Bantu Administration and Development) in its annual report for 1918[9]:

'There were two ways in which the law regarding such (urban) Natives might differ from colony to colony. In the first place the powers granted by statute to the local authorities varied to a very great extent, and in the second place, the policy of one central government, as demonstrated by its oversight of regulations, was to restrict the actions of local authorities, while that of another was to allow every latitude in the control of the Native population.'

When the Union of South Africa was formed, provision was made[10] for vesting control of municipal and other similar institutions in the provincial authorities, but all matters relating to the control and administration of Native affairs were assigned to the Governor-General-in-Council.[11]

The view at the time of Union was that the ultimate controlling authority should be the central government – firstly, to ensure uniformity of policy and, secondly, to improve conditions in the existing locations.

The Stallard Commission made the following recommendations which were embodied in the Natives (Urban Areas) Act, 1923[12]: (It is quoted in full because of its importance in the urbanization process.)

'It is agreed:

'1. That the treatment in regard to the housing and control of Natives in municipal areas has been extremely unsatisfactory in the past.

'2. That a statutory duty be placed on municipal bodies to provide adequate housing accommodation for all Natives within their area, and that suitable powers be given to these bodies to control the ingress of Natives into their area.

9. UG. 7-1919.

10. Section 85 of the South Africa Act.

11. Section 147 of the South Africa Act.

12. Act 21 of 1923 which was the precursor to the Bantu (Urban Areas) Consolidation Act, 1945 (Act 25 of 1945).

'3. That housing accommodation should take the form of:

(a) a house of reception of Natives immediately on their entering the area;

(b) the establishment of Native villages for those Natives whose residence is to be of some length, with buildings of Native kind;

(c) provision on an employer's premises, certified as suitable by the municipality.

'4. That an economic rent should be charged for housing accommodation.

'5. It is recognized that the existence of a redundant black population in municipal areas is a source of the gravest peril and responsible in a great measure for the unsatisfactory conditions prevailing. (By redundant Native is meant the Native, male or female, who is not required to minister to the wants of the white population, but does not include a Native who ministers to the legitimate needs of his fellow Natives within the municipal area). To combat this evil, the following practical measures are recommended:

(a) the provision of a rest-house, with suitable accommodation for male and female, where all Natives looking for employment will be housed;

(b) the prevention of any Native (male or female) living elsewhere than on his master's premises, in the Native village, or at the rest-house;

(c) the registration of Natives to remain in the hands of the Native Affairs Department, but in order to give the municipality the opportunity of discharging its duties, no Native to be registered to any employer or allowed to reside outside the rest-house or Native village without the certificate or visa of the municipality certifying that there is suitable accommodation for the employee.

'6. Native Advisory Boards to be established in every Native village, the boards to be so constituted and with such duties as may be fixed by by-law.

'7. The whole revenue from Natives derived by the municipality to be spent on their betterment.

'8. Trading within the Native village and rest-house to be confined to the Native residents or to the municipality: provided that the manufacture and sale of kaffir beer, if allowed, be a monopoly of the municipality.

'9. A special tribunal, on which there would be Native assessors, would be constituted, which should have power to deport, repatriate, or settle in labour colonies, idle, dissolute, or undesirable Natives in municipal areas.

'10. It is unanimously agreed that the placing at the disposal of all municipalities of adequate tracts of land is essential to the success of this or any other scheme for the betterment of the deplorable conditions prevailing in White urban areas. It is recommended that all powers possessed by the Government under the Gold Law be freely used for this purpose, and further that the compulsory purchase of any land required by a municipality be permitted at prices based on rateable value.

'11. The creation of a Native Affairs Department in all municipalities is highly desirable, the head of which must be a man of great experience of Natives and licensed or otherwise approved by the Native Affairs Department of the Union.

'12. It is recognized that the Native locations and townships form an integral portion of the town-planning problem of the whole community, and as such should be always subject to public control.'

Following the findings of the Young-Barrett Committee 'influx control' was introduced in 1937 in an effort to correlate labour supply with labour demand. The Bantu (Urban Areas) Consolidation Act, 1945 (Act 25 of 1945) embodies all the aforementioned cardinal principles but numerous amendments have been effected over the years.

Although the local authority is given extensive powers under current legislation[13] to regulate for the 'improved conditions of residence for Bantu in or near White urban areas and the better administration of Bantu affairs in such areas'[14], it is regarded as a creature of the Provincial Council which, having no inherent jurisdiction in respect of Bantu persons,[15] cannot, therefore, vest a local authority with such jurisdiction. The central government has, however, conferred on local authorities certain powers concerning the control of Bantu persons.[16] In exercising these powers local authorities act as the agent of the central government and therefore can never formulate separate policies of their own. The position was summarized as follows:[17]

13. Particularly under the Bantu (Urban Areas) Consolidation Act, 1945, and the Bantu Labour Act, 1964.

14. Long title of Act 25 of 1945.

15. Compare section 147 of the South Africa Act and the corresponding section III of Act 32 of 1961.

16. Particularly in Act 25 of 1945.

17. By the late Dr H.F. Verwoerd, then Minister of Native Affairs, in an address at the Congress of Administrators of Non-European Affairs on 17 September, 1956.

'The task of the urban authorities is to carry the policy of the country into effect, not to create basic policy for themselves or for the country. It is a very clear basis, laid down in our legislation from the outset, that it would only create confusion and disorder in the country if Native Affairs became subject to a diversity of policies . . . The State determines policy and the local authorities are the assistants in its application.'

It is a fundamental principle of the policy of multi-national development that the historic existence of the different Bantu nations with an own traditional Bantu homeland for each Bantu nation is acknowledged, and that the Bantu person enjoys full rights in his homeland. Insofar as the Bantu person's presence in the White urban or peri-urban area is concerned, the present and, in fact, the traditional, policy is in accord with the views of the Stallard Commission which were summarized as follows:[18]

'In these territories (Bantu homelands) the European has no claim to property and certain civil rights. There he is the temporary inhabitant who helps with the development of those areas, but they belong to the Natives. The rights of the Native are bound up with this fact. There the European remains without permanent rights of any sort. Just the opposite is the case in the European areas (homeland). There is the home of the European's rights and there the Native is the temporary resident and the guest, for whatever purpose he may be there . . . The Native residential area in the town is only a place where the European in his part of the country provides a temporary dwelling for those who require it of him because they work for him and thus earn their living in his service.'

NATIONAL IDENTITY OF BANTU IN WHITE HOMELAND

The Promotion of Bantu Self-government Act, 1959[19] provides for the political development of each Bantu nation in its homeland by means of the institution of its own government bodies. In the administration of the White urban areas due attention is paid to the distinction between different Bantu nations and homelands. The recent Bantu Homelands Citizenship Act, 1970,[20] provides for citizenship of each of the homelands. This Act also provides that every Bantu person in the Republic of South Africa,

18. By the late Dr H.F. Verwoerd at the Congress of Administrators of Non-European Affairs on 17 September, 1956.
19. Act 46 of 1959.
20. Act 26 of 1970.

who is not a prohibited immigrant, is entitled to a certificate of citizenship issued by the government of his homeland. These citizens will not be regarded as aliens in the Republic of South Africa but will, by virtue of such citizenship, remain citizens of the Republic of South Africa and be accorded full protection by the Republic of South Africa in terms of international law.

Government policy promotes the retention or renewal of the ties a Bantu person already has with his homeland. This is achieved in different ways: the work-seeker in the homeland is permitted to take up employment outside his specific homeland on the authority of a requisition and with the consent of the homeland authority for a limited period not exceeding one year. On the expiration of this period he has to return to his homeland and obtain authority from his homeland government for a further contract period.[21]

The governments of the various homelands are permitted to appoint urban representatives in the White homeland. Such representatives may in turn appoint assistants who may form boards to assist them in their functions, viz. to settle domestic disputes and to further the cultural, social and political interests of their homelands. Such representatives or their assistants advise their homeland governments in regard to all matters affecting the general interests of the members of the national unit concerned.[22]

Workers permitted to leave their homeland to take up employment in the White urban areas on a contract basis have to reside in single quarters, and every possible effort is made to ensure a visit by such a worker to his family in his homeland as often as circumstances may permit. With this in mind, special transport facilities are made available, especially over week-ends and long week-ends. Workers living within a commutable distance from White urban centres are required to live in their respective homelands and to commute daily on a heavily subsidized basis, as is also the case when they visit their families in the homelands on a weekly or monthly programme.

Policy thus aims at maintaining the urban Bantu worker's contact with his homeland, so that he is enabled to identify his aspirations with his homeland, of which he is a citizen and where he enjoys full citizenship, political and all other rights and privileges.

21. Bantu Labour Regulations (Bantu Areas) 1968 (Proclamation R74 of 1964).
22. Sections 4 and 5 of Act 46 of 1959.

Urban local authorities make substantial contributions by way of large sums of money for homeland development. Local authorities may also actively help in the development of a particular homeland by the building of towns or cities to cater for the needs of the workers traditionally employed in the area of their jurisdiction. It must be emphasized that a local authority does not in this way acquire any rights in the homeland. In carrying out any development works within a Bantu homeland a local authority in fact acts only as agent of the central government.

The migratory labour system as practised in the Republic of South Africa is by no means unique as it is general practice throughout the civilized world. The central government is, however, aware of the social problems attached to the system of migrant labour. Migrant labourers are housed in modern hostels or compounds and adequate recreational facilities are provided. A gigantic programme of decentralization of Bantu labour intensive industries to areas bordering on and in the Bantu homelands is at present being implemented. The decentralization of industries will enable a rapidly increasing number of Bantu workers to live with their families in their homelands. In the process migrant labour and its concomitant problems will be increasingly eliminated.

REVIEW OF LEGISLATION ON URBAN POLICY

The Bantu (Urban Areas) Consolidation Act, 1945[23] – which consolidated a series of laws passed since Union – is by far the most important measure regulating the presence of Bantu persons in urban areas in the White homeland. The long title of this Act summarizes its provisions as follows: 'To consolidate and amend the laws in force in the Republic which provide for improved conditions of residence for Bantu persons in White urban areas and prescribed areas, for the better administration of Bantu administration in such areas; for the regulation of the ingress of Bantu persons into and their residence in such areas; for the procedure to deal with idle or undesirable Bantu persons in areas outside the scheduled Bantu[24] and released areas[25] and with Bantu persons whose presence in prescribed areas is detrimental to the maintenance of peace and order; and for other incidental matters.'

23. Act 25 of 1945.

24. The Bantu homelands.

25. Areas defined (in the Schedule to Act 18 of 1936) with a view to their eventual incorporation in the Bantu homelands.

The urban local authority, as the controlling body, is required to set apart areas in the White homeland in which the Bantu have to reside. Regulations by the Minister of Bantu Administration and Development control such matters as the erection of houses and hostels by the local authority, the rental to be paid, the services to be rendered, the combating of slum conditions, the residence of unauthorized persons, etc. Funds may be obtained on a loan basis from the central government for building purposes. A Bantu person is not, however, permitted to acquire freehold title in the White homeland, just as much as a White person is not permitted to acquire freehold title in a Bantu homeland. A house in the Bantu residential area in the White homeland is allocated when both the head of the family and his wife qualify for residence in the White urban area. In all other cases, they reside in single quarters (hostels) provided by the local authority.

In terms of national policy, the Bantu (Urban Areas) Consolidation Act 1945 (Act 25 of 1945) and the Group Areas Act provide that a Bantu person may not reside in the urban area of the White homeland except in an urban Bantu residential area,[26] although an employer may obtain special dispensation from the local authority to house his Bantu workers in approved accommodation on his premises or in a compound specially approved for that purpose.

A Bantu person may be admitted into an urban or peri-urban area in the White homeland only with the approval of the local authority having jurisdiction over that area, such area being termed a prescribed area. The general rule is that a Bantu person may be in a prescribed area for a period not exceeding 72 hours unless he obtains special permission from the local authority. The following classes of persons are exempted from this rule[27]:

(i) a Bantu person who has lived in that area continuously from the time of his birth;

(ii) a Bantu person who has worked in that area uninterruptedly for one employer for longer than ten years or for more than one employer for fifteen years, without being convicted of a serious criminal offence;

(iii) the wife(unmarried daughter/son under the age of 18 years, or other dependant living with a Bantu person who qualifies under (i) or (ii).

A Bantu person who has any of these qualifications may apply for a

26. Compare section 9, Act 25 of 1945.

27. Section 10(1), Act 25 of 1945.

house in the urban Bantu residential area in the White homeland and he may change his employment in that area without jeopardizing his legal privilege to remain in that area.

All revenue which accrues from urban Bantu residents – whether it be in the form of rents paid for houses or accommodation in hostels, revenue from the sale of Bantu beer, fees paid by employees in respect of their registered workers, and fines imposed in respect of certain offences – is paid into a special account known as the Bantu Revenue Account which is controlled by the Minister of Bantu Administration and Development.[28]

There are a few areas where the Bantu Revenue Account is subsidized by the municipal general revenue account, but that is rather the exception than the rule.

Disbursements from the account are restricted to the urban Bantu residential area but the Minister may in certain circumstances sanction disbursements outside such an area, provided it is for the sole benefit of Bantu. The White taxpayer, therefore, does not benefit in any way from the revenue received from Bantu persons resident in his area.

To meet the costs resulting from the provision of link services to the urban Bantu residential areas the law[29] requires every White employer of adult Bantu males in a declared area[30] to make a monetary contribution[31] to the local authority which is then credited to the Bantu Revenue Account. Link services such as access roads, water, sanitation and lighting are financed from this source. These contributions are not payable in respect of private domestic servants or in respect of Bantu persons who are housed by their employers.

In addition provision[32] has been made for the payment of a further levy by White employers in declared areas, which is used to subsidize the cost of transport services for their Bantu employees.

Slum conditions are not tolerated. The relevant Bantu township regulations make provision for housing and hostel accommodation. Extensive powers are granted to the local authority to demolish unauthorized buildings.[33] In the event of Bantu persons squatting on unplanned land outside

28. Section 19, Act 25 of 1945.
29. Bantu Service Levy Act, 1952 (Act 64 of 1952).
30. Urban areas in which more than 20 000 Bantu reside or areas specially declared.
31. Usually 20c per week.
32. Bantu Transport Services Act, 1957 (Act 53 of 1957).
33. Compare also section 18, Act 25 of 1945.

an urban Bantu residential area special action may be taken under the emergency camp regulations[34] to regulate the accommodation on a temporary basis until permanent accommodation can be made available.

Special legislation was passed when it was found that existing legislation was inadequate to deal with slum conditions. An example of such legislation is the Bantu Resettlement Act, 1954[35] which was specifically designed to provide for the clearing of the slum areas of Sophiatown, Martindale and Newclare in Johannesburg and for the resettlement of the inhabitants in a properly planned township, Meadowlands, situated in the Johannesburg urban area. A statutory body known as the Bantu Resettlement Board was established to deal with this matter.

An urban local authority may establish an urban Bantu council for a Bantu residential area in the White homeland. This council is elected by the Bantu residents. Representatives of the Bantu nations within that area also elect a member or members on the council. The powers of an urban council are prescribed by regulation, but the council may, subject to the approval of the urban local authority concerned, exercise such additional powers relating to local administration in that residential area as may be assigned to it by the local authority with the approval of and subject to such conditions as may be determined by the Minister.[36] These include matters such as the lay-out of the area, the accommodation of Bantu persons in hostels, the erection and use of dwellings, the allotment of sites, the provision of sanitary, health and medical services, the moral and social welfare of Bantu persons living in the area, and the appointment of community guards. In this way the urban Bantu in the White homeland is represented and consulted in all matters affecting his welfare and the administration of the area in which he lives.

Bearing in mind that the Bantu's presence in the urban areas is justified by the service he renders in that area, legislation such as the Bantu Labour Act, 1964[37] and the Bantu Labour Regulations, 1965[38] provide the means for bringing the work-seeker and the employer in touch with each other. A local labour bureau is established in each urban area where work-seekers have to register and where employers must register all vacancies.

34. Prevention of Illegal Squatting Act, 1951 (Act 52 of 1951).
35. Act 19 of 1954.
36. Urban Bantu Councils Act, 1961 (Act 79 of 1961).
37. Act 67 of 1964.
38. Government Notice R.1892 of 1965.

A Bantu person in the White homeland must carry an identification document, commonly known as a reference book. This is provided for in the Bantu (Abolition of Passes and Co-ordination of Documents) Act, 1952.[39] In terms of this Act and its regulations a Bantu person, whether male or female, must on attaining the age of 16 years, acquire a reference book which serves as an identification document.

The urban Bantu person in the White homeland enjoys the same educational facilities as his counterpart outside the urban area. Educational matters are regulated by the Bantu Education Act 1953.[40] When determining monthly house rentals an amount on the average of 20c is included which accrues to the local authority for the provision of school buildings. The local authority has to provide school buildings and all town planning schemes make provision for school sites. The local Bantu population thus contributes towards the cost of school buildings.

All products, including Bantu beer[41] and liquor, are readily available to Bantu persons in the White homelands. They are entitled to buy freely in shops, and also to buy liquor and Bantu beer from any licensed bottle store in the White area of the town. Bantu beer is also sold in beer halls in the Bantu residential areas. All profits from Bantu beer sales are paid into the Bantu Revenue Account and are used for the benefit of the Bantu. Liquor outlets may also be provided inside the Bantu residential areas by the local authority in which case 80 per cent of the profits are paid to the central government for use for the benefit of Bantu. So far most of it has gone for the subsidization of daily transport costs of workers. Twenty per cent of the profits are retained by the local authority and paid into the Bantu Revenue Account for use to the benefit of the local Bantu residents.[42]

The number of Bantu workers in a White urban area is not restricted, but is regulated by the law of supply and demand and the availability of housing.

In terms of the Physical Planning and Utilization of Resources Act, 1967[43] and the proclamations issued thereunder, industries in certain urban areas may not increase their labour forces and no new Bantu labour inten-

39. Act 67 of 1952.
40. Act 47 of 1953.
41. Bantu Beer Act, 1962 (Act 63 of 1962).
42. Section 100 *bis,* Act 30 of 1928.
43. Act 88 of 1967.

sive industries may be established, except with the permission of the Department of Planning. This measure is designed to encourage decentralization of Bantu labour intensive industries and their establishment in areas bordering on or in the Bantu homelands.

Industrialists who transfer their factories from urban areas to areas bordering on or in the Bantu homelands themselves, receive certain concessions from the central government to cover their calculable net cost disabilities plus some additional concessions in respect of non-calculable cost disabilities. The concessions are calculated to compensate industrialists for their cost disabilities in decentralized areas, and to make it as attractive as possible for them to establish factories in the Bantu homelands or on the borders of Bantu homelands.

These concessions are in the form of cash grants, loans to purchase land (not granted within the Bantu homelands because a White person cannot own land in a Bantu homeland), loans for erection of dwellings for housing key White personnel, reductions on income tax and railage rebates, etc.

Industrialists establishing themselves within the Bantu homelands do so on an agency basis and receive more liberal concessions than those applicable in border areas.

Once the Decentralization Board has, with the authority of the Minister of Finance, approved of concessions in principle, the further administration of cash grants and loans is undertaken by the Industrial Development Corporation in the White area. The Bantu Investment Corporation administers grants and loans in connection with projects within the Bantu homelands, except in the Transkei-Ciskei area where the Xhosa Development Corporation undertakes this function.

The availability of family accommodation within the Bantu homeland makes it possible for the worker to live with his family and to travel to work daily in areas where border industries have been established.

The Bantu Administration Act, 1971: In order to establish more effective administrative machinery in respect of Bantu affairs in the White areas, the Bantu Administration Act, 1971 (Act 45 of 1971) has recently been passed by Parliament. Apart from its aims to achieve a more efficient administrative system through the establishment of Bantu Administration Boards, it provides for the greater mobility of Bantu workers within one or more White urban areas. Administration Boards will consist of persons with a wide knowledge of Bantu affairs and who have a keen interest in the Bantu worker. These persons will be drawn from local authorities, commerce, industry and agricultural organizations.

Bantu Administration Board areas are declared after consultation with local authorities and may include the areas of one or more local authorities. The Boards will be empowered to take over the administration of Bantu affairs in the White areas presently carried out by local authorities. These include *inter alia* the provision of housing, health services, recreational facilities, labour bureau matters, etc.

When one looks at the net result of this wide-ranging series of measures introduced over the years to implement Government policy in regard to the urban Bantu, it is safe to say that they systematically brought order to a situation which, initially, was chaotic and later tended to become explosive. It was only through influx control, for instance, that slum clearance and new housing projects could be tackled in a meaningful manner. It was through the labour bureaux that requirements of the economy could be reconciled with the necessity of providing decent living conditions and protection to Bantu workers already in the urban areas.

Measures designed to promote orderly administration led to the creation of a healthy and congenial environment in which hundreds of thousands of Bantu were able to enjoy amenities and a standard of living without parallel on the Continent of Africa.

'When I pass Croesus railway station,' the editor of the largest Bantu newspaper wrote recently, 'I see hundreds of Africans pouring out of the trains from Soweto to the factories of Croesus and Industria. They do not appear to be what you would call the down-trodden proletariat. They walk with their heads up. Their living standards are rising . . . '

In the urban areas large numbers of Bantu are acquiring the means, the know-how and the experience that can in due course be put to good use in the interests of the homelands of which they are citizens.

THE NEW PHASE OF URBAN DEVELOPMENT

As has been stated on various occasions in these pages, Government policy in relation to the Bantu in the urban areas remains orientated towards the Bantu homelands. It is therefore only reasonable and logical that Bantu businessmen, entrepreneurs, academicians, professional men and workers should be encouraged to apply their knowledge and skills in the homelands to which they belong, as and when the opportunity presents itself.

It is also reasonable and logical that, as citizens of a particular homeland, they are free and also entitled to exercise their political rights and to pursue their political ambitions in that homeland. In White South Africa, however, they cannot enjoy political rights although other rights or privileges, such as protection under the law, are fully guaranteed to them.

The Bantu of both sexes living and working in the White areas will, however, be able to exercise their votes in the elections of their homeland governments. In the case of the Transkei, the Xhosa living outside of the Transkei have on more than one occasion taken part in their Government's elections. The remaining seven homelands are now developing in line with the Transkei, so that in the near future many, or most, and eventually all Bantu living and working in the White areas, on attaining a certain age, will vote in the elections of their homeland governments.

Having disposed of the question of political rights in White South Africa, I can now turn to the new phase in Bantu urban development which will assume increasing importance in future.

Already in 1955, pointing to the lack of urban development in the Western sense, the Tomlinson Commission recommended the establishment of towns and villages in the Bantu areas. The Government concurred with this recommendation at the time and, with the first five-year development plan for the Bantu homelands in 1961, provided a large amount for the establishment of Bantu towns. An amount of R25 000 000 was actually spent. About sixty of a planned one hundred townships were fully or partly established. Today there are one hundred and sixty-nine townships in the Bantu homelands in some stage of planning.

During the second phase of this programme, which started in 1967, amounts allocated annually by Parliament for the establishment of townships and for housing in the Bantu homelands oscillated between more than R10 million and nearly R20 million per annum. During the last two fiscal years amounts of close on R5 million were allocated to the respective Bantu governing bodies. For the year 1971/1972 a sum of R18 million was set aside for Bantu urban development. In addition R4 760 000 has been allocated for this purpose to the various homeland administrations.

I visualize a shift in emphasis in the process of Bantu urbanization in the foreseeable future. The trend will be increasingly to transfer the responsibility for the establishment of Bantu urban communities to the governing organs of the homelands. As the homelands develop and find their feet they will be able to accommodate larger numbers of their citizens in urban communities. In fact, more than half a million Bantu have already been resettled in their respective homelands during the past seven years.

Although considerable numbers of Bantu will still be in the Republic of South Africa itself, one can distinguish more clearly in this development the ultimate aim of the policy of multi-national development : a community of nations that are politically independent and economically inter-dependent.

The Aspirations of the Urban African

M. T. Moerane

The author is the editor of World, *South Africa's top African daily. As a sophisticated African he has an intimate knowledge of the special problems of the so-called urban Bantu and is a recognized spokesman for this group.*

The Bishop of Zululand, the Right Rev. Alpheus Hamilton Zulu was arrested recently at Wilgespruit, Roodepoort near Johannesburg for failing to produce his pass book (reference book). In a raid by the municipal police conducted at 4.15 a.m. – a raid which the Town Clerk called 'one of the regular things' – Bishop Zulu was arrested, put into a police van and, at the police station, was charged and told he could pay an admission of guilt fine of five rand.

He preferred to appear in court as he felt he was not guilty. The Attorney General had the case withdrawn and Bishop Zulu had to show his reference book to the Bantu Affairs Commissioner in his home town of Eshowe when he returned from the conference on 'Black Theology' which he had been attending at Wilgespruit.

Thousands of Africans are arrested every month on this score. One of the important items in the reference book is a stamp which shows that the particular African is permitted to reside and work in the particular municipality. Without that permit an African is committing an offence if he is in an urban area for longer than 72 hours. Furthermore, he may not sleep in a White residential area. This permit is hard to come by and those of us who have it for an area like Johannesburg, where pay rates are comparatively higher, guard the right jealously.

Every African employee is permitted to be in this area as long as he works for the employer under whom he is registered. Should he lose his job with the particular employer, he forfeits his right to be in the area and has to go to the rural 'homelands'. He has no right to secure a job with any other employer. It is evident how insecure the urban African is, as anyone else would be in that position. It is the basic desire of the urban African to be free to live and work anywhere he can get a job and make a good living.

Recently Mrs Helen Suzman, the Progressive Party Member of Parliament, presented a charter of African women's rights to the House of Assembly in session in Cape Town. The charter demanded that the African woman should have the right to choose her marriage partner and to live with him throughout their life. This demand seems elementary enough. Yet the fact is that, in South Africa, if a young man who lives in an urban area marries a woman from the country, albeit just a few kilometres away, his wife has no right to join him and live with him in the urban area where he resides and works.

Another item of the charter demanded that an African woman who lives with her husband in an urban area should have the right to retain the home in which they live or to acquire property in her own right after the death of her husband. The law does not allow an African woman to become a registered tenant of a municipal house nor even to inherit the property that her late husband may have had. These items, which are only two of the six presented to the House of Assembly, serve to illustrate the disabilities that African women live under in the urban areas of this country. The anxieties and sufferings and frustrations that arise as a result of these policies are a sore point among the Africans. It means that families often are divided and at times are evicted to start a new life in new areas where the prospects are poor, sometimes at the hour of their greatest need after the death of a husband or after a divorce.

Yet all this stems from the basic policy of South Africa, which is that the African is a foreigner in the urban and industrial areas of South Africa. He is supposed to be in these areas as a temporary sojourner who is there merely to earn his living by serving the Whites and must be repatriated to the reserves when he ceases to fulfil that function. He cannot therefore have any economic or political rights in these so-called White areas.

THE REALITIES OF SOWETO

Soweto, the big complex, 67 square kilometres in area outside Johannesburg is the fourth largest city in South Africa. Like all the cities of South Africa, except Pretoria and Cape Town, the African population of this satellite city of Johannesburg is bigger than that of the mother city's Whites. Yet officialdom regards this Soweto complex not as an African city but as a dormitory where the Black workers who work for Johannesburg Whites are accommodated. They may not even aspire to engage seriously in trade even among their own people, beyond the most elementary levels of small grocery shops. Any who aspire to engage in real business are directed to the 'homeland' areas where they are loath to go for the population is sparse and the people poor.

In 1961, arbitrarily, in my opinion, the Government of South Africa under Dr H.F. Verwoerd, embarked on the policy of Balkanizing South Africa, apportioning 13 per cent of the land to the African people who today number 15 million, while allocating to the Whites who number $3\frac{1}{2}$ million, the rest of the 87 per cent of South Africa. This 13 per cent assigned to the Africans consists of the rural areas, which have been bypassed by industrial enterprise and have little hope of economic development.

In this discussion we are considering the aspirations of the 8 million Black people who live as displaced people without rights in the urban areas, outside the 13 per cent of land allocated to Africans. The United Party, which is the official Opposition in the White Parliament of South Africa, holds the view that urban Africans must be regarded as a permanent population in the urban areas, with full opportunities and rights within the locations set aside for their occupation. The urban African, too, claims no less than these basic rights, which common sense and elementary humanity, let alone justice, tell us ought to be granted. Considerable changes in the lot of the African would follow even this single concession.

The 800 000 strong community of Soweto does not have a single Teachers Training College and may not have it. Instead, parents of aspirant teachers must send them to the 'homelands', incurring transport and boarding fees they can ill afford. This, for reasons of ideological policy.

The right to own property and to engage in prosperous trade in the satellite townships would follow a change in policy and the frustrations and persecutions suffered under the influx control regulations would ease. A more contented community would arise to replace the present truculent population of Soweto, with its high rate of violent crime. The people there would become citizens, people of worth with human rights and obligations, and not the outcasts and objects of bureaucratic manipulation and paternalistic charity they feel themselves to be at present. They would have the satisfaction of taking part in the conduct and administration of their own affairs like adults. Now White city councillors run the affairs of these African townships and the Urban Bantu Councils or Advisory Boards meant to represent African interests are shadow bodies that have been termed 'toothless dogs' by the Africans.

In short, the urban African would desire simply to be free to earn an honest living, to be free to offer his services in an open market, to invest his earnings in enterprise in his own area among his people, to occupy or own his home and property with security of tenure and free title, and to secure the basic rights of education for his children and the social amenities of a decent society ensuring his health, security, survival and happiness. The influx control laws which bedevil the life of the African could be simplified so that if a person had a job and accommodation he would not need to be pestered about homeland histories and such considerations, if indeed the aim of influx control is to ensure that slums do not develop as a result of unemployed crowds swarming to the cities.

THE CLAIM TO POLITICAL PARTICIPATION

The United Party – not that it in itself has a high rating with the African people – has another pointer regarding the rights and aspirations of the African people. It believes that the African is a citizen of South Africa and must be represented in the Parliament that makes the laws that govern him. This is a lack that the urban African feels very keenly. His 'homeland' brother may derive some solace from the rudimentary institutions of self-government which the Government has been promoting during the last ten years. They may tolerate their present statelessness because of their hope of independent states-to-be. When it comes to the urban African, the award of citizenship of a distant ancestral homeland is a hollow, blurred concept.

The urban African desires the basic right of representation and participation in the Government that makes laws for him, where government shall be by consent and policies adopted by and with consultation and not by dictation. Only then will this country be run in the interests of all its people, contrasting with the present, when it is run in the interests of the Whites who alone have the franchise for the councils which make the laws and policies of South Africa.

If the African had political rights a situation would not arise where the country would be held to ransom against its own economic interests because the Government reserves skilled jobs for Whites only, although the chronic shortage of White workers threatens to ruin South Africa economically while African hands are waiting to do the job. You would not have thousands of eager Black faces roaming the streets for lack of classroom accommodation, while White children enjoy luxurious free schools. You would not have the state spending ten times as much on the education of White children and the White teacher earning twice and thrice as much as the African teacher.

It is a far cry to the day when South Africa will function as a united, democratic nation, with the participation of all, in the interests of all. But that is the destiny of this country, I am sure. How the process will be evolved will test the statesmanship of Black and White in this country. This is the big problem facing South Africa.

The White man, by devious techniques and rationalizations, has tried to contract out of his legitimate responsibility as a Government of this country. As long as the African was backward and simple, the White man was happy to rule over him and coerce him, even by imposing taxes, to enter his service and enrich him. No sooner had the African become modernized and sophisticated than he suddenly became a threat to the entrenched privilege which has always been the lot of the Whites in this land. He cannot bear to dispense equal justice to all, for he fears the preponderant numbers of the Black man. So he conjures up a new history that says South Africa has really never been one state, nor is the Black man a South African. While continuing to rule the Black man the White Government continues to declaim that the African is not really its responsibility.

This is a grave delusion. The White man, in his anxiety, wishes to go apart and yet is not prepared to pay the price of apartheid. He cannot go apart. It is too late in the day. The economic and social forces which have been set in motion in this country force us inexorably together. At present a huge array of legislation and sanctions thwart the free assertion of the will of those who do not share the views of the Government, directly or indirectly. The diversionary stratagems of Bantustan self-government and ethnic groups may help the Government to gain some time. However, we, the Africans, believe that the Bantustan policy which makes the African a foreigner in 87 per cent of the country of his birth is arbitrary and unjust.

The African regards all South Africa as his homeland. White South Africa must accept this and begin to restore justice to the Black man on this score. It must recognize the urban African as a permanent inhabitant of our cities with a rightful claim to economic and political rights in the urban African townships. The Bantustan policy must be regarded merely as a means to decentralize shared power between the races of South Africa in their common country. This means that the urban Bantu councils must be made full town councils for the Africans.

On the national level, a legislative assembly should be established for the urban Africans. Here we must stress that this assembly must represent all Africans in the urban areas and must avoid duplicating Bantustan tribal assemblies. Chief Minister Kaiser Matanzima visualizes – on the tribal level – a federation of all the Bantustan Legislative Assemblies.

According to my recommendation, then, there shall emerge a new constellation of legislative assemblies for :

(a) Tribal African groups – for the Zulu, Xhosa, Sotho, Pedi, Tswana, Shangaan and Venda.

(b) Urban Africans.

(c) Coloureds.

(d) Indians.

This constellation would accord *internal self-government* to these 'Black' segments of the South African population.

In the final analysis the real law-making and governing body in South Africa is the Cape Town Parliament. Unless and until the above 'Black' groups have representation in the Cape Town Parliament, South Africa is violating the fundamental tenets of democratic rule – rule by consent through elected representatives of the people. By what right does the White Parliament in Cape Town make laws for the Black people who are not represented in it?

The logical imperative is that the aforementioned legislative assemblies would send representatives to the Cape Town Parliament. How many each, is a detail. The important thing is the acceptance of this principle. The Government of South Africa may be shocked at the idea, but the fact is that the Black peoples of South Africa must be represented by their own people in the South African Parliament. What is more, we believe that most South Africans of all races in their heart of hearts know and accept the justice of such a course. It does not mean that when this measure has been implemented, the millennium will have come to South

Africa. All it will mean is that South Africa will have at last provided the machinery for consultation for all its peoples and for evolving realistic policies for the country. This would open a new road to this country's true destiny.

Together we have built a great country here. Its next phase of development will require the brawn, heart, will and mind of all its inhabitants. No-one can achieve this alone. Let us dare to stand for the right as God gives us to see the right. Sooner than we think, this country must go back to the true road of its destiny as one united nation.

There is frantic heart-searching even in circles close to the ruling group these days. Thinking people of all races know that our Government has not got the answer to the ordered and effective life of all in this country. Forces from within and from without are pressuring us to a new solution.

The Black people of this land seem to be going apart, but for reasons different from the Government's theories. They seek to find themselves. Tomorow they will assert their will. May it be sooner than late. For if it is sooner the confrontation will not be Black versus White; for right now agitation is building up to end the division of families in the urban areas; and the support for this campaign includes Black and White across the political lines.

Today we are finding ourselves or struggling to do so. Men of goodwill around the world can help us in the process. They can see us better than we see ourselves and they have a responsibility to speak out. They can help in counsel and material. The more dialogue we have with other nations the better. But in the final analysis the problems of this country will be solved by the people of this land.

The best thing our friends can do is to help us help ourselves. And the greatest aspiration of the urban African is to evolve a great, united, happy South Africa, with justice for all. He has the will, the faith and the patriotism to work for its realization.

As we go to print, a number of Black people at a conference in Soweto, Johannesburg, have decided to launch a new political movement. Their aims are to build Black solidarity and build a solid Black nation including Africans, Coloureds and Indians. The overall object is 'to build an egalitarian society which will give opportunity and equal treatment to all regardless of race or colour'. They will promote freedom from White domination, promote self-reliance within their own community and ' "conscientise" our people of the economic and political power they hold'. They will operate outside the Government framework of Bantustan policies. They do not recognize the Government creations of 'self-government' and Bantu Authorities and Urban Bantu Councils. They seek equality and freedom within South Africa as full citizens of the whole Republic.

This new movement could open a new chapter to a struggle that may be long and possibly even arduous. For Whites will not easily yield to surrendering their position of entrenched privilege, let alone correcting the imbalance in the distribution of power in all its diverse forms, which is the basic problem of this country.

It is not possible at this early stage to say whether we are engaged in the last battle for freedom for all in this country or the first battle of many to come before South Africa accepts equality and common citizenship for all, which I believe is our inevitable destiny, however much we may try to postpone its realization.

An African's View of Apartheid

W. F. Nkomo

The late Dr Nkomo was one of South Africa's best known Black leaders. A qualified medical practitioner, William Frederick Nkomo was recognized as a top spokesman of the urban African in general, and the African elite in particular. He was President of the South African Institute of Race Relations and had travelled widely in several Western countries.

History records that South Africa was first occupied by the Whites (Europeans) in what might pass as a permanent settlement in 1652. Tradition in the White circles of the country has it that these Whites occupied an open country and that they did not colonize or rob any people of their land. On the other hand, it is traditionally held by Blacks that the Whites robbed them of their land. It is even part of the folk-lore of the Xhosa that the prophet Ntsikana prophesied the coming of a people with long straight hair who would be ejected by the sea.

South Africa's historical background is of more than academic interest. Claims that the Whites were earlier arrivals than the Africans have often been made to justify the present grossly uneven division of the total land area. It is clear that the Western Cape was occupied only by Bushmen and Hottentot groups when the Whites first came. But elsewhere Bantu tribes were settled before Europeans landed at the Cape. In the course of their penetration of the interior, it not infrequently occurred that Whites annexed areas from which Africans had temporarily fled in the disruptions caused by the creation of the Zulu state and its aftermath. Elsewhere White settlers took over large areas as farms, oblivious to the existence of African families long resident there. Descendants of some of these families are now being evicted from such 'White' farms as redundant squatters or labour tenants.

HISTORICAL REALITIES – THE BLACK MAN'S PERSPECTIVE

Until recently, South Africa was generally regarded as having been 'discovered' on Christmas Day in 1497 by Vasco da Gama. Its history was regarded as having commenced when Jan van Riebeeck, together with a small group of servants of the Dutch East India Company, arrived at the Cape of Good Hope to set up a revictualling station for vessels on the long sea-route to the East Indies. All school-children used to be taught, and some are still being taught, that South African history is the history of the White man.

The latest *History of South Africa*[1] redresses this balance. 'This work', state the editors in the preface, 'derives from our belief that the central theme of South African history is inter-action between peoples of diverse origins, languages, technologies, ideologies, and social systems, meeting on South African soil.' They refer to certain other histories which 'are primarily concerned with the achievements of white people in South Africa, and their relations with one another. The experiences of the other inhabitants of South Africa are not dealt with at any length: they are treated mainly as peoples who constituted "Native", or "Coloured", or "Indian" problems for the Whites'.

This particular history, which takes into account the evidence of recent archaeological excavations, the writings of early travellers and other contemporary documents, as well as oral traditions and linguistic studies, records the history of the ancestors of the Africans of today, who were living in the area of the Republic long before the people from Europe arrived. It records the penetration and conquest of the present territory of the Republic by the Whites and the processes of contact with the African peoples. To us, the Bantu, this history is important. It supports our argument that the Whites colonized our country. It explains, I believe, why we Africans feel aggrieved and regard the Whites as being both our colonizers and conquerors.

It also explains, if such explanation be necessary, why African sensitivities are deeply wounded when they read a statement, such as the following:

'The first point is, therefore, that there was no colonization, only separate settlement by each group, nearly simultaneously and each had the chance for more than three hundred years to develop the country to serve

1. Monica Wilson and Leonard Thompson, Editors, *The Oxford History of South Africa,* Oxford University Press, 1969.

his growing population group. In fact, only in South Africa did the White man deliberately reserve land for the Bantu and endeavoured (mostly in vain) to train him to make the best use of it as he did with his own, and to such good purpose that the Black man came to him for employment, food and the good things of life. The White man, therefore, has not only an undoubted stake in, and right to, the land which he developed into a modern industrial state from denuded plains and empty valleys and isolated mountains, but according to all his principles of morality it was his, is his and must remain his.'[2]

I could, using similar terminology, invoke 'the principles of morality' to press the claims of the African people to sole ownership in the past and for the future. But this is a sterile approach.

We all share a common awareness that in the Cape Province there was throughout the nineteenth century a constant shifting of geographical boundaries in vain attempts to fix a definite dividing line between the European settlers moving in a north-easterly direction and the Bantu tribes moving southwards. Krüger who, unlike many of the politicians, concedes the fact that the Whites were colonizers, speaks of these attempts and says, 'This line was destined to disappear in the course of the nineteenth century'.[3]

Throughout a period of one hundred years of uneasy inter-action between the two groups, friction, mainly over the rights to land, culminated in recurrent fighting, followed by precarious peace agreements. Hence, although the final outcome was the South Africa we know today, struggle was the basis of our relationships. There was conflict after conflict following the meeting of Black and White in South Africa. And although missionaries later attempted to resolve this conflict, the memories of it have not completely been eradicated from our thoughts.

THE LAND PROBLEM SINCE UNION

The first point of conflict between Black and White was the land. Land is still today in the forefront of unresolved problems. Before Union, the four colonies had followed different policies in regard to African land rights. All four had set aside certain areas as 'Reserves' for African ownership and occupation, but the proportions so reserved differed markedly.

2. *Progress Through Separate Development,* Information Service of South Africa, New York, 1968, p. 11.

3. D.W. Krüger, *The Making of a Nation,* Macmillan, 1969, p. 5.

Moreover, the legal status of these Reserves and African rights of occupation were ill-defined. The Native Land Act passed in 1913 brought about uniformity of policy. Although it was only an interim measure, designed to maintain the status quo until Parliament made other provision, it made ominously clear what the final pattern was likely to be. The Act demarcated the existing Reserves and prohibited the transfer of such land by sale or lease to Whites. According to those who passed this Act, it was done for our protection. We do not regard it as a protection, but as a deprivation. For we were at the same time prohibited from buying land outside the Reserves. This deprived us of a right we had hitherto enjoyed.

It became the starting point of much agitation, as the people felt sorely aggrieved by this action on the part of the South African Parliament. All available legal channels were used to fight the measure. A court action succeeded in regaining for the Cape Africans their right to acquire land in areas other than the Reserves or those areas released by Parliament subsequent to the enactment of the 1913 Natives Land Act. There were many areas where Africans had acquired land either on individual tenure or in groups. There was also much land hunger amongst the Africans, who felt very strongly about the disproportionate distribution and allocation of the land of South Africa. This question of the inequitable distribution of land is a sore point with the Africans to this day. There will be no final peace of mind and restfulness on the part of the Africans until this matter is finally reviewed on an equitable basis, bearing in mind the population ratios of Black and White.

The land question was carried a stage further when in 1936 the Bantu Trust and Land Act was passed. In terms of this Act, the privileges enjoyed by the Africans in the Cape were taken away so that the restrictions which applied to Africans regarding the purchase of land outside the so-called Reserves now had Union-wide application. This, together with the removal of the African voters of the Cape from the common on to a communal roll, had the effect of uniting the Africans probably more than anything else had done in the past. The Africans called an *ad hoc* conference to deal with the new laws – the Land Act and the Representation of Natives Act, passed in the same year.

The emotions of the people ran high, and the peace and racial harmony of South Africa were threatened. A very moderate leader – the late Professor D.D.T. Jabavu – who was elected leader of the All African Convention, gave a very fiery and revolutionary presidential address. In his address the professor hinted at the possibility of a bloody and violent struggle to deal with the matter. The fact that the emotions of so balanced and moderate a personality as Professor Jabavu had reached this fever-pitch was an indication of the anger and the bitterness of the African people. This anger and bitterness still reverberates through the life of the people today. Yes, there is calm and apparent satisfaction with things as they are today, but I can state without any fear of contradiction that the situation, far from being one of acceptance, is one of enforced acquiescence.

The effect of the Bantu Trust and Land Act of 1936 was to take away land which Africans had outside the Reserves if this land was in areas surrounded by White land. The existing African farms there then became Black spots. Provision was made for additional land to be made available for African occupation. This was generally land in close proximity to the scheduled Reserves. According to the Act, an additional 6 132 283 hectares were to be released for African occupation. It should be noted that up to the present time the successive governments of South Africa have not yet provided all the promised additional land. Referring to land still to be made available, Muriel Horrell states: 'According to the Deputy Minister of Bantu Development its area as at the end of 1968 was 1 356 240 hectares. When one considers when the promise was made to the Africans, one is inclined to feel that there is no serious attempt to finalize this matter.'[4]

In the light of the fact that Africans form some 70 per cent of the total population of South Africa and that their reserves only constitute a little more than 12 per cent of the land surface of South Africa, it becomes clearly evident that great injustice is being done to the Africans. But let us leave the land question at this point in the hope that future generations of South Africans will be challenged to do something positive about the matter. As for the Africans, the refrain still rings in their ears 'Afrika Izwe Lethu' – Africa, our land.

WHITE PATERNALISM AND RACIAL SEGREGATION

When Union was established in the year 1910 the position of the Africans was radically affected as was that of the other racial groups of South Africa. The Africans now came under the direct control of the Central

4. *The African Reserves of South Africa,* S.A. Institute of Race Relations, 1969.

Government of the country. General Louis Botha made a speech in the House of Assembly on the 1st April, 1912, in which he said 'He did not wish to discuss the question of the Coloured people, but in regard to the Native question they were bound to act with the greatest caution. Some changes must be made, otherwise diffculties would arise. Were they to treat the races on a footing of equality, or must they try to find a solution which would give more satisfaction? . . . Personally, he thought the solution would be found in the increasing of the rights of the Natives who must have a certain measure of self-government under White supervision in order that they might work out their own salvation and be treated justly. In a social sense the two races could never become one. Marriages between Whites and Blacks were impossible and would only lead to sorrow and mischief. The Natives should be improved on their own national lines.' [5]

This enunciation of general policy and outlook towards the Africans on the part of the Prime Minister of the Union of South Africa – if pursued in the spirit in which it was uttered – could very well have become a sound corner-stone upon which to build the relationships between Black and White in South Africa. Whilst it was hesitant on the question of political equality, it yet appeared to accept as basic the principles of fair treatment and justice. One does appreciate the fact that there was the problem of differing cultural backgrounds, and that the Africans were mainly a primitive and illiterate people. With the background of the violent clashes between Black and White, there was bound to be fear and a degree of hatred and suspicion on both sides. These would naturally influence the direction of the policies which the country would follow.

It was clear that race separation or segregation would be uppermost in the thinking of the planners of the race policies of South Africa. Even a declaration such as that of General Botha was not free of the prejudices of race – as indicated in the words 'in a social sense the two races could never become one. Marriages between whites and blacks were impossible and would only lead to sorrow and mischief'. These prejudices are still dominant in the thinking of most Whites today. When White men take a bold stand for right and justice in the realm of race relations, they are often asked if they are prepared to let their daughters marry Black men. Self-preservation on the racial level is justifiable, but it must be rid of the prejudices that go with it. This has been a basic factor in the South African

5. D.W. Krüger, *South African Parties and Politics, 1910-1960,* Human and Rousseau, 1960, p. 361.

way of life. The result has been that whenever the advancement of the other racial groups has been considered, the planners have always wanted to know how such development or advancement would affect or prejudice the position of the Whites in the country.

One other factor in the declaration of General Botha was the question of granting the Africans a 'measure of self-government under White supervision'. In this utterance was entrenched the principle of paternalism. The Africans were to develop as wards or minors under White tutelage and supervision. There were already many enlightened Africans at the time of Union. These men were capable of being entrusted with the responsibility of leadership and government. It is true they would happily have accepted Whites as advisers, but not as supervisors. This meant to the Blacks that the Whites were determined to dominate the situation for all time. Mention must be made of the fact that the Africans at the time of Union felt they had been let down by the British. It had earlier been felt that at the conclusion of the Anglo-Boer War the British, in handing over the country to the Boers whom they had vanquished, paid hardly any attention to the Blacks and their aspirations. It was for this reason that when the National Convention was held, the Africans held their own convention where they stated their demands for equality and fair-play. They also felt, when General Louis Botha became the first prime minister, that it would have been better if John X. Merriman, prime minister of the Cape Colony prior to unification, had become the first prime minister of South Africa.

From the early days of the history of South Africa, the Africans had no say in the affairs of state. They were not represented at the National Convention, and they have not had any direct representation in any of the successive parliaments of the country. Cape liberalism succumbed to the principles of territorial separation and racial inequality characteristic of the other governments which preceded Union.

What we find obtaining today in the sphere of administration was practised in the governments of the republics prior to Union. For instance, in the Transvaal there was a policy of territorial separation and the administrator of the Transvaal was appointed the paramount chief of the Bantu. There was a superintendent of native affairs as well as native commissioners. The Africans had no vote. In the Free State, likewise, the Africans had no franchise rights. In Natal a limited number of Africans had the franchise. Only in the Cape Province had a colour-blind qualified franchise been introduced. At the National Convention of 1908 the question of the franchise for Non-Whites became the subject of heated debate. A compromise was reached which enabled Non-Whites, including the Africans who had the vote in the Cape Province, to retain that right. This was entrenched in the South Africa Act and it could only be changed by a two-thirds majority of both the House of Assembly and the Senate sitting together.

As early as 1926, General Hertzog published his Native Bills and one of these concerned the franchise. It was, however, only in 1936 that this Bill was passed, removing Africans from the common roll and providing for the creation of the Natives Representative Council. This body was to provide the forum where our views could be expressed. It proved a useless forum – just another advisory council – and it was doomed to failure. It was disbanded as a result of the Bantu Authorities Act of 1951.

THE ADVENT OF APARTHEID

The Bantu Authorities Act was passed by the present Nationalist Government, and with it began the apartheid era. In 1959 the Promotion of Bantu Self-Government Act was passed. In terms of this Act the country was fragmented into ethnic-territorial areas with various tiers of partially self-governing councils. These were to function under the supervision of White Commissioners General. Thus an old paternalistic practice was carried further. To us, this was a setback in the political development of the Africans. It entrenched the system of political separation. It meant that for all time we would be separated politically from the Whites. It also fragmented the Africans at a time when they had developed a national consciousness and a spirit of solidarity. It was the expression of White domination through the time-honoured strategy of divide and rule.

This innovation of the Nationalist Government under the leadership of Dr H.F. Verwoerd was detested by the Africans, who protested against it through whatever avenues were open to them. This finally led to the banning of African political organizations, followed by an era of strict police surveillance over the activities of African politicians. There was wide-spread intimidation. Through a network of police informers, those who dared to voice the grievances of their people were muzzled and gagged. Then followed a political calm which is misinterpreted as the acceptance of the status quo. People are compelled to acquiesce in a situation which they dislike and which is not of their choice or making. Today the ethnic territorial governments are seemingly well launched and it is believed that all is well. The leaders of these governments are mostly 'yes-men'. The Councils are dominated by Chiefs who are in the pay of the administration. There are not sufficient elected members to give full expression to the wishes of the people.

While most Chiefs adopt attitudes which will placate the authorities, an enlightened Chief speaks up forthrightly from time to time. Chief Gatsha Buthelezi is one such Chief. It is an open secret that Chief Buthelezi was for years a steadfast opponent of the whole concept of separate development. It was only his commitment to the service of his people, allied to his realization that at this stage there are no other options open to an African leader, which finally persuaded him to co-operate in the development of the Zulu homeland in accordance with government policy. He is an independent thinker, and even as Chief Executive Officer of the Zululand Territorial Authority, he does not hesitate to express his view. Speaking in Eshowe, he is reported as having said that 'Western and African cultural differences had been used to justify policies of differentiation. Implied in this one noticed a deliberate denial of human rights to other human beings on this basis'. He was speaking at a function to launch the Zulu Bureau of Language and Culture. He went on to say: 'We need to rediscover ourselves as a people and we can achieve this by looking at our past.'[6]

It is significant that while he states his claim strongly for the extension of human rights to us all, he still mentions this respect for the cultural heritage of the Zulu. He urges the Zulu to look 'at our past'.

It is often stated by those who want to deny us elementary human rights that we want to escape our colour and our culture. There is nothing of the sort. Far from that, there is a reverence of our past, customs, traditions and our culture as expressed in our music, language, folk lore and art. The trouble is that the paternalists and others want to tell us what they think is best for us. We, on the other hand, think and feel that the final decision must lie with us.

Even our young students and intellectuals respect their cultural background and heritage. The President of the Black South African Students' Organization (S.A.S.O.), Mr Barney Petyana, said, 'We must make Blacks independent of the Whites as far as possible and make them realize they

6. *Rand Daily Mail,* 27 January, 1971.

are on their own. In order for a group of people to bring about change there must be an identity which they seek to protect and promote. Black people must build themselves to a position of non-dependence on Whites. They must work towards a self-sufficient political, social and economic unit. In this manner they will help themselves towards a deeper realization of their potential and worth as a self-respecting people.'[7] But to allay the fears of those who may feel that he is in favour of apartheid or separate development, he goes on to say: 'Separate development dictates to us what we should have. We envisage a situation where we ourselves can make demands.'

A COMMON CULTURE

The Africans, no less than the Afrikaners, value their past and the cultural heritage that is theirs. But they are clearly aware that modern conditions generate continuing social change. They believe that in this process a common culture has evolved in South Africa, to which all groups have made their contributions. No group can develop on its own lines, uninfluenced by the total society of which it forms a part. Cultural isolation is not possible in the modern world – and this includes South Africa. It would impoverish us all if the young African intellectuals, goaded by rejection and recurrent humiliation, were to choose to opt out into an exclusive world and culture designed for Blacks. For this is as unrealistic as are the attempts of White supporters of separate development to exclude the Blacks from their White world and culture.

To make our exclusion more complete, there is a new Citizenship Act which gives Africans homeland citizenship and virtually deprives us of the citizenship of greater South Africa. Thus we are to become foreigners in the land of our birth: and soon we shall have to carry passports which give us a nebulous citizenship. This is an unhappy situation, which we do not accept, and against which we protest strongly. We have no alternatives along peaceful and constitutional channels. We are being driven to our extremity.

The latest development in the field of African administration is the Bantu Affairs Administration Bill, which will empower the Minister to take away from the local authorities the administration of the Africans in their area, and to hand it to goverment-appointed boards. It is a sugar-

7. *The Star*, 26 January, 1971.

coated pill in so far as it allows for some extensions of employment opportunities by allowing Africans to look for work in the larger areas, which may include several municipalities, under the control of a board. But we feel it is designed to help the government to expedite its programme of endorsing Africans out of the metropolitan areas and repatriating them to the homelands. It comes at a time when this whole question of urban Africans has become a burning issue.

The policy of repatriating Africans to the homelands has reached the point where urban Africans have become increasingly insecure. Under the Natives (Urban Areas) Act of 1945, as amended, it was legally possible for Africans to qualify for permanent residence in the urban areas. We fear that this right is gravely threatened. The trend is to abolish all political and other rights of Africans in non-Bantu areas. The argument is that with the abolition of rights in the so-called White areas, there will be the creation of opportunities in the homelands. But we are being stripped of rights long before the materialization of these opportunities.

Economic developments militate against ideological policies. The trend is towards urbanization. The pull will be to the towns where there is development and where there is employment. Repatriation to underdeveloped and even undeveloped areas means the condemnation of thousands of our people to starvation. This could lead to a volcanic situation. The country is anti-communist in its outlook, but it offers the frustrated and hungry millions on a platter to communism.

We are not opposed to the entrenchment of the existing reservations as African Reserves for all time. We also welcome the attempts to develop these areas so that they can produce more and be responsible for the well-being of as many people as possible. But surely these reserves are already overcrowded. On the present basis of life, where the people are mainly condemned to a peasant form of existence, more land is needed for those who are there now. There is naturally room for other development : and such development is urgently needed.

What we object to is the attempt to force people out of the towns by making life in those areas grimmer and harder for them. Mr Blaar Coetzee, whilst a deputy minister of Bantu Administration, always stressed that there should be a curtailment of amenities and rights for Africans in the urban areas so as to make them want to go to the homelands. The whole trend of policy is directed towards the curtailment of rights and enforcement of new restrictions. Some of the latest restrictions affect housing.

Whereas in the past it was possible for Africans to buy homes or the right of ownership of homes in their townships in the White areas, this right has been taken away. Those who have bought or built their own homes will be unable to sell such homes to Africans, but will be able to sell only to the local authorities.

Influx control is causing increasing hardship, particularly to young people. Young men are experiencing difficulty in securing permission for the entry of a bride from other towns, even neighbouring urban areas. This is practically impossible should a young man want to marry a girl from the homelands. In such cases, they are not permitted to establish a home in the urban areas. The number of disabilities affecting Africans in the towns seems to increase by the day. This appears to be part of a concerted effort to make the urban areas unpleasant for African settlement.

Even in the field of health services, an African doctor can only practise in an urban area if he is residentially qualified to live in that particular town – and then he must make his home in the area allotted to his ethnic group. Is it surprising that we cry out against such restrictions? We note that Whites are not subject to any of these curbs. It seems to us that a situation may arise when Africans will be denied the right to serve their own people in the towns. This will be a luxury in which they can indulge only in the homelands. To me this seems to be one – but certainly by no means the only – contradiction of apartheid. One notes, for example, that in many offices of the Department of Bantu Administration and Development, the officials continue to be White, and that there is a stringent application of apartheid – and sometimes of outright *baasskap.*

CONSTRUCTIVE DIALOGUE – NOT WHITE DOMINATION

The policies of the successive governments of South Africa have prepared the Whites for a place of supremacy and domination, and the Blacks for a place of subservience and permanent inferiority. It is held that apartheid will allow Africans to acquire or retain full control among their own people. 'It is on that point which I place emphasis', said Dr H.F. Verwoerd, 'that our struggle is not in the first place destructive but constructive. We want to build up a South Africa in which the Bantu and the White man can live next to one another as good neighbours and not as people who are continually quarrelling over supremacy.'[8]

8. House of Assembly, 27 January 1959.

But there will always be quarrelling whilst the basis is one of White supremacy. Only an honest change in approach, which makes it possible to involve all of us in dialogue, can lead us along the road towards ultimate peace.

We are of the opinion that it is wrong to evaluate people on the basis of colour. In South Africa, colour, rather than merit, has been the chief yardstick used to determine the treatment to be accorded to any people. It must be accepted that we shall live together for all times. The Bantu homelands cannot absorb all the Africans. Moreover, the areas in which the Africans are to develop their homelands are scattered throughout a wide arc of the country. The Tomlinson Commission found that there were 110 areas for Bantu habitation. There are also 154 so-called Black spots. This means that there can be no real geographical demarcation and that contact is bound to take place along an extended line.

It is increasingly urgent for us all to meet together in consultation and dialogue on the racial trends of South Africa. Of course, the response of those in the government will be to contend that their policies have been accepted by responsible African leaders and that these policies are working smoothly in practice. I repeat that most of those who welcome government policies are chiefs and headmen. Moreover, it must be remembered that many of the vocal Africans are either banned or behind bars. I wish to stress that those who are critical of official policies are not negatively so. Many of them are constructive and positive. They are ready for dialogue and consultation. They are patriotic in the truest sense, and they cherish the highest good for both Black and White in South Africa. What we need is to cultivate a spirit of mutual trust, and to banish the fears that are aroused when any one section stubbornly clings to what it considers to be right. We can arrive at understanding on the formula, what is right, not who is right.

A NEW FLUIDITY IN RACE RELATIONS

It is a new purpose, a new spirit and a new understanding that we require in our country. In common with a number of other observers, I sense a new fluidity in attitude and approach making itself evident. There appears to be greater awareness of the fact that we are part of a Black continent, and that our survival depends on our ability and preparedness to collaborate with people, irrespective of their colour or race. There also appears to be an increasing realization that South Africa is, in actual fact, a multi-racial country and that a *modus vivendi* must and can be evolved to bring into being what Professor S.P. Cilliers of Stellenbosch University called 'an equitable system of sharing economically and politically'. It is my belief that a shared society can be fashioned to bring all South Africa's peoples a greater measure of satisfaction.

Clearly, as Professor Cilliers states when discussing the difficulties confronting South Africa, 'We will never solve finally or perfectly the problems of human relationships. We can only strive to attain a *modus vivendi.*' No country has ever 'solved' the problems posed by the complexities and ever-changing inter-relationships of human beings and groups. But one is entitled to expect that there should be an acceptable direction and goal to which endeavour is channelled. Our present *modus vivendi* is basically unsatisfactory, and it cannot last. I, for one, would endorse the three-point policy set out by Professor Cilliers as his 'Wish for the New Year',[9] and believe its systematic implementation would set a course for the progress of the totality of South Africa's peoples. The three goals included in this policy are :

> A higher rate of development of the Bantu homelands than has been attained up to now, so as to accommodate economically as well as politically at least that section of the African population who still regard the homelands as their permanent homes.
> Movement towards full citizenship for the Coloured and Asian populations.
> The acceptance of those Africans who are permanently urbanized as part and parcel of the non-Bantu society.

South Africa could, if only the opportunity were given it, shape a pattern of racial harmony and co-existence. Our faith in the creation of a more just society based on the recognition of individual worth could be restored to us, making it possible for us once more to 'Go forward in faith' – the call made to the people of South Africa by J.H. Hofmeyr many years ago, at a time when it was easier to hope than now.

9. *Cape Argus,* 4 January, 1971.

The Coloured and Asian South Africans

The Coloured Policy of the National Party

W. B. Vosloo

The author is Professor of Political Science at the University of Stellenbosch. Holding a Ph. D. from Cornell University, Willem Benjamin Vosloo founded the Department of Political Science and Public Administration at the aforesaid university. He has a brilliant academic record and has visited the U.S.A. and the United Kingdom in the course of his training.

The year 1948 is a watershed in the political history of South Africa. It marks the victory of Afrikaner nationalism at the polls and the acceptance of apartheid as a comprehensive and articulate policy for the official regulation of the relationships between Whites and Non-Whites in all spheres of life on a nation-wide scale.

But policies of separation or segregation go far back into South African history and do not begin in 1948. For more than three centuries since the landing of Jan van Riebeeck at the Cape in 1652, the relationship between the races and ethnic groups has been based on some form of separation in the social, economic and political spheres. It was manifested by the mere social apartness of the early colonial years at the Cape, the no-equality-in-Church-and-State of the Boer Republics in the Orange Free State and Transvaal, as well as the more subtle but effective colour bar devised by British South Africans in Natal. Since Union in 1910, the great majority of White South Africans, whatever their political affiliations, have accepted White supremacy as the basis of policy. But the earlier segregation policies were more sporadic and pragmatic and allowed the forces of integration to operate in many fields – particularly the economic field – without much calculated planning.

The special significance of the National Party's success in 1948 was that it came to power largely on the platform of *apartheid* – a word which had been used as a slogan since 1943. In terms of what the Party considered as its electoral mandate, it was unequivocally committed to an elaborate policy programme directed towards the systematic disentanglement and separate development of the various racial and ethnic groups as far as practicable. This policy orientation was not new, but it interpreted the general attitudes and aspirations of a growing proportion of the White electorate in terms of a clear-cut formula.

At the root of the policy of apartheid lies the philosophy of differentiation which is deeply embedded in the history of the Afrikaner people. The Europeans who in the seventeenth century had come to settle in Southern Africa felt themselves different from the indigenous inhabitants they encountered – despite instances of miscegenation which contributed to the emergence of the Coloured population. Initially this distinction was between Christian and heathen, but in time the highly visible features of colour and race became the distinguishing marks between 'in' and 'out' groups. As a result of the obvious differences in culture and standards of living, a dark skin even came to be accepted as a sign of inferiority.[1]

The Afrikaner's sense of having a distinctive cultural heritage worth preserving asserted itself in the nineteenth century against the British cultural heritage, from whose domination they sought to escape by trekking into the interior. The *raison d'être* of the National Party needs to be interpreted in the same terms. The party was formed in 1914 to preserve the integrity of Afrikanerdom against the danger of obliteration by the potent, but significantly different, British cultural heritage. The same preoccupation with the needs of cultural differentiation gave birth to the policy of apartheid which had its rationale specifically in the threat of the numerically preponderant Non-Whites to the European-type White civilization which has been built up in South Africa in the course of three centuries.[2]

Although National Party policies are primarily directed towards the

1. See G.D. Scholtz, *The Origins and Essence of the Race Pattern in South Africa,* South African Information Service, Fact Paper 61, July 1958, pp. 4-9.

2. Some of the most cogent statements on apartheid by National Party leaders include the following: speech by Dr D.F. Malan at Party Congress in Bloemfontein on November 8, 1938; speech by Mr J.G. Strijdom in a debate on the Prime Minister's vote in House of Assembly on 20 and 21 April, 1955; speeches by Dr H.F. Verwoerd in the Senate on 3 September, 1948, and in the House of Assembly, 24 January, 1961; speeches by Mr B.J. Vorster in the House of Assembly, 23 September, 1966 and 24 April, 1971.

segregation of the Bantu peoples and their separate development in their traditional homelands, segregated patterns of development are also envisaged for the other major Non-White population groups, the Indians and the Coloureds.

THE ORIGIN AND COMPOSITION OF THE COLOUREDS[3]

The 'Coloured' population of South Africa is usually defined by a process of elimination. Within the context of the major population groups, this means that a Coloured person is someone of mixed descent who is not regarded as White (European descendants primarily of British and Afrikaner cultural heritage), or Bantu (Black Africans who are subdivided into several ethnic groups such as the Zulu, Xhosa, Swazi, Sotho, Tswana, Venda, and Tsonga) or Asiatic (mostly Indian descendants).

The origin of the Coloured population lies in the processes of contact and assimilation between the various racial and ethnic groups over the span of more than three centuries following the White settlement at the Cape in 1652. During the seventeenth and eighteenth centuries, three original elements were involved in the formation of the Coloured population: an aboriginal Khoi-Khoin element including largely the indigenous nomadic Hottentots and to a lesser extent the Bushmen; an important slave element including groups brought from West Africa, Madagascar and the East Indies; and a White element including a wide assortment of European settlers, seamen and soldiers. Since the last quarter of the nineteenth century an admixture of Bantu blood was brought into the Coloured mainstream, following the penetration of Bantu migrant workers into the Western Cape which is the traditional area of concentration of the Coloured people.

As a result of its diverse ethnic origins, the Coloured people is the most heterogeneous population group in South Africa. In physical features and in colour they vary from typically Khoi-Khoin and Negroid types to others which are virtually indistinguishable from Whites. But apart from this variation in physical types, it is highly significant to note that the peculiar ethnic composition of distinct sub-groups and the historical patterns of their settlement in particular areas or centres across the country produced certain identity groups such as the 'Cape Coloureds' largely concentrated

3. For a penetrating analysis of the origin, development and current situation of the Coloured people see S.P. Cilliers, *The Coloureds of South Africa,* Banier Uitgewers, Cape Town, 1963.

in the Western Cape, the 'Malays' in Cape Town and the Cape Peninsula, the 'Griquas' in the Northern and Eastern Cape Province, the 'Basters' of Rehoboth in South-West Africa and the North-Western Cape, as well as several family settlements such as the Dunns and Nunns in Natal, the Opperman and Carolus-Baatjies groups in the Orange Free State, and the Buys group in the Transvaal. In addition there are isolated small pockets of Coloureds in a number of scattered rural areas which were developed as mission stations and communal reserves for about two per cent of the total Coloured population. However, as a result of the constant urbanization process, these ethnographic distinctions are gradually disappearing so that all variations of Coloured types or 'Brown People' are found all over South Africa.

Due to their close association with the economic, religious and political structure of the dominant White pattern of life, the Coloureds gradually assumed also the social and cultural characteristics of the Western-oriented society. Basically they were integrated into the economy of White South Africa as part of the labouring class – but generally considered to be a cut above the Bantu population on the socio-economic ladder.

According to the 1970 census there are 2 018 533 Coloureds in South Africa, representing 9,4 per cent of the total population. The figures for the other groups are : Whites 3 750 716 (17,5%), Asians 620 422 (2,9%) and Bantu 15 057 559 (70,2%). Of the total Coloured population 86,7% live in the Cape Province, 47,1% live in the Western Cape and 29,6% live in the Cape Town metropolitan area. Only 7,5% live in the Transvaal, 3,3% in Natal, 1,8% in the Orange Free State and 0,7% in Bantu areas. This geographical concentration of Coloureds means that there are more Coloureds than Whites in all the economic regions of the Cape Province. The majority of Coloured people are urbanized (68% in 1960) which indicates that a growing proportion is moving from agricultural employment to the secondary and tertiary labour markets. As a population group, they exhibit all the demographic characteristics of an industrial and agricultural working class, particularly a high rate of natural increase.

EARLY POLITICAL HISTORY OF THE COLOUREDS[4]

The Coloured population has been subject to effective political control by Whites throughout South African political history. During the Dutch colo-

4. See W.J. de Kock, 'Konstitusionele Regte' in *Die Kleurlingbevolking van Suid-Afrika* (edited by Erika Theron), Stellenbosch, Universiteitsuitgewers, 1964.

nial period which ended in 1806, the political position of the emerging Coloured population was hardly a distinct problem since popular participation in government was strictly limited to the local level. The slaves, free half-breeds and Khoi-Khoin groups which were integrated into the economy, were essentially regarded as a socially differentiated appendage to the White settlers, but they were allowed access to the courts of law for protection of their persons, property and possessions. But as early as 1797 a pass system, imposing control on the movement of Hottentots, was introduced.

When the British colonial period started early in the nineteenth century, a new era began in the political history of the Coloureds. In 1809 all free Non-Whites were recognized as British subjects. The next major step was taken with Ordinance 50 of 1828, which recalled all pass laws and put all 'Free Persons of Colour' on an equal legal footing with Whites. Through their liberation in 1834, the slaves were put on a par with the Hottentot element, which enhanced the integration of these two elements into the emergent Coloured population. With the institution of local authorities in 1836, Non-Whites were treated equally with Whites.

These manifestations of the eighteenth century European humanitarian or philanthropic movement introduced by the British Government were diametrically opposed to the then already established pattern of differentiation between White and Non-White at the Cape and the deep-rooted views on White supremacy held by the largely Dutch-speaking settlers. A large exodus from the Cape Colony ensued from 1836 onwards, in which the Boers, by trekking into the interior, tried to escape both British rule and colour-blind practices. In the republics of the Orange Free State and the Transvaal there was no equality of Whites and Non-Whites, either in church or state.

In the subsequent constitutional developments of the Cape Colony, there was no colour bar. With the attainment of 'representative government' in 1853 and 'responsible government' in 1872, White, Coloured and Bantu males enjoyed the franchise on the same qualifications. These qualifications were raised in 1887 and again in 1892, but they were the same for all races. The main object of the changes was to restrict the number of Bantu voters, rather than to discriminate against Coloureds. It is important to note, however, that the Coloured voters hardly played a significant role in Cape politics during this period. Few Coloureds were registered as voters and there were no Coloured candidates who stood for election. When elective legislative government was introduced in the Natal Colony, measures were also taken to exclude the Bantu and Indian votes, but the Coloured vote was never restricted. After the Anglo-Boer War (1899-1902), the two Boer republics were initially governed as 'Crown Colonies', but when representative government was introduced, Coloureds were not given the franchise because of strong opposition from White citizens.

At the National Convention of 1908, the question of Non-White political rights, particularly those of the Coloureds, nearly shipwrecked the efforts to establish a Union of the four former colonies. The 'Cape Liberals' supported the extension of the Non-White franchise to the other provinces. Representatives of the 'Northern' provinces (including Natal) favoured the total restriction of all Non-White franchise rights. The franchise issue was resolved by maintaining the *status quo ante* in each province, i.e. retaining the Non-White franchise in the Cape and the Coloured franchise in Natal. The important limitation was added that all Non-Whites were excluded from being candidates for election to the Union Parliament. The existing Non-White franchise was entrenched by the proviso in Articles 35 and 152 of the South Africa Act of 1909, that it could be altered only by a two-thirds majority vote of a joint sitting of both Houses of Parliament.

In the period since Union in 1910 up to the National Party victory in 1948, there was a relative diminution of the Cape Coloured vote. The Women's Enfranchisement Act of 1930 halved the importance of the Cape Coloured vote for it enfranchised only White women. The Franchise Laws Amendment Act of 1931 lowered the voting age to 21 years, but it was extended to White persons only, thus weighing the scales in their favour in the Cape Province. In the 1940's several laws were enacted under the Smuts government, introducing onerous registration procedures for Coloured persons. Act 40 of 1945 made provision for the compulsory registration of White voters without similar references to Coloured voters. The Electoral Consolidation Act of 1946 made it possible to challenge Non-Whites on the voters roll to establish their voting qualifications at a Magistrate's Court under pain of being struck off the voters' list. The Electoral Laws Amendment Act of 1948 made it obligatory for Cape Coloured men applying for registration to fill in their application forms before a magistrate, police officer or electoral officer.

Although relatively few Coloureds were registered as voters, the Coloured vote was turned into a political football by the two major parties, the National Party and the United Party. In several constituencies the balance between the parties was held by the Coloured voters, accusations of fraudulent practices were common and pressures to remove the Coloureds from the common voters roll, as was done with the Bantu voters of the Cape in 1936, gradually gained momentum.

THE SEGREGATION OF COLOUREDS

In its early years, particularly under the leadership of General Hertzog (1914-1934), the National Party's policies on race relations were largely directed towards the segregation of the Bantu in view of what was generally termed the 'Black Peril' in election campaigns. In General Hertzog's view the Coloureds were akin to the White community culturally, although they were socially apart, and he held that they should be included in or allied to the White group.[5] He advocated the retention of the Coloured voters on the common voters roll in the Cape Province, the gradual extension of the Coloured franchise to the other provinces and the equal treatment of Coloureds in the economic field.[6] However, with the extension of the vote to women in 1930 under Hertzog's premiership, only White women were enfranchised, and the lowering of the voting age of 21 the next year was also limited to Whites.

When General Hertzog led a large proportion of National Party supporters into fusion with the South African Party (then under Smuts) to form the United Party in 1934, the remainder of the Afrikaner nationalists formed the 'Purified' National Party under the leadership of Dr D.F. Malan. The first clear indication of the Party's change of policy regarding the Coloured franchise was given in a speech by Dr Malan, as leader of the Opposition, during a Joint Session of both Houses of Parliament on 19th February, 1936.[7] He moved an amendment to the Bill for the Separate Representation of Natives, proposing the removal of the Coloureds from the common voters roll.

The National Party's policy on race relations was more fully outlined by Dr Malan prior to the general election of 1938 to include the following :

5. See Smithfield speech of November 13, 1925 quoted in C.M. van den Heever, *Generaal J.B.M. Hertzog,* Afrikaanse Pers Beperk, Johannesburg, 1943, p. 541.

6. These views were shared by Dr Malan as member in the Hertzog cabinet. See *Hansard,* 1928, col. 1882 (Afrikaans Text), *Hansard,* 1929, col. 242 (Afrikaans Text) and *Hansard,* 1931, col. 1035 (Afrikaans Text).

7. Quoted in full by D.W. Krüger, *South African Parties and Policies 1910-1960 – A Select Source Book,* Human and Rousseau, Cape Town, 1960, pp. 315-321.

the abolition of Bantu representation in the Union Parliament; the application of the principle of segregation to *all Non-Whites* in respect of residential areas, labour unions, work localities, and employment opportunities; and the removal of the Coloureds from the common to a separate voters roll.[8] These principles formed the foundation of the proposals of the 'Sauer Commission' which were incorporated in the Election Manifesto of the National Party in 1948.[9]

After coming to power in 1948, the National Party government embarked on a comprehensive legislative programme to put its policy of apartheid into practice. As far as the Coloured population was concerned, the basic objectives sought were the following: first, the prevention of further admixture of White and Coloured blood; second, the removal and regulation of points of contact between Whites and Coloureds; and third, the removal of Coloureds from the common voters roll in order to eliminate their influence in the power contest within the sphere of White party politics, and also to safeguard the White man's political control.[10]

AVOIDANCE OF RACIAL INTEGRATION

Several laws were enacted to prevent further miscegenation and to regulate matters incidental to this objective. The Prohibition of Mixed Marriages Act (1949) prohibited all future marriages between Whites and Non-Whites, that is, chiefly the Coloured. Its companion measure, the Immorality Amendment Act (1950), extended the prohibition of carnal intercourse between Whites and Bantu, which was enacted in 1927, to relations between Whites and Coloureds. In an effort to solve the difficulties involved in determining to which race a person might belong, the Population Registration Act (1950) was passed. It made provision for the compilation by the Director of Census and Statistics of a register of the population of South Africa and for the issue of identity cards to all persons included in the register. Every person included in the register is classified as either White, Coloured or Bantu and those classified in the latter two categories are further classified according to the ethnic or other group

8. *Die Burger,* April 5, 1938.

9. This manifesto appeared *inter alia* in *Die Burger,* 29 and 30 March, 1948. See also M.P.A. Malan, *Die Nasionale Party van Suid-Afrika: Sy Stryd en Prestasies,* Nasionale Party se Inligtingskomitee, Elsiesrivier, 1964, p. 224.

10. This summary of the main objectives is based on the speeches of the various Ministers during the second reading debates on the relevant bills.

to which they belong. A special administrative tribunal was established to hear objections to classifications with the additional possibility of appeal to a court of law. Initially the chief criteria of classification used were appearance and general acceptance or habitual association. These tests caused uncertainty and often great hardship particularly in respect of Coloured persons.[11] To reach more finality in classification the Population Registration Amendment Act (1967) was placed on the statute book, providing for descent as the crucial criterion of classification. A person is now classified as Coloured if both parents are Coloureds, or if one parent is White and the other is Coloured or Bantu.

REGULATION OF CONTACT SITUATIONS

In order to diminish points of friction between Whites, Coloureds and Bantu a series of laws were enacted to regulate situations of inter-group contact. The most far-reaching measure is the Group Areas Act (1950). Its main object is the demarcation of towns and districts into separate areas of residence or ownership for the different racial groups, and reserving all rights in such areas exclusively for their relevant groups. The Group Areas Development Act (1955) set up a Development Board with the powers to buy and sell property, to lay out townships and to build houses, and to delegate these powers to a local authority. These acts have been used over a number of years to remove and relocate clusters of Coloured or Bantu residents living close to or within proclaimed 'White' areas.[12]

For generations separate amenities and services have been provided in South Africa for Whites and Non-Whites by way of separate school facilities; separate accommodation in tramcars, buses, railway cars, etc.; separate counters in railway stations, post offices, police stations; separate entrances in public buildings; separate recreational facilities such as playgrounds, parks and theatres, and so forth. There was much litigation on the subject and many accusations were made of partial and unequal treatment to a substantial degree.[13] As a result the Reservation of Separate

11. The Minister of the Interior disclosed in Parliament that up to May 1956, 18 469 cases had been dealt with in which objections had been raised against classification. *Hansard* 15, cols. 5259/60.

12. See R.E. van der Ross, 'Group Areas Implications', *Cape Times,* 8 September, 1960 and also L.R. Dison and I. Mohammed, *Group Areas and their Development,* Butterworths, Durban, 1960.

13. See J.A. Centlivres in *Rex vs. Abdurahman,* 1950 (3) SA 136 (A.D.) and *Rex vs. Lusu,* 1953 (2) SA 484 (A.D.).

Amenities Act (1953) was enacted which declared that it is unnecessary when a separate amenity is provided for a particular class or race in any public premises or vehicle, to provide any or a substantially similar amenity for any other class or race. The Act covers all governmental or private premises or vehicles including schools, hospitals, clubs, hotels, theatres, restaurants, places of entertainment and taxis.

Until 1959 there was no legal colour bar in the various Acts establishing universities. Nevertheless, only two universities admitted Non-Whites, the universities of Cape Town and the Witwatersrand, and a third, the University of Natal, admitted Non-Whites to its medical school. The Extension of University Education Act (1959) provided for the establishment of separate university colleges for the Bantus, Indians and Coloureds, as well as the exclusion of Non-Whites from White universities with the exception of the University of South Africa (a correspondence university) and the medical school of the University of Natal.

The main statutory instrument for the regulation of the relationship between Whites and Coloureds in the economic field is the Industrial Conciliation Act (1956). In respect of labour unions with mixed membership the Act provides for separate branches for Whites and Non-Whites, separate meetings for Whites and Non-Whites, and the exclusion of Non-Whites from their executive committees. In addition, article 77 empowers the Minister of Labour, acting on the recommendations of the Industrial Tribunal, to reserve certain occupations for persons of a particular race. These powers have been largely used subsequently to protect White employees, but in respect of the clothing industry as well as most skilled employment opportunities in the Western Cape, job reservations for Coloureds have been made in order to protect them in their traditional area of concentration against the competition of the large supply of cheaper Bantu labour.

REMOVAL FROM THE COMMON VOTERS ROLL

The Nationalist Government came to power in 1948 with a minority of popular votes and a slim majority of five seats. Although less than 50 000 Coloureds were registered in the Cape Province at the time, their influence had been considerable in some twenty-five constituencies and decisive in about seven.[14] Since the Coloureds largely voted for the United

14. See Leo Marquard, *The Peoples and Policies of South Africa,* Oxford University Press, 1962, p. 80.

Party, their removal from the common voters roll potentially brought several seats within reach of the National Party. In addition, the National Party came to power on the mandate of apartheid, which included the creation of a separate political structure for the Coloureds. In view of these considerations, the Separate Representation of Voters Act (1951) was introduced which provided for separate representation in Parliament and in the Cape Provincial Council and for the creation of a Council for Coloured Affairs.

The Bill caused bitter controversy for six years. A constitutional crisis developed over the propriety of attempting to change the Coloured franchise by ordinary majority procedures in view of the constitutional requirement that the Non-White franchise could only be altered by a two-thirds majority vote of a joint sitting of both Houses of Parliament. When the Bill of 1951 was introduced, the two-thirds procedure was discarded. Four Coloured voters applied to the courts to have it declared invalid. The Appellate Division of the Supreme Court unanimously held the act void because it did not follow the two-thirds procedure for changing an entrenched clause (*Harris vs. Minister of Interior, 1952 (2) SA 428 A.D.*). Again Parliament passed an ordinary act which provided that judgments of the Supreme Court could be set aside by the 'High Court of Parliament', that is, Parliament constituting itself as the highest tribunal. It too was tested and unanimously declared invalid by the Appeal Court (*Minister of Interior and another vs. Harris and others, 1952 (4) SA 769 A.D.*). On three subsequent occasions the government called joint sessions in order to validate the 1951 Act, but failed to win a two-thirds vote. In 1955 an ordinary act enlarged the Appellate Division of the Supreme Court to eleven members for the hearing of constitutional cases. Another ordinary act enlarged the Senate and changed the method of election, with the result that the government acquired a sufficient majority in that body to gain a two-thirds majority in a joint session. In 1956 this majority, with Parliament meeting in joint session, removed the entrenchment of Non-White voting rights and validated the 1951 Act by the South Africa Act Amendment Act (Act No. 9 of 1956). In addition, the 1951 Act was revised by the Separate Representation of Voters Amendment Act (Act No. 30 of 1956). The validity of these acts was upheld by the Appeal Court (*Collins vs. Minister of Interior, 1957 (1) SA 552 A.D.*).

In terms of these enactments the Coloured population was given a limited qualified franchise on a separate voters roll for Coloured males living in the Cape Province. The Cape Province was divided into four constituencies to elect four White representatives to the House of Assembly and into two constituencies to elect two White representatives to the Cape Provincial Council. In addition provision was made for one senator to be appointed by the chief executive on the basis of his experience with regard to the special needs of all Non-Whites in the Cape Province.

These enactments also revived representation for Coloureds in an advisory council. The first Coloured Advisory Council was appointed as early as 1943 by the Smuts Government to advise the Government on matters pertaining to the interests of Coloured people. It resigned *en bloc* in 1950 as a result of conflicts with the National Party Government which came to power in 1948. The revived advisory council was called the Council for Coloured Affairs and was composed of 12 elected members (three members elected in each of the above-mentioned four constituencies by Coloureds on the separate voters roll) and 15 nominated members (8 members for the Cape Province, 4 for the Transvaal, 1 for the Orange Free State and 2 for Natal). Its main functions were to advise the government on Coloured affairs, to act as liaison between the government and the Coloured people, and to perform certain delegated executive tasks. The first Council for Coloured Affairs was constituted in 1959.

A NEW DISPENSATION: 'PARALLEL DEVELOPMENT'

During its first decade, the Nationalist Government's policy regarding the Coloured population was largely characterized by a series of segregationist measures. It was segregationist in that the main objective was to obtain a maximum of separation in the social, economic and political spheres in order to avoid further integration, to diminish points of contact or friction and to safeguard the White man's political control. A 'new vision' emerged around 1960 in which the emphasis shifted from segregation towards community development.[15] A new policy was framed which, in time, acquired the designation of 'parallel development' which is, in a developmental sense, community-directed in that it aims at the retention of the Coloured group's ethnic identity and at the promotion of its socio-economic

15. The 'new vision' was the outcome of a general public debate on Coloured Affairs which culminated in the appointment of a Cabinet Committee as well as a special committee by the Supreme Council of the National Party in the Cape Province. See *Die Burger*, 17 November, 1960.

development as a coherent, self-contained community managing its own affairs.[16]

In more concrete terms the new dispensation for the Coloured population had two basic aims: first, a comprehensive programme of socio-economic development, and second, the creation of separate governmental institutions for the Coloureds on both national and municipal levels.

SOCIO-ECONOMIC DEVELOPMENT

To implement its programme of socio-economic development the Government established the Department of Coloured Affairs as a fully-fledged government department under its own Cabinet Minister on August 3, 1961. The various government services for Coloured people, previously distributed amongst numerous institutions, were all brought under the auspices of the new department. Amongst these were community services, the development of rural areas, welfare services and education. Of special significance is the Coloured Development Corporation Act (1962) which created a development corporation with the specific task of promoting and financing Coloured entrepreneurs in the industrial, commercial and financial spheres.

A decision was made in 1962 to replace Bantu labourers with Coloureds in the Western Cape. A series of special committees were established to expedite this policy with the least amount of economic disruption. In addition, new programmes were started to provide large-scale housing and improved educational facilities.

Despite these efforts however, by 1971 it was still not possible to introduce compulsory education for Coloureds. Moreover, it was estimated that approximately two-thirds of all Coloureds in the Western Cape lived in overcrowded conditions, and that at least one-third lived in non-permanent or sub-standard housing.[17]

According to the 1960 census, farm workers (29,45%) and unskilled labourers (24,97%) were the two major occupational listings for economically active Coloured males. In the case of females, the majority (52,20%)

16. The 'new dispensation' was outlined by Dr Verwoerd in *Die Burger,* 8 December, 1960.

17. See S.P. Cilliers, *Socio-Economic Status of the Coloured Community and Implications for Education,* a paper read at the annual conference of the S.A. Institute of Race Relations, January, 1971.

were employed as domestic servants. Subsequently, however, a growing number of females were employed in factories as operatives, as waitresses in hotels, as shop assistants, as dressmakers and as nurses. Coloured men were increasingly employed in trades and crafts in the building industry, as skilled factory workers, as transport drivers, as postmen, as office clerks and as teachers. A growing number of Coloureds have started businesses as general dealers, transport contractors, green-grocers, butchers, outfitters, building contractors and barbers.

Although it is difficult to obtain a complete and accurate picture of the incomes of the various population groups, available statistics show a large discrepancy between the income levels of Whites and Coloureds. The income gap appears to be narrower in the case of skilled or white-collar workers in the private sector, but in the public sector the salaries of teachers, doctors, nurses, clerks, etc., are on the average between fifty and sixty per cent of those of Whites. On the whole, indications are that incomes for Coloureds are now on the average about a quarter of those of Whites.[18]

A SEPARATE 'PARLIAMENT' FOR COLOUREDS

The dual system of representation for Coloured people which existed since 1959, i.e. representation by nominated and elected Coloureds in the Council for Coloured Affairs on the one hand, and representation by four elected Whites in the House of Assembly and two elected Whites in the Cape Provincial Council on the other, gave rise to several difficulties in both Coloured and White political circles.

Coloured leadership was largely divided over the question of whether or not to co-operate within the framework of the system of separate representation created by the National Party Government. On the one extreme were those who refused to collaborate at all. Initially this group included Coloureds who were in alliance with the Congress Movement through the South African Coloured People's Organization (SACPO), founded in 1953 and later renamed the South African Coloured People's Congress, a Coloured teachers' organization known as the Teachers' League of South Africa, and those who were affiliated with the Non-European Unity Movement (N.E.U.M.) which was founded in 1943. They opposed all forms of separate consultative and administrative ma-

18. *Ibid.*

chinery for Coloured people and advised their followers not to register on the separate voters roll and to boycott elections. As a result only 14 694 Coloureds voted in the first election on the separate roll in April, 1958. At the other end of the spectrum another formation of Coloured groups emerged that was prepared to co-operate on the ground that there was more to be gained that way than by non-collaboration. The formally organized groups in this category included the Kleurlingvolksverbond, a rural group which supported the government, and the Coloured People's National Union, a small group led by Mr George Golding, which decided to make use of the existing legislation.

On the whole there was little interest on the part of the Coloureds to register as voters. The total number of registered voters declined from 29 281 in 1958 (out of a possible total of about 160 000 in the Cape Province) to 9 818 in 1963.[19] Apart from the above-mentioned isolated groups, there were at the time no Coloured political organizations that could play a decisive part in the elections. To the disenchantment of the National Party, this vacuum was to some extent filled by the United Party but more particularly by the Progressive Party. In the 1965 provincial election, Progressive candidates were returned in the two Coloured seats in the Cape Provincial Council.

Parliamentary debates on Coloured affairs in the early sixties were largely dominated by the question of the nature of Coloured representation in Parliament. Both major parties were internally divided on this issue. While agreeing that Coloured voters must remain on a separate voters roll, some Cape Nationalists felt that they should be allowed to elect Coloured representatives to Parliament.[20] Dr Verwoerd, supported by the Transvaal Nationalists, sternly opposed these proposals and announced 'self-government' for the Coloureds 'within the White state'.[21] Elaborating on this idea in a speech delivered to the Council for Coloured Affairs in 1961, Dr Verwoerd predicted that the Coloured people would be given full management of their own affairs by means of their own parliament, executive and administration within a decade.

The first step in this direction was the passage of the Coloured Persons

19. See *Report of the Commission of Inquiry into Improper Political Interference and the Political Representation of the Various Population Groups,* (R.P. 72/1967), p. 25.

20. See columnist 'Dawie' in *Die Burger,* 23 July, 1960.

21. *House of Assembly Debates,* 10 April, 1961.

Representative Council Act (No. 49 of 1964) which made provision for the replacement of the Council of Coloured Affairs at a date to be determined by the State President. The new Coloured Persons Representative Council was designed to consist of a majority of elected members and to be given more extensive legislative and executive powers. The franchise for Coloureds was to be extended to all adults above 21 years of age (i.e. in all Provinces) without any income, property or educational qualifications.

In view of the Government's aim to promote the development of the Coloured people as a distinct ethnic community with its own political structure, the existing parliamentary representation of the Coloureds by Whites and the role of the 'White' political parties in 'Coloured' politics remained as *casus belli.* The 'White' parties continued to play a major role in Coloured election campaigns and hampered the development of distinctly 'Coloured' parties. Under Dr Verwoerd's direction a bill was prepared to prohibit 'improper interference in Coloured politics'. This bill was strongly opposed by the United Party and after Dr Verwoerd's death in 1966, it was first referred to a Parliamentary Select Committee and then to a full commission of enquiry consisting of a majority of National Party M.P.'s. The Commission recommended *inter alia* the enlargement of the projected Coloured Persons Representative Council, the extension of its legislative and administrative powers, the discontinuation of the representation of Coloureds in Parliament and in the Cape Provincial Council, the introduction of a revised bill to prohibit the interference by one population group in the politics of any other population group, and finally, the appointment of a Parliamentary Select Committee to liaise with the Coloured Representative Council.[22]

These recommendations largely formed the basis of two bills which were passed the following year. The one, the Prohibition of Political Interference Act (No. 51 of 1968) made it an offence for a person who belongs to one population group to be a member of any party of which any person who belongs to any other population group is a member, or to render assistance as an agent to such parties or to address any assembly of persons organized by such parties. In addition it prohibits the receipt of financial assistance from abroad to parties and candidates. The other bill, the Separate Representation of Voters Amendment Act (No. 50 of 1968),

22. See Report, *op. cit.*, pp. xvi-xvii.

replaced the Act of 1951 and thereby abolished the system of Coloured representation in Parliament and in the Cape Provincial Council as of 1970. In addition, it enlarged the Coloured Persons Representative Council to 60 members of whom 40 were to be elected and 20 to be nominated. The constituencies were to be assigned on the following basis: Cape Province 28, Transvaal 6, Orange Free State 3 and Natal 3. The nominated members were to be selected partly on a provincial basis (Cape Province 12, Transvaal 2, Orange Free State 1 and Natal 1) and partly to give representation to specific sub-groups (Cape Malays 2 and Griquas 2).

In July 1969 the Council for Coloured Affairs was replaced by the Coloured Representative Council in terms of Proclamation 77 of April 3, 1969. Liaising between the government and the Coloured population, the Coloured Representative Council (C.R.C.) has been authorized to legislate on such matters as finance, local government and administration, social welfare and rural settlements.

All bills must, before they can be introduced in the C.R.C., be approved by the Minister of Coloured Affairs, and they must be ratified by the State President before coming into effect. Legislative acts passed by the C.R.C. repugnant to any Act of Parliament have no legal validity. The term of office of the C.R.C. is five years.

The executive functions of the C.R.C. are performed by a full-time Executive Committee of five members. The chairman is appointed by the State President and the remaining four members are elected by the C.R.C. from its own members. The Executive Committee generally acts as a 'cabinet', the chairman being entrusted with the portfolio of finance and the other four members with the portfolios of local government and administration, education, community welfare and pensions, and rural areas and settlements.

The Executive Committee is assisted in its task by the Administration for Coloured Affairs under direction of the government-appointed Commissioner for Coloured Affairs who has his offices in Cape Town. In 1971, 1 984 out of a total of 2 600 positions in the Administration (i.e. 75 per cent), were occupied by Coloured persons. Both White and Coloured officials in the Administration are members of the South African Public Service. Liaison with the Minister of Coloured Affairs and, through him, with other governmental institutions is maintained through the Department of Coloured Relations, which is one of the regular departments of the Central Government's administration. The main task of the Executive Committee is the budgetary allocation of its annual grant from the Central Government which amounted to R67 million for the financial year 1970-1971.[23]

The first elections for the Coloured Representative Council were held on 24th September, 1969. The following six parties nominated candidates:

(i) The Coloured People's Federal Party, a government-supporting party led by Mr Tom Swartz.

(ii) The Labour Party, an anti-apartheid party, established by Dr R.E. van der Ross in 1965, and led at that time by Mr M.D. Arendse (he was subsequently replaced as leader by Mr S. Leon).

(iii) The Coloured People's Republican Party, largely counting the Griquas amongst its followers and led by Mr Tom le Fleur.

(iv) The Coloured People's National Party, a Transvaal-based faction in favour of promoting a separate Coloured identity, and led by Dr C.L. Smith.

(v) The Conservative Party of South Africa, a pro-parallel development group led by Mr I.S. Petersen.

(vi) The Conservative Party, a Port Elizabeth-based faction also supporting parallel development and led by Mr R.H. Fischat.

The last-mentioned four parties formed an alliance against the Federals and the Labourites for the purposes of the election. Of the 570 000 Coloureds registered at the time, 293 348 went to the polls. The Labour Party won 26 constituencies and polled 135 202 votes, the Federal Party won 12 constituencies (three unopposed) and polled 90 025 votes, the National and Republican Parties each won 1 constituency. With a 47 per cent share of the votes the Labour Party won 65 per cent of the constituencies – mainly in the urban areas. The various parties in favour of parallel development polled a 53 per cent share of the popular vote but gained only a 35 per cent proportion of the constituencies. The Government packed the Council in its favour by appointing 20 members from the ranks of government-supporting candidates who lost in the election.

When the C.R.C. convened for its first brief session (20-21 November, 1969), the Federal Party majority elected its own Chairman and four members of the Executive Committee. Mr Tom Swartz was nominated by

23. For a general outline of the new political dispensation for the Coloured people see F. Gaum (Commissioner for Coloured Affairs), 'Die Nuwe Staatkundige Bedeling van die Kleurlinge', a speech made at Stellenbosch, 16 July, 1969.

the State President as Chairman of the Executive Committee. During its second session (November, 1970) the C.R.C. emerged as a highly significant political forum for the Coloured population. For the first time in the history of South Africa, Coloured representatives assembled for a frank public debate on the problems and obstacles faced by the Coloureds in the current South African setting. The Labour Party played the role of a vocal and vigorous opposition, giving vent to a wide array of grievances such as housing shortages, lack of educational facilities, differential pay scales, the shortage of recreational facilities, the employment conditions of farm labourers, the application of job reservation, the application of the Immorality Act and the Population Registration Act, as well as other related Government policies. It was a significant new experience not only for the Coloured leaders, but also for White society. In many ways it portends the end of an era of unilateral political control by Whites over Coloureds.

SEPARATE LOCAL GOVERNMENT INSTITUTIONS

Although Coloureds never qualified for voting rights on the municipal level in other provinces, in the Cape they could participate in theory on an equal footing with Whites since the beginnings of local government in that province. In actual practice, however, they played an insignificant role as voting qualifications were based on the ownership or occupation of taxable property – a qualification with which only a handful of Coloureds could comply.

In 1960 the Government appointed the Niemand Committee to investigate the participation of Coloureds in local government institutions. The committee recommended separate and parallel institutions for Coloureds. These recommendations were embodied in the Group Areas Amendment Act of 1962 (as amended by the Group Areas Act of 1966) and the Rural Coloured Areas Act, 1963. These enactments apply to two types of Coloured areas: first, densely populated Coloured areas which fall within the jurisdiction of adjacent White municipalities, and, secondly, densely populated areas which are classified as rural Coloured areas. In respect of both types of areas these Acts provide for the development of local government institutions for Coloureds in three stages. The first stage entails 'advisory committees' with nominated members but functioning under government officials as chairmen. The second stage involves 'management committees' with six elected and three nominated members, also chaired by government officials, but exercising certain prescribed executive functions of a local nature. The third stage culminates in full-scale 'municipal councils' functioning as ordinary elected local governments. At the end of 1970 there were a total of 43 Advisory Committees and 23 Management Committees in the Cape Province.

In view of the fact that the 1962/63 legislation did not remove the names of registered Coloured voters from the ordinary municipal electoral rolls, the issue was re-opened in 1970. To resolve the question of dual representation and in order to bring the system of representation on the local level in line with the system obtaining on the national level, it was decided to use the ordinary voting qualifications for Parliamentary elections also for municipal elections in the Cape Province. In effect, Coloured voters were thereby excluded from municipal elections. At the same time a commission of inquiry was appointed to investigate the feasibility of establishing full-scale municipalities in Coloured areas.

POLITICAL FUTURE OF THE COLOUREDS

The seventies inaugurated a new phase in the evolution of the National Party's Coloured policy in the form of an intense debate within Party circles on the ultimate political future envisaged for the Coloured population within the framework of the policy of 'parallel development'. Searching questions were raised on the proper relationship between the Coloured Representative Council and Parliament and on the feasibility of the creation of a homeland for the Coloureds which could form the territorial foundation of ultimate national independence.

The basic issue at stake is the position of the Coloured within the general framework of the policy of apartheid. In essence the chief exponents of the policy of apartheid have consistently aimed at the gradual and systematic disentanglement of the various Non-White groups from the social, economic and political structures of the Whites, enabling each group to exercise political rights and to create opportunities for progressive self-fulfilment in accordance with its own traditions and values within its own areas, and *where practicable* to develop into independent states. For the various Bantu ethnic groups the policy of apartheid gradually acquired the meaning of 'separate development', i.e. development in their traditional homelands with complete political – if not economic – independence as the ultimate objective. Bantu persons living outside the homelands are to be identified with the nation of their forebears and in 'White' South Africa are regarded as 'temporary sojourners' to whom property ownership and political rights are denied. For the Coloureds, the policy of apartheid gradually acquired the meaning of 'parallel development', i.e. a pattern of development which is basically community-directed but without a clear indication as to the ultimate political future of the Coloureds within the borders of what is called 'White' South Africa.

The issue became a potentially explosive one for the National Party because it is impossible to apply to the Coloured people both the logic and the moral justification of apartheid policies in the sense of 'separate development'. The Coloureds have no 'homeland' of their own and they are no separate 'nation'. They have no separate culture and are as South African as any population group can be.

At the root of the current controversy lies the basic dichotomy between the moderate (*verligte*) and the fundamentalist (*verkrampte*) schools of thought on all aspects of race policies within Afrikaner circles. In addition, the controversy has acquired the uneasy overtones of personality conflicts, of a North (Transvaal and O.F.S.)/South (Cape Province) bifurcation and of a deep rift within the National Party circles which involves the cabinet, the Party caucus, the Nationalist newspapers, Afrikaner cultural organizations (Broederbond, F.A.K., SABRA), Afrikaner academics and the party rank-and-file.

On the fundamentalist (and largely Northern) side are those who maintain that the logical consistency of the policy of apartheid requires the creation of a homeland for the Coloureds, i.e. that they should have their own national territory, their own national freedom and an independent destiny.[24] They foresee a future for the Coloureds 'further away' from the Whites and reject the phrase 'Brown Afrikaners' in referring to the Coloureds. They oppose any form of integration with the Coloureds on a permanent basis within the territorial boundaries of the same political system. As the only alternative to integration they propose the consolidation of the scattered rural and urban areas for Coloureds into a Coloured homeland consisting of fewer and larger pieces of land coinciding as far as possible with the various sub-groups within the Coloured population,

24. See report of speech by Mr M.C. Botha, Minister of Bantu Affairs, *Die Hoofstad*, 1 December, 1970. Two days later Dr C.P. Mulder, Minister of Information, referred in a public speech to the necessity of giving 'geographical content' to Coloured political institutions.

thereby giving 'geographical content' to Coloured political institutions.[25]

On the moderate side are those who reject the idea of a Bantustan-type homeland for Coloureds. It is maintained that White and Brown are 'destined to a parallel plural co-existence' which means neither independence in an adjacent homeland nor integration in the sense of uniting into a single nation.[26] The Coloured is regarded as the poltical 'ally' or 'junior partner' of the Whites within a framework of parallel development for White and Brown, both living as organic communities in 'twin-towns' on a permanent basis within the same homeland. The proposition that integration is the only alternative to separate (homeland) development is emphatically rejected on the grounds that there is a third choice in the form of 'parallelism' or a policy of 'good neighbourliness'. In terms of this approach the rural and urban Coloured areas are to be developed under the aegis of the Coloured Representative Council along the lines of a 'canton' system with close linkages to White institutions on the various levels of government.[27]

Outside the strictly Party circles a case has also been made by the Calvinist monthly in support of what is called an adapted 'three-stream' policy, using as analogy the 'two-stream' policy developed by General Hertzog to accommodate the Afrikaans and English groups as sub-cultures within the South African nation.[28] On the Afrikaans academic front a plea has been made for a two-pronged programme of pursuing the idea of separate development for the Bantu homelands with vigour on the one hand, while progressing towards 'full citizenship' for the Coloured, Asiatic and permanently domiciled Bantu persons together with Whites in the rest of the country at the same time.[29] Subsequently statements were signed by 29 Transvaal and 109 Cape Afrikaner academics and intellectuals in support of equal and full citizenship for the Coloured population.

25. See column by Dr A.P. Treurnicht in *Die Hoofstad,* 30 April, 1971. The same idea is propagated in a plan circulated by Mr J.A. Rabie, Transvaal secretary of the Coloureds' Federal Party as reported in *The Sunday Times,* March 28, 1971. See also speech at SABRA Youth Conference at Robertson by Prof. G. Viljoen, Rector of the Rand Afrikaans University, as reported in *Die Burger,* 7 April, 1971.

26. Editorial of *Die Burger,* 2 December, 1970.

27. See report of speech by Mr P.W. Botha, Minister of Defence and Provincial Leader of the National Party in the Cape, *Die Burger,* 24 April, 1971.

28. *Woord en Daad,* May 1971, p. 4.

29. 'A Sociological Perspective on the South African Situation', a paper read at a public meeting of the Institute of Citizenship, Cape Town, April 1, 1971 by Prof. S.P. Cilliers, University of Stellenbosch.

In an effort to resolve the uncertainty and confusion arising from the internal debate and conflicting statements made by Party influentials, the Cabinet issued a special public statement on its Coloured policy. The statement rejects both integration and the homeland idea. Integration is rejected on the grounds that it has been proved unsuccessful in the course of South African history. The idea of a homeland for Coloureds is rejected on the grounds that it is not 'practical politics'. The statement further reconfirmed the Government's policy of 'parallel development' for the Coloured people.[30]

In the 1971 Parliamentary debate on the Prime Minister's budgetary vote, Mr B.J. Vorster outlined his views on the political future of the Coloureds. He endorsed the contention that Whites and Coloureds will have to live side by side in one geographical area within a pattern of parallel devolpment. He rejected the view that the Coloureds should be regarded as an appendage of the Whites or be deprived of their leaders by a process of 'creaming off'. He claimed, instead, that the Coloureds must be seen as a 'nation' in the making – a 'nation in its own right'. On the question of liaison between the Coloured Representative Council and Parliament, Mr Vorster disclosed that the Coloured leaders themselves rejected the idea of joint consultative committees in favour of direct liaison between the Executive Committee of the C.R.C. and members of the Cabinet. Formal meetings are to be held with the Prime Minister shortly after the beginning of each annual Parliamentary session, and thereafter every two months in the presence of the Minister of Coloured Affairs or other Cabinet Ministers. The future evolution of and 'final formula' for this liaison between Coloured representatives and the Government, Mr Vorster contended, must be resolved by future generations.

CONCLUSION

The Coloured policy of the National Party evolved since 1936 as a sub-category of the general policy of apartheid. Initially, the main thrust of this policy was essentially segregationist in character in that the chief aim was to obtain a maximum of separation between Whites and all Non-Whites in the social, economic and political spheres. Some of the practical manifestations of the implementation of this policy, particularly since 1948, included the prohibition of carnal intercourse and marriage between

30. Statement by Mr J. Loots, Minister of Coloured Affairs, issued on behalf of the National Party Government, reported in ***Rapport,*** 6 December, 1970.

Whites and Non-Whites, separate residential areas, separate jobs and differential wage scales, separate labour organizations, separate recreational and health facilities, separate schools and universities, separate amenities in public premises and transport, separate churches and community organizations, and separate political structures.

After 1960 the policy shifted towards the development of the Non-White groups as coherent communities managing their own affairs. For the Bantu ethnic groups it meant separate development with their traditional homelands as focal points of their respective independent nationhoods. For the Coloureds it meant parallel development in some form of association with the Whites in the same homeland. At the moment there is a great deal of uncertainty as to the form this association might take.

In view of the momentum of the present constitutional developments in the direction of separate community-directed governmental institutions for Coloureds, a continuation of the present trends can be expected, i.e. extension of the powers and responsibilities of the Coloured Representative Council and the creation of further Management Committees and full-blown Municipal Councils for urban Coloured residential areas. The orthodox faction within the National Party which wants the Coloureds to move away from the Whites will continue to exert pressure for an 'unconsolidated' Coloured homeland. In view of the prominence of this group within National Party circles, something akin to a Coloured 'city-state' in the Western Cape with jurisdictional ties with other isolated Coloured areas elsewhere in the country, can be expected to arise. A separate and independent 'Coloured state' however, is totally impractical.

The Coloured Representative Council, as an example of community representation, must be taken seriously in patterning the future course of inter-group politics in 'White' South Africa. In contrast to the Bantu authorities which in their respective homelands are the embryo of national self-determination, the C.R.C. can be regarded as the embryo of community-based political sub-systems in the White-controlled part of South Africa. It portends the emergence of a new pluralistic pattern according to which political power could be transferred to the Non-White ethnic groups (Coloureds, Indians and detribalized urban Bantu) whose political aspirations are not likely to be absorbed by the system of 'separate freedoms' on a nation-state basis. The ultimate relationship of these 'community authorities' to the central government is a matter to be decided by the inter-group contest for power in the years to come.

Coloured Progress under Separate Development

Tom Swartz

The author, Chairman of the Executive of the Coloured Persons Representative Council (a partially elected body to serve the special interests of South Africa's Coloured population), is the leader of the Federal Coloured People's Party, and also chief spokesman of those Coloureds desirous of co-operating with the White Government on the basis of socio-political parallelism.

In terms of its policy of separate development the Government of the Republic of South Africa aims at encouraging each of the population groups to develop its own identity with a view to full self-realization.

For the purpose of overall implementation of this policy it has been decreed that members of each of the population groups as defined in the relative Act should be issued with identity cards. This aims at ensuring, *inter alia,* that facilities, such as those in the fields of housing, education, commerce, recreation, etc., are in fact enjoyed by the population group for which they are created.

The Coloured people regard it as their right to share the whole of the Republic of South Africa as their country. They enjoy freedom of movement as in the case of Whites, unlike the Bantu who are subject to influx control measures regulating their entry into areas outside those set aside for them.

For land, home ownership, business and residential purposes the Coloured people, as in the case of other population groups, are subject to the provisions of the Group Areas Act, which stipulates which areas shall be occupied by the various population groups. (This is apart from the vast rural areas available to Coloured persons only, in terms of the Rural Coloured Areas Act.)

The Coloured people occupy a very important position in the provision of manpower, especially in the Cape Province where many are employed in skilled work in the building and other trades, while a substantial proportion provide unskilled labour. An important feature in the Cape Peninsula is the very high percentage of women employed in the clothing industry. There are many other avenues of employment which absorb considerable numbers of Coloured workers. The Coloureds fulfil a similar role in the other three Provinces of the Republic although to a lesser degree than in the Cape.

At the present juncture, with an ever expanding economy, trade, industry and commerce are calling for more and more manpower – the demand virtually exceeding the supply. In the field of labour the provisions of the Industrial Conciliation Act No. 28 of 1956[1] apply, but because of the favourable economic and employment conditions which have prevailed for the past ten years and the end of which is not yet in sight, exemptions are granted where circumstances warrant it.

I cannot foresee a time when the labour and skill of the Coloured people will be redundant. Traditionally, their labour and skills have been used almost exclusively in the Western Cape since labour was introduced from the Far East in the days of the Dutch East India Company.

Besides providing labour and the skill for industry, Coloured contractors and master builders have also come into the field of development and are handling big contracts for other population groups and for the Government on a competitive tender basis. This in turn is creating a strong middle class from which an upper class is beginning to emerge. For this the Government's policy of separate development which insists on own identity and self-help must get the credit.

In order to encourage and promote the Coloured community's interests in the field of commerce and industry in their own areas the Government established the Coloured Development Corporation by an Act of Parliament, financed exclusively from Government funds. Whilst all other sources of financial assistance are still available to Coloured business enterprise on the same basis as for members of other population groups, the Coloured Development Corporation has been established as a measure of assistance and guidance exclusively for Coloured businessmen. With such assistance a considerable number of businesses have already arisen in Coloured areas, covering a variety of fields.

1. This Act formally entrenches South Africa's traditional colour bar in the labour sphere.

Apart from financial assistance the Corporation also provides expert guidance at all levels in the field of commerce and industry. Furthermore it also exerts itself in ensuring that Coloured businessmen attain the essential business know-how.

Another field in which considerable advances have been made is the liquor trade. Whereas Coloured enterprise (the same as in the case of members of other groups) could, in terms of the Liquor Act, previously only enter the liquor distribution trade on the 'quota' basis, the said Act was amended in 1963 to make special provision for the establishment by Coloured companies of restaurants with liquor licenses in Coloured areas. Coloured businessmen have come forward to make use of this special provision and, mainly with the assistance of the Coloured Development Corporation, a considerable number of successful licensed restaurants (also with off-sales facilities) have been established as a service to the Coloured community in their own areas. The provision of these facilities also aims at ensuring that decent refreshment amenities are provided where the Coloured person can relax in dignified surroundings, unlike the poor facilities which previously often existed.

The liquor trade for the Coloured businessmen has opened up new opportunities for the use of initiative in business undertaking and management, as well as offering remunerative employment for many persons. This development has been so favourable that certain liquor merchants have found it worthwhile to sponsor overseas tours for Coloured persons employed in managerial positions in the liquor trade for educational purposes, in catering, etc.

After these general observations, here are some details of the constitution of the Coloured Persons Representative Council, its Executive and its administrative organ.

During 1951 a Division of Coloured Affairs was created within the Department of the Interior of the Central Government. This Division attained full departmental status in April 1958, under the designation, Department of Coloured Affairs, and in July 1969, the Coloured Persons Representative Council was established in terms of the Coloured Persons Representative Council Act, No. 49 of 1964, as amended. Simultaneously, the Department of Coloured Affairs was abolished and succeeded by a newly created Administration of Coloured Affairs, henceforth to fulfil the bulk of the objectives and functions of that Department. The Council consists of forty members elected by registered Coloured voters and twenty members nominated by the State President. Only Coloured persons are eligible for nomination or election. A general registration of Coloured voters takes place every six years and a Coloured voters roll is prepared.

The Council has adopted standing rules and orders for the regulation and conduct of its proceedings and the despatch of business. There is freedom of speech and debate in the council.

The executive of the Council consists of five members of the Council of whom one is nominated by the State President as chairman, and four elected by the Council. The executive carries out the functions of the Council, except in so far as the making of laws is concerned, while the Council is not in session and also deals with the following matters in so far as they affect Coloured persons:

(i) finance;
(ii) local government;
(iii) education;
(iv) community welfare and pensions;
(v) rural areas and settlements for Coloureds;
(vi) such other matters as the State President may from time to time determine.

Except in the case of the chairman, to whom the management of finance is assigned, the executive designates, in respect of each of the remaining matters referred to above, one of its members to exercise and perform on its behalf and under its direction the functions and duties incidental to the matter in question.

The Council also has power, on request, to advise or make recommendations to the Government in regard to all matters affecting the economic, social, educational and political interests of the Coloured population of the Republic, or to make recommendations to the Government in regard to any planning calculated in the opinion of the Council to promote the best interests of the Coloured population, and generally to serve as a link between the Government and the Coloured population. The Government is represented by the Minister of Coloured Affairs. The Minister may attend any meeting of the Council or the Executive and take part in the proceedings thereof, but has not the right to vote at any such meeting.

The council can, with the approval of the Minister of Coloured Affairs, acquire and dispose of property, appoint servants, and do anything which it considers necessary in the exercise of its duties.

Cape Town is the headquarters of the Administration of Coloured

Affairs, and the Head of the Administration is the Commissioner for Coloured Affairs. For closer contact with the Coloured community the Administration has established regional offices at thirteen different centres in the four provinces of the Republic, each office having as its head a White Regional Representative and a staff consisting of White and Coloured officers. All these posts will eventually be filled by Coloureds.

STAFF OF THE ADMINISTRATION

Simultaneously with the creation of the Administration of Coloured Affairs, the Coloured officers of the abolished Department of Coloured Affairs were transferred to the Administration of Coloured Affairs, which was established to assist the Coloured Persons Representative Council in the execution of its functions. Owing to a shortage of experienced Coloured officers, sufficient numbers of White officers were made available and seconded to the Administration to assist in the professional, clerical, technical, teaching and other divisions. As experienced Coloured officers become available they will succeed the White officers who in turn will be absorbed in other Government departments. Eventually the staff of the Administration of Coloured Affairs will comprise Coloured officers only. For consistently outstanding services Coloured officers receive special recognition and promotion.

In order to achieve its aims and to carry out the functions of the Council, the organization of the Administration of Coloured Affairs comprises the following five Directorates:

1. The Directorate of Finance and Auxiliary Services;
2. the Directorate of Local Government;
3. the Directorate of Education;
4. the Directorate of Rural Areas and Settlements;
5. the Directorate of Community Welfare and Pensions.

The aims and functions of the respective Directorates are as set out briefly hereunder:

1. *The Directorate of Finance and Auxiliary Services*

Section 22 of the Coloured Persons Representative Council Act, No. 49 of 1964, as amended, regulates the financial arrangements of the Council.

In terms of section 22(1) of this Act the monies required for the exercise of the duties of the Council are made available annually out of monies appropriated by Parliament.

Section 22(2) determines that the estimates of expenditure by the Council shall be prepared by the Executive for submission to the Minister of Coloured Affairs, who shall in consultation with the Minister of Finance determine the amounts which shall be submitted to Parliament for appropriataion. The estimates of expenditure shall thereafter be submitted by the chairman of the Executive to the Council for the appropriation, by resolution, of the monies for the services specified in the estimates.

All financial transactions of the Council are accounted for by the normal state accounting procedures and the books and accounts are subject to audit by the Controller and Auditor General who then compile annual reports.

In terms of section 22(7) of the Act the Executive performs the functions of the Treasury in connection with the administration, control, disbursement and spending of the funds of the Council.

2. *The Directorate of Local Government*

Although the Coloured Persons Representative Council has as yet not taken over any powers by way of delegation in this field, an important role is nevertheless being played by them in conjunction with the Administration of Coloured Affairs and its Directorate of Local Government in the fulfilment of their main task, namely, to promote the development of the Coloured community to self-sufficiency. This task embraces assistance and advice to other authorities on matters such as:

(a) the establishment, composition and functioning of consultative and management committees for Coloured group areas;
(b) the demarcation and planning of group areas;
(c) industrial, commercial and private enterprise in and on the perimeter of Coloured areas;
(d) training of personnel;
(e) trading licences;
(f) development of community facilities including public amenities such as recreation resorts, sports and beach facilities;
(g) housing and conditions of occupancy;
(h) health services;
(i) resettlement of communities and disqualified persons;
(j) issuing of permits under the Group Areas Act.

3. *The Directorate of Education*

The aims are to promote by means of education the intellectual, mental and physical potential of the Coloured people. Because of its special significance in the development of the Coloured population, certain aspects in the sphere of education are discussed briefly.

Separate schools for Non-Whites and Whites are not the result of the present Government's policy but a continuation of the pattern which originated more than three centuries ago when the first school ever to be established in South Africa was opened in the year 1658 for the Non-White children of slaves.

In the year 1676 a Commissioner of the Dutch East India Company decreed that separate schools for White children had to be established. Although this decree was frequently ignored in subsequent years, it nevertheless set the pattern of parallel schools for Coloureds and Whites as it exists today.

The transfer of Coloured education in 1964 from the four Provincial Administrations and the Department of Higher Education to the former Department of Coloured Affairs did not result in any change with regard to separate schools, and affected only the control of existing schools. Coloured Education gained vastly from this transfer as it became the charge of a single controlling body responsible for the co-ordinated development of all facets. Under the previous system of divided control, certain aspects of education received either too much or too little attention.

The objections raised at the time of the above-mentioned transfer included accusations that a separate and hence inferior type of education was being planned for Coloureds. Time has proved this incorrect. In fact, the education of the Coloured people has benefited greatly as a result of the transfer. During the short period of seven years since 1964, the educational system has developed into a well-balanced system providing for the needs of all types of pupils and students, while the basic pattern of education in this country has been retained and the standards of education meticulously maintained.

As the aim of the transfer of 1964 was to co-ordinate the system and not to place the system under the control of the Coloured people, it was in line with the Government's policy of having a separate controlling body for the education of Coloureds.

The next important and logical step ensued in 1969 when the consolidated educational system was transferred to the control of the newly established Coloured Persons Representative Council. One of the members of the Executive Committee of this Council is responsible for education and, for the first time in history, the education of the Coloureds has been entrusted to Coloured persons whose bounden duty it is to provide the best possible education for their people.

The good faith of the Government has been proved by the fact that education has not been handed over merely to be administered as could best be accomplished, but to maintain standards at least at previous levels and then to improve upon them. For this purpose the Government is prepared to transfer the required number of White professional and administrative staff to tide the Administration over the interim period until all the posts from the lowest to the highest levels can be manned by suitably qualified and experienced Coloured personnel. In this respect it may be mentioned that Coloureds constitute the bulk of the teaching personnel. Towards the end of 1970 only 517 Whites were still employed, mostly in a temporary capacity, in a teaching force of more than 15 000 in educational institutions.

The following is a brief survey of the present educational system for Coloureds with indications of the progress made since 1964.

Pre-School Education – In this country pre-school education has always been considered a form of social service and therefore the concern of welfare organizations and private individuals. However, such schools, which are run on a non-profit basis, are subsidized by the Government.

In 1964 the number of such subsidized schools taken over was 32. In 1969 there were 42 such schools and subsidies were paid in favour of 3 054 infants.

Primary Education – Primary education is given in State-aided (church) schools and in Government schools. Since 1964 uniform curricula have been introduced throughout the country. The syllabuses are basically the same as those of the other Departments of Education. The standard of work done in the primary school is ensured by an inspectorate of highly qualified professional staff.

A new service was introduced in 1965 when adaptation classes were established for retarded pupils. By 1969 the number of these classes had grown to 96 with 1 337 pupils. This service is being extended continually.

Compulsory education has not as yet been generally introduced, except in one province and in a number of school districts, apart from a measure introduced in 1968 stipulating that henceforth all pupils enrolling at the beginning of the year must remain at school for the whole of the year concerned. However, it is our declared policy to introduce compulsory education in due course. This will be done in accordance with the availability of school accommodation and teachers.

Nevertheless, primary school enrolment has increased phenomenally since 1964. The increase of school facilities has undoubtedly contributed towards an awareness among the Coloured people of the importance of education. The number of primary school pupils has increased from 299 158 in 1965 to 375 361 in 1969. Various means are being employed to encourage and assist pupils to attend school. All pupils receive free schooling, free books and other school requisites.

The school is taken to the pupils. Primary schools are established whereever there are at least fifteen pupils. We have an extensive building programme and school accommodation is being provided with the greatest possible speed. During the period 1964-1969 additional and replacement accommodation was supplied for 100 669 pupils in 127 new government schools and extensions to 74 government schools.

When the school cannot be taken to the pupils, as sometimes happens in sparsely populated areas, hostels are erected or provision is made for transport to the nearest schools. Indigent pupils receive boarding grants or travelling allowances.

Secondary Education – In 1964 the percentage of pupils in the secondary Standards 6–8 was 10,3. In 1969 this percentage had grown to 11,9. This increase of 1,6 per cent is not phenomenal but significant in view of the large increase in the number of primary pupils.

The awareness of the need for secondary education is also growing apace and enrolment, especially in the lower secondary standards, is increasing in a gratifying manner. Pupils are encouraged in every way to continue their schooling to more advanced levels. For this purpose schooling, books and other equipment are provided free, hostels are erected in sparsely populated areas, transport and boarding grants are made available to indigent pupils.

The standard of secondary education is maintained at the national level by the moderation of all syllabuses and the Senior Certificate examinations by the Joint Matriculation Board, a statutory body responsible for the maintenance of standards at matriculation level.

There has been a marked improvement since 1964 in the results obtained by Junior and Senior Certificate candidates in the final examinations.

The most important development in secondary education since 1964 is undoubtedly the introduction of diversification. Whereas formerly the pupils in schools for Coloureds followed mostly the stereotyped academic course leading to a university course, all high schools have since 1964 introduced diversified courses to satisfy the interests, abilities and needs of the individual pupils.

A number of new subjects has been introduced and secondary school pupils are now able to follow any of the following courses: Academic, Commercial, Art, Hotel Catering, or a mixed course (including one or more vocational subjects in an academic course). In due course there will be a further choice of subjects such as Educational Theory and subjects related to the performing arts. All high schools offer Handwork for boys and Domestic Science and Needlework for girls.

Consideration is at present being given to the introduction of special courses for retarded pupils and slow learners at secondary level. Vocational guidance is an integral part of the secondary course. This was first introduced in 1967.

Technical Education – The development in this field since 1964 is outstanding. Whereas the training of apprentices had formerly been confined to a very limited number of classes attached to the technical colleges for Whites, five technical colleges have now been established for Coloured apprentices, using the most modern training methods. In addition to the normal theoretical tuition, workshop practice has also been included in the courses. In this respect we are further advanced than any other education department. The number of Coloured apprentices receiving tuition has increased from 951 in 1962 to 2 834 in 1969.

As has been stated, secondary school pupils can follow a course which includes technical subjects. This course is of a high standard and prepares pupils for more advanced technical education as well as for various types of apprenticeship.

The first College for Advanced Technical Training for Coloureds was established in 1967. This college has facilities for technical training beyond the Senior Certificate level. The whole range of technical courses will be offered in due course. At this stage, however, students are prepared for the National Building and Engineering Diplomas, Public Health Nursing, Health Inspection, Diplomas in Public Administration, Accounting and

Auditing. Facilities also exist for courses in Hairdressing, Domestic Science and Needlework.

The courses and syllabuses that are followed are prescribed, and the examinations conducted by the Department of National Education. The standard is the same for all population groups.

Special Education – These schools cater for physically and mentally handicapped children, such as the blind, deaf, epileptics and cerebral-palsied. Although the State can provide such schools, the five existing schools are state-aided to the extent of almost the full cost. A school for cripples is at present being considered.

Children's Act Schools – We have three reformatories and two industrial schools. Another industrial school is already in an advanced stage of planning. In these schools corrective education is given to delinquent children who have been committed to the custody of the schools. An intensive study of the educational programme of these schools has been made since 1964 and an improved programme will be introduced in 1972.

Adult Education – Immediately after the transfer of Coloured education in 1964, attention was paid to the planning and development of a comprehensive system of adult education. This has resulted in a system which is in advance of similar projects of other South African educational authorities. The aims of this service are to promote general literacy, to provide training for specific occupations, to improve qualifications, to promote cultural development and to provide recreational facilities.

A system of part-time classes was first introduced in 1966 and by 1969 the enrolment in these classes reached the very gratifying figure of 7 569. Special courses were also run to provide specific types of training. In collaboration with the Hotel Board short courses for table and wine stewards were conducted. Short courses were offered regularly to enable seamen to qualify as bo'suns, mates, skippers and engine-room personnel. The demand in this respect has proved to be constant and a School for Mariners has now been established. A training scheme introduced by the Cape clothing manufacturers for machinists has also been assisted financially.

Special attention is being paid to the promotion of activities of a cultural and recreational nature. The Minister has appointed a Council for Culture and Recreation to promote this aspect of education. The council is supported by committees in various specialized directions, such as music, drama, ballet, art, etc.

Very satisfactory progress has been made in all directions. Wherever possible, financial aid is given to interested cultural and recreational organizations to further their aims. More than R130 000 was spent during 1970 on this project.

Teacher Training – Successful implementation of the educational programme depends largely on the availability of adequately trained teachers. At present there is a serious shortage of teachers. Inadequate salaries do not account fully for this shortage. There are other important reasons, such as an insufficient number of candidates who have the entrance qualifications, remunerative posts readily available in other fields, and loss of interest in the teaching profession, which is a world-wide phenomenon.

Everything possible, however, is being done to increase the number of qualified teachers as the ultimate success of the whole venture depends on this. Bursaries are made available to all student teachers to enable them to obtain their training free. The teacher training courses have been revised completely since 1964 with a view to improving the standard of the training.

It is an accepted fact that the minimum academic requirement for primary teachers is the senior certificate. On account of the small numbers who actually obtain the senior certificate and the tremendous demand for teachers because of ever-increasing school attendance, we are still obliged to train female teachers for the lower primary standards at post-junior certificate level in five training schools and some of the colleges. This is a two-year course.

All male and some female teachers are trained in six training colleges to teach in the higher primary standards at a post-senior certificate level. This is a three-year course, but candidates who have successfully completed the second year of the course are awarded a Teachers' Certificate enabling them to commence teaching. The third year of the course is of a highly specialized nature and teachers who have completed this course are competent to teach subjects at secondary level. In this manner the training colleges help to augment the supply of secondary teachers.

Teachers of commercial and technical subjects are trained in three-year courses at the College for Advanced Technical Education. Secondary teachers are also trained at the University of the Western Cape where they are able to follow a degree course for two or three years and a professional course for one year. Higher teacher qualifications can also be obtained at the University.

Much has been done to improve facilities for training teachers. The buildings of the existing colleges are either being replaced with new buildings or being extended and modernized. An additional college is also being built. Because of the limited field from which recruits can be drawn the increase in the number of student-teachers has not been commensurate with the increase in the school enrolment. From 1964 to 1969 the number of teachers-in-training has increased from 1 857 to approximately 2 050. For this reason it is still necessary to draw on Whites for teaching personnel. The lack of teachers is the main deterrent to the introduction of complete compulsory education.

In addition to training new teachers a great deal is being done to improve the qualifications of teachers in service by means of study-leave grants and part-time courses at training colleges and at the University of the Western Cape.

Education at University level – The University of the Western Cape for Coloureds is an autonomous body that is not controlled by the Coloured Persons Representative Council. In spite of all the criticism that has been levelled at this institution by opponents of the policy of separate development, the University is proceeding from strength to strength and more and more students are graduating annually.

When this university was established in 1960 the student enrolment was 164 whereas in 1970 the enrolment was 936. More Coloured students now graduate annually at this university alone than used to graduate at all the other universities together in former years.

Faculties are being added as the demand for them arises. In the meantime students who wish to follow courses that are not being offered at this university are given permission to attend open universities. The future of the Coloured people depends largely on their acceptance and support of their own university.

Shortcomings in the educational system – The main shortcomings have mostly been indicated. They may be summarized as follows:

Complete compulsory school attendance has not yet been introduced.

In spite of every endeavour to catch up on the backlog, there is a shortage of school accommodation leading to overcrowded classes and double-shift classes, especially in the primary schools. There is a shortage of teachers.

All of these shortcomings originated mainly because Coloureds have awakened to the importance of education, and the school population has consequently increased phenomenally. All of these shortcomings are of a temporary nature and will be overcome in due course when every Coloured child will reap the benefit of a sound and enlightened educational system.

4. *The Directorate of Rural Areas and Settlements*

The aim of this Directorate is to promote the perpetuation of Coloureds in rural areas. The Directorate administers the Rural Coloured Areas Act (Act No. 24 of 1963), which makes provision *inter alia* for the efficient administration and development of incorporated rural areas, including the planning and lay-out of residential areas in accordance with accepted provincial standards, the development of the areas with State funds in accordance with previous determined programmes, the exploitation of the mineral wealth of the areas especially in the North West Cape Province to the greatest benefit of the Coloured inhabitants, the extension of self-government in the form of management boards similar to those of village management boards in White areas and the granting of registered ownership of land.

Special attention is also given to:

(a) agricultural planning;
(b) soil conservation in the form of stock watering schemes, grazing camps, boundary fencing and the reclamation and economic use of the soil according to scientifically proven methods;
(c) the erection of engines, windmills, building of bridges, weirs, reservoirs, supplying of implements and tractors, etc.

5. *The Directorate of Community Welfare and Pensions*

The aim of this Directorate is to promote the spiritual and material welfare of the less privileged and maladjusted in the Coloured community and to improve their lot by adequate social measures.

Where community welfare services have in the past been provided for the Coloured community, it is now the practice to activate each population group to promote its own services as far as possible. The present policy concerning welfare for the Coloureds is consequently directed at self-service and the cultivation of a welfare conscience and a sense of responsibility amongst the Coloured community to promote and organize its own welfare services, culture, sport and recreation.

THE HOMELAND ISSUE AND THE STRUGGLE AGAINST DISCRIMINATION

I now wish to refer briefly to two aspects of White-Coloured relations which have by their very actuality forced their way to the forefront of a debate which is currently exercising the minds of practically all informed South Africans, namely the so-called Coloured homeland issue and the very knotty problem of colour discrimination.

I reject unequivocally the idea of a Coloured homeland, whether a single geographically consolidated unit or a collective unit comprising a number of separate fragments. In this matter I enjoy the support of the Federal Party. The concept of an independent 'Colouredstan' is totally unfeasible and in complete disharmony with the hard-core realities of White-Coloured relations. South Africa has neither the land nor the financial resources to create an economically and politically viable Coloured nation state. Above all, the Coloureds feel that such a geo-political partition is unnecessary in view of the close economic, social, political and historical ties between the two groups. However, I am in favour of the creation of larger consolidated residential areas for the Coloured communities. These areas should be developed maximally but still as part and parcel of the Republic of South Africa.

Those Whites who advocate a Coloured homeland no doubt forget that the Western Cape, being the cradle of the Coloureds' emergence as a separate ethnic unit, is the only part of South Africa that could possibly form a true geographical basis for such a development. And it goes without saying that the Whites will not be amenable to a sacrifice of this magnitude. I am convinced that White and Brown in South Africa are destined to share a common fatherland for all time to come and any policy designed to handle White-Coloured relations must of necessity be geared to this inescapable fact. Admittedly, there are some Coloured leaders, several of whom are members of the Federal Party, who favour the Colouredstan concept, but they are in the minority. By rejecting the Coloured homeland concept I am not suggesting that a Coloured national consciousness does not exist. Such a consciousness is already emerging in Coloured ranks.

I also reject, in equally strong terms, the perpetuation of discriminatory practices determined and motivated by colour and racial differences. I have on several occasions warned the South African Government not to make enemies of the Coloureds by perpetuating outdated and unnecessary discrimination. We particularly favour the introduction of the colour-blind equal pay for equal work principle. By righting the present disparity in pay to Whites and Coloureds with equal qualifications the Whites could make loyal friends of the Coloured people. We also resent the hardship caused by job reservation. I have warned the Government that a fifth column could develop in South Africa if a situation which breeds injustice and discrimination is allowed to continue. The Whites must be sensitive to the reactions of Non-Whites with regard to their treatment. We must get away from the idea that everything must be assessed on the basis of a person's colour.

We welcome the Prime Minister's 'outward-going' policies, but the same sort of attitude should be applied to people inside this country. The Non-Whites of South Africa feel indignant when a Negro from the United States is given VIP treatment while the top local Coloured people – some of them 95 per cent White – cannot enjoy any of the White facilities simply because they are Coloured. I think the White man in South Africa at this stage must concern himself with these things. We love this country and it is essential that we should have this love for the country, and that we should stand together. If the Government does not concern itself with these matters – and what it does must be seen to be done – an unfavourable image will be created. We are particularly desirous to see the speedy end of the humiliating pinpricks to which the Coloureds are subjected in their day to day affairs. These 'petty apartheid' measures only cause ill-feeling and disturbed cross-racial relations. I am not suggesting that the identity of the Whites must be threatened in any way, but these petty apartheid injustices are not essential for the protection of the former's identity and way of life. In fact, their removal would be a better investment in White survival. But the White man has no more right than has any other citizen in the country to claim special privileges purely because of his White skin.

The aim of my party is to obtain for the Coloureds everything that the Whites enjoy in South Africa. I do not mean that we should obtain these things immediately, but within a qualified time. The Coloureds are advancing rapidly in all spheres and it seems to me that prospects are well set for peaceful co-existence in South Africa. We do not so much support parallel development as *equal* development, but this does not necessarily make us anti-government. We accept the Government's policy of parallel development, though we call it equal development. That is our policy – a policy of co-operation with all the races of South Africa, particularly the

Whites. I firmly believe that eventually the Coloureds will be accepted as part of the White nation in South Africa. Our destinies are inextricably enmeshed.

In terms of the Government's policy, the development of the Coloured people should as far as possible be on separate, parallel lines – that is the ideal. We have seen enough to have faith that this ideal can be realized. Everyone, both White and Coloured, must have this faith to make it possible.

The White man in South Africa will be challenged to demonstrate that faith by being fair and just in his dealings and attitudes towards the Coloured people and other Non-White groups in this country. Let me say straight out that the Coloured people demand the removal of all forms of discrimination on the basis of colour and will never be satisfied with anything less. I believe the White man is big enough to meet this demand, not only in his own interest but also in the general interest of all the citizens of our country.

The Frustration of being Coloured

David Curry

David M. Curry is the Deputy Leader of the Labour Party, the Coloured political party at present forming the Opposition in the Coloured Persons Representative Council. An able politician and a forceful debater, he is well-known for his forthright stand against the separate development policy

I have been asked to present a paper[1] regarding the place the Coloured people fill in present-day South African society. The term 'Coloured' is rejected by many of us; nevertheless I shall use the term so as to show how we are being discriminated against solely on the grounds of colour. I shall refer especially to the political situation, education for the Coloured community, wages and restrictions on job opportunities, housing and social conditions in Coloured areas.

THE POLITICAL SITUATION

The Coloured people have a history in South Africa as long as that of Whites. It has been said that if separate development was implemented in 1652 there would have been no Coloured people in South Africa. One of the first marriages performed at the fort of Jan van Riebeeck in 1656 was between a European and the daughter of Anthony of Bengal, a free Black.

The early mixing of the races must have affected the composition of the White group, but it certainly helped to establish the Coloured group. The introduction of slavery meant the importation of many people of colour and it was common for slave women to bear the children of White men. These would have been in the main regarded as Coloureds, but they

1. This article is based on a paper presented to the Peace and Justice Commission of the Archdiocese of Cape Town on September 14, 1971.

would also have been slaves. When slaves were freed in 1834, they numbered about 39 000 but there were also many thousands of free Coloured persons. In 1828, through Ordinance 50, all persons of colour, lawfully residing in the Cape Colony, were granted equality before the law and held the same rights as any British subject. In 1850 the Constitution Ordinance created a common suffrage for all male persons.

When the Union of South Africa was formed in 1910, the Coloureds and Africans were excluded from participating in central government bodies, and only those of European descent could become members of parliament. Coloured people could however become members of Municipal, Divisional and Provincial Councils. In 1930, the vote was given to White women but not to Coloured or African women. In 1936 African males were taken off the common roll. In 1956 Coloured males were finally taken off the common roll and separate parliamentary representation was established. This representation ended in 1970 with the first election of the Coloured Persons Representative Council, now commonly called the C.R.C.

Since the establishment of Union, when White South Africa began to whittle away our political rights, various Coloured organizations and political movements have fought not only to retain but to extend the rights of the Coloured people. This fight for full citizenship rights is still being continued today.

When Lord Crewe, Secretary of State for the Colonies, read the South Africa Bill for the second time on 27th July, 1909, these were some of the remarks he made:[2]

'When we come to the qualification for sitting in either House, we approach a point which has been the subject of much discussion and to which many protests have been made. Those who sit in either House of Parliament have to be of European descent. So far, the position is that in the Cape Colony no such restriction has hitherto existed. On the other hand no one not of European descent has ever sat in the Cape House of Assembly. I say frankly that there does seem to me to be a strong case against the insertion of such a provision in this Act or in any Act. There are men not of European descent who are of high standing, of high character, and of high ability. They regard this provision as a slight and

2. Lord Crewe, 'Second Reading South Africa Bill: House of Lords, July 27th, 1909', *International Society's Reading Course,* International University Society, Arboretum Street, Nottingham, pp. 139-140.

we regret that any loyal subject of the King should consider themselves slighted.

'On the other hand, the difficulties which have confronted those who have prepared this Bill were no doubt considerable . . . The fact which has decided us in not attempting to press this matter [of Coloured and African representation] against the wishes of the South African delegates has been that this is undoubtedly one of these matters which represent a delicately balanced compromise between themselves. As a government we cannot take – and personally I am not prepared to take – the responsibility for the wrecking of this Union measure altogether by a provision of this kind, and I am assured that such would be the result of any attempt to insert such a provision in the Bill. The cause of those who desire this change to be made has been pressed with deep feeling and much eloquence by some of the natives themselves and by those who specially represent their cause. But I do feel that if this change is to be made it must be made in South Africa by South Africans themselves and that it is not possible for us, whatever we may consider to be the special merits of the case, to attempt to enforce it upon the great representative body which with unanimity demand that it should not appear.'

From this quotation it is clear that the British Government connived with the various provincial governments of South Africa to take away the rights of both the Coloured and African people. In order to unite White South Africa, the Coloured and African people were offered on the altar of expediency.

Nevertheless, Lord Crewe had some prophetic things to say about the loss of voting rights – disfranchisement as he called it: I quote further.[2]

'It was ultimately decided that Parliament was to prescribe the form of franchise, it being however provided that the Cape vote should be saved to the native unless it was decided by a two-thirds majority of both Houses sitting together to abolish the native franchise there. This is said by those who desire to see the interests of the native in every way protected to involve a somewhat serious risk that the Cape franchise itself might be done away with. I think we may assume that, so far as the rest of the Union is concerned it will in future be a White franchise. It would require both Houses sitting together to abolish the franchise at the Cape. I think it may be assumed that it would require more than this, because it is not likely

3. *Ibid.*, pp. 140-141.

that the nominated senators, especially those who are appointed for their interest in the natives, would be likely to join in a venture of that kind. Therefore, from that point of view, as far as South Africa itself is concerned there does not seem to be much risk. Certainly it is not too much to say that the disfranchisement of a class who held this power of voting so long would be viewed with very deep disappointment.

'Disfranchisement is always an odious thing in itself, and if it were to be applied in this particular manner I am bound to say that it would assume a somewhat specially odious form. Consequently I myself refuse to believe that there is any probability that this particular provision will be carried into effect. Looking at it as a purely abstract question, we could wish that the safeguard might be even stronger, but such as it is I am prepared to consider it strong enough.'

I have quoted at length from Lord Crewe's speech to show that the fight to secure our rights is not a new development. In 1936, Generals Hertzog and Smuts formed the United Party and with a two-thirds majority removed the Cape Africans from the common roll. They received separate representation in Parliament which now also has been taken away. To use Lord Crewe's phrase, many 'odious forms' of disfranchisement have taken place in South Africa. The Coloured voters were removed from the common roll in the most immoral manner. I deliberately use the word immoral because it has always been said that the vote meant nothing to us. If this was so, why did the present government struggle for years to remove us from the roll? In 1951, the Separate Representation of Voters Act was passed but this was ruled invalid by the courts. The government then appointed its own High Court of Parliament, which the courts also declared invalid. The Senate was then enlarged and packed with National Party Senators which gave the Nationalist Government the necessary two-thirds majority to legally remove us from the common roll. When the present Coloured Council was formed the government reserved the right to nominate twenty members. Just as it packed the Senate to take our voting rights away, so it has packed the Coloured Council with nominated members. In South Africa the White man has performed many 'odious' acts to remove our rights. We will soon lose our last rights, the municipal franchise.

The loss of political rights has always put the Coloured man in a poor position. White South Africa, because it holds the reins of power, has always been able to stifle any opposition to its authority. The British

Government in 1910, against the wishes of the Coloured people, agreed not to allow Coloureds and Africans to sit in Parliament. This was done especially to satisfy the demands of the two former Boer Republics, the Orange Free State and the Transvaal. Coloured and African people in these two republics never held any voting rights, not even the municipal franchise.

The implementation of the policy of apartheid was greatly resented by the Coloured people. Due to the fact that the Coloured people are a heterogeneous society the laws of separation have had a terrible effect on our society. Apartheid notices and signs are taken as an insult to our dignity as persons. When the present government saw that it was not able to control South Africa through the traditional means of government it took on many powers not previously held: The laws regarding detention without trial are but one example of how the present government was able to force the policy of separate development on the Coloured people. The C.R.C. is an example of how White South Africa acts politically. In order to give the present policy 'a moral basis', elections to the C.R.C. were held. The Labour Party won twenty-six of the forty elected seats and the Federal Party led by Mr Tom Swartz, eleven. In order to give the Federal Party control of the Council, the twenty nominated members were all chosen from the Federal Party. Fourteen of the twenty nominated were defeated candidates in the election. Mr Tom Swartz, who nearly lost his deposit in the elections, was appointed Chairman of the Executive. The four members of the Executive Committee and the Chairman of the Council were all elected from Federal Party ranks because they had the majority of members in the Council. The Government clearly showed that even in this Council it would ignore the wishes of the Coloured people and thus appoint people who were prepared to work within the framework of its own policy. It is my firm conviction that the government's policy has no moral basis as far as the Coloured people are concerned. On most committees serving the Coloured community most, if not all, the members are nominated by the Government or by local authorities.

General Smuts's son, (J.C. Smuts) described the White man's attitude aptly when, in his book on the life of his father, he wrote.[4]

'The White came out to South Africa not merely to missionise and to settle on a trusteeship basis. He made it clear that he had come to stay.

4. J.C. Smuts, *Jan Christiaan Smuts,* Cassell, 1952, p. 304.

For three hundred years he has been here and he is determined to stay indefinitely. But with the advancement of civilisation and gradual evolution of the native the gap between White and Black has narrowed alarmingly. It is doubtful if the old master and servant relationship will be tenable for many more years to come. The White sees a grave danger for his children.'

With regard to the White man's approach to the problem of South Africa, he says:[5] 'It takes into account that the White man in the Union is outnumbered by four to one. It takes into account the fact that the Black man is increasing in numbers more rapidly than the White man. It assumes that two peoples cannot indefinitely go on living side by side without some major future eruption. For this day of reckoning we must prepare. We must see that we have in our power all those things which can ensure tactical and military superiority. We must prohibit non-Europeans from possessing firearms or in training of their use. Manufacturing industry, wealth and education must be kept in White hands. All these add up to military strength. We must frown upon trade unionism among the Bantu or upon the formation of political bodies for that leads to potentially dangerous consolidations. The emotional fear-complex is not to be construed with these military prerequisites.'

The White man in South Africa is afraid to grant us political rights because, so he thinks, it may endanger his position. The debate on the future political position of the Coloured people has come about not because some people have developed a sudden love for the Coloured (especially those in government circles) but because the Whites fear that even the present policy will lead to eventual integration, even to integration of political rights.

EDUCATION

Education is one of the chief means by which the White man ensures that he keeps the top position in all spheres in South Africa. According to the latest figures, R287 is spent on the education of every White child, R92 on every Coloured child and R15 on every African child. As far back as 1914, compulsory education was introduced for Whites. At present the system has not been implemented for Coloured pupils. It is to the credit of our community that they have always striven against great odds to give their children a sound education.

5. *Ibid.*, p. 306.

The Coloured population is expected to double between 1965 and 1985; the figure in 1965 was 1 791 900 and in 1985 it is expected to be 3 511 210. According to the 1970 census, there are two million Coloureds in South Africa. 50% of the Coloured population are under the age of 21; so we are a 'young' group in the demographic sense. In 1965 about 650 000 children (5-19 year age group) were of school-going age. Only 380 000 were actually at school, i.e. about 57%. In 1970, 520 000 children were at school out of a possible 810 000 (age group 5-19), i.e. about 63%. Close on 300 000 Coloured children are therefore not at school. About 500 000 Coloured people live on farms and nearly 90 000 farm children are not at school. Many factors militate against good school attendance, namely, lack of compulsory education, inadequate transport to school, living a great distance from the school, and shanty town conditions. Poor housing affects education because people who live in slums tend to be less interested in education. Many Coloured children leave school early in order to supplement the family income.

It is important to remember that in the age group 5-20 years the figure will double from 800 000 in 1965 to 1 600 000 in 1985. The number of Coloured children not at school will therefore increase and the position will deteriorate if the Government does not give the education authorities the necessary machinery to improve the situation considerably. During the last five years 127 new schools were built for Coloured pupils but many were closed down due to the area being declared White. At Stellenbosch four primary schools and one high school stand empty. All three new primary schools are on double shifts. The new high school is using six classrooms in a primary school because it cannot accommodate all the pupils. Generally, double-shift attendance has increased alarmingly. In 1970, 386 schools, 1 181 teachers and 41 350 pupils were involved in the system. In 1971 this increased to 1 539 teachers and 53 380 pupils, an increase of 12 000 pupils in one year. In order to solve the problem of double shifts alone 50 new schools will have to be built immediately. The annual increase in school attendance is estimated at 40 000 pupils. A further 50 new schools each year will have to be built to cater for new pupils.

With regard to the supply of teachers, it will be necessary for every Coloured student who passes matriculation to go into teaching just to cope with the increase in pupil attendance. To stress the point, I must state that, in order to cope with Coloured education, no Coloured teacher must die, get married or leave the profession. At present 944 unqualified teachers are employed in Coloured schools. Of these 821 teach in primary schools, 31 in secondary schools, 61 in high schools, 13 in training schools and 18 in training colleges. Between 1964-1969, 2 165 teachers resigned. In 1970, 656 have resigned. These resignations do not include those who left the service due to super-annuation (pension), marriage or death. In 1969, for example, 863 teachers left the teaching profession; of these 342 were resignations.

Coloured teachers leave primarily because of poor salaries and inferior service conditions. Let me give an example of a salary scale – Category D – for a university degree with a teacher's diploma (per annum):

White	R3 360 x 180 —	R4 800 x 300 =	R5 100
Coloured	R1 920 x 90 —	R2 640 x 120 =	R3 360
African	R1 200 x 60 —	R1 800 x 90 =	R2 520

Take a period of fifteen years and the White teacher would have earned R61 000 and the Coloured R33 880, a difference of R27 320. The position of the African teacher is even worse. The White teacher starts with R3 360 and the Coloured teacher ends with R3 360 after 15 years. After 10 years the White teacher is earning R155 more a month than his Coloured counterpart. There are many instances where White assistants teach at Coloured schools and earn more than the principal.

Regarding service conditions, here are some of the remarks made by Mr D.R. Ulster, a former president of the Cape Teachers Professional Association:

'(1) Some teachers get the feeling that they are "controlled" by some unknown force which constantly issues instructions that must be carried out. (2) Many teachers and principals confess that they get a feeling of being watched all the time. They are not given the feeling of being in the position of trust. The many inspectors (and believe me, there are many of them) certainly have positive aspects but then there is also the other side of the story. (3) The morale of the teacher is at a very low ebb today. If this is allowed to continue, there must emanate very serious results which will have a disastrous effect on the entire educational system at the tragic expense of our children.'

The drop-out rate in Coloured schools is high. This is of course because there is no compulsory education. If 100 pupils were in the first grade in 1965, 75 will have dropped out before completing the fourth grade (Std 2). In 1955, out of 100 pupils in the eighth grade (Std VI), only 31 reached the 10th grade (Std VIII) and only 9 reached the 12th grade (Std X).

As wages are generally low amongst the Coloured workers, children leave early to increase the family income. Large sums are spent on education for Whites but not for Coloureds and Africans. Education in South Africa is aimed chiefly at keeping the White man on top. It is used primarily for political ends.

WAGES AND WORKING CONDITIONS

Many Whites think that Coloured people receive high salaries. It is true that in some trades and professions the rate for the job is paid, but generally speaking wages are on a low level. Allow me to quote examples of monthly wages, published in the July 1971 issue of *Race Relations News*.[6] These figures were provided by the Department of Statistics for the last quarter of 1970.

	Whites	*Coloured*	*Indian*	*African*
Mining	R360	R75	R98	R18
Manufacturing	R307	R73	R77	R52
Construction	R325	R109	R150	R49
Electricity	R369	R76	—	R55
Banks and Building Societies	R298	R80	R106	R66
Government	R282	R114	R114	R44
Administration	R224	R59	R73	R35
Local Authorities	R293	R85	R60	R45
S.A. Railways	R295	R70	R53	R52

In most overseas countries the difference between the wages of skilled and unskilled is roughly 30%. If it is assumed that most White workers are skilled and most Coloured workers unskilled the difference in South Africa between skilled and unskilled is 400%. If again overseas rates are used as our point of departure, an African mine worker should earn R250 a month and a Coloured working for the S.A. Railways R200 a month. By employing cheap Coloured and African labour most employers save a

6. *Race Relations News*, July, 1971, S.A. Institute of Race Relations.

tremendous amount in wages. In South Africa the economic system has evolved to such an extent that nearly all industries operate on cheap labour. Here again it can be seen why Whites receive the best education possible and why Coloureds and Africans are denied the same facilities.

The White man in South Africa is always in a favourable position. It is the people termed 'Non-White' who carry the White men on their backs and not vice versa. The gold-mining industry is a very important outlet for manufactured articles. Gold is also our most important export. Without gold South Africa's economy would come close to collapse. The gold-mining industry depends not only on cheap African labour but also on the migratory labour system. One can clearly see what a price has to be paid to keep the White man in his privileged position.

The Coloured work force is mainly concentrated in the 'labour' spheres of employment as can be inferred from the following, based on 1970 data.

Artisans and apprentices	35 000
Teaching and allied professions	18 000
Medical and allied professions	1 500
Technicians	1 000
Administrative with executive powers	2 000
Clerical	17 000
Salesmen	6 000
Mining	9 000
Farming and fishing	128 000
Labourers	120 000
Operators and skilled trades	90 000
Transport, delivery and communication	30 000
	457 500

Out of a total labour force of 457 500, 63% can be classified as labourers earning an average of less than R60 a month. In a survey done by Market Research (Pty) Ltd of 181 Coloured households, it was found that the average Coloured family consists of 6 persons. Of the male heads of households 3% were professional workers, 5% did white collar work, 15% were employed in skilled jobs, the rest being semi-skilled or unskilled workers. The average income was R52 per month. In the urban areas 30% earned less than R50 per month, 28% earned between R50 and R109 and only 0,5% earned more than R210 a month. In the rural areas 84% earned less than R50 a month.

I do not think it is necessary to say much about job reservation. It is both legal and traditional in South Africa. The best jobs in nearly all forms of employment are reserved for Whites. It has been repeatedly stated that Coloured workers will not be employed at the expense of White workers. Education for Coloureds is deliberately stifled so that the Coloured worker cannot become a threat to the White man, especially in the economic field.

HOUSING AND LIVING CONDITIONS

Housing presents a major problem to our community. The Group Areas Act has caused not only bitterness but a severe shortage of houses. According to the Minister of Community Development (Feb., 1970) the number of families disqualified under the Act and those resettled were:

	Disqualified	*Resettled*
White	1 318	1 196
Coloured	68 897	24 240
Indian	37 653	21 939

The major social problems among our people centre around housing and poverty. We find ourselves in a vicious circle because poverty also causes other major social problems such as crime, juvenile delinquency and family disorganization. The lack of adequate housing and the growth of shanty towns are causing serious concern. If one looks at population figures, particularly regarding the Western Cape, one finds that between two-thirds to three-quarters of all Coloureds live in overcrowded conditions. Greater Cape Town contains over 750 000 Coloured persons, which means 130 000 families. Thus about 43 000 families are in need of homes. The authorities are already behind planned building programmes. Between 1970 and 1980, the Coloured population in Greater Cape Town will increase by another 320 000 and for them another 54 000 new dwellings will have to be provided. During the next ten years, 10 000 houses will have to be built every year to solve the housing problem in the Cape Town area alone.

This sad state of affairs has a depressing effect on the Coloured community. The threat of Group Areas removals remains constantly over our heads and this generates a feeling of insecurity. How can people who live in shanty towns or overcrowded homes be expected to be motivated to the better things in life? Loss of self-respect and dignity has trapped the

Coloured in a vicious circle. It is common knowledge that the incidence of crime is much higher amongst Coloureds than amongst Whites. In 1968, 13 out of every thousand Whites were convicted for an offence, while 69 out of every thousand Coloureds were convicted. There are no grounds to believe that we are inherently more inclined to lawlessness. When one compares the education, wages and the living conditions of Whites with Coloureds the reasons for lawlessness become only too obvious. If you have been moved into low-cost housing schemes where no stable community structure has as yet been developed and where the setting is conducive to crime, then you must expect trouble. Our areas lack effective policing, adequate street lighting, proper transport services, public amenities, schooling facilities and even simple things like public telephones. If Whites had to live under the same conditions, the same social problems would be part and parcel of their lives. Because of the general position awarded to us in South African society, because we are people of colour, Whites, generally speaking, do not look upon us as persons but as things.

Adam Small, the well known Coloured poet and lecturer, states the positions correctly when he comments in the *Cape Times* on the debate relating to the future of the Coloured people: 'I would call this debate about the so-called Coloureds a comedy of callous men. If I were a White politician perhaps I would not know how to look at myself in the mirror. How can a man who invariably speaks of other men as though they are a commodity, a kind of thing, face up to himself?

'I am not facetious, but very serious if I say that I feel pity for these men who speak of me, and people like me, as though we are things. I pity them because they lack humanity. Even the White academics who have come out on the side of the so-called Coloureds still speak only about these people.

'At the same time, therefore, as I salute them, I say to them also that the question they should have asked and that must be asked over and over again, is: What have those people themselves to say?

'After all, men can speak, and can speak for themselves. And these so-called Coloureds are men. Not even animals are mute.'

The policy of separate development really exposes itself when it comes to the solutions regarding the socio-economic position of the Coloured people. The Government knows very well what our problems are. The question can be asked, why don't they do something about it? Firstly, they have to consider the White electorate, whose interests always come first. Secondly, the system as a whole has become so entrenched that it is difficult even for the Government itself to find solutions because the real solution lies in establishing a truly democratic society. I will, for example, explain how the system in South Africa has led even to using prisoners as cheap labour.

The high crime rate has led to a high prison population. According to the Report of General J.C. Steyn, Commissioner of Prisons,[7] South Africa's daily average prisoner population – already the highest per capita in the world – rose another 3% in 1969-70 to reach 90 555. In the past nine years the daily prison average rose by 35 000. The total number of prisoners for the year was 484 661. Of these more than 416 000 were serving sentences up to four months and well over half – 268 584 – were in prison for one month or less. Penal reform in South Africa is long overdue. A total of 4 268 breast-fed babies were admitted to prison and 240 infants were born during their mothers' detention.

We thus have the staggering fact that more than 268 000 people are in prison for one month or less. Many are in prison for petty offences including the notorious pass laws. Many cannot afford to pay a fine. Low wages again come into the picture. Is it fair, when it comes to convictions, that Whites who earn five times as much should pay the same fine as Africans or Coloureds?

This is what Chief Justice Ogilvie Thompson said recently on the Springbok Radio programme 'Top Level': 'Statistics show that the ratio of our prison population to the total population of the country is strikingly high. Thus in 1969 – the last year for which internationally comparative figures are available to me – the number of incarcerated prisoners per 100 000 of our population was no less than 417 – a figure nearly six times the corresponding figure for that year in France with a total population just short of 2½ times our own and considerably more than five times the corresponding figure in England with a total population of more than double our own. The report of the Commissioner of Prisons for the year ending 30th June 1970 shows that more than 55% of all sentenced prisoners (excluding capital cases) for the year ending 30th June 1970 had been sentenced to imprisonment for only one month or less. The total of those who had been sentenced for four months or less actually constituted slightly over 86% of the aggregate of all sentenced prisoners during that

7. *Cape Times*, Cape Town.

year; and of that 86% a substantial porportion were first offenders. These figures are not indicative of any undue leniency on the part of the Courts, but show that a large number of crimes which are in themselves relatively unserious entail a prison sentence, and that a high proportion of all sentenced offenders is comprised by these short term prisoners. This is in an appreciable measure attributable to the composition of our population and the number of infringements of the Criminal Law associated with so-called pass offenders and breaches of what are sometimes generally designated "curfew regulations". Nevertheless, the cardinal fact remains that a strikingly high proportion of our prison population is comprised of those serving short-term sentences.'

Now comes the question again: Why is this allowed to continue? If so many people are in prison work must be found for them. Many of these prisoners are employed on farms. Prison labour is not new in South Africa. The practice to build farm jails was started in 1947 and became fully established when the Nationalist Government came to power. The costs of building each jail were met by local farmers, each of whom bought shares and able to draw labour according to his portion of share capital. Farmers were charged between 16 to 50c a day for each prisoner hired. Thirteen of these jails are situated in the Western Cape. By 1966 there were no less than 23 such prison out-stations with total accommodation for 6 000 long-term prisoners. It is clear that many farmers are becoming dependent on prison labour to run their farms.

In its defence, a former Minister of Justice, Mr C.R. Swart, contended that it was sensible to relieve the overcrowded city jails by sending some of their inhabitants out into the country districts where they could work constructively. Others argued that the private employment of casual convict labour should not lead to the systematic building of prisons with the primary object of providing farm labour. The argument that the latter system has led to a vested interest in crime is convincing. Surely farmers would resent having an empty farm jail which collectively would have cost them anything up to R50 000 to erect. In the Transvaal the right to draw convict labour even raised the value of land. In the Western Cape, the right to employ prison labour has been valued at R1 000 a convict.

It must be remembered that labour is being drawn to the cities through industrialization. Farmers are complaining of the shortage of labour. But why do Coloured people leave the farms? Because wages are generally low and housing conditions poor. It must also be remembered that it is Government policy to remove African labour from the Western Cape. The migratory labour system has become the backbone of the mining industry and South Africa's economy has become dependent on a morally evil system. Slowly, prison labour is becoming the backbone of the farming industry, because if the crime rate were to drop suddenly, many farmers, especially some of the wine farmers in the Western Cape, would be without labour. So the vicious circle continues: if you improve the living conditions of the Coloured people through education, proper wages and good housing your crime rate would drop, but so would your supply of farm labour. Again it can be seen how the White man's interests come first. But what a price the Coloured and African people must pay to keep the economy of this country moving.

WHAT ABOUT THE FUTURE?

There are two fundamentals I consider very important when I think of my country, South Africa. The one is that ours is a multi-racial society and that the rights of the individual are important. Some of the rights I believe in are that all men are born equal, that all are endowed by their Creator with certain rights which no man may take away, and that amongst these rights are life, liberty and the pursuit of happiness, and that to secure these rights governments are instituted amongst men, deriving their just powers from the consent of the governed; that whenever any form of government becomes destructive of these ends, it is the right of the people to alter or abolish it and to institute a new government invested with the aforesaid principles and with power organized in such a way that it shall promote the happiness, safety and freedom of all the country's inhabitants.

White South Africa, through its policies, whether you call it White leadership, apartheid, separate or parallel development, is trying to reach for the unattainable. Since 1909 some 200 laws have been adopted which seek to regulate the relationships between the various racial groups. It is most upsetting to see how these laws have multiplied.

From 1909 till 1948 – 49 laws in 38 years
From 1948 till 1960 – 53 laws in 12 years
From 1960 till 1971 – 98 laws in 10 years.

Yet, in South Africa this is called 'development'. You cannot escape seeing the writing on the wall – the tragedy of inhuman laws – White

South Africa reaching for the unattainable – groping for the Utopia in race relations. This system called 'development' has resulted in the riots of Sharpeville, Gelvandale and the cancellation of the planned 1971-72 cricket tour to Australia.

An example of these race laws is the Race Classification Act. Our population is divided into three main groups, White, Coloured and Bantu. Coloured and Bantu are divided into sub-groups but not Whites. The Coloured Group is divided into seven sub-groups : Cape Coloured, Malay, Griqua, Chinese, Indian, Other Asiatic and Other Coloured. In practice the term 'Other Coloured' on a Birth Certificate or Identity Card has created ill-feeling amongst the Coloured people. Under the Group Areas Act the population is divided into White, Coloured and Asiatic. An Indian therefore cannot live in a Coloured area. Marriage between Indians and Coloureds or even Coloureds and African creates deep wounds in race relations when it comes to the area in which these couples can live. If an African woman marries a Coloured man she may live with him in a Coloured area but if her husband leaves her she must return to her place of origin. But what happens now to the children who are perhaps registered as 'Other Coloured' ?

The Coloured community can be proud of one thing : White South Africans can find the solution to South Africa's problems in our own society. Moslems and Christians have lived in peace since the slave age. There has been social integration but there has never been loss of identity. Moslems have never asked for special laws or group areas to protect their 'identity'. I have said this before and I want to say it again. Has White South Africa become so spiritually bankrupt that its culture has to be protected by opera apartheid, bus apartheid, post office apartheid or even toilet apartheid? In 1899-1902, English-speaking South Africans and Afrikaners were involved in a war; in 1910 they formed the Union of South Africa. Why can the leaders of all racial groups not meet at another convention to work out a plan to make South Africa a country which could earn the respect of the world?

When we ask for full citizenship, the word 'integration' is always used to scare Whites. I want to remind White South Africans that they fathered the Coloured people. Economic integration is a fact in South Africa, yet it has not led to social integration. My argument is that if political integration takes place it does not mean that social integration will automatically follow. I believe that the mass of laws which enforce compulsory segregation should be scrapped. Social relationships must not be regulated by compulsion. They are best regulated by conventions of society and the attitudes of individuals. South Africans must be allowed to live their private lives as they see fit. Each man should be free to associate with whom he wishes provided that he does not exercise his freedom in such a way as to interfere with that of others.

Even today the English and Afrikaners are preserving their 'identities'; they live in their own 'group areas', go to their own schools, attend different universities, belong to different churches, and to a large extent have never integrated socially, but they enjoy the same political rights. As I said before, political integration does not mean social integration. Assimilation has never taken place between the English and the Afrikaner and by this I mean that neither group has absorbed the other. Coming back to the Coloured people: Moslems and Christians have lived together and neither group has been absorbed to the point of losing its 'identity'. But the 'integration' scarecrow influences White voters because the White man fears the Coloured and the African. He fears the loss of his privileged position; he fears having to share the good things in life we have helped him to obtain; he fears the loss of being 'Baas'. And yet, we have worked with him, fought with him in times of war, trekked with him in the days of the Voortrekkers, died with him at the hands of Dingaan, and yet he still fears us.

I was born in Cape Town but spent my childhood days in Cradock in the Eastern Cape. On a distant mountain you can see the grave of Olive Schreiner, the famous authoress. I would like to end by quoting her prophetic words written in 1908[8]: 'For the dark man is with us to stay . . . not only can we not exterminate him . . . but we cannot even transport him, because we want him. We want more and always more of him – to labour in our mines, to build our railways, to work in our fields, to perform our domestic labours.

'But if we fail? . . . If blinded by the gain of the moment, we see nothing in the dark man but a vast engine of labour, if he is to us not a man but a tool, if we force him permanently, in his millions, into the locations and compounds and slums of our cities . . . his own social organization broken up, without our having aided him to participate in our own?

8. Uys Krige (ed.), *Olive Schreiner – A Selection,* Oxford University Press, 1968, p. 189.

'If, unbound to us in gratitude and sympathy, and alien to us in blood and colour, we reduce this vast mass to the condition of a great, seething ignorant proletariat – then I would rather draw a veil over the future of this land.

'As long as nine-tenths of our community have no permanent stake in our land, and no right or share in our government, can we ever feel safe?

'Can we ever know peace?'

The Future of the Indian Community

H. E. Joosub

Hajee Ebrahim Joosub is one of South Africa's most respected Indian leaders. He is Chairman of the South African Indian Council (a statutory body created to serve the interests of the country's Indian population). A highly successful businessman, Mr Joosub founded the first Indian Bank in South Africa.

To sketch a present situation is relatively easy. It is less easy to predict what that situation will be in the distant and even near future. That is very much the case when one speaks of the place and future of the Indian community in South African society. One can at most base one's prediction of the future on past and present trends, although in a rapid changing world such as the one in which we live, even trends can be reversed overnight.

That is so especially in the case of the Indian South Africans, a minority group of about 600 000 persons in a total population of 21 447 230, of whom more than 15 millions are Bantu, 3 750 716 Whites, and 2 018 533 Coloureds.[1] These figures immediately highlight a very important truth that is too often overlooked by many, especially by Indian radicals, and that is that in view of the numerically strong Bantu group, the economically and politically strong White group, and the rapidly emerging Coloured group, the Indian South Africans will always be a minority, regardless of the political set-up in the country as a whole. Development in race relations in the rest of Africa, as well as in the United States and Britain, and indeed in India itself, have demonstrated beyond all doubt that no constitutional system, whether it be democratic or otherwise, has

1. Based on preliminary published data from the census of 6 May, 1970. The figures given for 'Asians' is 620 422. That includes also the Chinese, who would number at most 20 000.

so far eliminated either race consciousness or the way in which people are treated. In South Africa that means that the Indians will always be governed either by Whites or by the Bantu. The truth, however unpleasant it may be, can be disregarded only at one's own peril, and the truth for the Indian South African is that his choice lies between a South Africa governed by the Whites, or a South Africa governed by the Bantu.

Although since time immemorial Indians have settled on the African Continent, it was only in 1860 that, as a result of an agreement between the government of India and the colonial government of Natal, shiploads of Indians indentured for work on the sugar plantations landed in Durban, South Africa. In terms of the agreement, these Indian workers would be free to settle in the country, with all the privileges of the rest of the population. With the establishment of the Union of South Africa in 1910 the obligation to honour this contract devolved on the South African government. Simultaneously, with the arrival of the Indian workers, Indian traders came to Natal, mostly from East Africa, Mauritius and India, and very soon they spread all over the country. According to the 1970 census the distribution of the Indians in South Africa is as follows: Cape Province, 21 617; Natal, 514 803; Transvaal, 80 556; Orange Free State, 6; and Bantu homelands, 3 441. In Natal they outnumber the Whites by 72 704, but they are outnumbered by the Bantu even in that province by more than 2 500 000.

What has been the political, economic and social lot of the Indian community over the past century, and what are their prospects for the future?

In the political sphere the first restrictive legislation affecting the Indians was Act 3 of 1885 of the Transvaal. That Act deprived Indians of citizenship rights, and it also deprived them of the right to own fixed property, except in certain areas. But notwithstanding this Act, relations between the Indians and the Whites of the Transvaal were good at that time. Soon after the founding of the Transvaal Republic, 484 Afrikaner citizens presented a petition to the Volksraad or Parliament stating 'that withdrawal of the Indian traders would be a hardship', and in 1896 a member of the Volksraad said 'that the Indian traders sold the necessities of life at a lower price than the Whites, that these traders were beneficial to the whole country and that it would be unwise to legislate to their prejudice'.

The next fifty years was a period of steady and relatively untroubled development for the Indians. Custom, rather than legislation, kept them out of certain occupations and brought about a considerable measure of apartheid, but little was done for them in the way of education or the creation of avenues of employment. A large proportion of the economically active Indians found a livelihood in commerce, either as owners of shops, hawkers or shop assistants, and this period also saw the rise of the Indian wholesalers and importers. Others were occupied in the hotel trade, in peasant farming in Natal or in manual labour. During this period the South African Indians were not education-conscious, while their national and religious customs caused them to keep their women largely in the background, with the result that the percentage of economically active persons in the Indian group was lower than that of any other racial group in South Africa.

During all these decades, in fact until the year 1964, when the first South African Indian Council was established by the National Party government as an administrative body with advisory and consultative functions, the Indian community as such had no access to the government, nor had they any channel by which they could make their wishes felt, and the result was that when the first and almost fatal blow was struck at them in 1946, they had no redress.

INTRODUCTION OF STATUTORY SEGREGATION

This blow took the form of the Asiatic Land Tenure Act of 1946, popularly known as the Pegging Act. It was enacted by the United Party government under General J.C. Smuts, and it restricted any change in the racial character of the ownership or the occupation of land or premises as between Whites and Indians.

This was done two years before the National Party came to power and before apartheid became the policy of South Africa. It is true that the measure did not mean eviction of Indians from their homes or shops. There were no dramatic incidents, and the effects of the law were not immediately felt.

But it was in fact a sentence of lingering death. It meant that Indians could not occupy houses or premises which they had not occupied before. It forced young married couples to live with their parents. That led to congestion and slum conditions. It led to the exploitation of Indian tenants by rich landowners. The National Party was not responsible for this law.

Before the National Party came to power, and even during the first twelve years of their rule, there were no industrial areas where Indians could erect factories. They had to be traders, without the right to expand, or otherwise they remained manual workers in restricted fields. Indian subsistence farmers in Natal were refused loans. They had no university, and although in theory they could attend White universities, admission was so restricted that it did not signify much.

When the National Party came to power in 1948, matters initially became even worse for the Indian community. In 1950 the Group Areas Act was put on the statute book. In terms of the Act, premises for ownership and occupation were specified, and from the date of the proclamation of the Act no person could occupy any land or premises except under the authority of a permit in an area not lawfully occupied or deemed to have been occupied by a member of the same group.

The interim period between the proclamation of the Act and the actual proclamation of the areas to which Indians were ultimately restricted was the beginning of a time of uncertainty and suspense. This proved to be one of the facets of the policy of separate development, or apartheid, which notwithstanding the vast improvements that have since that time come about in the situation of Indian South Africans, has persisted. The sword of Damocles is today not nearly as sharp and as dangerous as it was then, but it is still hanging over our heads.

Throughout that period, and even today, the terms of the various proclamations affecting the lives of the Indian South Africans have always been far more severe than the implementation. Uncertainty as to the future and the consequent feeling of fear and insecurity have caused infinitely more harm than actual financial loss. In fact, as to that, it can with truth be said that the Indian South Africans have never been as prosperous as they are now, nor has there ever been a time when so many opportunities in different fields of economic activity have been opened to them as now, nor has their position in regard to housing, education, or medical and social services ever been as good as it is now. There is no country in Africa where we are so well placed as we are in the Republic of South Africa.

The first proclamations under the Group Areas Act are an example of what I mean. I shall take Pretoria as an illustration. Almost 70 per cent of the Indian population was affected. The 127 Indian shops in the central Prinsloo Street area, providing a livelihood for nearly 2 500 Indians, were given notice to vacate their premises within three years. Well over one hundred Indian shops in other parts of the city, including about forty stall-holders at the municipal market, were given one year. One hundred and seventy traders in the Indian Bazaar were told to quit within seven years. As alternate accommodation they were offered a bare piece of land about twelve kilometres west of the centre of the city, where there would be little or no opportunity for trading. It was tantamount to a sentence of death.

That was about fifteen years ago, but very few Indian shops have been vacated. Prinsloo Street is still predominantly an Indian trading area. The disappearance of a number of small Indian shops elsewhere has coincided with the disappearance of small White-owned businesses, following the general trend of the disappearance of small undertakings before the onslaught of the chain stores and supermarkets. Indian-owned properties that were sold under the Group Areas Act normally fetched fair prices. In the Diagonal Street Indian complex in Johannesburg some Indian owners voluntarily sold their buildings to property developers at high prices, and Indian tenants have to find other accommodation, because buildings are to be demolished, but that had nothing to do with the fact that they are Indians. In fact, the Minister of Community Development has publicly appealed to the property developers to assist the Indian businessmen whom they are forced to evict. He undertook that his department would then 'find business premises for them in their own group areas, or if that proves impossible, to make other arrangements which would necessitate their getting permits'.

However, in a number of places in Natal, especially Cato Manor and Riverside, compensation paid to Indians for properties expropriated under the Group Areas Act was so low that many Indians suffered considerable financial loss.

This kind of thing happened also in other parts of the country. In certain places Indian owners made a handsome profit by selling land and buildings to White companies who then increased the rentals very sharply. That hit the Indian tenants far more heavily than the White tenants, mainly because the trading pattern of the Whites makes a quick turnover possible, while the Indians operate on a slow turnover. But the government can hardly be blamed for that.

Unfortunately this is not the whole picture, but the undoubted discrimination against Indians would not be the whole picture either, and the true and unbiased picture could best be arrived at by sketching trends in the situation of the Indians in the sphere of politics, the economy and avenues of employment, education, housing and social services.

THE POLITICAL POSITION OF THE INDIANS

In the sphere of political rights it must be remembered that no South African government before 1961 recognized the South African Indian community as a permanent part of the population. The policy had always tacitly or openly been one of repatriation, although the vast majority of us have been in South Africa for several generations. When the National Party came to power in 1948 they took strenuous steps to implement that policy. A government commission in the late fifties, in the so-called Joint Report, recommended that in the case of the Indians there must be 'repatriation, failing which, boycott, to induce repatriation', while the then Minister of Interior said: 'We will endeavour to reduce the Indian people to the irreducible minimum.' That was followed by the proclamation of group areas for Indians.

Before August, 1961, when the Department of Indian Affairs was established, Indians had virtually no way of bringing their needs to the attention of the government. But in May, 1961, the Minister of the Interior in the late Dr H.F. Verwoerd's Cabinet made a statement which included these words: 'The Indians are here and the vast majority of them are going to remain here, and we must realize that the vast majority of them are South African citizens, and as such they are entitled to the necessary attention and the necessary assistance.'

In 1964 the government established the National Indian Council, which was replaced on September 1, 1968, by the South African Indian Council, a body nominated by the Minister of Indian Affairs, and consisting of 15 members from Natal, 7 from the Transvaal and 3 from the Cape Province. The Council has no more than advisory powers, but it is serving the important purpose of being a channel through which the Indian community can bring its needs and grievances to the attention of the government.

At first the Indian community did not accept either the Department of Indian Affairs or the nominated Indian Council as genuine gestures. Many Indians were so suspicious that they regarded the members of the Council as traitors to their cause and stooges of the government. It is largely due to this suspicion that the Indian Council is as yet not even a partially elected body. But the members of the Council are neither traitors nor stooges. They realize that the Indians are and always will be a minority group in South Africa, and that they can serve their people better by making use of available channels than making demands which they do not have the power to enforce. All that they would have achieved would have been loss of the significant and growing sympathy of the Whites.

It is significant, however, that there is no organized group or party among the Indians in South Africa that is opposed to the South African Indian Council. Criticism comes from individuals and newspapers, but the situation is quite different to that prevailing in the Coloured group, where the pro-government Coloured Federal Party in the Coloured Representative Council is opposed by the Coloured Labour Party, who are strongly represented in that Council. On the other hand it is also true that the Coloured Council is only partly a nominated body, while all the members of the Indian Council are as yet nominees of the government.

There was also a further consideration that weighed very heavily with thoughtful Indian South Africans. If the White government were to be overthrown by a political set-up involving universal franchise on the basis of one man one vote, and the present policy of separate development and self-determination for the numerically superior Bantu group, and with it the growing Bantu support for that policy were to be reversed, the Bantu would obviously be the dominant group. The political choice for us was a simple one – to be dominated by Whites or by Bantu. The argument that the rights of minorities could be safeguarded by entrenchments in the constitution did not sound very convincing. The states of Africa, including South Africa, have not proved to be fertile soil for constitutional entrenchment, nor could we disregard the lot of Indians in some Africa states – a lot far worse than our own. Apart from that we had to consider the several bloody riots in Natal, in 1949 and in 1959, when large number of Indians were killed in an outburst of Bantu fury. For those and other reasons we are not impressed by arguments used by expatriate Indian organizations that we are stooges and that we should not in any way co-operate with the government.

The outcome of events has proved that we were right. Although the Indian Council has no legislative powers, it has, by its free access to the government, been instrumental in bringing about so many improvements in the situation of the Indians in South Africa that the attitude of the Indian community to the Council has changed to such an extent that we are already looking forward to the time when the Council will be an elected body with certain legislative powers and administrative functions related to our community.

Obviously the poltical situation of the Indian South Africans will for the foreseeable future leave much to be desired. In the case of the Bantu the government's policy of separate development has some basis, in the sense that there are Bantu homelands where, in terms of that policy, the various Bantu races will develop towards complete political independence. But in the case of the Indian and Coloured communities there are no homelands, and at best we can expect to be residentially segregated and politically inarticulate, while we cannot see how the economy of our group can be developed as something apart from the economy of the country as a whole. In these matters we do not feel satisfied with government policy. But although many people in South Africa, especially Whites, would not agree that it is so, there is an evolutionary process at work in South Africa and this process is bound to be in the interest of all the racial groups, including the Indian group. Only short-sighted interference from outside by semi-informed or even openly hostile and extremist elements could halt this process, and whatever other racial groups in South Africa might stand to gain or lose by such interference, the country as a whole, and most certainly the Indian community, would definitely be the losers.

THE ECONOMIC SITUATION

However important political rights may be, it remains true that in many respects economy is the life-blood of a people. The populations of the Black African states, at least on paper, have complete political independence, but economically they are so backward that not one of the racial groups in South Africa, and definitely not the Indian group, would change places with them.

The South African Indians were initially almost all either indentured labourers on the sugar plantations in Natal, or traders. The traders gradually spread to the hinterland of Natal and the Transvaal, and they were welcomed everywhere, because they were able to supply the necessities of life to scattered White and Bantu communities, where White traders were not prepared to go. Many of these Indian traders settled in the cities and rural towns, and this gradually became a pattern of Indian life.

Many of the workers on the sugar plantations in Natal acquired small farms after their indenture was over, while others were employed as workers in other fields, especially in the catering industries. In the Transvaal they were mostly debarred from owning farms, with the result that except for Natal very few Indians were engaged in agriculture.

But many factors, such as restrictive laws and convention, militated against the economic progress of the Indians in South Africa. During the decades when the growth of the economy of the country as a whole was slow, they found it difficult to obtain employment. The government service was largely closed to them, and when the group as a whole reached the stage where a significant number of Indians could enter the professions, they were limited almost completely to the medical, legal and teaching professions.

A factor that slowed down the economic advancement of the Indian South Africans was that, in comparison with the Whites and the Coloureds, a very low proportion of them were economically active. In 1960 only 26,4 per cent of the Indians were economically active, as against 36,9 per cent and 35,7 per cent for the Whites and Coloureds respectively. One of the factors responsible was the fact that only 53,9 per cent of the Indian community fell in the working age of 15 to 64 years, as against 60,8 per cent of the Whites.

Apart from that, only about one half of these labour-age Indians were actually working. This was mainly due to the reluctance of Indians to allow their women to enter the labour force. These figures are found also in other African countries, where the same factors operate. In 1959 only 28 per cent of the Indians in Uganda were economically active.

Another factor militated against the Indians. Although, as will be shown, the situation is rapidly improving, educational facilities for Indians, especially before 1960, were not satisfactory, and that, together with economic necessity, caused the Indians to enter the labour market at an earlier age than, for example, the Whites. Consequently they were not as well qualified as the Whites, with the result that they were restricted to more menial and less lucrative work.

It was the National Party government, after 1961, that was the first to take active steps to alleviate this situation, and they did so by rapidly extending Indian education at primary, secondary and university level, and by taking active steps to provide employment for Indians.

The pattern thus far has been that the majority of Indians have found employment in the manufacturing industry. With the buoyant economy of the country and the improved training facilities for Indians, one can expect that more Indians will be employed in this sphere, and that their wages will show an upward curve. Many Indians – according to our critics, too many – are employed in commerce, either as owners or as assistants, but in comparison with other African states it is low, and the percentage is on the decrease. In 1960 only 21,8 per cent of the Indian labour force were engaged in commerce, as against 60 per cent in Mozambique and 40 per cent in Uganda. Indian farmers are, with few exceptions, poor subsistence farmers, and with increasing opportunities in other spheres the percentage and even the actual number of Indians deriving a livelihood from agriculture is on the decrease.

The following table confirms these trends. It includes only Indian workers in mining, manufacturing, construction, commerce, postal workers, railway workers, public servants and agriculture. The total number of Indian workers in these field were 63 794 for 1960 and 117 328 for 1970, although the figure for agriculture workers in the second column is for 1969 and not 1970.

	1960	*1970*
Mining	0,8%	0,6%
Manufacturing	48,7%	58,1%
Construction	1,1%	3,1%
Commerce	24,3%	20,1%
Postal Workers	0,1%	0,3%
Railways	1,0%	0,9%
Public Service	12,1%	10,8%
Agriculture	11,8%	6,1%

Economic changes do not take place overnight, but the trends illustrated in these figures calculated from census data are encouraging. Indians are increasingly active in manufacturing. Commerce shows a healthy decline, while nothing indicates the sustained improvement in the economic situation of the Indian so clearly as the sharp drop in the percentage of workers engaged in farming, which is mostly subsistence farming. As already indicated, the buoyant national economy with its growing demand for workers plus improved and ever improving educational and training facilities, will ensure a sustained increase in the wages of more and more factory workers, who already constitute 58,1 per cent of the Indian labour force. The figures for Indians in the professions and the services, e.g. catering, are not included in the table.

In the meantime much is being done by the government to create new careers for the Indian South Africans. In the M.L. Sultan Technical College for Indians courses are now being offered in secretarial practice, comptometry, public administration and other qualifications recognized by the Chartered Institute of Secretaries, the Institute of Commerce and Administration, and the Institute of Certified Bookkeepers. Enrollment is very high, and a very satisfactory response has already been received from firms who employ these graduates. As from 1970 an engineering course has been provided for at the University of Durban-Westville; at the M.L. Sultan Technical College a very successful course is being conducted in business management; the government provides training for Indians in the police force, and there are regular passing-out parades at the Chatsworth Training Centre in Durban. In 1970 a number of Indian policemen were promoted to officers' rank at Benoni in the Transvaal; there is a well-attended course for Indian women at the King Edward VIII School of Physiotherapy, while Indian students in secondary schools are being encouraged to take courses in physics and chemistry. To assist this project Indian teachers from 90 schools recently attended an orientation course in general science arranged by the Department of Indian Affairs. These are but some of the government-sponsored ventures that bode well for the economic future of the Indian community.

In addition to that the government-financed Industrial Development Corporation assists industrialists, including Indians, to establish or expand industries at low rates of interest.

The picture has also another side to it, but present trends and developments clearly speak of a growing part that will be played by Indians in the South African economy, to their own benefit as well as to the benefit of the country as a whole.

It is expected that a strong impetus will be given to the growth and diversification of industries and other undertakings by Indian entrepreneurs by the establishment late in 1970 of the all-Indian New Republic Bank, with its head-office in Durban. It is a general bank, and its main function will be to discount bills and hire-purchase agreements as well as to advance capital to Indian firms for the acquisition of capital equipment.

The government has ruled that only Indians can own shares in this bank, and although this was regarded by some as only yet another apartheid measure, it is in fact a protection, since otherwise the new bank would soon have been swallowed up by one of the large banking institutions in the country. There is no legal or other hindrance to an Indian buying shares in any other, White-controlled public company.

PROS AND CONS OF THE GROUP AREAS ACT

That does not mean that there are no legal restrictions on Indians in the economic sphere. Except under special permit no Indian can trade in a White proclaimed area, and although it is equally true that Whites are not allowed to trade in Indian proclaimed areas it has recently happened in Ladysmith, Natal, that Indians were first asked to move under the Group Areas Act from the centre of the town to the lower portion of the town, and that the rapid growth of this new Indian trading area led the Department of Planning to deproclaim the area and reproclaim it as a White area, while Indians will be moved further away, where they will have to start from scratch. It is true that they will be compensated, but this has created a feeling of insecurity among Indians all over the country.

But notwithstanding an assurance given by the Ministers of Indian Affairs and Planning that the deproclamation of an Indian group area would be considered only in exceptional circumstances and then only with the greatest circumspection, a government proposal for the rezoning of the already proclaimed Indian area in Newcastle, Natal, that would have meant a repetition of what has already happened at Ladysmith, was advertised in the newspapers.

However, no finality has been reached in Newcastle. In that town the White Town Council, as well as the majority of the White inhabitants, took up the matter on behalf of the Indians, and the enquiry that would have led to a second uprooting of Indians was postponed. An interdepartmental Steering Committee is at present investigating the situation. Apart from the fact that many Indians are in danger of being affected, much harm has already been done by the growing uncertainty and lack of security which these steps have caused.

The same cloud of uncertainty hangs over the Grey Street complex in Durban. It is almost predominantly Indian. Indians have invested large sums of money there. It is at the moment a 'controlled' area, which means that it can be proclaimed either a White or Indian area. If the Indians were to be removed from that area, it would adversely affect large numbers of our community, and it has even been said that the future of the South African Indian Council to a large extent depends on what is going to happen in Grey Street. But here also much harm has already been done by the feeling of insecurity caused by the uncertain future.

Another factor that has an adverse effect on the economic progress of the Indians is that the gap between the salaries of government-employed

White and Indian professional people, such as doctors, has, as a result of recent salary increases, widened instead of narrowing. This matter is also being dealt with by the Indian Council.

In fairness it must be said that the National Party has done much in the way of offering employment to Indians in the Civil Service, especially in the Department of Indian Affairs. In 1961 only 25 clerical Indian personnel were employed in three categories in that department. Very soon 306 were employed in 30 categories, involving higher-graded posts. That is true also in high professional posts in the Civil Service, including Inspectors of Education, Education Planners, and Welfare officers. Those posts did not exist for Indians before the Department of Indian Affairs was established.

Residential areas have also been affected by the Group Areas Act, and whereas government policy has always been as far as possible not to deprive Indian traders of their livelihood, the authorities have always been insistent that residentially Indians leave the areas that in terms of the Group Areas proclamation were closed to Indians for residential purposes. At the time it created a great outcry, and there were cases where people for reasons of principle refused to move, with the result that there were a number of court cases and evictions.

But this matter must be seen in its right perspective, and the first remark that must be made is that the residential removal of Indians to new Indian townships has brought about so vast an improvement in the situation of Indians that few of our community would want to have the old situation back. One must remember that prior to this change the Indians were still subject to the cruel restrictions of the Pegging Act. That meant that as young people grew up and married, they had no choice but to live in the already over-crowded house with their parents. That led to over-crowding and slum conditions. Accommodation was so scarce that Indian tenants were shamelessly exploited by landlords, whether White or Indian. Very few Indians owned houses. In Pretoria, to give but an example, the main concentration of Indians was in the Asiatic Bazaar, a backward area, where most of the houses were corrugated iron constructions. Even rich Indian professional people, who could afford spacious residences, were pegged down in shanties, because the law allowed for no development.

Today we are no longer pegged down. The government has laid out townships with all modern amenities. Indians in these places can own freehold land and build their houses to suit their needs. There wealthy

Indians have their elaborate and luxurious residences, and the middle-income group have their houses, in many ways more modern and convenient than the houses in some of the better White suburbs. Housing loans by the government are freely available, while houses are built for those who cannot afford to build their own houses. To date the government has spent more than R60 million on providing houses for these people. There is space for the young family to build its own house or rent one of the houses provided for this purpose. There are good roads, sports fields and shopping facilities in most of these townships. It is like a breath of fresh air compared with the smog-covered tin shanties with their narrow streets, their high rentals and their almost complete lack of amenities.

The objection has been raised that the scheme involves the residential segregation of the Indians, and that is an apartheid measure. That is true, but that also must be seen in its right perspective. The fact is that that is how we want it, and that is true of most Indians in Africa. Our customs and religion differ from those of the other racial groups, and we prefer to live with our own kind. We would, for example, not want our children to attend school with children of other racial groups, nor would we want our young people to belong to White or Black groups, and acquire their ways of life or adopt their habits.

This has been amply demonstrated in South Africa and elsewhere. Long before Indians in South Africa were required by law to live apart, the Indians in Durban of their own accord formed their own residential areas, as for example the Grey Street area. In Lourenco Marques, in Mozambique, there are even today no residential restrictions for Indians, but nevertheless they live apart, and they do so voluntarily.

The world must realize that apartheid is not always bad, however much the word may be used as a term of abuse against South Africa. In many societies and in many facets of life, apartheid may be the choice of the people, and forced integration, as is aimed at in the United States, may be regarded by a minority group as an intolerable injustice, against which we would rebel. There would, for example, without doubt be violent opposition by the majority of Indian South Africans if their children, as happens with the children in America, were to be forcibly transported to White or Black schools for the sake of integration.

The world would do the Indian South Africans a great service if they saw these things in sober perspective, instead of trying to foist ideologies on us that we do not want.

ADVANCEMENT IN INDIAN EDUCATION

Education is the life-blood of any community, and in this sphere only a blindly prejudiced person would dare say that the Indian South Africans are being neglected by the government. Under the Indian Education Act of 1965 Indian Education was tranferred from the Transvaal and Natal Provincial Administrations to the Department of Indian Affairs. A Division of Education was created within that Department. In the Cape Province Indian Education still falls under the Province, but here also the transfer is imminent.

There is a very strong Inspectorate, comprising three Chief Inspectors, 26 Circuit Inspectors, one Inspector in charge of Psychological Services, and 17 Subject Inspectors. Ten of these officials are Indians. In 1970 there were 162 976 Indian children in primary, secondary and other schools under the control of the Department in Natal and the Transvaal alone. If one keeps in mind that the total Indian population of South Africa is about 600 000, this is indeed a high percentage. Since 1966 the Department spent more than R13 million on school buildings for Indian children, and the building programme of the Department is still going on apace. The ideal aimed at is that approximately one third of the Indian population should be accommodated in government schools. The ratio of infant-primary to high school population is 7 to 4. Current planning by the Department indicates that some 2 000 primary school classrooms and 1 000 high school classrooms will be needed during the next ten years, at an estimated cost of R50 million. All education is free, and since the takeover by the Department, books are also supplied free of charge. The contents of the school subjects are the same for the Indian schools as for the other race groups. The same public examinations are held at the end of the secondary school course. In this respect they co-ordinate with the provincial administrations and with the Department of Education, Arts and Science.

Apart from primary and secondary education the Department of Indian Affairs provides technical education on a post-matriculation level. This work is mostly done by the M.L. Sultan Technical College in Natal, while negotiations for the establishment of an Indian Technical College in the Transvaal have reached an advanced stage.

There is also a brisk teacher-training programme. The Colleges of Education serving the Indian community offer full tuition fees, board, and books for trainee teachers, and these grants are repayable in service only.

The minimum training period is three years after the Matriculation examination. Special Education for handicapped pupils between the ages of three and twenty-three is provided, and this education is given at a number of subsidized schools run by the various organizations. There are special courses given on a part-time basis for Indians already in employment. These courses cover Business Management and a number of other fields.

In the sphere of university education the situation was not very rosy before 1961. Indian students had limited access to a few White universities, as well as to the Bantu College at Fort Hare, but the high tuition fees and the lack of available boarding facilities hampered the progress of the Indian student. The unfavourable state of affairs at that time is illustrated by the fact that in 1959 there were 3,07 Indian students at university per 1 000 of the Indian population as against 11,4 per thousand of the White population.

It was in 1961 that a university college for Indian students was established by the State at Salisbury Island in Durban. Initially the college fell under the control of the University of South Africa, which set the examinations and granted degrees. Only 114 students enrolled in the first year in the two faculties of arts and science. It then had 17 departments, offering 20 courses. Today the enrolment exceeds 1 700, with more than 30 departments under four faculties and offering more than 300 courses.

This progress led to the passing in 1969 of the University of Durban-Westville Act, and from the beginning of 1971 the College became an independent university. In the near future it will move into its multi-million rand campus at Chiltern Hills near Durban. A medical school and a faculty of engineering have recently been approved for the new university.

FAITH IN THE FUTURE

That does not mean that the position of the Indians in South Africa is ideal, notwithstanding the fact that his lot here is far better than in the African states to the North. There are still many legal restrictions, and there is also what some people call 'petty apartheid', often enforced by law and often the result of convention. Such petty measures do not really lead to progress or to separate development, and often they are rather ludicrous. A Coloured writer has recently pointed out that in the world of Coloureds it sometimes happens that all the clerks in a government office in a Coloured area are Coloureds, but nevertheless there are separate entrances and separate counters for Coloureds and Whites. We Indian South Africans experience similar unnecessary humiliations, and although the situation is improving, it is as yet very far from ideal.

In this and other matters referring to the situation of the Indian in South Africa a complete vindication of the government would be wrong, and a complete condemnation would be even more wrong. Our community can develop and is developing as a result of the devoted work done by both Indians and Whites, not by negative attitudes on the part of either of these groups. South Africa is our country and we have no other. It is our duty and privilege to criticize, where criticism is called for. But a blanket condemnation by people from outside is neither welcome nor helpful. The fact remains that the most dramatic progress in the situation of the Indian community in South Africa has been made since 1961, under a Nationalist government. That government deserves praise and criticism, but in many facets of life that affect us most intimately, they deserve more praise and less criticism than previous governments which, incidentally, were rarely, if ever, criticized by the outside world.

An Indian's views on Apartheid

Fatima Meer

Mrs Meer is an eminent Indian academician and leader. A sociologist attached to the University of Natal, Fatima Meer has conducted and initiated several research projects on the Indian population of Natal. She is well-known for her forthright opposition to the Government's apartheid policy.

Indians, Africans and Coloureds are grouped together as 'Non-Whites' in South Africa and held in subjection as such, yet the exploitation and the reaction to such exploitation of each Black group has never been the same. These have varied according to the historic origin of the particular Black group, the degree to which that group has been seen as threatening White domination and the perception that group has had of its own position in the power structure.

The status of Indians as Black South Africans, and their reactions to their inferior designation as such, has been influenced by the facts that they are not an indigenous Black people, that they were imported as indentured labourers from another Black country, that their import was due to agreements reached between the governments of Natal and India and that they continued to be imported throughout the latter half of the last century in large numbers. These facts contribute to the presence of the Indian as a distinct culture group, to the emergence of the Indian 'problem' as an international issue, and the isolation of the Indian resistance movement, almost up to the end of the last World War, from other Black resistance movements in the country.

The original conflict between Indian and White originated in the existing *disparity* between the Indian's evaluation of his status and the White colonist's evaluation of that status. The White colonist had imported the Indian as a labourer, and had expected him to remain as such;

the Indian saw himself as 'colonizer', for though the indentured labour system replaced slavery, it offered the 'indentured' full and equal citizenship rights in the colony. Thus the Indian on the expiry of his labour contract began exploiting Natal's virgin economy alongside the White colonist, thereby becoming the only segment of the Black sector seriously to threaten his economic monopoly. He became, on that score, the most hated of the Black communities. It is only since the last decade, following the effective isolation of Indian economic competition in Indian 'group areas', that overt White hostility against Indians has abated.

Discrimination against Indians began within thirty years of their arrival in South Africa. The Transvaal excluded them from citizenship rights, subjected their trade to a registration fee of twenty pounds, prohibited them from becoming license holders in any enterprise connected with mining, restricted their property rights to segregated wards, subjected them to the carrying of passes, and forbade them from walking on the pavements. The Orange Free State excluded them altogether by law in 1891; the Cape Colony subjected their immigration to an educational test. Natal disenfranchised them in 1895 (251 Indians had enrolled as voters by then), imposed a well-nigh impossible poll tax of £3 per annum on all Indian males of 16 years and over and on females of 12 years and over who refused to become reindentured or to return to India; checked the entry of free, that is non-indentured Indians to the colony, controlled the movement of all Indians across its boundaries through a permit system and restricted the issue of trade licences to them. The Act of Union confirmed all existing anti-Indian legislation, and passed new laws, so that by 1913 only the wives and minor children of Indians already domiciled in the Union were allowed into the country, and by 1953 even that was abolished. Successive laws made increasing inroads into Indian property and trading rights, culminating in the Group Areas Act of 1950, which deprived Indians of existing material assets in developed areas. They received negligible compensation and were confined to developing areas on the outskirts of the towns and cities, with no real assurance that this would be their final location.

Indian reactions to their growing problems of discrimination took a number of forms. Where discrimination was illegal, affected individuals tested it in court, often with good results, when the issues concerned land transactions or trading licences. Letters were written to the daily papers to protest against ill-treatment on the estates, or against personal humiliations. On a more organized level, groups of workers sought redress against their masters before magistrates, usually with poor result, or representations of businessmen waited upon government officials to present their grievances. With the establishment of the Natal Indian Congress in 1894 and the formal organization of Indian political life, petitions, memoranda presenting evidence before government-appointed commissions, holding consultations with the Prime Minister and as a last resort, passive resistance, became familiar modes of pressing claims.

Though the position of Indians deteriorated and their citizenship rights in the country dwindled, up to the coming into power of the National Party in 1948 there was sustained contact between Indian leaders and the Government. Problems were discussed in a mood of compromise and attempts were made to work out solutions. The attack on Indians moved from the municipalities and local areas to the centre, and the central government appeared reluctant to pass laws against them. This situation has now changed, and municipalities, particularly in respect of the Group Areas Act, have on occasions sought to restrain the zeal of the Nationalist Government in legislating against Indians.

THE INFLUENCE OF INDIA

The position of Indian South Africans as part of the Black group was unique in that up to 1946 they were, theoretically at least, protected by India. This was owing to the fact that their presence in South Africa was due to agreements reached between the governments of Natal and India, in terms of which Natal undertook, among other things, to extend full citizenship rights to the Indian immigrants. India intervened each time the agreement was violated. Her right to intercede on behalf of Indian South Africans was established in the laws of 1849 and reinforced by the fact that both countries were members of the British Empire and Commonwealth, and later of the United Nations Organization. Legally and morally, the commitments of the Natal government to the Indian citizens became those of the South African government at Union. South Africa recognized this and General Smuts confirmed it at the 1917 Imperial Conference when he said that 'the administrative problems that arose in respect of Indians in South Africa would be resolved in a peaceful and statesmanlike manner through friendly consultation and solution with India'. In terms of the Cape Town agreement of 1927, the two governments accepted an Indian Agent (later designated High Commissioner) who kept a watching brief on Indian affairs and kept the Indian Government alert and informed.

India intervened in the matter of the treatment of indentured labourers on the sugar estates in 1871, and applied labour sanctions against Natal until the situation was remedied; she stayed the passing of Dr Malan's Areas Regulation Bill in 1925 and had it replaced with the Cape Town Agreement of 1927 whereby South Africa accepted formal responsibility for Indians domiciled in the Union and pledged to raise their standards through educational, welfare and other facilities to accord with Western norms and to keep abreast with the rest of South Africa. A subsequent Round Table Conference of 1932 reiterated the principle of co-operation, and co-operation only ended in 1946, when General Smuts finally passed the long-threatened Land Act against Indians and refused further discussion in the matter through another Round Table Conference as requested by India. The Viceroy retaliated by recalling his High Commissioner and applying trade sanctions in an attempt to bring South Africa to her senses. From the Indian point of view, South Africa has not yet complied and so the deadlock remains.

India's withdrawal triggered off sanctions against South Africa by the newly emergent African states, and has led to her exclusion from international sport in a number of fields. There is little doubt that Indian South Africans have themselves suffered as a result of this withdrawal, and they would be among the first to benefit from a resumption of congenial relations between the two countries.

Though more Indians visit India today than they did in the past, they draw less strength from her now than they did previously. In 1947, the introduction of the issue of the treatment of Indians in South Africa in the United Nations Organization launched the newly liberated Indian Republic into the international field. In the years that followed her interest in Indian South Africans waned and she became just another of the countries in the Afro-Asian Bloc that agitated against racial discrimination in general.

In the last century and in the first decade of the present, Indians drew strength too, from the fact that they were British citizens and as such entitled to British equality. India during that period was not just India, but British India, and as such, was the more powerful. Compared to the Colony of Natal which was more a liability than a source of profit, India was 'the brightest jewel in the British crown'. Gandhi asserted with pride that most of the trade of the British Empire was carried on with the Indian Empire, that 'Every Britisher is agreed that the glory of the Empire depends upon the retention of the Indian Empire'.[1] This was no vain boast, for India was at the time 'the key to the imperial structure, politically (because of the size of the Indian army), and economically (because the country financed two-fifths of Britain's payment deficit)'.[2] Indians thus did not see themselves as quite the smallest South African minority, but as part of and supported by the hundreds of millions in a 'motherland' made the more powerful by her British affiliation. Spokesmen of the 'motherland' reciprocated by such statements as:

> 'The fate of the Empire and that of India is linked together, and India is an essential part of the Empire's greatness. For better or for worse, Indians are members of the Empire, they are subjects of the king and citizens of the Empire, and they decline to be treated like helots of the Empire.'[3]
>
> 'The treatment of Indians throughout the British colonies is deplorable and unless that is redeemed on a basis of justice there would be no contentment in India, but serious discontentment, which would grow and was bound to affect the internal administration of India.'[4]

The Indian 'presence' also imbued Indian South Africans with a sense of pride in their ancient culture so that far from developing feelings of inferiority they were capable of their own brand of ethnocentricism and when attacked they bristled with an anger generated by a 'six thousand year old civilization', and supported by 400 million people.

> 'We as the representatives of nearly 400 million people, subjects of the British Empire, have an inherent right to be treated in accordance with that sense of British fairplay and justice that has become traditional. We as members of a civilized race whose civilization dates back to a period of thousands of years before the Christian era, a

1. M.K. Gandhi, *Natal Advertiser,* 13 January, 1897.
2. George Lichtheim, *Imperialism,* Allen Lane, The Penguin Press, p. 73.
3. G.K. Gokhale, member of the Imperial Legislative Council of India during a state visit to South Africa at a reception on Oct. 30, 1912 in Johannesburg.
4. G.K. Gokhale, Oct. 1912, South Africa.

civilization that has stood the test of time while others have risen and fallen and disappeared into oblivion."[5]

ORGANIZED RESISTANCE AND POLITICAL BODIES

The first active group resistance of Indians against their treatment in South Africa occurred in 1862, when a group of workers downed tools and suffered several terms of imprisonment for refusing to work for their employer, Shire, at Umhlanga. Eventually they engaged a lawyer who submitted a petition on their behalf, and pressurized the government to appoint a commission to investigate their grievances. Though the commission found Shire guilty, the workers obtained no redress. They lost their wages and were ordered to return to their employer's estate on the ground that they had caused him to lose a season's crop, and to prevent further similar recurrences laws were passed making strikes on the estates illegal and prison conditions harder.[6]

In 1871, 143 of the first group of the expired indentured workers returning to India in the *Red Riding Hood* complained to the Indian government about serious breaches in labour regulations in Natal, and forced it to suspend all further emigration to that colony until Natal passed a reform law, which she did. The Indians complained, among other things, that the Natal Government had not paid them a gratuity of £10 each as promised when indenturing them, and they engaged a lawyer in Natal to represent them in the matter. Though Natal eventually admitted that she owed each returning worker 25s., she pleaded that this had been spent in providing him with board and lodging while awaiting his ship. Thus this cash amount was never paid out to them though certain other omissions were rectified.

Organized political activity on a mass level did not begin until 1894, when the Natal Indian Congress was founded with Gandhi as its first Secretary. That organization is still in existence though it has had a chequered career, reaching moments of brilliance through its founder at the end of the last and the beginning of the present century, under the leadership of A.I. Kajee and P.R. Pather during the late thirties and mid-forties and that of Doctors Dadoo and Naicker thereafter. It has been revived again recently, after having been put to bed by the National

5. Statement of the Natal Indian Congress protesting against their segregation at the Durban Turf Club in 1940.

6. Laws 21 and 22 of 1872.

Party following the banning of its entire executive in 1960. Congress became a countrywide organization in 1924 when the Transvaal Indian British Association founded by Gandhi in 1903, became transformed into the Transvaal Indian Congress. With the formation of a Cape wing under the leadership of Dr Abdurrahman, the three sectors became affiliated to the South African Indian Congress.

While Congress remained in the forefront of Indian political life, other organizations cropped up from time to time to oppose and to 'sharpen' it, and on occasions to push it into a second position. Thus in 1913, it played a conservative role, remaining aloof from Gandhi's passive resistance movement, and during the nineteen thirties and part of the forties the Natal Indian Association, dominated by Sohrabjee Rustomjee and S.R. Naidoo, replaced it as the formally recognized organ of Indian opinion by the South African and Indian governments. These organizations did not so much reflect differences in policies, as they did differences in personalities, and to some extent such sociological differences as indicated by religion, language, the original basis of immigration into the country – passenger or indenture – and the original area of emigration from India. Until 1946, regardless of organization, the active membership was drawn primarily from among the Gujarati-speaking group and thus from the commercial and passenger class. This bias was largely owing to the fact that until about the thirties, this group constituted the bulk of the relatively accessible, easily organizable, concentrated city dwellers. In 1941 of the 41 persons recorded in the top leadership of Congress, 26 were Gujarati-speaking Muslims, and only two were South Indians. Of 189 members reported at the 1948 Natal Indian Organization Conference,[7] 148 were Gujarati Muslims and 19 South Indians. This situation changed in the post World War II years, when as a result of industrialization and the consequent urbanization of the Indian worker, and his involvement in trade unionism, he became a decision-making force in the community. The officials of three Natal Congress branches taken at random in 1948 were by contrast predominantly South Indians and drawn from the descendants of indentured groups – Seaview: 19 South Indians, 2 Hindusthani-speaking and 2 Urdu-speaking Muslims; Pietermaritzburg: 11 South Indians, 5 Hindusthani, 2 Gujarati; Stanger: 10 South Indians, 4 Hindusthani-speaking, 2 Urdu-speaking. Gandhi had

7. This body was formed by the displaced leaders of the Indian Congress, Congress leadership having passed into the hands of a radical group in 1946.

on an action level broadened Indian political participation in 1913, when 5 000 mineworkers had struck in Northern Natal, and following their strike, the remaining Indian labour force of that province had come to a standstill. Gandhi, however, had not remained in the country to consolidate this new awakening on an organizational level.

The period marking the end of World War II brought radical changes in the quality of the Indian Congress, and it took on for the first time the character of a truly national organization, a claim which up to then had little factual support. Distinctions between indenture and passenger, or linguistic, or economic groups ceased, and the general membership and leadership became representative of a wide cross-section of the Indian community. The largely merchant and business oriented leadership of the old Congress formed the South African Indian Organization, and for the first time since Gandhi the differences between existing political groups were based on policy, rather than personality differences. Gandhi was obliged to form an alternate organization because of his ideological and tactical orientations. The South African Indian Organization, disagreeing with Congress's purist, non-compromise stand on segregation, its demand for full and equal citizenship rights on the basis of universal adult franchise, and its belligerent attitude towards the Government, pursued a policy of conciliation and compromise.

The political bodies and their programmes came alive each time the people were challenged by a new anti-Indian law. Thus the Congress became established in 1894 in response to the Indian Disenfranchisement Bill in the colony of Natal; the first passive resistance movement was launched in 1906 against the extension of passes to Indians in the Transvaal; the South African Indian Congress was established in the face of heightened anti-Indianism after World War I and the threat of Indian residential and commercial segregation following the report of the 1919 Lange Commission. The 1946 passive resistance and the breaking off of diplomatic relations with South Africa by India followed the passing of the Asiatic Land Tenure and Indian Representation Act, which finally legalized the residential and commercial segregation of Indians; and the 1952 Defiance of Unjust Laws Campaign in co-operation with the African National Congress was partly in protest against the Group Areas Act.

The Indian response to discrimination, though generally based on a common formula – memoranda, petitions, and when these failed, passive resistance – was modified each time by the mood of the government in power, the mood of the Indian people and the calibre of Indian leaders.

Towards the end of the nineteenth century, since Natal was still a colony, the Government in the last resort, was Britain; the potential for political action Indian shop keepers of the passenger class, and the leader, and Indian professional drawn from this class but cultivated in Britain and thereby, in many respects, thoroughly British.

The 'passenger' group considered itself distinct, different, and superior to the indentured. They spoke a different language, were lighter in complexion and better off both educationally and economically. The majority were Muslims and as such identified with the ruling class that had preceded the British in India. Seeing the servile conditions of the indentured, they had sought to identify themselves as Arab, but this had made no difference to the discrimination they had suffered, for the Whites had feared them even more than they had the ex-indentured. According to Gandhi the attitude of the passenger group as a whole had crystallized into one of 'pocketing' insults, so long as they made money.

Gandhi's political career began in this group; his political support came in the main from this group, and the political issues he championed were of pertinent concern to this group. This changed only in the last year of his South African phase, when he took up the issue of the poll tax which was peculiar to the ex-indentured class, and as a result became overnight a champion of the peasant and proletariat.

Gandhi succeeded with the Gujarati-speaking passenger group because he was part of it, and at the same time part of the Indian intelligentsia. This combined two complementary forms of conservatism. The Indian intellectual in the words of Gokhale, was a class that had been influenced 'by Western education, recognized the good work done by England, and accepted her as the trustee for the people of India whose aim was to gradually advance Indians to a position of equality with the people of England themselves'.[8] Gandhi, in addition, had developed a passion for British justice and British humanism and had transferred his great reverence for his deceased father to the British Empire. As a young man of 25 he could barely conceive of Britain doing wrong. The articulate ex-indentured Indians in Natal did not share these sentiments and were critical of the enthusiasm with which he attempted to involve them in the British war against the Boer, but the conciliatory approach this reflected was in

8. G.K. Gokhale, speaking at a reception in Kimberley, October, 1912.

accord with the shop-keeping community. They saw their Westernized, Western-oriented Gujarati countryman as the very necessary medium of communication with the Government, particularly in view of the fact that they did not speak its language nor understand its processes. Gandhi's philosophy of *Satyagraha,* as well as his technique of resistance, which was essentially an appeal to the beloved British authority to regain its values and in the process accept the Indian, was in accord with the Gujarati temperament. Shocked at what he saw as the violation of British values by Britishers, he felt duty-bound to correct the situation. But he could not as a trusting 'ward' behave with overt aggression against his 'guardian'. Thus his approach was one of humility and sacrifice, of pleading with the governments in Natal and the Transvaal, and this personal reaction led him with logical ease to the philosophy of *Satyagraha.* He came to represent 'Indian man' in South Africa and India, and his technique of dealing with racial domination became identified as the exclusively *Indian* reaction to domination, until in 1952 local Africans, supported by Indians used it in the Defiance of Unjust Laws Campaign. However, there were Indians who claimed that though Africans used the technique of passive resistance, they did not appreciate its philosophy, and there were Africans who claimed that their campaign was more aggressive and less passive and to that extent not Gandhian. In fact, there was hardly, if any, difference between the popular Indian and African approaches. The psychic and psychological content of Gandhi's approach and those of his close disciples, Indian and White, a selected elite group, was significantly different. These were people who had had material abundance and they 'sacrificed' it to live simple frugal lives. The African proletariat of 1952 and the peasants of India did not have to make such sacrifices, their lives being already simple and frugal. They concentrated on the technique and the promise of liberation from material want that it offered.

For all its conciliatory content, *Satyagraha* was a militant force which by 1913 had galvanized almost the entire Indian people into resisting acts of discrimination and withdrawing their labour and support from the Government. The result was that Smuts was obliged to compromise with Gandhi, and this resulted in some modification of the Indian status.

The leaders who succeeded Gandhi continued to be drawn from the Gujarati passenger group, augmented by a sprinkling of Hindu and Christian intellectuals, some of indenture origin. They took over Gandhi's main arguments in vindicating their rights to the colony on the grounds of their British citizenship, continued to appeal to the British and Christian conscience, to the liberal and democratic tradition of Western civilization, and continued to emphasize the importance of India to the Empire, though their enthusiasm for the last-mentioned lacked the ecstatic fervour of a Gandhi or Gokhale couched in such terms as: 'Behind all, behind the European community, behind the Indians – was the Empire, with the British flag floating over it, promising justice and equal opportunities for prosperity to the various members living under it.'[9]

They, however, abandoned Gandhian militancy, and leaned more heavily on Indian intervention. Their activity consisted chiefly of submitting memorandums, leading deputations and presenting expert evidence before commissions of inquiry in the intervals marking top level discussions between India and South Africa. The political atmosphere in which they lived was relatively congenial to this kind of activity as is observed in the facility with which local Indian leaders communicated with the government, with the Prime Minister and with Cabinet Ministers directly responsible for the issues in dispute, with the Administrator of Natal, and with heads of local governments. Thus, though Indians suffered residential segregation, a law to this effect was obviated through consultation and compromise and an undertaking by Indian leaders that though they reserved the right to invest in real estate, they would not penetrate 'White' areas.[10] In 1944, the secretary of the Indian Congress, Mr. A.I. Kajee, actually drafted an ordinance which was accepted by General Smuts for submission to the Natal Provincial Council.[11]

This type of strategy depended basically on placating White prejudices and White hostilities rather than opposing these, in allaying White fears, rather than exploiting them, to win demands. Thus Indian leaders up to 1946, including Gandhi, assured Whites, that though they were morally entitled to equality, they accepted White domination, understood the peculiar problems Whites faced in South Africa and in view of this, did not insist on absolute equality though they strove towards it. Thus Mr Gokhale said in 1912 that while a demand for absolute equality was theoretically sound, it was hardly tenable in practice and Indian South

9. G.K. Gokhale at the banquet organized in his honour by the British India Association at Johannesburg on 31 October, 1912.

10. The so-called Kajee assurance given to the Natal Municipal Association in the nineteen thirties.

11. This bill sought to institutionalize the so-called Kajee assurance, was accepted by the Prime Minister as the 'Pretoria Agreement'.

Africans should recognize the limitations with which the principles of justice and equal treatment could be applied in South Africa.[12] Gandhi negotiated on specific issues, and reacted strongly against laws which discriminated and thereby humiliated Indians, but was content with his compromise with General Smuts, though it left a substantial sector of his community dissatisfied. In the early forties, Indian leaders made such statements as:

> 'Indians would concede, as indeed they have done, political supremacy to Whites. They are not insensitive to the European's difficulties. They recognize his fears. They, however, denounce his prejudices.'[13]
>
> 'Indians have accepted European domination, but that should not degenerate into the attitude of the bully.'[14]
>
> 'I wish to emphasize that even in accepting control of residential occupation in terms of the Pretoria Agreement, the Indian community was making a concession to European racial attitudes, and that such a concession was not lightly undertaken, for it violated and violates the elementary rights of man.'[15]

While spokesmen of the community reluctantly engaged in such policies and heaved sighs of relief for temporary respites, the situation from the Indian South African point of view worsened and an understandable reaction built up against it. The official policies of the two competing political bodies of the time, the Indian Congress and the Indian Association began to be challenged from within, by trade unionists, students and professionals, and factions emerged in each calling themselves the Anti-Segregation Council and the Nationalist Bloc respectively. They were in turn supported by a number of 'Non-European' integrationist groups who exercised pressure from the outside. Where the 'old guards' evoked Indians in the name of India – 'in the name of your motherland',[16] the new radicals declared, 'We are eight million Indian, Coloured and Africans and we

12. G.K. Gokhale at a reception in Kimberley, October, 1912.

13. Leader editorial, March 29, 1941.

14. Leader editorial, April 1941.

15. A.I. Kajee, addressing the bar of the Natal Provincial Council, 30 Oct. 1944.

16. Sohrabjee Rustomjee of the Natal Indian Association, quelling a disturbance at a mass meeting in the Durban City Hall in 1941.

must stand solidly shoulder to shoulder.'[17] They criticized the existing policy as 'a futile policy of hat in hand negotiations in defence of the fast dwindling rights of the Indian people, a policy which has enabled the Government to introduce measure after measure of racially discriminating legislations that had continued for 32 years and replaced the positive struggle through passive resistance between 1907 and 1914'.[18]

This group had gained sufficient support at the end of the war to enable it to take over the leadership of the Indian people, consolidating it in the one mass organization of the Congress. The centre of gravity shifted from India to South Africa and from a concern with Indian discrimination to one with general Black discrimination. This shift was accelerated by the coincidence of India's withdrawal from South Africa which obliged Indian South Africans to become more self dependant and to seek alliances with their fellow oppressed, particularly Africans, for solutions. The new leadership and the new situation resulted above all in the replacement of a policy of appeasing White prejudices and pleading to the White government for redress, by one of consolidating Indian political consciousness on a mass level, linking it with general Black political consciousness, and demanding absolute equality in relatively aggressive tones. Leaders no longer spoke of 'We the Indian people', and of 'Indian discrimination', but 'We the Non-White people', and of 'Non-White discrimination'. Action-wise, Congress reverted to the Gandhian strategy of passive resistance and between 1946 and 1947 two thousand Indians served terms of imprisonment in deliberate violation of selected discriminatory laws.

The new Congress came into being about the same time that India gained independence, and local leaders entertained high hopes that its own militant stand, combined with India's strength, and India's growing influence in the international arena would lead to some redefinition of the Indian position in South Africa. However, these two positive developments from the point of view of Indian South Africans, were offset by the simultaneous 'liberation' of Afrikanerdom. Had the United Party remained in power, these expectations may have been met to some extent, but the National Party remained intractable. Moreover, while South Africa began reaping the harvest from the industrial infrastructure established during the war years and while its cheap labour policy yielding high profits

17. Speaker at a mass meeting of the Nationalist Bloc in 1941 at an open square in Durban.

18. Statement of the new Natal Indian Congress on assuming power in 1946.

attracted European and American investors, India soon became embroiled in conflicts with Pakistan, Portugal and China. These international tensions, combined with her own enormous problems of social and economic reconstruction, forced her to virtually withdraw all commitment to the cause of Indian South Africans.

The Indian Congress entered into a formal alliance with the African National Congress through a joint consultative committee, and organized nation-wide stay-aways from work (Gandhian *hartal*) in political protest, and launched a multi-racial passive resistance campaign, known as the Defiance of Unjust Laws in 1952. This was followed by a national convention – thc Congress of the People – and the formulating of the 'Freedom Charter' in 1956.

The drawing together of the Indian and African on the political front to offer joint resistance against what they began to recognize as common discrimination, was a slow process. It gained sudden momentum in the fifties and was then as suddenly snuffed out at the beginning of the sixties with the striking down of both Congresses by the Government. The fellowship that emerged in the political field had begun to extend into the social, 'cultural' and sporting fields and had legislation not intervened to suppress non-parliamentary political activity and to prevent inter-racial mixing in terms of the Group Areas Act, it may well have reached significant proportions by now. The potential for Indo-African solidarity exists, despite these laws, and is probably better now (1971) than it was at the beginning of the fifties, largely due to the greater opportunity for identification of interests in work and academic situations, in factories, and tribal universities.

In the last century, the African had viewed the Indian with contempt, for he had come to fill a labour position he, the African, had rejected. The Indian had learnt to fear the physical strength of the African, which his White employer had at times used against him, and had begun to see him as savage – '*jungle*' – and to call him '*kafrie*', Indianization of kaffir. The African reciprocated by calling him '*amakula*', Africanization of coolie. Resenting '*amakula*' and fearful of the violence that the term '*kafrie*' evoked, Indians replaced it with the less offensive Ravan, after the mythological opponent of the god Rama. Very little inter-marriage or sexual relations occurred between them despite the scarcity of Indian women, and to the extent that these did, they were more prevalent among the Gujarati Muslim – passenger group – than among the indentured.

While there is no record of Gandhi working with any African leader, he was sympathetically disposed to Africans. He saw the 'Zulu Rebellion', during which he, with a contingent of Indians, nursed wounded Zulus, as a massacre of the Zulus. He saw them as 'the tallest and most handsome of the negroes' and opined that the 'Creator did not spare Himself in fashioning the Zulu to perfection'.[19]

Despite the rigours of indenture on the one hand and the protection offered to the Zulus by Sir Theophilus Shepstone on the other, Indians were better placed than Africans in terms of their culture, their state of urbanization and their entree to modern business and farming techniques, to make progress in South Africa. Thus, with the expiry of their labour contracts the economic and culture gap between African and Indian widened and relations that had never been warm, cooled further. Indians realized, too, that as their conditions improved they became less acceptable to Whites than did the Africans.

The movement towards co-operation began during the war years when with industrial expansion large African populations moved into urban areas. In Durban, in particular, in the absence of any housing for Africans, they began renting rooms and sites from Indians and residential mixing became fairly common among the two groups. Added to this were the facts of sharing common transport, health, and recreational facilities and the discovery through bitter experience that the bargaining power of the Indian worker depended on the African worker realizing *his.* Thus integrated trade unions began to emerge. Complementing this was a growing intellectual understanding of the political identity of the two peoples, stimulated by such multi-racial study, discussion and debating societies as the Liberal Study Group, Asicolafrica, and the Non-European United Front, which emerged in the late thirties.

The vigorous application of the policy of separate development or apartheid destroyed the physical opportunities for Afro-Indian unity, and the banning of the African National Congress and the executive of the Indian Congress brought political unity to a halt.

THE NATIONALIST GOVERNMENT'S PROGRAMME FOR INDIANS

The National Party on coming into power refused to meet a deputation from the Congress, and although it accepted the conservatively led South

19. M.K. Gandhi, *op. cit.*, p. 9.

African Indian Organization, established by the displaced leaders of Congress as an acceptable channel for dealing with the Indian people, the first Minister of Indian Affairs said in 1962 : 'Our problem hitherto has been that we have not known whom we could approach to speak on behalf of the Indians. The Indian Organization has on occasion claimed that it is the mouthpiece and the Congress alleges that *it* is the mouthpiece.'[20] He went on to say that while the Congress movement was well organized, its influence was not as great as would appear from newspaper reports and accused it of resorting to victimization and terrorization. Accordingly, the South African Indian National Council, composed of 25 members nominated for three years and drawing remuneration[21] from the government was set up as the acceptable 'mouthpiece'.

This is in keeping with the Nationalist Government's policy of separate development, in terms of which each of the three Black groups have been compartmentalized into distinct departments presided over by the appropriate Minister (for Indian Affairs, Coloured Affairs, Bantu Affairs). These departments administer their lives in all respects save with regard to the crucial issues of land holdings and job reservation.

The councils representing the three Black groups are not identically structured. The rights of the wholly nominated Indian Council are less than those of the partly elected Coloured and African Councils which have in addition some executive powers. The Indian Council operates in a purely advisory capacity, and meets three times a year, its meetings being attended by departmental officials who may take part in discussions though they may not vote. A five-member executive elected by the council, and presided over by a chairman appointed by the Minister, is in continuous office. The government has stated that the Council will eventually be a democratically elected body with some executive functions, but there does not appear to be any move in that direction at present. As the supreme

20. Mr W.A. Maree, the Minister of Indian Affairs, in the Senate of the Parliament of the Republic of South Africa, 17 May, 1962.

21. The remuneration in 1970 was at the rates of R600 per annum for councillors, R800 for executive members, R900 for the chairman of the executive and R1 000 for the chairman of Council. Comparative rates for Coloured councillors were R1 500 per annum for executive members and for the chairman of Council R5 000 and R6 000 per annum respectively with provisions for an entertainment allowance, the use of a car for official purposes, and a house at nominal rent for each. The remunerations for the ministers and members of the Transkeian council were for chief minister R4 000 per annum, ministers R3 400 per annum and members of legislative assembly R800 per annum.

national political organ of the Indian people, it is supplemented by local affairs, or consultative, or management committees which begin from a nominated status and develop into an elected one.

Although council members are not entirely happy with their present restricted roles and nominated positions, they believe that they can and do serve a useful function on behalf of the community. They stress that for the first time Indians have been accepted as South African citizens and have official contact with the government through an officially constituted channel; that they have a measure of control over their education through appointments in the inspectorate and planning divisions and representation on the council of the Indian university, and that a large number of jobs have resulted in the civil service from the creation of a separate Indian Department. They argue that the new structure is a first step towards self-determination, and should be sympathetically accepted as such.

The Indian people by contrast are suspicious of the Department and see in it new and unprecedented machinery to curb their progress. They believe that the Council is in fact helpless and that any amelioration of the Indian position is due to the whim of the powerful government and is not the result of its mediation. They see the Council more as an instrument of the Government than as a body promoting their welfare. It has a bad press[22] and members have been the victims of public scorn and hostility on a sufficient number of occasions to have caused the Minister of Indian Affairs to announce publicly that Council members are not government stooges.[23] There is recognition that the government has provided greater Indian participation in some fields, especially in education, but there are grave misgivings about the quality and the intention of 'Indian education', separated from 'White education' and the suspicion exists that, like all segregated facilities, this must of necessity be of an inferior quality. The general hostility to the Department and the Council flows from the belief that all separate facilities bear the stigma of discrimination, and have the function of inferiorization.

Indian citizen rights which were implicit in the original laws of Indian

22. There are two Indian weeklies in Durban with approximate circulations of 12 000.

23. The Minister of Indian Affairs in his address to the first meeting of the second Statutory South African Indian Council, 14 October 1971, *Fiat Lux,* November 1971, Vol. 6, No. 9.

immigration in 1860 have never been as eroded as today. This is due to the many restrictive laws that have accumulated over a little less than a century. Some amelioration *appears* to have occurred in relation to local government but their political status in terms of the 1946 Asiatic Land Tenure and Indian Representation Act passed by the last government and abolished by the present was far more favourable, since it provided for four elected members in the Central Legislature – one to the Senate and three to the House of Assembly, albeit all White – and two elected Provincial councillors, who could have been Indian. Indians had previously also exercised franchise rights on the common roll at the Cape and served on Cape local councils. Yet Council members claim that the Nationalist Government is the first South African Government to accept Indians as South African citizens, basing this claim on the 1961 statement of the Minister of the Interior – subsequently confirmed by the Minister of Indian Affairs in 1962[24] – that Indians 'are here and the vast majority of them are going to remain here, and although repatriation is used on a very small scale, we must realize that the vast majority of them are South African citizens and as such they are also entitled to the necessary attention and the necessary assistance.'[25]

Their response to this statement differs significantly from that of every preceding generation of formal representatives, responding to similar statements by other heads of Government. The reason for this may be due to their eagerness to project a favourable image of the Government, to the extent that they see the implications of 'citizen' and 'national' to be identical. No South African government has ever denied that Indians are South African nationals. Their acceptance as such was implicit in the 1913 Gandhi-Smuts Agreement, and in the Cape Town Agreement of 1927 which elaborated the Government's responsibility to Indian South Africans. General Smuts found it convenient to declare to the world at the United Nations Organization in 1947 that Indian South Africans were Union nationals and their treatment in South Africa was therefore a domestic issue. They have, however, never enjoyed citizenship rights in the Union or Republic of South Africa, fundamentally because they have remained deprived of franchise rights. The Natal Indian Congress emphasized this in 1944, when in a letter to the Prime Minister it pointed out that whilst he, General Smuts, had publicly referred to Indians as 'our

24. Minister of Indian Affairs in the Senate, 17 May, 1962.
25. The Minister of Interior, in the House of Assembly, May, 1961.

fellow citizens', Indians in fact did not enjoy citizenship since they did not enjoy the franchise.[26]

Though the Indian Council operates as the first *Government* appointed channel of contact between the Indian people and the state, it is by no means the first official organ of such contact, since the United Party, and the Government of India, recognized the *elected* organ of the Indian people, which was in the main, the Natal Indian Congress. The Congress deliberated with a far greater measure of freedom and initiated discussions with any level of government, and with any official, from the Prime Minister downwards, and on any issue. Although there is a special Ministry for Indians today, the distance between the Government and the Indian people has never been greater. This is not only due to the fact that contact is rigidly defined and therefore rigidly narrowed, but also due to the fact that it occurs strictly on the initiative and the agenda approved by the Government.

This position is further aggravated by the arbitrary moods and incomprehensible logic of many officials, though these 'servants' may at times be 'humanized' by gifts. The predominant emotion that the Government evokes is that of fear and some of the fear felt towards it is extended to the Council. Like other Black South African populations, Indians have minute and hence easily observable 'elites'. A large Special Branch – it is reported that Durban alone has a staff of 70 – keeps a record of statements and movements, advises the Department of Indian Affairs on the issue of passports, and is especially watchful of students, who in addition are taken to task by the educational authorities for relatively small acts of insubordination, by threats and acts of expulsion.[27]

The Natal Indian Congress which had been put to bed in 1960, has been recently revived by a young group of students and professionals who have rejected the Indian Council and the Local Affairs Committees. The response from the Indian public has been spontaneous and strong. Its

26. Letter to the Prime Minister, General Smuts, written by the Natal Indian Congress on November 30, 1944.

27. The opposition of some students from the Indian University to the Republic Day celebrations resulted in the detention and interrogation of several students. Recent criticism by a student of the chairman of the executive of the Indian Council was followed by the security police searching his house. The university authorities, it was alleged, brought constraint upon the student to apologize to the Council member. An Indian girl was expelled from a high school because of her active part in opposing the Republican celebrations in 1971.

survival in its present form, however, depends very much on the attitude of the Minister of Indian Affairs and the reports of the Special Branch. Members of the *pro tem* committee have already been subjected to police raids, and its likely President has been banned.

In the past the ideological orientation of successive Indian leaders have been influenced by Gandhianism, liberalism, socialism and to a small extent communism. The first three influences remain today, augmented by American Black Powerism adopted by the South African Students Organization, which bands together Black student groups from the ethnic or tribal universities. Though Indian students are not allowed to join S.A.S.O. in terms of their University regulation, they are, however, attracted to it and S.A.S.O. officials have also been prominent on the Congress platform. S.A.S.O. claims to be working 'for the liberation of the Black man, first from the psychological oppression by themselves through inferiority complex, and secondly from physical oppression accruing out of living in a White racist society'. It defines Black people 'as those who are by law or tradition, politically, economically and socially discriminated against as a group in the South African society and identifying themselves as a unit in the struggle towards the realization of their aspirations'.[28] Its main thrust is to develop a Black consciousness and Black awareness; to reinterpret the whole concept of 'Black', so that from being a term evocative of a feeling of inferiority, it becomes one evoking pride and acceptance of the Black self. Its ultimate orientation is towards an open non-racial society in which both Black and White will live together freely; its technique of achieving this is for Blacks (i.e. Africans, Indians and Coloureds) to work together but to work separately from, and independently of Whites, since it holds that Black leaders working in collusion with White leaders tend to become in a sense 'White', and to compromise true Black interests. Thus 'before the Black people join the open society, they should first close their ranks, to form themselves into a solid group to oppose the definite racism that is meted out by the White society; to work out their direction clearly and bargain from a position of strength.' They hold that 'integration does not mean an assimilation of Blacks into an already established set of norms drawn up, and motivated by White society. Integration implies free participation by individuals in a given

28. South African Students' Organization, 2nd General Students' Council, July 1971, Policy Manifesto.

society, and proportionate contributions to the joint culture of that society by all constituted groups.'[29]

Stated thus, the policy finds ready acceptance among Indians, but the way in which it is articulated by some of its exponents and the amateurish manner in which it is often executed, raises simultaneously doubts and fears. The emphasis is too often too much on power, leaving the impression that it is more concerned with developing Black domination than Black consciousness. While Indians see themselves as part of Black consciousness, they doubt that they will ever be a part of Black domination, which by the very nature of the numerical balance between the 'races', will mean African domination. They believe that it is more than likely that in a position of domination the African will drop them as 'Brown men', and their subordinate position will not only continue, but may even worsen. Indians see their ultimate security in South Africa to be in a racially integrated society in which they will have the same rights and the same dignity as other South Africans.

The position of the Indian in South Africa is unique within the Black fold in that he is an immigrant who came to 'colonize' on the assumption that he had full and unfettered rights to do so, and brought with him a strong culture to which he was closely bound, and which energized him to exploit available agricultural, commercial, and later technological and professional opportunities. The White colonists baulked at the idea of a fellow Black colonizer and at the prospect of having for a co-equal a former 'colonized', so he set about unravelling the situation and redefining his status. The Indian has reacted consistently against this redefinition and the resultant deterioration of his social, economic and political status. He has used the ideological, tactical and commonsense means provided by his culture, but has modified these to accord with the intelligibility and responsiveness of a power which claims allegiance to a Western/Christian/liberal democratic tradition. He has been sensitive, too, to the changing moods of this power, and has adjusted his approach accordingly.

In the past, Indian South Africans have leaned on India, and up to the end of the last World War, India accepted responsibilty on their behalf and South Africa conceded as much. India's involvement in South Africa exposed the treatment of Indian South Africans and thus South African racism to the world, through imperial and commonwealth conferences and

29. *Ibid.*

later through the United Nations Organization. Thus Indian South Africans pioneered the present world censure against South Africa, which has had devastating effects in the field of sport. While this exposure hardened White attitudes against Indians it gave moral support to the local Indian resistance movement, which saw the world as being on its side.

In more recent times the relatively radical, student, professional and trade union elements have moved the community to depend on their own resources and to seek allegiance internally with all bodies espousing the cause of a non-racial democracy, seeing their salvation as a minority to lie in such an eventuality alone.

Their dominated status has never been as difficult as now, though they have never been as Westernized, as articulate and as skilled as today. Their deep frustrations are redeemed or masked only by the general economic stability of the country. They will be among the first to suffer in an economic recession, and anti-Indianism which became latent in the sixties, due largely to the restriction of their commercial and land-holding rights in their group areas, may flare up again in fresh explosions of racism. Probably the worst aspect of their domination is that though deprived and humiliated, legally and constitutionally, they may not meaningfully oppose and record their protest against such domination. 'Even a mother will not feed a hungry child unless it cries,' said Gandhi. Indians may not cry without exposing themselves to a series of severe punishments in terms of a number of security laws. They live today an intimidated existence in stark contrast to their past tradition of speaking out and hitting out and of taking up issues with the Government, often with the courage of martyrs.

Editor's note: In terms of the South African Indian Council Amendment Bill (1972), the erstwhile fully-nominated Indian Council is now a partly-elected body. The Bill provides for a maximum Council complement of 25 nominated and 5 elected members. This change elevates the Council to roughly the same politico-constitutional level as the Coloured Persons Representative Council.

The Church and Education in an Apartheid Society

The Churches and Race Relations

Denis E. Hurley

Dr Hurley is one of South Africa's senior church leaders. Internationally known for his ecclesiastical work, he is particularly recognized as a leading opponent of the Government's apartheid policy. At present Roman Catholic Archbishop of Durban, he took an active part in the Second Vatican Council of the Roman Catholic Church, serving on the Council Commission for Education and Priestly Training. He is a past President of the South African Institute of Race Relations.

The role of a church in the promotion of sound race relations is dependent upon the role it sees itself playing in human society generally. A quick glance at the way the churches have fared in influencing Western society during the past five hundred years will be helpful in this regard.

The West, as it moved into the turbulence of the Renaissance, carried with it an outlook on human society derived from mediaeval Catholicism. The mediaeval theologians, with Thomas Aquinas at their head, had put together a coherent structure of individual and social life impregnated with Christian faith and morality, consecrating the feudal system and dominated by Church authority, which saw itself as the divine agency entrusted with the task of maintaining the whole structure.

A vision of society produces a social ethic, that is, a moral system inspiring community relations in matters, for instance, of governing and being governed and of buying and selling. The two most important areas of social ethics are politics and economics. Included in the mediaeval social ethic was the conviction that no political power was absolute. The king was under God and under the law, like any other man, and the person to remind him of this was the pope, who as vicar of Christ had received the fullness of power. Economic life, too, fell within the scope of the religious vision. Mediaeval Christian teaching managed to make riches look more or less disreputable. No sincere Christian could really enjoy being rich. He was constantly being reminded of the camel and the eye of the needle and of the social obligations of wealth. Any excess of wealth accruing to him belonged by right to the poor, and interest on loans was sheer robbery. This was the theory anyway. We know how theory fares in practice.

The climax of the vision in regard to papal political control was reached at the beginning of the fourteenth century, when Pope Boniface VIII thought to bring King Philip the Fair of France to heel with the celebrated Bull, *Unam Sanctam.* Boniface claimed that there were two swords in the power of the Church, the spiritual and the temporal:[1] the former to be wielded by the priesthood of the Church, the latter by kings and soldiers on behalf and at the behest of the Church. Philip's rejection of this vision and his imprisonment of the Pope at Anagni illustrated dramatically how the vision had begun to crumble at the very climax of its formulation.

In any time of great social change it is not easy for men to distinguish between what can be legitimately discarded and what should be preserved. Renaissance Europe, in reacting against institutional control by the Church, unfortunately reacted too against much that was good in the general structure. One of these elements was the social ethic that had been created by the Church. A social ethic must be incarnated in institutions of one kind or another, and the danger is always present that when the institutions have grown old and need reform, they will be unceremoniously discarded along with the vision they incarnate and the ethics they enshrine. The baby goes out with the bath-water.

The Church was in a particularly poor position to preserve and promote its spiritual vision and social ethic in Renaissance Europe. It was a Church exhausted after the long haul out of the Dark Ages, compromised by involvement in the very institutions it had helped to create, and dissolving into the conflicts and divisions of the Reformation. The human society which it should have been educating was in no mood to listen to it. Even if the Church had been able to speak with a united and authoritative voice it would have had trouble with the self-confident humanism of the Renaissance. Without unity and authority it could do little to influence the emergence of the new Europe.

1. Referring to Luke 22:38.

It was a far cry from Boniface VIII at the beginning of the fourteenth century making his claim to be the spiritual father of Christendom, with the right to discipline and depose kings, to Machiavelli two centuries later proclaiming that ethics had no place in politics. Machiavelli had the ear of the future. What Machiavelli formulated had always been practised, of course, to a greater or lesser degree. No one would claim that politics was not politics even before he came on the scene; but rationalizing an abuse gives it power and prestige.

What made Renaissance humanism particularly averse to any kind of spiritual discipline exercised by the Church was the great new world of financial gain thrown open to it by the voyages of discovery. Christendom was suddenly in a position to rifle and exploit the wealth of Asia and America. For five hundred years it was to have this world at its feet, with Africa thrown in during the latter part of the period.

With colonialism, capitalism came into its own. The mediaeval vision of a church controlling the acquisitive instincts of man disappeared beneath the weight of the new wealth, the new methods of financing trade and the Puritan doctrine that worldly prosperity was the reward of diligence, sobriety and hard work. The crippled and divided Church tried for some time to impose Christian restraint on human cupidity, but it was a losing battle. By the time the Industrial Revolution burst upon the scene, the Church was powerless to curb its excesses.

As R.H. Tawney says: 'Surprise has sometimes been expressed that the Church should not have been more effective in giving inspiration and guidance during the immense economic reorganization to which tradition has assigned the not very felicitous name of the "Industrial Revolution". It did not give it, because it did not possess it. There were, no doubt, special conditions to account for its silence – mere ignorance and inefficiency, the supposed teachings of political economy, and, after 1790, the terror of all humanitarian movements inspired by France. But the explanation of its attitude is to be sought less in the peculiar circumstances of the moment, than in the prevalence of a temper which accepted the established order of class relations as needing no vindication before any higher tribunal, and which made religion, not its critic or its accuser, but its anodyne, its apologist, and its drudge. It was not that there was any relapse into abnormal inhumanity. It was that the very idea that the Church possessed an independent standard of values, to which social institutions were amenable, had been abandoned. The surrender had been made long before the battle began. The spiritual blindness which made possible the general acquiescence in the horrors of the early factory system was, not a novelty, but the habit of a century.'[2]

One of the worst excesses of the mercantilism that flourished in Europe after the Renaissance was slavery. Modern Western slavery came into existence in the fifteenth century when the Portuguese began to bring back slaves from their voyages down the west coast of Africa. After a few desultory attempts by leaders of church and state to stop the practice, it became firmly established and was vigorously prosecuted by whatever country was able to keep ships at sea : Portugal, Spain, Holland, England, France. How Christian nations got away with it so long is a puzzle to us now. The slave-trade was a particularly blatant example of social immorality and, apart from a few unavailing protests, the Church did nothing about it. In fact, its theology justified it. Ultimately it was the Quakers and the Evangelicals who led the battle for emancipation at the end of the eighteenth century, and they succeeded because a new element had entered Western culture : liberalism.

Liberalism grew out of the philosophical movement that dominated Western culture in the seventeenth and eighteenth centuries. It was a movement away from institutional Christianity and it began to assume the role that was slipping away from the enfeebled churches, that of promoting social ethics. The philosophers began by stressing the value of reason and ended by emphasizing the glories of freedom. The freedom of man was the dominant theme of liberalism. It was wholeheartedly embraced by the bourgeoisie who found in it the inspiration of their fight against kings and aristocrats.

Even as it reached its apogee in the aftermath of the French Revolution, two things happened to it : the source of its inspiration dried up and its Achilles' heel began to show. When the philosophy of reason had reached its climax in Kant and Hegel, it had played itself out. It was due to yield pride of place rapidly to science as the dominant intellectual influence in Western culture. Its Achilles' heel was its economic theory. Economic liberalism allied to the new technology of the Industrial Revolution produced some appalling horrors, in startling contrast with the gentle humanism that had been dreamed of. Intentionally or unintentionally the shady aspect of man that Christianity had labelled original

2. R.H. Tawney, *Religion and the Rise of Capitalism,* Penguin Books, p. 196.

sin had been overlooked. The field was wide open for a new vision and a new ethic. And this time it was socialism that filled the gap, with the lopsided genius of Karl Marx giving it its most systematic and penetrating expression.

The churches were still too feeble to provide a renewed Christian vision and to make a significant impact in the field of social ethics, though all due credit must be given for what was achieved by the Quakers and the Evangelicals of the eighteenth century, from whose ranks emerged the towering figure of John Wesley, just in time to give Christian inspiration to the labour movement in Britain.

It was not really until the end of the nineteenth century that churchmen began to think seriously and systematically about the relevance of Christian morality to social, political and economic life. Protestantism produced the 'social gospel', the 'religionless Christianity' of Bonhoeffer and the theology of secularization. Catholicism launched the movement known as 'social action' which was to evolve through 'Catholic action' and 'lay apostolate' to *The Church in the Modern World*.[3] The publication of Teilhard de Chardin's work after his death in 1955, added a luminous and visionary dimension to the unity in Christ of the secular and the sacred, of science and faith.

This renewed vision of the Church in the world is producing a new social ethic. It has been a hundred years a-growing and has by no means yet become an intellectual and moral force among the great bulk of Christian believers. The Church has been notoriously poor in mass communication in recent ages. The future, however, belongs to the new vision. With every year that passes, the old individualistic and pietistic view of Christianity gives way to the conviction that faith must have meaning for the totality of human life, the social as well as the personal. The young will accept no other religion than a religion concerned with man and his community, man with all his aspirations and miseries. Inevitably as this spiritual mutation accelerates so does the disorientation and confusion in the Church. But it is a creative confusion. The Church is pregnant with a new age, stirring under a new Pentecost.

One aspect of the confusion is the wild swing of the pendulum among some of the avant-garde to an extreme position on the mission and function of the Church. 'Politics', they say, 'is what religion is all about.'

3. The title of one of the documents produced by the Second Vatican Council.

But obviously religion can never be all about and only about politics. At the heart of religion is belief in a transcendent God, a God above humanity and politics, and yet present in them. To the Christian religion this God has given his presence a new expression through the incarnation of his Son, and the Christian concerned about politics must never forget that his concern is inspired, consecrated and energized by the death and resurrection of Christ and the sending of the Spirit and that its final aim is fulfilment in what Augustine called the 'total Christ'.

This divine mystery must carry on its illuminating and saving task among men, giving them a vision of what God expects of them and the strength to pursue the vision. It must do this for men in all the dimensions of their being, the individual and the social, the political and the economic. Politics and economics are made by human decisions, human attitudes, human behaviour. They have their own special values, no doubt, just as poetry and brick-laying have theirs, but these values in the men embodying them are inseparable from the values of Christian faith and morals. They all come together in that inmost citadel of human freedom : the conscience. A man can no more exclude from conscience his social, economic and political life than he can exclude his wife, his child, his brother, his neighbour. Politics and economics, because they are human, are matters of conscience.

But for a long time in Western Europe they were not – at least they were not among the major issues engaging the Christian conscience. But that period seems to be over now. The world of Western dominance launched by the Italian Renaissance and the Portuguese discoveries came to an end with the Second World War. Colonialism has all but disappeared. Communism is a fierce rival of capitalism. Some of the good things of liberalism still linger on, and, please God, will never die. And slowly and hesitantly, the Christian Church is recovering its sense of mission in the field of social ethics. One of the by-products of colonialism also lingers on in the form of a racial problem, most acutely felt in the United States and South Africa. The United States is tackling the problem in its own way, right out on the front lawn, as it tackles most of its family problems. But here we are dealing with the role of the churches in promoting sound race relations in the South African context.

THE CHURCHES AND SOCIAL CONSCIENCE IN SOUTH AFRICA

Not much of the social conscience that has been growing in the churches over the last hundred years is as yet manifest and effective in South Africa. The churches are aware of their duty to give a lead, but they are sadly unpractised in the art. The quarter-century that has elapsed since World War II has been filled with a great number of church reports, messages and statements and with a few vigorous acts of personal witness. But there has been very little popular response. Of moral theorizing there has been no lack; of true Christian action, very little. That long neglect in sensitizing the social conscience, that the South African churches inherited from Europe, is a paralyzing influence in a situation that is among the most painful in the world. And yet, even in South Africa, the churches are beginning to realize the social significance of their mission.

The Dutch Reformed Churches – The Dutch Reformed Churches exercise the greatest sway in South Africa because they command the allegiance of over fifty per cent of the White population.[4] They represent the soul of the Afrikaner people. It was once said of the Anglican Church that it was the Tory Party at prayer. It can be said with even greater justification of the Dutch Reformed Churches that they are the Afrikaner nation at prayer. It is a splendid thing in many ways for a church to identify itself with a people, because a certain amount of identification is essential. But total identification is a mortal danger. The result is usually that a church in this position is incapable of seeing beyond national interest to the broader demands of the Gospel. This is the problem of the Dutch Reformed Churches in South Africa. When they address themselves to the racial problem, they speak from within their commitment to the Afrikaner nation. They speak as its soul, with all the sense of divine destiny that Calvinism has imparted, with memories fresh and thick upon them of how that nation carved out its place in South Africa against the British and the Bantu, and with a determination, as steely as the sense of nationhood they inspire, that this nation will not lose its identity and perish from the earth.

The recent experience of the Dutch Reformed Churches in the field of

4. Under the general term 'Dutch Reformed Churches' reference is made to three distinct bodies of Dutch origin and Calvinist adherence: the Nederduitse Gereformeerde Kerk, known by the initials N.G.K., representing about 43% of the White population; the Nederduitsch Hervormde Kerk, representing 6%; and the Gereformeerde Kerk, representing 3%.

race relations has been of tension rising to a dangerous climax in the early sixties, then subsiding somewhat in the last few years – simmering probably beneath the surface until another and undoubtedly fiercer climax boils up.

The quarter-century review begins with the 1948 manifesto of the National Party that heralded its victory in the elections of that year. The hand of Dutch Reformed theologians is visible in this passage: 'At the same time the party rejects any policy of oppression and exploitation of the Non-European by the Europeans as being in conflict with the Christian basis of our national life and irreconcilable with our policy . . . The Non-European racial groups will have full opportunity for development in every sphere and will be able to develop their own institutions and social services whereby the forces of the progressive Non-Europeans can be harnessed for their own national development (*volksopbou*). The policy of the country must be so planned that it will eventually promote the ideal of complete separation (*algehele apartheid*) in a national way.'

Apartheid had been evolving in Afrikaner thought during the years preceding the election. Prominent Dutch Reformed churchmen had played an important part in this evolution. They had begun to realize that the old policy of segregation was politically unproductive and morally indefensible. So a new attempt was launched under the name of 'apartheid' to impose some sort of acceptable system on the co-existence of White and Black in South Africa. From the start it was ambiguous. While church leaders and intellectuals spoke in terms of pushing separation through to a morally acceptable territorial division, politicians thought mainly of a more rigidly enforced segregation in one undivided country. Through congresses, conferences and commissions, the Dutch Reformed Churches promoted the ideal of separate development. There was the Peoples' Congress of 1947, the 1950 Meeting of the Federal Council of the N.G.K. and the report of the Ad Hoc Commission on Race Relations of 1956.[5] Attempts were made to give separate development a scriptural justification, but there was too much theological opposition to this and in the end justification was sought more on pragmatic grounds.

The fairly universal and peaceful acceptance of separate development

5. Details of this brief survey of church attitudes, unless otherwise noted, have been taken from Lesley Cawood's, *The Church and Race Relations*, 1964, S.A. Institute of Race Relations, Johannesburg. For a full discussion of the apartheid idea, see *Apartheid* by N.J. Rhoodie and H.J. Venter, H.A.U.M., Cape Town, Pretoria.

by the Dutch Reformed Churches was to be rudely shattered in the next four years. In August 1958 the Fourth Reformed Ecumenical Synod brought together at Potchefstroom representatives of the N.G.K., the Gereformeerde Kerk and several Reformed Churches of other countries. The recommendations of the Committee on Race Relations sounded a warning of things to come. In 1959 a number of ministers of the three Dutch Reformed persuasions established an ecumenical study group on the Witwatersrand, and in the following year, the year of Sharpeville, some of them were involved in the publication of a book that denounced apartheid.[6] Things were happening now. A month later the Cottesloe[7] Consultation brought together six representatives of the World Council of Churches and 80 delegates from eight South African churches, 30 of them from Dutch Reformed Churches. Among the findings of the Consultation were the following:

> '1. We recognize that all racial groups who permanently inhabit our country are a part of our total population and we regard them as indigenous. Members of all these groups have an equal right to make their contribution towards the enrichment of the life of their country and to share in the ensuing responsibilities, reward and privileges.
> '5. The Church as the Body of Christ is a unity, and within this unity the natural diversity among men is not annulled but sanctified.
> '15. It is our conviction that the right to own land wherever he is domiciled and to participate in the government of his country, is part of the dignity of the adult man, and for this reason a policy which permanently denies to non-White people the right of collaboration in the government of the country of which they are citizens cannot be justified.'

The delegates of one of the Dutch Reformed Churches refused to accept the findings, but the others, representatives of the N.G.K., endorsed them. In the subsequent controversy they explained their attitude in these words:

'We wish to confirm that, as stated in the preamble, a policy of differen-

6. *Delayed Action.* See L. Marquard, *The People and Policies of South Africa,* fourth edition, Oxford paperbacks, p. 232.

7. Named after the Cottesloe Residence of the Witwatersrand University, Johannesburg, where the Consultation was held.

tiation can be defended from the Christian point of view, that it provides the only realistic solution to the problems of race relations and is, therefore, in the best interests of the various population groups. We do not consider the resolutions adopted by the Consultation as, in principle, incompatible with the above statement. In voting on resolution 15, the delegations of the two churches recorded their views as follows: The undersigned voted in favour of point 15, provided it be clearly understood that participation in the Government of this country refers, in the case of White areas, to the Africans who are domiciled in the declared White areas, in the sense that they have no other homeland.'

This concession to the Africans domiciled in White areas was dynamite. It rocked the Dutch Reformed Churches. The Hervormde Kerk repudiated most of the statement. Grave warnings were issued against divisions in the church. The N.G.K. delegates issued a press statement in which they said: 'If complete territorial separation is impossible, then full rights, including political rights, cannot be withheld indefinitely from them (Africans) living permanently in White areas. Those who do not agree with this must now give definite moral grounds for their point of view.'

In the fall-out after the explosion, professors lost their chairs, pastors resigned their pulpits, and the Dutch Reformed Churches that had been members of the World Council left it.[8]

A monthly publication, *Pro Veritate,* come into existence as the mouthpiece of the dissidents and their sympathizers, and in 1963 the Christian Institute was founded with the Rev. C.E. Beyers Naude as its first chairman. He had been elected Moderator of the Southern Transvaal Synod of the N.G.K. in April of that year, but now felt constrained to resign his ministry in order to accept the leadership of the Christian Institute. The Institute has come under heavy fire from both church and state; it has been subjected to synodal repudiation, police investigation and political condemnation; but so far it still survives and, under the dynamic leadership of Beyers Naude, provides a significant share of what Christian opposition there is in South Africa to apartheid. It endeavours to spread its influence through Bible Study and Christian Action groups and, in co-operation with the South African Council of Churches, has sponsored a scheme of theological training for ministers of the African Independent Churches.

8. L. Marquard, *op. cit.*, p. 232, and Lesley Cawood, *op. cit.*, pp. 130-134.

Another aspect of the ferment in Dutch Reformed circles that made itself felt about 1960 was the promotion by churchmen and others of the idea that the Coloured population should be given full recognition. This was practically the official policy of the South African Bureau of Racial Affairs until the then Prime Minister, Doctor H. Verwoerd, muzzled the organization.

Since those hectic days, the Dutch Reformed Churches have had little to say about race relations, apart from a detailed discussion on migratory labour in the Federal Council of the N.G.K. in January 1969. The analysis of the situation was excellent, but the Council had little to offer by way of solution except to urge the Government to study the system carefully in order to eliminate its disadvantages.[9]

The Other Churches – The other churches in South Africa had to wait until 1970 for their *crise de conscience,* and this, too, came through the World Council of Churches. The situation of these others churches is vastly different from that of the Dutch Reformed Churches, in that they are not identified with a nation that has been engaged in a continuous and bitter fight for existence throughout its brief and turbulent history. Again, quite considerable numbers of the White members of these churches are first generation South Africans without deep historical roots in the country, and a large proportion of their priests and ministers are immigrants. It is noteworthy that none of the Anglican churchmen who became prominent as opponents of apartheid, Bishop Ambrose Reeves, Father (now Bishop) Trevor Huddleston, Father Michael Scott and Bishop Edward Crowther are South Africans.

The story of the reaction of the so-called English-speaking churches ('so-called' because, in practically every case, the majority of their members are Africans), begins with a period of resolutions and statements.

The first in the field were the Methodists, with pronouncements of their governing body, the Methodist Conference, going back to 1947, and reiterated and enlarged upon in 1948 and subsequent years. The 1948 statement affirmed: 'In this multi-racial land we are bound to take account of the basic Christian principle that every human being is entitled to fundamental human rights and dignity and belongs to the family of God . . . No person of any race should be deprived of constitutional rights or privileges merely on the ground of race.'

9. ***A Survey of Race Relations in South Africa,*** 1969, S.A. Institute of Race Relations, p. 13.

In 1960 the Conference went beyond the statement stage and laid down a programme of education in race relations advocating mixed study groups and district conferences, exchange of pulpits and visits between church organizations. In 1963 the Methodist Conference elected as its president an African minister, the Rev. Seth Mokitini, and in 1968, another African, the Rev. R.A. Mtimkulu, was inducted as General President of the Triennial Conference.

The Anglican Church in South Africa, known as the Church of the Province of South Africa, has also been active in the publication of statements through its various organs of government: the Provincial Synod, the Synod of Bishops and Diocesan Synods. The Synod of Bishops had referred as early as 1930 to human rights being independent of race or colour. In 1949, at the beginning of the apartheid era, it took up the question again. Then in 1950, the Provincial Synod made an important statement incorporating a resolution of the Lambeth Conference of 1948, which reads as follows:

'The Conference is convinced that discrimination between men on grounds of race alone is inconsistent with the principles of Christ's religion. We urge that in every land men of every race should be encouraged to develop in accordance with their abilities; and that this involves fairness of opportunity in trades and professions, in facilities for travelling and in the provision of housing, in education at all stages, and in schemes of social welfare. Every churchman should be assured of a cordial welcome in any church of our Communion, and no one should be ineligible for any position in the Church by reason of his race or colour.'

This same message has been re-affirmed and applied to the South African situation in many subsequent pronouncements. The Anglican Church has also produced the strongest clerical opponents of apartheid and must easily hold the record for expulsions: at least three bishops and quite a few other clergy. It has elevated three of its African priests to episcopal rank, of whom the best known is Alpheus Zulu, Bishop of Zululand, and one of the six co-Presidents of the World Council of Churches.

It was in 1952 that the Roman Catholic Church entered the field of official utterances on race relations. In that year the Southern African Catholic Bishops' Conference issued its first statement on the subject, affirming that 'discrimination based exclusively on grounds of colour is an offence against the right of non-Europeans to their natural dignity as human persons'; and that 'justice demands that Non-Europeans be permitted to evolve gradually towards full participation in the political, economic and cultural life of the country.' Other statements followed at regular intervals, and, like the Anglicans, the Catholic Hierarchy had African bishops introduced into its ranks.

Similar statements have emanated from the Presbyterian, Lutheran, Congregational, Baptist and Apostolic Faith Churches, all calling for Christian love and justice and respect for human dignity and freedom. Most of these churches, too, were involved with the Anglican and Dutch Reformed Churches in the Cottesloe Conference of December 1961. The Presbyterians, like the Methodists, formulated a practical programme of inter-racial contacts. In 1969, the Congregational Union elected as its first African chairman, the Rev. Benjamin Ngidi.

Even as the church leaders published their statements, they were aware of the weakness in their own camp. The Anglicans said in 1950 : '(The Provincial Synod) recognizes that the Church has not in practice been always faithful to her own principle and has allowed herself to be infected by the racial prejudices prevalent in the world about her. It, therefore, calls upon all members of the church to re-examine their racial attitudes in the light of the Christian gospel, that in every parish witness may be borne to the equal standing of all churchmen before God, and to their brotherhood one with another in Christ.' Catholics also did some breast-beating in 1957 : 'The practice of segregation though officially not recognized in our churches, characterizes, nevertheless, many of our church societies, our schools, seminaries, convents, hospitals, and the social life of our people. In the light of Christ's teaching, this cannot be tolerated for ever. The time has come to pursue more vigorously the change of heart and practice that the law of Christ demands. We are hypocrites if we condemn apartheid in South African society and condone it in our own institutions.' There was an even more candid confession of failure by the Presbyterian Church in the report of the Church and Nation Committee to the General Assembly of 1962 : 'With a few exceptions that redound to the glory of God, contact between Black and White in the Church is so rare and superficial, that there can be no understanding of one another, no desire to pray for one another, no desire to bear one another's burdens. The contact is rare because the world has infected us with its own fear and suspicion, and has stifled that perfect love which can cast out fear. What kind of spiritual insight can be granted to a church where brotherly love is so conspiciously lacking?'

Faith in the ability of resolutions and statements to effect any significant change had pretty well evaporated by the beginning of the sixties. There were comments from many churchmen to this effect. The Rev. Robert Orr of the Presbyterian Church summed it up pretty well when he said: 'To the best of our knowledge, these statements and recommendations, piously noted by this Assembly, have had less effect than the rattling of tin cans tied to a cat's tail.'[10] Yet it was a stage the churches had to go through, just as there was a theoretical beginning to the modern revival of Christian social concern.

It was the realization that something more is wanted than statements launched into space that has inspired new developments in the last few years. Religious protest against hardship resulting from the implementation of apartheid policy has begun to assume more significant proportions. There always has been religious protest in the sense that church personalities have been involved; but in the last few years initiative and co-ordination have been slightly more conspicuous.

An instance of this was the outcry over population removals in 1968. Population removals had been going on for many years and voices had been raised in protest. But the removals that took place in Natal early in 1968 achieved almost world-wide notoriety because of the organized action initiated by some Catholic missionaries. In all these removals the Government had the habit of leaving itself wide open to criticism by removing African people from so-called 'Black Spots' in areas zoned for farming by Whites without proper preparation of the new settlements to which they were transferred. There were no houses to receive them; they were given tents to camp in until they could build new houses for themselves with the small financial compensation accorded them and the material they could salvage from their old homes. Water supplies were inadequate, and schools, stores and health facilities often non-existent. The name 'Limehill' became the symbol of this kind of heartless transfer of people. It was agitation stirred up by religious bodies that made it so. Religious groups were also the chief inspiration behind the efforts organized to supply food, blankets, clothing, firewood and medical care. A Division of Inter-Church Aid had been established by the South

10. Lesley Cawood, *op. cit.*, p. 95. See also pp. 52, 65, 79.

African Council of Churches shortly before and this became an important agent of co-ordination for these efforts.

Inter-Church Aid fulfilled a useful purpose in this field, but its principal aim has been to combat poverty in a more general way by means of feeding schemes and development projects. It has sponsored agricultural improvements, dam building and home industries. Schemes of this nature, not all directly connected with Inter-Church Aid, but inspired nevertheless by religious and humanitarian concern are proliferating around the country. They serve a useful purpose but, obviously, with the best will in the world, and all the money that church bodies can pour into them, they can only scratch the surface of the huge problem of poverty and under-development affecting the Non-White population. The ideal would be the co-operation of church bodies in development schemes planned and financed by the Government and the integration of church efforts into these; but this is hardly possible in present circumstances, except in isolated instances. At least what is done by church bodies is evidence of Christian concern and it helps to maintain sympathetic contact with the people.

There is need of such contact. All the indications are that at both ends of the social spectrum, the unsophisticated and the sophisticated, there is a fairly solid movement away from the White-controlled churches. The unsophisticated flock more and more to the Independent African Churches: the Ethiopeans, the Zionists and the African Messianic Movements. It appears that between 1946 and 1961 their total membership increased from 9,6 per cent of the African population to 20,1 per cent.[11] The sophisticated, educated and urbanized, conscious of their many privations in every sphere of life, find little to satisfy them in churches whose activities seem irrelevant to their needs and aspirations.

An attempt was made at the end of 1966 to solve the problem of relevance in regard to university students by the establishment of an ecumenical body, the University Christian Movement, designed to supplement the efforts of denominational student groups and relate Christian student activity more directly to South African conditions. However, church authorities have not been over-enthusiastic about some of the attitudes and practices of the Movement and White membership has tended to fall off with the growth of Black participation. But Black

11. *A Survey of Race Relations in South Africa,* 1967, S.A. Institute of Race Relations, p. 12.

participation itself seems on the decline and Black students seem more interested in a body recently formed for Black students only: The South African Student Organization. SASO promises to give Black students a stronger sense of their own identity as it pursues the 'Black is Beautiful' theme.

The tendency to assert their own identity is bound to grow among Black Christians who remain loyal to the old churches. There was a sign of things to come in the publication of a bill of grievances by a group of African Catholic priests in a Johannesburg daily paper in January 1970.

It was in the midst of such developments and with a sense of urgency and crisis that in September 1968, a theological commission of the South African Council of Churches, with a membership of Anglicans, Presbyterians, Catholics, Methodists, Lutherans, Baptists and members of the Dutch Reformed Churches, published a 'Message to the People of South Africa'. This Message was cast in a different style from that of the traditional church statement or resolution. It pulled no punches and spared no feelings and put the question squarely under the nose of every Christian: 'To whom or to what are you truly giving your first loyalty – to a sub-section of mankind, an ethnic group, a human tradition, or political idea – or to Christ?'[12]

It was the intention and the hope of the authors of the Message that it would serve as a prophetic call to all who really cared about their Christianity. It was widely disseminated and evoked a wide response. Some controversy was stirred up when the Prime Minister, Mr B.J. Vorster, warned church ministers not to turn their pulpits into political platforms. 'I want to say to them,' he said, 'cut it out, cut it out immediately, because the cloth you are wearing will not protect you if you try to do this in South Africa.' This was clear enough. Nevertheless, in one way or another all the governing bodies of 'English-speaking' churches, with the exception of the Baptists, supported the Message. Under the aegis of the South African Council of Churches and the Christian Institute, commissions have been set up to study the practical implications of the Message in the sphere of church, law, politics, economics, education and social relations. The undertaking is referred to as SPRO-CAS: Study Project on Christianity in Apartheid Society. Its reports have begun to appear.

12. *A Survey of Race Relations in South Africa,* 1968, S.A. Institute of Race Relations, pp. 21-24.

Has theory once more swallowed up practice? Has study once again become an excuse for inaction? At first sight it would appear so. And yet there are too many dedicated Christians in South Africa to allow this to go on indefinitely. They may not as yet understand too well how to translate thought into action in the excruciatingly complex South African situation, but they are resolved that this must be done. If they should be tempted to let their resolution flag, there are events afoot that will serve to temper it afresh.

One such event was the decision of the Executive Committee of the World Council of Churches in September 1970 to extend financial aid to the African liberation movements for non-military purposes.[13] This was a mighty shock for White Christians in South Africa, for few had realized what pressures had been building up since the Consultation at Mindola, Zambia, in 1961. No doubt it was at the same time a great encouragement to many Black Christians; though leaders like Bishop Zulu came out strongly against it. White South Africans were horrified to think that a responsible and widely representative Christian group could judge that there was so much 'institutional violence' in South Africa that practical encouragement could be given to movements designed to overthrow it by force. The average White South African would not know what you were talking about if you accused his country of 'institutional violence'. This is the measure of the churches' failure to communicate Christian concern to the great majority of their White members.

The judgment implied in all that has been said so far is that the churches have done very little to promote sound race relations. This is not a denial of the dedicated missionary efforts of the churches and their appreciable success in this field. Nor is it a denial of the courageous witness of individuals, and of the good work done in recent years in certain limited educational endeavours among both youth and adults. It is just a recognition of the fact that relations between the races in South Africa are anything but good and that the churches can point to very little that they have done to improve them. What significant groups of White church members are known for their practical communication and co-operation with their Non-White neighbours? What significant groups of African, Indian or Coloured Christians are united in bonds of understanding and friendship with their White fellow-Christians? One would

13. *A Survey of Race Relations in South Africa,* 1970, S.A. Institute of Race Relations, p. 15.

be hard put to find them; just as one would be hard put to find this kind of Christian communication in any country of mixed languages, nationalities or races. Let him who is without sin . . . But there is little comfort in this.

THE FUTURE ROLE OF THE CHURCHES

We have made a brief survey of the churches' attitude to race relations in South Africa over the past 25 years, the generation since the Second World War. We have observed the kind of spiritual paralysis that has prevented the churches from achieving anything substantial, a spiritual paralysis inherited from Christian experience in the West since Renaissance. Now we move into the decade of the seventies, which could well prove to be the truly critical one for South Africa, as foreign opposition gains momentum and the clash between economics and ideology erodes whatever credibility apartheid may ever have had. What role will the churches play? What role are they called upon to play? It is easier to answer the second question. The first is a matter of prophecy.

The role they are called upon to play is that of giving in the sphere of race relations a practical expression of the Christian faith they profess. It will require an enormous effort, a courageous effort, an effort that little in the recent history of the churches has prepared them to undertake. In their long alienation from social and cultural developments in the West, the churches became other-worldly and academic and almost exclusively concerned with the heavenly future of individual souls. Theology, in truth, cannot escape being other-worldly, for it is concerned with the transcendent; but it dare not become wholly other-worldly for it is concerned with the relevance of the transcendent to the here-and-now of human life, of human culture, politics, economics and social relations. Even in this field theology must be academic, but again, not wholly academic, for it must tell the Christian conscience what is expected of it in the here-and-now. If it fails to do this, it is not really theology: for it is not serving a living, active, concerned faith. For too long that has been the weakness of theology in the West; and when Western Christians are face-to-face with an agonizing situation, like the one in South Africa, they know what it is to have inherited that tradition. They know what it is to be on the threshold of a new age when the theology of that long retreat from reality is no longer adequate.

The Dutch Reformed Churches have two steps to take, the others one.

If the Dutch Reformed Churches can take the first, they could very well lead the others in the second, if the example of Beyers Naude and his colleagues is anything to go by. Both steps concern the passage from theory to practice.

The first step the Dutch Reformed Churches must take is a jump through the smoke-screen of separate development into the reality of South Africa. Up to now by remaining in the realm of theory they have been able to avert their eyes from the reality of Non-White poverty, humiliation, privation and degradation. The human mind is by nature and education selective. It has to select in order to concentrate and analyse. But selectivity is not its only characteristic. An even more important one is awareness of reality. Selectivity is only a means to this end and is useful only when the work of analysis is referred back to reality and promotes action: action related to reality. The Dutch Reformed Churches have been extremely selective in concentrating most of their attention on their service to the Afrikaner nation while throwing a smoke-screen over the condition of other people who share the same land with them. In arguing what separate development could achieve in a dream world they have prevented themselves from seeing what the politics they support are perpetrating in the real world. In the end we shall be judged not by the ingenious theories that have hidden reality from our eyes but by the practical Christian way in which we shall have faced the reality of the hungry, the thirsty, the naked, the sick, the imprisoned; the reality of human minds and hearts and personalities beyond the pale of our concepts and theories. The Christian standard is a terrifying one. And even as we take it upon ourselves to suggest where our brothers of the Dutch Reformed Churches may have fallen short of it, we dare not judge and condemn, for, in the same circumstances, would we have done better?

In the light of the behaviour of the other churches in South Africa, we would not. For these churches, too, have been hamstrung by their inability to break out of theory into practice. They have not had quite the same problem as the Dutch Reformed Churches. They have not suffered from an inadequate theory. They have just suffered from a paralysing incapacity to translate the right theory into practice. If the Dutch Reformed Churches ever come to accept a broader view of what Christianity means in South Africa, they will have to take this step, the second step for them, alongside their sister churches: the step of endeavouring to promote the practice of the Christian law of love in the South African situation.

One almost despairs, just thinking about it. For it would be an utterly new venture, that of promoting Christian standards of fraternal love between different racial groups sharing the same country. It is a terrible indictment of Christianity that South Africa has nowhere to look for an example. The efforts of the United States tell us something, but the situation is totally different, because in the United States it is a case of a powerful majority having to share its achievements with relatively small minorities. In South Africa a relatively small but politically omnipotent minority must share with others numerous enough to swamp it. This is what tempts one to despair and makes one realize why the World Council of Churches has apparently chosen to support the African liberation movements rather than continue backing an impotent Christian effort to change White South Africans.

But despair is a practical denial of Christian faith. It is incompatible with Christianity. A situation inducing despair is an opportunity for Christian hope. The next few years will tell if the churches in South Africa are prepared to face the challenge of hope, which is nothing less than this: to promote by practical teaching and example, and especially example, what so many of them have been saying in statements for the last twenty-five years; to promote this from within a legacy of Christian withdrawal from the field of social morality; in the face of apathy, incomprehension and opposition among their own members; under the menace of violence from without; and in the teeth of Government policy that looks upon Christian action in the racial field as subversion – and is well equipped to deal with subversion.

What it means is this: that the implications of the Christian gospel for South Africa must become the detailed, down-to-earth, day-to-day teaching of the churches; a regular feature of the Sunday sermon, the religion class, the guild meeting, the youth programme, the discussion group and every other church activity. The occasional lofty pronouncements of the governing body must become the frequent heart-to-heart communication of local ministers, youth leaders, Sunday school teachers. The exceptional witness of the lone prophetic figure must become the daily doing of every convinced Christian. The day of conferences and seminars dealing exclusively with intellectual principles and attitudes is over. Whatever conferences and seminars are held from now on must aim at communication and action: at what priests and ministers should be required to preach, and teachers to teach and Christian people – and their leaders before them – to do. The doing is important, for as one great South African with a universal heart has said: 'The only conquest that is ever valid is conquest by living example.'[14]

Is this possible? With faith all things are possible, even the moving of mountains – with faith motivated by a great vision of what Christianity should mean in a society like South Africa. Men do not move unless motivated. We need visionaries to inspire us, men and women who can write and speak and convince and paint for us a picture of an impossible human situation transformed by the love and sacrifice of Christ incarnated again in the lives of South African Christians of all colours. We must never forget the power of motivation and how important the intellectual vision is when oriented to action.

How will the Government react? There is bound to be a clash and a crisis. This is inevitable when Christianity is taken seriously in any social context where there is a vested interest in maintaining an unchristian situation. The churches have been warned by those in power both by word and by deed. A sudden flurry of passport and visa restrictions has affected church personnel of various denominations. It will be for every Christian leader and every member of every church to decide what part he should play in the crisis ahead. Conscience alone can dictate that, a conscience enlightened and supported by the grace of Christ.

There are passages in the gospel that seem remote for most of our lives, and then suddenly take on life and relevance. For growing numbers of Christians in South Africa one such passage may be this:

'You must not think that I have come to bring peace to the earth; I have not come to bring peace, but a sword. I have come to set a man against his father, a daughter against her mother, a young wife against her mother-in-law; and a man will find his enemies under his own roof.

'No man is worthy of me who cares more for father or mother than for me; no man is worthy of me who cares more for son or daughter; no man is worthy of me who does not take up his cross and walk in my footsteps. By gaining his life a man will lose it; by losing his life for my sake, he will gain it.'[15]

14. Laurens van der Post, *Journey into Russia,* Hogarth Press, London, 1964, p. 95.
15. Matthew 10:34-39.

Education in an Apartheid Society

Muriel Horrell

The author is Chief Research Officer of the South African Institute of Race Relations. She has written extensively on race relations and is internationally known for her research projects in this field. Her annual Survey of Race Relations in South Africa *has become a stock reference work. An outspoken opponent of apartheid, she has written many detailed critiques on this policy.*

Since one of the earliest manifestations of apartheid in South Africa was in the schools, and as education is now a field in which apartheid is well-nigh complete, it is of interest to look back to the origins of this separation.

In the earliest days of settlement in the Cape, it was the policy of successive governments that government schools, established primarily for Whites, should be open, too, to the children of slaves and of Hottentots (although, as far back as 1676, some White settlers objected). No colour bar existed in the schools that were founded by missions, primarily for Coloured or African pupils.

In 1834, however, school fees were introduced in government schools, and five years later the Department of Education ruled that all pupils 'should be decently clothed and of good deportment'. Many Coloured children were, in consequence, excluded. Finally the Appellate Division decided that an Act passed in 1905 had in effect removed the right of Coloured pupils to attend government schools. Coloured children were, thus, restricted to the mission schools, which provided primary classes only. The attendance of Whites at these schools dwindled and finally ceased as more government schools became available.

Professor J.S. Marais[1] wrote, 'It is quite impossible to assess the damage suffered by the Coloured people through their children being confined to the inferior mission schools.'

Until the first decade of the twentieth century, government schools in Natal accepted Coloured and Indian children who 'could conform in all respects to European habits and customs'. Lighter-skinned Coloured children were admitted to government schools in the Transvaal. Missions and church schools in the three northern territories, as in the Cape, followed a non-discriminatory policy. Gradually, however, the various governments established separate schools for Coloured and Indian pupils. As race consciousness grew among the Whites, Non-Whites were progressively excluded from their schools, this separation becoming well-nigh complete in Natal by 1905 and in the Transvaal and Free State in terms of laws of 1907.

In all four territories, African education was left almost entirely to the missions, which, especially in outlying districts, accepted Coloured children, too. As the subsidies payable were gradually augmented, the governments assumed increasing control. Between 1884 and 1904, the three northern territories introduced separate curricula for African primary schools.

Shortly before Union, compulsory education was progressively introduced for White children within defined age limits who lived reasonably close to a school.

1. For the sake of brevity, detailed lists of source material are omitted. These are contained in the author's booklets *African Education: Some Origins, and Developments until 1953; Bantu Education to 1968;* and *The Education of the Coloured Community in South Africa, 1962 to 1970;* all published by the S.A. Institute of Race Relations.

In addition, use has been made in this article of an account of Indian education by Professor A.L. Behr, published in the issue of *Fiat Lux* for November 1970; various books and articles on bilingualism by Dr E.G. Malherbe; and information kindly furnished over the years by the National Bureau of Educational and Social Research (now included in the Human Sciences Research Council).

THE PERIOD 1910 TO 1948

Control of Education

The Act of Union reserved higher education for the central government, while, later, vocational, technical and special education, too, became centrally controlled. Primary and secondary education and teacher-training remained the sphere of the four provinces.

Financing of Education

It was decided in 1925 that the State would pay educational subsidies to the four provinces on the basis of the average attendance of pupils. The amounts were fixed at R32 per White pupil per year in the three northern provinces, R28 per White pupil in the Cape, and R10,50 per Coloured or Indian pupil in all provinces.

The amount to be contributed from the Consolidated Revenue Fund for African education was pegged at the 1921-2 figure of R680 000 a year. To this was added increasing proportions (by 1943, the whole amount) of the sum paid by Africans in the general (or poll) tax. This money was administered by the provinces.

The financial system was changed in 1945. Each province would, in future, be paid a subsidy based on its actual expenditure on White, Coloured, and Indian education. All funds for African education would be drawn direct from the Consolidated Revenue Fund. Real progress resulted from these new arrangements.

In progressive steps, education became free for White, Coloured, and Indian pupils in government schools, although fees were charged in aided schools (including nearly all the schools for Africans).

Between 1942 and 1953, education was made compulsory for Coloured (but not Indian) children in Natal, and for Coloured children in six school board areas of the Cape, in respect of children who were between defined age limits and lived within reasonable distance of a recognized school. Natal provided boarding or travelling grants for rural Coloured children. Up to the time of writing, in 1971, compulsory education for Non-White children has not been introduced in any further areas.

A few excellent mission institutions existed for Africans, but, in general, the schools for Non-Whites were far less well-equipped than were those for Whites, and were very much overcrowded. A double-shift system in the use of classrooms was introduced in schools for Indians in Natal.

Expenditure on Education

Estimates of the per capita costs to the provinces *per pupil enrolled* in various years are:

	Whites R	*Coloured and Asian* R	*African* R
1925	40,48	9,00	4,05
1930	45,20	9,23	4,27
1940	51,42	11,55	4,43
1945	76,58	21,62	7,78

(Over this period the value of money declined substantially, nevertheless the progress made in terms of the new financial arrangements of 1945 is noteworthy.) The estimated costs to the provinces *per head of population* in 1945 were R14,46 for Whites, R3,97 for Coloured and Asians, and R0,60 per African.

The African and Indian communities themselves raised very large sums of money towards the capital costs of school buildings and the salaries of additional teachers.

School Enrolment

Accurate statistics are not available for early years, but at the end of the period under review, in 1949, the total enrolment in schools was:

Racial group	*Total enrolment*	*Percentage of pupils in secondary classes*
White	486 297	15,89
Coloured	200 947	2,34
Asian	55 457	3,44
African	786 978	2,51

As the last column indicates, the school life of the Non-White pupils was a very short one (averaging about four years).

Curricula

By the early twenties, all four provinces had special primary curricula for African schools, emphasizing practical subjects. Secondary school courses did not differ, except that students could offer their own languages as subjects. In the Cape, Natal, and Transvaal, the vernacular was used as the medium of instruction to the end of Standard II, religion and health being taught in Zulu to the end of Standard IV in Natal. Thereafter, English was more frequently used than was Afrikaans. Schools in the Free State used the vernacular to the end of Standard IV, while, in more senior classes, both official languages were employed.

The curricula and syllabuses in Coloured and Indian schools were the same as those used for White pupils, except that a more limited range of subjects could be offered because of a lack of equipment and suitably qualified teachers.

At the time of Union, varying policies were in operation in the four colonies in respect of the official language to be used as medium of instruction in schools for White, Coloured, and Indian pupils. By 1920, however, the official language with which the child was more familiar was usually compulsory up to the end of Standard VI in the Cape and Free State, and the end of Standard IV in the Transvaal. In Natal, parents had the right of choice, but schools were supposed to use the language that was not selected as the medium in teaching that language and as the partial medium in at least one other subject. Throughout South Africa, minority groups of not less than fifteen pupils in any standard were catered for by using both media, or by establishing parallel classes.

Technical and Higher Education

By 1950, 54 071 White, 1 090 Coloured, 1 679 Asian and 2 037 African students were attending full-time or part-time classes conducted by technical colleges – State-aided institutions. The classes for Non-Whites were segregated. One of the colleges, the M.L. Sultan Technical College in Durban, catered mainly for Indians. Its establishment in 1945 was made possible through donations by the Indian community and the Durban City Council.

Various government or aided trade and vocational schools existed: in 1949 they had 6 604 White and 3 351 Non-White students. There was a State agricultural school for Africans in the Transkei, and two aided schools of social work in Johannesburg and Bloemfontein respectively.

Ten universities or university colleges had been established. Seven of these were originally affiliated to the University of South Africa, but six of them had become independent by 1951. The University of South Africa then confined its activities to conducting correspondence classes and external examinations for students of all racial groups. The University College of Fort Hare (at first called the South African Native College) had been founded in 1916 by means of grants made by Africans themselves as well as various churches and the Government. In 1951 it became affiliated to Rhodes University. It admitted Coloured and Indian as well as African students.

From about 1909 the Universities of Cape Town and the Witwatersrand (the 'open' universities) accepted Non-White students on a basis of 'academic non-segregation'. In 1936 the University of Natal established a Non-White branch. Rhodes University admitted post-graduate African students for courses that were not available at Fort Hare. The University of Pretoria ran part-time, segregated classes for Non-Whites.

In 1949 there were 18 315 White, 149 Coloured, 289 Asian, and 421 African university students.

DEVELOPMENTS SINCE 1948

The National Party Government, which came into power in 1948, was the first government officially to promote the policy of apartheid (or separate development).

Control of Education

Africans: In January 1949 the Government appointed a Commission under the chairmanship of Dr W.W.M. Eiselen, its main term of reference being 'the formulation of the principles and aims of education for Natives as an independent race, in which their past and present, their inherent racial qualities, their distinctive characteristics and aptitude, and their needs under ever-changing social conditions are taken into consideration.' The Commission's recommendations formed the basis for the new system of Bantu education. In the course of a speech made in 1953 Dr H.F. Verwoerd (then Minister of Native Affairs) said[2], 'Education must train and teach people in accordance with their opportunities in life'. These remarks, and the Commission's recommendations, were strongly criticized by very many people, caused great antagonism among Africans to 'Bantu education', and led to unrest among many teachers and students.

2. *Assembly Hansard 10* of 1953, cols. 3576, 3585.

In terms of the Bantu Education Act of 1953, the control of school education and teacher-training for Africans was transferred from the provinces to the central government. A Division (from 1958 a separate Department) of Bantu Education was created. Missions were required to hand over teacher-training institutions to this Department. Subsidies to mission schools were progressively reduced, ending in 1957. Missions were urged to hand over their schools to the Government. Those that did not wish to do so could apply for registration of the schools as private, unaided institutions, but registration was not granted if the schools were situated in areas zoned for Whites under the Group Areas Act. The Roman Catholics, in particular, raised funds to continue some of their schools privately. Government schools that were staffed entirely by Africans were placed under the control of African school boards.

It became official policy that new high schools (providing the full matriculation course) should be sited in African rural areas rather than in the towns.

Since 1963 there have been further developments. The control of schools and teacher-training is progressively being delegated to African governing bodies (the Transkeian Legislative Assembly and Territorial Authorities in other African 'homelands' : legislative assemblies are planned for these other areas, too). The Transkei may make its own laws, subject to the State President's approval. Its students write the examinations of the Bantu Education Department. In other Bantu areas, for the foreseeable future, the Department will continue to determine general policy, prescribe syllabuses, control inspections, and administer examinations. White officials and senior educationalists have been seconded to assist the African governing bodies.

Coloured pupils: In terms of the Coloured Persons Education Act, the control of education for Coloured pupils was, from the beginning of 1964, transferred from the provinces to a Division of Education within the Coloured Affairs Department. *Inter alia,* the Act contained strict provisions governing the activities of Coloured teachers (many of whom had campaigned against the measure).

This Act, too, was bitterly opposed by most of the established Coloured organizations and churches, and by many others. Coloured people considered that they were being relegated to an inferior and subordinate status.

The Government established an Education Council for Coloured Persons, with nominated Coloured members, and Regional Education Boards and school committees, again with Coloured members, some appointed and some elected.

In 1968 a Coloured Persons Representative Council was established, with 40 elected and 20 nominated members, and an Administration of Coloured Affairs was created to administer matters assigned to the Council's control, including school education and teacher training. Again, senior White officials have been seconded to assist the Administration for the time being. The transfer of the control of education was effected in 1970. The control of the Coloured university (described later) was assigned to a newly-created Department of Coloured Relations.

Most of the schools in the Cape, and many of those in Natal, continue to be run by missions, as aided institutions, and subject to Departmental regulations and inspection.

Indians: An Indians' Education Act was passed in 1965, again providing for State instead of provincial control. It came into operation in Natal during 1966, in the Transvaal the following year, and in the Cape in 1971. (There are no Indians in the Free State.) This Act, too, was widely opposed.

Indian children in the Cape have up to the present attended the same schools as Coloured children; while in the Transvaal many mixed Coloured-Indian schools existed. Separate schools are gradually being built in the group areas allocated to members of these communities.

An Indian Council, with nominated members, was established in 1964, but thus far it has advisory powers only.

Technical and Vocational Education

An act of 1955 gave the State widely increased powers of control of technical colleges and subsidized continuation classes. Thereafter, the part-time classes that some of these colleges had conducted for Non-Whites were stopped, and the M.L. Sultan College was debarred from accepting African students. The Jan H. Hofmeyr School of Social Work in Johannesburg (catering for Africans) had to close because its subsidy was terminated. (The classes conducted in Bloemfontein had been discontinued earlier.)

In terms of a further act, in 1961 the Government removed the control of technical and vocational education for Non-Whites from the (then) central department of Education, Arts, and Science, assigning it, instead, to the Departments of Coloured Affairs, Indian Affairs, and Bantu Education, respectively.

University Education

The educational measure which met with the most widespread opposition was the Extension of University Education Act of 1959. It provided for the establishment of university colleges for Coloured, Indian, and African students, to fall under the respective Ministries. White students were prohibited from attending them.

Each university college would have a White Council and Senate and a Non-White advisory Council and Senate, the latter bodies gradually to be granted increasing executive powers. Examinations would be conducted, and degrees, diplomas, and certificates awarded by the University of South Africa, except that the colleges might themselves run courses in subjects not offered by this University. The 'conscience clause' was omitted. (This clause, contained in the charters of most South African universities, prohibits discrimination on religious or denominational grounds in the appointment of staff or admission of students.)

The respective Ministers were given very wide powers of control over the affairs of the colleges. They subsequently issued restrictive regulations governing student affairs, dealing *inter alia,* with the permission necessary before the students could join organizations, hold meetings, or produce publications or placards.

The Act provided that, after a date to be determined (the final date fixed was the end of 1961) no Non-White student could be admitted to a university or college catering for persons other than those of his own group, unless with special Ministerial approval. The medical school, which had earlier been established for Non-Whites by the University of Natal, was excluded from these provisions.

A companion measure, the University College of Fort Hare Transfer Act, transferred the control of this college from the governing council to the Minister of Bantu Education, and applied to it the provisions described above. Fort Hare was required to admit only Africans of the Xhosa-speaking groups, unless special exemption was granted.

Even before the Acts became law, the Government had commenced building a university college for Coloured students at Bellville near Cape Town, one for Indians in Durban, and two for Africans: one in Zululand for the Zulu and Swazi peoples and the other in an African area of the Northern Transvaal for Africans of the remaining ethnic groups.

Further legislation, passed in 1969, conferred full university status on the five Non-White colleges (i.e. including Fort Hare). For the time being external examiners and moderators will assist the staff.

Adult Education

Until 1955, all adult education fell under the central Department of Education, Arts, and Science, which subsidized evening or other classes conducted by a number of private organizations. Control of classes for Non-Whites was then transferred to the three Departments in charge of Coloured, Indian, and African affairs.

The Department of Bantu Education terminated the subsidies payable to classes for Africans that were conducted in 'White' areas, and insisted that private organizations should hand over to African school boards the control of classes held in African townships. All classes required annual Departmental approval and registration if they had ten or more students. Such approval was denied to a number of schools in 'White' areas.

Financing of Education

School education and teacher-training for Whites continues to be financed by the provinces, with the aid of State subsidies. Education for Coloured people and Indians is financed from the Consolidated Revenue Fund. All Coloured and Indian pupils now receive text books and stationery free of charge.

But in 1955 the Government created a Bantu Education Account, from which all education for Africans was to be financed. Into it would be paid a fixed amount of R13 000 000 a year from the Consolidated Revenue Fund, any recoverable advances made by this Fund, four-fifths of the general tax paid by Africans, and receipts from the management of schools. Africans were required to pay for the erection of lower primary schools, and to meet half the costs of building all other schools. School fees might be imposed. Except for readers in lower primary classes, parents had to pay for all text books and stationery.

In the years that followed, standards fell drastically. The per capita expenditure dropped from R17,08 in 1953-4 to R11,56 in 1962-3. Although parents contributed large sums voluntarily to pay for additional classrooms and teachers, and although the rates of African taxation were increased and the whole amount collected credited to the Bantu Education Account, the Government eventually conceded that more money was needed. From 1963 it paid an additional R1 500 000 a year for the maintenance of the university colleges. When the Transkei was granted partial self-government its educational services were subsidized without a reduction of the amounts paid to the Bantu Education Account for services in other areas. Interest-free advances were made to meet deficits in 1968 and 1969. Over the period 1970-72 inclusive an additional R17 500 000 a year is to be paid from the Consolidated Revenue Fund.

Final arrangements have not been decided upon at the time of writing. The Government is awaiting the results of a new system of taxing Africans. Meanwhile, the range of textbooks that are supplied free of charge has been widened.

Amounts Spent on Education

It would appear, from figures given in various official publications, that in 1970-1 about R48 762 360 will have been spent on education for the Coloured community, R27 284 000 on education for Indians, and R55 765 750 on Bantu education. This last figure does not include the costs of building schools in urban areas. Local authorities are now responsible for this – they may add amounts not exceeding 20 cents a month to the rentals of houses towards the costs.

In its *Newsletter* for February 1971, the Human Sciences Research Council estimated that the total cost of education to the State and the provinces would be about R371 000 000 in 1970-1. Subtracting the figures given above, it would appear that some R239 000 000 is to be spent on the education of Whites.

Estimated per capita figures are R228,38 for Whites[3] (1968), R70,30 for Indians (1969-70), R65 for Coloured students (1969-70), and R14,48 for Africans (1968-9).

Notes on Pupils and Teachers

The latest available figures showing the enrolment in schools are:

3. Estimation by F.E. Auerbach.

Group	*Number in school*	*Percentage in secondary classes*
Whites (1968)	812 961	32,53
Coloured (1970)	515 336	11,14
Indians (1970)		
(Natal and Transvaal)	157 891	23,89
Africans (1969)	2 545 755	4,20

It is clear that the drop-out rate is still very high, especially in African and Coloured schools. The position has been slightly improved in Coloured schools since 1968, when it became compulsory (unless exemption is granted) for a child who lives within five kilometres of a school and who enrols in any class at the start of a school year to attend regularly until the end of that year.

The numbers reaching the matriculation stage are far too low to meet the needs of industry and the professions. With the shortage of White workers, Non-Whites are increasingly being absorbed in semi-skilled and skilled work, very often at better rates of pay than professional workers receive. Hence the teaching profession is starved of well-educated recruits. This matter is discussed later. The table that follows indicates how few Non-White pupils do matriculate annually:

Group	*Number passing Matriculation*	*Of these, the number obtaining university entrance passes*
Whites (1968)	32 322	13 456
Coloured (1969)	1 446	413
Indians (1969)		
(Natal and Transvaal)	1 400	426
Africans (1969)	1 728	869

There is still an acute shortage of classrooms, especially for African and Coloured pupils. The use of the shared classroom or double-session system is steadily increasing in their schools. (There has been a slight decrease of this practice in schools for Indians.) In the Coloured schools each class involved has its own teacher; but in the Sub-Standards of African schools one teacher has to cope with two sets of pupils daily. In 1969, 750 428 African pupils (38 per cent of those in primary schools) and 30 531 Coloured (7 per cent) were in double-session classes. Especially in urban secondary schools for Africans, the pupil-teacher ratio is far too high.

Improved training courses and scholarship assistance have been made available for teachers, but far too few Non-White students are offering themselves for the more senior courses. In the years stated the percentages of teachers with university degrees were:

Coloured	1969	3,7%
Indian	1970	5,8%
African	1967	1,6%

Many of the better-qualified teachers of all racial groups are resigning from the profession.

Some of the Coloured have left the country, in frustration over their increasingly subordinate status in South Africa. Between 1965 and 1969, inclusive, an average of 360 Coloured teachers resigned annually for reasons other than superannuation or marriage. At the end of 1969, 991 Coloured students obtained teaching diplomas or certificates, but, of these, only 36 qualified for work in secondary schools.

One of the main reasons for the discontent and lack of an adequate number of recruits is the salary scales, which compare unfavouarbly with those offered in other sectors of the economy. White teachers are dissatisfied; but their scales are considerably higher than are those of Non-White teachers with equivalent qualifications and posts. One example is given, relating to a trained teacher with qualifications equivalent to matriculation plus three years' further education, who has been employed in a secondary school for four or more years. The scales reflect the position in 1971.

Men	*White*	*Coloured*	*African*
Salary range	R3 000–R4 800	R1 560–R3 000	R960–R2 340
Time taken to reach the top salary notch	11 years	15 years	21 years
Average annual salary over 20 years	R4 305	R2 397	R1 552,50
Percentage: Non-White to White	100%	55,7%	36,1%

Women	*White*	*Coloured*	*African*
Salary range	R2 640–R4 260	R1 380–R2 550	R840–R1 980
Time taken to reach the top salary notch	10 years	14 years	19 years
Average annual salary over 20 years	R3 855	R2 140,50	R1 414,50
Percentage: Non-White to White	100%	55,5%	36,7%

The salaries of Indian teachers approximate to those of Coloured members of the profession.

Syllabuses

During 1966, representatives of the various government and provincial education departments met to draw up 'basic or core' syllabuses for the various subjects that would form an adequate basis for the standard of work required in Standard X by the Joint Matriculation Board. The object was to modernize the syllabuses, especially in mathematics and science, and to help to close the gap between schools and universities.

These 'core' syllabuses were then adapted to the needs of the various departments, a special approach in their interpretation being followed where this was considered necessary, but a certain degree of uniformity nevertheless being maintained.

So far as Non-Whites are concerned, the greatest progress has been made in schools for Coloured pupils. The official plan is that in Standard VI (the first class of secondary schools) the teachers, with expert assistance, should try to discover the pupils' special aptitudes. Then, as facilities become available, the children will be streamed into academic, or technical, or commercial courses, provided in multi-lateral schools. Pupils who are not aiming at matriculation exemption (university entrance standard) may choose from a wide range of subjects for the Senior Certificate examination. By 1970, mainly because of the shortage of qualified teachers, only six schools were offering the technical secondary courses, however, and twenty-eight the commercial courses.

In schools for Indians, pupils are divided into advanced or ordinary level streams on the basis of their results in the Standard VI examinations. This Department, too, is planning more specialized courses for the final three years of schooling.

Media of Instruction

Decisions made since 1950 have had the effect, as Dr E.G. Malherbe has written, of 'artificially kraaling off' children from one another into unilingual schools during the most impressionable period of their lives, accentuating language differences, and diminishing opportunities for young people to associate with and learn to understand their fellow South Africans.

There is still some limited provision for parallel or dual-medium classes to cater for minority groups in schools; but in 1957 the Transvaal Administration ruled that single medium classes were to be preferred whereever possible in the White schools under its control, and a number of schools have been divided accordingly. The remaining right of parental choice of the medium was removed in the Transvaal in terms of ordinances of 1950 and 1957, except in cases where the education authorities decide that a child is equally proficient in both official languages.

In the Cape, Standard VI (to which class mother-tongue education was compulsory) was removed from primary to secondary schools in 1952. Two years later mother-tongue education was made compulsory for a further two years, i.e. to the end of Standard VIII. Parents retained the right to request that the other language should be gradually introduced as the medium of instruction in some subjects after that stage; but few, if any, wanted to make such a change towards the end of a child's school career.

Afrikaans was generally used in the Free State, and English in Natal, but in the latter province the parents retained the right of choice until 1969, when the Government decreed that, in all government and aided schools throughout the country, mother-tongue instruction was to be compulsory to the end of Standard VIII.

The home language is used as the medium, throughout, in schools for Coloured children (except in teaching the second official language itself). Schools for Indians use the official language with which a child is more familiar.

Dr Malherbe has pointed out that, according to census figures, the percentages of White and Coloured people who were bilingual decreased between 1951 and 1960. A survey he had conducted among 18 773 White pupils in the early forties had shown that, in parallel- or dual-medium schools, sectional prejudices receded as the children progressed to the higher standards, and the general standard of work actually improved.

In schools for Africans in the Republic, Standard VI is included in primary schools, and the vernacular is used as the medium of instruction (except in the official languages) to the end of that stage. A national conference on Bantu education, convened by the Institute of Race Relations in 1969, found that this arrangement was one of the most potent causes of continuing African mistrust of the system of Bantu education. It had caused a decline in their competence in the official languages, and it seriously handicapped children in learning subjects such as mathematics and science. Very soon after the Transkeian Government assumed control of education in its territory it re-introduced the system used in previous years, in terms of which, after Standard II, one of the official languages, as selected by parents, was gradually substituted for the African language as the medium of instruction. The Zulu Territorial Authority is pressing for a similar arrangement in its area.

Technical and Vocational Education

The Peninsula Technical College for Coloured students was opened at Bellville in 1967. By 1969 it had 68 full-time and 320 part-time students. Five trade schools for apprentices have been established at various centres, which are to have hostels; there are subsidized continuation classes in two other towns; and grants-in-aid are provided for indigent pupils who are attending vocational schools run by churches.

In 1968 the M.L. Sultan Technical College in Durban (for Indians) was declared a college for advanced technical education. It still runs a variety of classes below the Senior Certificate level, but these are gradually to be transferred to Departmental schools.

Thirteen trade schools and nine technical high schools exist for Africans. One of the latter, near Pretoria, provides certain advanced courses. A course for civil and agricultural engineering technicians has been started at a school near Pietersburg; and a technical college is being established at Umtata. Trade instructors are trained at a school near Mafeking. There are five agricultural or forestry schools.

University Education

In mid-1970 the enrolment at universities (including the University of South Africa, which provides correspondence courses) consisted of 73 204 Whites, 1 883 Coloured, 3 472 Asians, and 4 578 Africans.

Of the Non-Whites, 363 Coloured, 812 Asians, and 169 Africans were attending the Universities of Cape Town, Natal, Rhodes, and the Witwatersrand, a high proportion of them in the medical schools of three of these universities.

In 1969, 10 743 Whites, 121 Coloured, 350 Asians, and 315 Africans obtained university degrees or diplomas.

So far as the Non-White universities are concerned, there are Students' Representative Councils only at the Universities of the North and of Zululand and the Natal Medical School. Students of the remaining three universities have rejected plans for such bodies, claiming that the proposed constitutions are too restrictive, or that victimization of members is feared.

Two non-racial student organizations (the National Union of S.A. Students and the University Christian Movement) have been debarred from the Non-White campuses. As predicted by many people in the early fifties, the isolation of most Non-White students has led to a growth of nationalism. In 1969 a (Black) S.A. Students' Organization was formed, its constitution stating that the Black students believed that they had unique problems and aspirations, and that it was necessary for them to consolidate their ranks and reassert their pride and group identity.

CONCLUDING COMMENT

On the basis of the official policy of separate development, Non-White communities are participating in educational matters to a much greater extent than they did before 1948; but all major decisions relating to general policy and financial allocations remain in the hands of White politicians. On the other hand, private members of the White community have been actively discouraged from assisting with the education of Non-Whites, despite the fact that the State is making inadequate provision. This, and the separation of Afrikaans- and English-speaking White children, has inevitably led to a loss of mutual understanding, in a country that all must continue to share, whatever political policies are adopted.

There has been a very large growth in school enrolment; but for every 100 White children in secondary classes there are still only about 73 Indians, 34 Coloured children, and 13 Africans.

For every R100 spent annually on the education of White pupils, roughly R28 is spent on Indians, R26 on Coloured pupils, and R6 on Africans.

Except for Coloured children in Natal and in a few small areas of the Cape (and even in the areas mentioned it is not strictly enforced), education is not compulsory for Non-Whites.

In a paper given at a national conference dealing with education for the Coloured community, convened by the Institute of Race Relations in 1971,[4] Mr M.C. O'Dowd pointed out that in South Africa, the education of even the White group alone comes nowhere near the levels that are provided for the whole population in the United States and Japan. And the White population cannot hope to meet the demand for skilled manpower. In the interests of all, he said, every individual should be educated to the limit of his ability. The conference on Bantu education, referred to earlier, had resolved that economic and social realities demanded that all sections of the population should be educated so as to develop their innate potentials to the fullest extent.

This conference resolved that, 'Although it is recognized that the immediate educational and social needs of the different groups of the South African population may require, at different times and in different places, variations in educational control, provision, and administration, in teaching techniques and in language medium, Conference re-affirms the thesis that education is ultimately *not* divisible. Conference, therefore, looks forward to the time when the administration of education will be on a regional basis, with responsibility for the education of all the people in an area vested in one authority.'

It is significant that the main opposition to the legislative measures that divided the control of education on a racial basis came from those possessing first-hand experience of working together. However, these measures have been put into effect, and one must work in terms of present realities. What should the priorities be in improving South Africa's educacational system?

The first steps should clearly be to vote very greatly increased amounts for Non-White education, so that improved facilities can be offered. The main emphasis should then, perhaps, be placed on encouraging children to stay at school for much longer periods, with adequate scholarship assistance and boarding facilities. It is imperative that as many as possible should proceed to the matriculation stage, to meet the needs of the teaching profession as well as those of industry and other professions. The salaries of teachers must be improved.

4. RR. 147/1970.

Compulsory education must be introduced gradually; but an essential prerequisite is a large increase in the teaching staff.

The provisions relating to mother-tongue education throughout the African primary schools should be revised. Whether they work in the homelands or in towns, Africans need fluency in the official languages and knowledge of the skills of modern Western society, and present arrangements impede this. One of the official languages, most prevalent in the area concerned or as chosen by parents, should be introduced as the medium of instruction at a much earlier stage, the change-over being complete by Standard V or VI (except in the teaching of African languages themselves and, possibly, religion).

While there are practical reasons for having separate primary schools for children of different language groups and background, there seems to be every reason for discontinuing *compulsory* separation at the university level. It should again be left to each university to decide for itself whom to admit. Rigid separation at all stages undoubtedly makes for the growth of exclusive nationalism, which has very real dangers for South Africa. University students, who are likely to become leaders in their respective communities, should be enabled to develop tolerance and mutual understanding by meeting and learning to understand one another's point of view.

Bantu Education

H.J. van Zyl

A widely experienced anthropologist and educationist, Hendrik Johann van Zyl holds a Ph. D. degree from Pretoria University. He is an expert on African education and has written extensively on this subject, especially language manuals and guides for Bantu teachers. He is at present Secretary for Bantu Education in the South African Government.

In South Africa, as throughout the rest of Africa, the early history of education is a history of missionary endeavour. Apart from the significant efforts of the local Dutch Reformed Church, it was education brought by missionary bodies from Germany, Switzerland, France, England, Scotland, Sweden, Finland and the United States of America. It is commonly known that education in the hands of missionaries was a tool of evangelization. The establishment of the Christian faith and education, therefore, went hand in hand. From 1830 to the end of the century these missions established educational institutions spread over the country which were to become household names among the Bantu – *Lovedale* (Church of Scotland), *Healdtown* (Methodist), *Adams* (American), *Kilnerton* (Methodist), *Tigerkloof* (Anglican), *Botshabelo* (German), *Stofberg* (Dutch Reformed) – to mention but a few. These were training centres from which the early Bantu teachers and evangelists went out to start schools and churches.

Until the end of the nineteenth century the missions were mainly dependent upon their own financial resources. From 1904 onwards, however, subsidies from the State were progressively paid to them until, by 1954, just when the present educational system was introduced, over ninety per cent of the cost of 'native education' came from public funds. Control was then exercised by the provincial authorities, each province going its own way and inevitably giving the major part of its attention to White education. There was a lack of direction and purpose but in spite of this, 'native education' advanced and assumed amazing proportions. That so much was achieved in the first half of this century was due not only to the missions, but also to a small band of White professional educators who made the education of the Bantu their life work.

By 1950 it was clear that this task had become too great for the churches and the provinces, and that it was a national task requiring the resources and direction of the central government and the specialist attention of a state department equipped to provide the educational services increasingly being demanded by the Bantu peoples. Then, as now, Bantu parents prized education for their children above everything else and they wanted to be more closely involved in educational matters affecting their children.

The turning point came with the Eiselen Commission of 1949-51 followed by the Bantu Education Act of 1953. The changes brought about as a result of this Act may be summarized as follows:

over-all control passed from the hands of the provinces to the central government;
the professional administration of education became the responsibility of a special state department;
the local control and administration of education was taken over from the churches and placed under representatives of the Bantu communities by means of a school committee for each school and a school board for a number of schools which geographically or for other reasons (*inter alia,* ethnic) belonged together. The Catholic church chose to retain its own system of private church schools without state subsidy. The church still has 466 schools with a total enrolment of 86 000 pupils;
the education system was so constructed that the Bantu themselves could play an increasing part in the education of their own children, both as parents and as teachers. It has become generally known as the Community School System;
education ceased to exist in a vacuum and became closely co-ordinated with a definite and carefully planned policy for the development of the Bantu in all spheres, but in particular through the setting up of separate Bantu homelands.

THE TERMS 'BANTU' AND 'AFRICAN'

The schools which first came into existence were called mission schools. They were subsequently referred to as native schools and the service was called native education. The official present terminology is Bantu schools and Bantu Education. The term *Bantu* has for many years been used by anthropologists, sociologists, historians and, in fact, by all human scientists as a collective name for the African peoples occupying most of the African Continent south of the equator. They were described as a large group of people with related languages and cultural background, as distinct from other similar African groups like the Hamites, Nilotes, Negroes, Arabs etc.

For many years the sophisticated South African Bantu preferred this name to *native, kaffir, black,* and *African.* But to-day, in spite of its former pride of place and the scientific justification for its existence, many Bantu people seem to prefer the less meaningful term African; a phenomenon which may be ascribed to a pan-African ideology which dominated Bantu political activity about a decade ago. In their insistence on this name they are supported by the South African English language newspapers which invariably refer to the Bantu as Africans. Because there is no satisfactory scientific motivation for its use and also no suitable equivalent for the term in the Afrikaans language, Bantu remains the official term. In the different homelands it is being replaced by the particular name of the nation concerned, e.g. Zulu, Xhosa, etc. There is, however, no reason to believe that it will ever fall into disuse as a collective name in official government circles.

DIFFERENT ASPECTS OF BANTU EDUCATION

Growth Under the New System

When the Department of Bantu Education took over in 1954, it inherited about 5 700 schools, just over 21 000 teachers and 869 000 pupils. This represented only 40-45 per cent of the children of school-going age (7-15 years).

It was mainly because of the share parents were given in running the schools that soon after the new system of community schools was introduced, the Department was faced with an 'explosion' of the school population. This placed tremendous strains on the system even though school attendance is still voluntary. In 1970, 16 years later, there were 10 592 schools, 2 834 788 pupils and 48 033 teachers (including the privately paid staff). Because of these pressures, emergency measures such as double sessions in most Sub A & B classes and high pupil-teacher ratios are still in existence. In effect 48 000 teachers are doing the work of 60 000 and one can have nothing but admiration for what they have achieved. As far as can be established from the latest census figures (1970), approximately 80 per cent of the children of school-going age are in fact, attending school.

Courses Offered

The courses offered and the distribution of pupils and students enrolled for each course in 1970 are as follows:

Course	*Percentage of total enrolment*
(i) Lower Primary Course: 4 years (Sub-std A to Std II)	68,7%
(ii) Higher Primary Course: 4 years (Std III to VI)	26,5%
(iii) Junior Certificate: 3 years (Form I to III)	± 4,8% (iii)–(v)
(iv) Matriculation: 2 years (Form IV to V)	
(v) Trade and Vocational Training: 2 to 5 years	
Total	± 100%

(vi) Special schools for handicapped children	11 schools
(vii) Primary Teachers' Training	7 154 students
(viii) Secondary Teachers' Training	773 students
(ix) University Education	
(Bantu Universities)	2 022 students
(University of S.A.)	2 296 students
(x) Medical Training (University of Natal)	157 students
(xi) Engineering (University of the Witwatersrand)	4 students

Primary School Education

The Lower Primary Course : There is good reason for the large percentage of pupils enrolled for this course. The initial primary target for the first ten years was to ensure that every child who could benefit from education, was placed within reach of a school and could enjoy at least four years basic education. In order to accomplish this a rounded off lower primary course extending over four years as shown above has been introduced and where justified by the numbers, it is presented in separate lower primary schools. These schools have been entrusted with considerable success to staffs consisting of women only – including the principal. Due to the outstanding service of these women teachers, the lower primary schools are of the best-run and finest schools in the Department. Pupils who leave school after the lower primary course normally become farmers or workers on farms, in industry and commerce.

The Higher Primary Course : The lower primary course is followed by a higher primary course which extends over a further period of four years (Stds III-VI). This course is intended to prepare pupils for secondary education or to give them sufficient education to become a better class manual worker or, after some in-service training, reliable operatives in factories. The Std VI examination is a public examination and certificates are issued for first, second and third class passes. Those who obtain a third class pass are not allowed to proceed to secondary school. In 1970 approximately 130 000 candidates (including those from the Transkei) were entered for this examination. The curricula for both primary courses comprise the normal subjects taken in any South African school and include *inter alia* the vernacular, the two official languages (Afrikaans and English), arithmetic, science, environment studies, religious education, art and crafts.

Medium of Instruction : The medium of instruction in the primary school, i.e. for the first eight years of schooling is the mother tongue. Before 1954 it was English from Std I upwards, while a small number of schools then used Afrikaans. For the implementation of this sound educational principle, the seven recognized Bantu languages of the Republic were developed into fully-fledged school languages. A comprehensive list of 8 000 terms in each was prepared, thus placing at the disposal of the primary school teacher the terminology he needed for effective teaching. About 90 per cent of these terms were in existence. The list only recognized and gave them their rightful place. Others which were lacking were created by 'Bantuizing' English, Latin or Afrikaans terms or by introducing functional new terms.

With the aid of the main South African publishing houses excellent graded classbooks in all subjects for all standards have been produced in the various Bantu languages, thus advancing the school literature in these languages. Replacing English with the mother tongue as medium was not a popular step and initially there was much opposition against it on the part of teachers. Even today, after it has become clear that mother tongue instruction has contributed greatly towards a good foundation in the primary school resulting in much better achievement in the secondary and high schools, a large proportion of Bantu teachers are still dissatisfied with the policy and would like to return to English or Afrikaans as medium at the Std III level. Indeed, when the Transkei acquired self-rule, they abolished mother tongue education in the higher primary school and re-introduced English as medium. It remains to be seen whether the other homeland authorities will do the same when given the right to decide for themselves.

Problems facing the primary school teacher : In addition to coping with large classes, the primary school teacher in recent years has had to cope with the demands of new syllabuses, particularly in the field of languages, arithmetic and general science (which has taken the place of the former subject, nature study). The syllabuses based closely on the national 'basic' syllabuses, have been worked out in considerable detail in order to guide the teachers, most of whom have no more than the Junior Certificate plus two years professional training as teachers. Teachers' guides have been provided for most subjects while text books, particularly for the first four years, provide teaching material on a lesson-by-lesson basis. It is of interest to note that all text books (including graded classbooks), reading series, etc., are written specially for the department's own needs, and are geared to the syllabuses of Bantu Education.

Secondary Education

The Junior Certificate Course : This is the first post-primary course taken at a secondary school and extends over three years. The three standards are called Forms I, II and III. The syllabuses are prescribed by the Department of Bantu Education but again are based on national 'core' syllabuses which determine minimum requirements to be observed by all education departments in the country. The curriculum provides for a range of 30 school subjects, including commercial subjects, from which a course of seven subjects has to be taken. The vernacular, the two official languages, general science and mathematics are compulsory subjects. The Junior Certificate examination is conducted by the Department at the end of the course and certificates in the first, second and third class are issued. All who pass are allowed to continue their high school studies but where necessary priority is given to first and second class passes.

There has been a steady growth in the number of pupils enrolled for the J.C. course during the past ten years. In 1960 21 200 pupils were enrolled in Form I. After three years about 8 700 wrote the examination and 4 900 or 56,4 per cent passed. In 1970 there were 45 000 in Form I while 25 000 wrote the final examination and 17 200 or 68,8 per cent passed (figures to the nearest hundred).

Further statistics indicate a marked change in the attitude of parents towards secondary education. Whereas the completion of a primary school education was considered quite sufficient a few years ago, now the majority of pupils qualifying to enter the secondary school do in fact go on to Form I. This has caused a major problem of secondary school accommodation, particularly critical in the metropolitan areas such as Soweto, Johannesburg, but also with its effects on the boarding schools in the homelands. There are, at present, 373 secondary schools where the Junior Certificate course can be taken and an average of ten new such schools are registered annually. It is hoped that towards the end of the decade each of the 650 tribal areas will have its own secondary school with boarding establishment.

A survey conducted by the Department has shown that of the 12 450 candidates who passed the Junior Certificate examination in 1968, 4 700 proceeded to Form IV (see later) and 3 700 were enrolled for the Primary Teachers' Course. When one adds to these figures the girls who enter nursing at this level, the boys who join the police force or go on to trade and technical courses for which the entrance qualification is Junior Certificate, then it is clear that the majority of the successful J.C. candidates go on with some type of education or training. The remainder are readily absorbed by commerce and industry both in the homelands and White areas.

The medium of instruction in the secondary school is one or both of the official languages. In an effort to give equal treatment to these languages, two of the four content subjects taken are taught through the medium of Afrikaans and the other two in English. The implementation of this policy depends on the availability of teachers competent to teach in Afrikaans. After eight years of the official languages as subjects in the primary school, pupils normally do not experience much difficulty in switching from the mother tongue to another medium. Because of technical reasons such as the inadequacy of textbooks and other advanced literature in the Bantu languages, the Department is not in a position to introduce mother tongue instruction in classes beyond the primary school. *The Senior Certificate or Matriculation Course*: This is the final school course covered in two years and the classes are known as Forms IV and V. A course of six subjects must be taken from a range of more than 40 school subjects. Each high school offers a choice of 8 to 12 subjects depending on the size of the school and the number of teachers employed. The two official languages are compulsory for all and a third language (which may be a Bantu language) or mathematics must also be taken. Each education department has its own syllabuses which have to comply with requirements laid down by the Joint Matriculation Board. The Department of Bantu Education has not introduced its own matriculation examination yet and schools are allowed to choose between the examinations conducted by the Joint Matriculation Board itself or the Department of National Education. Because of the searchlight of public opinion which constantly rests on Bantu Education it was felt necessary to ensure that there could not be the slightest breath of suspicion that Bantu pupils were being measured by any other standards than those applied to all matriculants. However, there is now increasing support within the department for the idea of setting up its own senior certificate.

The number of pupils attempting the senior certificate course has increased considerably during the past decade. In 1960 there were 182 (25 per cent) candidates who passed the matriculation examination while in 1970 there were 1 842 (65,2 per cent) successful candidates. There are at present 105 schools offering the matriculation course and the standard of high school teaching has improved to such an extent that in 1970 there were 8 schools which obtained 100 per cent passes. At many others 80 per cent or more passed the examination.

The matriculation examination is the only recognized university entrance examination and the standard is therefore set by the Joint Matriculation Board on which all South African universities are represented.

University Training

There are three Bantu universities, viz. Fort Hare for the Xhosas, the University of Zululand for the Zulus and the University of the North for the remaining five national groups. In 1971 the enrolment at these universities was 783, 697 and 888 students respectively, giving a total of 2 368 students. A wide range of courses can be taken under faculties of arts, mathematics and science, education, law, agriculture, commerce and theology. For medical training Bantu students go to the University of Natal where the Wentworth Medical School enrols only Non-White students. There are at present 154 Bantu students undergoing medical training. An average of 10 to 12 doctors qualify each year.

Courses not offered by the Bantu universities can be taken at the so-called 'open' universities of the Witwatersrand and Cape Town with the permission of the Minister of Bantu Education. There are at present (1971) seven students taking engineering at the Witwatersrand University. Approximately 2 400 Bantu students taking correspondence courses are enrolled at the University of South Africa. In 1969 altogether approximately 230 students obtained a first degree.

Training of Teachers

Two teachers' courses are offered by the Department:

The Primary Teachers' Certificate: Junior Certificate plus two years professional training.

The Junior Secondary Teachers' Certificate: Senior Certificate plus two years training.

The Primary Teachers' Certificate may be taken at one of 33 Teachers Training Colleges in various parts of the country. The actual production of primary school teachers in 1970 was just over 3 000. To cope with the annual increases in enrolment, wastage from the existing teaching force because of retirement or resignations, and to eliminate all unqualified teachers over a ten year period, the production should be at least 3 500 per year. The target for 1975 is a minimum of 4 500 primary school teachers per year. The problem of insufficient teachers is clearly one that will remain with the Department for many years yet, particularly if it is taken into consideration that the yearly increase in pupils is creeping beyond the 150 000 mark.

In order to ensure an adequate supply of teachers for the ever increasing number of junior secondary schools the Department has instituted a Junior Secondary Teachers' Course at six of its training institutions. In 1970 131 teachers completed this course which extends over two years after matriculation. By 1975 it is hoped that at least 300 of these teachers will be produced per year. According to all reports those who qualified in 1969 and who have taught for a year are doing very satisfactory work.

The University Teachers' Diploma : This is a post-first-year or a post-degree course offered by the universities. In 1968 the three Bantu universities produced 32 graduate and 66 non-graduate secondary school teachers, whereas the estimated need was in the neighbourhood of 300-400. The introduction of the J.S.T.C. was therefore imperative.

In spite of their seemingly inadequate academic qualifications teachers at all levels are doing remarkably well.

Trade and Technical Training

The Department recognizes that the success of government policy for the Bantu homelands is fundamentally dependent upon the extent to which economic development takes place in these homelands. This in turn is partly dependent on skilled manpower, particularly on the artisan/technician levels. There are various ways in which this training is being provided :

Trade schools : In the building trades (bricklaying, carpentry, etc.) three-year courses following on Std VI are offered, while for motor mechanics and electricians the entrance qualification is Junior Certificate. In other trades the requirements for apprenticeship are completed after the trainee has left the trade school. In terms of government policy the status of artisan is recognized in the homelands only.

Technical schools : These schools offer a technical Junior Certificate which is a three-year course after Std VI and consists of the mother tongue, the two official languages, mathematics, a science, and the technical subject concerned to which 12 hours a week is devoted. The technical subjects include those required for the trade courses already mentioned, plus courses for radiotricians and watchmakers. At the conclusion of these courses the pupils may either continue to the Senior Certificate, take up a trade or take employment in industry at the operator level.

Technical Colleges: As yet there are only two of these colleges, offering post-matric courses for Health Inspectors, Engineering technicians and Survey-technicians. Further post-senior certificate courses will be offered in the near future.

Industrial Training: This is concerned with specific operations or processes required by border industries. There are two approaches to this, viz:

the subsidization of instructors at a training centre set up within a particular factory for workers in that factory;

the setting up of a 'centralized' training centre for a group of factories having similar needs, e.g. for textile factories.

Vocational courses for girls: These are in the main one-year courses in home management, dressmaking, and training as helpers in pre-school institutions for children such as crêches, places of safety, etc.

Psychological Services of the Department

Each year approximately 100 000 pupils at various levels are tested by the officers of this section. A battery of six achievement tests is used and the results are made available to the inspectorate and to schools. They are used,

to identify cases of individual under-achievement;

as a guide to Std VI teachers in helping them to assess the general standard of work of their classes in various subjects;

for vocational guidance purposes and to help with selection for post-primary education.

Other programmes have been developed at the lower levels of the primary school, and most important also at the Form III level, where the matter of selection for matriculation, teacher-training, technical, nursing and other courses arises.

Special Education

There are eleven special schools for physically handicapped Bantu children, with a total enrolment of about 1 200. Most of these schools are subsidized church schools and they cater for blind, deaf, dumb, crippled and cerebral-palsied children, as far as possible on an ethnic basis.

The Language Situation in Bantu Education

Although we have touched on this issue earlier on when dealing with media of instruction, it should be emphasized that the Department of

Bantu Education has to do with a rich and varied language situation. In addition to the seven officially-recognized Bantu languages in South Africa itself – Zulu, Xhosa, Northern Sotho, Southern Sotho, Tswana, Tsonga and Venda – it now has to concern itself with those indigenous to South West Africa (Nama, Ndonga, Kwangale, Herero, etc.) and Lozi in the Caprivi.

In Windhoek there is a Language Bureau which concerns itself with research, terminologies, readers, textbooks in the South West African languages, while at Head Office in Pretoria there is a strong section which does similar work for the Bantu languages of the Republic.

These Bantu languages are not mere local dialects but well-developed written languages, with effective orthographies, language manuals, dictionaries and a considerable literature. It is not generally realized that on the continent of Africa, omitting Arabic and Swahili, there are not more than five languages that are mother-tongues of more than three million people: two of these languages are Zulu and Xhosa.

The Bantu languages of South Africa are not 'primitive', limited means of communication but effective, living, developing languages: they are used by the people for every-day intercourse; they have a flourishing literature, particularly in poetry and drama; they are studied as full university subjects, and last but not least they are used as the media of instruction in Bantu primary schools.

Much has been said and written about mother-tongue instruction, and there may be genuine differences of opinion as to the stage when Western languages as media should be introduced in Africa, but there can be no doubt that it is necessary to give the child the foundation of his education in his own mother tongue. Education is more than an intellectual exercise: at the primary stage it should concern the emotional development of the child as well, and language is inextricably bound up with this.

Although the home language is given its rightful place of honour in the education of the Bantu child, this does not mean that English and Afrikaans are neglected. On the contrary. It is fully realized that these are imperative as tools of communication in the wider community of South Africa, as 'bread and butter' languages and as windows to the outside world.

From the moment the Bantu child enters school he starts to learn both English and Afrikaans. Throughout most of his primary school career he spends four hours a week on each of these languages.

Homeland Development and Decentralization

As we have said at the outset, the basic purposes of the Department of Bantu Education were to involve the Bantu themselves more deeply, both as professionals and as parents in the process and activities of education. Education was to be linked closely with the general development programmes aimed at greater self-realization for the various Bantu peoples.

Out of the experience of the last fifteen years has come a solid core of leaders, trained and responsible, both of local administrators of education and of professional educationalists, who have now taken on their shoulders further responsibilities. With the exception of the Zulus, a separate administration has now been set up for each homeland, with specific government responsibilities, among which one of the most important is education and cultural matters. For Bantu Education this has been a perfectly natural and logical step. It is the outcome of the planned objectives laid down in the Eiselen Report and the Bantu Education Act, and a recognition of the importance of education in the creation of self-reliant Bantu peoples.

Separate education departments have been set up for the Xhosa of the Ciskei (King William's Town), the Tswana (Mafeking), Southern Sotho (Witsieshoek), Northern Sotho (Pietersburg), Venda (Sibasa), Tsonga (Giyani) and for Ovamboland. Each of these departments is the responsibility of a Bantu executive councillor, and is headed by a White director assisted by not more than three White senior inspectors. The circuit inspectors, each responsible for 18-20 000 pupils, are all Bantu. They are experienced officers with years of sound training and experience behind them and the work in the field is safe in their hands.

The present distribution of schools, pupils and teachers in the homelands and White areas is as follows:

Area	*Schools*	*Pupils*	*Teachers*
(a) Tswana	643	252 207	4 093
(b) Northern Sotho	712	260 335	4 163
(c) Southern Sotho	20	8 569	113
(d) Ciskei (Xhosa)	529	156 467	2 563
(e) Zulu (not entrusted with partial self-government yet)	1 331	398 717	6 516
(f) Matshangana	201	60 190	934

Area	Schools	Pupils	Teachers
(g) Venda	246	69 492	1 070
(h) Transkei (Xhosa)	1 689	418 590	7 350
Total in Bantu Areas	5 371	1 624 567	26 802
(i) *White Area*	4 755	1 124 252	19 239
Grand Total	10 126	2 748 819	46 041
These figures include the following:			
Church schools	466	85 969	1 992

Financing of Bantu Education

It is government policy that all sections of the population should pay towards the education of their children. The provincial administrations, which are responsible for educational services for Whites only, impose a provincial tax and by it collect a substantial amount from the White population. A considerable portion of the funds so collected is used for education and should this prove to be inadequate, the taxes are invariably raised. Education is free and if a province spends lavishly on education, providing *inter alia* for high teachers' salaries, expensive school buildings, free books, etc., it is because the population is able and prepared to pay for it.

The same policy applies to the Bantu population. A separate Bantu Education Account has been established which is credited with a fixed amount from consolidated revenue, all direct taxes paid by the Bantu as well as certain other amounts which have been approved from time to time including over-head administration costs and salaries paid to White officials, inspectors and teachers which will decrease as homeland educational services progressively become the sole responsibility of Territorial Authorities.

For the financial year 1971/72 a total amount of R70 856 000 was made available for educational services in the Republic (including homelands), S.W.A., the Eastern Caprivi Strip, the Transkei, special education in all areas and university training (R4,48 m). This amount will be augmented by capital expenditure on school buildings by urban local authorities in White areas, the S.A. Bantu Trust (in homelands), owners of farm and factory schools, etc., bringing the total expected expenditure to about R75 million and a unit cost for primary and secondary education of approximately R25 or more.

The above sum provided for in the budget is derived from various sources, viz., a basic contribution from Revenue (R14 500 000), general and income tax payable by the Bantu (estimated to be R13 000 000 of which R6 000 000 is expected to come from income tax), special provision for South West Africa (R3 405 000), provision from Revenue for Special Education and the Caprivi (R807 000), separate provision for the Transkei (R9 580 000), cost of administration including White officials (R5 965 000), special advance to be derived from sales tax (R21 835 000).

Each homeland department budgets for itself but the funds are provided through the Bantu Education Account.

It is true that much more is spent per capita on White Education but this does not mean that Bantu Education is of an inferior nature. The comparatively limited funds are spent judiciously so that satisfactory standards are maintained. Luxurious buildings, which may be desirable but not indispensable, are almost non-existent. Good conventional utility school buildings are erected by Bantu workmen at reduced cost. Furniture is provided by factories in the homelands at a reasonable price. Teachers' salaries are lower than those paid to White teachers, but are determined by the economic position of the Bantu population. The adequacy of teachers' remuneration is in accordance with what it costs them to maintain an upper-middle class position in their community. The position is not static and changes continuously, however; the stage may soon be reached when Bantu economy will elevate the teachers to the same level as their counterparts in other population groups. If oil were to be discovered in a homeland, they might even be better off than all other teachers! It is interesting to note that the provision in 1960 was £9 400 000 or R18 800 000 with a per capita expenditure of R12,46. The maximum salary for a qualified high school assistant teacher with a degree was R1 540 in 1960 and R2 520 in 1970.

General Achievement

The following extract from the introductory remarks in the Annual Report (1969) of the Department of Bantu Education dealing with general achievement is of particular interest. Attention is drawn to certain matters, the significance of which is not always observed.

'The Department remains satisfied that good standards are being maintained in its schools, and attributes this to the application of proved teaching methods and its specialized approach to the work. Apart from the examination results there are other irrefutable proofs that the education service, in spite of its shortcomings, is equipping Bantu youth with certain basic abilities of which any education department rightly can be proud and which compare favourably with similar achievements anywhere in the world. We wish to draw attention to but a few aspects where the Department has achieved particular success, aspects which today are often regarded by education authorities as being too unimportant to warrant serious attention, but which usually are the basic requirements that, for example, are demanded in practical life of the young official in his first post.'

Bantu pupils who have reached matriculation standard, or have completed their training as teachers in a two-year course taken after Standard VIII, show proof of the following:

They have clear, neat, uniform and easily legible handwritings that are the envy of many a person and for which employers have the greatest appreciation. There is daily evidence of this.

They are in a position to write their own difficult mother-tongue well, fluently and correctly, and also of course to speak it faultlessly. In addition to their own language most of them are also able to converse freely in at least one other Bantu language.

They have no reason to be ashamed of their knowledge of both the official languages, whether in written or in spoken form; they can boast of a bilingualism that has frequently surprised many a hearer.

When they work with figures they are neat and accurate, to such an extent that they have already gained recognition for the outstanding quality of the work they perform in this sphere.

They have a sound understanding of any instructions in Afrikaans and English which they may be required to study, and can carry out these instructions. In 1970, the Department of Statistics for the first time made extensive use of Bantu teachers as census officials and the results were extremely satisfactory.

As is fairly generally acknowledged, the Bantu has achieved considerable success in the field of choral singing.

There is general praise for those pupils who leave school on the completion of Junior Certificate (Standard VIII) to be trained, for example, as nurses, to take up an apprenticeship in a trade or employment as factory workers in industry. According to the evidence of employers they measure up in every respect to the expectations that have been entertained of them. It is even maintained that the Bantu woman factory worker with a good school background can be compared with the best of her kind in the world.

Those pupils who leave school before reaching Standard VI become useful workers who can read, write and do figures, while those who complete Standard VI become employees who rise to the position of foremen, to whom considerable responsibilities are often delegated.

Boys who qualify as artisans (particularly in the building industry) give proof in practice that they are capable of producing top-grade workmanship. In the Bantu homelands, Bantu artisans solely are responsible for the erection of buildings and their work compares very favourably with any other building work.

At the three vigorous young universities 2 400 students are receiving higher education – a further contribution to the preparation of Bantu youth for playing their part in progressive communities in each homeland.

Editor's Note: In terms of the Bantu Education Account Abolition Act (1972), the separate Bantu Education Account was abolished and the method of financing this educational service changed. In terms of the Act, Bantu Education is now financed from the Consolidated Revenue Fund by way of a Bantu Education Vote for White areas and a separate budget for each homeland Department of Education and Culture. Direct Bantu taxes collected will be divided *pro rata* among the different homeland governments for general development purposes.

Sources

W.M.M. Eiselen, Unpublished speech to Bantu Education Board, 23rd March, 1970.

K.B. Hartshorne, Unpublished notes prepared for Department of Bantu Education, 1970.

H.J. van Zyl, Unpublished notes, Department of Bantu Education, 1970.

Bantu Education Journal 1960-61, Department of Information, Pretoria.

Report: *Commission on Native Education (1949-51)*, Gov. Printer, Pretoria.

Annual Report 1969, Department of Bantu Education, Gov. Printer, Pretoria.

The Verkramp/Verlig Dichotomy

The Concepts ,Verkramp' and ,Verlig'

W.J. de Klerk

Willem Johannes de Klerk is Professor of Philosophy and Pastoral Psychology at the Potchefstroom University for Christian Higher Education. A brilliant speaker and original thinker, he has attained international recognition for his views on contemporary socio-political trends in South Africa. He is one of Afrikanerdom's most objective students of separate development.

The two Afrikaans terms 'verlig' and 'verkramp' have become internationally known. It is difficult to translate the term 'verkramp'. The nearest word in English would be 'cramped' or 'ultra-conservative'. The German word 'verkrampfen' also conveys something of the meaning of the Afrikaans word, i.e. 'to become rigid or motionless as the result of a cramp'. The word is used in a metaphorical sense to indicate a specific outlook on life. Expressing an attribute, the word becomes 'verkrampte'.

'Verlig' may be translated by 'enlightened' (either a person or point of view). However, in the context of South African politics, the word was originally used in a negative sense. Used attributively the word becomes 'verligte'. The original Afrikaans terms have been used throughout this article.

When writing this article I had a choice of two methods, both of which, from a psychological point of view, have their respective pros and cons.

The first method was to write in vague and evasive terms, to formulate problems and to leave it to the reader to draw his own conclusions.

The second method, and the one I decided to follow well aware of the risks involved in such a choice, was to take up a direct standpoint, to make a clear choice and to commit myself to an *a priori* at the risk of being accused of dogmatism.

This article was written from a theoretical, or shall we say philosophical, angle. It operates on the basis of attitudes and points of view rather than on the basis of empiric data. At the root of facts and policies there is always a central motive, a guiding idea, and it was this particular aspect which I wanted to bring into focus. Consequently, I have avoided detail and tried only to indicate lines of thought.

I have taken as framework for my article two premises which can be briefly summarized as follows:

1. As the original formulator of the terms 'verkramp' and 'verlig' (words which have subsequently also been used in the world press in referring to South African political concepts), I have used these two words in this article in their original meaning. With these two words I aimed at a formulation of two viewpoints or schools of thought in South Africa:

'Verkramp' is the word which designates the attitude and school of thought manifesting itself in hostility towards all that is new; an attachment to the existing; a resistance to renewal and passion to continue with and extend patterns belonging to the past; negation, condemnation and suppression of new demands which in the march of history continually lead to new situations calling for creativeness and adaptation. In short: 'Verkramp' is a traditionalistic attitude which elevates tradition as such to principle and norm.

'Verlig' represents the other extreme. This term has a positive meaning, but when I originally used the word, I did so in a negative sense.

I want to state clearly that 'verlig' as such, according to the meaning attributed to the word in the languages of the world, is not a suspect concept, but in South African politics the word had originally the negative meaning of leftist, anti-traditional, a propelling towards renewal and progression in so radical a manner that existing social patterns and recognized frameworks of principle were thrown overboard.

This school of thought aspires to unprincipled openness; to compromise and pragmatism; to a reckless innovation of new patterns based on experimental thinking.

Although the word *'verlig'* originally conveyed a negative meaning, it gradually acquired a positive content in the South African sphere. For that reason I will use the word in its *positive* sense.

A distinction must be made between 'verkramp' and integrationist on the one hand, between 'verkramp' and 'verlig' on the other.

Applied to the context of race relations in South Africa, 'verkramp' is the rigid and inflexible traditionalism which pushes to extremes the pattern of separation of races on the basis of a master/servant, more/less relationship and which seeks the perpetuation of this relationship. Integration is the concept of complete or absolute integration of the nations in South Africa. The identity of nations is of secondary importance – of primary importance is the establishment of a new society of all races, in the synthesis of one nation.

As first premise: I reject – and so do numerous other South Africans, Whites and Non-Whites alike – both these concepts.

2. I want to advocate a third possibility in regard to the relationship between South African races, which may be termed *equality in diversity.*

The two main fundamentals here are: The equality of peoples and nations and the diversity of peoples and nations. These two concepts are reciprocal, viz. diversity determines the character of equality and the measure of equality is determined by the degree of diversity.

I shall now proceed to a more detailed discussion of these premises.

I shall, in the first instance, give a critical survey of the 'verkrampte' attitude; then of the integration attitude and, finally, I propose to set out the third school of thought, equality in diversity, which may be applied to race relations in South Africa.

'VERKRAMP' AND RACE RELATIONS IN SOUTH AFRICA

I intend analysing this on the basis of four concepts:

1. A racial theory of superior/inferior is at the root of the 'verkrampte' attitude

This is a hierarchical conception of nations based mainly on the following three motives:

The motive of colour, the chauvinistic motive and the motive of civilization.

The motive of colour. Colour, in the context of 'verkrampte' thinking, is a barrier between nations, ordained by God; miscegenation across this colour bar is a *per se* transgression of the existing structure of nations and as such of principle and divine ordinance. The Coloureds, to the 'verkrampte' person, are of a lower order, intellectually and otherwise. The

Coloureds, to this school of thought, are, in contrast with the Whites who are the bearers of Christianity, exponents of an anti-Christian way of life. The curse of Noah, pronounced upon his son Ham, is applicable to the Coloured nations. Miscegenation is a betrayal of identity, as being White is seen as the conclusive factor of identity. The genetic results of miscegenation are thought to lead to a biologically inferior race.

The chauvinistic motive. In 'verkrampte' thinking, the chauvinistic motive functions in the form of a disguised 'herrenvolkism' where the own nation and the purity of the own race relies on superiority of the own nation. A clear distinction must be made between chauvinism and a sound and an essential nationalism which endeavours to preserve and develop its own particular national identity.

The motive of civilization. This motive also plays a role in the racial theory of the 'verkrampte' in that generalization is brought into play and all Coloureds are stereotyped as uncivilized, immature, and for the Whites, as belonging to a foreign culture.

This racial theory is untenable and unacceptable and is explicitly rejected by the majority of South Africans. It is not supported by biblical principles or Christian traditions. It is not borne out by psychological, sociological and genetic research. It does not find support in the practical situation.

Colour and chauvinism should never form the basis of South African racial policy and where these motives become evident, they should be resolutely opposed, as has been done up to the present.

The motive of civilization holds good up to a certain point, but it is wrong to generalize as the standard of civilization amongst the Non-White races is steadily being raised and as there is abundant proof of their gradual acceptance of Western patterns of living and thinking. It is perhaps necessary to comment on the question of whether or not all races command the same potentialities for development. Answers to this question reveal a major irreconcilability. In refutation of the 'verkrampte' attitude, it does, however, seem to be scientifically tenable to state that racial differences are basically determined by culture, education and environment and not by genetics. In the words of Klineberg: 'As the environmental opportunities of different racial or ethnic groups become more alike, the observed differences in test results also tend to disappear.'[1]

1. *Race and Psychology*, p. 24.

It would appear that different races command equal potentialities, although they stem from different cultures.

2. The 'verkrampte' conception of guardianship is suspect

The 'verkrampte' explains guardianship as a perpetual subordination of the Non-Whites to the Whites in a father/child relationship. That is, the Non-White is a child, must remain a child and must be kept a child because his created state is that of a child. It is the duty of the White guardian to guide this child and, up to a point, to care and think for him. It is in the interests of the Non-Whites (and Whites?) to live in this state of guardianship. Although gradual emancipation is advocated, the granting of self-government is postponed.

This concept of guardianship is false. In the 'verkrampte' school of thought, this is a pious word for domination and control.

This does not imply that guardianship as such is wrong. The correct view of guardianship, which is also the one generally accepted in South Africa, is that guardianship is a responsible attitude of Christian charity and, in accordance with this, a more developed nation (White) accepts responsibility for a less developed nation (Non-White). Seen in this context, the motive of guardianship is education and training in order to guide the less developed nation to maturity and co-existence. This concept of guardianship is the one generally accepted in South Africa and this fact is borne out by the policy of the South African government which plans to give full autonomy to the various Bantu nations as soon as they are ready to accept this responsibility.

3. The third concept on which the 'verkrampte' attitude is based, is that of discrimination

Here groups are stereotyped on the basis of the underlying racial theory. In the 'verkrampte' camp it is argued that preferential treatment should be given to Whites on the basis of their membership of the White nation. That this type of preferential treatment creates double standards, does not trouble the 'verkrampte' person.

By double standards is meant the fact that the Non-Whites have to be satisfied with less, as regards quantity and quality, in the different spheres of labour, wages, public amenities, cultural activities and recreational facilities.

There is a sharp reaction against this type of attitude in South Africa.

There is a growing insistence on equal treatment, equal facilities and equal opportunities for all in South Africa. This equality must be qualified as an equality that does not eliminate diversity; equality must take into account the factual situations of differences in standard of living and civilization.

Considerable prejudice still has to be overcome and much capital and energy will have to be expended by Whites and Non-Whites to wipe out forms of intentional and unintentional discrimination which have become part and parcel of our history. With this is bound up skill and economic capacity – where these are not equal it follows that a higher and lower standard of living should not summarily be labelled as discrimination. Fortunately, it is official policy in South Africa to open up all possible channels to enable the Non-Whites to attain full and equal development. However, this development remains a process which is co-determined by the initiative and planning of the Non-Whites.

4. To isolate the various groups of the population, is a favourite idea of the 'verkrampte'

The existence of a structure of parallelism in South Africa, i.e. a pattern of segregation between Whites and Non-Whites in regard to residential areas, transport services, places of amusement, education, etc., is part of South African tradition. The continued existence of this pattern cannot summarily be called 'verkramp'. The fundamental reasons for this tradition are that it affords protection against friction, insult, violence and embarrassment to two groups who in general stem from different cultural backgrounds and maintain different standards of living. It also guarantees order and facilitates social organization and, in many cases, both groups prefer this arrangement. It also serves to preserve separate identities and is, as indicated, up to a certain point, based on the standard of civilization and numerical proportions.

The 'verkrampte' school of thought, however, elevates this to a principle by insisting on the rigorous application of this structure of parallelism without any exceptions whatsoever. Here again, the motive of colour is the deciding factor.

A tendency to assume that the essence of co-existence is communication, and that it is absurd to push isolation to extremes, is spreading in South Africa. Similar interests, adaptability, civilization and cultural and social standards are more and more accepted as determinants of patterns of contact.

Communication will always have to take into account the South African tradition of parallelism and non-integration as a basic principle for racial peace.

In the discussion of these four concepts, I have endeavoured to draw a profile of the 'verkrampte' attitude and to indicate the answers to and criticism of this school of thought.

The reader may now rightly ask: How strong is the 'verkrampte' attitude in South Africa?

Although never a majority attitude, the 'verkrampte' school of thought was stronger a decade or two ago. Today its only adherents are isolated individuals and small groups. There is not a single political party in South Africa which subscribes to the 'verkrampte' concept as set out above. The traditions of the Afrikaner do not include the racial rejection of the Non-Whites. Although there were numerous clashes between Whites and Non-Whites in the history of South Africa, the basic tendency was one of openheartedness and readiness to further the development of the Non-Whites.

And yet a certain amount of estrangement did take place. This can, in part, be attributed to a reaction against integrationists who at times played an active role in our history with no regard for the feelings, culture and standard of living of the two parties. Reaction often causes the pendulum to swing to an extreme opposite. Such a swing gave rise to the 'verkrampte' way of thinking. On the other hand, the Afrikaner is very strongly tradition-bound. Under the influence of the Anglo-Saxon world of the eighteenth and nineteenth centuries, during which time South Africa was part of the British Empire and under the political influence of Britain, the Afrikaner accepted the racial concepts which were prevalent during this period of colonization. A small minority of Afrikaners is still being fed from this climate of thought and has not yet experienced the influence of the twentieth century on race relations, and this also gives rise to ultra-conservatism.

Fear also plays a part in the 'verkrampte' attitude – fear of being wiped out as a result of the fact that the Whites form a small minority; fear of the 'uhuru' of Africa and extremistic 'Black powers'; fear of losing an identity which was only gained through much hard work after many years of struggle against Anglo-Saxon domination. The 'verkrampte' attitude is thus essentially a form of self-preservation.

It can thus not be denied that there are Afrikaners who, sometimes wittingly, sometimes unwittingly, sometimes in regard to one aspect, sometimes all along the line, show a tendency towards adhering to the 'verkrampte' school of thought, but it also cannot be denied that they meet with very strong opposition.

What can be emphatically denied is that the majority of Afrikaners subscribe to these concepts or that government policy is based on a 'verkrampte' attitude. I mainly accentuated the 'verkrampte' attitude as conceived by the Afrikaners. A considerable number of English-speaking South Africans have been and are inclined towards the 'verkrampte' attitude, although this concept has been formulated in different ways. Superficially, these formulations create the impression of being liberal, but a closer analysis reveals the presence of the above-mentioned four motives in a disguised form.

The last twelve years have seen a radical swing away from 'verkrampte' elements. In political, cultural and academic circles there is a perceptible change in attitude which manifests itself in antagonism towards the 'verkampte'. And this is also true of the man in the street and especially of the younger generation. A certain measure of resistance is still encountered on some points, even in statements of policy by authorities. However, there is a clearly perceptible movement in the direction of true, more realistic and equal racial and human relations. Government policy, public opinion and the acceleration of this movement under the influence of various leaders in public opinion, justify the statement that there is no future in South Africa for the 'verkrampte' school of thought. It seems appropriate to draw a conclusion at this stage:

The concept 'verkramp' as used in this article in relation to race relations, is fundamentally, practically, and seen from our situation, unacceptable, without any reservation whatsoever. 'Verkramp', in the context of this article, was never a general manifestation in South Africa although tendencies of the attitude appeared and still appear, sometimes in good faith, very seldom in bad faith; the tendency of thought in influential circles is a swing away from 'verkrampte' stagnation. Many South Africans have no ties with the 'verkrampte' school of thought, others are straining hard to break the ties with which they are bound to this way of thinking, while only a very few place their hopes on this concept.

INTEGRATION AND RACE RELATIONS IN SOUTH AFRICA

There are variations among integrationists, the main difference being the degree of integration.

The exponents of complete integration desire to abolish the national barriers of the various nations in South Africa, and their concept is based on an anti-national motive which wants to substitute humanity for nationality.

According to them, a separate nationalism for every nation in a multi-racial community is impossible. Therefore, it is necessary to create a constitutional nationalism to oppose individual nationalism. The ideal is gradual growth in the direction of a civilized Western community in a single state in which one and all enjoy political rights. The exponents of partial integration are prepared to recognize national identities. The various nations must, however, enjoy joint political authority (to be determined with the aid of various formulae) in a single country under a single state, which, despite the various nations, is to rely on economic, social and political integration.

While the 'verkrampte' concept relies on a racial theory leading to an extremistic separatist ideology, the integrationist school of thought relies on a racial theory leading to an extremistic integration ideology of compulsory equalization and unification. The 'verkrampte' theory disregards the close connections between the nations of South Africa and the integration theory disregards the fundamental diversity of nations in South Africa.

The latter approach is unacceptable for the reasons stipulated below:

1. The diversity of nations in South Africa is no theory of ideology, but an objective fact. Should we tamper with this fact in imitation of the ideology of equalization prevalent elsewhere in the world, we would be tampering with reality in South Africa. The diversity of nations is an empiric fact which cannot be manipulated by ideology. In accordance with our Christian view of life, we maintain this empiric fact as a principle.

2. The human race is an entity, but this does not mean sameness or similarity. The identity of a nation, as expressed in its own language, own culture and country, should be maintained. Integration aims at bringing together cultures which are not assimilable. This does not mean that there is a total absence of common characteristics. The Bantu culture has on

many points been influenced by Western culture. Separate identities, cannot, however, be wiped out by these common elements.
3. Territorial separation is one of the essential factors which counteracts the undesirable mixing which threatens the various national identities. Where there is considerable difference in the cultures and standards of civilization of nations, the idea of a multi-racial nation in a single country can only lead to friction, disorderliness and exploitation. The independence, freedom and self-expression of Whites and Non-Whites would be seriously impaired by integration.
4. In the interim, before complete territorial separation has been finalized, steps should be taken to eliminate friction in the multi-racial society and to afford protection to the various nations and their cultures.
5. Negation of the diversity of nations by the introduction of artificial and forced integration has never yet been successful. Where attempts have been made to integrate, racial conflicts have continued to exist to a greater or lesser extent and this led to discrimination, the swallowing up of the one group by the other, or the suppression of justifiable national aspirations.
6. The differences in numbers, standards of civilization and socio-economic-technical development are so marked that integration cannot bear positive fruits but can only delay the independence and development of the Non-White.

HOW STRONG IS THE INTEGRATIONIST ELEMENT IN SOUTH AFRICA?

The results of political elections have up to now always shown a clear rejection of the concept of integration. The historical social pattern accepted by Whites and Non-Whites, is that of segregation. The leading political parties have always declared themselves against complete integration. Non-White leaders in all spheres of life have at all levels indicated that the Non-White ideal is still independence of the nation in its own territory. The major Bantu nations in South Africa have indeed made much headway on the road to independence and the realization of national identity.

There are groups and individuals, also amongst the Non-Whites, who are fierce supporters of integration. However, their ideas seems to gather little momentum.

In conclusion to this section, I want to formulate the viewpoint of integration in nearly the same words used to formulate 'verkramp' : *That which has been indicated as integration in race relations, is in principle and practice, and from our situation, unacceptable; integration has never been a general manifestation in South Africa, although minorities have become adherents to this theory.*

THE THIRD BASIS FOR RACE RELATIONS IN SOUTH AFRICA

I have already, in my criticism of previous viewpoints, drawn attention to many of the elements of this third concept. In conclusion, I am going to draw the broad outlines of this concept. You can call the point of view which follows 'verlig'. This meaning, with reference to race relations, is being increasingly attached to this word in South Africa.

The third basis for race relations may be termed *equality in diversity.* It is based on three premises already discussed in this article.

1. The preservation of the diversity of nations in South Africa as national identities with their own cultural capacities and territorial boundaries. In contradistinction to the world's ideology of integration, and its passion for its particular type of equality, we regard the diversity of people as a system which allows for individual group identity, freedom, national development, for the fulfilment of all peoples in South Africa. The history of Africa has shown that nationalism tends to be exclusive. There is a call for Africanization in opposition to pseudo-Europeanization.
2. Equality in diversity demands the elimination of discrimination; of subjection of one nation to another; of continued guardianship which does not lead to independence and freedom. Equality in diversity means equal treatment, equal opportunities to develop in the political, economic and social fields. The emphasis on social justice is a universal appeal to which we must give increased attention. South Africa must take note of the fact that the climate of present times calls for equal rights; that White supremacy and colour prejudice will not be tolerated; that double standards and yardsticks will not be accepted. Woe to us if we disregard these appeals. We reject integration but the alternative is not perpetual discrimination.
3. We have to accept the facts of the present situation, viz. that there are numerous inequalities with regard to standards of development. In this context the Whites are called upon to stimulate the less developed nations to full development and, in just ways, to lead them to full independence.

These three premises find embodiment in the following:

(a) The determined development, in all fields, of the countries of the various Bantu nations. This includes, *inter alia,* the consolidation and expansion of their territories in order to accommodate the nations; economic, agricultural and industrial development; professional development in all sectors; general educational development not only to expand their own culture but also to enable them to integrate Western culture with their own.

(b) Full political independence as soon as a country reaches a stage of development where it is able to shoulder the task of self-governmnet.

(c) Maintenance and expansion of inter-state co-existence as independent nations in partnership and co-operation.

(d) Elimination of discrimination while Whites and Non-Whites are still living together in one country, and later in inter-state and inter-group communication between the various independent countries. It will be difficult to eliminate the pattern of parallelism at the various levels in the first-mentioned stage, as this pattern ensures law and order and obviates conflict and exploitation, as well as furthering the development and preservation of the various identities. The elements of discrimination and injustice of one group against the other, should, however, be replaced by a pattern of equal opportunities within the framework of diversity.

(e) Emphasis should be placed on interaction, communication and participation at various levels so that connectedness, common interests, interdependence and co-operation can be realized in spite of differences. The form of co-existence should not be negative, humiliating, 'cramped' and discriminatory. The immediate task for White, Brown and Black is to prove that they are willing to live and build together in a spirit of democratic justice. The Whites in South Africa are not colonialists. Like the Coloureds and Bantu, they are of Africa, and with the Coloureds and Bantu have a right to their fatherland. I want to emphasize that the Afrikaner nation is of Western origin, but is *of Africa*, and its people are not part of a colonial settlement. As the other peoples of Africa we know no other fatherland and therefore we are inseparably connected to the other nations of Africa and with them we have to seek our destiny.

(f) The national-cultural identity of certain groups such as the Indians and Coloureds, who are more or less permanent inhabitants of the

> Whites' country, should be maintained. But here also an arrangement should be made to enable these groups to participate in political and economic activities and to guarantee their political and economic growth within the framework of diversity.

This third concept of race relations is the road to which South Africa is turning. Progress has been made in connection with the development of the Bantu homelands, legislation has been passed in connection with the future independence of these countries and in the furthering of healthy race relations based on human rights. Public opinion in South Africa favours the above-mentioned six points and the authorities are continually stimulated to extend our relationship policies on the basis and within the framework of equality in diversity.

It would be naïve to suggest that this theory does not encounter opposition. There is the ideological resistance of the 'verkrampte' and integrationist schools of thought; there are resistances stemming from the practical situation with its complicated racial composition. Some of these problems are dealt with in other articles.

My article is a philosophical analysis of the situation in regard to race relations in South Africa. I have tried not to be dogmatic, but realistic; not to be opportunistic but to point out fundamental principles; not to present a rationalization or apology but an honest report; not to suggest a compromise, but to indicate a third solution based on the best principled methods of approach and common sense.

This article is an attempt to reveal the untenability of the extreme poles.

I can declare with a clear conscience that South Africa has not accepted a 'verkrampte' attitude in regard to race relations and is also avoiding the chaos of the integrationist point of view. We have embarked on, and are gaining momentum in the development of our own great society, a society based on equality in diversity.

Trends in Afrikaner Race Attitudes

Otto Krause

A brilliant writer and a perspicacious observer of local politics, Otto Krause is well-known for his objective, original and avant garde style of evaluating South African political affairs. He read Law at Stellenbosch, Oxford and Yale, and has travelled widely in African and Western Countries. He edited the former News/Check *magazine for many years.*

South African politics is perhaps best likened to a game of three-dimensional chess. It is a complicated matter of interrelationships affecting interrelationships, and one cannot look merely to one surface without taking the others into account. The game is constantly upset by moves from unexpected quarters.

Possibly the most besetting harm done to South African politics is that too many people, within South Africa and even more so without, view it as operating on one single surface. White South Africans, looking only to the power framework of the White democracy, see *that* as the one that counts. Too often do they forget that even within White society there are two distinct sets of politics, that of Afrikanerdom and that of English-speaking South Africa. The outside observer, seeing South Africa as a whole, as a country of many people shading from White through to Black, assumes too easily that *that* is the operative plane and immediately puts upon it the stamp of conventional politics throughout the world – the usual pattern of Right shading into Left. And of course according to this view White is Right and Black is Left.

The facts are different. South Africa, as a country of many peoples, is in truth a country of many sets of politics; all are distinct, and are becoming more and more distinct as new power bases are erected, and yet all interact with each other. Within each grouping, English, Afrikaner, Indian and the various African groupings – the Coloureds are perhaps the one exception here – there is a spectrum of opinion which relates to the conventional left/right pattern *as well as to* the question of the maintenance of the group structure.

Thus an Afrikaner Nationalist can be liberal in his outlook about what he feels the character of Afrikaner society should be and also liberal in his attitude towards Non-Whites, but the latter exactly because he is fiercely conservative when it comes to the preservation of his nationhood. An English liberal may be similarly jealous about the preservation of English rights. A Black nationalist most likely will be liberal in that he looks to the modernization of his people, yet hotly exclusivist – and hence conservative – when he looks to the opportunities of Black power.

So are attitudes determined by what one wants for one's group and by what one feels the group relationship should be towards others. And the Coloureds are possibly the exception because they, least of all, look to maintaining their group as such . . . By and large the Coloureds want in with the Whites, but if the door is not opened they could well fall back into the typical group political pattern of South Africa, differing among themselves about internal group matters and lining up otherwise when interacting with other groups.

SOUTH AFRICAN PARTICULARITY

South African politics, then, are something unique – a fragmented system of baffling, ever-changing patterns. They refuse to fit into the conventional view of politics, and this can only be misleading. Yet to complicate matters further, there is no denying that the conventional left/right view imported from outside *does* affect many South Africans in their thinking about themselves . . .

However, it was to describe this unique South African situation, and with particular reference to Afrikaner politics, that the new coinages *verlig* and *verkramp* of Prof. Wimpie de Klerk of Potchefstroom were taken up so readily in common political parlance in the years after 1966. These words have turned out to be most useful labels or instruments for describing the special kind of politics in South Africa, and they have already gathered themselves an impressive content, emotionally as well as intellectually.

Moreover, their usage has spilled over from Afrikanerdom and led to their being applied to other groups – and applied accurately, for the fact is that other groups' politics are or are likely to be very similar to Afrikanerdom's in the special South African context.

To plumb the meaning of *verlig* and *verkramp* and their meaning for South African politics it is perhaps best to look to the competition for power in South African society – for that is, I feel, the key to much understanding of politics – and to recent political happenings and the considerations attached to them.

POWER COMPETITION

Contrary to what first meets the eye, the competition for power in the Republic is essentially a battle between English-speaking and Afrikaners, with Britain having been in the wings to a lesser and lesser degree ever since Union in 1910. At first sight it is of course natural to say that competition for power should be between Black South Africa and White South Africa, for after all Blacks greatly outnumber Whites in a ratio of 4 : 1, and they seemingly have a whole continent behind them. This racial view of where the power struggle should lie does not however fit the tough fact.

That is that White South Africa's power, in real terms, is basically unchallenged – despite all the talk and all the propaganda. White power has been challenged in minor ways in the past – hark back to 1960 – and it will be increasingly challenged in future; but for now the truth is that White South Africa can afford the luxury (one may say) of competing among itself for power, and moreover in such a way as would radically change the relationship between Black and White.

White South Africa is relatively strong enough to do so; it is furthermore very concerned with doing so, for much is at stake. At stake is the control of South Africa, with all its riches; and the prize and the circumstances are such that both English and Afrikaners want to and can reach out for that control.

This is clearly the prime motivation of White South African politics. It is language which determines the vote (perhaps never so much as in the general election of 1970); there are manifestly two linguistically-defined establishments competing with each other, and behind this struggle lies as much tradition as history.

But it is a competition for power which is never spoken of in straight terms which obfuscates matters all the more. For the truth is that it suits neither English South Africa nor Afrikanerdom to speak of a power struggle between the two White groups. Afrikanerdom because it looks forward to English South Africans joining it in a nation distinct from Black South Africa, English South Africa because its traditional appeal has been to woo Afrikaners away from an Afrikaner consciousness. This latter consideration arises from the simple arithmetic of White South Africa's demography: English-speakers are in a minority with respect to Afrikaners, and therefore if Afrikaners are united politically the English must lose out. Thus to gain political power it is self-evident that English South Africa should divide Afrikanerdom.

This political minority status of a group which in well-nigh every other respect – economically, socially and culturally – is South Africa's most powerful body of people, is a matter which lies at the heart of the Republic's White politics. For most of the years before 1948, English South Africa did indeed rule the country; and it did this by successfully putting forward the idea and idealism of 'broad South Africanism' which would encompass Afrikaners, as well as a Commonwealth idealism, of South Africa belonging to a greater whole, to the British family of nations.

These idealisms cracked in 1948, and in the fifties and sixties they were further buried, particularly with the decline of British power throughout the world – the power prop to the idealism was lost.

However, as a minority group, English South Africa did not have only one card – the dividing of Afrikanerdom – to play. There was also the prospect of alliance with Non-Whites. This English South Africa did indeed have, and employed, in the form of the Coloured vote; for until the late fifties Coloureds voted alongside Whites in the same electoral constituencies. And that, simply, was the main power consideration which led an Afrikaner Nationalist government to remove the Coloured voters from the common voters' roll (much as many Afrikaners today may rue the day their government did it).

This act, however, successfully prevented English South Africa from expanding its alliance with Non-Whites to a point where Afrikaners could one day be lifted from the seats of power. With the Coloureds off the roll and a solid Afrikaner electoral unity backing the National Party, English South Africa was properly boxed in.

This, nonetheless, still does not mean that English South Africa – or at least today the establishments of its two parties – has given up hope of someday, somehow, calling in a Non-White vote to redress the balance against the numerically preponderant Afrikaner voters. And on paper, still today, both opposition parties propound policies which would do exactly that. The United Party looks to giving Non-Whites a certain fixed number of seats in the central parliament; the Progressive Party wishes to open the franchise to Non-Whites on a qualified basis.

It is significant that both these parties wish to open the door to Non-Whites only so far . . . Neither relish the prospect of Non-Whites flooding the electorate; in fact both parties (despite protestations) would firmly resist any such flooding. Again it is a matter of the English/Afrikaner power struggle. The English-based parties would only allow in sufficient Non-White votes to overturn Afrikaner political power: anything more would deprive *them* of their control.

TIME OF CHANGE

The fifties were a time when Afrikanerdom seemed to move inexorably to the Right, as seen in conventional terms. Not only were the Coloureds politically negated, but increasing apartheid measures designed to bring about personal segregation appeared to mould Afrikanerdom permanently in a rightist shape. That indeed was the high tide of *baasskap* policies, even defined as such by the government.

The other side of the coin was an English South Africa seemingly moving left, opposing all government measures to separate off Non-Whites, its bosses (though less and less the man in the street) still looking to Non-White alliances. The upshot was that English South Africa well-nigh cornered the market in humanitarianism, in wishing well to the Non-Whites.

Meanwhile though, during the fifties too, Afrikaner thinkers were growing more and more restless with the prospect of *baasskap* apartheid. It was obvious to many that a horizontal division with Whites on top and Non-Whites below was morally wrong and untenable in the long run. Particularly with Afrikaners seeing themselves essentially as yet another nation in Africa did this thesis of dominance not wash. Thus did the Tomlinson Commission, Afrikaner churchmen and Afrikaner intellectuals (operating mainly through the S.A. Bureau for Racial Affairs) fashion the policy of separate development – looking to a South Africa of many equal nations, each based on its traditional territory and all regarding the others' people in terms of equal human dignity.

This concept, growing out of old-style apartheid, was ironically opposed in the fifties by the Nationalist government, in particular by the then

Minister of Native Affairs, Dr Verwoerd. However, on his accession to the Premiership, Verwoerd performed a notable *volte face*. Not only did he accept separate development as official government policy, but he embellished it and added further glosses. And Verwoerd declared, as much as any other proponent of separate development, that the policy must ultimately lead to a situation in which there was no discrimination between Black and White, as little as between people of any nations, for all except the vote.

Thus did the National Party arrive at a position in which it ran two policies concomitantly which in the final essence denied each other – segregationist apartheid as against an open-minded and tolerant separate development.

TWO POLICIES AT ONCE

For a normal political party to run two mutually exclusive policies at the same time would appear to be vastly inconsistent and untenable. But because South Africa has a series of group politics, each with its own spectrum, this was perfectly in order and understandable. If anything, this duality of Nationalist policy was political genius. And after all, the National Party is not founded on the rock of apartheid (as many outsiders see it), but on the rock of Afrikaner unity, Afrikaner nationalism and Afrikaner nationhood – the latter being simply the other side of the coin of separate development.

Still, it was out of this dualism of policy that the concepts of *verlig* and *verkramp* grew. Verligte Afrikaners are essentially separate development people; verkramptes essentially believe in *baasskap* apartheid. And when it comes to appraising the self-interest of the Afrikaner nation, as a new nation living among other nations in Africa, verligtes see themselves simply as being wiser and more enlightened about that self-interest; they see verkramptes as being closed-minded and narrow in weighing up that self-interest. Apart from self-interest, it is also true that verligtes are more tolerant people, verkramptes more intolerant.

With English South Africa having cornered the market in humanitarianism and tolerance, verligtes have had a tough row to hoe. For seemingly, and in terms of the tradition the National Party had built since 1948, it was 'un-Nationalist' to appear tolerant or speak tolerance. This looked too much like playing into English hands and admitting the English argument. For the typical Nationalist it had become correct practice to talk separate development but not be overly concerned about either its implementation or its implications.

But when Prof. de Klerk launched his coinages, matters had developed sufficiently within Afrikanerdom for everyone to know that his polarizations were remarkably true. They did indeed reflect accurately a division within Afrikanerdom.

CONVENTIONAL VIEW

A curious aspect of the verligte/verkrampte issue is that English South Africa did not for several years take it seriously. In its battle of words against Afrikanerdom, English South Africa has preferred to put over the conventional view of South African politics, namely, that there is only one spectrum for the whole country, only one plane on which politics operate. That spectrum would put Afrikaners on the ultra-right; next, moving leftwards, would come English-speakers, then Coloureds, Indians and Blacks. In what seemed a leftward-minded world it looked like suiting the English book to categorize Afrikaners as ultra-rightists. But this belied the facts.

The truth of South African politics, if one is to adopt the conventional view to look at them, is that English-speakers are probably the most conservative group in the country. In every sphere except politics, and most of all in the economic field, they are the 'haves', and it is natural that they should wish to hold. Subconsciously they know that Afrikaners are a revolutionary group out to upset their power base: Afrikaners have done so politically, and are a threat in other spheres. But this subconscious realization is not admitted . . . it is preferable to tab Afrikaners as *the* conservatives.

Yet, in reality, Afrikaners, however conservative in the matter of preserving their nationhood, are at least in their policy of separate development the true radicals among the Whites. For they would upset things: they would dissolve White dominion over the Black areas of the country, they would give the Blacks power – real, administrative power, not merely a minority voice in Parliament as would the opposition parties – and they would on this basis countenance a sharing of power with Blacks in the territory which is now South Africa.

As it has dawned on English-speakers that Afrikaners are indeed intent on carrying out this policy, that they are perfectly serious, and that the verligte/verkrampte division within Afrikanerdom is something that does exist, so have English-speakers, one feels, come to realize the validity of such patterning in South Africa's group-fragmented politics. Thus the words *verlig* and *verkramp* have gradually become more and more a part of English South African parlance; and curiously, English South Africans have come around to discerning verligtes and verkramptes even among themselves.

One notices too, an incipient line-up in English politics between verligtes and verkramptes, and this possibility was given further reality by the Progressive Party's recent toying with the idea of separate development. There will hence be a conflict between verligte and verkrampte Progressives (the latter, ironically, being those Progressives of the traditionally 'liberal' stripe, those who still look to 'One South Africa'); and within the United Party a similar division has recently been apparent, though deftly swept beneath the carpet.

PATTERN FOR ALL GROUPS?

It appears then, that group-oriented politics, as South Africa has, fall naturally, for each camp, into verligte/verkrampte polarizations. One already notices a similar phenomenon among Blacks. Verligtes are notable for their concern about relations with other groups, and so South Africa is seeing the rise of Black verkramptes, militant exclusivists who want no truck with any other groups, as well as Black verligtes who see self-interest as best being served by co-operation with other groups and tolerance towards them.

All these patterns are still in the formative stage, for South Africa's multiple power structure has not yet unfolded fully. But that the country should have a multiple power structure now seems inevitable, simply because White South Africa, which now holds the power, knows (or is coming to know) that it will go under if power is not shared out separately in this way.

Yet still, there will always be the question of interrelationships between the power structures and between the groups on a personal level: for whatever happens, Black, White and Brown will still live geographically mixed.

And so, for South Africa, will the verligte/verkrampte polarizations have meaning: does a group wish to bottle itself up, or does it wish to survive with healthy interrelationships between all the multifarious groups that live in the land?

Apartheid and International Relations

South Africa's Outward Policy: from Isolation to Dialogue

John Barratt

C. J. A. Barratt is Director of the South African Institute of International Affairs. A recognized expert on South Africa's position in the international context, he has written authoritatively on South Africa's external relations. Prior to taking up his present post, he served abroad with the South African Permanent Mission to the United Nations.

The trend towards South Africa's isolation in international politics began at the end of World War II. At that time the country appeared to enjoy considerable prestige. As one of the victorious allies, it became a founder member of the United Nations. Its Prime Minister, General J.C. Smuts, was among the world's prominent elder statesmen, and the San Francisco Conference accepted his draft for the Preamble to the Charter of the new world organization. But from the first session of the U.N. General Assembly in 1946 the South African Government found itself under attack on two issues, namely its refusal to enter into a trusteeship agreement with the United Nations over the territory of South West Africa and the question of its domestic racial policies.

These two issues, which were not at first as prominent as they later became in U.N. debates, were symptoms of a changing world situation, in which South Africa's position was to be drastically affected. Two factors in particular were relevant to South Africa's position in the world community. One was the reaction to nazism and racism. The revelation of the inhuman practices of the Nazi regime in Germany, including its racist policies, caused a widespread concern in the Western world about the infringement of individual human rights. Thus, for example, the U.N. Charter, in its Preamble, expressed the determination of the member states 'to reaffirm faith in fundamental human rights, in the dignity and worth of the human person . . .' Moreover, in Article 55 of the Charter, member states agreed to promote 'universal respect for, and observance of, human rights and fundamental freedoms for all without distinction as to race, sex, language or religion', in addition to promoting such ideals as higher standards of living and full employment.

These provisions of the Charter provided the grounds for international consideration of matters normally falling exclusively within the province of national governments, in spite of another Charter provision which excludes U.N. intervention 'in matters which are essentially within the domestic jurisdiction of any state' (Article 2, para. 7). The stage was, therefore, set for South African domestic policies to become an international issue.

The other relevant factor in the fast-changing post-war world was anti-colonialism. The drive for self-determination and independence throughout Asia and Africa gathered increasing momentum, and brought the Western and White colonial powers into conflict with the Non-White peoples of the world. In this confrontation White South Africa was an outpost of the Western world in a Black continent, and, as the Western powers withdrew from their colonies, South Africa became increasingly isolated. Moreover, White South Africans were, and still are, widely regarded as a remnant of colonialism, and as an embarrassment to the Western powers who wish to rid themselves of the stigma of their colonial past.

South Africa's position was aggravated by the coming to power in 1948 of a political party, under Dr D.F. Malan, which formulated South Africa's traditional practice of racial segregation in a positive governmental policy of strict separation of the races – a policy identified by the new word *apartheid* which had been coined as an election slogan.

During the fifties the attention paid to South African domestic policies in the United Nations General Assembly increased, while the Government consistently maintained that even discussion of these policies, let alone the passing of resolutions, was illegal in terms of the U.N. Charter (Article 2(7) in particular). But South Africa's international position was not acute, even in the U.N. There was, for instance, no serious attempt to raise the South African situation in the Security Council as a threat to world peace, and the country's membership of the Commonwealth was not threatened.

The Commonwealth provided valuable links with the world community, and it constituted a buffer against the gathering threats of isolation.

Negotiation of the Simonstown Agreement with the United Kingdom in 1955, including the British undertaking to supply naval weapons, raised no international outcry, and in 1959 South Africa benefited even in the United Nations from its membership of the Commonwealth group, when its Foreign Minister, Mr Eric Louw, was elected to a Vice-Presidency of the General Assembly, as the agreed Commonwealth candidate.

SOUTH AFRICA AND THE WINDS OF CHANGE

At the same time the Government was beginning to realize the need to come to terms with the changes taking place in Africa. The granting of independence to their colonies by the Western powers had not at first been supported by the South African Government which regarded the withdrawal of these powers from Africa as premature. However, in 1955 the Prime Minister, Mr Strijdom (who had succeeded Dr Malan towards the end of 1954), said that South Africa should behave towards the Non-White states in such a way that they and South Africa would not face each other as enemies, 'but as peoples and governments which recognize and honour each other's right to exist'.[1] By 1957, when Ghana, Sudan, Tunisia, Morocco and Libya had gained their independence (Liberia, Ethiopia, Egypt and South Africa had previously been the only independent African States), Mr Strijdom recognized that 'the whole position has changed in Africa'. He recognized, too, that, as the new countries in Africa developed, there would have to be contact in economic and other matters, and he added: 'In the course of time there will have to be ordinary relations and even diplomatic relations.'[2] The Minister of External Affairs, Mr Eric Louw, also spoke of his policy to maintain contact with other states in Africa whether they were European or African controlled.[3]

These indications of changing attitudes and of a recognition of the new international situation, especially in Africa, were perhaps the small beginnings of an 'outward' policy by the Government and of an attempt to prevent South Africa's complete isolation internationally. But the be-

1. Quoted by political commentator, 'Dawie', in *Die Burger,* Cape Town, 27 August 1955.

2. Gail-Maryse Cockram, *Vorster's Foreign Policy,* Academica, Pretoria and Cape Town, 1970, p. 116.

3. *Ibid.*

ginning of the new decade saw a dramatic turn for the worse in South Africa's international position. This was marked by the speech of British Prime Minister Harold Macmillan to both Houses of Parliament in Cape Town in February, 1960, in which he warned that a 'wind of change' was blowing through Africa. In March racial disturbances occurred in various parts of South Africa, associated ever since with the name of Sharpeville. The U.N. Security Council was, as a result, asked for the first time to consider South African racial policies as a possible threat to world peace. Throughout the world criticism of the South African Government reached new heights of violence and emotion, and South Africa's membership of the Commonwealth was threatened. The South African economy suffered, and there was an outflow of capital from the country.

The force of the attacks on the South African Government was due not only to events within South Africa, but also to the fact that 1960 was the peak year of the anti-colonialism campaign. In that year alone sixteen African states achieved independence and were admitted to the United Nations. The colonial powers, with the exception of Portugal, had now in effect given up all attempts to resist the pressures on them to withdraw from Africa, and, as fast as they were able to, they were handing over authority to African governments. In this process they had no inclination to defend South Africa. The threat of isolation which had been building up during the fifties now became very real for South Africa, both in Africa and in the international community generally.

This isolation was manifested most clearly in the United Nations where even the Western powers withdrew their earlier support of the South African arguments concerning the illegality of U.N. interference in domestic affairs. The Security Council considered the situation in South Africa on several occasions between 1960 and 1964; the U.N. Secretary General visited South Africa for discussions with the Government; and towards the end of 1962 the General Assembly for the first time recommended that member states should enforce economic sanctions and other measures designed to isolate and put pressure on the South African Government.

South Africa's participation in other international organizations and at international conferences was also made increasingly difficult, and it was forced to withdraw from some important organizations, such as the International Labour Organization and the Food and Agriculture Organization. It was no longer possible for the country to participate in any African organization, including the Committee for Technical Co-operation in Africa (CCTA) and the Scientific Council for Africa (CSA), in which South Africa had been playing a leading role, as well as the U.N. Economic Commission for Africa, which had only been formed at the end of the fifties.

At the same time South Africa was forced, by the pressure of the Non-White members, to withdraw from the Commonwealth when it became a republic in 1961. It thus ceased to belong to any grouping or alliance of states, regional or otherwise. Membership of groups had become an important factor in international politics, especially within the United Nations, and the only other country in the world to find itself in this isolated position internationally was, and still is, Israel.

Membership of the Commonwealth had been a basic ingredient of South African foreign policy since Union in 1910. In fact, association with the Commonwealth, which meant in effect association with the United Kingdom as a great power, removed any real incentive for South Africa to develop a distinctive foreign policy of its own. The National Party Government which came to power in 1948 had been adopting a more independent stance, but it was nevertheless still very dependent on Britain for contacts in Africa and throughout the world, in those countries where it had no diplomatic or trade representatives of its own. This dependence was now suddenly broken, and South Africa was forced, without much time for preparation and in a hostile world, to look after itself without any outside help.

During the early sixties the initial reaction within South Africa was to go on to the defensive, which further increased the political isolation. The mood among the electorate was not one which encouraged talk of contact with Black African states. White South Africans to a great extent turned in on themselves behind a psychological wall of reaction against the potential threat of Black Africa and a generally hostile world.

At the same time, however, life in the modern world had to go on for South Africa, and, with Commonwealth membership ended, those in charge of the conduct of foreign relations and those engaged in external trade were forced to be more self-reliant and to establish their own contacts abroad. The threat of sanctions and the torrent of hostile criticism from outside, intended to isolate South Africa, also had the effect of unifying the two main White groups – the Afrikaans and English – and of developing more of a common purpose. The establishment of the Republic, too, had removed a bone of contention which had for years divided these two groups. Then, as the country's economic power increased during the middle and latter sixties, a sense of confidence returned, and it was possible for the Government to speak and act from a position of greater strength.

The most serious threat in the first half of the sixties concerned the issue of South West Africa – often referred to as South Africa's 'Achilles' heel'. This issue had been taken to the International Court in 1960 by Ethiopia and Liberia, former members of the League of Nations, and it was widely expected that the judgement would go against the South African Government, and that this would provide a legal basis for intervention by the United Nations, either by means of mandatory sanctions or even by the use of force. This threat was regarded with some seriousness within South Africa, and, while the proceedings before the International Court dragged on for over five years, the Government moved energetically to develop the Republic's military strength and to reduce its dependence on outside sources for such strategically important materials as oil.

THE GENESIS OF THE OUTWARD POLICY

The judgement of the International Court, which was eventually given in July, 1966, was after all a technical victory for the South African Government, and this unexpected result removed the most serious external threat to South Africa. In fact this judgement marked a turning point in South Africa's foreign policy. Although the campaign against the Government was still widening in the United Nations and elsewhere, attitudes in South Africa became more relaxed and, with the Republic's greater economic and military strength, the threats from outside were no longer regarded so seriously.

Another factor in these changing attitudes was that the policy of 'separate development' (more positive in its content than 'apartheid'), as defined more clearly by the late Dr H.F. Verwoerd during the early sixties, tended to remove the ideological objections to independent African states. The wide-spread disapproval of the policies of self-determination and independence for African peoples gave way to a greater acceptance of the facts of the anti-colonial upheaval, and a realization that, if nationalism was justified for Whites, it should not be suppressed in the case of Black Africans. As a result, the coming independence of the British territories of Basutoland, Bechuanaland and Swaziland was accepted as part of an emerging pattern for all Southern Africa, which would eventually include independent states formed out of the Bantu 'homelands' within the Republic. This was a notable change from the policy which had existed not many years previously, and which sought rather the incorporation of these territories into South Africa, and it was the starting point of a new policy towards the rest of independent Black Africa.

In his study of South African foreign policy, Professor Amry Vandenbosch states: 'The foreign policy of South Africa has become almost totally a defense of its racial policy against the hostile pressure of nearly the whole world.'[4] This was perhaps true in the first half of the sixties, but, although the hostile pressure has remained and in some areas increased, a new 'outward' trend developed in the Government's foreign policy during the second half of the sixties. It developed as a conscious effort to break out of the increasing isolation described above.

The word 'outward' appears to have been first used in respect of South Africa's external relations, in September, 1965, when an article appeared in the periodical *News/Check,* entitled 'The Choice before South Africa – look inwards or look outwards'. This article stated, *inter alia*: 'To grow means looking outwards, to the other peoples of South Africa, to the outside world. This is modernity's inescapable logic – an interwebbing of men and things. And to grow is to survive. Yet this also means change, adaptation, tolerance, and a committed acceptance of the new, and employing of the new to one's own advantage.' The comment in the concluding paragraph of the article was: 'For building a nation is a pragmatic task; it is a matter of looking wisely to self-interest, to growth and to long-term prospects. Above all, in a modern world it is a business of looking outwards, to building contact and thriving on the exchange. This is the choice to be made.'[5]

While it was some time before the phrase 'outward movement' became an accepted term, and while the Government at first refused to acknowledge that there was any change in its foreign policy, the signs of a new direction in attitudes and policy were discernible in the mid-sixties. As the decade proceeded the movement became clearer. It involved not only government policy, but also the thinking and action of scientists, academics, businessmen and other groups who increasingly looked outwards for new contacts – out of necessity and because they could not thrive in isola-

4. Amry Vandenbosch, *South Africa and the World,* The University Press of Kentucky, 1970, p. 13.

5. *News/Check,* Vol. 4, No. 6, 24 September 1965, Johannesburg.

tion. This widening movement provided the backing for the Government to develop the new positive, and less defensive, trend in its foreign policy.

In February, 1967, the Prime Minister, Mr Vorster, said in an important speech that South Africans did not have a spirit of isolation and were prepared to go out into the world so that South Africa could play its role there – in spite of all the problems which had to be met. He then defined his own task as one of leading South Africa towards becoming fully part of the international community.[6] A weekly newspaper, supporting the Government, stated in regard to this speech that its central message was that South Africa was on the brink of a major effort to fight against isolation. Behind Mr Vorster's words, it said, was a desire among many Nationalists to break outwards in various fields.[7]

The development of this outward policy has been slow. The Government has moved with extreme caution, appearing always to be looking over its shoulder for an anticipated reaction from the electorate. Within the National Party there was in fact a reaction which formed part of the so-called 'verligte/verkrampte' struggle, involving various aspects of government policies, including the outward movement. This struggle reached a peak in 1969 when a small section of the National Party broke away to form a new right-wing party, under the leadership of Dr Albert Hertzog.

The struggle during the years 1967 to 1969 no doubt inhibited the Government in the pursuit of its outward foreign policy, as well as in the development of the more positive aspects of its internal policies, because there was apparently a fear that Dr Hertzog had considerable support among the rank and file members of the National Party. However this fear was proved to be largely groundless in the elections of April, 1970, when Dr Hertzog's party received very little support and gained no seats in Parliament.

The outward movement has not been concerned only with Africa. It has involved efforts to expand trade and diplomatic contacts in Asia and Australasia, and moves to establish new links in various fields with Latin American countries. There has also been a more pragmatic attitude in recent years towards the United Nations and in general a less defensive attitude towards criticism. Attempts have been made to explain South

6. J.H.P. Serfontein, *Die verkrampte Aanslag,* Human and Rousseau, Cape Town and Pretoria, 1970, p. 119.

7. *Die Beeld,* Johannesburg, 19 February, 1967.

Africa's problems and policies in terms more appreciated in the modern world, and even a willingness, at least in some government quarters, to re-examine the official position *vis-a-vis* the concept of human rights as reflected in the U.N. Declaration on Human Rights and other international instruments.

But it is mainly in respect of South Africa's relations with Africa that the outward policy has become known. It is here that the results of the policy have been most significant when judged against South Africa's complete isolation in Africa early in the sixties. Moreover, if progress can be made in co-operative relations with Black African states, South Africa's image will be favourably affected and its relations with countries outside Africa may well be eased as a result. Less tension in Africa generally may also have a positive effect on relations between groups within South Africa.

IMPACT OF AFRICAN POLITICS ON THE OUTWARD MOVEMENT

It is worth looking, therefore, in more detail at how this outward movement in Africa has evolved during the past few years. As will be seen it is not a one-sided affair. What progress there has been has depended as much on initiatives and changes in attitude of other African leaders as on the policies of the South African Government.

As indicated above, the change in attitude towards independent African states was initiated by Dr Verwoerd's acceptance of the approaching independence of the British territories within and on the borders of the Republic. He gave expression to this acceptance by inviting Prime Minister Leabua Jonathan of Lesotho to visit him in Pretoria in September, 1966, shortly before Lesotho achieved independence. This was a gesture of immense significance in bringing home to South Africans the change that was taking place. For people and governments overseas, unfamiliar with South Africa, the importance of this event was perhaps difficult to grasp. It was the last major act of Dr Verwoerd before his assassination in the same month, and it broke the ground on which his successor, Mr Vorster, was to build.

Lesotho became independent on October 3rd, 1966. At his first press conference after independence, Chief Jonathan referred to his meeting with Dr Verwoerd the previous month, and said that this had 'marked the beginning . . . of a new relationship between our two countries'. He

8. Cockram, *op. cit.*, p. 123.

continued: 'South Africa and Lesotho have much to gain from peaceful co-existence, provided this is based on mutual respect for our respective national policies. No country is an island unto itself, and no country can grow and prosper in isolation.' Dr Hilgard Muller, South African Foreign Minister, after attending the independence celebrations, commented that he was more convinced than ever that South Africa should maintain its friendship with her newly independent neighbouring states.[9]

In January, 1967, Chief Jonathan visited the new Prime Minister, Mr Vorster. This was in fact the first visit of the Head of an independent Black African State to a South African Prime Minister. A joint communique said that the South African Government would, as soon as possible, investigate proposals for economic aid and technical assistance to Lesotho, and Chief Jonathan commented after his return to his country that he believed his visits to South Africa had broken the 'race relations curtain' and that peaceful co-existence had been put into practice.[10]

Botswana became independent a few days before Lesotho, on 30th September, 1966. Botswana's leader, Sir Seretse Khama, said that his country fully appreciated 'that it is wholly in our interests to preserve neighbourly relations with the Republic of South Africa. Our economic links with South Africa are virtually indissoluble. We are tied directly to South Africa – for communications, for markets for our beef, for labour in the mines, and in many other respects.'[11]

Swaziland, the third British territory bordering on South Africa, did not become independent until September, 1968, but in 1966 the Prime Minister, Prince Dlamini, spoke about the foreign policy which he said his country would follow when it became independent, and this included the cultivation of understanding with neighbouring states and non-interference in their internal affairs, as well as the maintenance of economic ties with South Africa, to change which 'would result in economic chaos'.[12]

With some variations the co-operative relations between South Africa and its three small neighbours have continued since their independence. There has been technical assistance from governmental and private sources to Lesotho in particular and also to Swaziland. Botswana has gradually adopted a more independent stance, and Sir Seretse Khama has become

9. *Ibid.*
10. *Ibid.*, p. 124.
11. *Ibid.*, p. 123.
12. *Ibid.*, p. 127-128.

more critical of South African internal policies in public statements. But he has not allowed any use at all of Botswana territory by guerilla movements aiming to infiltrate into South Africa. This is of considerable significance because of Botswana's strategic position in relation to the Republic. Although the Botswana government has not sought financial assistance from the South African Government, South African companies are playing a role in the exploiting of Botswana's mineral deposits which may give that country in the future a fair degree of economic independence to match its political independence in the Southern African region.

All three territories are in a customs and monetary union with South Africa. Probably the most important development in relations between the four States was the lengthy but successful negotiations leading to a revised customs agreement in 1969. During the negotiations there were suggestions that the South African Government was being insensitive to the interests of the weaker parties. But the negotiations were amicably concluded, and the new agreement, which substantially improves the position of the three small states in the customs union, has been welcomed by all concerned.

It should be said in respect of these three immediate neighbours that they had little choice regarding their relations with South Africa when they became independent. The existing facts of their economic links to their powerful neighbour, including the employment of so many of their nationals in the Republic, as well as their dire poverty, have allowed them no real alternative to maintaining good working relations with the South African Government. But from the South African side it is to the credit of the outward movement that the Government and private organizations are willing to aid these states and encourage their development. The attitude towards the independence of these states, which is one of full acceptance of their sovereign independence and of non-interference in their internal affairs, is also important.

The Republic of Malawi, which became independent in 1964, is in a different position. It is not an immediate neighbour and therefore not as dependent on South Africa, although it has one important factor in common with the neighbouring states, namely the employment of a large number of Malawians in South Africa, which is a considerable source of income for Malawi. Dr Hastings Banda, the President of Malawi, has evolved a very individualistic and pragmatic foreign policy which includes cordial relations with South Africa, in spite of the almost unanimous disapproval in the past of the rest of Black Africa. The position *vis-a-vis*

South Africa began to become clear in 1966. For instance, in October of that year, when the U.N. General Assembly passed a resolution purporting to revoke South Africa's mandate in respect of South West Africa, Malawi was one of only three countries to abstain – the others being the U.K. and France. In that same year South Africa gave financial assistance to Malawi for the building of a sugar mill which came into operation early in 1967.

In March, 1967, three Malawian Ministers paid a goodwill visit to South Africa, during which a trade agreement was signed. One of the Ministers, Mr Aleke Banda, commented that, although Malawi and South Africa had different internal policies, there were areas in which there could be mutually rewarding co-operation, trade being one of these, because 'politics and trade are completely separate matters'. Dr Hilgard Muller said that the visit would serve 'as an example to others that peaceful co-existence is possible in Southern Africa between the various nations and groups whose internal policies may not necessarily be the same'.[13] Subsequently President Banda condemned those countries which had criticized the trade agreement with South Africa. He said that 'while they are criticizing me for trading with South Africa openly, they themselves are trading with South Africa secretly'. He also commented on this occasion that 'there must be a start on a dialogue between political leaders in the rest of Africa and those in South Africa'.[14]

In regard to these new developments Mr Vorster said in the course of a speech in May, 1967, that it was not his intention to try to build Rome in one day, but slowly and systematically to establish relations with neighbouring states in Southern Africa and further north as saner attitudes prevailed – relations which would be to the benefit of the Republic and of the other states concerned.[15]

Towards the end of 1967 it was announced that there would be an exchange of diplomatic representatives between Malawi and South Africa. At first Malawi was represented by a White Charge d'Affaires, with a Black deputy, but in 1971 a Black Ambassador was appointed. In view of the earlier hesitation on the part of the South African Government, as well as the outright opposition from some quarters, regarding the possibility of establishing diplomatic relations with Black African states, this develop-

13. *South African Digest,* 23 March 1967, p. 1.
14. Cockram, *op. cit.,* p. 138.
15. *South African Digest,* 9 June 1967.

ment was indicative of a significant change. The presence in South Africa of a Black African enjoying full diplomatic privileges and immunities has had to be handled with extreme care and has necessitated some special arrangements, in view not only of legislation involving segregation of the races, but also of traditional social practices. However, this situation has not proved as difficult as many expected; it has not given rise to incidents affecting the relations between the two countries; and there is no doubt that this small beginning will lead to the presence of more diplomats from African states in South Africa.

There has been since 1966 considerable assistance, financial and technical, to Malawi for various purposes, which has been more substantial than to any other country. Especially notable has been the R8 million loan for the building of Malawi's new capital at Lilongwe and the financing in the form of an even larger loan of the new railroad providing Malawi with a second outlet to the sea at the port of Nacala in Mozambique. There have also been many visits of Ministers and officials between the two countries. In 1970 the South African Prime Minister, Mr Vorster, paid an official visit to Malawi, and President Banda paid a state visit to South Africa during the second half of 1971.

The four states mentioned above were, until 1970, the only ones with which South Africa had open co-operative relations, although in May, 1969, the Foreign Minister, Dr Muller, said in Parliament that the Government was in direct contact with many more African states than he was able to mention.[16] One of these was no doubt Madagascar, as there had been visits by officials and businessmen to that country, and during 1969 President Tsiranana of Madagascar indicated that he wished to encourage closer economic relations. Then in 1970 Dr Hilgard Muller paid an official visit to Madagascar, and it was reported that negotiations regarding South African financial assistance in developing the tourist industry and other projects, were proceeding.

By early 1970 economic links with Mauritius were increasing, and some contacts had been made with Gabon. Increasing contacts by South African businessmen and companies in other African countries were reported, although for political reasons these were seldom openly admitted.

While there had, therefore, been a significant change in South Africa's position in Africa since the first half of the sixties, it appeared by mid-

16. *House of Assembly Debates (Hansard)*, 7 May 1969, col. 5450.

1970 that the outward movement was bound to be limited mainly to Southern Africa, and that it had reached an almost impenetrable political barrier in the rest of the continent. However, in the second half of 1970 the movement developed a new dimension. Early in November President Felix Houphouët-Boigny of the Ivory Coast announced that he was planning to urge other African leaders to undertake direct talks with South Africa, because he considered that force would not solve the problem of apartheid. He commented in a subsequent interview that to obtain peace there was only one weapon – negotiation. 'We hope to succeed by dialogue. For seven years we have had nothing but grand and violent speeches, with tragic and sometimes ridiculous results. We cannot make threats without the means to apply them.' The President went on to argue that the threats encouraged South Africa to accumulate more arms, together with a defensive reaction which would be vented against the Black states to the north. He went on: 'My opinion is that we shall obtain nothing by the use of force. How can we reach a solution if we refuse all talk with South Africa?'[17]

President Houphouët-Boigny received immediate support from the leaders of Madagascar, Gabon, Dahomey and the Central African Republic, as well as from Prime Minister Jonathan of Lesotho and President Banda of Malawi. The latter two indicated that they had been advocating the same policy for some time.

Support came also from Ghana, although this should perhaps be regarded as an independent initiative, because the Prime Minister, Dr Busia, had tentatively raised the possibility of dialogue at an earlier date. He encountered considerable opposition in Ghana, however. After President Houphouët-Boigny's statement, Dr Busia said that neither trade embargoes nor guerilla warfare was likely to break the rule of the White minority government in South Africa. Instead he suggested African states should negotiate with the South African government while encouraging 'constitutional and moral change' from within the White-ruled country.[18]

In December, 1970, Dr Busia spelt out his philosophy in more detail in a statement to parliament in Accra,[19] during which he said:

17. *Malawi News,* 17 Nov. 1971.

18. *The Times* (London), 11 Nov. 1971.

19. Extracts reproduced in *The Star* (Johannesburg), 23 March 1971.

> 'We would like to see in South Africa a multi-racial society in which every citizen, whatever his origin, race, colour or creed, enjoys the same human dignity, rights, privileges and opportunities, as every other citizen, a society in which every citizen has an equal and unfettered opportunity both for individual development and for service to his country in justice and freedom, according to his ability and capacity.'

Dr Busia argued that this aim could not be achieved through the policies of force so far adopted by the OAU which were 'woefully and hopelessly inadequate' for a successful struggle against a strong South Africa. In view of the failure of the policies of force and isolation, Dr Busia asked whether the African states were right in maintaining these policies, and he indicated that a policy of dialogue might be more successful.

President Houphouët-Boigny indicated from the start that he did not wish to act unilaterally, and he set about attempting to gain the support first of the OCAM group of French African states, with the apparent aim of subsequently trying for wider support within the OAU itself. However, he was opposed by important leaders within OCAM, notably Leopold Senghor of Senegal and Amadou Ahidjo of Cameroun, as well as President Mobutu of Zaire. As a result the important OCAM meeting held in Chad in January, 1971, did not deal with the matter, but instead simply took note of communications from the Ivory Coast and Madagascar in this connection.

Apart from the opposition of the influential leaders mentioned above, President Houphouët-Boigny's strategy was probably affected by the militant reaction amongst African states to the alleged invasion of Guinea towards the end of November, 1970. The mood of militancy was not conducive to talk of dialogue with the White South. Nevertheless, the supporters of dialogue continued to argue their case in public, and even within the OAU, in spite of strong majority opposition.

In spite of the considerable attention given to President Houphouët-Boigny's initiative in the South African press, which talked of a 'breakthrough' for South Africa, official reaction in South Africa was very reserved. The initiative, which had no doubt been preceded by private contacts, was welcomed, but there was awareness of the difficulties involved. In March, 1971, the Prime Minister, Mr Vorster, stated clearly that he was willing to meet other African leaders on an equal footing.

Ghana's Foreign Minister responded immediately that he would be prepared to come to South Africa for discussions with the government. A two-day debate in the Ghanaian Parliament ended with support being given to Dr Busia's approach – in spite of strong objections from the opposition. The government motion, however, approved of a dialogue which would be 'based on the philosophy underlying the Lusaka Manifesto', and which would be 'one of the weapons which could be used in the struggle to eliminate apartheid'.[20]

THE LUSAKA MANIFESTO

The Lusaka Manifesto has been mentioned by President Houphouët-Boigny, too, as a basis for discussions with South Africa. Although approved by the OAU, and eventually by the U.N., this Manifesto originated with the East African States in 1969 and reflects the philosophy of Presidents Kaunda of Zambia and Nyerere of Tanzania. While it expresses preference for negotiation rather than the use of force, it supports the 'liberation movements' in Southern Africa, and, while it recognizes all the peoples who have made their homes in Southern Africa as Africans, it argues strongly for the isolating and ostracizing of South Africa. There is no suggestion anywhere in the Manifesto that any sort of dialogue would be possible with the present South African Government. On the contrary it says, in calling for South Africa's isolation : 'The South African Government cannot be allowed both to reject the very concept of mankind's unity and to benefit by the strength given through friendly international relations.'[21]

It is difficult to see, therefore, how the Lusaka Manifesto can form the basis for a fruitful dialogue; it would seem rather to constitute a stumbling block in the way of any discussions at all. As indicated in the Manifesto, Presidents Nyerere and Kaunda have adopted a policy of confrontation towards the White-ruled states, and have made clear their opposition to the dialogue proposals – in spite of the fact that President Kaunda was, between 1968 and 1971, himself privately negotiating with the South African Prime Minister about the possibility of a meeting between them

20. *Ibid.*

21. Quotations from text of Manifesto as reproduced in *24th Session of the U.N. General Assembly*: *Questions Affecting South Africa*, South African Institute of International Affairs, 1970, Annexure 1.

and about other matters.[22] President Kaunda has always expressed opposition to South African internal policies, but he has become more extreme in his public statements since the Rhodesian declaration of independence in November, 1965. It is possible that, if it had not been for the Rhodesian dispute, his approach to the problems of Southern Africa might have been generally more moderate. He might have been in favour of the concept of dialogue, in order both to maintain the obvious economic advantages of links with South Africa (which Zambia still enjoys), and to bring an influence to bear on internal policies of the South African Government.

DOMESTIC AFFAIRS AN INTERNATIONAL ISSUE

It appears from the statements of all the African leaders who have supported the idea of a dialogue with South Africa, that they see this as a means of influencing the course of events within South Africa itself. It must be taken into account, however, that the more extreme statements in this regard, in which the dialogue, for instance, is referred to as a 'weapon' in the struggle against apartheid, are made partly in order to ward off criticism from other African leaders who do not support dialogue. In other words there are some things which have to be said, because to give an impression that the South African government's racial policies are being supported, would be to destroy any influence these leaders might have in Black Africa. Although expressing strong objections to apartheid, some of these African leaders no doubt see the possibility of material advantages, in the way of trade, as well as financial and technical assistance, for their own countries. They are probably genuinely motivated, too, by a desire to lessen friction in Africa, in order that more attention can be paid to the urgent needs for development, and there is a fear among some of them that continued conflict opens the way for communist influence – of both the Russian and Chinese varieties. This latter point is one that President Houphouët-Boigny, for instance, has stressed.

At the same time, taking all this into account, South Africans have to accept that the main point of difference to be reconciled in the proposed dialogue, concerns in fact aspects of South Africa's domestic policies. This is an illustration of South Africa's dilemma, namely that its domestic affairs are an issue in its international relations, and this creates

22. See Mr Vorster's statement in the House of Assembly on 21 April 1971, and the texts of letters released by the Zambian Government on 23 April 1971.

particular difficulties. However, the South African Government clearly recognizes that the dialogue will concern its internal policies, and at his press conference in March, 1971, Mr Vorster said:

> '. . . as far as the policy of separate development is concerned, it can be discussed, and I take it as a matter of course that it will be discussed. I will welcome the opportunity to discuss the policy with each and everybody concerned for the simple reason that more nonsense has been written and spoken about the policy of separate development than any other subject I know of. And I will gladly take the opportunity to explain the policy for what it is and not what people think it is.'[23]

On an earlier occasion, in July, 1969, in a speech on the Government's outward policy, Mr Vorster spoke of his desire to establish friendly relations with other countries on the basis of non-interference in internal affairs. They 'must accept us as we are,' he said. At the same time he recognized that in contacts with other countries, which he was seeking, there would be attempts to influence South Africa. 'People can and will of course, try to influence you. There is no law against it. All countries, in fact, try to influence each other, because that is what diplomacy is for. But one must not try to *reform* another country.'[24]

This acceptance of the fact that South Africa's domestic policies will be an issue in the proposed dialogue amounts to a significant concession to the views of other African governments, because it is contrary to normal international law and practice that any sovereign state's domestic affairs should be subject to interference by other governments, and because the South African Government has always adopted a very rigid stand against attempts at interference in its domestic affairs. This has in fact been a cornerstone of its foreign policy. It remains to be seen how the dialogue will proceed, if the 'separate development' policy becomes a major issue, on a resolution of which further progress in the dialogue depends. Possibly there will be visible and constructive progress in domestic policies while the dialogue proceeds, which will help to satisfy other African leaders, at least to some extent, on this score. But it cannot be expected that the

23. *The Star* (Johannesburg), 30 March 1971.

24. Suid-Afrikaanse Akademie vir Wetenskap en Kuns, *South Africa in the World*, Tafelberg-Uitgewers, Cape Town and Johannesburg, 1970, p. 98.

Government will make concessions in its internal policies simply to please other countries, even though it must be realized that relations with the rest of Africa will never become normal, until discriminatory practices, which are not defensible, have disappeared from South African society.

Under these unusual circumstances the conduct and development of the proposed dialogue will call for very careful planning and skilful handling. While there is no doubt that South African foreign policy and diplomacy have entered a new and exciting phase, in contrast to the period of increasing isolation described above, it will not be an easy phase for those who conduct our foreign relations. The risks which will have to be taken are great; and in any case the progress is bound to be slow. But the positive response so far from some African leaders to South Africa's attempts to move outwards, holds out hope that dialogue may lead away from confrontation and isolation towards co-existence and co-operation in Africa.

South Africa's Reactions to External Criticism

Denis Worrall

One of South Africa's best qualified political scientists, Denis Worrall can write and speak authoritatively on South African affairs in the context of international politics. He holds an M.A. from the University of Cape Town and a Ph.D. from Cornell University and is Editor of the Southern African intellectual review, New Nation. *He is at present attached to the Department of International Relations at the University of the Witwatersrand.*

SOUTH AFRICA AND THE CHANGED POST-WAR WORLD

World War II marked something of a revolution in South Africa's position within the community of nations. From being a respected member of the international community, it became, in the words of a leading Afrikaans newspaper, 'the polecat among nations'. From being welcomed as a member of international organizations and a participant in international activities at all levels, the Union after the war faced concerted challenges to its membership of international organizations, and increasing isolation. Professor Ben Cockram, formerly Jan Smuts Professor of International Relations at the University of Witwatersrand, points out that the change in attitude towards South Africa was clearly reflected in attitudes towards General J.C. Smuts, the then South African Prime Minister, at the San Francisco Conference in 1945.[1]

1. 'At San Francisco Smuts was revered for his contribution to the making of the League, honoured for his contribution to victory, respected and listened to whenever he intervened in debate, but he left the impression of being a relic of the past. Almost alone of the delegates he wore military uniform – "General" Carlos Romulo, the Philippine journalist, was the only other to do so whom I can call to mind at this date – and his age was apparent among the younger generation who had emerged into prominence during World War II.' – Professor Ben Cockram, *General Smuts and South African Diplomacy,* South African Institute of International Affairs, Johannesburg (roneod), 1970, p. 7.

The reasons for this change have less to do with conditions in South Africa (which remained more or less constant), than with the very changed circumstances of the post-War international system. Prior to World War II the structure of the South African governmental system had been oligarchic and official policy with respect to race relations was discriminatory. But this had not hindered South Africa, and White South Africans, from playing a normal role in international affairs. Conflict was inevitable in the greatly altered circumstances of the post-War world, with its commitment to humanism as expressed in such documents as the Universal Declaration of Human Rights and the various conventions against racial and other forms of discrimination, and with the coming to independence of the countries of Asia and the rest of Africa.

The first indications of this conflict were present during the opening session of the General Assembly of the United Nations in 1946, when it rejected a South African proposal to be permitted to incorporate the mandated territory of South West Africa. The General Assembly recommended instead that South West Africa be placed under the Trusteeship System of the United Nations.[2] Also during the first session of the General Assembly of 1946, the Indian delegation raised the question of the treatment by the South African government of persons of Indo-Pakistani descent.[3] With the exception of the 1949 session, this issue appeared on the agenda of the General Assembly until the sixteenth (1961-1962) session, when it was fused with the so-called apartheid issue. This first appeared on the agenda during the seventh session (1952-1953) and became a permanent item on the General Assembly's agenda after this. By

2. For a full statement of the South African point of view, see *South West Africa Survey, 1967,* Department of Foreign Affairs, Pretoria, 1967. A critical view is set out in Ronald Segal and Ruth First, (eds.) *South West Africa,* London, 1967. For a concise treatment of South Africa at the United States, see Gerrit Olivier, "South African Foreign Policy", in Denis Worrall (ed.), *South Africa: Government and Politics,* Van Schaik, Pretoria, 1971.

3. Professor Cockram, who was present at the San Francisco conference and the first few sessions of the United Nations, graphically describes the occasion. 'Mrs Pandit, spotlighted in a beautiful sari, and using her wonderful, resonant voice to perfection, said that she was not a famous soldier, nor an experienced statesman, she could speak only as a woman, but as a woman she could feel for the oppressed wherever they were, and particularly if they were her own fellow countrymen. As she stood with her arms uplifted, tears glistened on her cheecks, and the Assembly broke into a thunder of applause. In such an environment the cards were stacked against Smuts, as they have remained stacked against South Africa to this day.' *Op. cit.,* p. 7.

1962 the General Assembly had set up a Special Committee on Apartheid.[4]

While international criticism of South Africa was spearheaded at the United Nations, disapproval of the situation in South Africa and criticism of that country's policies were not limited to the world organization. In fact, by the early sixties external criticism of South Africa was expressed in a variety of proposals which ranged from simple expressions of disapproval of apartheid to proposals for the armed invasion of South Africa. The more important forms of criticism might be catalogued as follows:

(a) The organization of activist groups, particularly in Western countries with strong trade relations with South Africa, which championed the application of economic sanctions and boycotts. The British Anti-Apartheid Movement, which is probably the best known, was established in 1960. Its aims and objects are:

> (1) to inform the people in Britain and elsewhere about apartheid and what it means to the people of South Africa; (2) to campaign for international action to help bring the system of apartheid to an end; (3) to co-operate with and support South African organizations campaigning against apartheid.[5]

The Anti-Apartheid Movement took the initiative in organizing the International Conference on Sanctions Against South Africa of 14-17 April, 1964.[6] These bodies have managed to forge close links with churches, universities, trade unions, and youth groups in several Western countries.

(b) Formulation of blueprints of change in South Africa along lines amenable to that country's international critics. Two examples are the report of the Myrdal committee (so called after its chairman Alva Myrdal) which was appointed following the adoption on 4 December, 1963 by the Security Council of a resolution (S/5471) which requested the Secretary-General to establish

4. For a reasonably detailed statement of the goals of the Committee, see Ram C. Malhotra, "Apartheid and the United Nations", in *The Annals,* American Academy of Political and Social Science, Philadelphia, July, 1964.

5. Harold Soref and Ian Greig, *The Puppeteers,* London, 1965, p. 14.

6. Ronald Segal (ed.), *Sanctions Against South Africa,* London, 1964.

'. . . a small group of recognized experts to examine methods of resolving the present situation in South Africa, through full, peaceful, and orderly application of human rights and fundamental freedoms for all inhabitants of the territory as a whole, regardless of race, colour, or creed, and to consider what part the United Nations might play in the achievement of that end . . . ;'[7]

and the British Council of Churches' study.[8]

(c) Pressure on South Africa to withdraw from international organizations. The most noteworthy instance of this was South Africa's enforced withdrawal from the Commonwealth of Nations in 1961. On the eve of becoming a republic, South Africa, following the precedent of India, Ceylon and Ghana, had wished to continue as a member of the association. However, as a result of criticism of South Africa's internal policies at the Commonwealth Prime Ministers' conference in January, 1961, South Africa withdrew its application for continued membership.[9]

(d) Outside of the United Nations, South Africa's policies have been condemned by the governments of numerous countries. Thus the United States Assistant Secretary of State for African Affairs, Mr David Newsom, and his Deputy, Mr Beverly Carter, Jnr. during a visit to Southern Africa in November, 1970, stated their country's attitude towards the South African situation in a press conference in Johannesburg as follows:

'The American official attitude toward the policy of racial discrimination in South Africa has been constant. We abhor racial policies which by law separate men, and deny them rights solely on the basis of the colour of their skin. There is no question of the United States condoning or acquiescing in these policies. We stand on the side of fundamental human rights in southern Africa as we do at home and elsewhere.'[10]

7. See *Report by the Secretary General in Pursuance of the Resolution by the Security Council at its 1078th Meeting* on 4 December, 1963 (S/5471), UN Doc., S/5658, 20 April, 1964, p. 7.

8. *The Future of South Africa: A Study by British Christians,* British Council of Churches, London, 1965.

9. See Gerrit Olivier, *op. cit.,* pp. 291-294, for a brief but informative account.

10. *Transcript of Proceedings: Report on African Trip* by Assistant Secretary David D. Newsom and Deputy Assistant Secretary W. Beverley Carter, Jnr., December 4, 1970, Department of State, Washington, D.C., p. 2.

This statement is fairly typical of the stance adopted by those Western countries which have expressed themselves on the South African situation.

Some countries have gone further, and prohibited trade with South Africa, refused facilities to South African-registered vessels, denied landing rights and the use of air-space to South African civilian aircraft, and refused entry to South African passport-holders. (Ghana requires South Africans to sign a declaration of opposition to apartheid as a condition for the grant of a visa.) In terms of a Security Council resolution of 7 August, 1963, member-states are required to refuse to supply South Africa with arms and ammunition and all types of military equipment. This resolution has only very partially been complied with.

(e) Assistance of different kinds to the liberation movements sponsored by the Organization for African Unity. Examples are the grants of money by the World Council of Churches, the Netherlands head of state, and the Israeli government.[11] However, no Western country has declared itself in favour of externally mounted violence directed at the South African government. Thus Mr Newsom, on the same occasion referred to earlier, expressed his government's attitude on this question when he said:

> 'The United States has always sought a non-violent and evolutionary solution to these problems. While recognising worldwide concern over these matters, we believe that the solutions must ultimately be worked out by the peoples concerned. Similarly, we do not inject ourselves into the question of relations between South Africa and the remainder of the continent; this matter is essentially one for Africa."[12]

Again, this is fairly typical of the position adopted by most Western countries and an increasing number of African states. The idea of change through violence is, however, canvassed, perhaps less so today than a decade ago, in Western countries by various activist groups. Probably the most comprehensive study of the feasibility of coercive action against

11. The Israeli grant was not immediately accepted by the OAU and was subsequently withdrawn largely as a result of tremendous pressure from South African Jews.

12. *Transcript of Proceedings, op. cit.*, pp. 2-3.

South Africa was prepared under the auspices of the Carnegie Endowment for International Peace in 1964. Although no general conclusions or policy recommendations were made, the obstacles to such a course appeared to be very considerable.[13]

(f) Physical attacks on South African official and semi-official facilities in other countries. Known examples of this kind of action against South Africa are the bomb attacks against the South African Consulate General in New York and the attempted attack (also in New York) on the office of the South African Tourist Corporation.

(g) Apart from having been expelled from international sporting organizations (notably the Olympic Games), organized attempts have been made to disrupt tours abroad of South African teams and individual South African sportsmen have been harrassed in overseas competition.

(h) Prominent visitors to South Africa – politicians, academicians, journalists, churchmen, businessmen – have been openly critical during their stay of prevailing conditions and policies. Thus the syndicated columns (which were on South Africa) of both C.L. Sulzburger and Carl Rowan were published in certain South African newspapers while they were still in the country; and the criticism of visitors of the standing of Congressman Charles Diggs, Chairman of the House Sub-Committee on Africa, Ramsey Clark, former US Attorney General, Denis Healey, former Minister of Defence in the Labour Government in Britain, and the Archbishop of Canterbury, have been widely publicized in South Africa.

(i) Race relations in South Africa has been the subject of considerable academic writing (much of it critical) and a great deal of multi-media reporting (much of it one-sided). Obviously these are risky judgements for an academic to make, but with respect to scholarly literature on South Africa in the field of political science, in particular, scholars have tended to regard South Africa as wholly *sui generis* and thus, for example, where they would sympathetically view the problem population diversity presents Nigeria and other African countries in terms of political integration, their examination of the South African situation is focussed on the race

13. Amelia C. Leiss, *Apartheid and United Nations Collective Measures,* The Carnegie Endowment for International Peace, New York, 1965.

relations aspect, and is suffused with value-judgments.[14] As far as the news media are concerned, there is a tendency to publish only that which conforms with the well-established image of this country. So, for example, a decision to introduce a television service which caters to the different language groups was presented by *Time* magazine as an instance of segregation.[15]

International disapproval of conditions in South Africa and official policies with respect to race relations is thus widespread and assumes many varied forms. However, that South Africans in general, and White South Africans in particular, are conscious of this criticism is undeniable. Little attempt is made to suppress the criticism,[16] as even a casual reading of the headlines of a South African newspaper will show. For example, *The Star* (the biggest circulating daily newspaper in the country) of 22 July, 1971 contained no fewer than eight news items dealing (in some form or other) with international attitudes towards South Africa.[17] Moreover,

14. Typical of the sort of writing referred to is Pierre L. van den Berghe's *South Africa: A Study in Conflict,* Middletown, Conn., 1965. It abounds with statements like: 'White South Africans were, however, quick to perceive that cultural assimilation would be accompanied by social integration and "bastardization" of the *Herrenvolk*' (p. 225), and 'A South Africa divided against itself awaits the impending and inexorable catastrophe. The Whites claim a right to survival which hardly anybody denies them. But in claiming to assert that right they have set themselves against the course of history, and have become an arrogant, oppressive albinocracy. Their pride and prejudice may well be their undoing. *Quos vult Jupiter perdere, dementat prius.*' (p. 264). Offsetting this, however, is the pioneering scholarship of American-based scholars like Carter, Feit, Karis, Kuper, Munger, Stutz, Walshe, and, more recently, Adam and Grundy.

15. *Time,* New York, 10 May, 1971, p. 31.

16. Censorship in South Africa, although a source of irritation and anger to a very considerable section of the English- as well as Afrikaans-speaking intelligentsia, does not affect news reporting.

17. The items were – 'Plebiscite Plan Had Court in Quandary' – a reference to South Africa's proposal to the International Court of Justice that it direct that the future status of South West Africa be determined by a plebiscite of the local population; 'Letter to Kennedy on US Policy' – a reference to a letter Senator Edward Kennedy received from the US State Department regarding a cocktail party the American ambassador had held in Cape Town and at which no Non-Whites were present; 'Small "Go Home" Party for the Boks' – a reference to the hostile reception which awaited a South African rugby team during its tour of Australia; 'Minority Body Stops Tour' – a reference to the Labour and Liberal minority on the Birmingham City Council managing to put a stop to a lecture tour of South Africa by the City Librarian; 'Cassius Clay To Visit South Africa?' – a reference to the possibility of the American boxer visiting South Africa with a statement from the Minister of Interior that his application for a visa would be treated on merit; 'South Africa Making New Friends through Africa' – a report of a speech by Dr F.J. de Villiers of the Africa

overseas newspapers, particularly British newspapers like *The Times, The Daily Telegraph, The Observer,* and *The Sunday Times* (all of which are well-represented in South Africa and carry a surprising amount of news about South Africa), as well as news magazines like *Time* and *Newsweek,* are freely available in South Africa.

Furthermore the demonstrations against touring South African sports teams (in particular rugby and cricket) have ensured that the awareness of South Africa's unpopularity in the world has percolated down from the intelligentsia. In fact, the pervasiveness of the criticism, its persistence, and its comprehensiveness, are important factors in the assessment of the impact of overseas criticism on White South Africans.

WHITE SOUTH AFRICAN RESPONSE TO CRITICISM

A precise or even remotely scientific assessment of the impact of external criticism of racial policies and practices in South Africa on White South Africans is simply not possible. Opinion surveying, except of the soaps and cereals variety, is virtually non-existent in this country; and no studies along the lines of Gabriel Almond's *The American People and Foreign Policy*[18] have been made. At best, therefore, one has to infer reactions (and probable reactions) from newspaper and radio reports, and from the public pronouncements of politicians and other conscious fashioners of public opinion. The natural reluctance of politicians to admit that overseas criticism has influenced any particular policy decision renders even more difficult an accurate determination of the impact of overseas criticism on South Africa's domestic policies. As will be seen presently, this is nicely exemplified in the case of South Africa's international sporting relations.

The White South African response to overseas criticism has been neither uniform nor passive. White society is hardly monolithic, and in fact much of the overseas criticism is shared by a sizeable segment of the White intelligentsia – both English- as well as Afrikaans-speaking. Moreover, the non-racial, shared or common society which is the recipe for justice and racial harmony of the overwhelming majority of South Africa's

Institute; 'Breezes of Change in South African Society' – an editorial page article about the United States-South Africa Leader Exchange Programme's conference in Johannesburg, attended by several prominent black Americans; 'Cricket Tour on – Bedford Insists' – a reference to the possibility that a scheduled cricket tour of Australia would be cancelled as a result of demonstrations.

18. Gabriel Almond, *The American People and Foreign Policy,* New York, 1960.

overseas critics, is also espoused by the English-speaking intelligentsia, with the result that many critical overseas pronouncements – particularly where they are 'informed' and 'sensible' (in the South African context) – are used by sections of the White opposition to corroborate the validity of their own position. So, for example, when the Foreign Ministers Conference of the Organization for African Unity in June, 1971 decided by majority vote against dialogue with South Africa, *The Rand Daily Mail* (probably the most consistent supporter among English language newspapers of the common society position) in an editorial – 'A Message from Addis Ababa' – in its issue of 21 June, 1971, declared:

> 'It is all very well for Mr Vorster to tell the good citizens of Naboomspruit [the South African equivalent of Hicksville] that he will do all he can to win African friendships – but what do African states make of the fact that he seems reluctant to extend the same opportunity to a Black man within his own country? When Chief Buthelezi, a potential Prime Minister of the Zulus, admitted the other day that he had never met Mr Vorster, he revealed our vulnerability. We cannot wriggle out of it – dialogue with Africans begins at home.'[19]

The reaction to overseas criticism is not uniform and neither is it passively received. In the first place it is interpreted in terms of the views and values of the beholder; and secondly, there is a reaction. Moreover, the evaluation of the criticism, even at a relatively unsophisticated level, occurs in terms of a framework of reference in which knowledge (or a certain kind of knowledge) of circumstances in the country from which the criticism originates figures. This may be illustrated in relation to the visit to South Africa of Mr Ramsey Clark. The former United States Attorney General was invited to South Africa by the National Union of South African Students (NUSAS), an organization mainly representative of English-speaking students in South Africa and having a political commitment to multi-racialism and a common society. For several years now NUSAS has invited to South Africa to address NUSAS audiences prominent persons who may be expected to associate themselves with this point of view. Although Mr Clark's speeches were widely reported in the South African press, the South African Broadcasting Corporation in its daily

19. *The Rand Daily Mail*, Johannesburg, 21 June, 1971.

programme *Current Affairs* helped to defuse his criticism of South Africa in a talk which was broadcast shortly after his departure from the country.

> 'Mr Clark is a former Attorney General of the United States, and he is seen by some Americans as a Democratic candidate for the Presidency. During the six days he was in this country, he proferred advice on a wide range of the nation's affairs. And it should be noted that Mr Clark is not merely a theorist: through eight years during the sixties he was in a key position to put his ideas into practice . . . There is the record of his own performance against which to judge the worth of what he said. He criticized while he was here the recent legislation to curb the danger of drugs. While he was in office in the United States drug addiction in that country reached unprecedented proportions . . . Mr Clark chose to advise us on law-enforcement. While he was in office in the United States crime in that country reached unprecedented proportions . . . Mr Clark said while he was here that millions of Black and White Americans were enraged by apartheid, and he advocated total integration as the only answer to the country's problems. While he was in office in the United States racial hatred in that country reached unprecedented proportions.'[20]

Rugby football being South Africa's national game, virtually every adult White would have been made conscious of the campaign against South Africa as a result of the rugby tour of Australia in 1971. Quite apart from press reports, which dealt almost as much with the demonstrations against the team as with the actual competition, running commentries of all the matches were broadcast, and in the background listeners could hear the chants (generally 'Go home, racists!') of the 'demos'.[21] Yet almost as many South Africans are aware that Australia is not blameless in the field of race relations; and in the midst of all the publicity which the demonstrators against the tour were receiving in South Africa appeared a report that Mr Peter Hain, a former South African who has made something of a career out of opposing South African sporting tours of Britain, and

20. South African Broadcasting Corporation Survey: *Current Affairs,* Johannesburg, 18 May, 1971.

21. It should be added that the Afrikaans commentator punctuated his commentary of the play itself with savoury references to the demonstrators of the kind – 'One has nothing against long hair, if only it were clean!'

who had been invited out to Australia to give the anti-tour forces there the benefit of his wisdom, had hit out at 'racism' in Australia on his return to London. 'Australia,' Mr Hain was reported as having said, 'should pay more than lip service to non-racialism otherwise its international image and internal policies could justifiably be termed racialist.'[22] Racial unrest anywhere in the world is news in South Africa, and most South Africans know that countries like the United States and Britain have their problems. The fact that South Africa is the only country which officially condones discrimination is a subtle point which escapes most of them.

Apart from the fact that external criticism of the South African situation will be interpreted in terms of a certain framework of reference, the sophisticated South African reaction reveals an intense desire to show that the situation is not nearly as bad as it is made out to be. However, something more specific should be said about official and non-official reactions to overseas criticism.

As the storm clouds mounted on South Africa's international horizon, the official reaction was a granite-like insistence that the issues involved were nobody other than South Africa's business. This posture was most clearly evident at the United Nations, where the South African reaction to criticism was solidly based on article 2, paragraph 7 (the so-called domestic jurisdiction clause) of the Charter.[23] Some idea of the South African position during the fifties and the early sixties is obtained from the following speech delivered by Mr Eric Louw, the South African Foreign Minister, before the General Assembly on 15 November, 1956. On this occasion Mr Louw was protesting the inclusion on the agenda of the General Assembly of two items, namely the treatment of Indians in South Africa, and the South African government's apartheid policy.

> 'On behalf of the Government of the Union of South Africa, I wish to object to the inclusion of item 24 (treatment of Indians) and 61 (apartheid policy) in the agenda of this Assembly. The objection of my Government is based on the ground that the Assembly is precluded by article 2, paragraph 7, of the Charter from either consider-

22. *The Star,* Johannesburg, 23 July, 1971.

23. Article 2, paragraph 7, of the Charter states: 'Nothing contained in the present Charter shall authorize the United Nations to intervene in matters which are essentially in the domestic jurisdiction of any state or shall require the members to submit such matters to settlement under the present Charter . . .'

ing or discussing these items. It is further the contention of the Union Government, if these items were to be placed on the agenda, such action in itself would constitute interference in the domestic affairs of a Member State of the United Nations, and that it would therefore be in conflict with the provision of article 2, paragraph 7 of the Charter. For the past ten years, since the first meeting of this Organization, the Union of South Africa has strongly opposed the inscription of item 24. During those years the Sovereign State of South Africa has not only had to resist interference in its domestic affairs, but our delegations have in that connection had to submit to unjust, baseless, and often malicious attacks on their country. I submit that South Africa has borne these attacks with exemplary and commendable patience, and has throughout these years consistently adhered to the principle contained in article 2, paragraph 7, also when it was sought to interfere in the domestic affairs of other countries.'[24]

On 27 November, 1956 Mr Louw announced the South African government's decision to withdraw its delegation from the General Assembly, and to maintain only a token representation at the United Nations. The South African government's attitude towards external criticism at this time comes across clearly in the following excerpt from his address:

> 'May I remind this Assembly that South Africa, like some other countries that shall be nameless, is faced with difficult racial problems which we are trying our utmost to solve in a manner which will take account of both the interests of the European and the Non-European peoples, and which, if carried out in the right spirit of both sides, will provide the basis for harmonious co-operation between the two sections of South Africa's population.
> The continued interference of the United Nations in South Africa's problems, accompanied as it is by baseless charges of oppression and ill-treatment, made from the rostrum of this Assembly, have had the effect of aggravating racial tensions and of seriously disturbing racial relations in South Africa . . . We are not willing any longer to be even an unwilling partner to the continued interference in South Africa's domestic affairs – interference moreover which is detri-

24. H.H.H. Bierman (ed.), *The Case for South Africa,* New York, 1963, p. 21.

> mentally effecting the maintenance and the promotion of harmonious racial relations in our country.
>
> It has therefore been decided that until such time as the United Nations is prepared to act in accordance with the San Francisco Conference of 1945, and to conform to the principles laid down by the founders of the Organization in article 2, paragraph 7 of the Charter, the Union of South Africa, while as yet continuing to be a member of the United Nations, will in future maintain only a local representation or a nominal representation at the meeting of the Assembly and at the Headquarters of the Organization.'[25]

The obvious disadvantage of this posture is that denying others the right to discuss conditions in South Africa precludes a detailed defence of South Africa. But this was the position South Africa adopted throughout the fifties and early sixties. In fact, the South African decision to withdraw its application for continued membership of the Commonwealth in 1961, once it became a republic, was also justified in these terms.[26]

CHANGED ATTITUDES IN THE SIXTIES

A distinct change is discernible in the official reaction to overseas criticism by the mid-sixties. While still insisting that South Africa's problems are an internal matter, at the United Nations and elsewhere South African spokesmen explained the South African situation in detail and embarked upon spirited defences of South Africa's policies. Nowhere is the difference in tone and approach so evident as in the address Dr Hilgard Muller, successor to Mr Eric Louw as Foreign Minister, delivered in the General Assembly on the 21st December, 1964. Dr Muller prefaced a detailed defence of South Africa's race relations policies as follows:

> 'It is against this immediate background of what is fundamental in our Charter – the recognition of basic differences of culture, tradition, and forms of government, coupled with emphasis on the right of each people to attain nationhood – that I deem it necessary to refer to certain aspects of our national life. In doing so I must, however, repeat what we have constantly stated, namely that my government does not regard itself accountable to the United Nations for

25. *Ibid.*, pp. 37-38.
26. See Gerrit Olivier, *op. cit.*

the manner in which it governs the country. If I feel obliged to speak about our domestic affairs it is simply to place before all those who are prepared to listen objectively the facts of our position – the facts as they really are and not as some believe them to be.'

The South African Foreign Minister then went on to deal with what he described as 'the main objection to the policy of the South African government, namely . . . that it is alleged to be or believed to be one of perpetual domination by one section of the population over the others. I want to state most categorically that this charge is completely unfounded and unjustified'. The rest of his speech (about two-thirds of the total address) was devoted to explaining South Africa's race relations policy and answering criticisms which had been levelled at it.[27] A similar advocacy of South Africa's policies was evident from around this period in the activities of the South African Department of Information, which had been considerably expanded.

By the late sixties official reaction was remarkably relaxed. Policy with respect to known and likely critics, as reflected for example in the issue of visas, was fairly flexible; and organizations like the South Africa Foundation and the United States-South Africa Leader Exchange Programme have been encouraged to invite to South Africa very improbable sympathizers with government policy.

This change in official attitude and policy is probably due to the steady improvement from the mid-sixties onwards of the international climate as far as South Africa is concerned. For one thing, the economic boom experienced by that country in the mid-sixties put it high up on the list of important trading countries, a fact which, combined with its greater military strength and armament self-sufficiency, put an end, for the time being at any rate, to talk of military invasions and economic sanctions. Racial tension in Britain and elsewhere, and the slow-down of the civil rights movement in the United States as it had been conceived in the years following the US Supreme Court decision in *Brown vs. Board of Education* of 1954,[28] was another factor favouring South Africa: without implying

27. *Text of Address Delivered in the General Assembly on December 21, 1964* by Dr The Hon. Hilgard Muller, Minister of Foreign Affairs of the Republic of South Africa, Permanent South African Mission to the United Nations, New York.

28. See Denis Worrall, 'The Coloureds: Lessons from America', *New Nation,* September, 1971, Pretoria, for an elaboration of this view.

approval of South African policy, these developments underlined the intractability of race problems and the unlikelihood of 'instant' solutions.[29] The failure of the African states to realize the early hopes held out for them should be added to this factor.[30]

Furthermore the development of super-tankers, the closing of the Suez Canal, and the determined Soviet penetration of the Indian Ocean, focused attention on the importance of the Cape sea route; and although there is disagreement about its strategic importance in a nuclear age, an old argument for meaningful co-operation with the Republic was given new substance.[31] Also among the factors which changed the international environment as far as South Africa is concerned was the development to independence of Black states in and around the Republic. Apart from the fact that their dependence on South Africa was not lost on her detractors, a situation was created which forced policy-makers in the Republic to face up to the question of relations with Black African states; and an important objective of South Africa's 'outward policy' was the establishment of diplomatic and other ties in Africa itself. South Africa has been encouraged in this regard by the division which has developed within African states over the so-called 'dialogue with South Africa' issue.[32]

Finally, there is the fact that by the late sixties, official race relations policy in South Africa had reached the stage where the government could point to certain tangible achievements – something which its critics (both internal and external) were forced to acknowledge.[33]

These are some of the reasons for the rather significant change in the

29. This much was admitted by Assistant Secretary of State for Africa, Mr David D. Newsom in his statement before the House Sub-Committee on Africa and in several of his speeches following his return to the United States from his visit during November, 1970 to southern Africa.

30. See Professor C.W. de Kiewiet, 'The Revolution that Disappeared', in *South Africa International,* Vol. 1, No. 3, January, 1971, Johannesburg. This article originally appeared in *The Virginia Quarterly Review,* Vol. 46, No. 2, Spring, 1970.

31. The British in 1970 cited the importance of the Cape sea route, particularly in view of Soviet naval activity in the Indian ocean, to justify the sale of military equipment to South Africa.

32. See in this regard John Barratt, 'A new Wind of Change in Africa', *New Nation,* July 1971.

33. See Alan Paton, 'Thoughts on the Common Society' in Peter Randall (ed.), *South Africa: Directions of Change* (SPROCAS, 1971); Edwin S. Munger, 'South Africa: Are there silver linings?', *Foreign Affairs,* January, 1969, Washington, D.C.; and George F. Kennan, 'Hazardous Course in Southern Africa', *Foreign Affairs,* January, 1971.

official attitude towards overseas criticism which has occurred since the mid-sixties. From regarding the question of race relations in South Africa as essentially a matter of internal and domestic concern, and therefore no business of outsiders – whether governments, organizations, or individuals – the Prime Minister at a press conference in March 1971 declared his willingness to discuss South Africa's policies with the leaders of other African countries. (During his very successful five-day visit to South Africa in August, 1971, President Banda of Malawi on all occasions made it clear that he did not accept the segregational aspects of South African policy. However, he was always quick to add that he believed that the way to change was through contact, discussion, dialogue, etc., rather than confrontation and force.[34])

So much for the official attitude in general towards overseas criticism. How has the government responded to specific criticisms? In the first place, much criticism has simply been ignored. Thus there was no official reaction to the criticism of persons like Mr Denis Healey, the Archbishop of Canterbury, Mr Carl Rowan, and Mr Ramsey Clark, during their visits to South Africa.[35] A second distinct reaction has been the substantive answer. Perhaps the best illustration of this is the South West African case, where, apart from arguing the technically-legal aspects, the government countered the charges of oppression with a very detailed brief and (apparently) actually forced the applicants (Ethiopia and Liberia) to abandon this part of their case.[36] Thirdly, a great deal of criticism is rejected out of hand on grounds of questionable *bona fides* (for example, that the critics are communists or fellow-travellers) or by pointing out that a double standard is involved in the criticism. So, for example, the Prime Minister in a speech on South Africa's role within Southern Africa at an international relations symposium held at Potchefstroom University in August, 1971 observed that migratory labour is a fairly common phenomenon in Western Europe; yet, he said, ministers of religion from these countries come to South Africa and criticize the practice here.

Finally, international criticism is used by South African politicians to justify existing policies. It is presented as a threat and variously used to

34. See 'Banda Tells Press: I'm Running Show', *The Star,* 20 August, 1971.

35. Although the fact is that in these and similar cases the government could rely on the Afrikaans press and the South African Broadcasting Corporation to express more or less its sentiments.

36. See in this regard *South West Africa Survey, op. cit.,* pp. 142-152.

rally party followers or to mobilize them in support of the general course the government has charted. So Mr Theo Gerdener, the Minister of the Interior, in a speech in July, 1971, used the international threat to justify the acceleration of progressive change. According to *The Star* of 20 July, 1971

> '(Mr Gerdener) warned Whites that they would have to adopt more supple and more humane attitudes towards Non-Whites and that the campaign of dialogue with black states would have to gain impetus and be accepted. The decade of the seventies would be "final". South Africa would not get a second chance to put her house in order. It was vital that priority be given to the development of the Bantu homelands.'[37]

Non-governmental reactions to criticism, with the exception of instances already referred to where overseas criticism is actually used to bolster local political positions, correspond more or less to the government's. However, White South African reactions tend to be unanimous where the criticism is of a radical nature and, for example, affects basic security or where it entails a very obvious interference in South Africa's affairs. Thus when Israel announced the grant of R2 000 to the OAU's liberation committee, *The Rand Daily Mail* editorialized:

> 'In some ways Israel's donation to the African "liberation movements" is even more distateful than other such gestures of moral support made recently. This is because it is so patently more an act of political expediency. The purpose obviously is to curry favour with the militant African states and so hopefully prevent them from supporting the Arab cause against Israel. Understandable perhaps. But how would Israel feel if we were to give money to Al Fatah in the hope that this would take some of the political heat off us . . . We find it sad that a country founded on such high ideals should resort to such cheap expediency. We accept that Israel disapproves strongly of apartheid. But we thought that it, of all countries, would disapprove of terrorism too.'[38]

Proposals for the withdrawal of investments from South Africa by overseas based companies have similarly met with opposition from Progressive

37. 'Big Changes on the Way – Gerdener', *The Star,* 20 July, 1971.
38. 'Act of Expediency', *The Rand Daily Mail,* 4 June, 1971.

and Liberal quarters. So Dr Ellen Hellmann, a leading South African liberal and articulate exponent of the common society point of view, described the action of Mr Neil Wates, a British businessman who decided against investing in South Africa on political grounds, as '. . . the most negative option offering'.[39]

Of the private organizations involved with South Africa's image in the world, the most important by far is the South Africa Foundation. Established eleven years ago by businessmen who were alarmed at the exodus of capital from the country which followed the disturbances associated with Sharpeville and Langa, the Foundation's main goal is '. . . to promote international understanding of South Africa – her achievements, her problems, and her potential, and by so doing, to advance the welfare of all her peoples . . .'[40] The South Africa Foundation aims to influence through elites, and now has offices in London, Paris, Bonn and Washington, and committees of notables in Australia, Belgium, Canada, Israel, the Lebanon, New Zealand, the Scandinavian countries, Switzerland and the United States. It is mainly responsible for bringing to South Africa prominent personalities from different countries and assisting other visitors to South Africa with their itineraries, contacts, etc. The South Africa Foundation claims to be non-political (it draws its support from businessmen right across the political spectrum), and in presenting South Africa's case it stresses the non-political aspects. It has sounded warnings of developments overseas which are inimical to South Africa's interests, but in its comments on developments in South Africa it is very discreet.[41] It prefers to make personal representations at the ministerial level.

Beside businessmen, Afrikaans churchmen as a group have responded quite vigorously at times to overseas criticism. In view of their close association with churches and universities in the Netherlands – a significant

39. Dr Ellen Hellmann, 'Boycotts and the Economy: What Mr Neil Wates Forgets', in *New Nation,* September, 1971.

40. *South Africa Foundation: Annual Report, 1970,* Johannesburg, p. 1.

41. A good example of this is the address the Foundation's President, Major-General Sir Francis de Guingand, delivered at the eleventh annual general meeting of the body in Durban on the 24th March, 1971. After warning that 'I will not disguise the fact that in my view the pressures against South Africa in some ways are increasing and becoming more dangerous,' he went on to mention '. . . a few facets of our discriminatory legislation where I suggest some rethinking might be appropriate.' For details, see *South Africa Foundation: Presidential Address by Major-General Sir Francis de Guingand, K.B.E., C.B., D.S.O.,* South Africa Foundation, Johannesburg, 1971.

number of Afrikaans ministers of religion have received and continue to receive their training in the Netherlands – the main Afrikaans churches have a kind of love-hate relationship with their Dutch counterparts, and they are quick to counter criticism emanating from church circles in Holland.[42]

THE ROLE OF OVERSEAS CRITICISM

There can be no doubt that overseas criticism figures in the process of change in South Africa, but what its precise effect is or its extent is not easy to determine. This point may be illustrated in relation to South Africa's international sporting relations. Sport involves masses, and is therefore politically a highly sensitive area – a fact which also South Africa's critics know.[43] The issue is also fairly simple: sport in South Africa has been organized on segregational lines, and in international competition the teams representative of South Africa have been selected exclusively from the White organizations. Overseas opposition to this state of affairs first began to make itself felt in the mid-fifties. The objectives of critics have varied: sometimes they have insisted simply on integrated teams; sometimes they have wanted to see the teams selected on a competitive basis; and sometimes their goal has been the integration of all sport in South Africa.

Although pressures have been directed at bilateral sporting relations, (South Africa's long-standing cricket ties with England and Australia, and its rugby football ties with the British Isles, New Zealand and Australia), the main focal point has been South Africa's membership of international sporting bodies and the Olympic Games in particular. In 1955 the South African Soccer Federation (a Non-White organization) made representations to the Federation of International Football Associations (FIFA) that it replace the White Football Association of South Africa (FASA) as the representative national body. The matter dragged through several years with various compromise arrangements being suggested (at one point FASA offered to recognize the Non-White body as an affiliate, but without voting rights), until at the FIFA conference in 1961 FASA's international status was withdrawn, which meant that South African

42. A good example is W.A. Landman (ed.), *A Plea For Understanding: A Reply to The Reformed Church in America,* Cape Town, 1968.

43. This point was made in *The Future of South Africa: A Study by British Christians, op. cit.*

soccer teams could not compete in international competitions. The same pattern of events has occurred in other sports.

South Africa's membership of the Olympic Games was terminated fifty days before the Tokyo Games of 1964, following protracted negotiations between the South African Olympic and National Games Association (SAONGA) and the International Olympic Committee. A factor in the IOC decision was the South African Non-Racial Olympic Committee (SANROC) which, from its founding in October 1962, mounted an intensive campaign to be recognized in the place of SAONGA.

At a meeting of the IOC in Rome in April, 1966, South Africa's suspension was confirmed. In 1967, following a meeting of the IOC in Teheran, a fact-finding commission of three members visited South Africa and subsequently presented a report in terms of which the IOC decided to settle the matter by a postal vote of all its seventy members. The result (announced at an IOC meeting in Grenoble in February, 1968) was a majority in favour of South Africa of 38 to 27,[44] and South African sportsmen went ahead with preparations to participate in the 1968 Mexico City Games. However, on 26 April, as a result of pressure on the IOC and the fear that South Africa's presence would cause demonstrations and possible violence, the IOC announced that the invitation to South Africa had been withdrawn by a vote of 46 for, 14 against, with two abstentions.

Throughout these developments, the South African government did not remain passive. At crucial points it intervened with policy statements which either reiterated existing policy with respect to colour and sport or which actually involved reformulations of policy. So in June, 1956, when South Africa's policies and practices in sport were first drawing serious international attention, the Minister of the Interior declared that

> '. . . while the government was most sympathetic towards, and anxious to help, "legitimate non-European sporting activities", these must accord with the policy of separate development. Whites and Non-Whites should organize their sporting activity separately, there should be no inter-racial competitions within South Africa, the mixing of races in teams should be avoided, and sportsmen from other countries should respect South Africa's customs, as she respected

44. The main reason for this favourable vote were the concessions which the new Prime Minister had made. See Muriel Horrell, *South Africa and the Olympic Games* (SAIRR, Johannesburg, 1968), p. 23. This is a most useful publication.

> theirs. In that framework Non-White sportsmen from outside would not be debarred from entering South Africa to compete with Non-Whites."[45]

Early 1963, in the middle of the argument about South Africa's participation in the Olympic Games, the Minister of the Interior again reiterated official policy as follows:

> (1) Whites and Non-Whites must not compete against one another within the borders of South Africa. Outside of these borders South Africans might compete with sportsmen of racial groups different from their own who came from other countries.
> (2) Sporting bodies would not be allowed to send mixed teams to represent South Africa as a whole in international events. If Whites participated in overseas competitions they must do so as representatives of the Whites in South Africa, and if Non-Whites took part, they must do so as representatives of the South African Non-Whites.
> (3) Each Non-White association should develop alongside the corresponding White body. The White executive committee should co-ordinate the work of both, and representation in the international organization concerned should be through members of the White body.
> (4) One or two members of the White executive committee might attend meetings of the Non-White committee, when requested, to maintain liaison. If this method appeared impracticable in a particular instance, one or more members of the Non-White body should be elected or co-opted to the White executive in an advisory capacity when matters affecting the Non-White were being discussed.[46]

A similar statement was made stressing the same points shortly before the 1964 Tokyo Games, with the effect of completely undermining the position of South Africa's representatives at the IOC.[47]

In 1965 attention turned to another facet of South Africa's sporting relations, when, with a South African rugby football team touring New Zealand at the time, the South African Prime Minister declared (in the

45. Horrell, *op. cit.*, p. 9.
46. *Ibid.*, pp. 13-14.
47. *Ibid.*, p. 16.

so-called Loskop Dam speech) that Maoris would not be welcome in a New Zealand touring team of South Africa. Later in 1965 the government was reported to have rejected pleas from the President of the South African Rugby Board that his board be allowed to invite its counterpart in New Zealand to send a truly representative team to tour South Africa in 1967. This tour did not take place as a consequence.

With South African sport embattled on all sides, the new Prime Minister in April, 1967 re-stated government policy in far more flexible terms. Although no mixed sport between White and Non-White South Africans would be tolerated, according to Miss Horrell,

> '. . . he said that a very clear distinction should be drawn between personal relations on the one hand and inter-State relations on the other. In regard to international sporting events, Mr Vorster adopted a more flexible approach than that of Dr Verwoerd. Mr Vorster's policy so far as the Olympic Games are concerned is that South Africa will have to comply with the requirements that only one team from each country may participate, and that the sportsmen selected must form one contingent under their country's flag.'[48]

With regard to rugby and cricket the new Prime Minister said that South Africa could not prescribe to these countries the composition of future visiting teams. In relation to New Zealand rugby teams, Mr Vorster specifically made the point that Maoris had been included in past teams and there had been no discrimination against them in South Africa.[49]

In line with this new policy a fully representative New Zealand rugby team (it included two Maoris) toured South Africa in 1970. It was followed by a French rugby team, one member of which was Coloured. Also in 1971, Yvonne Goolagong, the Australian Aborigine, competed in and won the South African national tennis championship.

In April, 1971, on the eve of a South African rugby tour of Australia, and with a cricket tour scheduled to follow shortly afterwards, Mr Vorster made another significant policy statement. The government felt that

> '. . . the time had arrived for the Non-Whites to be afforded the opportunity of participating in international sport; they had to be

48. *Ibid.*, p. 19.
49. *Ibid.*

> afforded the opportunity of not only participating in international sport, but also of improving the standard of their sport in South Africa . . . I believe the matter has to be improved within the national context of each of those groups.'[50]

Towards this end, the Prime Minister said, visiting national teams would be encouraged to compete against all communities in South Africa. An invitation to this effect, he said, had already gone out to the British Rugby Board which was due to send a team to South Africa in 1972. Further opportunities for Non-White sportsmen would be opened up by the staging of international competitions in South Africa in all the Olympic sports and tennis. Participation would be without regard to race or colour. Thus, as government policy stands at the present time, although no mixed sport will be permitted at the club, provincial, or national level, White and Non-White South Africans may now compete against each other for the first time in open competition in South Africa at 'international competitions'. (An 'international' athletic competition was held late in 1971.)

Official sport policy has been dealt with at some length for two reasons: firstly, it illustrates how South African race relations evolve; and secondly, it demonstrates how overseas pressure in one particular (although important) area has escalated over the last fifteen years. There can be no doubt that overseas criticism has influenced government policy. But apart from the fact that politicians are adept at concealing their motives,[51] several other factors of change are present in the South African situation. So, for example, there are the views of South Africa's White sportsmen. Quite apart from the disappointment which is felt and expressed at their exclusion from international competition, not a few of them have taken up

50. *Hansard,* Second Session – Fourth Parliament (No. 11), Pretoria, Col. 4999.

51. This point is made in its general sense by Maurice Cowling of Cambridge, where he writes '. . . there is a tendency to suppose that by studying "the structure of contemporary government" light will be thrown on the way in which governments work – as though those who govern make public the factors which determine the decisions they take. Not only is it unlikely that their explanations will reveal their intentions: it is likely, on the contrary, that they will conceal them. And not only in trivial or unimportant matters but in important matters also: and the more important the matter, the more likely is concealment to occur.' – Maurice Cowling, *The Nature and Limits of Political Science,* Cambridge, 1963, pp. 20-21. In the South African government's case, even a very close reading of the *Hansard* report of Mr Vorster's speech on sport (and the following speeches) fails to uncover any trace of an admission of the influence of external criticism or pressure.

what amounts to 'political' positions. So, for example, early in 1971 a team, which included some of South Africa's top international cricketers, staged a walk-off in protest of government policy. There is also the fact that attitudes in regard to inter-racial sport reflect the changes which are taking place in race relations in general.

The question of whether or not outsiders have a right to concern themselves in the South African situation seems academic, considering that they are involved and will continue to be involved. Their view that outside pressure on South Africa is imperative if it is to change, is justified partly in moral terms and partly on grounds of expediency. As Dennis Austin puts it:

> 'It is stated, on the one hand, that apartheid is an evil which the rest of the world community has a moral duty to eradicate. But it is also argued that a fundamental conflict exists in South Africa which is absolutely beyond the ability of either side to resolve and the outside world will one day be forced to intervene. The question, therefore, is not whether the United Nations or the West should act against South Africa, but whether they should intervene on their own terms now, or wait until they are forced to do so later. If not, there may be a chance of the peaceful dismantling of apartheid . . . In sum, it is a plea for preventive action by the West not only to end a particularly cruel form of government – although that would be a justifiable end in itself – to avert the danger of a small "race war" or a communist victory among the Afro-Asian states, or both. These are the primary arguments behind the advocacy of sanctions, by which the Nationalist government is to be forced either to abandon its racialist policies, and to accept the demand for a "multiracial Convention", or be replaced by leaders who are prepared to move in that direction.'[52]

CRITICISM AND THE THRUST OF CHANGE

Ironical, however, is the fact that, all the pressure notwithstanding, the thrust of change in South Africa has been in the opposite direction from that demanded by the country's critics – a point which possibly requires elaboration.

52. Dennis Austin, *Britain and South Africa,* Oxford, 1966, pp. 12-13.

In 1958 Professor Gwendolen Carter, in the last chapter – 'Where is South Africa going?' – of her monumental work *The Politics of Inequality,* suggested two radical courses of change South Africa could take. The first of these is territorial separation – what, it is suggested, might be called partition; and the second is the liberal course of integration in a common society.[53] This choice of alternatives is also suggested by practical considerations. Looking at the White South African political spectrum, of the established political parties there are two which accept radical change as necessary if not also desirable. They are the Progressive Party, which espouses some form of adult suffrage leading in the direction of a common society, and the National Party, which advocates a transfer of power on territorial lines in the direction of separate states.

While South Africa's external critics have overwhelmingly supported the common society alternative, official policy has steered change in the other direction, and towards the end of 1971 South Africa stands on the threshold of partition.[54] In fact, as the seventies deepen, South African politics are likely to focus increasingly on the size of the homelands and their share of the wealth of South Africa, on ways of linking Africans in the urban areas with their homelands, on the position of the Coloured and Asian minority groups within 'White' South Africa, on ways of eradicating discrimination on grounds of colour, and on the nature of the over-all constitutional configuration of Southern Africa (in other words, what form will the emerging southern African regionalism take – a commonwealth, a confederation, or a loose federation?).

Can external criticism reverse this course? It would probably be a factor in such a process were there to be a major change in government in South Africa or were there to be a revolution. However, the first possibility seems very unlikely: the Progressive Party in the more than ten years of its existence has never won more than four per cent of the total

53. Gwendolen M. Carter, *The Politics of Inequality,* London, 1958, p. 407.

54. Following tremendous pressure from several English language newspapers and *The Sunday Times* in particular, the Leader of the Opposition, in a policy statement on 4 September, 1971, admitted that the 'momentum towards Bantustan independence may well become irreversible'. According to *The Sunday Times,* Sir de Villiers Graaff declared: 'We may be faced with the fact that, while some Bantustans have reached independence, others will be on the verge of it, will have prepared themselves for it, and will want it.' (*The Sunday Times,* 5 September, 1971). Sir de Villiers was of course speaking of what the situation might be should the United Party be voted into power.

poll or returned more than one candidate.[55] And Austin's conclusion regarding the second possibility, namely that '. . . revolution was not and has never been "just round the corner",'[56] is, if anything, more true in 1971 than it was in the mid-sixties.

Has external criticism, therefore, no role in the South African situation? It has – and there are few enlightened White South Africans (and this includes supporters of government policy) who would deny this. But if external critics are to exercise any significant influence they will have to re-examine their premises in important respects. In the first place, they have tended to see the South African situation almost exclusively as a problem of race conflict and ignored the more enduring element of nationalism. They have also paid only slight attention to the point of view and interests of the White African and other two minorities. In this regard, quite rare in the commentary of external critics is George Kennan's observation that

> 'It should be recognized, first of all, that the South African Whites and the Afrikaners in particular, are confronted with a very real problem when it comes to maintaining, in the face of a large black African majority, their own historical and cultural identity. It is a remarkable identity, forged and affirmed over the course of centuries, at times in struggle and diversity, and against a background of circumstances in some respects different from that which any other people has ever had to face. It is an identity in which, as in the case of the Israelis, national components are mixed, for better or for worse, with religious ones; and the Afrikaners are not more inclined to jeopardize it, by placing themselves entirely in the power of a surrounding foreign majority, than are their Middle Eastern counterparts. They would die rather than do so; and it is simply useless to come at them with demands which suggest that it is this that is expected of them.'[57]

55. The Progressive Party's sole representative in Parliament is the doughty Mrs Helen Suzman, the Member for Houghton (a suburb of Johannesburg).

56. Austin, *op. cit.*, p. 7.

57. George F. Kennan, 'Hazardous Courses in Southern Africa', in *Foreign Affairs*, January, 1971, New York, p. 220.

Secondly, South Africa's external critics have failed to examine the constitutional and political implications of their demand for a common society, given the tremendous pluralism – cultural, ethnic, and nationalist – of the South African situation. As Austin puts it:

> 'Criticism of the Nationalist Government, often implies that there is a just solution to the country's racial problems lying close at hand if only the government would move towards it. But what is a "just solution" in terms of the plurality of South African society? What measures need to be introduced in South Africa in order to produce a free and prosperous community in which racial attitudes are subordinated to national needs? Where is the model in other parts of the world from which South Africa could take its copy? . . . The answer is clear. There is none, and it is difficult to see any agreement between the USSR and the West, or between the South African leaders and the powers imposing sanctions on the nature of the regime which could hold power in the new republic.'[58]

And in demanding a single political system in a common society, how do external critics explain away in the South African context Professor Rupert Emerson's observation that 'Where there is a clear separation, as between Negro and White, Chinese and Malay, there must be a strong presumption that the knitting together of a single nation with actual equality for all will be a long and hazardous project at the best'?[59]

It may be that Kennan's advice to South Africa's external critics to the effect that

> 'Let the friends of the various South African peoples hold the White rulers of that country to the recognition that to the outside world the present pattern of South African apartheid is abhorrent in aspect and unconvincing in rationale. But beyond that let it be the task of those rulers, who know their own situation better than any outsider can, to find the conceivable alternatives,'[60]

places limitations on their self-perceived responsibilities to the Non-White

58. Austin, *op. cit.,* p. 15.
59. Rupert Emerson, *From Empire to Nation* (Boston, 1960), p. 335.
60. Kennan, *op. cit.,* pp. 226-227.

peoples of South African which few would be prepared to accept. But less easily quibbled with is Kennan's observation that

> 'The foreign critic . . . in weighing South Africa's problems, has to remember that the question of racial discrimination represents by no means the totality of them, and that there are some, including a few of the most profound and bitter ones, that could not possibly be mastered without the continued enthusiastic commitment – and this in many respects means the leadership of the White South African community on whose shoulders the responsibilities of government now rest. The two communities are mutually dependent in a way that White and Blacks further north in Africa never were; and the problems of neither can be solved by the destruction or permanent frustration of the other.'[61]

This is something thinking White South Africans do not have to be told.

61. *Ibid.*, p. 224.

South Africa's Racial Policies — A Threat to Peace?

C.A.W. Manning

Charles Anthony Woodward Manning is at present Emeritus Professor of International Relations after occupying this post with distinction at the London School of Economics for 32 years. He has written profusely on his subject, amongst others, The Nature of International Relations, *in 1962. A Fellow of New College, Oxford, and a Laura Spellman Rockefeller Fellow, Charles Manning has had wide experience in the field of international relations,* inter alia *as Personal Assistant to the Secretary-General of the League of Nations.*

In times as queer as these in which we are living queer questions can be put. And this is surely one. Yet what a topic for a school debate! South Africa's 'racial' policies a threat to the peace? The question is worded as if pertaining to a matter of fact, and admitting, in principle, of an answer which if correctly given would be objectively apt. And yet in reality it involves an inherently contentious matter of opinion, calling, in the first place, for clarification of the language employed. What, in particular, for the purpose of the inquiry, is to be understood by a racial policy – and what by a threat to the peace?

South Africans appreciate that, while there is probably no community in the world about which shocking things could not be reported, there must be many more kindly commentators, holy men among them, currently engaged vis-à-vis South Africa in what, were its object a person not a people, would only be describable as cold-blooded character-assassination, than can ever have been the case with any other country. Whether South Africa's policies for the mitigation of human suffering in an often drought-afflicted land are as resourceful and farsighted as they might be is itself a question that could be put. But this article concerns not South

Africa's policies for promoting welfare but her distinctively 'racial' policies – whichever these may be. And though her adversaries, in speaking of them, do not as a rule specify which they are, they doubtless know.

Concisely stated, the basis of South Africa's policies, whether classed as racial or not, is that the country has been assigned, by history, a job to do. 'We're not going to be pushed around by anybody,' declared Mr Harold Wilson, as British Prime Minister, 'We've got a job to do.' South Africa has equally little disposition to be pushed around. The nature of her policies, like those of any other intelligently-administered state, answers to that of the problems they are designed to meet. Military policies, communications policies, educational, public health and other social policies – which of these has one to categorize as 'racial' for the purpose of this inquiry?

Every government has its tasks. These in America's case, as in South Africa's, are conditioned by the ubiquity of more races than one. This gives to many of South Africa's, as of America's, problems a racial dimension. But, while keeping this in mind, she must also hold it in perspective and, viewing her problems in their many-sided complexity, deal with them appropriately as the economic, social, educational, etc., problems that they ultimately are. Calling them racial does not make them any simpler to solve.

The problems of South Africa are further affected by the fact that, while the make-up of the population is multi-racial, the government is formally responsible through an all-White parliament to an all-White electorate. In Switzerland, too, while the population is both male and female, it had been to an all-male electorate that government had hitherto owed responsibility, at least in form. There, though problems are influenced by the presence of more sexes than one, and politicians must keep this fact in mind, the policies followed are never commonly referred to even by the unsympathetic as the sexual policies endorsed by an all-male electorate.

The policy in South Africa of providing hospital services for Blacks virtually gratis, while charging Whites the cost of what they get, is a public health policy, not a racial one. Discrimination in the matter has not heretofore been picked upon internationally for censure. Yet might it not involve some sort of a slur upon the dignity of the Blacks? Are South Africa's educational policies racial? They certainly presuppose the differentiation between the races. Are her military policies racial? These too are discriminatory, laying upon the Whites burdens which the Blacks are not called upon to share. Is it possible in a country like South Africa to have any policies *not* related to, and reflective of, the division of the population into sections having physical origins and civilizational taproots in Asia, in Europe, and in Africa respectively – not to mention a section of mixed descent?

Did Britain's South Africa Act of 1909, distinguishing as it did between persons of European descent and other persons, come within the category of 'racial' legislation? Or was not the fact of its recognizing of racial differences sufficient in itself to put it there? Does legislation perhaps become racial by virtue of being that of a parliament in which persons of European descent alone can sit? Would legislation artificially ensuring equality of opportunity to those of every race, by arrangements specially favouring the less well-endowed, be racial? Or is legislation racial only when its *less* beneficent impact happens to be on those of certain races? The laws determining in which areas particular sections of the population shall be suffered to reside – are these to be seen as a matter of 'racial' policy, and if so, why? Could it not simply have been that social peace and public order were judged likely to be less in danger if the several races were housed apart?

Most often probably what is complained against as 'racial' is no more than an aspect of the White government's practice for maintaining the authority of the law. That it may be appropriate, if not inevitable, in time of serious disorders, for the military to be called upon in support of the police, events in, for example, the United States have recently reminded us. But suppose that in South Africa there were tomorrow to be riots on the scale of those lately witnessed in the United States, and suppose that these were to be quelled, as in the United States, with the aid of the troops, can one not imagine what an uproar at the United Nations there would be? The policy followed in such a situation, that, namely, of resolutely restoring order irrespective of the racial classification of those found in active defiance of the law, would not necessarily escape censure in New York. It might even be invoked there as constituting a threat to the peace. And not merely for the purposes of an academic debate.

SOUTH AFRICA'S POLICIES AND THE UNITED NATIONS

For the real importance of the question about South Africa's policies is that, while it may be examined, by a connoisseur of politics, as if simply a question of fact, it may also be posed as a political problem at the table of the Security Council of the United Nations. Indeed, it has already from time to time been mooted there by interested parties, parties interested not in the question of fact but in the alignment of states on what had better be done in regard to South Africa. For each state represented on the Security Council, the question at such time is, what line shall we instruct our man to take when this matter is put to a vote? Shall we charge him to say yes to the question, thereby accepting our share of the responsibility for the consequences of a formal finding by the Security Council that there exists a threat to the peace? What line its man is to take is for each state a question of political choice in what may be a highly complex diplomatic conjuncture. And the problem is less likely to be that of how to avoid acknowledging a state of manifest danger than that of whether purportedly to see danger when this is less manifestly there. For the proposal is in practice more likely to be met with when the degree of danger is not obviously great than in the hypothetical circumstances of South Africa's policy being palpably a threat to the peace.

The philosopher Bambrough makes a good distinction between inquisitive, and deliberative, questions. As examined by the political connoisseur our question is in principle inquisitive. But as faced by the government of a United Nations member state it is necessarily deliberative. For the judgment to be arrived at is a judgment not of what to think but of what to do.

The United Nations is not in general an organization for the taking of action. Rather is it an elaborate mechanism for the formulating and propagating of views. But in certain circumstances the Security Council has competence to organize active measures, which may typically take the form of mandatory sanctions against some selected country. If there are states represented on the Security Council who, for whatever reasons, would be pleased to see hostile measures concerted against a given country, the procedure for securing this is there. What they must do is persuade the Security Council to determine, that is, to find, the existence of a threat to the peace.

Whether A was a saint, or B a genius, or whether C's conversation is crude – these are matters that may or may not matter very much: but characteristically they are matters not of fact but of opinion. How crude is crude? It is all very well to quote *De gustibus* . . . It is precisely *de gustibus* that the liveliest disputation may be prone to occur. Sometimes it is fair to say of such a discussion that it has been enjoyable but essentially academic.

But if we may ask how crude is crude, we may also ask how academic is academic. The answer here may well be that it depends upon the circumstances. Whether my conduct is uncouth may be debatable: but this question too becomes practically important, at least for me, if for my alleged uncouthness I may be excluded from my club.

In the old League of Nations days, a topic for much earnest head-scratching was how, in the event of war, to determine who was the 'aggressor'. The idea might almost be thought to have been that without an aggressor there couldn't be any war, and that, if being deemed an aggressor was likely to entail disagreeable consequences, no-one would want to be taken or mistaken for one, and so there wouldn't be any war. Nowadays the idea is different. As before, you have a formula for making things disagreeable for someone, this time for use when peace is considered to be in peril. Whereas in the old days you asked, for example, Has Italy resorted to war in disregard of her covenants? what nowadays you ask is, Is there a threat to the peace? And whereas in the old days each member state was expected to answer the crucial question for itself, nowadays it is for the Security Council to take a view. So the question, Is there a threat to the peace? may be more than merely academic if the circumstances are such that the Security Council might be led to answer it in a particular manner.

When, in an English court, it is asked, Was there negligence? what is meant is, Was there negligence in the sight of the law? But by contrast when, at the United Nations, the question is, Is there a threat to the peace? what is meant is, Shall there be declared to exist a threat, in the sight of the Security Council? It is proper to consider how very different a question this could be. For now, instead of being concerned with what was essentially a question of opinion, we are looking at what may in practice be a matter of something else, namely, the collective official policy of a number of member states.

For light upon the nature of this question we have not far to go, no further indeed than to what occurred in the single instance of sanctions being prescribed by the Security Council: namely, in the case of Rhodesia.

In the Rhodesia case the reality was that a colonial power, now with few colonies left to dominate, was seeking vainly to assert its colonialist authority over an area never theretofore a part of its colonial domain. And ironically enough it was the typically anti-colonialist elements that in this instance were most insistent that it should. But it was not of course the inability of Mr Wilson to humble Mr Smith that formed the alleged danger to peace, but the manners at the Commonwealth conference table of the spokesmen of governments allergic to the appearance in the seats of power in Salisbury of the likes of Mr Smith. Like George Washington, and indeed like some of them, Mr Smith had rebelled against British rule, or the prospect of it. And this was what the anti-colonialists affected to find so intolerable, so intolerable indeed that the situation as conditioned by their show of indignation was to be accepted by the Security Council as involving a threat to the peace.

What it at this point becomes relevant to discuss is the basis, if any, on which the affirmative finding of the Security Council will in this case have been arrived at. Two views, or three, may here be distinguished, the third a sort of compromise between numbers one and two. The first would be that the situation was indeed so full, intrinsically, of imminent danger that the Security Council had no effective option but to say so. The second, that it was expedient to assert that there was danger whether there was danger or not – and, this being so, who was to say the Security Council nay? The third view would be that there was danger just sufficient to provide the Security Council with a colourable excuse for doing what its members, or enough of them, were in any event only too happy to do. And it was their need for happiness that tipped the scale.

No proposal for holding South Africa's racial policies a threat to peace has ever as yet attracted quite enough support. But this is not by any means to say that some similar initiative might not on some future occasion succeed. It is germane, therefore, to consider how likely this is to come about. Do the facts first require to become more shocking than they apparently are taken to be? How shocking must they reputedly be in order to warrant a formal finding that they are a danger to peace? That this is an unanswerable question the reader will already know. For while it is one thing to consider with respect to particular policies whether they in fact amount to a threat to peace, it is another thing to consider whether they fall within the class of threats to the peace as this expression might come to be interpreted in the practice of the Security Council.

Before determining that something was a source of danger a court of judges could be expected to hear evidence to that effect. A political body need not. That peace was in peril in the Rhodesia situation appeared rather to be taken for granted than established by studious attention to the facts. The ominous thing in that instance was the apparent ease with which so many Security Council members were found able to fall into line. What the episode suggested was the Security Council's capacity, at need, to cut its calculations loose from the historicity standard and let its assumptions float. All too easily this *modus operandi* might take on the aspect of a habit. The Gibraltarians, especially, who have seemingly little taste for any Goa-pattern 'liberation', may rejoice that, luckily for them, Britain, unlike South Africa, has always the vital power of veto in the Security Council.

In the old days the questions were, Would the member states play ball? Would they recognize a breach of the Covenant when they saw it? Would they act accordingly? And would they stay on the job? In the test case, in 1935-36, all but three of them did recognize the *casus foederis.* And all but four did purport to act accordingly. But it was not very long before a voice was heard opining that it was 'midsummer madness' to keep the sanctions going any longer. And South Africa was alone in protesting against this failure to stay on the job. (For this the South African delegate was personally thanked by the Emperor Haile Selassie, arch-adversary of South Africa today!)

In the Rhodesia case there was near-unanimity in purporting to play ball. And since sanctions are still officially on, they presumably are still by way of doing so. And presumably there is still, in the official theory of the matter, a threat to the peace. Or *is* there? Meanwhile neither in South East Asia nor in the Middle East has there ever yet been comparable recognition of any threat to the peace!

What has been the value of this probing into the past? The point of it has been to highlight the difference between the reporting of a factual perception and the adoption of a political stance. It is the difference between a judicial appreciation of what is indeed the case and the presentation in quasi-judicial fancy-dress of a strategic decision. As so often, the Greeks had their words for what it is being sought to say. They differentiated between what was the case intrinsically (*phusei*), and what was so as a matter of convention (*nomo*) – the difference, in the present context, between down-to-earthness, and indulgence in diplomatic make-believe. In another context it is the difference between Greenwich Mean, and British Summer Time.

The mechanics of the process of collective opinion-formulation at the United Nations are scarcely such as to guarantee much necessary connection between the findings to be arrived at and the facts with which ostensibly they deal.

There is a world of difference between an ordinary trial, in which facts are established – in the light of evidence given, and tested by cross-examination, in open court – by a jury, and the type of political trial of which Europe has furnished all too many examples even in a relatively recent past. The idea in a political trial, Dr Goebbels is said to have said, is that 'this man must go!' Thus in a political trial, though the procedure is, in form, judicial, the decision-making is not. The Security Council in the Rhodesia case was not a body of judges and cannot be considered to have acted like one. More important, it was not required to do so by the Charter. The question was not whether peace was actually in peril but whether enough of the representatives had instructions to support the formal finding that it was. Fiction has played a role in the historical development of many institutions.

Meanwhile, artificialities apart, what of South Africa's 'racial' policies? Are they *phusei* a danger to peace? The reader is invited to appreciate that there is a real sense, but at the same time a strictly trivial sense, in which the answer should be yes. It is trivial in that it turns not upon the inherent quality of the policies but on the context, both general and special, in which they are pursued. In a general way they are the policies of a state co-existing with others in the world of sovereign states. In a special way they are a contribution to a dialogue in which others have something to say. It was the posturings of others, not the attitude of either Mr Wilson or Mr Smith, that lent its particle of plausibility to the finding in the Rhodesia case. In the presence of a madman my slightest movement may elicit a lethal response. It may be unwise to fondle, however affectionately, a rattlesnake.

And as for the world of sovereign states it is not a scene from which South Africa has effective freedom to withdraw. A car is a dangerous implement only when out on the road. South Africa must always be out on the road: she cannot lay herself up in a shed. It is of the very essence of the human condition that in going about even their most blameless occupations states may inescapably cause inconvenience to other states. Protectionist policies are a case in point.

In a confrontation between the super powers, involving unavoidably the practice of brinkmanship by both, every slightest move by either party may quite rationally be seen by its opponent as a threat to the peace. In the armed camp which was the Europe of 1914 steps were forced upon every government which were open to be so construed. That policy is, as by definition, a threat to the peace which, in the circumstances in which it is followed, is susceptible of eliciting a bellicose response. Such policies need have no positive content. The merely negative posture of a refusal to yield to diplomatic blackmail may have the same effect. Serbia's rejection of the Austro-Hungarian ultimatum was in this sense, to say the least, a risking of the peace. And no blame to Serbia either. She did no more than was required of her by the situation into which the grim imperatives of international politics had landed her. For what was Chamberlain criticized if it was not precisely for his reluctance in a crucial hour to risk the cause of peace? And for what, in the Cuba crisis, has Kennedy been lauded if not for his wise readiness, at need, to put that cause in jeopardy?

The life of states is by its nature a life of danger. The mere will of Czechoslovakia to live, there in the heart of Europe, was, in Hitler's day, a threat to the peace, to the extent that Hitler chose so to see it. In a hysterically hostile environment, beset, in the one case by Arab, in the other by Afro-Asian, ill-wishers, it is unneccessary to ask what Israel's, or South Africa's, policies actually are. Be they what they may be, if they amount to nothing more combative than a cool-headed response to the logic of an inherited situation, a threat to the peace they inevitably are. For whether a given gesture endangers peace is largely a function of the authenticity, the intensity, and the whereabouts, of the indignation it excites.

It is true that Mr Vorster is reported as having intimated that were South Africa to be attacked, she would hit back hard. If in so saying he became a threat to the peace then that is what Scotland can never not have been, from time immemorial. *Nemo me impune lacessit*! Individuals may have been known to commit hara-kiri at the bidding of their peers. Peoples less commonly do. For the Israeli people to carry conciliation of their Arab adversaries beyond a certain point would, at least for them, be tantamount to their suicide as a state. Their state is not so constituted as to have an aptitude for that particular exercise. And so it is with South Africa. It is indeed a mercy for her that some of those in whose diplomatic vicinity she perforce must pursue her way are as yet not formidably armed. For it is essentially on the ground of her reluctance to scupper herself that the Security Council has before now been exhorted to see her policies as a threat to the peace.

SEPARATE DEVELOPMENT AND THE DICTATES OF LOGIC

What then are these 'racial' policies of South Africa's of which so exalted a body has been invited to take so alarmist a view? As has above been suggested, they are largely those dictated to her by the logic of the situation in which she has, by history, been put. 'Our generation,' wrote Ben Marais, 'did not create the colour problem in South Africa. We inherited that problem . . . '

Out of six Australian colonies Britain had in 1900 created the great new colony of Australia. Out of four South African colonies she created in 1909-10 the great new colony of South Africa. The South African ship of state was launched into existence loaded down with problems enough to presage disaster should it encounter heavy weather early on. It did.

Britain's involvement, involving South Africa with it, in war with Germany aggravated immeasurably the problems with which South Africa had been born. And when post-war South Africa seemed on the way towards solving some of these, Britain for a second time got into war with Germany. This time South Africa could perfectly well, like the Irish Free State, have stood aloof. But, led by General Smuts, she rallied, days ahead of, for example, Canada, to Britain's side. And, when consulted, her electorate endorsed the participation policy of General Smuts. It is now the fashion to forget how close Britain came to defeat. What chance of victory she would have had had South Africa not rallied to her support is a question not often enough considered.

Once more the domestic problems of South Africa were enormously aggravated by her involvement in war with Britain's foe. And, as if that were not enough, Britain underwent meanwhile, politically, socially and even spiritually, a veritable revolution. And presently the setting in which South Africa had to persevere in her attack upon her problems was transformed by the withdrawal of British authority from much of Africa. And, with respect to South Africa's difficulties, there emerged in Britain a generation which endorsed with near-unanimity a speech, in Cape Town of all places, about the wind of change. What Smuts's comments, had he been there to make them, would have been on such a speech is sobering to wonder.

South Africa, abandoned by the Britain that she on two occasions had not abandoned, is still dourly wrestling with the problems with which in 1909-10 she had begun. This in a world which, expressly or by implication, condemns what Britain did in creating the great new colony of

South Africa as a system, full of problems, in which the responsibility for dealing with these was in effect to be the burden of the White minority alone. The policy of not devolving that responsibility upon the population as a whole, but of emulating instead the British example of providing self-determination for peoples long subject to European domination, is not expressly based upon objection to the principle of the self-determination of peoples, but simply on the fact that this policy is not the one that those critics would have preferred, that, namely, of transferring the responsibility for coping with all South Africa's problems to the population as a whole.

At more than one point the United Nations Charter refers with apparent approval to the principle of the self-determination of peoples. Consistently with this, the United Kingdom made known its intention to bring to independence the peoples of Basutoland, Bechuanaland and Swaziland; as in due time she did. British policy in doing this was probably not even on Cairo Radio described as 'racial'. Still less was it denounced as a denial of self-determination. In offering self-determination to the Zulus and the other subject peoples in South Africa, the Afrikaner leaders are merely following the example of the British, who had of course previously allowed it successively to *inter alios* the Australians, the Irish and the Indians. Does anyone suggest that the granting of independence to the Indians was not in accord with that principle of the self-determination of peoples which the Charter itself enshrines? Yet in offering the same solution to comparably dependent peoples South Africa is seen as denying the self-determination principle and endangering peace. Whatever else might be said for a transfer of powers to the African majority, this would scarcely be the self-determination of 'peoples'. For, though racially akin, the Africans are not collectively *a* people. There are a number of African peoples, each, like the Whites, a minority, within the perimeter of the South African state.

The problems and policies of the United Kingdom are those of a multiracial democracy, and difficult enough they are coming to be found. The problems of South Africa are those, not of a democracy, but of an oligarchy, and a White-ruled one at that. That South Africa's policies should differ from those of Britain need, in the circumstances, surprise nobody. The inhabitants of South Africa compose by long tradition not one community but a mingling of four communities within the framework of a single state.

In Britain now the talk is of 'community', rather than of 'race', relations: but this is not because there now are recognized more communities than one. With the local equivalent of the American philosophy of the melting pot, the British are working for more harmonious inter-personal relations between elements as of a single community. A difficulty in Britain is that various distinct elements within the supposedly single community will persist in feeling and seeing themselves as communities distinct. And it is not assumed that were you to take more care of the relations between self-conscious communities perceived as such the relations between their individual memberships might largely be found to take care of themselves.

The standards and methods of the West are the well-ripened fruit of the centuries-long experience of the West, accumulated in the conditions obtaining in the West. Those of the Afrikaners are correspondingly the fruit of a radically different experience, in radically different conditions. It is hardly astonishing that the standards of the Afrikaners should be found to differ in some respect from those of the West. What would, however, be surprising would be if the West felt it necessary to adapt its own well-matured standards to bring them into similarity with those of the Afrikaners. The latter would never ask them to. For the Afrikaners, for all their other human failings, are at least not guilty of that ideological imperialism which moves people to seek to impose their own standards upon those whose experience has been different. Whereas the assumption of some folk seems to be that other countries which are far from having found the answer to their own problems must at least know the answers to South Africa's, and that for not accepting these from them, but relying rather upon her own judgment, South Africa is internationally at fault. 'We don't do such things in *our* country: *ergo,* you can have no respectable reason for doing them in yours.' This is the sort of pseudo-rational moralistics that would condemn a heart-transplant operation on the ground that some people were not in need of one.

The writer is not himself a Catholic, but when he saw and heard on television a Prelate in Northern Ireland upholding the education of Catholic children in schools of their own he felt he understood the sanity of separate development better than ever before. Lately too he heard a domestic opponent of the South African government regretting the way in which he and his associates had left it to the Nationalists monopolistically to do justice in their programme to the patently multi-ethnic composition of South African society. The result had been that it was now scarcely possible to refer to the rationale of separate development without the risk of being rated as a racist. (It must have taken courage for such a man to say such a thing. There are many who would be tempted to deny that two and two made four if there were evidence of their political rivals having been the first to see it.)

There may from time to time in history have been peoples so situated that they could, or at least they thought so, envisage the future with equanimity. 'We live,' said once a Canadian statesman, 'in a fireproof house.' Not every people has ever felt so secure. South Africa has never. But, while many countries must reflect with anxiety on the risks of failure to keep sweet their relations with other countries, in South Africa's case there is also unavoidable apprehension lest the bases be imperilled of peace within. Indeed a great part of the country's unpopularity stems from the fact that where public security at home and reputation abroad are in tension, security at home has claims to prior place.

Politics are in a sense no more than a surface manifestation compared with the inertia of ingrained social habit, as well as with the ground swell of spontaneous change, in a country's way of life. If this is to alter fundamentally, it must be through developments at the grassroots level rather than in the rituals of the political tug-o'-war. As in other countries so also in South Africa new emphases are forever suggesting themselves in the structure of social thought. These may be nurtured, but they may also be neutralized, by pious admonitions from abroad.

MOTIVES FOR DIFFERENTIATION

A familiar habit of South Africa's critics is to attribute the policies that they find incomprehensible to motives which everyone must abhor. Differentiation between White and Non-White in South Africa is imputed, as if as a matter of course, to the White man's dislike or contempt for the Black, to belief in the latter's innate inferiority, in his lack of the needed capabilities for utilizing the sort of opportunities that he is being denied. The decision of the Boers, in founding their republics, that these should in effect be offshoots of the civilization of Europe, with no equality of White and Black – meaning of European and Non-European – meaning of civilized man and barbarian – provided a root for the outlook that marks the Afrikaners as a people to this day. History has now placed them in legitimate control of the whole of a far-stretched land. But at no point have circumstances, or even the dictates of a conqueror, required them to forgo their cherished idea – that theirs, though a part of Africa, remains at the same time in a sense a part of Europe and that those not of European descent are not 'we' but 'they'.

Given, however, the difference in colour it was probably inevitable that the notion of European-ness and that of Whiteness should from the first have been confounded. And though lines came to be drawn among the Non-Whites – the Asians, the Africans and the Coloureds – it was the White-Non-White distinction which remained basic to the social and political thinking of the typical Afrikaner. And to differentiate-between comes only too easily to be vulgarly equated with to discriminate-against.

Yet can anyone suppose that were South Africa's several communities, while remaining otherwise such as they respectively are, to wake up one fine morning all of them equally black, or equally red, white or blue, the need to differentiate between them would be found to have disappeared? The situation, sociologically speaking, of potential conflict would still be there.

It is, too, a fact of international life, an aspect indeed of the universal human predicament, that situations come about in which sections of humanity are as it were constrained by history and circumstances to view each other with resentment, with envy, with suspicion and with fear. Given the special structure of South Africa, and given the need of the Afro-Asian peoples for confirmation of their re-established self-esteem, it would be strange if the very existence of such a set-up as South Africa's were not viewed, officially, by the politicians of the lately emancipated countries as an affront to the pride and dignity of themselves and those they claimed to speak for. The idea of a country, the home of many peoples, grouped administratively in four communities, where one of these last is by constitutional entitlement 'on top' – more especially if its pigmentation does not happen to be dark – is understandably abhorrent to the newer states. So constituted, no country could hope to be the object, universally, of affection. South Africa has indeed been described as the most loudly and systematically (sic) hated country in the world today. But this does not of itself render her policies either reprehensible or inimical to peace. Jews and Christians at least should understand and concede that unpopularity is no proof of ill-desert. The first man in the Old Testament story to suffer death at the hands of an angry brother was the inoffensive Abel, because his sacrifice had been pleasing to the Lord.

And it is the very reasonableness of South Africa's programme, and the promise it holds of a brighter future, that may cause her bitterer critics pain. To those whose wish it is to see it founder, it can afford little joy to perceive that the country's ship of state is proceeding upon so even a keel. It is the well-functioning, not the ill-functioning, of the South African system which must the more infuriate some. When these declare that the situation is 'explosive', they are voicing their wishful thoughts. Reformism was ever anathema to the partisans of revolution.

Regretting the pattern given by a Liberal-dominated Britain to South Africa in 1909-10, the vocal preponderance of the United Nations General Assembly reject the means relied on by South Africa for making the enterprise a success. People speak of 'racial' policies without explicit mention of anything in particular. But if from general indications it is sought to deduce what they really are objecting to it commonly seems to be the very survival in its inherited form of South Africa as a state. 'So long,' declared the late Tom Mboya, 'as any part of Africa remains under European rule we do not feel that Africans will be regarded in the right way.' It is hard to doubt that, in the context, Mboya, by European, meant White. *Carthago est delenda.* In Soekarno's day it was Malaysia that was scheduled for demolition. In Nasser's it was Israel. Soekarno is no more. So too is Nasser. And so, alas, is Mboya.

What sort of changes in South Africa are these people seeking to promote? A speeding up of the industrial and agricultural development of the homelands? Improvements in African housing in the urban areas? Relaxation of job reservation, of pass laws, of laws against mixed marriages? What is it that they are wanting in South Africa? Is it peace? Or is it turmoil? Were civil war to break out in South Africa would this, for these critics, be good news or bad? What do they really wish for? One answer was provided years ago by a delegate at the United Nations. 'The position of the African countries,' he said, 'is clear. What they are asking for must necessarily and typically take the form of a transfer of power to the African population. This excludes any idea of partitioning the country.' Whereas the Afrikaners, like the British under Churchill, have opted to survive in independence as a people distinct.

What Communism dislikes about social democracy in capitalist contexts is that it aims at making people happier when for the purposes of Communism it is more desirable that their miseries increase. Only what is bad news from South Africa is good news for those who can be content with nothing less than the replacement of White minority rule. Hence no doubt the apparent relish with which a British church dignitary was heard declaring that things in South Africa were getting not better but worse. Is there in all the world a country where nothing is getting worse? Was his own Britain such a country? How about the crime figures?

Things getting worse. Friends of South Africa know that, using true information only, a gloomy enough picture could be presented of conditions there today. But there is reassurance for them in the apparent implied recognition by their adversaries that a strong enough case against South Africa could not be caused to rest upon verifiable allegations only. And should South Africa's policies come ever to be classed by the Security Council as threatening to peace, it is likely to be those policies as misconceived or skilfully misrepresented, and not as they actually are. These are, admittedly, designed to meet the necessities of the peoples of South Africa rather than to satisfy the preferences of the peoples of the world. And admittedly they seek to exploit the possibility of making things better rather than to overcome the impossibility of making them perfect. But they are not the policies imputed to her in the popular mythology of New York. There the wickedness of White South Africa has by now become with many a veritable article of faith, an ingredient in that drive-ideology which prescribes the idiom of their perennial disfavour. The test of this is the apparent distaste with which they will entertain even the thought of their having possibly been deceived. The true seeker after truth is by contrast ever alert to learn of where he may inadvertently have let himself be misled.

For popular ignorance in the West of 'the principles and practices of political warfare' has been described, and very justly so, as 'a tremendous and terrifying liability'.

The merit, and the magic, of the activating myth lies not so much in any intrinsic truthfulness it may incidentally possess, but in what a writer of discernment once called its 'existential adequacy', its potency, that is, for sounding, so to say, a bell in the unconscious of those to whom it spoke. How such an element gets infiltrated into the conventional wisdom of a whole society has been partly explained as follows: 'If you repeat a false accusation often enough; if you tell enough half-truths in the context of what is irrelevant; if you create enough confusion in people's minds; if by such means you can manoeuvre your opponent on the defensive, you have a fair chance of persuading the world that what you say is true, what you stand for is good.' The writer, a political parson, of those words was not avowedly reporting on the evangelistic procedures of himself and friends. But his testimony is revealing even so. And the build-up of Pavlovian disapproval of South Africa among the highminded is now so formidable as to recall the comparable animus in Nazi Germany against the Jews, an animus engendered and kept ardent, in the main, by similar techniques.

SEEING THE WHOLE PICTURE

'To understand why some things are done,' wrote Ben Marais, 'it is necessary to see the whole picture: and the true South African picture is very different from the caricature as seen by the world.' The caricature: yes. A police state, administered by fascists, with censorship of the press and imprisonment without trial and with denial of a proper education to the underdog, where to comment adversely on government policies is to invite incarceration, where avoidable malnutrition and disease are rife among the majority, and where the idea is to herd that majority into the most impoverished corners of the land – how many normally quite ungullible people have not some such image of South Africa as this?

That harsh things happen in South Africa no-one can deny. Some are inseparable from the application of laws enacted in the general interest of all the country's peoples. As an American sociologist has pointed out, governments deal with 'issues' and in so doing cause 'troubles' for individuals – and this even in the best-run states. Stories of troubles make good journalistic reportage, especially when maliciously embellished. But as every young lawyer is taught, 'hard cases' make 'bad law'.

If South Africa's more militant critics could detect anything sufficiently objectionable in her policy of separate development they might presumably content themselves with pointing it out. Instead, in seeming despair of proving it inhumane or otherwise anti-social, they resort to the sorry and ignominious expedient of misconstruing it. They portray it as a policy geared to the perpetuation of racial domination. Since this is something that the world can be counted upon to deplore, it is as racial domination that South Africa's policy is depicted. Rarely are there quoted the words of Dr Verwoerd in London in 1961: 'The essential condition to a stable and prosperous country is that racial domination will have to be removed. So long as domination of one race by another exists there will be resistance and unrest. Consequently the solution should be sought by means of a policy which is calculated to eliminate domination in every form and in every respect.'

It was of separate development that, writing soon after then, Sir Penderel Moon declared that it was difficult to see how anyone could object in principle to such a policy, if it was honestly and fairly carried out. The 'extraordinary thing' was that 'at the United Nations and elsewhere', the 'whole principle of such a policy' was assailed as if there were something intrinsically immoral about it. 'As if . . . immoral'. This is the key idea. For the recognition that historically South Africa has developed as more communities than one is indeed assailed as if immoral. Yet there is surely nothing immoral in the recognition of what social philosophers have referred to as 'relevant differences'. If the differences between the communities of the Bushmen, the Namas and the Herero in South West Africa were not relevant for the purpose of doing the best thing possible, administratively, for all of them, what would be? It was not Pretoria, it was the two peoples themselves that insisted that they, the Venda and the Tsonga, should retain their respective identities and not be merged together into one. There was separate development in South West Africa long before the advent of the Whites. Wise and humane administration pays heed to relevant differences.

But what South Africa's extremer critics appear to be interested in is not the wisdom or unwisdom of her administration but the ending in South Africa of White minority rule. The so-called 'racial' policy to which they take exception is the policy, of the European-descended community, of persisting in the exercise of that stewardship for the well-being of the entire population which they assumed with the launching of the Union. It is the policy of the conservation of that aspect of the social structure of South Africa which identifies the individual with the ethnic group which is his.

As John Hatch, of the *New Statesman*, wrote in 1964, 'Any relevant solution must start from a recognition that South Africa is not a nation, but a collection of communities.' Certainly the country's present policies do have the merit of so starting. It is precisely this necessary recognition, counselled by John Hatch, that South Africa's ill-wishers still persist in deprecating and eschewing. Such folk think only in terms of colour, and in particular of whiteness and non-whiteness. Their formula for toppling the White minority from the position that it constitutionally holds is to demand the introduction of democracy, the merging of all the peoples into one. It was this idea that Chief Matanzima, addressing White undergraduates at Rhodes University, described as 'the silliest imaginable thing'. And so it very obviously would be.

For a land in which inequalities and injustices between different sections of society have come to be accepted and endured as if part of some inexorable natural order one need look no further than to Soviet Russia or to Franco's Spain. It may be that there exist countries – is Sweden perhaps one? – where all blessings are fairly shared and each is the equal of his neighbour. South Africa is not such a country and never has been. 'The dilemma,' it has been declared, 'of the South African political system is that while it is in dire need of reforming itself it is structurally incapable of doing so.' The question is not whether the South African system is indeed in need of reforming itself but whether it is in fact so incapable, by its very structure, of doing so. It is after all in process of doing so at this very time. Lenin's revolutionary strategy is said to have depended upon the premise that parliamentary procedures and reformist politics were incapable of achieving anything substantial for alleviating the condition of the workers. And the campaigning of South Africa's opponents depends comparably upon the assumption that the only policy to be hoped for from a White minority regime is that of the perpetuation of the domination of one race by another. This is the false doctrinal baseline to which they most resolutely cling. The fact that at a recent election in South Africa the party of reaction was wiped, if only for the time being, from the parliamentary map, means nothing to these folk. Their strategy continues to necessitate the contrary assumption.

THE BLIGHT OF IGNORANCE

How much does the otherwise relatively well-educated man-in-the-street in Western countries know about South Africa's domestic policies, the nature of the various measures adopted, and the reasons, or even the merely ostensible reasons, for which they were judged appropriate? Why are conditions in South Africa not more candidly and comprehensively reported, were it only in order then to be uncharitably discussed? Why, instead, are they so almost exclusively portrayed in snide caricature?

Recently after the writer had been addressing some presumably literate British adults, there arose one who said: 'Professor, you told us that there were in South Africa universities for the Blacks. Frankly, Professor, I don't believe you.' Barely two weeks later, when speaking at one of the universities in question, the writer was able to cite this little incident as illustrative of how poorly the British public had been served in the relevant respects by its customary sources of information.

It would be easier for a government to reflect in its policies what could appear to be a decent respect for the opinion of mankind, if in forming those opinions mankind could be seen to have reflected a decent respect for the evidence. When, by contrast, mankind as represented by, for instance, the American leadership can be heard denouncing South Africa's policy – of offering self-determination to her subject peoples – as a denial (sic) of self-determination, it must be difficult for the average South African to feel for such an opinion anything but the profoundest *dis*-respect.

Nevertheless, the fact must be faced that there is nothing – except their sense of what is seemly or expedient – to prevent the relevant assortment of states from some day instructing their representatives to support at the Security Council a purported finding that this or that policy, being applied by South Africa, is now, if only now for the first time, a threat to the peace. The finding could be arbitrary, unrealistic, cynical, a subterfuge of diplomatic make-believe, an exercise in unblushing appeasement, but once reached it could provide the sufficient formal basis for a recourse to the sanctions provisions of the Charter.

It is not as if the finding of a threat to peace need even have the air of being more than a requisite, but empty, form of words. It would be the alleged iniquity, not the threatening nature, of the policies in question that would be thought to confer a semblance of respectability on the Security Council's decision. It would be in the name of righteousness rather than of strategic prudence that the United Nations would shoulder its distasteful responsibility. The preamble, many paragraphs if not many pages of it, would as likely as not be from the pen of a Kenneth Kaunda rather than of some soldier on the United Nations staff. And the conscience of mankind, nourished on the output of the apartheid unit in UNO's bureaucracy, would give thanks that at long last war was to be waged against those 'evil things'.

Political warfare is largely a matter of the manufacture and distribution of suppositions strategically opportune from the standpoint of the producer and distributor. Any child should be competent to draw up a set of beliefs respecting South Africa which it must suit the strategic interests of, say, the Kremlin to render prevalent in the capitalist West. It is remarkable how many of these opinions would be found to be precisely those which in recent decades have become part, in the West, of the conventional wisdom.

Given a state of political war between West and East, the likely intentions of the East are most feasibly deducible from the apparent strategic interests of the East. And as elements relatively amenable to eastern influences are now enthroned in Cairo and at Aden, so must it presumably be in Russia's strategic interest that the friends and allies of the West be extruded from seats of power at the Cape. Those whom Communism plans to assimilate, it first has a bash at making mad. And the West is in some respects a little bit mad already. A wind of ideological change is permeating even the corridors of Western power.

When in the late thirties the expansionist ambition of Nazi Germany made the absorption of Czechoslovakia its target, there was patently a threat to the peace. Though the United Nations was then as yet non-existent, the danger was duly contained. This was achieved when Britain and France, with Italian connivance, brought about a situation such that President Benes had no effective choice but to capitulate to the Nazi demands. It was the sort of thing which, given the needed *sang froid,* might tomorrow be attempted at the expense of some other ethnically-composite sovereign state. As the Czechoslovakia, in whose founding Britain and France had nineteen years earlier concurred, had now to be dismantled, so might the South Africa of whose creation Britain had once been proud have to be dealt with in say 1984. Given, that is, a sufficient degree of cynicism – Munich-style – in the appropriate centres.

What distinguishes the South African situation from that of Czechoslovakia in 1938 is that, while the covetousness is hardly less ('We must liberate South Africa,' wrote Kwame Nkrumah, 'so as to regain (sic) our wealth and resources in that area . . . '), the power for effective action of the hostile OAU is as yet not so great as was that of Adolf Hitler. The point of the analogy lies in the fact that had the United Nations existed in 1938 all that might need to have happened would have been for the Security Council to be persuaded to determine the Central European situation a threat to the peace. Concerted pressures could then have been brought to bear upon Benes, who might even have succumbed without a struggle. As indeed he had to. Whether South Africa faced with action by the United Nations would similarly succumb is another matter entirely.

'THREAT' ACCUSATION EXPLOITED BY ENEMIES OF WEST

It is true that South Africa's treatment of her subject peoples is widely considered to be oppressive, as was the treatment by Benes of the Sudetendeutsch. Even so, from the *Times Literary Supplement* (6.7.1967) there may be quoted the following : 'At last when he (Group Captain Christie) met Henlein in Zurich in August, 1938 . . . Henlein said to Christie quite frankly that even if there were no Germans in Czechoslovakia Germany could no longer tolerate its existence : the authority for this is a Communist report backed by one from the German Ambassador in Paris.' Had there been no Blacks in Southern Africa would Nkrumah have desired those resources less, or Moscow that footing at the Cape?

The model for the proceedings in 1938 might have been found in Chapter 21 in the first book of the Kings. In the story, that is, of Naboth's vineyard. 'The Lord forbid it me that I should give the inheritance of my fathers unto thee.' So, like Benes in 1938 and like South Africa today, Naboth was given a bad press. A smear-mythology about him was put into circulation. And, like Benes, he became sufficiently discredited for it to be possible, without provoking an uncontrollable volume of public hullaballoo, to liquidate Naboth, and to liberate his vineyard. It is small consolation to reflect that mankind now feels a certain retrospective tenderness both for Naboth and for Benes.

Not that anything of the sort here suggested is really so very likely to happen tomorrow. The overthrow or collapse of the South African system is so obviously to the interest of the enemies of the West that the United States, in particular, save in a moment of almost inconceivable loss of poise, would hardly be eager to promote it.

Meanwhile, one inference that South Africans may have been prompted to draw from the Rhodesia object-lesson is this, namely, that, while it must at all times be wise so to frame one's policies as to cause least distress to one's friends, and whereas in the olden time it was prudent so to act as not to be taken by one's contemporaries for a covenant-breaking aggressor, it would in present conditions be pointless to take thought lest one's policies should come peradventure to be labelled, and libelled, as a danger to the peace. They will be if they will be, and they won't be if they won't. If it suits the Security Council to call them such, then such will they be called. All one can hope is that if the calling were to be too blatantly implausible some states might be found unwilling to play ball. And this no doubt the Security Council might itself be expected to fear.

Index